Computer Simulation Experiments
with Models of Economic Systems

Computer Simulation Experiments with Models of Economic Systems

£5.70 Eng
Sales
prod

oks are tc   before

Thomas H. Naylor

Director, Social System
Simulation Program
Duke University

WITH CONTRIBUTIONS BY:

James M. Boughton

Donald S. Burdick

J. M. Finger

Daniel A. Graham

E. Philip Howrey

H. H. Kelejian

Philip J. Kiviat

Marilyn Manser

William A. Moy

Norfleet W. Rives

W. Earl Sasser

John M. Vernon

Kenneth Wertz

Thomas H. Wonnacott

JOHN WILEY & SONS, INC.,
New York | London | Sydney | Toronto

848,669

Preface

This book is concerned with the methodology for designing computer simulation experiments with models of economic systems. It is the sequel to an earlier book by Naylor, Balintfy, Burdick, and Chu entitled *Computer Simulation Techniques* (Wiley, 1966).

For our purposes, simulation is defined as a numerical technique for conducting *experiments* with certain types of mathematical models that describe the behavior of a complex system on a digital computer over extended periods of time. An emphasis, unique to this book, is placed on the experimental aspects of simulation. But, since a computer simulation is indeed an experiment, it follows that careful attention must be given to problems of experimental design and data analysis.

The starting point of any computer simulation experiment is a *model* of the system to be simulated. That is, we assume that a model has already been formulated and that its parameters have been specified. In this book, we focus on models of economic and management systems. However, the methodology that is described is completely general and easily may be adapted to social, political, psychological, biomedical, or engineering systems.

The reader is assumed to have some knowledge of differential and integral calculus, mathematical statistics, and computer programming. Although the book stands alone as a self-contained text, it includes appendixes on pseudorandom number generators, random variable generators, and simulation languages for readers who are not already familiar with these techniques.

In Chapter 1 simulation is defined and a rationale is set forth for the use of computer simulation as a tool of analysis. A six-step methodology for the design of computer simulation experiments is described in Chapter 2. These steps are (1) the formulation of the problem, (2) the formulation of a mathematical model, (3) the formulation of a computer program, (4) validation, (5) experimental design, and (6) data analysis.

Chapter 3 contains a collection of management science models that includes Markov chain models, queueing models, inventory models, marketing models, production models, financial models, corporate models, and management games. Models of the firm and industry and macroeconometric models are presented in Chapter 4.

Chapters 5 and 6, respectively, are concerned with the problems of validation and experimental design. Analysis of variance, sequential sampling, and spectral analysis are the subject matter of Chapters 7 to 9.

In Chapters 10 to 12, special attention is given to three methodological problems: variance reduction, stopping rules, and simulation versus analytical solutions. We conclude with the analysis of three specific simulation experiments in Chapters 13 to 15—a simulation of the tobacco industry, a simulation of the effects of alternative governmental resource allocation policies, and a simulation of the monetary sector of the economy of the United States.

Throughout this book we make extensive use of numerical examples and of actual simulation experiments to illustrate specific techniques and methodological problems.

We are grateful to the editors of the following journals for permission to reproduce this material: *Applied Economics, Communications of the ACM, Econometrica, Management Science, Journal of the American Statistical Association, Review of Economics and Statistics, Review of the International Statistical Institute, Southern Economic Journal*, and *Simulation*. We also acknowledge the support provided by the National Science Foundation to the Social System Simulation Program at Duke University. Chapter 10 was written by William A. Moy, Chapter 12 by E. Philip Howrey and H. H. Kelejian, and Appendix C by Philip J. Kiviat. Chapters 10 and 12 are based on papers by Moy, Howrey, and Kelejian that were published originally in *The Design of Computer Simulation Experiments*, edited by Thomas H. Naylor and published by the Duke University Press in 1969. The paper by Philip Kiviat is reproduced with the permission of the RAND Corporation.

Alan G. Merten contributed a number of incisive comments and Stephanie Thorn typed the numerous drafts of the manuscript. Finally, I am especially grateful to the University of Wisconsin for providing the time and atmosphere for one to bring this book to its completion.

Thomas H. Naylor
October 1, 1970

Contents

Chapter 1. Computer Simulation Defined   1

Introduction 1

A Definition of Simulation 2

Why Simulate 6

**Chapter 2. Computer Simulation Experiments with Models
of Economic Systems**   11

Methodology 11

    Formulation of the Problem 11

    Formulation of a Mathematical Model 12

    Formulation of a Computer Program 15

       Computer Program 15

       Data Input and Starting Conditions 16

       Data Generation 16

    Validation 21

    Experimental Design 22

       The Problem of Stochastic Convergence 24

       The Problem of Size 26

       The Problem of Motive 27

       The Multiple Response Problem 28

    Data Analysis 29

       F-Test 34

       Multiple Comparisons 34

       Multiple Rankings 34

       Spectral Analysis 35

       Sequential Sampling 35

       Nonparametric Methods 36

Bibliography 36

Chapter 3. Management Science Models 40

Introduction 40

Properties of Computer Models 40

Markov Chain Models 42

Queueing Models 44
    A Single-Channel, Single-Station Model 44
    A Single-Channel, Multistation Model 48
    A Multichannel, Multistation Model 48

Inventory Models 52

Production Models 57

Marketing Models 59
    The Pillsbury Model 59
    The Anheuser-Busch Model 59
    The Corning Glass Model 61
    Other Marketing Models. 61

Financial Models 61
    The Clarkson Model 61
    The Hertz Model 62
    The Mattessich Model. 64
    The Sun Oil Model 64
    Other Financial Models 65

Corporate Models 68
    The Anheuser-Busch Model 68
    The IBM Model 70
    The Pillsbury Model 70
    The XEROX Model 72

Management Games 73

Bibliography 83

Chapter 4. Economic Models 89

Introduction 89

Models of the Firm 89
    Cobweb Models 89
        Cobweb Model 1 89

Cobweb Model 2 91
Cobweb Model 3 92
A Model of a Competitive Industry 93
A Duopoly Model 96
Behavioral Models 99
Duopoly Model 100
Oligopoly Model 101
Department Store Model 101
Monopoly Model 105
Bonini Model 105
Industrial Dynamic (DYNAMO) 107
Reflections on Computer Models of the Firm 111

Industry Models 113

A Model of the Textile Industry 113
Endogenous Variables 114
Exogenous Variables 114
Status Variables 115
Identities 115
Behavioral Equations 115
Apparel Demand 115
Apparent Output 115
Demand for Textile Mill Products 115
Output of Textile Mill Products 116
Employment of Production Workers 116
Earnings 116
Prices 116
Profit 116
Investment 117
A Model of the Shoe, Leather, Hide Industry 119
A Model of the Lumber Industry 124

Macroeconometric Models 126

Introduction 126
An Example Model 128
Problem Formulation 128
Model Formulation 128
Parameter Estimation 130
Computer Program Formulation 130
Experimental Design 133
Data Analysis 133

Solving Econometric Models 136
   Linear Models 136
   Nonlinear Models 139
   PROGRAM SIMULATE 141
Large-Scale Econometric Models 142
   Brookings Model 142
   OBE Model 142
   Wharton Model 142
Some Unresolved Problems 143
   Simulation Versus Analytical Solutions 143
   Perverse Simulation Results 143
   Inadequate Estimation Techniques 146
   Unstable Coefficients 147

Bibliography 147

Chapter 5. Validation
    by Thomas H. Naylor and J. M. Finger   153

The Problem of Validation 153

Three Positions on Validation 154

   Rationalism 154
   Empiricism 155
   Positive Economics 155

Multistage Validation 156

Goodness of Fit 159

   Analysis of Variance 160
   Chi-Square Test 160
   Factor Analysis 160
   Kolmogorov—Smirnov Test 160
   Nonparametric Tests 160
   Regression Analysis 160
   Spectral Analysis 160
   Theil's Inequality Coefficient 161

Summary 161

Bibliography 163

Chapter 6. The Design of Computer Simulation Experiments   165

Experimental Design 165

An Example Model 165

Data Analysis 167

Exploratory Experiments 167

     Full Factorial Designs 167
     Fractional Factorial Designs 168
     Rotatable Designs 171
     Response Surface Designs 172
     Other Designs 175

Optimization Experiments 175

Some Pitfalls and Contingencies 180

     The Problem of Sample Size 180
     The Problem of Too Many Factors 180
     The Multiple Response Problem 181
     The Problem of Nonlinearity 181
     The Problem of Convergence 181
     Constrained Optimization 182

Summary 182

Bibliography 183

Chapter 7. Analysis of Variance   185

Introduction 185

A Model of the Firm 186

The Computer Program 190

Validation 195

The Experiment 196

Data Analysis 200

     F-Test 201
     Multiple Comparisons 203
     Multiple Rankings 205

An Econometric Model 209

The Computer Program 211

Validation 212

The Experiment 212

Data Analysis 215

    F-Test 215
    Multiple Comparisons 216
    Multiple Rankings 218

Summary 218

Bibliography 219

Chapter 8. Sequential Sampling
by W. Earl Sasser, Daniel A. Graham, Donald S. Burdick, and Thomas H. Naylor   223

Introduction 223

An Inventory Model 224

The Experiment 227

Sequential Analysis 230

    Testing a Hypothesis Regarding the Mean 230
    Comparing the Means of K Experimental Categories
      with a Control 231
    A Multiple-Decision Procedure for Selecting the Best
      One of Several Populations [9] 232
    A Heuristic Approach to the Bechhofer Procedure 233

Analysis of Simulation Results 234

    Testing a Hypothesis Regarding the Mean 234
    Comparing K Experimental Categories with a Control . . . 240
    A Multiple-Decision Procedure for Selecting the Best
      One of Several Populations 242
    A Heuristic Approach to Selecting the Best One of
      Several Populations 243

Conclusions 243

Bibliography 243

Chapter 9. Spectral Analysis
by Thomas H. Naylor, Kenneth Wertz, and
Thomas H. Wonnacott   247

Introduction 247

An Example Model 248

Simulation Runs 250

    Run 1 250
    Run 2 251
    Run 3 251

Theory of Spectral Analysis 251

Statistical Properties of Spectra 255

Spectral Analysis: A Larger Role? 265

Summary 266

Bibliography 266

Chapter 10. Variance Reduction
by William A. Moy   269

Introduction 269

Problem Formulation 270

Regression Sampling 271

Antithetic-Variate Sampling 274

Stratified Sampling 275

Importance Sampling 278

Experimental Results 282

Conclusions 287

Bibliography 287

Chapter 11. Stopping Rules   290

Introduction 290

Independent Observations 291

    Fixed Sample Size Rules 291
        Estimation of the Population Mean 291

Testing a Hypothesis about the Mean 292
F-Test 292
Multiple Ranking Procedures 292
Sequential Sampling Rules 293
Estimation of the Population Mean 293
Testing a Hypothesis about the Mean 294
Comparing the Means of K Experimental Categories . . 294
A Multiple Ranking Procedure 294

Autocorrelated Observations 295

Bibliography 296

Chapter 12. Simulation Versus Analytical Solutions by E. Philip Howrey and H. H. Kelejian

299

Introduction 299

Simulation of Linear Models 301
Nonstochastic Simulation 301
Stochastic Simulation 303

Simulation of Nonlinear Models 305
Reduced-Form Equations 306
Nonstochastic Simulation 308

Dynamic Properties of Stochastic Linear Systems 310
Final Form and Solution of a Linear Model 311
Spectral Representation of Solution 312
Application of Spectral Method 314
Spectral Representation in Validation 316

Conclusions 317

Bibliography 318

Chapter 13. A Computer Model of the Tobacco Industry by John M. Vernon, Norfleet W. Rives, and Thomas H. Naylor

320

Introduction 320

Description of the Industry 320

The Model 323

1. Leaf Production 326
2. Leaf Price 330
3. Cigarettes 332

Simulations 333

Bibliography 335

Chapter 14. Effects of Alternative Policies for Allocating
Federal Aid for Education to the States
by Marilyn Manser, Thomas H. Naylor and
Kenneth Wertz   338

Introduction 338

The Model 338

The Policy Alternatives 343

Policy Simulations 345

Data Analysis 346
F-Test 346
Multiple Comparisons 348
Multiple Ranking 349

Bibliography 350

Chapter 15. A Model of the United States Monetary Sector
by James M. Boughton and Thomas H. Naylor   353

Introduction 353

Variables 354

The Model 357

Analysis of the Model 361

Validation 363

Policy Simulations 366

Bibliography 379

Appendix A. Pseudorandom Number Generators   381

Introduction 381

Congruential Methods 382

The Multiplicative Method 383
Binary Computers 384
Decimal Computers 386
The Mixed Method 387
Binary Computers 388
Decimal Computers 388
The Combination Method 389

Autocorrelation 390

Statistical Tests 391

Bibliography 392

Appendix B. Random Variable Generators   396

Introduction 396

Continuous Probability Distributions 396

Uniform Distribution 397
Normal Distribution 397
Multivariate Normal Distribution 397
Exponential Distribution 399
Gamma Distribution 399
Other Distributions 400

Discrete Probability Distributions 400

Geometric Distribution 400
Pascal Distribution 401
Binomial Distribution 401
Hypergeometric Distribution 402
Poisson Distribution 402

Bibliography 403

Appendix C. Simulation Languages
by Philip J. Kiviat   406

Introduction 406

Some Definitions 407
Principal Features of Simulation Languages 409
Reasons for Having SPL's 410
Reasons for Using Existing POL's 411

Simulation Programming Concepts 413

Describing a System: The Static Structure 413
Identification of Objects and Object Characteristics . . 414
Relationships between Objects 415
Generation of Objects 416
Describing a System: The Dynamic Structure 417
The Concept of Simulated Time 417
The Structure of Simulation Control Programs 417
Event Selections Procedures 420
The Activity Scanning Approach 420
The Event Scheduling Approach 421
The Process Iteration Approach 422

Simulation Programming Language Features 425

Specifying System Structure 425
Representating Statical Phenomena 425
Data Collection, Analysis, and Display 429
Data Collection Specification 429
Data Collection Facilities 430
Data Analysis 430
Display Media 431
Specification of Display Formats 432
Monitoring and Debugging 433
Initialization 434
Other Features 435

Some Examples of SPLS 436

SIMSCRIPT II 436
The Model 436
Initiating a Task 440
Review of Secretarial Task 443
Executive Available at the End of a Task 445
Secretary Available at the End of a Task 447
Description of the Program 447
SIMULA 456
The Model 456
The Program 458
Description of the Program 459
CSL: An Activity-Oriented Language 466
The Model 466
Description of the Program 466

GPSS/360: A Transaction-Flow Language 473
The Model 474
The Program 474
Description of the Program 475
Summary 478

Current SPL Research 478

Research on Simulation Concepts 479
Research on Operating Systems and Mechanisms 481
Interactive Languages 481
Time-Sharing 482
Graphics 482

The Future of SPLS 483

Bibliography 486

Index

Chapter 1 | Computer Simulation Defined

INTRODUCTION

Three alternatives are available to economic policy makers for evaluating the effectiveness of economic policies. First, at least in theory, it may be possible to perform controlled experiments with the given economic system, where the economic system may be a firm, an industry, or the economy of a country. Usually, institutional, political, and other practical constraints make this alternative impossible in the case of an industry or the economy as a whole. Occasionally, it may be feasible for a firm to experiment with, say, different advertising and marketing policies and then to compare the results. However, even in the limited number of cases where actual experiments are conducted with economic systems, it is unlikely that all variables can be held constant so as to obtain meaningful comparisons of alternative economic policies.

Second, if cross-section data are available over time it may be possible to perform a type of *ex post* experiment with an economic system. Suppose, for example, that we have time series data available by states for some economic variable such as per capita income, and that we assume that differences in per capita income among states can be explained by two or three policy instruments and a relatively small amount of random error. We may then be able to evaluate the effects of alternative economic policies on per capita income. Frequently, cross-section data are not available over time and, even when sufficient data are available, the assumption that differences among endogenous variables over the cross-section are due primarily to controllable policy variables is likely to be highly questionable, since the data were not generated from a controlled experiment. Therefore, we may find that random error or "noise" is the principal cause of differences among endogenous variables over time. When this is the case, we shall not be willing to place much confidence in our evaluations of different economic policies that use cross-section data.

When controlled experimentation is impossible or impractical and cross-section data are unavailable (or cross-section data are available but random error is excessive), then the policy maker is left with only one alternative. He may formulate (and estimate the parameters of) a model of the given economic system that relates the endogenous (dependent) variables of the system to the exogenous (independent) variables and policy instruments. If, for example, the model takes the form of a relatively small number of first- or second-order, simultaneous, linear differential or difference equations, then analytical techniques may be used to evaluate the effects of alternative economic policies. If, on the other hand, the model consists of a larger number of higher-order, simultaneous, nonlinear differential or difference equations with stochastic error terms included, then analytical techniques may exist in theory only. When this is the case, we must resort to numerical analysis or simulation to evaluate alternative economic policies.

In recent years computer simulation has become increasingly popular among economists and management scientists as a tool for analyzing the behavior of complex economic systems. The range of applications of computer simulation now extends from specific activities of business firms, for example, inventory control and production scheduling, to simulations of entire corporations and even the economy of the United States (as well as other countries). As a tool for testing the effects of alternative managerial or governmental policies on the behavior of particular economic systems, simulation has achieved a noteworthy record in only a short period of time.

Before turning to the methodology of designing a computer simulation experiment with a model of an economic system, it is appropriate that we define exactly what we mean by simulation.

A DEFINITION OF SIMULATION

We shall define simulation as *a numerical technique for conducting experiments with certain types of mathematical models which describe the behavior of a complex system on a digital computer over extended periods of time.* The starting point of any computer simulation experiment is a model of the system to be simulated. That is, we assume that a model has already been formulated and its parameters have been specified. The principal difference between a simulation experiment and a "real world" experiment is that, with simulation, the experiment is conducted with a model of the real system instead of with the actual system itself.

In order to fully appreciate this definition of simulation, the following conceptual framework will be useful.[1]

---

[1] This conceptual framework for simulation was developed by Professor J. S. Hunter of Princeton University.

Let Y denote some output (endogenous) variable of a system that we wish to study, and let $\mathbf{X}$ denote the k variables (exogenous variables and policy variables) that are thought to influence Y according to the functional relationship:

$$Y = \phi(\mathbf{X}) \tag{1-1}$$

In the experimental design literature, Y is said to be a *response* and the X_i's ($i = 1, 2, \ldots, k$) are said to be *factors*. The function ϕ is called a *response surface*. A special case of (1-1) is the simple linear model

$$Y = \sum_{i=1}^{k} \theta_i X_i \tag{1-2}$$

where the θ_i's are parameters. If experimentation were possible, one could vary the $\mathbf{X}$, observe Y, determine the estimates of the parameters $\boldsymbol{\theta}$, and then interpret the fitted model

$$\hat{Y} = \sum_{i=1}^{k} \hat{\theta}_i X_i \tag{1-3}$$

where $\hat{\theta}_i$ and $\hat{Y}$ denote estimates of θ_i and Y, respectively.

Unfortunately, it is frequently impossible or impractical to perform controlled experiments with business and economic systems. However, it may be possible to perform a type of quasi experiment with a model of the system through the use of computer simulation techniques. In our example, if experimentation were impossible, the response could be simulated by varying either, or both, the $\boldsymbol{\theta}$ and $\mathbf{X}$.

The additive model (1-3) that we have proposed is altogether too simple to be analyzed with simulation techniques. That is, it could probably be solved by straightforward analytical techniques and would not require the use of numerical analysis or simulation. To make the model more realistic, we might add a random variable ϵ and rewrite the model as

$$Y = \sum_{i=1}^{k} \theta_i X_i + \epsilon \tag{1-4}$$

where the probability density function of ϵ is given by $f(\epsilon, \mathbf{\mu})$ and $\mathbf{\mu}$ represents the parameters of the distribution. To introduce further realism (and complexity), transformations $g(Y)$ and $h(X_i)$ on the response or on one or more of the $\mathbf{X}$ could be included in the model. Some of these transformations might involve nonlinearities as well as additional parameters. Additional random variables γ_j, each entering with its own weight β_j and each with its own distribution and parameters $\psi(\gamma_j, \mathbf{\mu}_j)$, also could be introduced into the model. A time dependence, denoted by the subscript t, could also be employed. In general, the model would then be specified as follows:

$$g(Y_t) = \sum_{i=1}^{k} \theta_i h(X_{it}) + \sum_{j=1}^{m} \beta_j \psi(\gamma_{jt}, \mathbf{u}_j) + f(\epsilon, \mathbf{u}) \tag{1-5}$$

Dummy variables δ_{ijt}, consisting of ones and zeros, could be used to represent the presence or absence of certain variables at certain times, and to identify blocks of variables that are used together. Constraints may also be imposed on the variables and parameters of the model. Dynamic feedback mechanisms may be built into the model by letting Y_t be a function of $Y_{t-1}, Y_{t-2}, \ldots, Y_{t-n}$. Finally, we might modify the additivity aspects of the model or might introduce other response variables, thus, converting the model into a multiple response model. Clearly, at this point we would have a model that cannot be solved by analytical techniques. Then we would have to resort to simulation as a mode of analysis.

In summary, a model that lends itself to analysis by simulation is characterized by the following.

1. Many variables $\mathbf{X}$, and their functions.
2. Random variables γ and ϵ and their distributions.
3. Many parameters θ, β, and $\mathbf{u}$.
4. Many linkages δ between elements of the model.
5. Nonlinearities.
6. Assorted constraints.
7. A response (or responses) that may or may not have a time path.

There is one other characteristic of a simulation model that should be mentioned—a computer is usually an essential adjunct.

There are several key words in the definition of simulation which was set forth at the beginning of this section.

First, the fact that simulation is a *numerical technique* implies that it is a technique of "last resort" to be used only when analytical techniques are not available for obtaining solutions to a given model. Being a technique of last resort by no means implies that simulation will be of limited usefulness in management science and economics, since it is well known that only a small number of problems in the social sciences give rise to mathematical models for which standard analytical techniques exist for finding solutions. For example, although classical optimization techniques and mathematical programming techniques indeed, are powerful analytical tools, the number of real world problems that can be formulated in a manner consistent with the assumptions underlying these techniques is relatively small. In macroeconomics, if we are fortunate enough to be able to represent the actual economic system in terms of a set of simultaneous linear difference or differential equations, then analytical techniques exist for solving these systems of equations. But, if we are faced with systems of nonlinear difference or differential equations characterized by complex lag structures and the inclusion of random variables, then analytical solutions are out of the question. For many problems in economics and management science, simulation may be the only technique that is available to the analyst. However, in some cases, even if we suspect that an analytical solution may exist to a particular model (although we are not familiar with it), it may be less costly in terms of the time of the analyst and of the computer time to run a simulation. That is, the additional information gained for an analytical solution (if one exists in the first place) may not be sufficient to justify the search time for the analytical technique and the set-up time for implementing it. But having made this statement, we must add that the question of when to use simulation rather than analytical techniques is by no means an easy question to answer. At best, we can only answer the question for specific classes of problems. We shall devote an entire chapter to this question later (Chapter 12).

Second, a computer simulation is an *experiment*. With the advent of the high-speed digital computer, economists and management scientists can now perform controlled, laboratory-like experiments in a manner similar to the one employed by physicists and other physical scientists, only by using a mathematical model programmed into a computer instead of a physical process such as a nuclear reactor. The only difference between a simulation experiment and a "real world" experiment is that, with simulation, the experiment is conducted with a model of the real system rather than with the real system. Since a simulation is an experiment, special consideration should be given to the problems of *experimental design and the analysis of output data*—a point that, too often, has been ignored by economists and management scientists. In this book we place major emphasis on the problems of experimental design and data analysis. Chapter 6 is devoted to problems of experimental design, and Chapters 7, 8, and 9 are concerned with the analysis of output data, generated by computer simulation experiments.

Third, although a *computer* is not a necessary tool for carrying out a simulation experiment with a mathematical model of an economic system, it certainly speeds up the process, eliminating computational drudgery, and reduces the probability of error. For these reasons, we concentrate only on computer simulation experiments. Although it is indeed possible to conduct simulation experiments with models of economic systems on analog computers, the programming flexibility that one gains by using digital computers is sufficient to induce most analysts to restrict themselves to digital computers.

Fourth, with computer simulation we can conduct experiments with our model at a *particular point in time,* or we can conduct experiments over *extended periods of time.* In the former case, the simulation is said to be a *static* or *cross-section* simulation. In the latter case, the simulation is said to be a *dynamic* or *time-series* simulation. A static simulation is achieved by replicating a given simulation run, that is, by changing one or more of the conditions under which the simulation is being conducted. A dynamic simulation results when we simply extend the length of a given simulation run over time without changing any of the conditions under which the simulation is being run. The concept of static and dynamic simulations raises two important questions. First, how many times must a particular simulation experiment be replicated in order to achieve a given level of statistical precision? Second, how long must we run a dynamic simulation so that any statistical inferences that we might make about the behavior of the system will not be influenced by the *initial conditions* or *starting conditions* of the system? These are difficult methodological problems. They are discussed briefly in Chapters 7, 8, and 9, and in more detail in Chapters 10 and 11.

Fifth, most simulation experiments with models of economic systems are stochastic[2] simulations as opposed to a purely deterministic simulation. Models of business and economic systems frequently include *random variables* over which decision makers can exercise little or no control. By including these random or stochastic variables in the model, a simulation experiment can be used to make inferences about the overall behavior of the system of interest that is based on the probability distributions of these random variables. Sometimes the term *Monte Carlo* technique is used as a synonym for stochastic simulation. Deterministic simulations are characterized by the absence of random error, that is, all stochastic variables are suppressed.

WHY SIMULATE

To outline the rationale underlying the use of computer simulation as a vehicle of analysis for models of business and economic systems, we must point out an obvious, but very important, similarity between computer simulation and several standard analytical techniques such as differential

---

[2] The term stochastic implies the presence of a random variable that is distributed over time.

calculus, mathematical programming, and calculus of variations. In general, the principal motivation for using any one of these tools of analysis (with models of economic systems) is the pursuit of scientific knowledge about the behavior of a given economic system. When it is applied to economic systems, the scientific method follows this well-known four-stage procedure: (1) the observation of the system; (2) the formulation of a mathematical model that attempts to explain the observations of the system; (3) the prediction of the behavior of the system on the basis of the model by using mathematical or logical deduction, that is, by obtaining solutions to the model; and (4) the performance of experiments to test the validity of the model.

Computer simulation becomes a relevant tool for analyzing economic systems when it is not plausible to carry out one or more of the four steps of the scientific method. Frequently, with economic systems it is simply impossible, impractical, or uneconomical to conduct controlled experiments. When this is the case, some form of simulation may prove to be an acceptable substitute for the step (or steps) in the scientific method that is causing the difficulty. That is, simulation may permit the possibility of conducting a type of quasi experiment with economic systems.

Considering first the *observation stage* of the scientific method, we find frequently in economics that it is either impossible or extremely costly to observe the actual behavior of an economic system. For example, certain historical data such as sales data, cost data, and production data simply may not exist for a particular business firm. Or data on wages, investment, population, and productivity may be virtually nonexistent in an underdeveloped country. However, in both of these cases we may have sufficient information to formulate "meaningful" hypotheses about the probability distributions of some of these variables over time or about the estimates of their trends over time. We may then use a computer to generate data (pseudo-observations) for the economic system of interest on the basis of the assumed probability distributions or time trends. The pseudo-observations, in turn, may be used by the analyst in formulating, manipulating, and testing models that describe the behavior of the system as a whole. That is, we merely substitute the computer-generated data for the missing actual observations of the economic system. In many cases, this simulated data may prove to be completely adequate, particularly if the model of the economic system under study is sensitive only to large changes in the magnitude of the values of the simulated input data.

To be sure, in the second step of the scientific method, one would want to completely avoid *formulating mathematical models* that describe the behavior of a complex economic system such as a firm, based entirely on simulated data. However, we may be willing to place considerable confidence in models of the firm which have been formulated with the aid of data collected from empirical observations that have been supplemented by simulated data (in the case of missing data), provided that the model is subjected to extensive statistical testing in the fourth step of the scientific method.

However, it is the third step of this method that provides most of the impetus for using computer simulation as a tool of analysis in economics. Even though a mathematical model can be formulated to describe a dynamic economic system operating under conditions of uncertainty, it may not be possible to obtain a solution to the model by standard analytical techniques such as the Lagrangian multiplier method or mathematical programming methods and, in turn, make *predictions* about the behavior of the system. Most of the problems in economics are of such a complex nature that solution techniques do not exist for solving them or, if solution techniques do exist, they may very well exceed the capabilities of our present-day computers. Models used in the development of theories of the business cycle and market behavior both give rise to difficulties of this type. Since the 1930's, economists have relied on solutions to differential and difference equations as the standard analytical techniques for investigating the behavior of business cycles and competitive markets. But as non-linearities, higher-order equations, and stochastic variates are introduced into these models, solutions by straightforward analytical techniques become increasingly difficult, if not impossible. Although it may be conceptually possible to formulate a mathematical model describing the behavior of a dynamic, multiprocess firm operating under uncertainty, present-day mathematics is simply incapable of yielding solutions to a problem of this magnitude. Under these circumstances, economists have almost been forced to turn to numerical analysis or to computer simulation as an alternative mode of analysis.

Computer models . . . can be made as complex and realistic as our theories permit, for analytical solutions to these models are unnecessary. No matter how complicated the formulation of the model, simulation techniques enable us to trace out the consequences of the model. Hence, economic theories can be cast into a precise model without distortion of the meaning embodied in the theories, and the descriptions of the world implied by these theories can be determined.[3]

Finally, it may be either impossible or very costly to perform experiments to *test the validity* of mathematical models that describe the behavior of an economic system. Obviously, this problem is merely a mirror image of the first problem that we discussed regarding the implementation of the

---

[3] Kalman J. Cohen, *Computer Models of the Shoe, Leather, Hide Sequence* (Eaglewood Cliffs, N.J.: Prentice-Hall, Inc., 1960, p. 82).

scientific method. In both cases, there exists a problem of insufficient data. In the first case, data available for the purpose of formulating hypotheses about the system was insufficient. However, in the fourth step of the scientific method, the problem lies in obtaining numerical data to verify the mathematical model and its solution. In fact, the only difference between these two problems is in the use to which the simulated data is to be put. For example, in the first case, we may be interested in simulating next year's sales data to facilitate the *formulation of a mathematical model* describing the behavior of a firm that uses sales data as one of its inputs. However, in the fourth case, we may be interested in simulating next year's sales data for an entirely different reason. That is, simulated data may be used to *test* alternative *hypotheses* concerning the operation of the firm during the forthcoming year. These hypotheses are usually called decision rules. In other words, simulation provides us with a tool for tracing out the effects of alternative decision rules on the behavior of the firm within the confines of a tightly controlled laboratory experiment. Of course, it may be argued that one can do the same thing with more traditional analytical techniques, but with computer simulation we can experiment with more variables, more decision rules, more complex models, and models that more nearly approximate the actual behavior of business firms; and we can do all of these things with speeds that heretofore were unattainable.

Although the principal reason for choosing computer simulation may be its ability to overcome the above-mentioned difficulties in implementing the scientific method, there are several other reasons for using simulation. It should be obvious that most of these additional reasons are not unrelated to our previous discussion. Furthermore, these reasons are by no means intended to be mutually exclusive.

1. Simulation makes it possible to study and experiment with the complex internal interactions of a given system whether it be a firm, an industry, an economy, or some subsystem of one of them.

2. Through simulation, one can study the effects of certain informational, organizational, and environmental changes on the operation of a system by making alterations in the model of the system and by observing the effects of these alterations on the system's behavior.

3. A detailed observation of the system being simulated may lead to a better understanding of the system and to suggestions for improving it, which otherwise would be unobtainable.

4. Simulation can be used as a pedagogical device for teaching both students and practitioners basic skills in theoretical analysis, statistical analysis, and decision making.

5. The experience of designing a computer simulation model may be more valuable than the actual simulation itself. The knowledge obtained in designing a simulation study frequently suggests changes in the system being simulated. The effects of these changes can then be tested via simulation before implementing them on the actual system.

6. Simulation of complex systems can yield valuable insight into which variables are more important than others in the system and how these variables interact.

7. Simulation can be used to experiment with new situations about which we have little or no information, so as to prepare for what may happen.

8. Simulation can serve as a "preservice test" to try out new policies and decision rules for operating a system, before the risk is run of experimenting on the real system.

9. For certain types of stochastic problems the sequence of events may be of particular importance. Information about expected values and moments may not be sufficient to describe the process. In these cases, Monte Carlo methods may be the only satisfactory way of providing the required information.

10. Monte Carlo simulations can be performed to verify analytical solutions.

11. Simulation enables one to study dynamic systems in either real time, compressed time, or expanded time.

12. When new elements are introduced into a system, simulation can be used to anticipate bottlenecks and other problems that may arise in the behavior of the system.

Chapter 2 | Computer Simulation
Experiments with Models of
Economic Systems

METHODOLOGY

Following the definition of computer simulation and our discussion of some of the reasons why one might choose to use this tool to analyze the behavior of complex business and economic systems, we now summarize briefly the methodology of computer simulation.[1]

Computer simulation experiments with models of economic systems usually involve a procedure that consists of these six steps:

1. The formulation of the problem.
2. The formulation of a mathematical model.
3. The formulation of a computer program.
4. Validation.
5. Experimental design.
6. Data analysis.

A description of each of these steps follows.

1. Formulation of the Problem

Not unlike other forms of scientific inquiry, computer simulation experiments should begin with the formulation of a problem or with an explicit statement of the objectives of the experiment, since there is little benefit to be derived from experiments that involve simulation for the sake of simulation. These objectives usually take the form of (1) questions to be answered, (2) hypotheses to be tested, and (3) effects to be estimated.

---

[1] For a comprehensive treatment of the methodology of computer simulation see Thomas H. Naylor, Joseph L. Balintfy, Donald S. Burdick, and Kong Chu, *Computer Simulation Techniques*) N.Y.: John Wiley, 1966).

If the objective of a simulation experiment is to obtain answers to one or more specific questions, then, obviously, one must attempt to specify these questions with a high degree of detail at the outset of the experiment. Among the questions or decision problems that might be solved by computer simulation in economics are the following: What effect will a change in the discount rate by the Federal Reserve Board have on the price level and the rate of unemployment? Will a change in Federal import quotas adversely affect the profitability of a given business firm? What effect will a particular production scheduling rule have on the production costs of the firm? Needless to say, it is not sufficient just to specify the questions that are to be answered by a simulation experiment, but we also must specify objective criteria for evaluating possible answers to these questions. For example, in international trade we must define exactly what we mean by an "optimum" trade policy if we are to expect to recognize such a policy when we are confronted with it. Unless we specify precisely what is meant by a "suitable" answer to a question that has been raised, we cannot hope to achieve meaningful results from computer simulation experiments.

On the other hand, the objective of a simulation experiment may be to test one or more hypotheses about the behavior of a complex economic system. Will a guaranteed annual income affect the rate of unemployment in the United States? Will a decrease in the defense budget lead to a recession? Is there any significant difference in the effects of five alternative advertising policies on the sales of a firm? What effects do population control programs have on economic growth in underdeveloped countries? In each case, the hypotheses to be tested must be stated explicitly, as well as the criteria for "accepting" or "rejecting" them.

Finally, the objective of a simulation may be to estimate the effects of certain changes in the controllable decision variables of an economic system on the endogenous or dependent variables that describe the behavior of the system. For example, we may wish to estimate the effects of alternative monetary and fiscal policies on GNP. Generally, we would want to construct confidence intervals for the parameter estimates of endogenous variables that are generated by simulation experiments, where these output variables represent the results of the use of alternative policies, decision rules, parameters, etc.

2. Formulation of a Mathematical Model

Having formulated our experimental objectives, the next step in the design of a simulation experiment is the formulation of a mathematical model relating the endogenous variables of the system to the controllable variables and exogenous variables of a system. The exogenous variables are assumed to be determined by forces outside the system. Some of the exogenous variables may be random variables; others may be expressed in the form of time trends. As we shall soon observe, the inclusion of random or stochastic variables in a computer model gives rise to a number of unique methodological problems that do not exist with deterministic methods.

One of the first considerations that enters into the formulation of a mathematical model of an economic system is the choice of variables to be included in the model. As a general rule, we encounter little or no difficulty with regard to the endogenous variables of a model because these variables are usually determined at the outset of the experiment when we formulate the objectives of the study. For example, the endogenous variables of a socioeconomic model of a city might include per capita income, employment, the level of education, the crime rate, the age distribution of the population, etc. However, the real difficulty arises in the choice of the input (exogenous and controllable) variables affecting the output variables. Too few input variables may lead to invalid models whereas too many exogenous and decision variables may render computer simulation impossible because of insufficient computer memory or may make computational procedures unnecessarily complicated.

A second major consideration in the formulation of mathematical models is the complexity of the model. On the one hand, it can be argued that business and economic systems are indeed quite complicated and that mathematical models that claim to describe the behavior of these systems also must be complicated necessarily. To a certain extent this is true but, on the other hand, we would not want to go to the extreme of constructing these complex models, regardless of how realistic they may be, as they require an unreasonable amount of computation time. In general, we are interested in formulating mathematical models that yield reasonably accurate descriptions or predictions about the behavior of economic systems while they minimize computational and programming time. The complete interdependence of these characteristics of mathematical models cannot be overemphasized. For example, the number of variables in a model and its complexity are directly related to programming time, computation time, and validity. By altering any one of the characteristics of a model we, in turn, alter all of the other characteristics.

Computer programming time represents a third area of consideration in formulating mathematical models for computer simulation. The amount of time required to write a computer program for generating the time paths for the endogenous variables of a particular mathematical model depends, in part, on the number of variables used in the model and the complexity of the model. If some of the variables used in the model are stochastic in nature, then both programming time and computation time are likely to be increased significantly. The amount of effort one expends in attempting to reduce programming time, of course, must be balanced against the questions of validity and of computational speed. If the costs in terms of realism are not too great, it may even pay the analyst to formulate his model in such a manner that it satisfies the requirements of one of the simulation languages such as SIMSCRIPT II [34], GPSS [30,31,55], DYNAMO [52], or SIMULATE [27]. The gains made in terms of reduced programming time may completely offset the loss in validity that may result from such a modification.

The fourth area of interest in model building is the validity of the model or the amount of "realism" built into it. That is, does the model adequately describe the behavior of the system being simulated in future time periods? Unless the answer to this question is "yes," then the value of our model is reduced considerably, and our simulation experiment becomes merely an exercise in deductive logic.

The fifth and final consideration in formulating a computer simulation model is its compatibility with the type of experiments that are going to be carried out with it. Since our primary objective in formulating mathematical models is to enable us to conduct simulation experiments, thought must be given to the particular type of experimental design features that must be built into our models.

After we have formulated a mathematical model that describes the behavior of an economic system, we then must estimate the values of the parameters of the model and must test the statistical significance of these estimates.

Once we have formulated a model that describes the behavior of our system and have estimated the parameters of the model on the basis of observations taken from the real world, we then must make an initial value judgement concerning the adequacy of our model. That is, we must test the model. Clearly, there is very little to be gained by using an inadequate model to carry out simulation experiments on a computer because we would merely be "simulating our own ignorance."

Among the questions that we may wish to raise at this point in our procedure are the following.

1. Have we included any variables that are not pertinent in the sense that they contribute little to our ability to predict the behavior of the endogenous variables of the system?

2. Have we failed to include one or more exogenous variables that are likely to affect the behavior of the endogenous variables in our system?

3. Have we inaccurately formulated one or more of the functional relationships between the system's output and input variables?

4. Have the estimates of the parameters of the model's operating characteristics or behavioral equations been estimated properly?

5. Are the estimates of the parameters in our model statistically significant?

6. On the basis of hand calculations (since we have not yet formulated a computer program), how do the theoretical values of the endogenous variables of our model compare with the historical or actual values of the endogenous variables?

If, and only if, we can answer all six of these questions satisfactorily should we proceed to step 3 and the formulation of a computer program. Otherwise, we should repeat steps 1 and 2 until we can achieve satisfactory answers to these questions.

3. Formulation of a Computer Program

The formulation of a computer program for the purpose of conducting simulation experiments with a model of a complex system requires that special consideration be given to three activities: (1) the computer program; (2) the data input and starting conditions; and (3) the data generation.

Computer Program

The first step in writing a computer simulation program involves the formulation of a flow chart that outlines the logical sequence of events to be carried out by the computer in generating the time paths of the model's endogenous variables. The importance of flow charting in writing computer programs cannot be overemphasized. Next we must consider the matter of writing the actual computer code that will be used to run our experiments. In general, there are two alternatives available to us. We can either write our program in a general purpose language such as FORTRAN, ALGOL, or PL/I, or we can use a special purpose simulation language such as GPSS/360 [30,31,55], SIMSCRIPT II [34], DYNAMO [52], or SIMU-LATE [27]. The principal advantage of using special purpose simulation languages is that they require less programming time than general purpose compilers. These languages have been written to facilitate the programming of certain types of systems. For example, SIMULATE was designed primarily for simulating large-scale economic systems that have been formulated as econometric models consisting of large sets of equations. On the other hand, GPSS/360 and SIMSCRIPT are particularly well suited for queueing problems. Although we can reduce programming time by using a simulation language, we must usually pay a price for this benefit in terms of reduced flexibility in models and of increased computer running times. Another important advantage of special purpose simulation languages is that they usually provide error-checking techniques that are far superior to the ones provided by FORTRAN, ALGOL, etc. One final consideration in the development of a computer program for a simulation experiment is the kind of output reports that are needed to provide the required information about the behavior of the simulated system. If we use a general purpose language such as FORTRAN, then there will be a minimum number of restrictions imposed on the format of our output reports. However, if we use a special purpose simulation language such as SIMSCRIPT II, then we must adhere to the output format requirements of the language.

Data Input and Starting Conditions

Another aspect of the computer-programming phase of the development of simulation experiments is the matter of input data and starting conditions for the simulation experiments. Since simulation experiments are by their very nature dynamic experiments, a question arises as to what values should be assigned to the model's variables and parameters at the point in time when we begin simulating the system. That is, we must break into the system at some particular point in time. When we do so, what assumptions should we make about the state of the system being simulated? Of course, this question is not easily answered for most systems, and the investigator must usually resort to trial-and-error methods to determine a set of initial conditions for the system which will not lead to biased results in future time periods.

Data Generation

A problem directly related to the one of writing computer simulation programs is the development of numerical techniques (which can be programmed on a computer) for data generation. Data used in computer simulation experiments can either be read into the computer from external sources, such as punched cards and magnetic tapes, or it may be generated internally by special sub-routines. If one or more of the exogenous variables included in our model is a stochastic variable with a known probability distribution, we are confronted with the problem of devising a process of random selection from the given probability distribution; hence, the results of the repetition of this process on a digital computer will give rise to a probability distribution of sampled values that corresponds to the probability distribution of the variable of interest.

In considering stochastic processes that involve either continuous or discrete random variables, we define a function $F(x)$, called the *cumulative distribution* function of x, which denotes the probability that a random variable X takes on the value of x or less. If the random variable is discrete, then x takes on specific values and $F(x)$ is a step function. If $F(x)$ is continuous over the domain of x, it is possible to differentiate this function and to define $f(x) = dF(x)/dx$. The derivative $f(x)$ is called a probability density function. Finally, the cumulative distribution function may be stated mathematically as

$$F(x) = P(X \leq x) = \int_{-\infty}^{x} f(t) \, dt \qquad (2\text{-}1)$$

where $F(x)$ is defined over the range $0 \leq F(x) \leq 1$, and $f(t)$ represents the value of the probability density function of the random variable X when $X = t$.

Uniformly distributed random variables play a major role in the generation of random variables drawn from *other* probability distributions. We shall denote uniform variables by r, when $0 \leq r \leq 1$, and $F(r) = r$. Appendix A contains a survey of methods for generating uniformly distributed random variables on the interval $(0,1)$. These numbers are called pseudorandom numbers because, although they are generated from a completely deterministic recursive formula by a computer, their statistical properties coincide with the statistical properties of numbers generated by an idealized chance device that selects numbers from the unit interval $(0,1)$ independently and with all numbers equally likely. As long as these pseudorandom numbers can pass the set of statistical tests (frequency test, serial test, lagged product test, runs test, gap test ,and so on) implied by an idealized chance device, then these pseudorandom numbers can be treated as "truly" random numbers, even though they are not. Chapter 3 of [42] contains a comprehensive treatment of the theory and methods for generating pseudorandom numbers as well as the statistical tests for randomness.

Since pseudorandom number generators (in the form of subroutines) are available for all computers, we shall not go further into the topic. (See Appendix A for several FORTRAN subroutines for generating pseudorandom numbers.) It will be assumed that the pseudorandom numbers used in the subroutines described in the following pages will be generated by a preprogrammed FORTRAN subroutine. This subroutine can be called by the FORTRAN statement CALL RAND(R).

If we wish to generate random variables, x_i's, from some particular statistical population whose distribution function is given by $f(x)$, we first obtain the cumulative distribution function $F(x)$ (see Figure 2-1). Since $F(x)$ is defined over the range 0 to 1 we can generate uniformly distributed

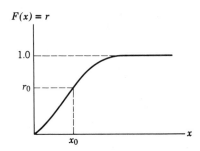

Figure 2-1   A cumulative distribution function.

random numbers and set $F(x) = r$. It is clear that x is uniquely determined by $r = F(x)$. It follows, therefore, that for any particular value of r, say r_0, which we generate, it is possible to find the value of x, in this case x_0, corresponding to r_0 by the inverse function of F if it is known,

$$x_0 = F^{-1}(r_0) \qquad (2\text{-}2)$$

where $F^{-1}(r)$ is the inverse transformation of r on the unit interval into the domain of x. We can summarize this method mathematically by saying that, if we generate uniform random numbers corresponding to a given $F(x)$,

$$r = F(x) = \int_{-\infty}^{x} f(t)\, dt \qquad (2\text{-}3)$$

then

$$P(X \le x) = F(x) = P[r \le F(x)] = P[F^{-1}(r) \le x] \qquad (2\text{-}4)$$

and, consequently, $F^{-1}(r)$ is a variable that has $f(x)$ as its probability density function. This is equivalent to solving (2-3) for x in terms of r. This procedure is called the inverse transformation method.

Perhaps the simplest continuous probability density function is the one that is constant over the interval (a,b) and is zero otherwise. This density function defines what is known as the uniform or rectangular distribution. The principal value of the uniform distribution for simulation techniques is in its simplicity and in the fact that it can be used to generate random variables from numerous other probability distributions.

Mathematically, the uniform density function is defined as follows,

$$f(x) = \begin{cases} \dfrac{1}{b-a}, & a < x < b \\[2mm] 0, & \text{otherwise} \end{cases} \qquad (2\text{-}5)$$

Here X is a random variable defined over the interval (a,b). The graph of the uniform distribution is illustrated in Figure 2-2.

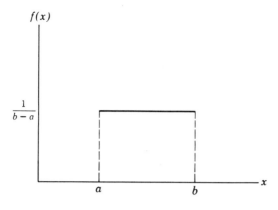

Figure 2-2.

The cumulative distribution function, $F(x)$, for a uniformly distributed random variable X is

$$F(x) = \int_a^x \frac{1}{b-a}\, dt = \frac{x-a}{b-a} \qquad 0 \leq F(x) \leq 1 \qquad (2\text{-}6)$$

To simulate a uniform distribution over some given domain (a,b) we must first obtain the inverse transformation for (2-6), according to (2-2).

$$x = a + (b-a)\, r \qquad 0 \leq r \leq 1 \qquad (2\text{-}7)$$

We then generate a set of pseudorandom numbers corresponding to the range of cumulative probabilities, that is, uniform random variables defined over the range 0 to 1. Each random number r determines uniquely a uniformly distributed variable x.

A graphical explanation will perhaps serve to clarify the issues here. Figure 2-3 illustrates the fact that each generated value of r is associated with one and only one value of x. For example, the specific value of the cumulative distribution function at r_0, fixes the value of x at x_0. Obviously, this procedure may be repeated as many times as one desires, each time generating a new value of x.

Figure 2-4 contains a FORTRAN subroutine for generating a uniform distribution for a given interval (a,b). The first statement in the subroutine is an initialization statement that identifies the particular subroutine as the one called by the main program. The second statement in the subroutine is a library function that causes the variable R to be set equal to a pseudorandom number generated by the subroutine RAND. Each time the subroutine is called, a new value of R will be generated. The variable R is the FORTRAN symbol for r. The third statement in the FORTRAN sub-

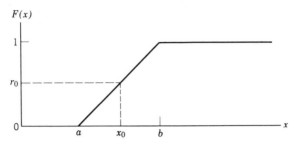

Figure 2-3.

1. SUBROUTINE UNIFRM (A,B,X)
2. CALL RAND (R)
3. X = A + (B-A)*R
4. RETURN

Figure 2-4. Generation of uniform variables FORTRAN subroutine.

routine transforms R from the $(0,1)$ interval to the (a,b) interval by use of FORTRAN arithmetic and (2-7). The fourth statement returns the generated value of X and the program control back to the main program.

Techniques for generating other probability distributions can be derived directly from the procedure described above, for generating uniform variates.[2] For example, the Central Limit Theorem can be used to derive a generator for normally distributed random variables (with given mean and variance) by simply taking the sum of N uniform variables (See [42, Chapter 4]). Below is a FORTRAN subroutine for generating normally distributed random variables X with mean EX and standard deviation STDX.

Techniques for generating χ^2, t, and F distributions can be derived from the previously mentioned procedure for generating normal variables [42].

[2] See Appendix B for a collection of FORTRAN subroutines for generating random variables on a computer.

1. SUBROUTINE NORMAL (EX,STDX,X)
2. SUM = 0.0
3. DO 5 I = 1,12
4. CALL RAND (R)
5. SUM = SUM + R
6. X = STDX* (SUM-6.0) + EX
7. RETURN

Figure 2-5. A FORTRAN subroutine for generating normally distributed random variables.

We conclude this section by describing a somewhat more general method that can be used to simulate: (1) any empirical distribution, (2) any discrete distribution, and (3) any continuous distribution that can be approximated by a discrete distribution. Let X be a discrete random variable with $P(X = b_i) = p_i$. Suppose, for example, that X could be described by the following distribution.

b_i	$P(X = b_i) = p_i$
b_1	0.273
b_2	0.037
b_3	0.195
b_4	0.009
b_5	0.124
b_6	0.058
b_7	0.062
b_8	0.151
b_9	0.047
b_{10}	0.044

In memory locations 1–1000 of the computer store 273 b_1's, 37 b_2's, 195 b_3's, . . . , 44 b_{10}'s. Then generate a 3-digit, uniform random number $r = d_1d_2d_3$ where $0 \le r \le 1000$. The number in location r will be the value of x. This process may be repeated for as many times as is required.

Appendix B contains FORTRAN subroutines for generating random variables from the following distributions: exponential, gamma, multivariate normal, Pascal, binomial, hypergeometric, and Poisson.

4. Validation

The problem of validating simulation models is indeed a difficult one, because it involves a host of practical, theoretical, statistical, and even philosophical [44] complexities. Validation of simulation experiments is merely part of a more general problem, namely, the validation of any kind of model or hypothesis. The basic questions are: What does it mean to validate a hypothesis? What criteria should be used to establish the validity of a hypothesis?

In general, two tests seem appropriate for validating simulation models. First, how well do the simulated values of the endogenous or output variables compare with known historical data, if historical data are available? Second, how accurate are the simulation model's predictions of the behavior of the actual system in future time periods?

We view computer simulation methods as a form of the scientific method, and like Reichenbach we take the position that the scientific method represents a "functional concept of knowledge, which regards knowledge as an instrument of prediction" [53, p. 252]. Yet we do not consider either computer simulation techniques or the scientific method as a means of achieving complete certainty in forecasting because the foundation on which they both rest is probability theory not "truth."

The concept of posit is the key to the understanding of predictive knowledge. A statement about the future cannot be uttered with the claim that it is true; we can always imagine that the contrary will happen, and we have no guarantee that future experience will not present to us as real what is imagination today. This very fact is the rock on which every rationalist interpretation of knowledge has been wrecked. A prediction of future experiences can be uttered only in the sense of a trial; we take its possible falsehood into account, and if the prediction turns out to be wrong, we are ready for another trial. The method of trial and error is the only existing instrument of prediction. A predictive statement is a posit; instead of knowing its truth we know only its rating, which is measured in terms of probability [53, p. 241].

What are some of the practical considerations that one faces in validating computer simulation models? We must define meaningful criteria to indicate when the time paths generated by a computer simulation agree sufficiently with the actual or the observed time paths so that agreement cannot be attributed merely to chance. In Chapter 5, we shall consider specific measures and techniques for testing the "goodness of fit" of a simulation model, that is, the degree of conformity of simulated time series to observed data. An interesting reference on the validation of computer simulation models is the paper by Richard Van Horn [58].

5. Experimental Design[3]

In a computer simulation experiment, as in any experiment, careful attention should be given to the problem of experimental design. Our objective in this section and in the following one is to show the relationship between existing experimental design and data analysis techniques and the design of computer simulation experiments with models of economic systems. Chapter 6 treats the problem of experimental design in much greater detail. Then in Chapters 7, 8, and 9 we discuss the relevance of three specific data analysis techniques to the analysis of data generated by simulation experiments. The reader may also wish to consult the papers by Hunter and Naylor [41], Smith [56], Gupta [22], Chernoff [10], and Watts [61] in the book entitled *The Design of Computer Simulation Experiments* [41].

[3] This section and the following section are based on two papers by Donald S. Burdick and Thomas H. Naylor [6,43].

Before we consider a number of specific experimental design problems, it is appropriate that we define several terms.

The two most important terms in the language of experimental design are *factor* and *response*. Both terms refer to variables. Whether a variable in a particular experiment is a factor or a response depends on the role played by the variable in the experiment in question. To illustrate the difference between a factor and a response, suppose that we have two variables, X and Y. If our experiment is designed to answer the question of how a change in X affects Y, then X is a factor and Y is a response. In an experiment with a computer model of an economic system, a response must of necessity be an endogenous (output) variable, whereas a factor will normally be an exogenous or policy (input) variable.

For example, with a computer model of a firm profit, output or utility might be response variables. On the other hand, advertising expenditures, labor inputs, capital outlays, GNP, and per capita income might be treated as factors.

A large percentage of the terms and concepts in the theory of experimental design results from the classification of the factors in the experiment by the following dichotomous questions.

1. Is the factor in question controlled or not?
2. Are the values (levels) of the factor observed or not?
3. Is the effect of the factor a subject for study or is the factor included merely to increase the precision of the experiment?
4. Are the levels of the factor quantitative or qualitative?
5. Is the factor fixed or random?

A factor is *controlled* if its levels are purposefully selected by the experimenter. In the case of economic models, the experimenter is usually called a policy maker or a decision maker. Again, using the business firm as an example, production scheduling rules and inventory control policies are subject to the control of managerial decision makers. Wars, foreign competition, labor strikes, and national disasters are factors that affect the firm but that may not be controllable by the firm's policy makers.

A factor is *observed* if its levels are observed or measured and recorded as part of the data. More often than not the observed factors consist of just the controlled factors in a particular experiment, but there are frequent exceptions. It is unwise to control a factor without observing it, but an uncontrolled factor may often be observed. For the firm, wars and strikes, although uncontrolled, can be observed. Observations on uncontrolled factors are often called *concomitant* observations. In the analysis of data the concomitant observations should be treated differently from the observations on controlled factors. The *analysis of covariance* is a technique of data analysis that utilizes concomitant observations. Although concomitant observations are useful, in the real world it is never possible to observe *all* the factors that might affect a given response.

The distinction between factors that are of basic interest and the ones that are included to increase precision is an important distinction, since it emphasizes the fact that, for almost all experiments, the factors of basic interest are not the only ones to significantly affect the outcome. In the literature the controlled factors that are included to increase precision are often called block factors, and their levels are called blocks. In simulation experiments one never has uncontrolled or unobserved factors. The role that uncontrolled and unobserved factors play in the real world is played in a computer simulation model by the random character of exogenous variables. The effects or variations in response that these factors cause in the real world have been incorporated in the computer simulation model in the form of experimental errors or random deviations. Once we have a model, the factors are determined, and it is not possible in an experiment on the model to identify additional factors as sources of variation.

A factor is *quantitative* if its levels are numbers that are expected to have a meaningful relationship with the response. Otherwise, a factor is *qualitative*. The amount of money spent on advertising and the size of the work force might be among the quantitative factors for a model of the firm. If part of the input to a simulation model consists of a decision rule or policy, and if several policies are under consideration, the policy could be a qualitative factor.

When an experimenter is investigating the effect of a factor on a response, he will be interested in drawing inferences with respect to a certain range or population of levels for the factors. If all the levels of interest of a particular factor are included in the experiment, that factor is said to be *fixed*. If, however, the levels of a factor that actually are included in the experiment constitute a random (or representative) sample from the population of levels in which the experimenter is interested, then the factor is said to be *random*. The notion of random factors permits inferences of a probabilistic nature to be made about factor levels that do not actually appear in the experiment.

Next we describe four problems that arise in the design of simulation experiments and identify some of the techniques that have been developed to solve them. The four experimental design problems include: (1) the problem of stochastic convergence, (2) the problem of size, (3) the problem of motive, and (4) the multiple response problem.

(1) The Problem of Stochastic Convergence

Most simulation experiments are intended to yield information about population quantities or averages, for example, the average level of income in the case of a model of the economy of the United States. As estimates of population averages, the sample averages we compute from several runs on a computer will be subject to random fluctuations and will not be exactly equal to the population averages. However, the larger the sample (that is, the more runs we observe), the greater the probability that the sample averages will be very close to the population averages. The convergence of sample averages for increasing sample size is called *stochastic convergence*.

The problem of stochastic convergence is that it is slow. A measure of the amount of random fluctuation inherent in a chance quantity is its standard deviation. If σ is the standard deviation of a single observation, then the standard deviation of the average of n observations is $\sigma/\sqrt{n}$. Thus, in order to halve the random error, one must quadruple the sample size n; to decrease the random error by a factor ten, one must increase the sample size by a factor of one hundred. It can easily happen that a reasonably small random error requires an unreasonably large sample size.

The slowness of stochastic convergence causes us to seek methods other than increasing sample size to reduce random error. In real world experiments the error reduction techniques usually involve including factors such as blocks or concomitant variables that are not of basic interest to the experimenter. If some of these factors, instead of being uncontrolled and unobserved, can be controlled or observed, then their effects will no longer contribute to the random error, and the standard deviation σ of a single observation will be reduced.

In a computer simulation experiment on a given model it is not possible to include more factors for error reduction purposes. The inclusion of more factors requires a change in the model. Once the model has been specified, all the uncontrolled factors have been irretrievably absorbed in the probabilistic specification for the exogenous inputs.

There are, however, error reduction techniques that are suitable for computer simulation experiments. They are called Monte Carlo techniques. The underlying principle of Monte Carlo techniques is the utilization of knowledge about the structure of the model, the properties of the probability distributions of the exogenous inputs, and the properties of the observed variates actually used for inputs to increase the precision (that is, reduce random error) in the measurement of averages for the response variables.

Hammersley and Handscomb [23] have written an excellent book on Monte Carlo techniques. Some of the techniques they discuss are importance sampling, control variates, correlation (that is, regression methods and antithetic-variate methods), and conditional Monte Carlo. The book also contains an extensive bibliography.

In Chapter 10, we describe four Monte Carlo techniques in detail: (1) regression sampling, (2) antithetic-variate sampling, (3) stratified sampling, and (4) importance sampling. We apply each of these techniques to an example model and compare the simulation results.

See also the papers by Handscomb and Kleijnen in [41].

② *The Problem of Size*

What we have called the problem of size arises in both real world and simulation experiments. It could as easily be called "the problem of too many factors." In a factorial design for several factors the number of cells required is the product of the number of levels for each of the factors in the experiment. Thus, in a four-factor experiment with a model of a firm, if we have 6 different employment policies, 5 alternative marketing plans, 5 possible inventory policies, and 10 different equipment replacement policies, then a total of $6 \times 5 \times 5 \times 10 = 1500$ cells (or factor combinations) would be required for a full factorial design. If we had a ten-factor experiment and if we only used two levels for each of these factors the full factorial experiment would require $2^{10} = 1024$ cells. Clearly, the full design can require an unmanageably large number of cells if more than a few factors are to be investigated.

If we require a complete investigation of the factors in the experiment (including main effects and interactions of all orders)[4] then there is no solution to the problem of size. If, however, we are willing to settle for a less than complete investigation (perhaps, including main effects and two-factor interactions), then there are designs that will accomplish our purpose and that require fewer cells than the full factorial. Fractional factorial designs, including Latin square and Greco-Latin square designs, are examples of designs that require only a fraction of the cells required by the full factorial design. More will be said about fractional factorial designs in Chapter 6. Three references on this topic are the book by Cochran and Cox [11] and the papers by Hunter and Naylor [41] and Overholt [49].

Thus far the problem of size reduction has been discussed in an analysis of variance framework. This collection of techniques for data analysis (that is, the analysis of variance) is appropriate when the factors are qualitative. However, if the factors $X_1, X_2, \ldots, X_k$ are quantitative, and the response Y is related to the factors by some mathematical function f, then regression analysis, rather than the analysis of variance, may be an appropriate method of data analysis. The functional relationship $Y = f(X_1, \ldots, X_k)$ between the response and the quantitative factors is called the *response surface* [4,5,7,8,25,26,29]. Least squares regression analysis is a

---

[4] The terms "main effect" and "interaction" will be defined when we discuss the analysis of variance later in this chapter.

method for fitting a response surface to observed data in such a way as to minimize the sum of squared deviations of the observed responses from the value predicted from the fitted response surface.

For an experiment that uses regression analysis to explore a response surface, a factorial design or a fractional factorial design may not be optimal. Several authors, primarily George Box, have developed designs called *response surface* designs that are appropriate when response surface exploration via regression analysis is the aim of the experiment. An important advantage of the response surface designs in comparison with comparable factorial designs is the reduction in the required size of the experiment without a corresponding reduction in the amount of information obtained.

Response surface designs have not received the attention they deserve in most of the books on experimental design. An exception is Chapter 8A in the second edition of the book by Cochran and Cox [11]. The recent paper by Hill and W. G. Hunter [26] contains a survey of response surface designs and a complete bibliography. Response surface designs were used by Hufschmidt [29] to design a computer simulation experiment with a model of a water-resource system.

In Chapter 6, we consider the use of response surface designs with an example inventory model. The two papers by Burdick and Naylor [7,8] on the use of response surface designs with simulation experiments and the paper by Herzberg and Cox [25] will be helpful to the reader.

③ *The Problem of Motive*

The experimenter should specify his objectives as precisely as possible to facilitate the choice of a design that will best satisfy his objectives. Two important types of experimental objectives can be identified: (1) the experimenter wishes to find the combination of factor levels at which the response variable is maximized (or minimized) in order to optimize some process, (2) the experimenter wishes to make a rather general investigation of the relationship of the response to the factors in order to determine the underlying mechanisms governing the process under study. The distinction between these two aims is less important when the factors are qualitative than it is when the factors are quantitative. Unless certain interactions can be assumed to be zero, the only way to find the combination of levels of qualitative factors that will produce an optimum response is to measure the response at all combinations of factor levels (that is, the full factorial design). Even if interactions are assumed neglibible in an experiment with qualitative factors, the design is likely to be the same whether the aim is to optimize or to explore.

In an experiment with quantitative factors the picture is quite different. Hence, the continuity of the response surface can usually be used to guide us quickly and efficiently to a determination of the optimum combination of factor levels. There are two generally used sampling methods for finding the optimum of a response surface: systematic sampling and random sampling. Systematic sampling methods include: (1) the uniform-grid or factorial method, (2) the single-factor method, (3) the method of marginal analysis, and (4) the method of steepest ascent. The article by Hufschmidt [29] contains a case study that involves the use of both systematic and random sampling methods for the design of a simulation experiment. A detailed description of several of these methods can be found in Cochran and Cox [11].

When the general exploration of a response surface is the aim, it is difficult to identify a "best" experimental design because general exploration is usually a less precisely specified goal than optimization. However, we can state a guiding principle: when the aim of an experiment is to further general knowledge and understanding, it is important to give careful and precise consideration to the existing state of knowledge and to the questions and uncertainties on which we desire the experimental data to shed light.

④ The Multiple Response Problem

This problem arises when we wish to observe many different response variables in a given experiment. The multiple response problem occurs frequently in computer simulation experiments with economic systems. For example, salary, security, status, power, prestige, social service, and professional excellence, to mention only a few, might all be treated as response variables in a simulation experiment with a model of an organization.

Often, it is possible to bypass the multiple response problem by treating an experiment with many responses as many experiments, each with a single response. Or several responses could be combined (for example, by addition) and treated as a single response. However, it is not always possible to bypass the multiple response problem; often multiple responses are inherent to the situation under study. Unfortunately, experimental design techniques for multiple response experiments are virtually nonexistent.

Any attempt to solve the multiple response program is likely to require the use of utility theory. Gary Fromm [19,20] has taken an initial step in this direction by using utility theory to evaluate the results of policy simulation experiments with the Brookings Model. The specific problem with which Fromm was confronted was how to choose among alternative economic policies that affect a large number of different response variables in many different ways. He treated utility as a response variable and developed a discounted utility function over time that depends on the values of the endogenous variables of the model, as well as on the mean, variance, skewness, and kurtosis of these variables.

6. Data Analysis

In a well-designed experiment, consideration must be given to methods of analyzing the data once it is obtained. Most of the classical experimental design techniques described in the literature are used in the expectation that the data will be analyzed by one or both of the following two methods: analysis of variance and regression analysis. The analysis of variance is a collection of techniques for data analysis that are appropriate when qualitative factors are present, although quantitative factors are not excluded. Regression analysis is a collection of techniques for data analysis that uses the numerical properties of the levels of quantitative factors. From a mathematical point of view the distinction between regression analysis and the analysis of variance is somewhat artificial. For example, an analysis of variance can be performed as a regression analysis by using dummy variables that can assume only the values zero or one. An excellent treatise on the application of regression analysis has been written by Draper and Smith [15]. The paper by Smith [56] contains a useful comparison of the analysis of variance and regression analysis as tools for analyzing the data from simulation experiments.

The great bulk of experimental design techniques described in the literature have the analysis of variance as the intended method of data analysis. As an illustration of the analysis of variance, let us consider a computer simulation experiment with a national income model in which monetary policy and fiscal policy are qualitative factors, and national income is the response variable. Suppose that there are six monetary policies and six fiscal policies under consideration. The monetary policies are denoted by $M(1), \ldots, M(6)$ and the fiscal policies by $F(1), \ldots, F(6)$. In other words, the monetary policy and fiscal policy factors have six levels each. A basic experimental design calls for the collection of data (generated by the computer) for each of the six monetary policies in combination with each of the six fiscal policies. This basic design is called the factorial design for two factors. It is customary to present this design in a two-way table as in Figure 2-6.

Each one of the 36 cells or boxes in Figure 2-6, corresponding to the 36 combinations of monetary policies with fiscal policies, represents a population of possible observations. For example, if monthly national income is

Monetary Policy	Fiscal Policy					
	F(1)	F(2)	F(3)	F(4)	F(5)	F(6)
M(1)						
M(2)						
M(3)						
M(4)						
M(5)						
M(6)						

Figure 2-6.   Layout for two-factor factorial design.

the response variable, we might imagine a population of monthly national income data for all months during which fiscal policy F(4) might conceivably be used with monetary policy M(2). Of course, the actual experimental data will contain only a sample (for example, 24 months' data from this population).

If we are interested in investigating the effects of the factors on the response, a logical first question to ask is: Do the factors have any effect at all on the response? The statement that the factors have no effect is a statement about the 36 populations in the experiment. It says that these 36 populations are all the same. Therefore, we can rephrase our logical first question to: Do the (36) populations of our experiment differ, or are they all the same?

We still may not have the question we really want to ask of the data. There are many ways in which populations can vary, and we usually are not interested in all of these ways. The population mean is an aspect of populations in which we are likely to be interested. A more suitable question might be: Do the means of the (36) populations of our experiment differ, or are they all the same? The analysis of variance is a tool for answering this question.

To answer questions about means of populations, one can and usually does look at means of random samples from these populations. However, one cannot conclude that population means differ simply by observing that the corresponding sample means differ. The random character of sample means makes it virtually certain that two sample means will differ even when the corresponding population means are the same. To infer that the population means differ, we must first measure the magnitude of random fluctuations. This measurement is obtained from the variation between observations in the same sample or cell (the within-cell variance). If the population means, in fact, are equal, then these limits will seldom be exceeded by the sample means of the cells. Therefore, if our data shows that these limits are exceeded, we can infer that the population means are probably different. This type of inference, established by comparing between-cell variance to within-cell variance, is the essence of the analysis of variance.

Of course, it is not enough to state that the factors *in toto* affect the response. We are very much interested in identifying and in measuring the effects that individual factors have on the response. For example, suppose that the population means for all the cells in any one column are the same but that the population means differ from column to column. In our example, if columns represent fiscal policies, as in Figure 2-6, this would mean that different monetary policies in combination with the same fiscal policy would result in the same national income, but that different fiscal policies yield different national incomes. In this case, we would say that the fiscal policy factor affects the response but that the monetary policy factor does not.

To separate the effects due to the two factors, it is customary to consider row and column means. In our example, a row mean would be the average national income associated with a particular monetary policy (row) when used with all six fiscal policies (columns). A column mean would be the average national income associated with a particular fiscal policy and all six monetary policies.

We have reached a point from which it is difficult to continue without introducing some notation. Let $\overline{Y}_{ij}$ denote the average national income associated with monetary policy i when combined with fiscal policy j. Let $\overline{Y}_{i.}$ denote the average national income associated with monetary policy i in combination with all six fiscal policies (the ith row mean), and let $\overline{Y}_{.j}$ denote the average national income associated with fiscal policy j for all six monetary policies (the jth column mean). The average for all 36 cells, $\overline{Y}_{..}$, is called the grand mean.

The *main effect* for a particular row (or column) is defined to be the deviation of the corresponding row (or column) mean from the grand mean. Thus, the main effect for monetary policy i is $\overline{Y}_{i.} - \overline{Y}_{..}$, and the main effect for fiscal policy j is $\overline{Y}_{.j} - \overline{Y}_{..}$. Suppose, as suggested above, that for any one fiscal policy the average national income for each of the six monetary policies is the same. If the means are the same for the six monetary policies in combination with any one fiscal policy, they will be the same for the six monetary policies when averaged over fiscal policies. Therefore, we shall have $\overline{Y}_{1.} = \overline{Y}_{2.} = \overline{Y}_{3.} = \overline{Y}_{4.} = \overline{Y}_{5.} = \overline{Y}_{6.}$. Since all row means are equal, they will also be equal to their average $\overline{Y}_{..}$, the grand mean and, therefore, $\overline{Y}_{i.} - \overline{Y}_{..} = 0$ for each i. In other words, the row main effects are all zero. On the other hand, if national income varies from fiscal policy to fiscal policy, the averages over monetary policies will also, and the column means will differ. Since the column means differ, they cannot all be equal to their average, the grand mean; hence, some column mean effects must be nonzero. Thus, by looking at main effects, we can obtain information regarding the relative importance of the factors.

If the main effects told the whole story, then each cell mean could be represented as the sum of the grand mean, a row main effect, and a column main effect [that is, $\overline{Y}_{ij} = \overline{Y}_{..} + (\overline{Y}_{i.} - \overline{Y}_{..}) + (\overline{Y}_{.j} - \overline{Y}_{..})$]. The fact that this is not true in general, can be simply illustrated. Suppose that the even numbered monetary policies result in above average national income when they are used with even-numbered fiscal policies but that they result in below average national income when used with odd-numbered fiscal policies; whereas odd-numbered monetary policies yield above average national income when used with odd-numbered fiscal policies. (This example is admittedly artificial and unrealistic, but it serves well to illustrate the point in question.) Each monetary policy will yield above average national income for half the fiscal policies and below average national income for the other half. Therefore, the national income averaged over fiscal policies will be the same for each monetary policy, and the row main effects will be zero. Similarly, each fiscal policy will yield above average national income for half the monetary policies and below average national income for the other half, which implies that the column main effects are also zero. If the equation $\overline{Y}_{ij} = \overline{Y}_{..} + (\overline{Y}_{i.} - \overline{Y}_{..}) + (\overline{Y}_{.j} - \overline{Y}_{..})$ held true, in general, then each cell mean would have to be equal to the grand mean whenever all main effects are zero. In the example just discussed, however, some cell means are above the grand mean and others are below it, even though all main effects are zero.

The difference between a cell mean and the value predicted from the grand mean and the main effects, given by $\overline{Y}_{ij} - \overline{Y}_{..} - (\overline{Y}_{i.} - \overline{Y}_{..}) - (\overline{Y}_{.j} - \overline{Y}_{..}) = \overline{Y}_{ij} - \overline{Y}_{i.} - \overline{Y}_{.j} + \overline{Y}_{..}$, is called an *interaction effect*. Customarily, we also speak of a *two-factor interaction between the fiscal policy and monetary policy factors*. This terminology is redundant in an experiment involving only two factors. However, in experiments with more than two factors, interactions involving three or more factors can occur, and two-factor interactions can occur between any pair of factors in the experiment.

In the absence of interaction the equation $\overline{Y}_{ij} = \overline{Y}_{..} + (\overline{Y}_{i.} - \overline{Y}_{..}) + (\overline{Y}_{.j} - \overline{Y}_{..})$ will hold true. If the average national income associated with monetary policy i is 3 billion dollars above the overall average, and if the average national income associated with fiscal policy j is 2 billion dollars below the overall average, then, in the absence of interaction, we can predict that the average national income associated with monetary policy i in combination with fiscal policy j will be 3-2 = 1 billion dollars above the overall average. In other words, the performance of monetary policy i *in combination with* fiscal policy j can be predicted from a measurement (that is, main effect) on monetary policy i only and a measurement on fiscal policy j only. Thus, the absence of interaction implies that the factors have a certain kind of independence. This independence is not statistical independence, but an independence in the way in which the factors affect the response. Thus, the absence of interaction means that the effect it has on the response may be studied and measured separately for each of the factors, and these separate or independent determinations may be used to predict the response at any combination of levels for the factors in question. When this independence fails [as it did in the above example, since an average monetary policy in combination with an average fiscal policy could produce an above (or below) average result], then interaction will be present.

The absence of interaction implies even more than independence of the factors. It implies that the effects of the factors are additive. In other words the average national income associated with monetary policy i in combination with fiscal policy j is the *sum* of an overall average, an effect for monetary policy i, and an effect for fiscal policy j. If, instead, the average national income were the *product* of an overall average, an effect for monetary policy i, and an effect for fiscal policy j, then interaction would be present even though the factors retain their independence.

An interaction which is caused by nonadditivity of independent factors can often be removed by a suitable transformation of the data. For example, if effects are multiplicative when output data is used, then additivity can be restored by using logarithms of outputs as the mode of expression for the data.

Many experimenters habitually conclude that the presence of interaction implies that the factors are not independent without giving any consideration to the possibility of independent but nonadditive factors. This practice is inadvisable and should be avoided.

From our consideration of the two-factor example it should be clear that three-factor and higher-order interactions can be defined in a strictly analogous manner (although the algebra becomes increasingly complex).

In the following paragraphs we briefly summarize some of the important features of several special cases of the analysis of variance including: F-test, multiple comparisons, multiple rankings, spectral analysis, sequential sampling, and nonparametric methods. The F-test, multiple comparisons, and multiple ranking procedures will be treated in greater detail in Chapter 7. Sequential sampling and spectral analysis will be the topics of Chapters 8 and 9, respectively.

F-Test

Suppose that we are interested in testing the null hypothesis that the expected value of per capita income associated with each of five economic development policies (for an underdeveloped country) are equal. The F-test is a straightforward procedure for testing hypotheses of this type. If the null hypothesis is accepted in our example experiment, then one tentatively concludes that the sample differences between policies are attributable to random fluctuations rather than to actual differences in population values. On the other hand, if the null hypothesis is rejected, then further analysis, such as multiple comparisons and multiple rankings, is recommended. The F-test rests on three important assumptions: (1) *normality,* (2) *equality of variance,* and (3) *statistical independence.* Chapter 7 contains two different applications of the use of the F-test to analyze data that are generated by simulation experiments. Chapter 14 contains a third application of this technique.

Multiple Comparisons

Typically, social scientists are interested not only in whether alternatives differ but also in *how* they differ. Multiple comparison and multiple ranking procedures often become tools relevant to meeting the latter query, since they have been designed specifically to attack questions of how the means of many populations differ.

In contrast with the analysis of variance, multiple comparison methods [54] emphasize the use of confidence intervals instead of the testing of hypotheses. For example, if one is interested in comparing the means of different populations, then a number of $(100\text{-}\alpha)\%$ confidence intervals for the differences between population means may be constructed. Chapters 7 and 14 contain examples of the application of multiple comparisons to the analysis of data from simulation experiments.

Multiple Rankings

Frequently, the objective of computer simulation experiments with models of business and economic systems is to find the "best," "second best," "third best," etc. alternative. Although multiple comparison methods of estimating the sizes of differences between policies (as measured by population means) are often used as a way of attempting, indirectly, to achieve goals of this type, multiple ranking methods represent a more direct approach to a solution of the ranking problem.

A good estimate of the rank of a set of alternatives is simply the ranking of the sample means associated with the given alternatives. Because of random error, however, sample rankings may yield incorrect results. With what probability can we say that a ranking of sample means represents the true ranking of the population means? It is basically this question that multiple ranking procedures attempt to answer.

Bechhofer, Dunnett, and Sobel [1] have developed a procedure for selecting a single population and of guaranteeing with probability P that the selected population is the best, provided that some other condition on the parameters is satisfied. This procedure assumes normality, statistical independence, and a common *unknown variance*. In Chapter 7, we apply the Bechhofer, Dunnett, and Sobel [1] procedure to a model of a multiprocess firm and to a macroeconomic model of national income. A third example of the use of multiple ranking procedures appears in Chapter 14. For two references on the application of multiple ranking procedures to simulation experiments, see the papers by Gupta [22] and Kleijnen and Naylor [35].

Spectral Analysis

Spectral analysis is a technique that is particularly useful for analyzing time series data which are characterized by the presence of autocorrelation. The information content of spectral analysis is much greater than that of sample means and variances. With spectral analysis it is possible to decompose the total variance of a time series into cyclical components and to assess the importance of cycles of different lengths. Spectral analysis can be used to construct confidence bands to test hypotheses for the purpose of comparing two or more alternative simulation runs. Spectral analysis can also be used as a validation technique. In Chapter 9, we apply spectral analysis to several simulation runs with a macroeconomic model. The paper by Watts [61] is a particularly readable paper on the use of spectral analysis to analyze output data from simulation experiments.

Sequential Sampling

With sequential sampling [59] the sample size n (or number of replications) is treated as a random variable that is dependent on the outcome of the first n-1 observations (replications) of the experiment. Instead of fixing the sample size in advance, with sequential sampling we make one of the following decisions at the end of the ith replication: (1) to accept a given hypothesis, (2) to reject the hypothesis, or (3) to continue sampling, that is, to replicate the experiment one more time. With sequential sampling it is possible to achieve substantial reductions in sample size when compared with conventional fixed sample-size methods. In Chapter 8, we apply several different sequential sampling methods to a multi-item inventory model. Chernoff's papers [9,10] on this topic also will be of interest.

Nonparametric Methods

Another class of data analysis techniques is also available to analyze data from simulation experiments—nonparametric methods. The book by Walsh [60] is an excellent handbook on nonparametric statistical techniques.

BIBLIOGRAPHY

1. Bechhofer, Robert E., Dunnett, C. W., and Sobel, M. "A Two-Sample Multiple Decision Procedure for Ranking Means of Normal Populations with a Common Unknown Variance," *Biometrika*, **XLI** (1954), 170–176.
2. Blackman, R. B., and Tukey, J. W. *The Measurement of Power Spectra.* New York: Dover Publications, Inc., 1958.
3. Bonini, Charles P. *Simulation of Information and Decision Systems in the Firm.* Englewood Cliffs, N. J.: Prentice-Hall, Inc., 1963.
4. Box, G. E. P. "The Exploration and Exploitation of Response Surfaces: Some General Considerations and Examples," *Biometrics*, **X** (1954), 16-60.
5. Box, G. E. P., Wilson, K. B. "On the Experimental Attainment of Optimum Conditions," *Journal of the Royal Statistical Society B*, **XIII** (1951), 1-45.
6. Burdick, Donald S., and Naylor, Thomas H. "Design of Computer Simulation Experiments for Industrial Systems," *Communications of the ACM*, **IX** (May 1966), 329-339.
7. Burdick, Donald S., and Naylor, Thomas H. "Response Surface Techniques in Economics," *Review of the International Statistical Institute*, No. 2 (1969).
8. Burdick, Donald S., and Naylor, Thomas H. "The Use of Response Surface Methods to Design Computer Simulation Experiments with Models of Business and Economic Systems," *The Design of Computer Simulation Experiments*, Thomas H. Naylor (ed), Durham, N. C.: Duke University Press, 1969.
9. Chernoff, Herman. "Sequential Design of Experiments," *Annals of Mathematical Statistics*, **XXX** (September 1959), 755-770.
10. Chernoff, Herman. "Sequential Designs," *The Design of Computer Simulation Experiments*, Thomas H. Naylor (ed). Durham, N.C.: Duke University Press, 1969.
11. Cochran, W. G., and Cox, G. M. *Experimental Designs.* New York: John Wiley & Sons, 1957.
12. Cyert, Richard M. "A Description and Evaluation of Some Firm Simulations," *Proceedings of the IBM Scientific Computing Symposium on Simulation Models and Gaming.* White Plains, N. Y.: IBM, 1966.
13. Cyert, Richard M., and March, James G. *A Behavioral Theory of the Firm.* Englewood Cliffs, N. J.: Prentice-Hall, Inc., 1963.
14. Dahl, O. J., Myhrhaug, B., and Nygaard, K. "Some Features of the SIMULA 67 Language," *Proceedings of the Second Conference on Applications of Simulation*, New York, December 2-4, 1968.

15. Draper, N. R., and Smith H. *Applied Regression Analysis*. New York: John Wiley & Sons, 1966.

16. Evans, Michael. "Computer Simulation of Nonlinear Econometric Models," *The Design of Computer Simulation Experiments*, Thomas H. Naylor (ed), Durham. N. C.: Duke University Press, 1969.

17. Fishman, George S., and Kiviat, Philip J. "The Analysis of Simulation-Generated Time Series," *Management Science*, **XIII** (March 1967), 525-557.

18. "Fractional Factorial Designs for Factors at Two and Three Levels," U. S. Department of Commerce, National Bureau of Standards, *Applied Mathematics Series 58*, U. S. Government Printing Office, Washington 25, D. C. (September 1, 1961).

19. Fromm, Gary. "Utility Theory and the Analysis of Simulation Output Data," *The Design of Computer Simulation Experiments*, Thomas H. Naylor (ed). Durham, N. C.: Duke University Press, 1969.

20. Fromm, Gary, and Taubman, Paul. *Policy Simulations with an Econometric Model*. Washington, D. C.: The Brookings Institute, 1968.

21. Granger, C. W. J., and Hatanaka, M. *Spectral Analysis of Economic Time Series*. Princeton, N. J.: Princeton University Press, 1964.

22. Gupta, S. S. and Panchapapkesan, S. "Multiple Ranking Procedures," *The Design of Computer Simulation Experiments*, Thomas H. Naylor (ed). Durham, N. C.: Duke University Press, 1969.

23. Hammersley, J. M., and Handscomb, D. C. *Monte Carlo Methods*. New York: John Wiley & Sons, 1964.

24. Handscomb, D. C. "Variance Reduction Techniques: Theoretical," *The Design of Computer Simulation Experiments*, Thomas H. Naylor (ed). Durham, N. C.: Duke University Press, 1969.

25. Herzberg, A. M., and Cox, D. R. "Recent Work on the Design of Experiments: A Bibliography and Review," *Journal of the Royal Statistical Society A*, **CXXXII** (1969).

26. Hill, William J., and Hunter, William G. "A Review of Response Surface Methodology: A Literature Survey," *Technometrics*, **VIII** (November 1966), 571-590.

27. Holt, Charles C., *et al. PROGRAM SIMULATE II*, Social Systems Research Institute, Madison, Wisconsin, April, 1967.

28. Howrey, Philip, and Kelejian, H. H. "Computer Simulation Versus Analytical Solutions," *The Design of Computer Simulation Experiments*, Thomas H. Naylor (ed). Durham, N. C.: Duke University Press, 1969.

29. Hufschmidt, M. M. "Analysis of Simulation: Examination of Response Surface," *Design of Water-Resource Systems*, Arthur Maass *et al*. (eds). Cambridge: Harvard University Press, 1966.

30. IBM, *General Purpose Simulation System/360, Application Description*, H20-0186-1, 1966.

31. IBM, *General Purpose Simulation System/360 User's Manual*, H20-0326-2, 1967.

32. Jenkins, G. M. "General Considerations in the Analysis of Spectra," *Technometrics*, **III** (May 1961), 133-166.

33. Kiviat, Philip J. *Digital Computer Simulation: Computer Programming Languages*, The RAND Corporation, RM-5883-PR, Santa Monica, California, January, 1969.

34. Kiviat, P. J., Villanueva, R., and Markowitz, H. M. *The SIMSCRIPT II Programming Language*. Englewood Cliffs, N. J.: Prentice-Hall, Inc., 1968.

35. Kleijnen, Jack P., and Naylor, Thomas H. "The Use of Multiple Ranking Procedures to Analyze Business and Economic Systems," *Proceedings of the American Statistical Association* (August 1969).

36. Krasnow, Howard S. "Simulation Languages: Facilities for Experimentation," *The Design of Computer Simulation Experiments*, Thomas H. Naylor (ed). Durham, N. C.: Duke University Press, 1969.

37. Ling, Timothy Y. "A Statistical Concept of Statics and Dynamics," *The Design of Computer Simulation Experiments*, Thomas H. Naylor (ed). Durham, N. C.: Duke University Press, 1969.

38. Malone, J. M. *SILLY*. Pittsburgh, Pa.: United States Steel Corporation, 1968.

39. Moy, William A. "Variance Reduction Techniques: Practical," *The Design of Computer Simulation Experiments*, Thomas H. Naylor (ed). Durham, N. C.: Duke University Press, 1969.

40. Naylor, Thomas H. "Bibliography on Simulation and Gaming," *Computing Reviews*, (January 1969), 61-69.

41. Naylor, Thomas H. (ed). *The Design of Computer Simulation Experiments*. Durham, N. C.: Duke University Press, 1969.

42. Naylor, Thomas H., Balintfy, Joseph L., Burdick, Donald S., and Chu, Kong. *Computer Simulation Techniques*. New York: John Wiley & Sons, 1966.

43. Naylor, Thomas H., Burdick, Donald S., and Sasser, W. Earl. "Computer Simulation Experiments with Economic Systems: The Problem of Experimental Design," *Journal of the American Statistical Association*, **LXII** (December 1967), 1315-1337.

44. Naylor, Thomas H., and Finger, J. M. "Verification of Computer Simulation Models," *Management Science*, **XIV** (October 1967), 92-101.

45. Naylor, Thomas H., Wallace, William H., and Sasser, W. Earl. "A Computer Simulation Model of the Textile Industry," *Journal of the American Statistical Association*, (December 1967), 1338-1364.

46. Naylor, Thomas H., Wertz, Kenneth, and Wonnacott, Thomas. "Methods for Analyzing Data from Computer Simulation Experiments," *Communications of the ACM*, **X** (November 1967), 703-710.

47. Naylor, Thomas H., Wertz, Kenneth, and Wonnacott, Thomas H. "Some Methods for Evaluating the Effects of Economic Policies Using Simulation Experiments," *Review of the International Statistical Institute*, **XXXVI** (1968), 184-200.

48. Naylor, Thomas H., Wertz, Kenneth, and Wonnacott, Thomas. "Spectral Analysis of Data Generated by Simulation Experiments with Econometric Models," *Econometrica*, **XXXVII** (April 1969), 333-352.

49. Overholt, John L. "Factorial Designs," *The Design of Computer Simulation Experiments*, Thomas H. Naylor (ed). Durham, N. C.: Duke University Press, 1969.

50. Parzen, Emanuel. "Mathematical Considerations in the Estimation of Spectra," *Technometrics*, **III** (May 1961), 167-190.
51. Pritsker, A. A. B., and Kiviat, Philip J. *GASP II: A FORTRAN Based Simulation Language*. Department of Industrial Engineering, Arizona State University, September 1967.
52. Pugh, Alexander L. *DYNAMO User's Manual*. Cambridge, Mass.: The M. I. T. Press, 1963.
53. Reichembach. Hans. *The Rise of Scientific Philosophy*. Berkeley: University of California Press, 1951.
54. Scheffé, Henry. *The Analysis of Variance*. New York: John Wiley & Sons, 1959.
55. Schriber, Thomas J. *General Purpose Simulation System/360: Introductory Concepts and Case Studies*. New York: John Wiley & Sons, 1970.
56. Smith, Harry. "Regression Analysis and Analysis of Variance," *The Design of Computer Simulation Experiments*, Thomas H. Naylor (ed). Durham, N. C.: Duke University Press, 1969.
57. Tukey, John W. "Discussion Emphasizing the Connection Between Analysis of Variance and Spectral Analysis," *Technometrics*, **III** (May 1961), 191-220.
58. Van Horn, Richard. "The Problem of Validation," *The Design of Computer Simulation Experiments*, Thomas H. Naylor (ed). Durham, N. C.: Duke University Press, 1969.
59. Wald, Abraham. *Sequential Analysis*. New York: John Wiley & Sons, 1967.
60. Walsh, John E. *Handbook of Nonparametric Statistics*, I and II. Princeton, N. J.: D. Van Nostrand Co., 1962, 1965.
61. Watts, Donald. "Spectral Analysis," *The Design of Computer Simulation Experiments*, Thomas H. Naylor (ed). Durham, N. C.: Duke University Press, 1969.

Chapter 3 | Management Science Models

INTRODUCTION

In this chapter we survey a number of different types of computer models that have been used in the field of management science. Our objective is not to provide a comprehensive treatment of each type of model but, instead, to provide several examples of the different types of management-science computer models that are presently available.

Before discussing specific models, we briefly summarize some of the properties of computer models in general, We then treat Markov chain models, queueing models, inventory models, production models, financial models, marketing models, corporate models, and management models.

PROPERTIES OF COMPUTER MODELS

Before we describe a number of specific computer models, it is appropriate that we specify exactly what we mean by a computer model. A scientific model can be defined as an abstraction of some real system that can be used for purposes of prediction and control. The purpose of a scientific model is to enable the analyst to determine how one or more changes in aspects of a modeled system may affect other aspects of the system or the system as a whole. To be useful, a scientific model must necessarily embody elements of two conflicting attributes—realism and simplicity. On the one hand, the model should be a reasonably close approximation of the real system and should incorporate most of its important aspects. On the other hand, the model must not be so complex that it is impossible to understand and to manipulate. Unfortunately, realistic models are seldom simple, and simple models are seldom realistic. Since in this book our primary interest in model building is limited to mathematical models, we shall now concentrate on the design of mathematical models for computer simulation instead of continuing this somewhat general treatise on the philosophy of model building.

Mathematical models of business or economic systems consist of four well-defined elements: components, variables, parameters, and functional relationships.

The components of an economic model are, in fact, simply models of the various subsystems of a total economic system. The components of business and economic models tend to vary widely depending on whether the system being simulated is the total economy of a country, an industry, a firm, or some component thereof. For example, major sectors such as the household, business, and government sectors have been used as components in a number of macroeconomic models. Among the models that use major sectors of the economy as components are the Wharton Model [33] and the Brookings Model [29]. The shoe industry and the tobacco industry were used as basic components in simulation studies by Cohen [18] and Vernon et al [88]. The firm has served as a component in the computer models of Bonini [9], Chu and Naylor [14], and Cyert and March [25]. The inventory and production systems of a firm were components in the studies by Dzielinski [30,31,32], Geisler [37,38], Naddor [64], and Muth and Thompson [62].

The variables that appear in business and economic models are used to relate one component to another and can be conveniently classified as endogenous variables, status variables, exogenous variables, and policy (or decision) variables.

Endogenous variables are the dependent or output variables of the system and are generated from the interaction of the system's exogenous and policy variables according to the system's behavioral equations and identities. There must be one equation in the model for every endogenous variable. The endogenous variables for a business firm might include cost, output, sales, and profit. Sometimes it is convenient to classify a special subset of output variables as status variables. Status variables are output variables about which the policy maker has little or no intrest but which must be included to complete the specification of the model. Frequently, status variables are actually intermediate output variables that are needed to calculate final values of the endogenous variables of the system.

Exogenous variables and the policy variables are the independent or input variables of the model. The exogenous variables are assumed to have been predetermined and given independently of the system being modeled. These variables may be treated as though they act on the system but are not acted on by the system. The direction of causality is assumed to flow one way from the exogenous variables to the system.

The policy variables or decision variables are those variables that can be manipulated or controlled by the policy makers or decision makers of the system. The policy variables for the economy of a country might include monetary policy, fiscal policy, and population policy variables. Decision variables for a firm might include the rate of production, the size of the labor force, and the dividend rate.

In the language of experimental design, exogenous and policy variables are classified as *factors*. In conducting computer simulation experiments with a model of a given system, we are concerned with the effects that different levels of the various factors have on the endogenous or *response* variables. That is, a computer simulation experiment consists of a series of computer runs in which we test empirically (using data from the simulation) the effects of alternative factor levels on the values of the response variables.

The functional relationships that describe the interaction of the variables and components of a model of a business or economic system are twofold—identities and behavioral equations. Both identities and behavioral equations are used to generate the behavior of the system. Identities may take the form of either definitions or tautological statements about the components of the model. For the firm, total profit is defined as the difference between total revenue and total cost, and total assets are equal to total liabilities plus net worth. A behavioral relationship is a hypothesis, usually a mathematical equation, relating the system's endogenous and status variables to its exogenous variables. Consumption and investment functions for an economy, demand functions for an industry, and production functions for a firm are examples of equations of economic systems. Behavioral equations for stochastic processes take the form of probability density functions. Unlike components and variables, which can be directly observed from the real system, the parameters of behavioral equations can only be derived on the basis of statistical inference. Moreover, the accuracy of the results of a simulation depend to a great extent on the accuracy of these estimates of the system's parameters.

MARKOV CHAIN MODELS

Perhaps, the simplest example of a computer model that has proved useful in management science is the so-called Markov chain model. A Markov process is a process that can be described by a finite number of different states. At any particular point in time, the process will be in one of M different states. The probability that the process will be in state j $(j = 1, 2, \ldots, M)$ at the end of a particular time period depends only on the state of the process i $(i = 1, 2, \ldots, M)$ at the end of the preceding period. Such a process can be fully described by a transition matrix P whose elements p_{ij} denote the probability of going from state i to state j.

$$P = \begin{bmatrix} p_{11} & p_{12} & \cdots & p_{1M} \\ p_{21} & p_{22} & \cdots & p_{2M} \\ \cdot & \cdot & & \cdot \\ \cdot & \cdot & & \cdot \\ \cdot & \cdot & & \cdot \\ p_{M1} & p_{M2} & \cdots & p_{MM} \end{bmatrix} \tag{3-1}$$

where

$$\sum_{j=1}^{M} p_{ij} = 1 \qquad i = 1,2,\ldots M \tag{3-2}$$

Markov chain models have been used frequently in marketing to simulate the brand preferences of consumers. In this case, the states would correspond to different brand preferences for a particular product.

Galliher [36, p. 237] has developed a very simple technique for simulating a Markov process on a computer which uses the rows of the transition matrix P. If the last state of the process was i, then the next state will be j when

$$\sum_{k=1}^{j-1} p_{ik} < r \le \sum_{k=1}^{j} p_{ik} \tag{3-3}$$

where r is a pseudorandom number on the $(0,1)$ interval. Each pseudorandom number generated will cause a transition from state i to state j.

Figure 3-1 contains a FORTRAN program for generating a Markov process on a computer, where M denotes the number of states, N is the number of transitions or length of the Markov chain required, and I is the arbitrary starting state. The Q matrix is a matrix derived from the P matrix such that it contains the cumulative probabilities in each row. The program prints out the state of the process at the beginning of each period and repeats this procedure N times.

```
1. READ ( ), M, N, I
2. READ ( ), Q
3. DO 9 L = 1, N
4. CALL RAND(R)
5. DO 7 J = 1, M
6. IF (Q(I,J) — R) 7,8,8
7. CONTINUE
8. I = J
9. PRINT ( ), I
10. END
```

Figure 3-1. Simulation of Markov process, FORTAN program.

QUEUEING MODELS

Many industrial systems are characterized by the arrival of some type of input unit to one or more service stations. These inputs may be sales orders, production orders, machine breakdowns, aircraft arriving at an airport, or automobiles arriving at a gas station. Service stations may be a battery of machines (in series or in parallel), stages in a production process, an airport, or a theater ticket booth. In many cases the time interval between inputs and the service time intervals themselves are random variables or, at least, can be assumed to be random.

From the standpoint of economic theory, a queueing problem is essentially a problem in balancing the marginal cost of waiting against the marginal cost of idle time for all service stations in a system. The costs associated with waiting include the loss of customers or potential customers as well as in-process inventory costs such as storage costs, handling costs, depreciation, deterioration, and the opportunity cost of dollars invested in inventory, etc. Idle time costs represent imputed or opportunity costs, that is, the cost of having resources tied up in a nonproductive asset instead of in an asset earning a positive return. Unfortunately, neither economists nor mathematicians have been able to develop straightforward analytical techniques for determining the conditions under which the marginal cost of waiting is equal to the marginal cost of idle time for complex, multichannel, multistation queueing systems.

In this chapter, we describe three different queueing models—a single-channel, single-station model, a single-channel, multistation model, and a multichannel, multistation model. In each case, after defining the model, a computer flow chart of the model is presented in such a manner that the reader can treat the flow chart as a computer subroutine and can perform various experiments with the model, depending on his particular interests.

A Single-Channel, Single-Station Model[1]

The simplest of all possible queueing models is the one that is characterized by a single service station in which units arrive at the service station and are served on a first-come, first-served basis when the station becomes free. The time interval between arrivals and the service time are both assumed to be random variables with given probability distributions.

[1] This model was first published by Kong Chu and Thomas H. Naylor in a paper entitled, "Two Alternative Methods for Simulating Waiting Line Models," *Journal of Industrial Engineering* (November–December 1965). The model was later reproduced in [67].

The variables and equations describing this model are listed below:

ENDOGENOUS VARIABLES

$\overline{WT}$ = the mean waiting time.   (3-4)
$\overline{IDT}$ = the mean idle time.   (3-5)

STATUS VARIABLES

WT_i = the amount of time the ith arrival unit spends waiting to
enter the service station, $i = 1, 2, \ldots, m$.   (3-6)
IDT_i = the amount of time the service station remains idle while
waiting for the ith arrival unit to arrive, $i = 1, 2, \ldots, m$.   (3-7)

EXOGENOUS VARIABLES

AT_i = the time interval between the arrival of the ith unit and
the $(i + 1)$th unit, $i = 1, 2, \ldots, m$.   (3-8)
ST_i = the service time for the ith arrival unit, $i = 1, 2, \ldots, m$.   (3-9)

BEHAVIORAL RELATIONSHIPS

$f(AT)$ = the probability density function for the time interval
between arrivals.   (3-10)
$f(ST)$ = the probability density function for service time.   (3-11)

IDENTITIES

$$\overline{WT} = \sum_{i=1}^{m} WT_i/m = TWT/m \tag{3-12}$$

$$\overline{IDT} = \sum_{i=1}^{m} IDT_i/m = TIDT/m \tag{3-13}$$

Figure 3-2 contains a computer flow chart for our model of a single-channel queueing system. In block 1 of Figure 3-2 arrival time, waiting time, idle time, total waiting time, and total idle time are all set equal to zero, indicating that the first unit has arrived at the service station. A second unit is assumed to arrive at the system, and an arrival time (that is, the time between the arrival of the first and second input units) is generated by the appropriate stochastic subroutine in block 2. Waiting time, which is equal to zero on the first iteration, is subtracted from arrival time in block 3. Next, a service time is generated and compared with the adjusted arrival time recorded in block 3. If service time exceeds arrival time, the second or $(i + 1)$th input unit arrives before service is completed on the first or ith unit. Therefore, waiting time occurs, and idle time is set equal to zero. Waiting time is set equal to the difference between service and arrival time and accumulated in blocks 7 and 8, respectively. On the other hand, if service time is less than arrival time, idle time results, and waiting time is equal to zero. Idle time is then set equal to the difference between arrival time and service time and accumulated. If service time and arrival times are equal, neither waiting time or idle time occur.

This procedure can be repeated for as many arrivals as are required or for as long a period of time as is necessary. For each subsequent iteration, the waiting time of the previous input unit is subtracted from the arrival time before the comparison of arrival time and service time is made. At the end

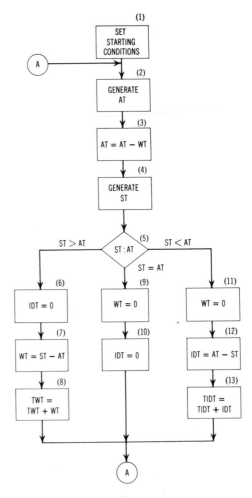

Figure 3-2.   The flow chart for a single-channel, single-station queueing model.

of each simulation run, statistics such as mean waiting time, mean idle time, etc., can be computed and compared with the known theoretical values of these parameters.

To check the validity of our queueing model, experimental runs can be made on the basis of certain special assumptions about the probability distributions of arrival time and service time for which there exist theoretical values for parameters of the system such as expected waiting time, expected idle time, etc. For example, we can show that for the case in which arrival time and service time both have negative exponential distributions with expected values equal to $1/\lambda$ and $1/\mu$, respectively, that the following relationships hold true when $\mu > \lambda$ [81, pp. 131-133]:

$$\frac{\lambda}{\mu(\mu - \lambda)} = \text{expected waiting time.} \tag{3-14}$$

$$(1 - \lambda/\mu) = \text{CLOCK} = \text{expected idle time (CLOCK} = \text{total time).} \tag{3-15}$$

$$\frac{\lambda^2}{\mu(\mu - \lambda)} = \text{expected queue length.} \tag{3-16}$$

$$\frac{\mu}{\mu - \lambda} = \text{expected length of nonempty queues.} \tag{3-17}$$

$$\frac{\lambda}{\mu - \lambda} = \text{expected number of units in the system.} \tag{3-18}$$

$$\frac{1}{\mu - \lambda} = \text{expected waiting time of an arrival that waits.} \tag{3-19}$$

$$\frac{1}{\mu - \lambda} = \text{expected time an arrival spends in the system.} \tag{3-20}$$

$$1 - \lambda/\mu = \text{expected fraction of total time service station is idle.} \tag{3-21}$$

$$\lambda/\mu = \text{expected fraction of total time service station is occupied.} \tag{3-22}$$

$$\left(1 - \frac{\lambda}{\mu}\right)\left(\frac{\lambda}{\mu}\right)^n = \text{probability that there are } n \text{ units in the system, } n \geq 0. \tag{3-23}$$

To say anything about the statistical precision of our estimates of the expected values of the variables mentioned above, we also must estimate the variance of these variables. Estimates of the variance of a simulated random variable can be obtained by replicating the given simulation experiment, using different starting values in the multiplicative congruential random number generators of the model for each replication. In addition, experiments can be performed to test the effects of changes in either the probability distribution, expected value, or variance of arrival times and service times on mean waiting time, mean idle time, etc. We can also experiment with alternative queue disciplines and restrictions on maximum queue length. However, the principal value of this model is its ability to be used as a subroutine in simulating more complex multichannel, multistation queueing systems.

A Single-Channel, Multistation Model

Our second queueing model consists of N different stations in series (see Figure 3-3). An arrival unit must pass through all N stations in the sequence indicated in Figure 3-3 before leaving the system.

A mathematical model of this single-channel, multistation queueing system is described in Chapter 7. A flow chart, FORTRAN program, and simulation output from the model also are included in Chapter 7.

Figure 3-3.   A single-channel, multistation queueing system.

A Multichannel, Multistation Model[2]

Consider a system consisting of n service stations operating in parallel (Figure 3-4). Input units arrive at the system and are admitted to the first vacant service station on a first-come, first-served basis. The time interval between arrivals is a random variable with a known probability distribution. The service time for each of the n service stations is a random variable, with each station having its own given probability distribution for service time.

When an input unit arrives at the system, the n service stations are checked to determine whether any one of them is vacant at the moment. If all n are occupied, then waiting time occurs until one station becomes vacant. When a service station becomes vacant before another unit arrives at the system, idle time occurs until a unit arrives and enters the vacant service station.

[2] This model was developed by Professor Kong Chu and was first published in [15, pp. 154-159].

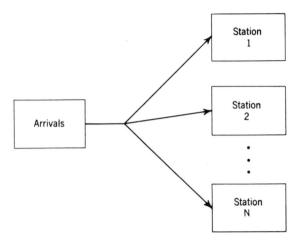

Figure 3-4.   A multichannel, multistation queueing system.

The variables describing this system are identical to the ones used in the first model with the following exceptions:

TAT_i = total arrival time when the ith arrival unit arrives at the system, $i = 1,2, \ldots$.   (3-24)

$T_{ij} = \text{ST}_{ij} + \text{IDT}_{ij}$,

= the time interval between the departure of the $(i - 1)$th unit and the ith unit from the jth service station, $i = 1,2, \ldots$ and $j = 1,2, \ldots, n$.   (3-25)

TT_{ij} = total time that has elapsed at the jth service station when the ith arrival unit departs from the jth service station, $i = 1,2, \ldots,$ and $j = 1,2, \ldots, n$.   (3-26)

SMIN = the minimum $\text{TT}_{i-1,j}$ over all j $(j = 1,2, \ldots, n)$.   (3-27)

When the first unit arrives at the system, these relationships are assumed to hold true:

$$\text{AT}_1 = 0 \tag{3-28}$$

$$\text{IDT}_{1,j} = 0 \qquad j = 1,2, \ldots, n \tag{3-29}$$

$$\text{WT}_{1,j} = 0 \qquad j = 1,2, \ldots, n \tag{3-30}$$

$$\text{TT}_{11} = \text{ST}_{11} \tag{3-31}$$

$$\text{ST}_{1j} = 0 \qquad j = 2, \ldots, n. \tag{3-32}$$

For all subsequent arrivals the following relationships describe the system for that j for which TT_{1ij} is a minimum. If

$$TAT_i > SMIN \qquad i = 1,2, \ldots , \tag{3-33}$$

then

$$IDT_{ij} = TAT_i - SMIN \qquad i = 1,2, \ldots , \tag{3-34}$$

and

$$WT_{ij} = 0 \qquad i = 1,2, \ldots . \tag{3-35}$$

If on the other hand,

$$TAT_i \leq SMIN \qquad i = 1,2, \ldots , \tag{3-36}$$

then

$$WT_{ij} = SMIN - TAT_i \qquad i = 1,2, \ldots , \tag{3-37}$$

and

$$IDT_{ij} = 0 \qquad i = 1,2, \ldots . \tag{3-38}$$

Notice that the subscript i has been used in two different ways in (3-24) to (3-38). In the case of AT_i and TAT_i, the subscript i has been used to denote the sequence of arrivals to the system as a whole. In the case of ST_{ij}, IDT_{ij}, T_{ij}, TT_{ij}, and WT_{ij}, the subscript i has been used to denote the sequence of arrivals at the jth service station.

Figure 3-5 contains a flow chart for simulating a multichannel queueing system. We begin by reading into the computer M (the total number of arrivals to be simulated), N (the number of parallel service stations), the expected value and variance of arrival time, and the expected value and variance of service time for each of the service stations. Next total arrival time and idle time for station 1 are set equal to zero. The DO-loop, which encompasses blocks 3 through 6, generates N-1 additional arrival times, as well as initial idle time values for stations 2 to N. N units must arrive before the possibility exists for waiting time. The initial idle time for the jth station is simply the total arrival time that has been accumulated before a unit is assigned to the jth station.

In the block 7 we indicate that N units have arrived. Next we generate N service times, one for each station. Notice that at this point each station has received only one input unit. In block 9 the total idle time and service time are accumulated for each station according to (3-25) and (3-26).

Blocks 10 through 15 represent a well-known computer subroutine for finding the minimum of a sequence of numbers. In this case, we are interested in finding the minimum value of TT(J), which we call TT(L), where L is the station that becomes vacant first or, equivalently, has the minimum value of TT(J), which we previously defined to be SMIN.

The index I is then incremented by 1, indicating the arrival of a new unit into the system. A check is then made to determine whether M arrivals have been simulated. If I is equal to M, then the simulation has been completed, and the appropriate statistics, such as expected waiting time and idle time, are computed.

However, if I is less than M, a new arrival time is generated and added to the previous total arrival time. Then following (3-33) through (3-38), we take the difference (DIF) between total arrival time for the system and total idle time plus service time for the Lth station, that is, the first vacant station. Depending on whether this difference is negative, zero, or positive, waiting time and idle time are then computed according to the appropriate rule.

Finally, a new service time is generated for the vacant station, and it is added to the updated total time for the Lth station in block 37. The procedure of searching for a vacant station, generating a new arrival time, checking for waiting time or idle time, and generating a new service time is then repeated until a total of M units have arrived.

An analytical solution has been developed for a special case of this model. If we have n service stations, Poisson arrivals with expected arrival rate λ, and exponential service times with expected service rate μ, then the following formulas can be derived for given values of λ, μ, and n [81, pp. 137-138]:

$$\frac{\lambda\mu(\lambda/\mu)^n P_0}{(n-1)!(n\mu-\lambda)^2} = \text{expected queue length,} \tag{3-39}$$

$$\frac{\lambda\mu(\lambda/\mu)^n P_0}{(n-1)!(n\mu-\lambda)^2} + \frac{\lambda}{\mu} = \text{expected number of units in the system,} \tag{3-40}$$

$$\frac{\mu(\lambda/\mu)^n P_0}{(n-1)!(n\mu-\lambda)^2} = \text{expected waiting time of an arrival,} \tag{3-41}$$

$$\frac{\mu(\lambda/\mu)^n P_0}{(n-1)!(n\mu-\lambda)^2} + \frac{1}{\mu} = \text{expected time an arrival spends in the system,} \tag{3-42}$$

where

$P_0 =$ the probability that there are no units in the system at a particular time

$$= \frac{1}{\left[\displaystyle\sum_{k=0}^{n-1} (1/k!)(\lambda/\mu)^k\right] + (1/n!)(\lambda/\mu)^n n\mu/(n\mu-\lambda)}. \tag{3-43}$$

Simulated values of these statistics can be compared with the theoretical values to provide a check on the validity of our computer model.

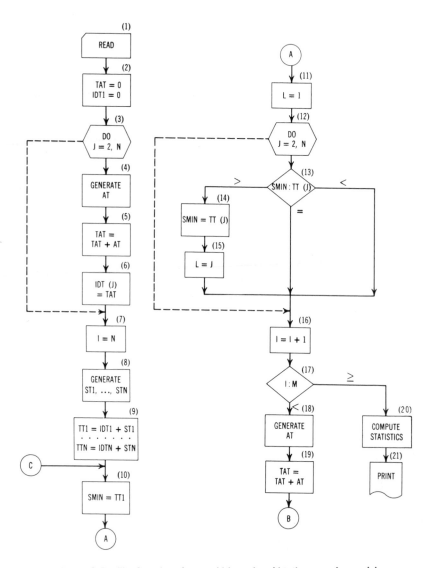

Figure 3-5.   The flow chart for a multichannel, multistation queueing model.

INVENTORY MODELS

A third general classification of industrial systems for which computer simulation has been found to be a useful analytical tool is the area known as inventory systems. Since our objective in this chapter is to present a col-

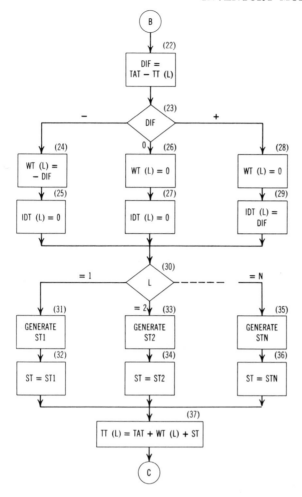

Figure 3-5 (continued).

lection of computer models taken from a number of different applications, we make no attempt to treat the subjects of inventory control and inventory system analysis exhaustively in this section. Instead we have elected to formulate only one model of a particular inventory system. Hopefully, the system chosen for illustrative purposes contains a representative sample of some of the more important elements usually found in inventory systems.

A number of inventory simulation studies have been described in the literature, including the work of Berman [8], Brenner [10,11], Dzielinski, Baker and Manne [30,31,32], Geisler [37,38], Monty [60], Muyen [63], Naddor [64], and Packer [72]. In Chapter 8 we make use of a multi-item inventory model to illustrate the use of sequential sampling techniques.

For the most part, inventory problems are concerned with the determination or order quantities and reorder points. How much should the firm produce (or order) and how often should the firm produce (or reorder) so as to minimize the sum of the following costs?

1. Carrying costs.
2. Set-up costs.
3. Shortage costs.

Consider an inventory system in which daily demand and production lead time (in days) are both random variables with known probability distributions. The inventory level is reduced each day by the total demand for that day. When the inventory level becomes less than or equal to the reorder point (ROP), then a production order is issued for an "optimum" order quantity (EOQ). When a production order is filled, the number of units of the product ordered are added to the inventory stock.

Our inventory system can be described by the following variables and functional relationships.

ENDOGENOUS VARIABLE

TC = total inventory cost.   (3-44)

STATUS VARIABLES

TC1 = total carrying cost.   (3-45)
TC2 = total set-up cost.   (3-46)
TC3 = total shortage cost.   (3-47)
CLOCK = clock time.   (3-48)
T = time at which production order will be filled.   (3-49)
V1 = inventory level.   (3-50)

EXOGENOUS VARIABLES

D_i = daily demand for the ith day, i = 1,2, ...   (3-51)
PLT_j = production lead time (in days) for the ith order,
$\qquad j$ = 1,2, ...   (3-52)

DECISION VARIABLES

EOQ = economic order quantity.   (3-53)
ROP = reorder point.   (3-54)

PARAMETERS

C1 = carrying cost per unit per unit time.   (3-55)
C2 = set-up cost per order.   (3-56)
C3 = shortage cost per unit.   (3-57)
BI = beginning inventory level.   (3-58)
TT = total time period of the simulation run.   (3-59)

BEHAVIORAL RELATIONSHIPS

$f(D)$ = the probability density function for demand.   (3-60)

$f(PLT)$ = the probability density function for lead time.   (3-61)

IDENTITY

$$TC = TC1 + TC2 + TC3. \tag{3-62}$$

Suppose that we are interested in either exploring the effects of alternative values of EOQ and ROP on total cost or in finding the values of EOQ and ROP which will minimize total cost TC. Chapter 6 describes several experimental designs which may prove useful in designing a computer simulation experiment that will achieve either of these objectives. Figure 3-6 contains a computer flow chart for simulating the behavior of our inventory system.

We begin in Figure 3-6 by reading into the computer EOQ, ROP, C1, C2, C3, BI, TT, and the parameters describing the probability density functions of D and PLT. Then we set CLOCK, T, TC1, TC2, TC3, and TC equal to zero. The inventory level is then set equal to the beginning level, and a daily demand is generated by the appropriate subroutine. The CLOCK is incremented by one unit of time (one day). In block 7 a check is made to determine whether or not the computer run has been completed. If clock time exceeds TT, the total time period of the simulation run, then the simulation run will be terminated, total cost TC will be calculated, and the final output report will be printed. If clock time is less than or equal to TT, we check the clock to determine if sufficient time has elapsed for an outstanding production order to be filled. If sufficient time has elapsed, the inventory level is increased by an amount equal to EOQ. If no order has been filled, the inventory is merely reduced by the amount of daily demand.

If the level of inventory becomes negative, a shortage occurs and a shortage cost is computed. When a shortage occurs, the sale is assumed to be lost entirely. (This is just one of many possible assumptions we might make about the nature of shortages.) Hence, the inventory level must be reset to zero in block 15. Total carrying charges are then updated in block 16. If the level of inventory has not fallen to the reorder point level, then a new daily demand is generated in block 5, and the procedure is repeated. But if the inventory level is either less than or equal to the reorder point, we then proceed to block 18, where we check to see if there is an outstanding production order. If a production order remains unfilled then we return to block 5. On the other hand, if there is no outstanding unfilled order at this time, we place a production order in block 19 and update total set-up (order) costs. A lead time is then generated for the new order. The new lead time is then added to clock time indicating when the new order will be filled. We then proceed to block 5 and a new daily demand.

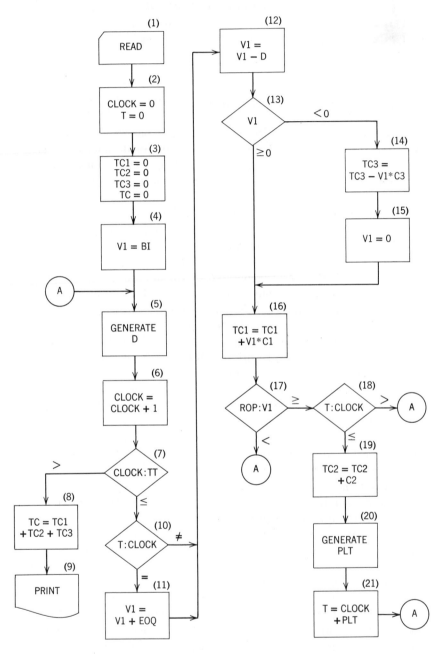

Figure 3-6.   The flow chart for an inventory model.

In addition to experimenting with different values of EOQ and ROP, the two decision variables, the analyst may also be interested in simulating the effects on TC of different values of the parameters C1, C2, C3, and BI. Changes can be made in any combination of these parameters or distributions, and the effects can be observed on total inventory cost, thus providing the analyst with a wide range over which he can experiment with the system.

Under certain assumptions about the distributions of D and PLT it is possible to derive an analytical solution to this model that can be used to check the validity of our simulation results. The book by Manne [55] describes such an analytical procedure.

PRODUCTION MODELS

The term "production scheduling" has been used to describe a wide variety of industrial problems involving decisions on the allocation of manufacturing resources at each instant of time during a given planning period.

Industrial scheduling problems differ greatly from one firm to another. Sometimes the manufacturing process consists of a series of ⚡ operations at one work station on only one physical part; sometimes operations require very different labor skills and equipment on each of many thousands of sub-assemblies. Sometimes inventories of finished goods must be maintained to satisfy customer demands; sometimes such inventories are impossible to keep under all conceivable circumstances. Unique features of the firm's organization, of the market, of plant capabilities are always present [62, p. ix].

Among the more important factors in analyzing production scheduling problems are included the availability of resources (machines, raw materials, and manpower), process times, machine breakdowns, due dates, and demand fluctuations. Any solution to a production scheduling problem necessarily involves a compromise in satisfying the following objectives.

1. To complete all orders on time.

2. To minimize the sum of capital investment expenditures, operating costs, and in-process inventory charges.

3. To achieve an even distribution of workloads among all production facilities and a smooth (as opposed to a fluctuating) production rate.

Production scheduling problems can conveniently be partitioned into three phases: loading, scheduling, and dispatching [76, pp. 103-104].

Loading involves the comparison of demand (measured in production hours) with the capacity of the factory at a given time period. If demand exceeds capacity for a given time period, then standard operating rules cannot be applied to production scheduling. In these cases the firm can either reject the excess demand (that is, not produce or adjust its capacity by working overtime), subcontracting orders to other firms, or extending delivery schedules.

Scheduling involves assigning production orders to specific time periods. That is, specfic orders or jobs are assigned to particular days according to one or more scheduling priority rules. Among the possible scheduling rules that the firm's decision makers might use are the following ones.

1. First-come, first-served.
2. First-come, first served within priority classes.
3. Sequential rule.
4. Minimum imminent processing time.
5. Maximum imminent processing time.
6. Earliest start date [76, p. 118].

The dispatching phase of production scheduling is concerned with the assignment of each order to specific machines or groups of machines at specific times within a given time period. For the multiproduct, multiprocess firm the dispatching phase of production scheduling is, indeed, the most complicated phase. Poor dispatching may lead to extensive waiting times for orders to be processed on particular machines, idle time and excess capacity on other machines, and a failure to meet due dates on some orders.

A special subset of scheduling problems known as the "job shop" problem has been the subject of numerous simulation studies since the early days of computer simulation [48]. The job shop problem, in its simplest form, consists of the random arrival of jobs requiring work to be done in some given sequence by a set of processing facilities. The process times associated with each facility are different and, usually, are assumed to be random variables. Associated with each job is a routing defined on a subset of facilities. The objective is to assign jobs to facilities over time in a manner consistent with the goals of the organization.

The underlying theoretical structure of job shop production systems is basically a queueing model with two or more sequential servers. The usual performance measures of queues such as state probabilities, waiting times, and facility utilization are all relevant to job shops. Typically, job shop simulations are concerned with experiments with various queue disciplines and priority rules as means of optimizing some performance index.

The book by Naylor, Balintfy, Burdick, and Chu [67] contains several computer models of production systems. There is an extensive literature describing particular simulations of job shop problems and production systems. Some of the more interesting references include: Ackerman [2], Baker and Dzielinski [5], Bulkin et al [13], Conway [23,24], Gere [39], Heller [42], Hurst [46], Jackson [48], Muth and Thompson [62], Nelson [69], Pritsker [73,74], Salveson [78], Sandeman [80], Thompson [84], Tonge [86], and Trilling [87].

MARKETING MODELS

Marketing is another area of management science in which simulation has found extensive use. The book by Montgomery and Urban [59] contains an excellent survey of recent management science models in marketing. Since many of the computer models that have been developed for use in the marketing area have focused on consumer behavior and product demand, we briefly describe three models of this type: (1) the Pillsbury Model, (2) the Anheuser-Busch Model [7], and (3) the Corning Glass Model.

The Pillsbury Model

The Pillsbury Company has developed a consumer behavior model to simulate the effects of alternative marketing and promotion strategies on consumer movement and purchasing behavior in various points of sale environments. The exogenous variables and parameters of this model include the demographic characteristics of consumers and retail outlets in various market areas, consumer attitudes toward and awareness of various brands, the characteristics of different products (for example, package type, size, quality, price, etc.), and the inventory level on retail shelves. The decision variables include the marketing strategy, promotional price, discount coupon, type of advertising, retail display, and companion sales. The endogenous variables are total market, market location, and market share. The behavior of each consumer is simulated over a sequence of steps leading to a purchasing decision. The inventory level of each product is updated after each purchasing decision. Simulation runs of up to one year are generated and compared with actual data for the industry and the company.

The Anheuser-Busch Model [7]

Anheuser-Busch has developed a model for forecasting the industry demand for beer. The total industry demand for beer is a function of the per capita consumption of beer and the population of people of drinking age. The logic of the model is outlined in Figure 3-7. The population projections are achieved through the use of conventional demographic projection techniques. Per capita consumption of beer is a function of per capita real disposable income and consumer spending habits. The output of the model is a projection of the annual industry demand for beer.

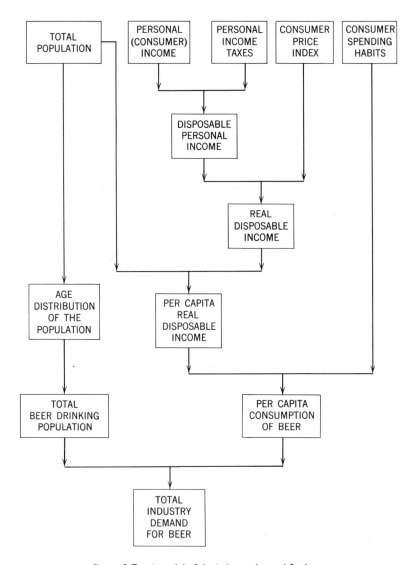

Figure 3-7. A model of the industry demand for beer.

The Corning Glass Model

Corning Glass simulates future sales for black-and-white and color television sets with a simultaneous equation econometric model of the market for television sets. (This type of model is described in more detail in Chapter 4.) Some of the exogenous variables of the model are generated by simulations with the Wharton Model of the United States economy. Management uses the simulation results for intermediate-range planning.

Other Marketing Models

The literature on marketing simulation models is now extensive. The following publications will be of interest to the reader: Amstutz [4], Day [26], Kuehn [50,51], Weiss [89], Weitz [90], and Wells [91].

FINANCIAL MODELS

Finance is another management science area in which simulation has been employed quite extensively in recent years. We shall summarize four different financial models in which simulation has been applied effectively: (1) Clarkson's [16,17] simulation of trust investment, (2) Hertz's [44] model of capital budgeting under risk, (3) Mattessich's [56,57] budgeting model of the firm, and (4) the Sun Oil Corporate Financial Model [40].

The Clarkson Model [16]

One of the earliest examples of the use of simulation in the field of finance was G. P. E. Clarkson's simulation of the investment decisions of a trust officer in a bank. The model simulates the decision processes used by the trust officer in "choosing investment policies for particular accounts, in evaluating the alternatives presented by the market, and in selecting the required portfolios." The behavioral model developed by Clarkson attempts to make use of the same information that is available to the trust officer when he makes his portfolio decisions. The information considered in Clarkson's model includes the following.

Information abounds on the operation of firms and the market valuation of their stocks, and published reports make predictions about the future state of the general economy and the stock market. When an investor acts in an agency or fiduciary capacity, legal restrictions and the desires of the client must also be considered. These factors, when evaluated and combined into an investment program, ultimately result in a decision to buy specific quantities of particular stocks and bonds. Thus, an investor choosing a portfolio is processing information: he sorts the useful from the irrelevant and applies the parts of the total information flow that are most important [25, p. 254] and [16].

The Hertz Model [44]

David Hertz has proposed an interesting approach to investment decisions under risk [44]. To illustrate the Hertz model we use the example of a manufacturing firm taken from [68, pp. 415-417]. The objective is to determine the probability distribution of the present value of a proposal to construct a new plant.

First, the decision maker must select the variables that are important to the present value calculation. For simplicity, suppose that the following three variables are selected: (1) operating cost, OC; (2) share of the market, SM; and (3) market size, MS. Next, the decision maker obtains estimates of these three variables (Table 3-1).

Table 3-1   Estimates of Relevant Variables

	Expected Value	Standard Deviation
Operating Cost, OC	\$ 110,000	\$ 11,000
Share of Market, SM	10%	2%
Market Size, MS	\$2,750,000	\$250,000

For convenience, we express the present value of the proposal in the following general functional form,

$$PV = PV(OC, SM, MS, \ldots) \tag{3-63}$$

where OC, SM, and MS denote the *crucial* variables in the present value calculation and the dots imply that there are other variables that may have some small effect on PV, but they are being ignored.

In addition to assuming that the decision maker knows the expected value and standard deviation of the three crucial variables in the present valuation calculation, Hertz also assumes that the probability density functions of OC, SM, and MS are known. The density functions are shown in Figure 3-8. There are no restrictions imposed on the shape of these density functions. (For the moment, we assume that OC, SM, and MS are independent.)

Hertz then proposes that we generate values for the three random variables OC, SM, and MS on a computer and that we substitute these values

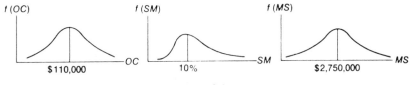

Figure 3-8.

into (3-63) to obtain a single value of PV. By repeating this process, say 1000 times, we can generate an empirical distribution of PV of the type illustrated in Figure 3-9.

Notice that the present value equation (3-63) is likely to be nonlinear in the variables OC, SM, and MS. Thus, the mean of the PV distribution in Figure 3-9 is unlikely to be the same value of PV that would be obtained by simply substituting the expected values from Table 3-1 into (3-63).

Hertz used an internal rate of return criterion in his model instead of the present value criterion that we have used. However, in reporting the results of his example, he observed a rather large difference between the rate calculated with expected values only and the rate determined via simulation.

> . . . management had been informed, on the basis of the "one best estimate" approach, that the expected return was 25.2% before taxes. When we ran the new set of data through the computer program, however, we got an expected return of only 14.6% before taxes. This surprising difference not only is due to the fact that under the new approach we use a range of values; it also reflects the fact that we have weighted each value in the range by the chances of its occurrence. (44, p. 183].

The Hertz model can also handle *dependency* among the random variables. For example, it is reasonable to view our variables OC and SM as being interdependent. That is, it can be argued that the lower the firm's operating costs, the higher will be its share of the market.

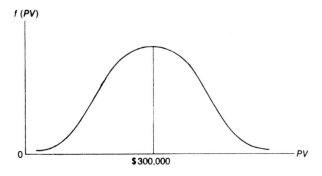

Figure 3-9.

The method for handling the dependency of SM on OC is straight-forward. The firm could develop a number of probability distributions of SM, each corresponding to a different *range* of values of OC. As an example, suppose that only two distributions of SM are constructed, one with an expected value of 8 percent and the other 12 percent. Now, the computer generates a random variable from the OC distribution first. If the random variable happens to fall in the *lower half* of the range of OC values, the computer then generates a random variable from the SM distribution with the 12 percent expected value. The rest of the procedure is the same as was described previously.

The Mattessich Model [57,58]

The Mattessich model describes the firm in terms of a set of conventional accounting identities. The exogenous variables and input data of this deterministic model include standard labor hours, operating expense rates, overhead rates, sales rates, production rates, number of products, number of raw materials, number of departments, and so on. At the end of each time period the model generates an income statement, a balance sheet, and a set of budgets (sales, production, raw materials, labor, factory overhead, operating expenses, cash, etc.).

The Sun Oil Corporate Financial Model [40]

The Sun Oil Company's Corporate Financial Model [40] developed by George Gershefski represents a major contribution to computer model building in general and to the field of finance in particular. The objective of the Sun Oil model is, "to provide management with a fast, reliable method for forecasting the financial performance of the company based on any specific set of anticipated conditions" [40, p. 5]. The model is used to develop revised projections of net income, cash flow, and balance-sheet accounts whenever significant changes occur in important variables that affect the performance of the company. The model is also used for long-range planning and to develop budgets that are consistent with corporate objectives.

The model consists of 1500 inputs per year and includes these kinds of variables:

1. Product prices and volumes.
2. Raw material costs.
3. General economic conditions.
4. Investments.

5. Subsidiary company incomes.
6. Discretionary expense items.

The model generates the following output reports (see Figure 3-10).

1. An income statement.
2. The capital investment schedule.
3. A source and use of funds statement.
4. A statement of earnings employed and stockholder's equity.
5. A tax report.
6. A rate of return analysis.
7. A financial and operating summary.

The Sun Oil Model consists of more than 2000 equations of which over 60 were estimated by regression analysis. The equations are grouped into a series of blocks or subroutines. "Each block represents a specific aspect of company operations and considers the physical operations performed, operating alternatives available, the relationship between costs and volumes, and the accounting procedure followed" [40, p. 23]. The blocks that are interrelated to determine consolidated net income are illustrated in Figure 3-11.

The model was originally programmed in FORTRAN IV for the GE 635 computer and required 38,000 words (36-bit) of core space. Fourteen seconds of central processor time were required to generate one year of simulated experience on the GE 635. The model also has been programmed for time sharing. Recently, the model has been converted to the CDC 6400 computer.

The first working version of the model required 13 man-years of effort to complete. This consisted of 10 man-years of analytical time and 3 man-years of computer coding effort. An additional 10-man years was spent to familiarize management, at various levels, with the operation of the model, to solicit their comments for improvement, and to incorporate their suggestions. The total elasped time for development and implementation was two and one-half years [40, p. 3].

Other Financial Models

Several other financial models may also be of interest: (1) the Pillsbury Corporate Capital Expenditure Model, (2) the Boise Cascade Pacific Northwest Investment Planning Model [27], (3) the Corning Glass Multinational Investment Model, and (4) the Dow Chemical Corporate Financial Planning Model [52]. The Pillsbury Model is a time-shared model for testing the effects of alternative investment decisions on rate of return, depreciation, and profit. The Pacific Northwest Investment Planning Model

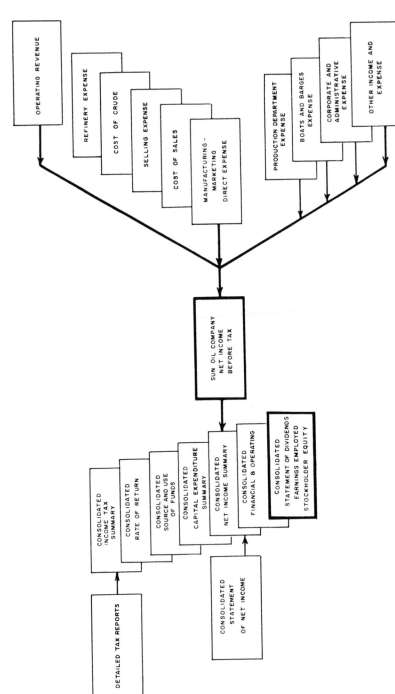

Figures 3-10. Reports generated by the financial model [40, p. 22].

66

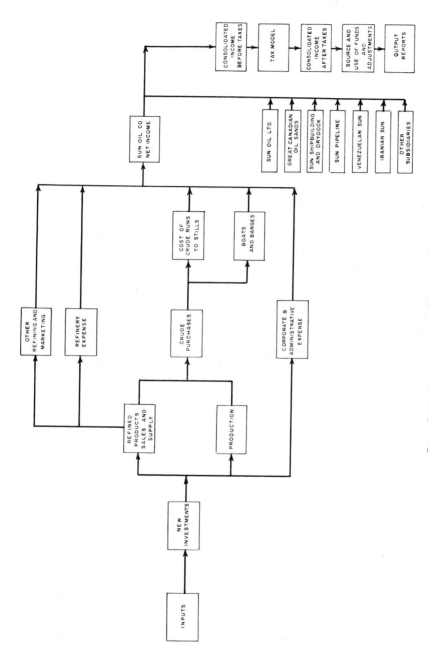

Figure 3-11. The financial model flow chart [40, p. 26].

67

has been used by Boise Cascade to simulate the effects of timber land purchases and capital expenditures on profits. The Corning Glass Model is used to evaluate the effects of proposed international investments on gross margins, operating margins, net profit, cash flow, return on investment, and so on. The Dow Chemical Model provides another example of a deterministic accounting model that calculates income and expense statements, consolidated balance sheets, cash flow balances, and performance measures of future years.

CORPORATE MODELS [82]

In the preceding sections of this chapter we have examined several computer models of specific functional areas of business—production, marketing, and finance. Recently, a number of large corporations in the United States have embarked on an entirely new approach to computer model building: corporate simulation models. Instead of treating production, marketing, accounting, and finance as though they were separate, independent functions, corporate simulation models treat the business firm as a *total system*. That is, corporate simulation models represent an attempt to model the behavior of an entire corporation. With corporate models the firm's distribution, finance, production, information, and control subsystems are treated as though they were completely interdependent. Here we describe briefly some of the properties of four corporate simulation models: (1) the Anheuser-Busch Model, (2) the IBM Model, (3) the Pillsbury Model, and (4) the XEROX Model.

The Anheuser-Busch Model [7]

The Anheuser-Busch Model consists of 10 different submodels and is basically a simulation of the flow of materials and dollars through the beer division of the company. Figure 3-12 contains a flow chart of the logic of the model.

The components of sales demand, industry demand, and Anheuser-Busch market share, are combined to come up with a sales demand projection for Anheuser-Busch. Existing capacity and capacity additions dictated by expansion strategy are combined to arrive at the production capacity for the company. Demand is matched against capacity to get projected sales volume. The components of price and the components of cost are combined to come up with an average price per unit and an average cost per unit. Multiplying these by sales volume gives total revenue and marginal costs. After deducting the fixed cost of operations we have determined the operating profit. At this point the physical activities resulting from producing

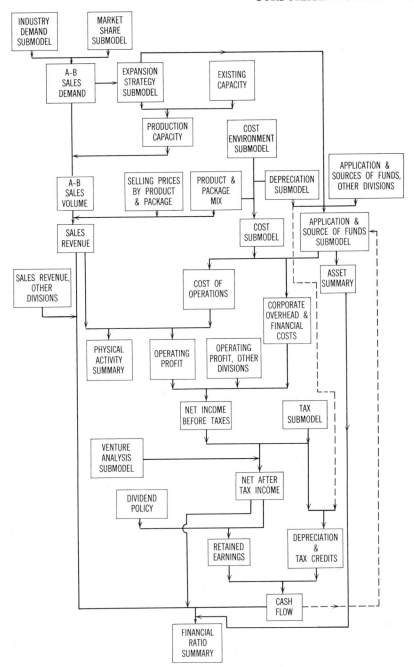

Figure 3-12. The Anheuser-Busch Model.

and selling a given volume can be summarized. Adding together the operating profit from all divisions and deducting corporate overhead and corporate financial cost leaves net income before taxes. Deduct taxes to get net after tax income. After taking into account dividends, depreciation, and tax credits, cash flow can be calculated. Some major financial ratios can be calculated with the values of revenue, assets, equity, cash flow, and income generated by the model [7, p. 9].

The Anheuser-Busch Model was designed for use on the IBM 1130 computer. It cost approximately $100,000 to develop and required five and one-half man-years.

Figure 3-13 contains a 3^4 factorial design for a simulation experiment with the model to test the effects of four different factors (demand level, price, cost, and expansion level) on the average rate of return over a ten-year period.

The IBM Model [82]

The IBM Systems Research Institute has developed a computer model of a "hypothetical growth company" that has the following characteristics:

(1) The company produces a single product.
(2) The demand for the company's product grows over time.
(3) The firm can sell and/or lease its product.
(4) Inventories can be accumulated or reduced.
(5) Production capacity can be expanded.
(6) The firm is affected by inflation and technological change.
(7) Capital expansion can be financed by the sale of stocks and bonds.

The input variables of the model include (1) the purchase and lease prices of the product, (2) the production volume, (3) the amount of capital expansion, and (4) the amount of money to be raised through the borrowing and selling of stock. The output of the System/360 computer program yields balance sheets, income statements, and statements of sources and uses of funds for each year. "In addition, the program provides measurements of corporate performance. By varying the input factors, the user can gain insight into the relative profitability of leasing the company's product versus selling it outright, financing through debt rather than equity, and varying the time at which new plant and equipment are introduced."

The Pillsbury Model

Pillsbury has developed a time-sharing model to analyze proposed business acquisitions. Whenever Pillsbury is considering the acquisition of a company, a complete history of the proposed acquisition is read into the

		EXPANSION STRATEGY 1			EXPANSION STRATEGY 2			EXPANSION STRATEGY 2		
		Cost 1	Cost 2	Cost 3	Cost 1	Cost 2	Cost 3	Cost 1	Cost 2	Cost 3
Demand Level 1	Price 1									
	Price 2									
	Price 3									
Demand Level 2	Price 1									
	Price 2									
	Price 3									
Demand Level 3	Price 1									
	Price 2									
	Price 3									

Figure 3-13. A factorial design for the Anheuser-Busch Model.

computer which includes data on sales, costs, cash flow, and profit. The model is then used to make projections for several years into the future of these output variables. These simulation results then are compared with the projections provided by the owners of the firm that is being considered for acquisition and, thus, they provide Pillsbury's management with a check on the validity of the projections given by the owners of the business that is being considered. The model is run by the planning department of Pillsbury under a wide variety of different input conditions. Then at the meeting of the executive committee of Pillsbury a terminal is placed in the room and, as questions are raised by committee members, the model can be interrogated directly from the terminal, and it provides immediate response in terms of capital requirements, cash flow, return on investment, and profits.

The XEROX Model [12, 82]

The XEROX Model was developed by the XEROX Corporation to facilitate the formulation of long-range plans. It consists of submodels of the company's major operating functions: marketing, manufacturing, and distribution. The principal input of the model is the revenue forecast, and the major outputs include financial reports and manpower and facilities summaries. Among the uses of the XEROX Model are the following:

1. Test feasibility of strategies.
2. Anticipate and identify future problems.
3. Evaluate financial effects of strategies.
4. Measure impact of new proposals.
5. Diagnose corporate maladies.
6. Show effect of environmental changes.
7. Investigate results of timing of strategies.

Among the major decisions in which the XEROX Model has been particularly useful are the following:

1. Should the company offer XEROX machines for sale or continue to lease them?
2. Should the supplies required for the use of each machine be sold or given away, with their costs being hidden in the lease price?
3. Should the company continue to offer more kinds of copiers, or should it go into the duplicating or printing market?
4. Increased drum life on XEROX machines will result in reduced drum revenue, but it also will result in reduced manufacturing costs and in reduced service call costs. Should this technological improvement be instituted?

The management of the XEROX Corporation contends that a number of important lessons have been learned through their experience with the XEROX Model. Some of these lessons are worth passing on to the reader:

1. Thorough top management support must be obtained if efforts such as the XEROX Model are to succeed.

2. A single group should be given full responsibility for the effort.

3. The objective of the model should be clearly stated and should be limited in nature at the very outset of the project.

4. Some form of model should be pressed into limited, but online, use as soon as possible.

5. An investment in the development of a corporate model commits the firm to a heavy investment in model and data-base maintenance once an operational status is achieved.

6. The modular design used in the development of the XEROX Model should be used in any comparable effort because of the flexibility it provides.

7. Large-scale corporate models should be supported by software that is capable of providing random access to the data base.

MANAGEMENT GAMES

We conclude this chapter on management science models with a discussion of a special type of simulation called a *management game*. A management game is a simulation in which human participants act as decision makers within the framework of the system being simulated. Although the concept of gaming originated many centuries ago in the form of military war games (used for training purposes), its use in business and economics only goes back to 1956 when the American Management Association developed the first so-called management decision-making game, called the Top Management Decision Game. Since 1956, hundreds of management games have been developed by various universities, business firms, and research organizations, both for research purposes and for training persons in diverse disciplines such as management, business operation, economics, organization theory, psychology, production management, finance, accounting, and marketing. These games range in degree of complexity from simple competitive games to the extremely complex Carnegie Tech Management Game [19,20,22]. The degree of realism and the level of abstraction also vary considerably among the existing management games. However, most games involve decisions that would be made only by fairly high level executives as opposed to operating employees.

Most business games are built around a hypothetical oligopolistic industry consisting of three to six firms, whose decision makers or managers are the "players" of the game. At the outset of the game, each firm or "team" is allocated a specified amount of resources in the form of cash, inventories, raw materials, plant and equipment, and so forth. Then before each operating period (usually assumed to be a quarter) the players make decisions concerning price, output, advertising, marketing, raw material acquisition, changes in plant capacity, and wage rates, to mention only a few possibilities. Then this information is read into a computer that has been programmed on the basis of a set of mathematical models that provide a link between the operating results of the individual firms (for example, sales, profits, and levels of inventory) and the individual firms' operating decisions, as well as the external environment (the market). On the basis of (1) a set of behavioral equations, such as demand and cost functions, and a set of accounting formulas that have been programmed into the computer and (2) the individual decisions of each firm, operating results are generated by the computer in the form of printed reports, for example, profit and loss statements, balance sheets, production reports, sales reports, and total industry reports at the end of each operating period. Usually, the environment can be changed by the administrator of the game by altering the parameters of the operating characteristics of the game. For example, it may be possible to change parameters that affect the rate of growth of the economy, the rate of taxation, the rate of depreciation of fixed assets, the industry wage rate, the prices of raw materials and production lead time. In each case, the firms find it necessary to react according to the magnitude and the nature of the change imposed by the external environment, that is, by changing the parameters of the game. Some of the more complicated and more realistic games even permit multiple products, plants, and marketing areas, stochastic production periods, stochastic demand, labor negotiations, and the sale of common stock.

In this section a simplified version of a well-known management game, which has been widely used by colleges and universities and businessmen alike as a training tool—the International Business Machines Management Decision-Making Game,[3]—will be outlined. Since we are merely attempting to survey several different types of applications of computer simulation in managerial science in this chapter, it is not possible to present a highly complex game within the confines of a few pages. Although this scaled-down version of the IBM Game is not nearly as realistic or as complicated as, for instance, the Carnegie Tech Management Game, it does contain most of the basic features of business games. Furthermore, after careful study of the description of this game, anyone who is knowledgeable in economic theory

[3] Based on "IBM Management Decision-Making Laboratory Administrator's Reference Manual," IBM, B20-8099 (1963). Reproduced with the permission of IBM.

and standard accounting techniques should be able to design his own management game, incorporating whatever degree of realism is desired, subject to the constraints imposed by computer technology and the analyst's knowledge of the mathematical forms and the parameter estimates of the operating characteristics of the real world.

Our reduced form of the IBM Game consists of three firms that are producing a single homogeneous product for sale in a single marketing area. Each firm begins the period of play with equal endowments of cash, inventory, and plant capacity. The net worth of each firm is equal to the total assets of the firm, since firms are not permitted to borrow money or to incur debts in this game. At the beginning of each operating period, the three firms make separate decisions about the following:

1. Price.
2. Marketing expenditures.
3. Plant improvement expenditures.
4. Production expenditures.
5. Research and development expenditures.

However, the total expenditures of a firm in a particular period cannot exceed the amount of cash that the firm has available at the beginning of the period. The decisions are punched into cards and read into the computer, which processes the decisions according to the flow chart in Figure 3-16. The computer simulates the behavior of each firm and generates reports showing the operating results of the activity in the period. This cycle can be repeated for as many periods or quarters as are desired.

At the start of play, each firm receives an identical set of reports—a confidential report and an industry report. Figures 3-14 and 3-15 contain sample copies of a confidential report and an industry report for the start of play. After each period of play, the three firms receive a new set of confidential and industry reports. After the first period of play, the confidential reports are no longer identical for each firm because they depend entirely on the decisions made by the three firms in preceding periods, as well as any changes that have been made in the parameters of the operating characteristic functions by the administrator of the game. However, the industry reports are always identical for each firm in a particular period.

A total of 37 variables and more than 30 parameters are required to describe this game. The variables have been categorized as decision variables, status variables, and output variables and are specified below. We have not listed the parameters or specified their initial values because to a large extent, they are arbitrary. The set of mathematical equations describing the behavior of this hypothetical industry consists of 15 be-

Firm 1 Report

Sales Analysis

Orders	253
Sales	253
Unit Price	$40
Sales revenue	$10,119
Marketing expenses	$600

Production

	Inventory	Plant Capacity	Current Production
Quantity	9	260	216
Unit cost	$35.49	$34.44	$35.49
Total cost	$304	$8,955	$7,650

Profit and Loss Statement

Total revenue		$10,119
Cost of goods sold	$8,881	
Marketing	$600	
Research and development	$100	
Depreciation	$104	
Total expenses		$9,685
Profit before taxes		$434
Taxes		$217
		———
Net profit		$217

Cash Statement

Old balance		$8,500
Total revenue		$10,119
Production cost	$7,650	
Marketing	$600	
Research and development	$100	
Plant improvement	$104	
Taxes	$217	
Total outlay		$8,671
		———
New cash balance		$9,948

Balance Sheet

Cash balance		$9,948
Current inventory		$304
Old plant	$5,200	
Depreciation	$104	
Plant improvement	$104	
New plant		$5,200
		———
Total assets		$15,452
Net worth		$15,452

Figure 3-14. A sample firm report.

Industry Report

Firm 1 Balance Sheet

	Cash	$ 9,948
	Inventory	304
	Plant	5,200
	Total assets	$15,452

Firm 2 Balance Sheet

	Cash	$ 9,948
	Inventory	304
	Plant	5,200
	Total assets	$15,452

Firm 3 Balance Sheet

	Cash	$ 9,948
	Inventory	304
	Plant	5,200
	Total assets	$15,452

Total Market Survey

	Total orders	759
	Total sales	759
	Total marketing expenditure	$ 1,800
	Firm 1 price	$40
	Firm 2 price	$40
	Firm 3 price	$40

Figure 3-15. A sample industry report.

havioral equations and 18 accounting formulas. We shall not attempt to elaborate on the assumptions underlying the equations for the behavioral equations or to discuss the accounting formulas. The behavioral equations are based on a set of fairly arbitrary assumptions about the real world, which are self-evident on careful examination of the equations. The accounting formulas, based on standard accounting practices, are relatively easy to interpret.

DECISION VARIABLES

P_i = Price of the ith firm. $\qquad$ (3-64)

M_i = Marketing expenditure of the ith firm. $\qquad$ (3-65)

PI_i = Plant improvement expenditure of the ith firm. $\qquad$ (3-66)

PC_i = Production expenditure of the ith firm. $\qquad$ (3-67)

RD_i = Research and development expenditure of the ith firm. $\qquad$ (3-68)

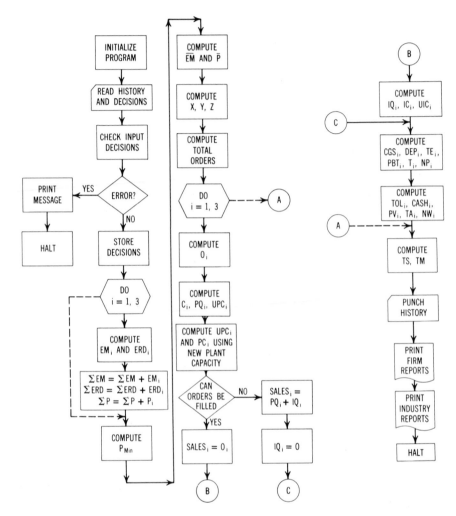

Figure 3-16.   The flow chart for a management decision-making game.

STATUS VARIABLES

X = Effect of research and development expenditures on total orders for the industry.   (3-69)

Y = Effect of marketing expenditures on total orders for the industry.   (3-70)

Z = Effect of price on total orders for the industry.   (3-71)

EM_i = Effective marketing expenditure of the ith firm.   (3-72)

ERD_i = Effective research and development expenditure of the ith firm.   (3-73)

V_i = Share of market of the ith firm.   (3-74)

W_i = Overall order-producing effect of decisions of the ith firm.   (3-75)

S = Research and development factor.   (3-76)

V = Quantity factor.   (3-77)

F = Penalty factor for producing less than capacity.   (3-78)

OUTPUT VARIABLES

O_i = Number of orders received by the ith firm.   (3-79)

$SALES_i$ = Number of units actually sold by the ith firm.   (3-80)

$SERV_i$ = Sales revenue of the ith firm.   (3-81)

IQ_i = Quantity of inventory of the ith firm.   (3-82)

UIC_i = Unit cost of inventory of the ith firm.   (3-83)

IC_i = Total cost of inventory of the ith firm.   (3-84)

C_i = Production capacity (in units) of the ith firm.   (3-85)

UPC_i = Unit production costs of the ith firm.   (3-86)

PQ_i = Production quantity of the ith firm.   (3-87)

CGS_i = Cost of goods sold of the ith firm.   (3-88)

DEP_i = Depreciation charges of the ith firm.   (3-89)

TE_i = Total expenses of the ith firm.   (3-90)

PBT_i = Profit before taxes of the ith firm.   (3-91)

T_i = Taxes of the ith firm.   (3-92)

NP_i = Net profit of the ith firm.   (3-93)

$CASH_i$ = Cash balance of the ith firm.   (3-94)

TOL_i = Total outlay of the ith firm.   (3-95)

PV_i = Plant value of the ith firm.   (3-96)

TA_i = Total assets of the ith firm.   (3-97)

NW_i = Net worth of the ith firm.   (3-98)

TS = Total sales for the industry.   (3-99)

TM = Total marketing expenditures for the industry.   (3-100)

BEHAVIORAL EQUATIONS

Total Orders

$$TO_T = rT_1 X_T Y_T Z_T. \tag{3-101}$$

Marketing Effects

$$Y_T = b_1 - \frac{sT_3 b_2}{x_2 \sum_{i=1}^{3} EM_{i,T}} \quad \text{if} \quad \sum_{i=1}^{3} EM_{i,T} > 125{,}000 \tag{3-102}$$

$$= \frac{\sum_{i=1}^{3} \text{EM}_{i,\text{T}}}{125,000} \quad \text{if } \sum_{i=1}^{3} \text{EM}_{i,\text{T}} \leq 125,000.$$

$$\text{EM}_{i,\text{T}} = a_1 \text{M}_{i,\text{T}} + a_2 \text{M}_{i,\text{T}-1} + a_3 \text{M}_{i,\text{T}-2}. \tag{3-103}$$

Research and Development Effects

$$\text{X}_\text{T} = b_3 + \frac{\sum_{i=1}^{3} \text{ERD}_{i,\text{T}}}{b_4}. \tag{3-104}$$

$$\text{ERD}_{i,\text{T}} = g\text{ERD}_{i,\text{T}-1} + \text{RD}_{i,\text{T}}. \tag{3-105}$$

Price Effects

$$\text{Z}_\text{T} = \frac{x_1 \text{T}_2}{P_{\text{Min}}}. \tag{3-106}$$

Market Share

$$\text{O}_{i,\text{T}} = \text{V}_{i,\text{T}} \text{TO}_\text{T}. \tag{3-107}$$

$$\text{V}_{i,\text{T}} = \frac{\text{W}_{i,\text{T}}}{\sum_{i=1}^{3} \text{W}_{i,\text{T}}}. \tag{3-108}$$

$$\text{W}_{i,\text{T}} = \left(\frac{\text{EM}_{i,\text{T}}}{\text{EM}_\text{T}} - y_1\right)\left(\frac{\overline{\text{P}}_\text{T}}{\text{P}_{i,\text{T}}} - y_2\right)\left(c_1 + y_3 \frac{\text{ERD}_{i,\text{T}}}{\text{SALES}_{i,\text{T}-1}}\right). \tag{3-109}$$

Plant Capacity

$$\text{C}_{i,\text{T}} = \frac{0.98\text{PV}_{i,\text{T}-2} + \text{PI}_{i,\text{T}-1}}{20}. \tag{3-110}$$

Production Quantity

$$\text{PQ}_{i,\text{T}} = \frac{(\text{PC}_{i,\text{T}}/\text{T}_4) - \text{SK}_2 - \text{C}_{i,\text{T}}\text{K}_3}{\text{SK}_1 - \text{K}_3}. \tag{3-111}$$

$$\text{S} = d_3 - \frac{\text{Z}_2\text{ERD}_{i,\text{T}}}{d_4}. \tag{3-112}$$

Unit Production Cost

$$\text{UPC}_{i,\text{T}} = \text{T}_4(\text{VS} + \text{F}). \tag{3-113}$$

$$\text{V} = \left(d_1 + \frac{d_2}{\text{PQ}_{i,\text{T}}}\right)\text{Z}_1. \tag{3-114}$$

$$\text{F} = \left(\frac{\text{C}_{i,\text{T}} - \text{PQ}_{i,\text{T}}}{\text{PQ}_{i,\text{T}}}\right)\text{K}_3. \tag{3-115}$$

ACCOUNTING FORMULAS

Sales

$$\text{SALES}_{i,\text{T}} = \text{O}_{i,\text{T}} \qquad\qquad \text{if } \text{O}_{i,\text{T}} \leq \text{PQ}_{i,\text{T}} + \text{IQ}_{i,\text{T}-1}$$

$$= \text{PQ}_{i,\text{T}} + \text{IQ}_{i,\text{T}-1} \quad \text{if } \text{O}_{i,\text{T}} > \text{PQ}_{i,\text{T}} + \text{IQ}_{i,\text{T}-1}. \qquad (3\text{-}116)$$

Sales Revenue

$$\text{SREV}_{i,\text{T}} = \text{P}_{i,\text{T}} \cdot \text{SALES}_{i,\text{T}}. \qquad\qquad (3\text{-}117)$$

Inventory Quantity

$$\text{IQ}_{i,\text{T}} = \text{PQ}_{i,\text{T}} + \text{IQ}_{i,\text{T}-1} - \text{SALES}_{i,\text{T}}. \qquad\qquad (3\text{-}118)$$

Inventory Cost

$$\text{IC}_{i,\text{T}} = [(\text{PQ}_{i,\text{T}} + \text{IQ}_{i,\text{T}-1}) - \text{O}_{i,\text{T}}] \, \text{UPC}_{i,\text{T}}, \qquad\qquad (3\text{-}119)$$

when

$$\text{IQ}_{i,\text{T}-1} \leq \text{O}_{i,\text{T}} < (\text{IQ}_{i,\text{T}-1} + \text{PQ}_{i,\text{T}}).$$

$$\text{IC}_{i,\text{T}} = [(\text{IQ}_{i,\text{T}-1} - \text{O}_{i,\text{T}}) \, \text{UIC}_{i,\text{T}-1}] + \text{PC}_{i,\text{T}},$$

when

$$\text{O}_{i,\text{T}} < \text{IQ}_{i,\text{T}-1}.$$

$$\text{IC}_{i,\text{T}} = 0,$$

when

$$\text{PQ}_{i,\text{T}} + \text{IQ}_{i,\text{T}-1} < \text{O}_{i,\text{T}}.$$

Unit Inventory Cost

$$\text{UIC}_{i,\text{T}} = \frac{\text{IC}_{i,\text{T}}}{\text{IQ}_{i,\text{T}}}. \qquad\qquad (3\text{-}120)$$

Cost of Goods Sold

$$\text{CGS}_{i,\text{T}} = \text{IC}_{i,\text{T}-1} + (\text{SALES}_{i,\text{T}} - \text{IQ}_{i,\text{T}-1}) \, \text{UPC}_{i,\text{T}}, \qquad (3\text{-}121)$$

when

$$\text{IQ}_{i,\text{T}-1} \leq \text{SALES}_{i,\text{T}} < (\text{IQ}_{i,\text{T}-1} + \text{PQ}_{i,\text{T}}).$$

$$\text{CGS}_{i,\text{T}} = \text{SALES}_{i,\text{T}} \cdot \text{UIC}_{i,\text{T}-1}$$

when

$$\text{SALES}_{i,\text{T}} < \text{IQ}_{i,\text{T}-1}.$$

$$\text{CGS}_{i,\text{T}} = \text{IC}_{i,\text{T}-1} + \text{PC}_{i,\text{T}}$$

when

$$\text{SALES}_{i,\text{T}} = \text{IQ}_{i,\text{T}-1} + \text{PQ}_{,\text{T}}.$$

Depreciation

$$\text{DEP}_{i,\text{T}} = 0.02\text{PV}_{i,\text{T}-1}. \tag{3-122}$$

Total Expenses

$$\text{TE}_{i,\text{T}} = \text{CGS}_{i,\text{T}} + \text{M}_{i,\text{T}} + \text{RD}_{i,\text{T}} + \text{DEP}_{i,\text{T}}. \tag{3-123}$$

Profit Before Taxes

$$\text{PBT}_{i,\text{T}} = \text{SREV}_{i,\text{T}} - \text{TE}_{i,\text{T}}. \tag{3-124}$$

Taxes

$$\text{T}_{i,\text{T}} = 0.5\text{PBT}_{i,\text{T}}. \tag{3-125}$$

Net Profit

$$\text{NP}_{i,\text{T}} = \text{PBT}_{i,\text{T}} - \text{T}_{i,\text{T}}. \tag{3-126}$$

Total Outlay

$$\text{TOL}_{i,\text{T}} = \text{PC}_{i,\text{T}} + \text{M}_{i,\text{T}} + \text{RD}_{i,\text{T}} + \text{PI}_{i,\text{T}} + \text{T}_{i,\text{T}}. \tag{3-127}$$

Net Cash Balance

$$\text{CASH}_{i,\text{T}} = \text{CASH}_{i,\text{T}-1} + \text{SREV}_{i,\text{T}} - \text{TOL}_{i,\text{T}}. \tag{3-128}$$

Plant Value

$$\text{PV}_{i,\text{T}} = \text{PV}_{i,\text{T}-1} - \text{DEP}_{i,\text{T}} + \text{PI}_{i,\text{T}}. \tag{3-129}$$

Total Assets

$$\text{TA}_{i,\text{T}} = \text{CASH}_{i,\text{T}} + \text{IC}_{i,\text{T}} + \text{PV}_{i,\text{T}}. \tag{3-130}$$

$$\text{NW}_{i,\text{T}} = \text{TA}_{i,\text{T}}. \tag{3-131}$$

Industry Totals

$$\text{TS} = \sum_{i=1}^{3} \text{SALES}_i. \tag{3-132}$$

$$\text{TM} = \sum_{i=1}^{3} \text{M}_i. \tag{3-133}$$

Figure 3-16 shows a computer flow chart for our modified version of the IBM Game. The input data for this computer program consist of history cards and decision cards. The history cards contain the values of the lagged output and decision variables required by (3-101) through (3-133). For the first period of play, a set of initial values must be specified and punched on cards that become the starting history deck. However, at the end of each computer run a new history deck is punched by the computer. This output deck then becomes part of the input data for the next period.

For those who are interested in developing their own business game, the following procedure may be helpful. Begin by writing a computer program for the game described in this section, using the flow chart in Figure 3-16 as a guide. Experiment with the game by observing the effect on operating results of various changes in the parameters of the operating characteristics. Finally, gradually, step by step, relax some of the assumptions of the model by making the appropriate changes in the operating characteristics and accounting formulas. By following this simple procedure it may be possible to develop a fairly realistic management game. Undoubtedly, those readers who elect to develop their own game will find the experience an extremely rewarding one, since one cannot possibly write a computer program for a business game without a clear understanding of the complex interactions involved in the operation of a business firm. Such an experience is highly recommended for students in business administration and economics who want to test their real knowledge of the behavior of business firms in a dynamic world.

Several excellent books are available that describe particular management games, including the Carnegie Tech Game [19,20,22], the Harvard Game [54], and the U.C.L.A.-Michigan State Game [43]. The concept of gaming is now being extended to many other disciplines, including state and local government and population policy.

BIBLIOGRAPHY

1. Abe, D. K. "Corporate Model System for Planning," TIMS XVI International Meeting, New York, March 22, 1969.
2. Ackerman, S. S. "Even-Flow, A Scheduling Method for Reducing Lateness in Job Shops," *Management Technology*, **III** (May 1963), 20-32.
3. Amstutz, A. E. "Management Games," *Industrial Management Review*, (Fall, 1963), 29-63.
4. Amstutz, A. E. *Computer Simulation of Competitive Market Response.* Cambridge, Mass.: M. I. T. Technology Press, 1967.
5. Baker, C. T., and Dzielinski, B. P. "Simulation of a Simplified Job Shop," *Management Science*, **VI** (1960), 311-323.
6. Baumol, William J. *Economic Dynamics.* New York: The Macmillan Co., 1959.
7. Beracha, Harry H. "Strategic Planning Systems," presented at the American Management Association Seminar on Corporate Financial Models, December 16-18, 1968, New York.
8. Berman, E. B. "Monte Carlo Determination of Stock Redistribution," *Operations Research*, **X** (July-August 1962), 500-506.

9. Bonini, Charles P. *Simulation of Information and Decision Systems in the Firm.* Englewood Cliffs, N. J.: Prentice-Hall, 1963.

10. Brenner, M. E. "Selective Sampling—A Technique for Reducing Sample Size in Simulation of Decision-Making Problems," *Journal of Industrial Engineering,* **XIV** (November-December 1963), 291-296.

11. Brenner, M. E. "A Relation Between Decision Making Penalty and Simulation Sample Size for Inventory Systems," *Operations Research,* **XIII** (May-June 1965), 433-443.

12. Brown, David E. "The XEROX Planning Model," presented at the American Management Association Seminar on Corporate Financial Models, December 16-18, 1968, New York.

13. Bulkin, Michael H., Colley, John L., and Steinhoff, Harry W. "Load Forecasting, Priority Sequencing, and Simulation in a Job Shop Control System," *Management Science,* **XIII** (October 1966), 29-51.

14. Chu, Kong, and Naylor, Thomas H. "A Dynamic Model of the Firm," *Management Science,* **XI** (May 1965), 736-750.

15. Chu, Kong, and Naylor, Thomas H. "Two Alternative Methods for Simulating Waiting Line Models," *Journal of Industrial Engineering* (November-December 1965).

16. Clarkson, Geoffrey, P. E. Portfolio Selection: *A Simulation of Trust Investment.* Englewood Cliffs, N. J.: Prentice Hall, Inc., 1962.

17. Clarkson, Geoffrey P. E., and Simon, H. A. "Simulation of Individual and Group Behavior," *American Economic Review,* **L,** No. 5 (December 1960), 920-932.

18. Cohen, K. J. *Computer Models of the Shoe, Leather, Hide Sequence.* Englewood Cliffs, N. J.: Prentice-Hall, Inc., 1960.

19. Cohen, K. J. *et al.* "The Carnegie Tech Management Game," *Simulation in Social Science,* Harold Guetzkow (ed). Englewood Cliffs, N. J.: Prentice-Hall, Inc., 1962.

20. Cohen, Kalman J., *et al. The Carnegie Tech Management Game.* Homewood, Ill.: Richard D. Irwin, 1964.

21. Cohen, Kalman J., and Elton, E. J. "Inter-Temporal Portfolio Analysis Based on Simulation," *Management Science,* **XIV** (September 1967), 5-18.

22. Cohen, Kalman J., and Rhenman, Eric. "The Role of Management Games in Education and Research," *Management Science,* **VII** (1961). 171-176.

23. Conway, R. W. "An Experimental Investigation of Priority Dispatching," *Journal of Industrial Engineers,* **XI** (1960), 221-230.

24. Conway, R. W. "Priority Dispatching and Job Lateness in a Job Shop," *Journal of Industrial Engineering,* **XVI** (July-August 1965), 228-236.

25. Cyert, Richard M., and March, James G. *A Behavioral Theory of the Firm.* Englewood Cliffs, N. J.: Prentice-Hall, Inc., 1963.

26. Day, R. L. "Simulation of Consumer Preference," *Journal of Advertising Research,* **V** (September 1965).

27. Dickens, J. H. and Frazier, G. D. "Linear Programming in Corporate Simulation," TIMS College on Simulation Symposium on Corporate Simulation Models, University of Washington, March 23-25, 1970.

28. Dill, William R., and Doppelt, Neil. "The Acquisition of Experience in a Complex Management Game," *Management Science*, **X** (October 1963), 30-46.

29. Duesenberry, James S., Fromm, Gary, Klein, L. R., and Kuh, Edwin. *The Brookings Model: Some Further Results.* Chicago: Rand McNally, 1969.

30. Dzielinski, B. P., Baker, C. T., and Manne, A. S. "Simulation Tests of Lot-Size Programming," *Industrial Scheduling.* Edited by John F. Muth and Gerald L. Thompson. Englewood Cliffs, N. J.: Prentice Hall, Inc., 1963.

31. Dzielinski, B. P., Baker, C. T., and Manne, A. S. "Simulation Tests of Lot Size Programming," *Management Science*, **IX** (1963), 229-258.

32. Dzielinski, B. P., and Manne, A. S. "Simulation of a Hypothetical Multi-Item Production and Inventory System," *Journal of Industrial Engineering*, **XII** (1961), 417-421.

33. Evans, M. K., and Klein, L. R. *The Wharton Econometric Forecasting Model.* Philadelphia: Wharton School, University of Pennsylvania (second edition), 1968.

34. Forrester, Jay W. *Industrial Dynamics.* New York: The M. I. T. Press and John Wiley & Sons, 1961.

35. Fromm, Gary, and Taubman, Paul. *Policy Simulations with an Econometric Model.* Washington, D. C.: The Brookings Institution, 1968.

36. Galliher, Herbert P. "Simulation of Random Processes," *Notes on Operations Research 1959.* Cambridge: The Technology Press, Massachusetts Institute of Technology, 1959.

37. Geisler, M. A. "Appraisal of Laboratory Simulation Experience," *Management Science*, **VIII** (April 1962), 239-245.

38. Geisler, Murray A. "The Sizes of Simulation Samples Required to Compute Certain Inventory Characteristics with Stated Precision and Confidence," *Management Science*, **X** (January 1964), 261-286.

39. Gere, William S. "Heuristics in Job Shop Scheduling," *Management Science*, **XIII** (November 1966), 167-190.

40. Gershefski, George W. *The Development and Application of a Corporation Financial Model.* Oxford, Ohio: Planning Executives Institute, 1968.

41. Gross, Donald, and Ray, Jack. "A General Purpose Forecast Simulator," *Management Science*, **XI** (April 1965), 119-135.

42. Heller, J. "Some Numerical Experiments for an M x J Flow Shop and Its Decision Theoretical Aspects," *Operations Research*, **VIII** (March-April 1960), 178-184.

43. Henshaw, R. C., and Jackson, J. R. *The Executive Game.* Homewood, Ill.: Richard D. Irwin, 1966.

44. Hertz, D. B. "Risk Analysis in Capital Budgeting," *Harvard Business Review*, **XLII** (January-February 1964), 95-106.

45. Hicks, J. R. *Value and Capital.* Oxford: Clarendon Press, 1939.

46. Hurst, E. G. *et al.* "Heuristic Scheduling in a Woolen Mill." *Management Science*, **XIV** (December 1967), 182-203.

47. IBM. *The Job Simulator.* New York: IBM Mathematics and Applications Dept., 1960.

48. Jackson, J. R. "Queues with Dynamic Priority Discipline," *Management Science,* **VIII** (October 1961), 18–34.
49. Kagdis, John, and Lackner, Michael R. "A Management Control Systems Simulation Model," *Management Technology,* **III** (December 1963), 145-159.
50. Kuehn, Alfred A. "Complex Interactive Models," *Quantitative Techniques in Marketing Analysis,* Ronald E. Frank (ed). Homewood, Ill.: Richard D. Irwin, Inc., 1962.
51. Kuehn, Alfred A., and Hamburger, Michael J. "A Heuristic Program for Locating Warehouses," *Quantitative Techniques in Marketing Analysis,* Ronald E. Frank (ed). Homewood, Ill.: Richard D. Irwin, Inc., 1962.
52. Lawless, Robert M. "The Dow Chemical Corporate Financial Planning Model," TIMS College on Simulation Symposium on Corporate Simulation Models, University of Washington, March 23-25, 1970.
53. LeGrande, E. "The Development of a Factory Simulation System Using Actual Operating Data," *Management Technology,* **III** (1963, 1-19.
54. McKenney, James L. *Simulation Gaming for Management Development.* Boston: Graduate School of Business Administration, 1967.
55. Manne, Alan S. *Economic Analysis for Business Decisions.* New York: McGraw-Hill, 1961.
56. Mattessich, R. "Budgeting Models and Systems Simulation," *Accounting Review,* **XXXVI** (July 1961), 384-397.
57. Mattessich, Richard. *Simulation of the Firm Through a Budget Computer Program.* Homewood, Ill.: Richard D. Irwin, 1964.
58. Meir, Robert C., Newell, William T., and Pazer, Harold L. *Simulation in Business and Economics.* Englewood Cliffs, N. J.: Prentice-Hall, Inc. 1969.
59. Montgomery, David B., and Urban, Glen L. *Management Science in Marketing.* Englewood Cliffs, N. J.: Prentice-Hall, Inc., 1969.
60. Monty, G. "Practical Applications of Simulation in the Area of Stock Management," *Digital Simulation in Operational Research,* S. H. Hollingdale (editor). New York: American Elsevier Publishing Co., 1967.
61. Moss, John H. "Commentary on Harling's Simulation Techniques in Operations Research," *Operations Research,* **VI** (July-August 1958), 591-593.
62. Muth, John F., and Thompson, Gerald L. *Industrial Scheduling.* Englewood Cliffs, N. J.: Prentice-Hall, Inc., 1963.
63. Muyen, A. R. "Optimum Lot Size Policy if Tools Breakdown Frequently," *Operational Research Quarterly,* **XII** (May 1967), 41-53.
64. Naddor, E. "Markov Chains and Simulations in an Inventory System," *Journal of Industrial Engineering,* **XIV** (1963), 91-98.
65. Naylor, Thomas H. "Bibliography on Simulation and Gaming," *Computing Reviews,* **X** (January 1969), 61-69.
66. Naylor, Thomas H. "Corporate Simulation Models," Econometric System Simulation Program, Working Paper No. 32, Duke University, March 1, 1969.
67. Naylor, Thomas H., Balintfy, Joseph L., Burdick, Donald, and Chu, Kong. *Computer Simulation Techniques.* New York: John Wiley & Sons, 1966.

68. Naylor, Thomas H., and Vernon, John M. *Microeconomics and Decision Models of the Firm*. New York: Harcourt, Brace, and World, Inc., 1969.

69. Nelson, Rosser T. "Labor and Machine Limited Production Systems," *Management Science*, **XIII** (May 1967), 648-671.

70. Orcutt, Guy H. "Simulation of Economic Systems," *American Economic Review*, **L** (December 1960), 893-907.

71. Orcutt, Guy H. "Views on Simulation and Models of Social Systems," in *Symposium on Simulation Models*, Austin C. Hoggatt and Frederick E. Balderston (editors). Cincinnati: South-Western Publishing Co., 1963.

72. Orcutt, Guy H. *et al. Microanalysis of Socioeconomic Systems: A Simulation Study*. New York: Harper & Brothers, 1961.

72. Packer, Arnold H. "Simulation and Adaptive Forecasting as Applied to Inventory Control," *Operations Research*, **XV** (July-August, 1967), 660-679.

73. Pritsker, A. A. B. "The Monte Carlo Approach to Setting Maintenance Tolerance Limits," *Journal of Industrial Engineering*, **XIV** (May-June 1963), 115.

74. Pritsker, A. A. B. "Applications of Multi-Channel Queueing Results to the Analysis of Conveyor Systems," *The Journal of Industrial Engineering*, **XVII** (January 1966), 14-21.

75. Robinson, Joan. *Economic Philosophy*. Chicago: Aldine Publishing Co., 1963.

76. Rowe, Alan J. "Towards a Theory of Scheduling," *Contributions to Scientific Research in Management*. Los Angeles: School of Business, 1959.

77. Saaty, Thomas L. *Elements of Queueing Theory*. New York: McGraw-Hill Book Co., 1961.

78. Salveson, M. E. "A Computational Technique for the Scheduling Problem," *Journal of Industrial Ehgineering*, **XIII** (January-February 1962), 30-41.

79. Samuelson, Paul A. *Foundations of Economic Analysis*. Cambridge, Mass.: Harvard University Press, 1948.

80. Sandeman, J. "Empirical Design of Priority Waiting Times for Jobbing Shop Control," *Operations Research*, **IX** (July-August 1961), 446-455.

81. Sasieni, Maurice, Yaspin, Arthur, and Friedman, Lawrence. *Operations Research*. New York: John Wiley & Sons, 1959.

82. Schrieber, Albert N. *Corporate Simulation Models*. Seattle: University of Washington, 1970.

83. Sprowls, R. C., and Asimow, M. "A Computer Simulation Business Firm," *Management Control Systems*, D. G. Malcolm and A. J. Rowe (eds). New York: John Wiley & Sons, 1960.

84. Thompson, G. L. "Recent Developments in the Job Shop Scheduling Problem," *Naval Research Logistics Quarterly*, **VII** (1960), 585-589.

85. Thorelli, Hans B., and Graves, Robert L., *International Operations Simulation*. New York: The Free Press of Glencoe, 1964.

86. Tonge, Fred M. *A Heuristic Program for Assembly Line Balancing*. Englewood Cliffs: Prentice-Hall, Inc., 1961.

87. Trilling, D. R. "Job Shop Simulation of Orders Not on Networks," *Journal of Industrial Engineering*, **XVII** (February 1966).

88. Vernon, John, Rives, Norfleet, and Naylor, Thomas H. "An Econometric Model of the Tobacco Industry," *Review of Economics and Statistics*, **LI** (May 1969), 149-157.
89. Weiss, D. L. "Simulation for Decision Making in Marketing," *Journal of Marketing*, **XXVIII** (July 1964), 45-50.
90. Weitz, H. Simulation Models in Marketing. Yorktown Heights, New York: IBM, 1966.
91. Wells, W. D. "Computer Simulation of Consumer Behavior," *Harvard Business Review*, **XLI** (1963), 93.

Chapter 4 | Economic Models

INTRODUCTION

Having described a number of different computer simulation models for management science applications in the preceding chapter, we now consider economic models. We begin by presenting several economic models of the firm including the cobweb model, a model of a competitive industry, a duopoly model, several behavioral models, and an *Industrial Dynamics* model. Next we describe in some detail a computer simulation model of the textile industry. Models of the shoe, leather, and hide industry and the lumber industry are also summarized. We conclude the chapter with a discussion of Macroeconometric models, including an example model with simulation results, and a discussion of the techniques for solving nonlinear econometric models.

MODELS OF THE FIRM

Cobweb Models

Perhaps the simplest dynamic model of firm and market behavior is the so-called "cobweb" model. Although there are many variations of this familiar model, all have certain basic characteristics. Typically, the quantity demanded of a particular product (usually assumed to be an agricultural product) in a specified time period depends on the price (and other factors) in that time period. The quantity supplied is assumed to depend on the price in the preceding time period. And, finally, the market is assumed to be cleared at the end of each period. We shall consider three separate variations of the cobweb model—a stochastic model, a learning model, and a model with stocks.

Cobweb Model 1

The variables, behavioral equations, and market clearing condition for the stochastic model are given as follows.

EXOGENOUS VARIABLES

U_T = a random variable with a known probability distribution, expected value equal to zero, and variance VU. (4-1)

V_T = a random variable with a known probability distribution, expected value equal to zero, and variance VV. (4-2)

W_T = a random variable with a known probability distribution, expected value equal to zero, and variance VW. (4-3)

ENDOGENOUS VARIABLES

P_T = price in period T. (4-4)

D_T = quantity demanded in period T. (4-5)

S_T = quantity supplied in period T. (4-6)

BEHAVIORAL EQUATIONS

$D_T = A - BP_T + U_T.$ (4-7)

$S_T = C + DP_{T-1} + V_T.$ (4-8)

MARKET CLEARING CONDITION

$S_T = D_T + W_T.$ (4-9)

The constants A, B, C, and D are assumed to have been estimated by standard econometric estimating techniques.

The behavioral equations can be interpreted as follows. The quantity demanded in period T is a linear function of the price in period T and a random variable U_T. This random variable is assumed to reflect changes in consumers' tastes and income as well as any other random element that might affect the quantity demanded in period T. The quantity supplied in period T depends on the price in period T-1 and a random variable V_T. The random variable is assumed to represent the net effect on the supply quantity of weather conditions, technology, production efficiency, and so forth. The supply quantity in period T is assumed to be cleared subject to random fluctuations in the error term W_T.

By substituting the values of D_T and S_T in (4-7) and (4-8) into (4-9) and solving for P_T, we obtain

$$P_T = 1/B(A - C - DP_{T-1} + U_T + W_T - V_T) \qquad (4\text{-}10)$$

Then for a given initial price P_0 and known probability distributions for U_T, V_T, and W_T, we can generate time paths for P_T, S_T, and D_T. A flow chart for generating the time paths for Model 1 appears in Figure 4-1.

It is interesting to compare the time path of P_T generated by Model 1 with the well-known theoretical results for the nonstochastic version of this model, that is, when U_T, V_T, and W_T are assumed to be equal to zero. Under complete certainty the time path of P_T is completely determined

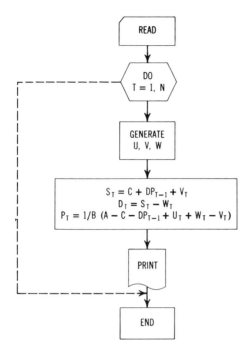

Figure 4-1   The flow chart for Cobweb Model 1.

by the magnitude of the constants D and B. Whether P_T oscillates in a manner that is explosive, regular, or damped depends entirely on D and B,

If $D > B$, then oscillations of P_T are explosive.
If $D = B$, then oscillations of P_T are regular.   (4-11)
If $D < B$, then oscillations of P_T are damped.

Cobweb Model 2

Model 1 was based on the implicit assumption that suppliers never learn In each period the supplier behaved in a manner consistent with the expectation that the price of the previous period would continue in the next period. Yet this expectation was continuously disappointed each period. In this model we alter Model 1 only slightly. We now assume that the supplier is capable of learning or that the expected price of the supplier is $P_{T-1} - \rho \, \Delta P_{T-2}$, where

$$\Delta P_{T-2} = P_{T-1} - P_{T-2} \qquad (4\text{-}12)$$

and ρ is a constant $(0 \leq \rho \leq 1)$, indicating the importance the supplier attaches to the tendency of price movements to be reversed (or continued). Equation (4-9) therefore becomes

$$S_T = C + D(P_{T-1} - \rho \Delta P_{T-2}) + V_T. \tag{4-13}$$

Since all of the other assumptions of Model 1 are assumed to hold true, the procedure for generating time paths for P_T, S_T, and D_T differs only slightly from that of Model 1 and will not be repeated [3, pp. 13-14].

Cobweb Model 3

In Models 1 and 2 the price was set to clear supply, implying that either there was no inventory on hand (for example, a perishable good) or that inventory was maintained at a constant level. In this model we introduce a third group of individuals called "merchants," whose function is distinguished from that of the buyers and suppliers. Merchants can hold inventory and make sales. For notational convenience, we assume complete certainty in this model. We let

$$Q_T = \text{the level of inventory at the end of period T,} \tag{4-14}$$

and

$$\Delta Q_T = Q_T - Q_{T-1} = S_T - D_T. \tag{4-15}$$

The merchants are assumed to set the price in period T according to the rule that the price is set higher if inventories in the previous period fall and the amount of the increase is proportional to the decrease in inventory [3, pp. 15-16]. That is,

$$P_T = P_{T-1} - \lambda \Delta Q_{T-1}, \tag{4-16}$$

where λ is a positive constant. The supply and demand functions are expressed as

$$S_T = C + DP_T, \tag{4-17}$$

$$D_T = A + BP_T. \tag{4-18}$$

But, since

$$\Delta Q_{T-1} = Q_{T-1} - Q_{T-2}$$

$$= S_{T-1} - D_{T-1}$$

$$= (C - A) + (D - B) P_{T-1}, \tag{4-19}$$

then by substitution

$$P_T = P_{T-1} - \lambda(C - A) - \lambda(D - B) P_{T-1}$$

$$= \lambda(A - C) + [1 - \lambda(D - B)] P_{T-1}. \tag{4-20}$$

The procedure for generating the time paths of P_T, S_T, D_T, and Q_T would follow a straightforward process (see Figure 4-2). Once we specify starting values for P_0 and Q_0, then P_T, S_T, D_T, and Q_T are completely determined for any value of $T(T = 1, \ldots, N)$.

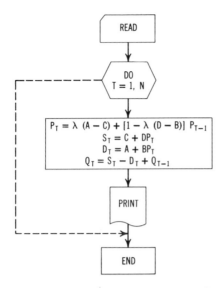

Figure 4-2.   The flow chart for Cobweb Model 3.

A Model of a Competitive Industry

This model provides us with an example of a simulation of a three-firm competitive industry in which each firm must decide each period how much it is going to produce and to sell. That is, the output the firm produces each period is considered as a controllable variable. The output decision for each firm is made by the individual firms themselves instead of by a mathematical decision rule that has been programmed into the computer. This is in contrast to the cobweb models in which output decisions were controlled entirely by mathematical formulas based on particular behavioral assumptions as to how firms or industries make their output decisions. Variables that are subject to human control of this type are said to be "instrumental" or "decision" variables. This model is a variation of a small-scale experimental game developed by Austin C. Hoggatt [45]. The variables, behavioral equations, and identities for this model are outlined below.

DECISION VARIABLE

X_{iT} = the quantity produced and sold by the ith firm in the Tth
period, i = 1, 2, 3.   (4-21)

EXOGENOUS VARIABLES

U_{iT} = a stochastic variate with a given expected value, variance,
and probability distribution.   (4-22)

V_T = a stochastic variate with a given expected value, variance, and probability distribution. $\qquad$ (4-23)

PARAMETERS

A_i = a scale parameter for the ith firm, i = 1, 2, 3. $\qquad$ (4-24)
B = a technological parameter. $\qquad$ (4-25)
C = a technological parameter. $\qquad$ (4-26)
D,E,F,G = constants. $\qquad$ (4-27)

ENDOGENOUS VARIABLES

S_T = quantity supplied by the entire industry in period T. $\qquad$ (4-28)
D_T = quantity of the industry's output demanded in period T. $\qquad$ (4-29)
P_T = industry price in period T. $\qquad$ (4-30)
C_{iT} = total cost of production of the ith firm in the Tth period. $\qquad$ (4-31)
Π_{iT} = total profit of the ith firm in period T. $\qquad$ (4-32)

BEHAVIORAL EQUATIONS

$$C_{iT} = (X_{iT} - A_i)^2 + BA_i^2 + C + U_{iT}. \qquad (4\text{-}33)$$
$$P_T = D - ED_T - FD_{T-1} - GD_{T-2} + V_T. \qquad (4\text{-}34)$$

IDENTITIES

$$S_T = \sum_{i=1}^{3} X_{iT}. \qquad (4\text{-}35)$$

$$S_T = D_T. \qquad (4\text{-}36)$$

$$\Pi_{iT} = P_T X_{iT} - C_{iT}. \qquad (4\text{-}37)$$

In making its output decisions, each firm is assumed to have the following information available to it.

1. Each firm knows the coefficients of its own cost function.

2. Each firm knows the functional form of the cost functions of other firms but not the coefficient values.

3. Each firm knows the demand function facing the industry and the values of its parameters.

4. Each firm knows the total industry output for the two previous periods.

5. Each firm knows the industry price of the previous period.

Since collusion is not permitted, the information available to each firm is strictly limited to the five items listed above. After each firm makes its output decision on the basis of the given information available, the outputs of the three firms are added together to obtain the total quantity supplied by the industry as indicated by (4-35). The market is forced into short-run equilibrium each period by the identity (4-36). Once the quantity demanded D_T, is established by (4-36), then (4-34) (the industry demand function) yields P_T the market clearing price. The industry demand curve expresses price as a function of the quantity actually sold in periods T, T-1, and T-2, as well as a random variable. Once the industry price is determined, total profit is computed for each firm according to (4-37). Therefore, a firm's profit depends on the industry price, the firm's output, the scale of the plant as measured by the parameter A_i, the present state of technology as measured by B and C, and the random variable U_{iT}. (The values of B and C are the same for all three firms.)

A flow chart for this three-firm industry simulation can be found in Figure 4-3. The data which must be read into the computer include X_{iT}, A_i, B, C, the mean and variance of U_{iT} and V_T, and the constants D,E,F,G.

This simulation can be easily extended to an N-firm industry. Experiments can also be performed on the birth and death of firms. That is, we might begin with, say, ten firms in the industry. In each period when, at

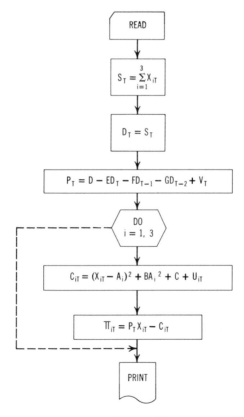

Figure 4-3. The flow chart of a three-firm competitive industry.

least, one firm operates at a loss (that is, has negative profit), the firm that has the greatest loss is eliminated from the industry. In each period when, at least, one firm has a positive profit, then a new firm will enter the industry. This new firm enters the industry at an optimum scale (as measured by A_i) based on the assumption that the price in the previous period will continue in the future. Another way in which the model could be modified would be to use mathematical decision rules to determine each firm's output in a particular period. One possible rule might be stated as follows: each firm assumes that its competitors will not change their output in the following period. That is, each firm assumes that the only changes in output for the industry in the next period (over the previous period) will be attributed only to its changes (the particular firm's changes) in output and not to that of its competitors. Each firm would then produce at the optimum level each period, based on its cost function and the industry demand function in which the output of the firm's competitors is held constant. Such a rule can easily be determined by applying simple differential calculus to (4-37). It also is possible to make interesting comparisons between the behavior of our simulated industry and that of industries whose behavior is based on classical duopoly and oligopoly models as well as that of industries in the real world.

A Duopoly Model

One of the most fertile fields for the application of computer simulation in economics is in the area of economic theory known as oligopoly theory. The theory of oligopoly, of which duopoly theory is a special case, is one of the oldest of all economic theories that are concerned with competition and monopoly and the behavior of the individual firm. Although the theory of oligopoly began with the work of Cournot in 1838 and Edgeworth in 1897, its usefulness in economics has until recently been limited primarily to that of a pedagogical device rather than as a theory that describes or predicts the behavior of firms in the real world. Before the advent of the computer, practical necessity dictated that theories of oligopoly and duopoly be based on fairly strong (and frequently unrealistic) assumptions, since to do otherwise would lead to models of such a complex nature that they would be impossible to solve or to interpret. Nevertheless, there has not been a very high degree of correlation between the behavior of actual business firms and the behavior of the hypothetical firms described by the mathematical constructs of classical oligopoly and duopoly theory. However, with the arrival of the computer, the necessity of basing oligopoly and duopoly theories on assumptions that are completely incompatible with the real world no longer exists, as the recent work of Cyert, Feigenbaum, and March demonstrates [19]. These researchers, by using a set of highly detailed assumptions about the behavior of the decision processes of firms, and by specifying particular values for the parameters of their model, have achieved a relatively high degree of success in simulating some aspects of the behavior of the tin can industry from the time when the Continental Can Company entered as a competitor to the American Can Company.

To illustrate the applicability of computer simulation to oligopoly and duopoly theory, we have chosen to use a slightly modified version of Cournot's duopoly model as an example. Although the model is quite unrealistic and is based on a set of rather gross assumptions, it easily can be extended to include more detailed and more realistic assumptions. Several possible extensions of the model are suggested following the explanation of the model and the simulation procedure. Furthermore, our only purpose in restricting the model to the special case of duopoly is to conserve time and space in explaining the model. The model works equally well for any number of firms.

The following assumptions underlie our particular interpretation of the Cournot model.

1. The industry consists of two firms, A and B.
2. Both firms are profit maximizers.
3. Both firms decide in each time period how much they will produce during that time period. This is the only decision made by the firms.
4. The demand function for the industry as a whole is known by both firms.
5. The industry demand function is a linear function in which price is expressed as a function of total industry output plus a random variable.
6. Firm A assumes that Firm B's output in period T will be the same as it was in period T-1. Firm B assumes that Firm A's output in period T will be the same as it was in period T-1.
7. The total output of Firm A and Firm B combined is sold each period at the market price, that is, the price at which the market can absorb the entire industry output.
8. Unit costs are constant for both firms and equal.
9. The firms produce a perfectly homogeneous product, in no way differentiated.
10. There are no limitations on the production capacity of either firm. The variables and functional relationships for our model are specified below.

EXOGENOUS VARIABLES

U_T = a stochastic variate with a given mean and variance and a
known probability distribution.   (4-38)

PARAMETERS

$$C = \text{unit cost for Firm A and Firm B.} \tag{4-39}$$

$$D \text{ and } E = \text{constants.} \tag{4-40}$$

ENDOGENOUS VARIABLES

$$A_T = \text{output of Firm A in period T.} \tag{4-41}$$

$$B_T = \text{output of Firm B in period T.} \tag{4-42}$$

$$Q_T = \text{industry output in period T.} \tag{4-43}$$

$$P_T = \text{industry price in period T.} \tag{4-44}$$

$$\Pi A_T = \text{profit of Firm A in period T.} \tag{4-45}$$

$$\Pi B_T = \text{profit of Firm B in period T.} \tag{4-46}$$

BEHAVIORAL EQUATIONS

$$P_T = D - EQ_T + U_T. \tag{4-47}$$

$$A_T = \frac{D - EB_{T-1} + U_T - C}{2E}. \tag{4-48}$$

$$B_T = \frac{D - EA_{T-1} + U_T - C}{2E}. \tag{4-49}$$

IDENTITIES

$$Q_T = A_T + B_T. \tag{4-50}$$

$$\Pi A_T = P_T A_T - CA_T. \tag{4-51}$$

$$\Pi B_T = P_T B_T - CB_T. \tag{4-52}$$

A word of explanation is in order concerning the derivation of (4-48) and (4-49). Firm A's expected profit is given by the expression:

$$\Pi A_T = P_T A_T - CA_T. \tag{4-53}$$

By substituting the value of P_T in (4-47) for P_T in (4-53) ,we obtain

$$\Pi A_T = (D - EQ_T + U_T)\, A_T - CA_T. \tag{4-54}$$

or, equivalently,

$$\Pi A_T = DA_T - EQ_T A_T + U_T A_T - CA_T. \tag{4-55}$$

But Firm A assumes that Firm B's output in period T will be equal to B_{T-1}. Therefore,

$$Q_T = A_T + B_{T-1} \tag{4-56}$$

represents Firm A's expectation concerning total industry output in period T. By substituting (4-56) into (4-55), we obtain

$$\Pi A_T = DA_T - EA_T(A_T + B_{T-1}) + U_T A_T - CA_T. \tag{4-57}$$

Taking the first derivative of (4-57) with respect to A_T and setting it equal to zero, we obtain

$$\frac{d(\Pi A_T)}{dA_T} = D - 2EA_T - EB_{T-1} + U_T - C = 0. \qquad (4\text{-}58)$$

And solving for A_T we arrive at Firm A's output decision,

$$A_T = \frac{D - EB_{T-1} + U_T - C}{2E}. \qquad (4\text{-}59)$$

Firm B's output quantity (4-48) can be derived in a similar manner.

A flow chart for generating the time paths for this hypothetical industry over N time periods appears in Figure 4-4. Given the values of C, D, E, A_0, and B_0, as well as the parameters describing U_T, the simulation of the behavior of this industry follows a straightforward process.

Behavioral Models

Recently, Cyert and March [20] and others have proposed several extensions to the traditional economic theory of the firm which attempt to integrate organization theory into the existing theory of the firm. In *A Behavioral Theory of the Firm* [20] Cyert and March have developed a theory that centers on the organizational decision-making process of the firm with special emphasis given to decisions such as price, output, and resource allocation. Their theory consists of four subtheories:

1. *A theory of organizational goals* to consider how goals arise in an organization, how they change over time, and how the organization attends to them.

2. *A theory of organizational expectations* to treat the questions of how and when an organization searches for information or new alternatives and how information is processed through the organization.

3. *A theory of organizational choice* to treat the process by which the alternatives available to the organization are ordered and the decisions made among them.

4. *A theory or organizational control* to explain the differences between managerial choice in a firm and the decisions actually implemented [20, p. 21].

Cyert and March have applied their theory of the firm to the development of several computer models of the firm, including a duopoly model, an oligopoly model, and a model of a department store. In the following paragraphs, we shall describe these three models as well as the behavioral models developed by Cohen and Cyert [16] and Bonini [9].

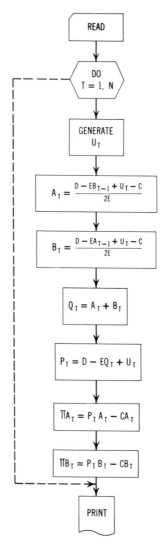

Fgure 4-4. The flow chart for a duopoly model.

Duopoly Model

The duopoly model developed by Cyert, Feigenbaum, and March [19] is one of the most interesting recent extensions of classical oligopoly theory from the standpoint of the degree of detail incorporated into the assumptions underlying the model. Their model is considered by some economists as an indication of the direction that research on the theory of oligopoly will take in the future. The assumptions of the model are summarized as follows:

> In rough outline, each firm is assumed to: (1) forecast the reactions of its competitor, (2) revise its estimate of the demand curve, (3) revise its estimate of its own cost curve, (4) specify its profit goal (on the basis of its profit achievement in the past), (5) evaluate the alternatives available to it. If no alternatives which meet its goal are available, the firm (6) searches for opportunities for cost reduction, (7) re-examines its estimates of demand, and (8) lowers its profit goal to a more modest level. Finally, the firm (9) sets its output for the coming period [14, p. 926].

In contrasting behavioral duopoly models with classical duopoly models, Cyert, Feigenbaum, and March have stated:

> (1) The models are built on a description of the decision-making process. . . . (2) The models depend on a theory of search as well as a theory of choice. They specify under what conditions search will be intensified. . . . They also specify the direction in which search will be undertaken. . . . (3) The models describe organizations in which objectives change over time as a result of experience. . . . (4) Similarly, the models describe organizations that adjust forecasts on the basis of experience. Organizational learning occurs. . . . (5) The models introduce organizational biases in making estimates. . . . (6) The models all introduce features of organizational slack [19, pp. 93-94], [14, p. 926].

Oligopoly Model

The oligopoly model is essentially an extension of the duopoly model and represents an attempt to describe and to analyze a general behavioral theory of price and output determination for an oligopoly.

> The model portrays the process of decision making in terms consistent with a behavioral theory of the firm. The firm uses multiple, changing, aspiration-level goals; it solves problems in each of its decision areas more or less independently; it searches for solutions in a manner learned from experience. Decisions on price, output, and sales strategy are made on the basis of profit, inventory, production-smoothing, sales, market share, and competitive position goals [20, p. 182].

A unique feature of this model is the use of multiple regression analysis "to determine the extent to which behavior in the model is sensitive to variations in various internal parameters" [20, p. 173].

Department-Store Model

The department-store model was used by Cyert and March to illustrate the applicability of their general behavioral theory of the firm to a particular type of firm, namely, a large retail department store. The modeled firm is a part of an oligopoly that consists of three large downtown department stores. Although each of the firms in the market operates one or more suburban stores, attention is focused on the downtown market, where each firm makes most of its sales. The firm in question has several merchandizing groups, each of which has several departments. The department store has more than 100 departments.

The model assumes that price and output decisions are made independently of each other. For the most part, price and output decisions are made on the basis of different goals and different stimuli. Each department in the firm is assumed to pursue two general goals:

(1) *A sales objective;* the department expects (and is expected by the firm) to achieve an annual sales objective; (2) *a mark-up objective;* the department attempts to realize a specified average mark-up on the goods sold [20, p. 129].

Decisions are made in response to actual problems and perceived potential problems with respect to one or the other of the above-mentioned goals.

A flow chart of the decision-making process of a department with respect to the sales goal is outlined in Figure 4-5.

The organization forms sales "estimates" that are consistent with its sales goal and develops a routine ordering plan for advance orders. These orders are designed to avoid overcommitment, pending feedback on sales. As feedback on sales is provided, results are checked against the sales objective. If the objective is being achieved, reorders are made according to standard rules. This is the usual route of decisions. . . .

Suppose, however, that the sales goal is not being achieved. Under such circumstances a series of steps is taken. First, the department attempts to change its environment by negotiating revised agreements with either its suppliers or other parts of its own firm or both. Within the firm, it seeks a change in the promotional budget that will provide greater promotional resources for the goods sold by the department. Outside the firm, the department seeks price concessions from manufacturers that will permit a reduction in retail price. If either of these attempts to relax external constraints is successful, reorders are made according to appropriately revised rules.

Second, the department considers a routine mark-down to stimulate sales generally and to make room for new items in the inventory. . . . The department ordinarily has a pool of stock available for mark-downs and expects to have to reduce the mark-up in this way on some of the goods sold. It will attempt to stimulate all sales by taking some of these anticipated markdowns. Once again, if the tactic is successful in stimulating sales, reorders are made according to slightly revised rules.

Third, the department searches for new items that can be sold at relatively low prices (but with standard mark-up). Most commonly such items are found when domestic supplies are eliminating lines or are in financial trouble. A second major source is in foreign markets.

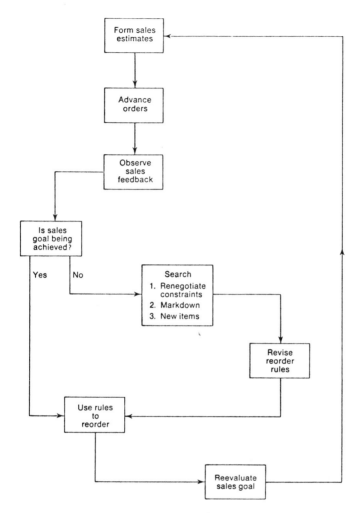

Figure 4-5. The general form of reaction to sales-goal indicators.

In general, the department continues to search for solutions to its sales problems until it finds them. If the search procedures are successful, all goes well. In the long run, however, it may find a solution in another way. The feedback on sales not only triggers action, but also leads to the re-evaluation of the sales goal. In the face of persistent failure to achieve the sales goal, the goal adjusts downward. With persistent success it adjusts upward [20, pp. 129-131].

The flow chart in Figure 4-6 describes the departmental decision process with respect to the markup goal.

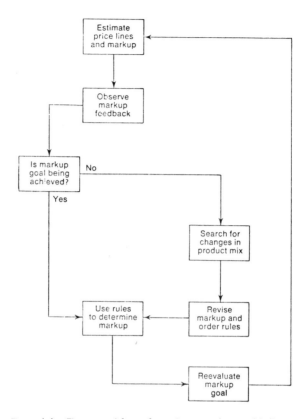

Figure 4-6   The general form of reaction to markup goal indicators.

On the basis of the mark-up goal (and standard industry practice), price lines and planned mark-up are established. Feedback on realized mark-up is received. If it is consistent with the goal, no action is taken and standard decision rules are maintained.

If the mark-up goal is not being achieved, the department searches for ways in which it can raise mark-up. Basically, the search focuses on procedures for altering the product mix of the department by increasing the proportion of high-up items sold. For example, the department searches for items that are exclusive, for items that can be obtained from regular supplies below standard cost, and for items from abroad. Where some of the search efforts led to price reduction (and maintenance of mark-up) when stimulated by failure on the sales goal, here they lead to maintenance of price and increase in mark-up. At the same time, the organization directs its major promotional efforts toward items on which high mark-ups can be realized. In some instances, the department has a reservoir of solutions to mark-up problems (e.g., pressure selling of high mark-up items). Such solutions are generally reserved for problem solving and are not viewed as appropriate long-run solutions

Finally, as in the case of the sales goal, the mark-up goal adjusts to experience gradually [20, p. 131].

Following this general description of their department-store model, Cyert and March then developed a detailed model of the major price and output decisions for the modeled firm and compared the results of computer simulation experiments with the model with actual results from the organization being investigated.

Monopoly Model

Another behavioral model (which is also a computer model) has been proposed by Cohen and Cyert [17]. Their model describes the behavior of a monopolist in the absence of a well-defined objective function which it is trying to maximize.

This model assumes behavior by the firm which is characterized by an aspiration level mechanism defining when satisfactory performance has been attained and by the existence of organizational slack which allows members of the firm to absorb part of the profits as costs.

The model embodies a single type of dynamic behavior: it is a sequence of one-period decisions in which the environment at the start of each period is affected by the firm's past behavior. The internal climate of the firm and its mechanism for making decisions are also affected by past behavior. The firm makes its decisions on a one-period basis, however, ignoring any implications for the future which may be implicit in its present behavior.

The demand function facing the monopolist is the same each period, except for the addition of a random term which varies over time. The firm's aspiration level equals its profits last period. Over time the firm tries to increase its profits. If it succeeds, organizational slack increases and it becomes less precise in determining output. Thus, in good times there is less pressure on the managers of the firm, and they have more freedom to pursue their own aims independent of the firm's profit goal. During any period that the firm fails to increase its profits, the reverse effect occurs. Organizational slack decreases and the managers become more attentive to business and set the firm's output more precisely [17, pp. 363-364].

Bonini Model

Another interesting behavioral model was developed by Bonini for his doctoral dissertation entitled "Simulation of Information and Decision Systems in the Firm" [9]. This model of a hypothetical business firm represents a synthesis of some of the important theories from a number of disciplines, among which are economics, accounting, organization theory, and behavioral science. The Bonini model consists of a series of difference equations which are used in the following way:

... specify in quantitative terms the behavior of individuals or groups within the organization as a function of the behavior of other individuals and of the information available, both past and present. The sum of these behavior parts for individuals represents the total model [9, p. 11].

The essential elements of the Bonini hypothetical business organization include decision centers, information centers, decision rules, information links, information systems, and decision systems. The purpose of the model was to study the effects of three types of changes on the behavior of the firm-changes in the external environment, changes in the information system, and changes in the decision system. This analysis was accomplished by a factorial experimental design in which the main effects and the various interactions of eight specific changes in the model on prices, inventory levels, costs, sales, profits, and organizational pressure were estimated. In addition, the factorial experimental design yielded estimates of the effects on the behavior of the firm of differences in the initial starting conditions of the firm. The eight types of alterations that were made on the model and whose effects on firm behavior were analyzed included:

1. Low versus high variability in the external environment of the firm. More specifically, we are interested in the effect of small versus large standard deviations in the probability distributions for sales and production costs.

2. Two different market trends for the firm: one a slow (2 percent per year) growth upon which is imposed a three-year cycle; the other a fast (10 percent per year) but irregular growth.

3. A "loose" versus "tight" industrial engineering department in the matter of changing standards.

4. An organization that is contagious to pressure as opposed to one that is not.

5. An organization in which the individuals are sensitive to pressure as opposed to one in which they are not.

6. An average cost method of inventory valuation versus a LIFO method.

7. Knowledge on the part of the sales force about the inventory position of the company versus the absence of such knowledge.

8. The reliance primarily on present versus past information for control within the firm [9, pp. 86-87].

Bonini then tested null hypotheses according to which these changes taken both one at a time and two at a time had no significant effect on the behavior of the firm as measured by changes in prices, inventory levels, costs, sales, profits, and organizational pressure.

Industrial Dynamics (DYNAMO)

Industrial Dynamics [33] has been defined by its author, Jay Forrester, as follows:

> . . . the study of the information-feedback characteristics of industrial activity to show how organizational structure, amplification (in policies), and time delays (in decisions and actions) interact to influence the success of the enterprise. It treats the interactions between the flows of information, money, orders, material, personnel, and capital equipment in a company, an industry, or a national economy [33, p. 13].

Forrester has developed his own set of flow chart symbols and special-purpose simulation language, DYNAMO, to simulate the behavior of business and economic systems that can be described in terms of a set of recursive difference equations.

In his book entitled *Industrial Dynamics* [33], Forrester describes three *Industrial Dynamics* models of the firm including a production-distribution model, an advertising model, and a customer-producer-employment model. The DYNAMO output for these models takes the form of a series of graphs of the time paths of the endogenous variables of the models. In addition to the hypothetical models included in Forrester's book [33], *Industrial Dynamics* has also been applied to a number of simulations of firms and industries in the real world, for example, the Sprague Electric Company [33, p. ix], the shoe, leather, hide industry [91], and the textile industry [92]. Several excellent papers have been written that describe specific applications of *Industrial Dynamics*. They include the work of Carlson [10], Fey [30], Forrester [31,32,34], Jarmain [51], Roberts [80], and Wismer [90]. Other important applications of *Industrial Dynamics* include Nord's (72) study of interaction between a company's capacity acquisition policy and the growth rate of new products, Packer's [76] study of research acquisition in corporate growth, and Holland and Gillespie's [47] simulation of the Indian economy. The paper by Ansoff and Slevin [5] contains a useful critical appraisal of *Industrial Dynamics*. Almost without exception, the papers that have been written describing specific simulation experiments with *Industrial Dynamics* have completely ignored the problems of experimental design and data analysis.

The special-purpose simulation language, DYNAMO, was written as a companion language to *Industrial Dynamics* by Alexander Pugh [78] at the Massachusetts Institute of Technology. DYNAMO bears a close resemblance to FORTRAN. A special set of flow chart symbols and figures have been developed by Jay Forrester for writing flow charts for economic and industrial systems that are to be converted into DYNAMO simulation programs. DYNAMO makes use of two different types of instructions (equations and directions) to obtain step-by-step (recursive) numerical solutions to the set of difference equations describing the system under study. The basic components of the DYNAMO language are almost identical to those found in FORTRAN because they include:

1. Variables.
2. Constants.
3. Subscripts.
4. Equations.
5. Functions.

However, in DYNAMO variables are further subdivided into levels, auxiliaries, rates, supplementary variables, boxcar trains, and initial values. DYNAMO equations are classified as either levels, ratios, or boxcars. The special functions or subroutines that are available with DYNAMO include:

1. Exponential.
2. Logarithmic.
3. Square root.
4. Trigonometric.
5. Uniform variates.
6. Normal variates.
7. Third-order delays.
8. Step functions.
9. Ramp functions.
10. Samplers.
11. Maximum and minimum functions.
12. Limiting functions.
13. Switch functions.
14. Table functions.
15. Summing functions.

A DYNAMO run consists of the following six phases.

1. The *input phase* reads the cards that describe the model specifications and generates tables in preparation of later phases.

2. The *generation phase* transforms the model specifications into computer instructions.

3. The *running phase* computes the values of the model variables, thereby generating data for printing and plotting.

4. The *printing phase* tabulates the data in the form requested on PRINT cards.

5. The *plotting phase* plots the data in accordance with the PLOT card requests.

6. The *rerun phase* modifies constants in preparation for rerunning a model by the running phase [78, p. 44].

DYNAMO programs consist of the following steps.

1. The formulation of a mathematical model of the system under study in DYNAMO notation.

2. The specification of the initial values of the system.
3. The provision of input data.
4. The assignment of values to constants in the model.
5. The specification of variables to be printed or plotted.
6. The identification of the model.
7. The specification of the required length of a simulation run.

The state of the system at the beginning of the simulation run is specified by the initial values or starting conditions included in the DYNAMO equations. Then the computer determines the values of the endogenous variables of the system at the end of each time interval. Since DYNAMO is a fixed-time-increment simulation language, each time interval is of equal length. Time can be advanced over as many time intervals as are required by the investigator. The values of the variables of the model of the system can be printed either in graphical or tabular form at the end of each iteration. Both the print-out procedure and the length of the simulation run are communicated to the computer by means of a set of direction instructions.

Although space does not permit a detailed description of the DYNAMO language, insight can be gained into the rudiments of DYNAMO by reference to the following example program. (For a complete treatment of DYNAMO the reader should consult the *DYNAMO User's Manual* [78] by Alexander Pugh.) The example program contained in Figure 4-7 is a DYNAMO version of Cobweb Model 1, which was described previously in Figure 4-1. The numbers found on the right-hand side of Figure 4-7 are strictly for expository purposes and should not be considered as part of the program.

The DYNAMO equations for the Cobweb Model are listed as (4-63) through (4-71). Equations (4-63) through (4-65) are subroutines for generating values for the stochastic variates U, V, and W, which are assumed to have expected values equal to 0.0 and standard deviations equal to 1.0. The letter K is a subscript that is analogous to T in Figure 4-1. K denotes the present time period. The symbol 34A denotes the type of DYNAMO equations found in (4-63) through (4-65). It is necessary to specify the exact type of all equations by a similar coding procedure, as is implied by the left-hand columns of the DYNAMO listing. Equation 4-66 is a "boxcar" function used to permit the storage and later use of historical data. In this example P_T is stored in the memory location denoted by the variable $P*1.K$, and P_{T-1} is stored in the location denoted by $P*2.K$. After each iteration is completed the value stored in location $P*1.K$ is shifted into $P*2.K$, and the number zero is stored in $P*1.K$. Equations 4-67 and 4-68 correspond to the supply equation in Figure 4.1. Equation 4-69 is the equilibrium condition for the model, and (4-70) is the price

RUN	1980TN	(4-60)
NOTE	COBWEB MODEL I	(4-61)
NOTE	NOTE	(4-62)
34A	U.K. = (1) NORMRN (0.0, 1.0)	(4-63)
34A	V.K. = (1) NORMRN (0.0, 1.0)	(4-64)
34A	W.K. = (1) NORMRN (0.0, 1.0)	(4-65)
37B	P = BOXLIN (2, 1.0)	(4-66)
12A	DP.K = (D) (P * 2.K)	(4-67)
8A	S.K. = A + DP.K + V.K	(4-68)
7A	D.K. = S.K − W.K	(4-69)
24A	X.K = (1/B) (A − C − DP.K + U.K + W.K − V.K)	(4-70)
56A	P * 1.K = MAX (X.K, 0.0)	(4-71)
NOTE		(4-72)
NOTE	INITIAL CONDITIONS	(4-73)
NOTE	NOTE	(4-74)
C	P * = 0/25	(4-75)
NOTE		(4-76)
NOTE		(4-77)
NOTE	CONSTANTS	(4-78)
C	A = 100	(4-79)
C	B = 2	(4-80)
C	C = 50	(4-81)
C	D = 3	(4-82)
NOTE		(4-83)
PRINT	1) S/2) D/3) P * 1	(4-84)
PLOT	S = S, D = D, P * 1 = P	(4-85)
SPEC	DT = 1.0/LENGTH = 50/PRTPER = 2/PLTPER = 1	(4-86)

Figure 4-7. A DYNAMO listing of Cobweb Model 1.

equation. Equation 4-71 is a subroutine for checking negative prices. If the price falls below zero, (4-71) automatically sets price equal to zero. The initial conditions and constants for the model are given by (4-75) and (4-79) through (4-82), respectively. The starting price is assumed to be 25, and A, B, C, and D are given by

$$A = 100$$
$$B = 2$$
$$C = 50$$
$$D = 3.$$

Equation 4-84 contains a print instruction indicating that variables S, D, and P * 1 should be tabulated. Equation 4-85 indicates that these same three variables should be plotted graphically. Finally, (4-86) specifies the length of each time interval (one year), the total number of time intervals to be simulated (50), the frequency with which the output variables should be tabulated (every other year), and the frequency with which the output variables should be plotted (every year).[1]

Reflections on Computer Models of the Firm

In December of 1960, *The American Economic Review* published a symposium on simulation which consisted of papers by Orcutt, Shubik, Clarkson, and Simon. The central theme of the latter two papers was that with the advent of computer simulation techniques, economists could look forward to some major innovations in the theory of the firm resulting from the use of simulation to develop more realistic, less aggregative, dynamic models of the firm. Shubik concluded his article with the following optimistic forecast:

Simulation studies promise to provide the way to add the richness (in terms of explicit consideration of information costs, marketing variables, organizational structure and so forth) needed to obtain adequate theories of the firm, pricing and market structure. The promise is two-fold. The new methodology is beginning to offer the opportunity both to construct more complex theories and to validate them [84, pp. 917-918].

Similar prognoses were made by Cohen and Cyert [16] and Clarkson and Simon [14].

Surprisingly enough, very few innovations in the theory of the firm have appeared in the published literature since 1960. Although Cyert and March's book was not published until 1963, most of the results that appeared in the book had been published previously in the form of journal articles and were well known in 1960. In fact, their work was cited by Shubik [84], Clarkson and Simon [14], and Cohen and Cyert [16]. Since 1960 (and particularly since 1963) the number of articles published in the leading economic journals on computer models of the firm has been small indeed. Given these developments, it is quite natural to ask why the theory of the firm has not been significantly modified beyond the initial perturbations injected by the work of Cyert and March? Why have computer simulation techniques had so little influence on the theory of the firm? Is this pattern likely to continue in the future?

[1] We are indebted to Gary McKay and Jerry Yurow of the Civilian Industrial Technology Program in Textiles (United States Department of Commerce) in Washington, D.C., for a number of helpful suggestions regarding our DYNAMO program and the discussion of the DYNAMO simulation language in general.

Although we do not claim to have answers to all of these questions, we, perhaps, can shed light on a number of problems that have tended to impede the development of computer models of the firm.

First, there is the problem of adequate data. If there is one general underlying characteristic of all of the computer models described thus far, it is the fact that they have a strong empirical base. But if one is going to construct an empirical model based on the behavior of one or more actual firms, he must have adequate data. Typically, data of the type required to build a highly disaggregative computer model of the firm is simply not available to professional economists. In part, this problem results from the fact that business firms simply are not willing to make their data available to "outsiders." This is likely to be particularly true of firms in a highly competitive industry. Although a number of large corporations such as Xerox, Sun Oil, Anheuser-Busch, Philadelphia Electric, IBM, Pillsbury, Wells Fargo Bank, and others have constructed large scale corporate models, these firms usually do not make available to outsiders detailed information about their models that would include data, behavioral assumptions, or output results. Although some of these models contain interesting extensions of the theory of the firm, thus far, the results of these simulation studies have not been widely circulated among economists.

Second, computer models require a detailed knowledge of the decision processes actually followed by firms. To obtain knowledge of this type, the economist must not only possess empirical data about the decision processes of actual firms but he must have a thorough grasp of the contributions to decision theory, the theory of group behavior, and so forth of a number of behavioral science disciplines, including psychology, sociology, political science, business administration, and economics. Unless the economist has both empirical data and a sound theoretical base on which to build, he is likely to encounter difficulty in constructing realistic behavioral models. Although economists have shown an increasing willingness to participate in interdisciplinary studies in recent years, they are still somewhat reluctant to engage in these projects. This type of behavior is in an extreme form among those economists who find it necessary to construct narrow definitions as to what constitutes "economics." As long as this type of economic provincialism exists, it will be a constraint on the future development of computer models of the firm.

Third, in a computer simulation experiment with a behavioral model of the firm, as in any experiment, careful thought should be given to the problem of experimental design. Although a number of researchers have considered the need to use experimental design techniques in computer simulation experiments and have noted the extensive literature on the subject of experimental design, economists have had little or nothing to say about the problem of designing simulation experiments with models of the firm. For this reason, the results of many of the existing simulation experiments with models of the firm have proved to be inconclusive and difficult to interpret. Clearly, there is need to devote more careful attention in the future to problems of experimental design and data analysis in conducting simulation experiments with computer models of the firm. Unless this is done, one should completely avoid making generalizations on the basis of poorly designed simulation experiments with models of the firm. Unfortunately, this rule has been violated too many times in the past and is, perhaps, a major source of the skepticism of some economists about the usefulness of computer models of the firm.

Fourth, it may be that, in some cases, computer models have been applied where traditional methods would have been more appropriate. For example, Machlup has argued that the simple marginal formula based on profit maximization is suitable where the following is true:

(1) *large groups* of firms are involved and nothing has to be predicted about particular firms, (2) the effects of a *specified change* in conditions upon prices, inputs, and outputs are to be explained or predicted rather than the values of the magnitudes before or after the change, and nothing has to be said about the "total situation" or general developments, and (3) only *qualitative answers*, that is, answers about directions of change, are sought rather than precise numerical results [60, p. 31].

Of course, one should avoid applying a particular type of model or analytical technique to a situation in which the facts are in direct conflict with the assumptions underlying the particular model or technique. In the case of models of the firm, one should never use numerical or simulation techniques when analytical techniques exist for analyzing the properties of the model.

INDUSTRY MODELS

In the preceding section we described several computer models of the firm. We now consider computer models of entire industries rather than a single firm. We begin by describing a computer model of the textile industry, developed by Naylor, Wallace, and Sasser [71]. Simulation results with this model also are presented. Next we provide summary descriptions of Cohen's [15] model of the shoe, leather, hide sequence and Balderston and Hoggatt's [6] model of the lumber industry.

A Model of the Textile Industry

Naylor, Wallace, and Sasser [71] have developed a model of the United States textile industry that attempts to explain the behavior of nine endogenous variables describing the textile industry between 1953 and 1962. The time paths of these endogenous variables for the period 1953 to 1962 are generated through the use of the model and computer-simulation techniques.

Monthly adjusted data was used to estimate the parameters of the model and to provide the observed values of the exogenous variables in the simulation runs. The data sources included the Office of Business Economics (OBE), the United States Department of Labor, the Federal Trade Commission, the Securities and Exchange Commission (SEC), and the American Textile Manufacturers Institute (ATMI). Nevertheless, the exogenous variables and lagged endogenous variables that appear in the model are but a sample of the total number of such variables considered in the study. A multiplicity of other variables were rejected because their parameter estimates were found to be statistically insignificant.

The model consists of the following endogenous, exogenous, and status variables, identities, and behavioral equations.

ENDOGENOUS VARIABLES

D_A = Apparel retail sales in millions of dollars (*Source.* OBE).

O_A = Index of production of apparel products (*Source.* OBE).

D_T = Shipments of textile mill products, in billions of dollars (*Source.* OBE).

O_T = Index of production of textile mill products (*Source.* OBE).

N_{PT} = Production and related workers on the payrolls in textile manufacturing in thousands (*Source.* OBE).

$E_{\overline{w}/m}$ = Average weekly gross earnings per production worker in textiles, in dollars (*Source.* OBE).

P_T = Index of prices of textile products and apparel (*Source.* United States Department of Labor).

II_T = Net profit after taxes in textile mill products quarterly in millions of dollars (*Source.* SEC).

I_T = Investment in new plant and equipment quarterly in billions of dollars (*Source.* SEC).

EXOGENOUS VARIABLES

DPI = Disposable personal income in billions of dollars (*Source.* OBE).

CPI = Consumer price index (*Source.* United States Department of Labor).

A_D = Magazine advertising for apparel and accessories in millions of dollars (*Source.* OBE).

INV_A = Inventories of apparel retail stores in millions of dollars (*Source.* OBE).

IP_{DG} = Index of production of durable goods (*Source.* OBE).
INV/UO = Ratio of inventories to unfilled orders for textile mill products (*Source.* ATMI).
P_W = Index of wool prices (*Source.* OBE).

STATUS VARIABLES

M = Monthly dummy variables, numbered 1 for January, 2 for February, . . . , and 12 for December.
T = Trend dummy variable numbered 1 through 144.
AD_A = Moving average of D_A.
AO_A = Moving average of O_A.
AD_T = Moving average of D_T.

IDENTITIES

$$AD_A(t) = \frac{1}{3} \sum_{r=1}^{3} D_A(t - r) \tag{4-87}$$

$$AO_T(t) = \frac{1}{6} \sum_{r=7}^{12} O_A(t - r) \tag{4-88}$$

$$AD_T(t) = \frac{1}{12} \sum_{r=1}^{12} D_T(t - r) \tag{4-89}$$

BEHAVIORAL EQUATIONS

Apparel demand.

$$D_A(t) = -552.71 + 300.81 \left[\frac{DPI(t - 1)}{CPI(t - 1)} \right] + 96.94[A_D(t - 1)]$$

$\theta =$

$$(48.8) \qquad\qquad (12.7) \tag{4-90}$$

$$-55.19[A_D(t - 2)] + 94.38[A_D(t - 3)] + 34.83[M]$$
$$(11.3) \qquad\qquad (12.2) \qquad\qquad (4.5)$$

R = .835.

Apparel output.

$$O_A(t) = -4.38 + .01824[AD_A(t)] + 30.70[INV_A(t - 1)]$$
$$(.0056) \qquad\qquad (3.10) \tag{4-91}$$

R = .786

Demand for textile mill products.

$$D_T(t) = .3029 + .0014[AO_A(t)] + .00064[IP_{DG}(t - 1)] + .0083[M]$$
$$(.00068) \qquad\qquad (.00011) \qquad\qquad (.0027)$$
R = .610
$$\tag{4-92}$$

Output of textile mill products.

$$O_T(t) = 58.99 + 41.20[D_T(t)] - 14.45\left[\frac{INV}{UO}(t-1)\right]$$
$$(3.2)(2.4)$$

$$- .515[M] + .082[T] \tag{4-93}$$
$$(.106)(.009)$$

$$R = .894$$

Employment of production workers.

$$N_{PT}(t) = 1684.29 + .4745[O_T(t)] + .9623[O_T(t-1)]$$
$$\phantom{N_{PT}(t) = 1684.29 + }(.21)(.33) \tag{4-94}$$

$$+ .6041[O_T(t-2)] + .7305[O_T(t-3)]$$
$$(.32)(.32)$$

$$- 411.72\left[\frac{DPI(t-1)}{CPI(t-1)}\right]$$
$$(14.84)$$

$$R = .936$$

Earnings.

$$E_{\overline{w}/m}(t) = .3153 + .0427[N_{PT}(t)] + .2421[T]$$
$$\phantom{E_{\overline{w}/m}(t) = .3153 + }(.0025)\phantom{.0427[N_{PT}(t)] + }(.0072) \tag{4-95}$$

$$R = .980$$

Prices.

$$P_T(t) = 169.07 - 8.41\left[\frac{INV}{UO}(t-1)\right] + .5722[E_{\overline{w}/m}(t)]$$
$$(2.13)\phantom{8.41\left[\frac{INV}{UO}(t-1)\right] + }(.1522) \tag{4-96}$$

$$+ .7986[P_T(t-1)]$$
$$(.0267)$$

$$+ .0342[P_w(t-1)] - .0682[T]$$
$$(.0093)(.0245)$$

$$R = .983$$

Profit.

$$II_T(t) = -463.43 + 1.80[P_T(t)] - 1.39[P_T(t-1)] + 41.28[D_T(t)]$$
$$(.33)(.31)(15.72) \tag{4-97}$$

$$- 58.65 \left[\frac{\text{INV}}{\text{UO}} (t - 1) \right] + 1.78[\text{E}_{\overline{\text{w}}/\text{m}}(t)]$$
$$ (9.91) (.42)$$

$$R = .851$$

Investment.

$$I_T(t) = -.1869 + .2524[\text{AD}_T(t)] + .000075[\text{T}]$$
$$ (.0138) (.000029) (4\text{-}98)$$

$$R = .90$$

This model of the textile industry is completely recursive. With a recursive model, ordinary least squares and full-information maximum likelihood methods are identical and in theory yield unbiased estimates. The parameters of the nine behavioral equations listed above were estimated by ordinary least squares. The standard errors of the parameter estimates are listed below the corresponding parameter estimates and are enclosed in parentheses. R denotes the multiple correlation coefficient. All of the parameter estimates are significant at the .05 level except the coefficient of $O_T(t - 2)$ in the employment equation which is significant at the .06 level. Most of the parameter estimates are significant at the .01 level.

Not unlike other econometric models, this model is at best merely a partial representation of the actual economic system whose behavior it attempts to explain, namely, the United States textile industry. In this section we shall provide a brief interpretation of the model, point out some of its obvious shortcomings, and indicate several possible ways to improve on it.

The apparel demand equation indicates that apparel retail sales depend, in part, on real disposable income, magazine advertising in the three preceding months, and the month of the year. The relationship between apparel sales and disposable income simply reflects the fact that the demand for apparel is influenced by the general state of the United States economy. The negative coefficient of $A_D(t - 2)$ does not lend itself to a simple explanation.

The apparel products production index is positively related to the moving average of apparel retail sales in the preceding three months and apparel inventories in retail stores in the preceding month.

The textile mill products demand equation represents, perhaps, the most serious deficiency of the model in the present form, since it does not provide for the impact of imports or exports on the total demand for textile mill products. The demand for textile mill products is explained by a moving average of the apparel production index for months $t - 7$ through $t - 12$, the index of production of durable goods in the previous month, and the monthly dummy variable. The inclusion of the durable goods production index represents an attempt to explain the portion of demand that is not derived from apparel demand but, instead, depends on the demand for industrial products such as automobiles, trucks, tires, and furniture. It, perhaps, would have been more appropriate to include some of these variables in the equation.

The textile mill products production index varies positively with the demand for textile mill products and the trend variable but varies negatively with the ratio of inventories to unfilled orders in the preceding month and the monthly dummy variable. Neither of these negative signs represents a surprise.

Employment in textiles varies positively with output in the present month and the three preceding months but varies negatively with real disposable personal income in period $t - 1$. The negative sign is consistent with, at least, two hypotheses. First, employment in textiles showed a downward trend in the 1950's as a result of automation and the substitution of capital for labor. During this same time period, real disposable personal income was going up. Hence, a negative relationship would be expected between the two variables. Second, wages in the textile industry are among the lowest in the country. To the extent that an increase in real disposable personal income reflects the ability of other industries to bid away the lower-paid textile workers from the textile industry during times of prosperity, textile employment would tend to vary negatively with real disposable income. One possible criticism of the employment equation is that it does not include a measure of the wage rate as an explanatory variable. It could be argued on the basis of economic theory that the level of employment and the wage rate are jointly determined. If this is the case, then the parameters of the employment and earnings equations should be estimated simultaneously by a technique other than least squares to avoid the problem of simultaneous equation bias.

The price equation yields the highest value of R for the nine equations. The textile and apparel price index is explained by the ratio of inventories to unfilled orders in period $t - 1$, the wage rate, the value of the textile and apparel price index in the preceding month, the price of wool in the preceding month, and the time trend. Surprisingly, the price of cotton failed to make a significant contribution to the variance of P_t when it was included in the regression equation. Hence, it was deleted from the final form of the equation.

Profit depends on the price of the product, the number of units of product sold, and the cost of the factors of production used in producing the product. Our profit equation includes explanatory variables that reflect the price of the product and the quantity sold, but the only factor cost that is included is the wage rate. It does not include the direct cost of raw materials. However, the cost of raw materials is indirectly reflected by the value of inventories in the ratio of inventories to unfilled orders. The most serious problem arising in conjunction with the profit equation is the fact that profit data are not available on a monthly basis and must be approximated from quarterly data.

Investment is explained in terms of a three-month moving average of demand and a time trend. It seems likely that other variables can be found to explain investment in new plant and equipment.

The method used to generate the time paths of the endogenous variables for our model is similar to the method employed by Kalman J. Cohen [15] with his "process" model of the shoe, leather, hide industry. The simulation run begins in February 1953 and terminates in December 1962.

The observed time paths of the exogenous variables are assumed to be given as well as the starting values for the lagged endogenous variables. The values of M and T are generated sequentially, as implied by their respective definitions. Each month the simulated values of the nine endogenous variables are determined by the nine behavioral equations, the three identities, the given values of the exogenous variables, and the values of the lagged endogenous variables. The values of the lagged endogenous variables are simply the simulated values of the endogenous variables generated in the preceding months and not the actual observed (*ex post*) values of the endogenous variables.

The time paths of the endogenous variables are plotted graphically in Figures 4-8 to 4-16 with the broken lines representing the simulated values. A total of 119 observations has been generated for each of the nine endogenous variables, that is, one observation for each month between February 1953 and December 1962. In their original paper, Naylor, Wallace, and Sasser [71] used spectral analysis and analysis of variance to test the validity of the simulation results.

A Model of the Shoe, Leather, Hide Industry

In his doctoral dissertation, entitled *Computer Models of the Shoe, Leather Hide Sequence*, Kalman Cohen formulated and experimented with two mathematical models—a "one-period-change model" and a "process model," describing the aggregate behavior of shoe retailers, shoe manufacturers, and cattlehide leather tanners between 1930 and 1940 [17]. The principal exogenous variables included in Cohen's models were the Bureau of Labor Statistics consumers' price index, disposable personal income,

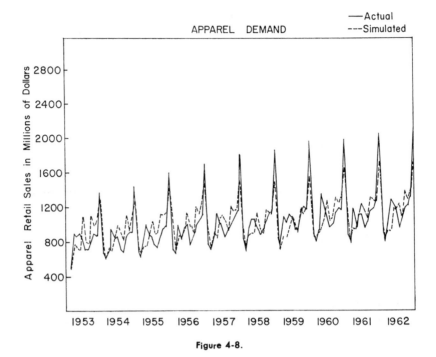

Figure 4-8.

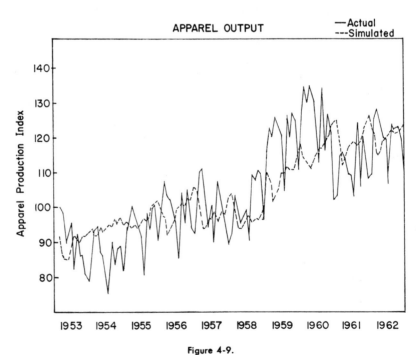

Figure 4-9.

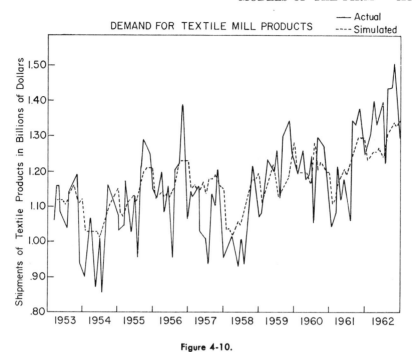

Figure 4-10.

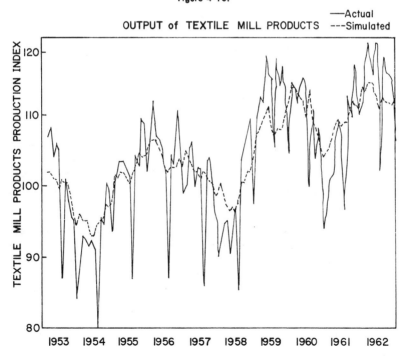

Figure 4-11.

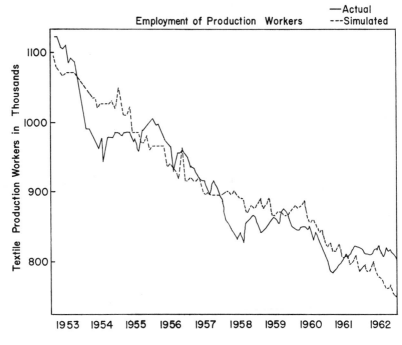

Figure 4-12.

and the stocks of hides held by hide dealers. After dividing the industry vertically into five segments—consumers, shoe retailers, shoe manufacturers, cattlehide tanners, and hide dealers—two major classes of endogenous variables were defined: price and physical flow. Among the endogenous variables analyzed by Cohen were the retailers' selling price, sales, and shoe receipts, the manufacturers' selling price, production, and leather receipts, the tanners' selling price, finished production, hide wettings, and hide receipts, and the hide dealers' selling price [17, p. vii]. Both of Cohen's models consisted of lagged simultaneous nonlinear difference equations subject to boundary constraints, with one month used as the unit of time.

. . . A "one-period-change model," is intended to explain the values of the endogenous variables for only one time period ahead into the future; this model assumes, as is usually done in econometrics, that lagged endogenous variables refer to their actually observed values. . . . A "process model" is designed to explain the determination of the endogenous variables for the arbitrarily large number of future time periods. The equations of the process model, together with the observed time path of the exogenous variables, are treated as a closed dynamic system; each month, the values of the predetermined endogenous variables are the values generated by the model, not the actually observed values [17, p. vii].

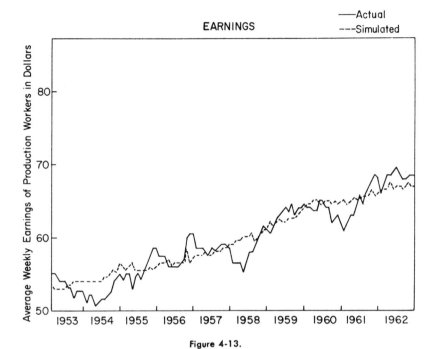

Figure 4-13.

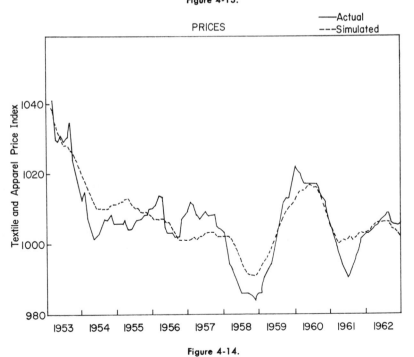

Figure 4-14.

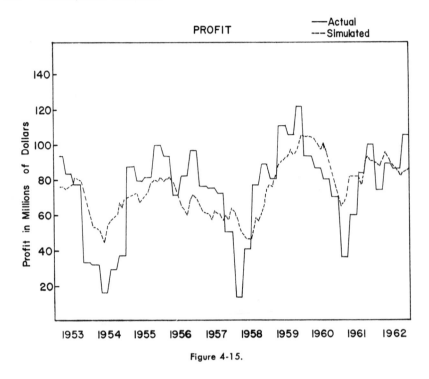

Figure 4-15.

A computer was used to generate the time paths from 1930 to 1940 of each endogenous variable for each of the two models. These results were in turn compared with the actual time paths of these variables. A very close correspondence was found between the simulated time paths and the actual time paths on an annual basis.

A Model of the Lumber Industry

The joint work of Balderston and Hoggatt [6,7] is a simulation study of the United States' West Coast lumber industry and attempts "to show how limits on market information, decentralization of market decisions, and institutional alignments affect and are affected by economic forces" [7, p. 183]. This study grew out of the initial investigations by Balderston of the communication networks in intermediate markets of the West Coast lumber industry and Hoggatt's doctoral dissertation "Simulation of the Firm" which employed simulation techniques to analyze several problems in traditional microeconomic theory.

Three sets of participants were involved in this industry model—manufacturers, wholesalers, and retailers. The FORTRAN computer program

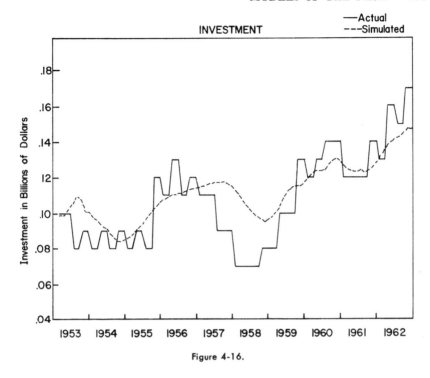

Figure 4-16.

for this model used six different classes of variables (of which there were 16,000) and functional relationships: economic, physical commodity flow, accounting and cash flow, decision, information, and institution. Manufacturers are assumed to sell to wholesalers who resell to retailers who, in turn, sell to final consumers according to explicit decision rules concerning price and output. However, physical shipments go from the manufacturer directly to the retailer (bypassing the wholesaler) and from the retailer to the final consumers. Complete accounting records (balance sheet, cash flow, net revenue, etc.) are maintained for each firm in the industry. Manufacturers and retailers obtain information from wholesalers in the form of "messages" that concern possible transactions. Messages are a prerequisite for a transaction to occur and must be paid for by the manufacturers and the retailers. They are analogous to long-distance telephone calls and telegraph messages between manufacturers and wholesalers, and retailers and wholesalers concerning prices and commodity supplies. Decision making is autonomous and completely decentralized among firms that follow a set of institutional decision rules for all transactions.

The principal value of this study lies not in its empirical accuracy in describing the behavior of the West Coast lumber industry but rather in the information it yields concerning the effects of changes in two key experimental parameters: "(1) the unit cost of sending a message . . . and (2) the choice of a method for setting the preference ordering by each firm on its potential partners in transactions" [7, p. 187]. This type of information could not have been otherwise obtained, if at all, without copious and laborious computations. Although this study provides a valuable linkage between economics, sociology, and marketing, it possesses four features that are of primary interest to economists in particular.

(1) It represents a multi-stage rather than a single-stage market; (2) the firms constituting the market face uncertainty and operate with limited information; (3) transactions occur by means of sequences of steps that are reminiscent of the Walrasian "tatonnements" though not identical with them; and (4) the system is dynamic in the strict, technical sense that its path develops, period by period, as a consequence of the interactions that occur [6, p. 16].

Recently this model has been extended by Preston and Collins to include a final-demand stage in the marketing process. A number of parameters and decision rules have been modified in the revision of the model, so as "to eliminate certain features of particular relevance to the study of the West Coast lumber industry and to replace these features with others of greater conceptual simplicity and more general theoretical interest" [77, p. 5]. One unique feature of this study is the use of response surface techniques to analyze the output data of the simulations.

MACROECONOMETRIC MODELS

Introduction

In the previous sections of this chapter we concentrated on simulation models of the firm and industry. However, now let us consider an even more difficult problem—namely, the problem of simulating the entire economy of a sociopolitical unit such as a state or a country. From a strictly technical standpoint the mechanics of simulating an economy on a computer are no different from the techniques that are required to simulate a firm, an industry, or some component thereof. That is, we still have to define the economic system, to define the pertinent exogenous and endogenous variables, to formulate mathematical models describing the system, to formulate a computer flow chart of the simulation procedure, and to write a computer program. But a number of big differences remain between simulating the behavior of an economy and simulating the behavior of a microeconomic system, and all of these differences are related to the problem of obtaining meaningful mathematical formulations of the behavioral equations of an economy.

First, the endogenous variables of a macrodynamic system, such as national income, national product, and total employment, are likely to depend on the magnitude of a very large number of significant variables (both exogenous and endogenous to the system)—considerably more than are usually found in microeconomic models. Second, if aggregative variables are used to describe the behavior of the system, then an acceptable theory of aggregation must be developed for the system, relating microeconomic variables to their aggregative counterparts. The so-called aggregation problem in economics has continuously plagued economists, both theoreticians and empiricists alike, throughout the history of economic thought. Third, there are likely to be complicated interactions and feedback effects among the endogenous variables of a macrodynamic system. Fourth, the formulation of realistic hypotheses concerning the behavior of a dynamic economy requires a considerable knowledge of macroeconomic theory. The analyst who attempts to use simulation techniques as a substitute for a thorough grounding in macroeconomic theory is very likely to find that he has simulated his own ignorance rather than the real world. Fifth, the econometric problem of estimating the parameters for multiple-equation, dynamic, aggregative models is indeed a formidable one. Sixth, suitable data for constructing mathematical models of macrodynamic systems may be even more difficult to obtain than data for microeconomic systems.

In a book of this kind we cannot possibly attempt to solve these problems or even to elaborate on them to any extent, since volumes have been written on each of them. However, we are obligated, at least, to forewarn the reader of the potential pitfalls he may face in attempting to simulate macrodynamic systems unless he has first acquired more than a superficial knowledge of macroeconomic theory, mathematical economics, and econometrics.

In this section, we begin by describing a simple, six-equation linear econometric model of the economy of the United States. We then give the results of a simulation experiment with the model. Next we consider the problem of simulating the behavior of macroeconomic systems which have been expressed in terms of nonlinear models. The Gauss-Seidel method and PROGRAM SIMULATE then are described as techniques for simulating the time paths of the endogenous variables of nonlinear econometric models. Next we present summary descriptions of the Brookings [23,39,40], OBE [43], and Wharton [28,29] econometric models of the United States economy. We conclude by defining a number of unresolved problems associated with macroeconometric simulation experiments.

An Example Model [83]

Problem Formulation

Suppose that we are interested in testing the effects of one or more governmental fiscal policies on the behavior of the economy of the United States. To be more specific, suppose that we are interested in the effects that (1) the governmental wage bill, (2) governmental demand, and(3) business taxes have on (1) consumption, (2) wages, (3) profits, (4) investment, (5) capital stock, and (6) national income.

Model Formulation

Given the above-mentioned objective, it follows that we should formulate an econometric model that relates the six endogenous variables defined above to the three policy variables. Needless to say, a realistic model explaining the behavior of these six endogenous variables would probably be quite complex. Clearly, these six endogenous variables are going to be influenced by variables other than the three policy variables listed above. For this reason, a valid model of the economy of the United States would probably require as many as 100 equations. The Wharton Model and the Brookings Models are examples of models of this type. In these models our six endogenous variables would be explained in terms of a multiplicity of other endogenous, policy, and exogenous variables. However, for expository purposes we shall consider a somewhat less complex six-equation econometric model of the United States economy that was developed by Klein [53]. This model has two principal attributes. First, it is a relatively simple model and well known to economists. Second, although an analytical solution exists for certain special cases of this model, it still possesses many of the characteristics of more complex econometric models which do not lend themselves to straightforward analytical solutions.

Specifically, the model consists of the following policy variables, output variables, and functional relationships:

POLICY VARIABLES

$W2_T$ = governmental wage bill in period T.
G_T = governmental demand in period T.
TX_T = business taxes in period T.

OUTPUT VARIABLES

C_T = consumption in period T.
$W1_T$ = private wage bill in period T.
Π_T = non-wage income (profits) in period T.
I_T = net investment in period T.
K_T = capital stock at end of period T.
Y_T = national income in period T.

BEHAVIORAL EQUATIONS

Consumption function.

$$C_T = a_1 + a_2(W1_T + W2_T) + a_3\Pi_T + a_4\Pi_{T-1} + \mu_{1T} \qquad (4\text{-}99)$$

Investment function.

$$I_T = b_1 + b_2\Pi_T + b_3\Pi_{T-1} + b_4K_{T-1} + \mu_{2T} \qquad (4\text{-}100)$$

Demand-for-labor function

$$W_{1T} = c_1 + c_2(Y_T + TX_T - W2_T)$$
$$+ c_3(Y_{T-1} + TX_{T-1} - W2_{T-1}) + c_4T + \mu_{3T} \qquad (4\text{-}101)$$

IDENTITIES

National income equation.

$$Y_T = C_T + I_T + G_T - TX_T \qquad (4\text{-}102)$$

Profit equation.

$$\Pi_T = Y_T - (W1_T + W2_T) \qquad (4\text{-}103)$$

Capital stock equation.

$$K_T = K_{T-1} + I_T \qquad (4\text{-}104)$$

The disturbance terms μ_1, μ_2, and μ_3 are assumed to have a multivariate normal distribution with expected values $E(\mu_1)$, $E(\mu_2)$, and $E(\mu_3)$ equal to zero and a variance-covariance matrix given by

$$\sum = \begin{bmatrix} \sigma_{11} & \sigma_{12} & \sigma_{13} \\ \sigma_{21} & \sigma_{22} & \sigma_{23} \\ \sigma_{31} & \sigma_{32} & \sigma_{33} \end{bmatrix} \qquad (4\text{-}105)$$

where σ_{ij} denotes the covariance between the contemporaneous disturbances in the ith and jth equation $(i, j = 1, 2, 3)$.

There are at least three reasons why one might want to include stochastic disturbance terms in simulation experiments with macroeconometric models. *First*, as Phil Howrey has pointed out in an unpublished paper entitled, "Dynamic Properties of Stochastic Linear Econometric Models," if the long-term properties of an econometric model are to be investigated,

. . . it may not be reasonable to disregard the impact of the disturbance terms on the time paths of the endogenous variables. Neither the characteristic roots nor the dynamic multipliers provide information about the magnitude or correlation properties of deviations from the expected value of the time path.

Second, Howrey and Kelejian [49] have demonstrated that, "the application of nonstochastic simulation procedures to econometric models that contain nonlinearities in the endogenous variables yields results that are not consistent with the properties of the reduced form of the model." *Third*, by including stochastic error terms, one can then replicate the simulation experiment and make statistical inferences and test hypotheses about the behavior of the system being simulated that are based on the output data generated by the simulation experiment.

Parameter Estimation

The parameters of the behavioral equations of our model were estimated by three-stage least squares and are given by

$$C_T = 16.44 + .7901(W1_T + W2_T) + .1249\Pi_T + .1631\Pi_{T-1} + \mu_{1T}$$

(4-106)

$$I_T = 28.18 - .01308\Pi_T + .7557\Pi_{T-1} - .1948K_{T-1} + \mu_{2T} \qquad (4\text{-}107)$$

$$W1_T = 15.08 + .4005(Y_T + TX_T - W2_T)$$
$$- .1813(Y_{T-1} + TX_{T-1} - W2_{T-1}) - .1497T + \mu_{3T} \quad (4\text{-}108)$$

The variance-covariance matrix $\sum$ can be estimated by the formula,

$$\sum = 1/N \; \hat{U}' \; \hat{U} \qquad (4\text{-}109)$$

Where $\hat{U}$ is the $N \times M$ matrix of least squares structural disturbances, N is the number of observations in the sample, and M is the number of behavioral equations.

Computer Program Formulation

Before formulating a computer program for simulating the behavior of our econometric model we shall introduce some matrix notation. By rearranging equations (4-99) through (4-104) and using the appropriate parameter estimates our system of equations becomes,

$$C_T - .7901W1_T - .1249\Pi_T = 16.44 + .7901W2_T + .1631\Pi_{T-1} + \mu_{1T}$$

(4-100)

$$I_T + .01308\Pi_T = 28.18 + .7557\Pi_{T-1} - .1948K_{T-1} + \mu_{2T} \qquad (4\text{-}111)$$

$$W1_T - .4005Y_T = 15.08 + .4005(TX_T - W2_T)$$
$$+ .1813(Y_{T-1} + TX_{T-1} + W2_{T-1}) + .1497 + \mu_{3T} \quad (4\text{-}112)$$

$$Y_T - C_T - I_T = G_T - TX_T \qquad (4\text{-}113)$$

$$\Pi_T + W1_T - Y_T = W2_T \qquad (4\text{-}114)$$

$$K_T - I_T = K_{T-1} \qquad (4\text{-}115)$$

The left side of the system contains terms associated with the current values of the endogenous variables; the right side contains all of the other terms including the lagged endogenous variables, the policy variables, the constant terms, and the disturbance terms. The left-hand side of the system of equations can be represented as follows:

$$
\begin{array}{l}
1C_T + 0I_T - .7901 \ W1_T + \quad 0 \ Y_T - .1249 \ \Pi_T + 0K_T \\
0C_T + 1I_T + \quad 0 \ W1_T + \quad 0 \ Y_T + .01308 \ \Pi_T + 0K_T \\
0C_T + 0I_T + \quad 1 \ W1_T - .4005 \ Y_T + \quad 0 \ \Pi_T + 0K_T \\
-1C_T - 1I_T + \quad 0 \ W1_T + \quad 1 \ Y_T + \quad 0 \ \Pi_T + 0K_T \\
0C_T + 0I_T + \quad 1 \ W1_T - \quad 1 \ Y_T + \quad 1 \ \Pi_T + 0K_T \\
0C_T - 1I_T + \quad 0 \ W1_T + \quad 0 \ Y_T + \quad 0 \ \Pi_T + 1K_T
\end{array}
\tag{4-116}
$$

In matrix form this can be denoted by $A \ X$ where A is the 6×6 coefficient matrix and X is the 6×1 column vector of the output variables.

$$
A = \begin{bmatrix}
1 & 0 & -.7901 & 0 & -.1249 & 0 \\
0 & 1 & 0 & 0 & .01308 & 0 \\
0 & 0 & 1 & -.4005 & 0 & 0 \\
-1 & -1 & 0 & 1 & 0 & 0 \\
0 & 0 & 1 & -1 & 1 & 0 \\
0 & -1 & 0 & 0 & 0 & 0
\end{bmatrix}
\quad X = \begin{bmatrix}
C_T \\ I_T \\ W1_T \\ Y_T \\ \Pi_T \\ K_T
\end{bmatrix}
$$

Next, we set the right-hand side of our system equal to the 6×1 column vector B.

$$
B = \begin{bmatrix}
16.44 + .7901W2_T + .1631\Pi_{T-1} + \mu_{1T} \\
28.18 + .7557\Pi_{T-1} - .1948K_{T-1} + \mu_{2T} \\
15.08 + .4005(TX_T - W2_T) + .1813(Y_{T-1} + TX_{T-1} \\
\qquad\qquad\qquad\qquad + W2_{T-1}) + .1497T + \mu_{3T} \\
G_T - TX_T \\
W2_T \\
K_{T-1}
\end{bmatrix}
$$

We can now represent our system in matrix form as

$$
A \ X = B. \tag{4-117}
$$

To generate the time paths of the endogenous variables of the system we just solve for X each time period,

$$
X = A^{-1}B. \tag{4-118}
$$

Figure 4-17 contains a computer flow chart for simulating the behavior of our system for N time periods. We begin by reading in the initial values of the lagged endogenous variables Π, K, and Y. Next we read in the coefficient matrix A and calculate the inverse of A. Blocks 4 to 6 of Figure 4-17 represent a DO-loop for calculating X. This procedure is repeated N times, where N denotes the length of the planning horizon. To calculate B, we must read in the appropriate values of the policy variables each period and generate the disturbance terms through the use of a multivariate normal subroutine (see Appendix B). The current values of the endogenous variables for each period are calculated from (4-118). The lagged endogenous variables that are used to calculate B are the values of the endogenous variables generated by the model in preceding periods. Thus, the simulation represents a closed-loop system in which values of the endogenous variables generated in one period are fed back into the system in future time periods. This procedure is repeated N times, and at the end of each period the results are printed out.

Once we have completed the computer flow chart of the logic of our simulation experiment we then can write a computer program for our

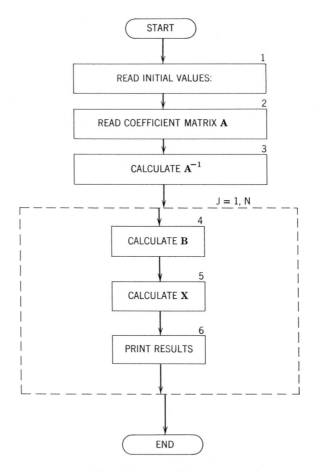

Figure 4-17. A flow chart of the example model.

model. In this case FORTRAN, PL/1, or ALGOL would be suitable programming languages or, perhaps, PROGRAM SIMULATE [48], which we describe later in this chapter.

Experimental Design

Suppose that we are interested in determining the effects of four different fiscal policies on the behavior of the economy as measured by national income. The four policies include these procedures:

1. Maintaining government spending, the government wage bill, and taxes at their present levels.
2. Reducing taxes by 5 percent.
3. Increasing government spending by 5 percent.
4. Increasing the government wage bill by 5 percent.

Suppose that the objective of the simulation experiment is to determine which policy yields the highest sample mean for national income over a 20-year planning horizon. We then would conduct an initial control run (Run 1) in which all three policy variables are held constant at their present levels. Three additional runs would then be made, each time changing one of the policy variables while holding the other two constant. Runs 2, 3, and 4 correspond, respectively, to increased government spending, an increased government wage bill, and decreased taxes.

Data Analysis

Figures 4-18 to 4-21 contain a graphical representation of the output data generated by Runs 1 to 4 of our simulation experiment. The values of national income for each period are tabulated in Table 4-1 for each of the four simulation runs. Sample means and variances are also recorded. We observe in Table 4-1 that the policy of increased government spending gives rise to the largest sample mean for national income among the four simulation runs. However, if our objective has been to determine the policy that induces the greatest degree of stability in national income, then we would select the policy associated with the smallest variance of Y_T, namely, an increase in the government wage bill.

If we wish to test hypotheses or to construct confidence intervals using the output generated by the experiment, we should consider statistical methods such as analysis of variance, multiple comparisons, multiple rankings, and spectral analysis. If our experimental objective is to test the hypothesis that there is no difference between two or more policies, then analysis of variance is an appropriate analytical tool. If the objective is to obtain estimates of the sizes of these differences, then multiple comparisons are more appropriate. But if the object is to find the best policy, second

Table 4-1   Tabular Representation of Simulation Output

YEAR	Run 1 CONTROL	Run 2 INCREASED GOV'T SPEND.	Run 3 INCREASED GOV'T WAGE BILL	Run 4 DECREASED TAX
1	52.37	60.06	54.17	54.48
2	76.29	85.63	81.60	82.98
3	99.18	101.36	98.96	104.06
4	115.27	114.70	108.08	112.46
5	118.94	113.76	104.52	113.00
6	107.81	106.64	97.56	105.08
7	85.06	93.72	84.51	89.37
8	61.91	84.83	76.37	70.28
9	49.32	71.12	72.85	56.13
10	39.89	72.88	73.51	49.53
11	42.91	75.38	75.34	52.12
12	47.86	76.66	77.32	60.71
13	46.00	79.26	71.67	62.73
14	53.95	82.05	76.55	63.82
15	61.50	87.42	85.27	70.03
16	62.62	95.63	89.28	76.69
17	63.51	100.25	94.45	79.22
18	64.93	108.69	95.22	80.86
19	59.70	114.36	95.99	79.71
20	61.29	121.99	86.70	76.17
$\Sigma.X$	1370.32	1846.39	1699.93	1539.43
$\overline{X}$	68.52	92.32	85.00	76.97
s^2	583.75	303.07	174.74	386.51

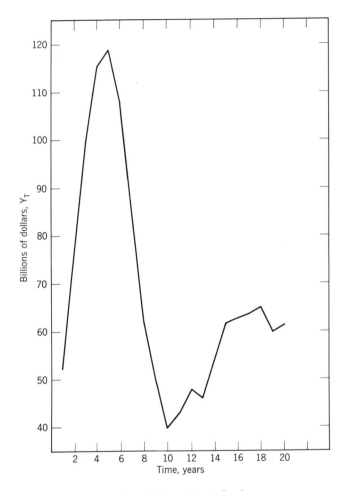

Figure 4-18.   Control—Run 1

best policy, and so on, then multiple ranking procedures represent the most direct approach. Spectral analysis is a statistical technique used by economists to analyze the behavior of economic time series which are usually highly autocorrelated. These data analysis techniques are discussed in Chapters 7, 8, and 9 and are applied to specific simulation experiments.

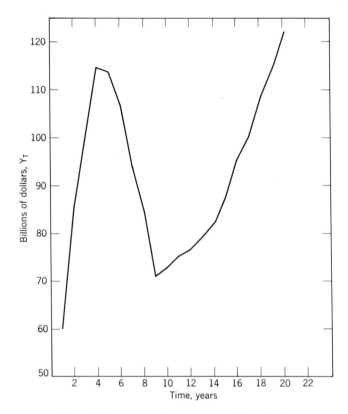

Figure 4-19. Increased government spending—Run 2.

Solving Econometric Models

Linear Models

The most general form of an econometric model is given by the set of equations [40, p. 364],

$$f_i(y_{i,\mathrm{T}},\ y_{i,\mathrm{T}-j},\ z_{k,\mathrm{T}}) = \mu_{i,\mathrm{T}} \qquad (4\text{-}119)$$

where

$\quad y_{i,\mathrm{T}}$ = endogenous variables, $i = 1, \ldots, n$
$\quad y_{i,\mathrm{T}-j}$ = lagged endogenous variables, $j = 1, \ldots, p$
$\quad z_{k,\mathrm{T}}$ = independent (exogenous and policy) variables, $k = 1, \ldots, m$
$\quad \mu_{i,\mathrm{T}}$ = random disturbance variables

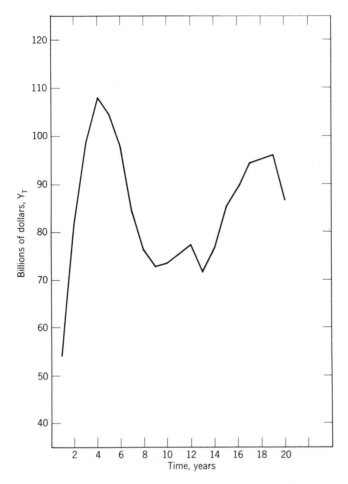

Figure 4-20. Increased government wage bill—Run 3.

If the equations of the model are linear, then the system will be of the following form,

$$a_i + \sum_{j=0}^{p} \sum_{h=1}^{n} b_{i,h,j} y_{h,\mathrm{T}-j} + \sum_{k=1}^{m} c_{i,k} z_{k,\mathrm{T}} = \mu_{i,\mathrm{T}} \qquad (4\text{-}120)$$

where $i = 1, \ldots, n$. Equation system 4-120 may be expressed in matrix notation as follows:

$$\mathbf{A} + \mathbf{B}\mathbf{Y}_\mathrm{T} + \sum_{j=1}^{p} \mathbf{B}_j \mathbf{Y}_{\mathrm{T}-j} + \mathbf{C}\mathbf{Z}_\mathrm{T} = \mathbf{U}_\mathrm{T} \qquad (4\text{-}121)$$

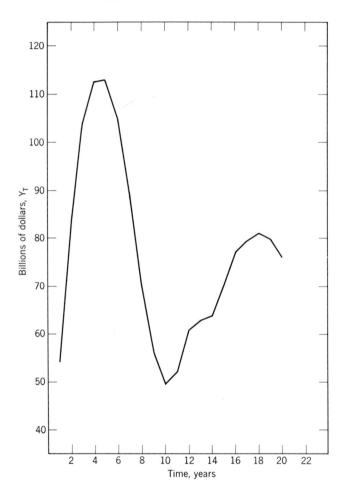

Figure 4-21.   Decreased tax—Run 4.

The coefficient matrices $\mathbf{A}$, $\mathbf{B}$, $\mathbf{B}_j$, and $\mathbf{C}$ are assumed to be known (or have been estimated by standard econometric techniques). With simulation at time period T, the values of $\mathbf{Y}_{T-j}$, $\mathbf{Z}_T$, and $\mathbf{U}_T$ are also known. $\mathbf{Y}_{T-j}$ was generated by the model j periods ago, the $\mathbf{Z}_T$'s are given, and $\mathbf{U}_T$ can be generated by the appropriate computer subroutine. Therefore, it is possible to solve (4-121) for $\mathbf{Y}_T$ and to express $\mathbf{Y}_T$ in terms of a set of coefficient matrices and variables that are completely known:

$$\mathbf{Y}_T = -\mathbf{B}^{-1}\mathbf{A} - \mathbf{B}^{-1}\sum_{j=1}^{p} \mathbf{B}_j\mathbf{Y}_{T-j} - \mathbf{B}^{-1}\mathbf{C}\mathbf{Z}_T + \mathbf{B}^{-1}\mathbf{U}_T \qquad (4\text{-}122)$$

Since it is possible to invert very large matrices on today's digital computers in only a few seconds, it is relatively easy to generate the time paths of the endogenous variables of *linear* econometric models through the use of computer simulation techniques.

Nonlinear Models

Unfortunately, realistic econometric models are seldom linear. One example of nonlinearity that arises frequently in econometric models is the use of price times quantity terms in the identity defining Gross National Product in current prices. The Wharton Model of the United States economy contains several other examples of nonlinearities including: (1) relative prices in the consumption functions, (2) logarithmic treatment of the production function, and (3) nonlinearity of the wage rate and capacity term in some of the price formation equations.

The Gauss-Seidel method is one of the easiest methods available for solving nonlinear econometric models. The paper by Evans [25] and the book by Klein and Evans entitled *Econometric Gaming* [56] provide complete descriptions of the Gauss-Seidel method. We briefly summarize the procedure by using the notation and example model suggested by Klein and Evans [25, 56].

For expository purposes, we consider a model which consists of only two equations, two endogenous variables, and two exogenous variables. We begin by writing each equation in the following form:

$$y_{1T} = f_1(y_{1T}, y_{2T}, y_{1,T-1}, y_{2,T-1}, z_{1T}, z_{2T})$$
$$y_{2T} = f_2(y_{1T}, y_{2T}, y_{1,T-1}, y_{2,T-1}, z_{1T}, z_{2T}).$$

$$(4\text{-}123)$$

Notice that each endogenous variable appears one and only one time on the left side of the system. For expository purposes, we assume a one-period lag structure for the endogenous variables. The method can easily be extended to include more equations, more variables, and more complex lag structures.

Next, we choose starting values for y_{1T} and y_{2T}. These starting values, $y_{1T}^{(0)}$ and $y_{2T}^{(0)}$, may be based on informed guesses or on recent observed values of y_{1T} and y_{2T}. We then substitute these starting values into (4-123) and obtain

$$y_{1T}^{(1)} = f_1[y_{1T}^{(0)}, y_{2T}^{(0)}, y_{1,T-1}, y_{2,T-1}, z_{1T}, z_{2T}]$$
$$y_{2T}^{(1)} = f_2[y_{1T}^{(0)}, y_{2T}^{(0)}, y_{1,T-1}, y_{2,T-1}, z_{1T}, z_{2T}].$$

$$(4\text{-}124)$$

Then continuing this iterative procedure we calculate

$$y_{1T}^{(2)} = f_1[y_{1T}^{(1)}, y_{2T}^{(1)}, y_{1,T-1}, y_{2,T-1}, z_{1T}, z_{2T}]$$
$$y_{2T}^{(2)} = f_2[y_{1T}^{(1)}, y_{2T}^{(1)}, y_{1,T-1}, y_{2,T-1}, z_{1T}, z_{2T}].$$

$$(4\text{-}125)$$

Notice that $y_{1,T-1}$, $y_{2,T-1}$, z_{1T}, and z_{2T} are fixed and known for each time period and do not change from iteration to iteration of the Gauss-Seidel method.

After r interations, the equation system will be of the following general form.

$$y_{1T}^{(r)} = f_1[y_{1T}^{(r-1)}, y_{2T}^{(r-1)}, y_{1,T-1}, y_{2,T-1}, z_{1T}, z_{2T}]$$
$$y_{2T}^{(r)} = f_2[y_{1T}^{(r-1)}, y_{2T}^{(r-1)}, y_{1,T-1}, y_{2,T-1}, z_{1T}, z_{2T}]$$

(4-126)

A useful "stopping rule" for terminating this procedure is to stop the process when the following inequalities are satisfied,

$$\left| \frac{y_{1T}^{(r)} - y_{1T}^{(r-1)}}{y_{1T}^{(r-1)}} \right| < .001$$

and

$$\left| \frac{y_{2T}^{(r)} - y_{2T}^{(r-1)}}{y_{2T}^{(r-1)}} \right| < .001$$

(4-127)

That is, we terminate the interative procedure when the endogenous variables change by less than .1 percent on successive interations, or when we have obtained a numerical solution with an arbitrarily chosen degree of accuracy.

We can increase the speed of convergence by substituting a value obtained during one interation into later equations in the same iteration. That is, we simply replace $y_{1T}^{(r-1)}$ by $y_{1T}^{(r)}$ in the second equation of the rth iteration. By using this modified procedure, the equations become

$$y_{1T}^{(r)} = f_1(y_{1T}^{(r-1)}, y_{2T}^{(r-1)}, y_{1,T-1}, y_{2,T-1}, z_{1T}, z_{2T})$$
$$y_{2T}^{(r)} = f_2(y_{1T}^{(r)}, y_{2T}^{(r-1)}, y_{1,T-1}, y_{2,T-1}, z_{1T}, z_{2T})$$

(4-128)

Two factors influence convergence in this algorithm. The first is the procedure of normalization; i.e., the choice of the variable in each equation to be written on the left hand side with unit coefficient and expressed as a function of all other variables. In almost all equations this normalization procedure can be carried out in a variety of ways. Some normalizations lead to convergence and some to divergence.

The other factor affecting convergence is the ordering of the equations in the case where we substitute in a given iteration a value computed earlier in the same iteration. This is not of any consequence if there are only two equations, but is important if there are several. As with normalization, some orderings lead to convergence while others cause divergence. No simple rule is available for the optimal ordering, and some experimentation may be necessary to find an ordering which will give a convergent solution. This is a consequence of the particular iterative procedure used here and not of the exact solution of the model itself. In particular, even if a fully simultaneous solution of the model always converges, an attempt to solve by iteration with an erroneous ordering will lead to divergence. This was actually the case in some early trials of solution for the Wharton Model [25, 56].

Program Simulate

An alternative to the use of the Gauss-Seidel method to solve nonlinear econometric models is to use a special purpose simulation language developed by Charles Holt [48] and his associates at the University of Wisconsin called PROGRAM SIMULATE II.

The original version of SIMULATE was written for a CDC 3600 and later adapted to the IBM 360/75 and the UNIVAC 1108. It was designed to solve a maximum of 200 linear or nonlinear difference equations with a maximum of 100 exogenous variables. SIMULATE is capable of performing the following functions:

(1) The manipulation of data used to validate the model and test its performance.

(2) The debugging of the model and the data.

(3) The analysis of the block recursive ordering of the equations of the model so that the simultaneous equation system of minimum size can be identified.

(4) The solution of the equation system.

(5) The calculation of measures of performance of the system.

This program is heavily user-oriented and provides numerous checks to detect various errors and prints out useful diagnostics.

SIMULATE is a two-stage program. SIMA analyzes a given model in terms of its lag structure and simultaneity and orders the model for solution. SIMB simulates the system over time by means of a user-specified procedure and calculates residuals for individual equations. In addition to the Gauss-Seidel method, the user may specify seven other methods for solving the nonlinear equations of the model including Newton's method, the Newton-Raphson method, the modified Newton-Raphson method, the relaxation method, and the modified relaxation method. All of these methods of solving nonlinear econometric models are described in [48].

For a given econometric model, the procedure is to run the model first through SIMA to determine the relevant ordering and then through SIMB for solution. Since the objective of most simulation experiments with econometric models is to explore the effects of alternative model formulations, parameter estimation procedures, and economic policies, the econometric model often will need to be altered between successive simulation runs and the results will have to be compared. To facilitate changes of this type, the program allows the user flexibility to make local changes in the model by adding, deleting, or modifying equations and variables.

Large-Scale Econometric Model

A number of large-scale econometric models have been developed in the past few years for the economy of the United States as well as for the economies of many other countries, including Brazil, Chile, England, France, Holland, India, Israel, Japan, Peru, Taiwan, and Thailand. Probably, the best-known models of the United States economy are the Brookings [23,39,40], OBE [43,58], and Wharton [28,29] quarterly econometric models. These models have been the object of numerous computer simulation experiments that have been described in the literature [23,25,27,29,35,36,37,38,39,40,43].

Brookings Model

The Brookings Model is the largest of the econometric models of the United States. It was developed originally by a team of 20 different economists. More recent developments with this model have been under the direction of Gary Fromm [38] at the Brookings Institution. The latest version [38] of the model consists of 230 equations of which 118 are behavioral equations. The model contains 104 exogenous and policy variables. A flow chart of the logic of the Brookings Model is given in Figure 4-22.

OBE Model

The OBE Model [43] is the first large-scale econometric model built by and for the use of the United States Government. The model was developed by the Econometric Branch of the Office of Business Economics of the U. S. Department of Commerce. It contains 56 behavioral equations, 46 identities, and 75 exogenous variables and is an outgrowth of an earlier [58] 36-equation model.

Wharton Model

The Wharton Econometric Forecasting Model [28] developed by Michael Evans and Lawrence Klein at the Economics Research Unit of the Wharton School at the University of Pennsylvania is probably the most widely used econometric model today. Quarterly forecasts from the Wharton Model are published in *Business Week*. In addition, a number of large business firms in the United States that have their own corporate models and industry models use the forecasts generated by the Wharton Model to conduct simulation experiments with their own models. Output variables from the Wharton Model serve as exogenous input variables to these corporate and industry models.

Like the Brookings Model and the OBE Model, the Wharton Model also is a Keynesian type model that determines the aggregate level of output and employment. It extends the usual effective-demand type model to include price determination, wage rate determination, aggregate supply, and factor shares. The Wharton Model is essentially a real sector model but does include a six-equation monetary sector. It contains 76 equations, including 47 behavioral equations and 29 identities.

Some Unresolved Problems

We conclude this section by summarizing a number of methodological problems associated with policy simulation experiments with macroeconometric models for which solutions do not presently exist.

Simulation Versus Analytical Solutions

Explicit analytical solutions for the reduced form of simultaneous, nonlinear, stochastic difference equations are frequently difficult, if not impossible to obtain. For this reason, economists have found it necessary to resort to numerical techniques or to computer simulation experiments to validate these models and to investigate their dynamic properties. Howrey and Kelejian [49] have recently raised some very interesting questions concerning the use of computer simulation techniques with econometric models. In general, they have suggested that the role of computer simulation as a tool of analysis with econometric models should be reconsidered. They have argued, "that once a *linear* econometric model has been estimated and tested in terms of the known distribution theory concerning parameter estimates, simulation experiments . . . yield *no additional* information about the validity of the model." In addition, Howrey and Kelejian [49] have pointed out that, "although some of the dynamic properties of linear models can be inferred from simulation results, an analytical technique (spectral analysis) based on the model itself is available for this purpose." Since any nonlinear econometric model can be approximated by a linear model through the use of an appropriate Taylor series expansion, the arguments of Howrey and Kelejian also can be extended to include nonlinear econometric models. The questions raised by Howrey and Kelejian are important ones and merit further theoretical and empirical consideration. In general, the whole question of when to use simulation rather than standard mathematical techniques is a question that needs further investigation, not only with econometric models but with economic models of all types. We shall treat this topic in more detail in Chapter 12.

Perverse Simulation Results

Econometric models that have been estimated properly and are based on sound economic theory may yield simulation results that are nonsensical.

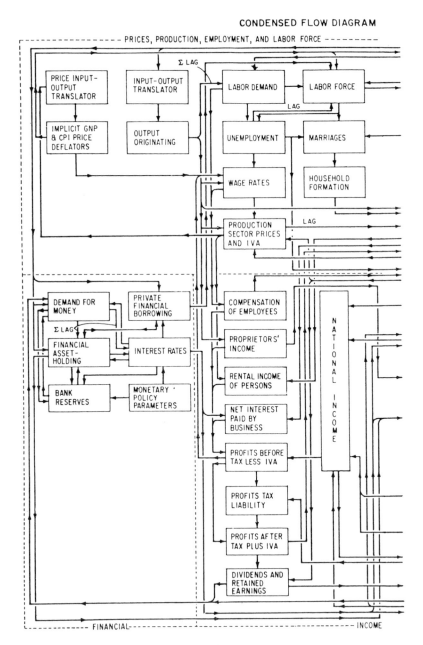

Figure 4-22a.

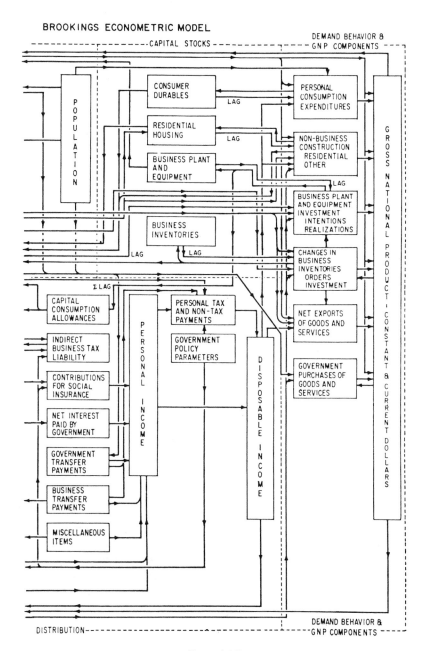

Figure 4-22b.

That is, the simulations may "explode," and inherently positive variables may turn negative, leading to results that are in complete conflict with reality. We must learn more about the mathematical properties of our models with the hope of devising techniques that will enable us to spot these problems with our models analytically before running simulations with them. For example, Howrey and Kelejian [49] have shown that the application of simulation techniques to nonstochastic econometric models that contain nonlinearities in the endogenous variables, "yields results that are not consistent with the properties of the reduced form of the model." What other information can be gleaned from the structure of econometric models prior to conducting simulation experiments?

There appears to be a definite need to combine the approaches of the econometrician and the systems analyst in formulating models of complex economic systems. To the systems analyst an economic model consists of a set of mathematical inequalities which reflect the various conditional statements, logical branchings, and complex feedback mechanisms that depict the economy as a dynamic, self-regulating system. Although economists have made considerable progress in building econometric models and developing techniques to estimate their parameters, little or no attention has been given to alternative model structures such as the ones used by systems analysts. The possibility of developing models of the economy as a whole that consist of structures other than simultaneous difference equations needs to be explored more fully. Special attention should be given to the types of logical models that have been developed by systems analysts. To use systems analysis to build macroeconometric models that accurately reflect the underlying decision processes of the total economy, it may be necessary to draw heavily on other disciplines, including sociology, psychology, and political science.

Inadequate Estimation Techniques

Although the static properties of simultaneous equation estimators, such as two-stage least squares, limited-information methods, full-information maximum likelihood methods, and three-stage least squares [42,52,61], are well known, we have no assurance whatsoever from econometric theory that a model whose parameters have been estimated by one of these methods will yield valid, dynamic, closed-loop simulations. That is, it is quite possible for a model which has been estimated by one of the above-mentioned techniques to yield simulations which in no sense resemble the behavior of the system that they were designed to emulate. What is needed is a new estimation technique that uses as its criterion of goodness-of-fit, "How well does the model simulate?" rather than "How well does the static model fit the historical data based on one-period predictions?" The question of whether poor simulation results with econometric models are because of improper methods of estimation or a misspecified model is a question that calls for further research.

Unstable Coefficients

The simulation experiments of the Adelmans [1,2] and others have demonstrated the effects of including additive stochastic error terms in econometric models. Howrey and Kelejian [49] also have treated this question from a theoretical standpoint. What has not been considered is the question of what happens if we treat the coefficients of an econometric model as random variables in simulation experiments. Yet we know very well that these coefficients are, indeed, random variables and that they are not likely to remain constant over long periods of time. Preliminary experiments with this problem indicate that, by shocking the coefficients of the Klein-Goldberger Model [57], we encounter two different problems. First, we encounter serious difficulty in solving the model. Second, the results are quite different from the deterministic simulations as well as the simulations with additive shocks. Finally, the structure of the model may in reality evolve over time, and the assumption of constant coefficients, independent of time, may require review.

BIBLIOGRAPHY

1. Adelman, Irma. "Long Cycles-A Simulation Experiment," *Symposium on Simulation Models*, Austin C. Hoggatt and Frederick E. Balderston (eds). Cincinnati: South-Western Publishing Co., 1963.
2. Adelman, Irma and Frank. "The Dynamic Properties of the Klein-Goldberger Model," *Econometrica* (October 1959), 596-625.
3. Allen, R. G. D. *Mathematical Economics*. New York: Macmillan and Co., 1960.
4. Ando, Albert K., Modigliani, Franco, and Rasche, Robert. "Economic Theory in the FRB-MIT-PENN Model," Conference on Econometric Models of Cyclical Behavior, Harvard University, November 14-15 1969.
5. Ansoff, H. Igor, and Slevin, Dennis P. "An appreciation of Industrial Dynamics," *Management Science*, **XIV** (March 1968), 383-396.
6. Balderston, F. E., and Hoggatt, Austin C. *Simulation of Market Processes*. Berkeley: Institute of Business and Economic Research, 1962.
7. Balderston, F. E., and Hoggatt, Austin C. "Simulation Models: Analytic Variety and the Problem of Model Reduction," *Symposium on Simulation Models*, Austin C. Hoggatt and Frederick E. Balderston (eds). Cincinnati: South-Western Publishing Co., 1963.
8. Baumol, William J. *Economic Dynamics*. New York: The Macmillan Co., 1959.
9. Bonini, Charles P. *Simulation of Information and Decision Systems in the Firm*. Englewood Cliffs, N.J.: Prentice-Hall, Inc., 1963.

10. Carlson, Bruce R. "An Industrialist Views Industrial Dynamics," *Industrial Management Review*, **V** (Fall 1964), 21-29.

11. Chow, Gregory C., Burns, Arthur F., and Moore, Geoffrey, H. "An Econometric Model of Business Cycles," Conference on Econometric Models of Cyclical Behavior, Harvard University, November 14-15, 1969.

12. Christ, C. F. "Aggregate Econometric Models," *American Economic Review*, **XLVI** (June 1956), 385-408.

13. Chu, Kong, and Naylor, Thomas H. "A Dynamic Model of the Firm," *Management Science*, **XI** (May 1965), 736-750.

14. Clarkson, G. P. E., and Simon, H. A. "Simulation of Individual and Group Behavior," *American Economic Review*, **L**, No. 5 (December 1960), 920-932.

15. Cohen, K. J. *Computer Models of the Shoe, Leather, Hide Sequence*. Englewood Cliffs, N. J.: Prentice-Hall, Inc. 1960.

16. Cohen, Kalman J., and Cyert, Richard M. "Computer Models in Synamic Economics," *Quarterly Journal of Economics*, **LXXV** (February 1961), 112-127.

17. Cohen, Kalman J., and Cyert, Richard M. *Theory of the Firm: Resource Allocation in a Market Economy*. Englewood Cliffs, N. J.: Prentice-Hall, Inc., 1965.

18. Cooper, Ronald L., and Jorgenson, Dale W. "The Predictive Performance of Quarterly Econometric Models of the United States," Conference on Econometric Models of Cyclical Behavior, Harvard University, November 14-15, 1969.

19. Cyert, Richard M., Feigenbaum, E. A., and March, J. G. "Models in a Behavioral Theory of the Firm," *Behavioral Science*, **IV** (April 1959), 81-95.

20. Cyert, Richard M., and March, James G. *A Behavioral Theory of the Firm*. Englewood Cliffs: Prentice Hall, Inc., 1963.

21. De Leeuw, Frank. "Financial Markets in Business Cycles: A Simulation Study," *American Economic Review*, **LIV** (May 1964), 309-323.

22. DeLeeuw, Frank, and Gramlich, Edward. "The Federal Reserve-M.I.T. Econometric Model," *Federal Reserve Bulletin* (January 1968), 1-40.

23. Duesenberry, James S., Fromm, Gary, Klein, L. R., and Kuh, Edwin. *The Brookings Model: Some Further Results*. Chicago: Rand McNally, 1969.

24. Engle, R. F., and Liu, T. C. "Effects of Aggregation over Time on Dynamic Characteristics of an Econometric Model," Conference on Econometric Models of Cyclical Behavior, Harvard University, November 14-15, 1969.

25. Evans, Michael. "Computer Simulation of Nonlinear Econometric Models," *The Design of Computer Simulation Experiments*, Thomas H. Naylor (ed). Durham, N. C.: Duke University Press, 1969.

26. Evans, Michael K. *Macroeconomic Activity*. New York: Harper & Row, Publishers, 1969.

27. Evans, M. K., Haitovsky, Yoel, and Treyz, George I. "An Analysis of the Forecasting Properties of U.S. Econometric Models," Conference on Econometric Models of Cyclical Behavior, Harvard University, November 14-15, 1969.

28. Evans, M. K., and Klein, L. R. *The Wharton Econometric Forecasting Model.* Philadelphia: Wharton School, University of Pennsylvania (second edition), 1968.

29. Evans, M. K., and Klein, L. R. "Short and Long Term Simulations with the Wharton Model," Conference on Econometric Models of Cyclical Behavior, Harvard University, November 14-15, 1969.

30. Fey, Willard R. "An Industrial Dynamics Case Study," *Industrial Management Review,* **IV** (Fall 1962), 79-99.

31. Forrester, Jay W. "Industrial Dynamics: A Major Breakthrough for Decision Makers," *Harvard Business Review,* **XXXVI** (July-August 1958), 37-66.

32. Forrester, Jay W. "Advertising: A Problem in Industrial Dynamics," *Harvard Business Review,* **XXXVII** (March-April 1959), 100-110.

33. Forrester, Jay W. *Industrial Dynamics.* New York: The M.I.T. Press and John Wiley & Sons, 1961.

34. Forrester, Jay W. "Industrial Dynamics—After the First Decade," *Management Science,* **XIV** (March 1968), 398-414.

35. Fromm, Gary. "Recent Monetary Policy: An Econometric View," *National Banking Review,* **III** (March 1966), 299-306.

36. Fromm, Gary. "An Evaluation of Monetary Policy Instruments," *The Brookings Model: Some Further Results,* J. S. Duesenberry *et al* (ed). Chicago: Rand McNally, 1969.

37. Fromm, Gary. "Utility Theory and the Analysis of Simulation Output Data," *The Design of Computer Simulation Experiments,* Thomas H. Naylor (ed). Durham, N. C.: Duke University Press, 1969.

38. Fromm, Gary, and Klein, Lawrence R. "The Brookings-SSRC Quarterly Econometric Model of the United States: Model Properties," *American Economic Review,* **LV** (May 1965), 348-361.

39. Fromm, Gary, and Klein, Lawrence R. "Short and Long Term Simulations with the Brookings Model," Conference on Econometric Models of Cyclical Behavior, Harvard University, November 14-15, 1969.

40. Fromm, Gary, and Taubman, Paul. *Policy Simulations with an Econometric Model.* Washington, D.C.: The Brookings Institution, 1968.

41. Geraci, Vincent J. "On the Simulation of Dynamic Econometric Models," Econometric Systems Simulation Program, Duke University, Durham, N. C., August 15, 1969.

42. Goldberger, Arthur S. *Econometric Theory.* New York: John Wiley & Sons, 1964.

43. Green, George. "Short and Long Term Simulations with the OBE Econometric Model," Conference on Econometric Models of Cyclical Behavior, Harvard University, November 14-15, 1969.

44. Hicks, J. R. *A Contribution to the Theory of the Trade Cycle.* Oxford: Clarendon Press, 1950.

45. Hoggatt, Austin C. "An Experimental Business Game," *Behavioral Science,* **IV** (1959), 192-203.

46. Hoggatt, Austin C. "A Simulation Study of an Economic Model," *Contributions to Scientific Research in Management.* The Proceedings of the Scientific Program Following the Dedication of the Western Data Pro-

cessing Center, Graduate School of Business Administration, U.C.L.A., January 29-30, 1959.

47. Holland, Edward P., and Gillespie, Robert W. *Experiments on a Simulated Underdeveloped Economy: Development Plans and Balance of Payments Policies.* Cambridge: The M.I.T. Press, 1963.

48. Holt, Charles C. *et al. PROGRAM SIMULATE II*, Social Systems Research Institute, Madison, Wisconsin, April 1967.

49. Howrey, Philip, and Kelejian, H. H. "Computer Simulation Versus Analytical Solutions," *The Design of Computer Simulation Experiments*, Thomas H. Naylor (ed). Durham, N. C.: Duke University Press, 1969.

50. Howrey, E. Philip. "Dynamic Properties of a Condensed Version of the Wharton Model," Conference on Econometric Models of Cyclical Behavior, Harvard University, November 14-15, 1969.

51. Jarmain, W. Edwin. *Problems in Industrial Dynamics.* Cambridge: The M.I.T. Press, 1963.

52. Johnston, J. *Econometric Methods.* New York: McGraw-Hill Book Co., 1963.

53. Klein, L. R. *Economic Fluctuations in the United States, 1921-1941.* New York: John Wiley & Sons, 1950.

54. Klein, L. R. "An Econometric Analysis of the Tax Cut of 1964," *The Brookings Model: Some Further Results*, J. S. Deusenberry *et al.* (ed). Chicago: Rand McNally, 1969.

55. Klein, L. R. "Solutions of the Complete System," *The Brookings Model:* Some *Further Results*, J. S. Duesenberry *et al.* (ed). Chicago: Rand McNally, 1969.

56. Klein, L. R., and Evans, M. K. *Econometric Gaming.* New York: The Macmillan Co., 1969.

57. Klein, L. R. and Goldberger, A. S. *An Econometric Model of the United States, 1929-1952.* Amsterdam: North-Holland Publishing Co., 1955.

58. Liebenberg, M., Hirsch, A. A., Popkin, P. "A Quarterly Econometric Model of the United States," *Survey of Current Business*, **XLVI** (May 1966), 13-39.

59. Liu, Ta-Chung. "A Monthly Recursive Econometric Model of the United States," *Review of Economics and Statistics*, **LI** (February 1969), 1-13.

60. Machlup, Fritz. "Theories of the Firm: Marginalist, Behavioral, Managerial," *American Economic Review*, **LVII** (March 1967), 1-33.

61. Malinvaud, E. *Statistical Methods in Econometrics.* Chicago: Rand McNally & Co., 1966.

62. Moore, Geoffrey H., Boschan, Charlotte, and Zarnowitz, Victor. "Business Cycle Analysis of Econometric Model Simulations," Conference on Econometric Models of Cyclical Behavior, Harvard University, November 14-15, 1969.

63. Nagar, A. L. "Stochastic Simulations of the Brookings Econometric Model," *The Brookings Model: Some Further Results*, J. S. Duesenberry *et al.* (ed). Chicago: Rand McNally, 1969.

64. Naylor, Thomas H. "Simulation as a Planning Tool," Working Paper No. 19, Econometric System Simulation Program, Duke University, Durham, N. C., March 29, 1968.

65. Naylor, Thomas H. "Computer Simulation Models for Designing and Evaluating Alternative Population Planning Policies," *Proceedings of the American Cybernetic Society* (1969).

66. Naylor, Thomas H. (ed). *The Design of Computer Simulation Experiments.* Durham, N. C.: Duke University Press, 1969.

67. Naylor, Thomas H., Balintfy, Joseph L., Burdick, Donald S., and Chu, Kong. *Computer Simulation Techniques.* New York: John Wiley & Sons, 1966.

68. Naylor, Thomas H., and Vernon, John M. *Microeconomics and Decision Models of the Firm.* New York: Harcourt, Brace, & World, Inc., 1969.

69. Naylor, Thomas H., Wertz, Kenneth, and Wonnacott, Thomas H. "Some Methods for Evaluating the Effects of Economic Policies Using Simulation Experiments," *Review of the International Statistical Institute,* **XXXVI** (1968), 814-200.

70. Naylor, Thomas H., Wertz, Kenneth, and Wonnacott, Thomas. "Spectral Analysis of Data Generated by Simulation Experiments with Econometric Models," *Econometrica,* **XXXVII** (April 1969), 333-352.

71. Naylor, Thomas H., Wallace, William H., and Sasser, W. Earl. "A Computer Simulation Model of the Textile Industry," *Journal of the American Statistical Association,* **LXII** (December 1967), 1338-1364.

72. Nord, Ole C. *Growth of a New Product: Effects of Capacity-Acquisition Policies.* Cambridge: The M.I.T. Press, 1963.

73. Orcutt, Guy H. "Simulation of Economic Systems," *American Economic Review,* **L** (December 1960), 893-907.

74. Orcutt, Guy H. "Views on Simulation and Models of Social Systems," in *Symposium on Simulation Models,* Austin C. Hoggatt, and Frederick E. Balderston (eds). Cincinnati: South-Western Publishing Co., 1963.

75. Orcutt, Guy H. *et al. Microanalysis of Socioeconomic Systems: A Simulation Study.* New York: Harper & Brothers, 1961.

76. Packer, D. W. *Resource Acquisition in Corporate Growth.* Cambridge: M.I.T. Press, 1964.

77. Preston, Lee E., and Collins, Norman R. *Studies in a Simulated Market,* Research Program in Marketing, Graduate School of Business Administration, University of California, Berkeley, 1966.

78. Pugh, Alexander L. *DYNAMO User's Manual.* Cambridge, Mass.: The M.I.T. Press, 1963.

79. Reichenbach, Hans. *The Rise of Scientific Philosophy.* Berkeley: University of California Press, 1961.

80. Roberts, Edward B. "New Directions in Industrial Dynamics," *Industrial Management Review,* **VI** (Fall 1964), 5-20.

81. Robinson, Joan, *Economic Philosophy.* Chicago: Aldine Publishing Co., 1963.

82. Samuelson, Paul A. *Foundations of Economic Analysis.* Cambridge, Mass.: Harvard University Press, 1948.

83. Sasser, W. Earl, and Naylor, Thomas H. "Computer Simulation of Economic Systems: An Example Model," *Simulation*, **VIII** (January 1967), 21-32.

84. Shubik, Martin. "Simulation of the Industry and the Firm," *American Economic Review*, **L**, No. 5 (December 1960), 908-919.

85. Stekler, H. O. "Forecasting with an Econometric Model: Comment," *American Economic Review*, **LVI** (December 1966), 1241-1248.

86. Stekler, H. O. "Forecasting with Econometric Models: An Evaluation," *Econometrica*, **XXXVI** (July-October 1968), 437-463.

87. Suits, Daniel B. "Forecasting and Analysis with an Econometric Model," *American Economic Review*, **LII** (March 1962), 104-132.

88. Treyz, George I. *Computer Problem Booklet for Economics*. New York: The Macmillan Company, 1969.

89. Vernon, John, Rives, Norfleet, and Naylor, Thomas H. "An Econometric Model of the Tobacco Industry," *Review of Economics and Statistics*, **LI** (May 1969), 149-157.

90. Wismer, David A. "On the Use of Industrial Dynamics Models," *Operations Research*, **XV** (July-August 1967).

91. Yance, J. V. "A Model of Price Flexibility," *American Economic Review*, **L** (June 1960), 401-418.

92. Yurow, Jerome A. "Analysis and Computer Simulation of the Production and Distribution Systems for a Tufted Carpet Mill," *Journal of Industrial Engineering*, **XVIII** (January 1967).

Chapter 5 | Validation[1]

THOMAS H. NAYLOR AND J. M. FINGER

THE PROBLEM OF VALIDATION

Analysts, in discussing procedures and techniques used in designing computer simulation experiments with economic systems, have had little to say about how one goes about validating a simulation model or the data generated by such a model on a digital computer. In part, the reason for avoiding the subject of validation stems from the fact that the problem of validating computer models remains today perhaps the most elusive of all the unresolved methodological problems associated with computer simulation techniques. Yet we know very well that, "validation is a necessary constituent of the theory of meaning. A sentence the truth of which cannot be determined from possible observations is meaningless" [23, pp. 256-257].

Likewise, simulation models based on purely hypothetical functional relationships and contrived data which have not been subjected to empirical validation are void of meaning. Referring to computer models of management control systems which have not been validated, Clay Sprowls has said that, "I am prepared to look at each of them as an interesting isolated case which can be described to me but from which I shall draw no conclusions" [26, pp. 148]. Although the construction and analysis of a simulation model, the validity of which has not been ascertained by empirical observation, may prove to be of interest for expository or pedagogical purposes (for example, to illustrate particular simulation techniques), such a model contributes nothing to the understanding of the system being simulated.

To validate any kind of model (for example, economic models) means to prove the model to be true. But to prove that a model is "true" implies (1) that we have established a set of criteria for differentiating between

---

[1] This chapter is based on a paper by Thomas H. Naylor and J. M. Finger entitled "Verification of Computer Simulation Models," *Management Science*, **XIV** (October 1967), pp. 92-101.

the models that are "true" and the models that are "not true," and (2) that we have the ability to readily apply these criteria to any given model.In view of the difficulty which arises in attempting to agree on a set of criteria for establishing when a model is validated, Karl R. Popper [22] has suggested that we concentrate on the degree of confirmation of a model instead of whether or not the model has been validated. If, in a series of empirical tests of a model, no negative results are found but the number of positive instances increases, then our confidence in the model will grow step by step. "Thus, instead of validation, we may speak of gradually increasing confirmation of the law" [3].

The rules for validating computer simulation models and the data generated by these models are sampling rules resting entirely on the theory of probability. Both the simulation models that have been programmed into a computer and the data that have been generated from these models represent the essence of inductive reasoning, since they are the joint conclusions of a set of inductive inferences (behavioral assumptions or operating characteristics) about the behavior of a given system. The validity of a model is made probable, not certain, by the assumptions underlying the model; the inductive inference must be conceived as an operation belonging in the calculus of probability [23, p. 233].

In the following section we explore three major methodological positions concerning the problem of validation in economics which are relevant to the problem of validating computer models of economic systems.

THREE POSITIONS ON VALIDATION

1. Rationalism

Rationalism holds that a model or theory is simply a system of logical deductions from a series of synthetic premises of unquestionable truth "not themselves open to empirical validation or general appeal to objective experience" [1, p. 612]. Immanuel Kant (1724-1804), who believed that such premises exist, coined the term *synthetic a priori* to describe premises of this type. The classical arguments in support of rationalism in economics have been outlined below:

These are not postulates the existence of whose counterparts in reality admits of extensive dispute once their nature is fully realized. We do not need controlled experiments to establish their validity: they are so much the stuff of our everyday experience that they have only to be stated to be recognized as obvious. Indeed, the danger is that they may be thought to be so obvious that nothing significant can be derived from their further examination. Yet, in fact, it is on postulates of this sort that the complicated theorems of advanced analysis ultimately depend [24, pp. 80].

Thus the problem of validation has been reduced to the problem of searching for a set of basic assumptions underlying the behavior of the system of interest.

Unfortunately, any attempt to spell out literally and in detail all of the basic assumptions underlying a particular system soon reveals limitations to their obviousness [16, p. 136]. Reichenbach goes so far as to deny the very existence of a synthetic a priori.

Scientific philosophy . . . refuses to accept any knowledge of the physical world as absolutely certain. Neither the individual occurrences, nor the laws controlling them, can be stated with certainty. The principles of logic and mathematics represent the only domain in which certainty is attainable; but these principles are analytic and empty. Certainty is inseparable from emptiness; there is no synthetic a priori [23, p. 304].

2 · Empiricism

At the other end of the methodological spectrum in complete opposition to rationalism is *empiricism*. Empiricists regard empirical science, and not mathematics, as the ideal form of knowledge. "They insist that sense observation is the primary source and the ultimate judge of knowledge, and that it is self-deception to believe the human mind to have direct access to any kind of truth other than that of empty logical relations" [23, pp. 73-74]. Empiricism refuses to admit any postulates or assumptions that cannot be independently verified. This extreme form of logical positivism asks that we begin with facts, not assumptions [1, pp. 612-613].

T. W. Hutchison, a leading proponent of empiricism as a means of validation in economics, has said that " 'propositions of pure theory' is a name for those propositions not conceivably falsifiable empirically and which do not exclude or 'forbid' any conceivable occurrence, and which are therefore devoid of empirical content, being concerned with language" [14, p. 161]. Continuing, Hutchison has added that, "Propositions of pure theory, by themselves, have no prognostic value or 'causal significance' " [14, p. 162].

However, Blaug suggests that throughout the history of economic thought some economists have been willing to compromise on these two extreme points of view—synthetic a priority and empiricism. The controversy is over matters of emphasis, and economists have always occupied the middle ground between extreme a priority and empiricism [1, pp. 612-613].

3 · Positive Economics

Milton Friedman argues that critics of economic theory have missed the point by their preoccupation with the validity of the assumptions of models.

According to Friedman, the validity of a model depends not on the validity of the assumptions on which the model rests (as Hutchison would have one believe) but, instead, on the ability of the model to predict the behavior of the dependent variables that are treated by the model.

The difficulty in the social sciences of getting new evidence for this class of phenomena and of judging its conformity with the implications of the hypothesis makes it tempting to suppose that other, more readily available, evidence is equally relevant to the validity of the hypothesis—to suppose that hypotheses have not only "implications" but also "assumptions" and that the conformity of these "assumptions" to "reality" is a test of the validity of the hypothesis different from or additional to the test by implications. This widely held view is fundamentally wrong and productive of much mischief. Far from providing an easier means for sifting valid from invalid hypotheses, it only confuses the issue, promotes misunderstanding about the significance of empirical evidence for economic theory, produces a misdirection of much intellectual effort devoted to the development of consensus on tentative hypotheses in positive economics [13, p. 14].

Although the notion that conformity to observed behavior is a desirable check on the validity of an economic model is, indeed, an appealing methodological position, Friedman has by no means escaped criticism for maintaining this position. "Friedman's position is unassailable until it is realized that he is insisting on empirical testing of predictions as the sole criterion of validity; he seems to be saying that it makes no difference whatever to what extent the assumptions falsify reality" [1, pp. 612-613].

Critics of Friedman's brand of positive economics as applied to "validation by accuracy of predictions" argue that to state a set of assumptions, and then to exempt a subclass of their implications from verification, is a curiously roundabout way of specifying the content of a theory that is regarded as open to empirical refutation [16, p. 139]. "It leaves one without an understanding of the reasons for the exemptions" [16, p. 139].

MULTISTAGE VALIDATION

Computer simulation suggests yet a fourth possible approach to the problem of validation—multistage validation. This approach to validation is a three-stage procedure, incorporating the methodology of rationalism, empiricism, and positive economics. Multistage validation implies that each of the above-mentioned methodological positions is a necessary procedure for validating simulation experiments but that neither of them is a sufficient procedure for solving the problem of validation. Although multistage validation may be applicable to the validation of models, in general, we shall argue in this section that multistage validation is applicable particularly to the validation of computer simulation models of economic systems.

The first stage of this procedure calls for the formulation of a set of postulates of hypotheses describing the behavior of the system of interest. To be sure, they are not just any postulates, for what is required in stage one is a diligent search for Kant's "synthetic a priori," using all possible information at our disposal.

Like the scientists, the scientific philosopher can do nothing but look for his best posits. But that is what he can do; and he is willing to do it with the perseverence, the self-criticism, and the readiness for new attempts which are indispensable for scientific work. If error is corrected whenever it is recognized as such, the path of error is the path of truth [23, p. 326].

We would not object to the argument that this set of postulates is formed from the researcher's already acquired "general knowledge" of the system to be simulated or from his knowledge of other "similar" systems that have already been successfully simulated. The point we are striving to make is that the researcher cannot subject all possible postulates to formal empirical testing and, therefore, must select, on essentially a priori grounds, a limited number of postulates for further detailed study. Of course, he also is rejecting an infinity of postulates on the same grounds. The selection of postulates is taken here to include the specification of components and the selection of variables as well as the formulation of functional relationships. But having arrived at a set of basic postulates on which to build our simulation model, we are not willing to assume that these postulates are of such a nature as to require no further validation. Instead, we merely submit these postulates as tentative hypotheses about the behavior of a system.

The second stage of our multistage validation procedure calls for an attempt on the part of the analyst to "validate" the postulates on which the model is based subject to the limitations of existing statistical tests. Although we cannot solve the philosophical problem of "what does it mean to validate a postulate?" we can apply the "best" available statistical tests to these postulates.

But in economics we often find that many of our postulates are either impossible to falsify by empirical evidence or extremely difficult to subject to empirical testing. In these cases we have two choices: (1) we may either abandon the postulates entirely, arguing that they are scientifically meaningless, since they cannot be conceivably falsified, or (2) we may retain the postulates merely as "tentative" postulates. If we choose the first alternative, we must continue searching for other postulates that can be subjected to empirical testing. However, we may elect to retain these "tentative" postulates which cannot be falsified empirically on the basis that there is no reason to assume that they are invalid just because they cannot be tested.

The third stage of this validation procedure consists of testing the model's ability to predict the behavior of the system under study. C. West Churchman states flatly that the purpose of simulation is to predict, and he considers the point so obvious that he offers no defense of it before incorporating it into his discussion of the concept of simulation [4]. This point does indeed seem obvious. Unless the construction of simulation models is viewed as a game with no purpose other than the formulation of a model, it is hard to escape the conclusion that the purpose of a simulation experiment is to predict some aspect of reality. In order to test the degree to which data generated by computer simulation models conform to observed data, two alternatives are available—historical validation and validation by forecasting. The essence of these procedures is prediction, since historical validation is concerned with retrospective predictions and forecasting is concerned with prospective predictions.

If one uses a simulation model for descriptive analysis, he is interested in the behavior of the system being simulated and, thus, would attempt to produce a model which would predict that behavior. The use of simulation models for prescriptive purposes involves predicting the behavior of the system being studied under different combinations of policy conditions. Then the experimenter would decide on the most desirable set of policy conditions to put into effect by picking the set that produces the most desirable set of outcomes. When a simulation model is used for descriptive analysis, the actual historical record produced by the system being simulated can be used as a check on the accuracy of the predictions and, hence, on the extent to which the model fulfilled its purpose. But prescriptive analysis involves choosing one historical path along which the system will be directed. Hence, only the historical record of the path actually traveled will be generated, and the historical records of alternative paths corresponding to alternative policies will not be available for comparison. Although, in this case, the historical record cannot be used as a direct check on whether or not the model did actually point out the best policy to follow, the actual outcome of the policy chosen can be compared with the outcome predicted by the simulation model as an indirect test of the model. In either case, the predictions of the model are directly related to the purpose for which the model was formulated, but the assumptions that make up the model are only indirectly related to its purpose through their influence on the predictions. Hence, the final decision concerning the validity of the model must be based on its predictions.

GOODNESS OF FIT

Thus far, we have concerned ourselves only with the philosophical aspects of the problem of validating computer simulation models. What are some of the practical considerations that the economist and management scientist face in validating computer models? Some criteria must be devised to indicate when the time paths generated by a computer simulation model agree sufficiently with the observed or historical time paths, so that agreement cannot be attributed merely to chance. Specific *measures* and *techniques* must be considered for testing the "goodness of fit" of a simulation model, that is, the degree of conformity of simulated time series to observed data. Richard M. Cyert has suggested that the following measures might be appropriate [10].

1. The number of turning points.
2. The timing of turning points.
3. The direction of turning points.
4. The amplitude of the fluctuations for corresponding time segments.
5. The average values of variables.
6. The simultaneity of turning points for different variables.
7. The average values of variables.
8. The exact matching of values of variables.

To this list of measures we would add the probability distribution and variation about the mean (variance, skewness, kurtosis) of variables.

Although a number of statistical techniques exist for testing the "goodness of fit" of simulation models, for some unknown reason, management scientists and economists, more often than not, have restricted themselves to purely graphical (as opposed to statistical) techniques of "goodness of fit" for validating computer models [5,19]. The following statement by Cyert and March concerning the validity of their duopoly model is indicative of the lack of emphasis placed on goodness of fit by many practitioners in this field.

In general, we feel that the fit of the behavioral model to data is surprisingly good, although we do not regard this fit as validating the approach [11, p. 97].

This statement was made on the basis of a graphical comparison of the simulated time series and actual data. Not unlike most other simulation studies described in the literature, Cyert and March did not pursue the question of validation beyond the point described in this statement.

Within the confines of this chapter it is impossible to enumerate all of the statistical techniques that are available for testing the goodness of fit of simulation models. However, we list some of the more important ones and suggest a number of references that describe these tests in detail.

1. *Analysis of Variance.* The analysis of variance is a collection of techniques for data analysis which can be used to test the hypothesis that the mean (or variance) of a series generated by a computer simulation experiment is equal to the mean (or variance) of the corresponding observed series. The use of this technique is based on three important assumptions—normality, statistical independence, and a common variance. The paper by Naylor, Wallace, and Sasser [19] describes the use of the analysis of variance to validate a computer simulation model of the textile industry.

2. *Chi-Square Test.* The Chi-square test is a classical statistical test which can be used for testing the hypothesis that the set of data generated by a simulation model has the same frequency distribution as a set of observed historical data. Although this test is relatively easy to apply, it has the problem of all tests that use categorical type data, namely, the problem of selecting categories in a suitable and unbiased fashion. It has the further disadvantage that it is relatively sensitive to nonnormality.

3. *Factor Analysis.* Cohen and Cyert have suggested the performance of a factor analysis on the set of time paths generated by a computer model, second factor analysis on the set of observed time paths, and a test of whether the two groups of factor loadings are significantly different from each other [6].

4. *Kolmogorov-Smirnov Test.* The Kolmogorov-Smirnov test is a *distribution-free* (nonparametric) test concerned with the degree of agreement between the distribution of a set of sample values (simulated series) and some specified theoretical distribution (distribution of actual data). The test involves specifying the cumulative frequency distribution of the simulated and actual data. It treats individual observations separately and, unlike the Chi-square test, does not lose information through the combining of categories [25].

5. *Nonparametric Tests.* The books by Siegel [25] and Walsh [29] describe a host of other nonparametric tests which can be used for testing the "goodness of fit" of simulated data to real world data.

6. *Regression Analysis.* Cohen and Cyert have also suggested the possibility of regressing actual series on the generated series and of testing whether the resulting regression equations have intercepts that are not significantly different from zero and have slopes that are not significantly different from unity [6].

7. *Spectral Analysis.* Data generated by computer simulation experiments are usually highly autocorrelated. When autocorrelation is present in sample data, the use of classical statistical estimating techniques (which assume the absence of autocorrelation) will lead to underestimates of

sampling variances (which are unduly large) and inefficient predictions. Spectral analysis considers data arranged in a series according to historical time. It is essentially the quantification and evaluation of autocorrelated data at which spectral analysis is aimed, after the data have been transformed into the frequency domain. For purposes of describing the behavior of a stochastic variate over time, the information content of spectral analysis is greater than that of sample means and variances. Spectral analysis provides a means of objectively comparing time series generated by a computer model with observed time series. By comparing the estimated spectra of simulated data and by corresponding real-world data, one can infer how well the simulation resembles the system it was designed to emulate [12,20,21]. Naylor, Wallace, and Sasser [19] have used spectral analysis to validate a model of the textile industry. In Chapter 9 of this book we describe in detail how one goes about applying spectral analysis to validate a computer simulation model.

8. *Theil's Inequality Coefficient.* A technique developed by Theil has been used by a number of economists to validate simulations with econometric models [28]. Theil's inequality coefficient U provides an index which measures the degree to which a simulation model provides retrospective predictions P_i of observed historical data A_i:

$$U = \frac{\sqrt{1/n \sum (P_i - A_i)^2}}{\sqrt{1/n \sum P_i^2} + \sqrt{1/n \sum A_i^2}}$$

U varies between 0 and 1. If $U = 0$, we have perfect predictions. If $U = 1$, we have very bad predictions. Theil gives an alternative definition of the inequality coefficient in [30] and generalizes the technique to the multivariate case in [29].

SUMMARY

Although we *have* argued that the success or failure of a simulation experiment must be measured by how well the model developed predicts the particular phenomena in question, we *have not* argued that care exercised in selecting assumptions and in the statistical testing of these assumptions are purposeless or wasteful activities. Our defense of the first two stages of the three-stage process of validation, we have proposed, rests solidly on the law of scarcity. Any hypotheses that can be rejected on a priori grounds should be so rejected because testing by this procedure is *cheaper* than formal statistical testing. Only if the experimenter had an unlimited budget could he afford to subject *all* possible hypotheses to statistical testing. Likewise, testing assumptions is cheaper than deriving and testing predictions; hence, any increase of validity that we can obtain at an early stage is cheaper than an additional validity gained at a later stage.

Having described multistage validation, it is appropriate that we point out that this approach to validation is by no means limited to simulation models. For example, suppose that we were interested in validating a simple econometric model of consumer demand for a particular commodity, the model consisting of one or two equations. First, we might study the rationale or the a priori assumptions underlying the model. These assumptions might take the form of postulates about the shape of individual marginal utility functions, the sign and magnitude of income and substitution effects, the shape of indifference curves, and so on. Are these assumptions in accordance with the body of knowledge known as economic theory? Second, if we are satisfied with the model on purely a priori grounds, we then may atempt to verify one or more of the assumptions underlying our model empirically, if data are available. Third, we then might subject the model to further testing by comparing theoretical values of consumer demand (as indicated by the model) with actual or historical values.

However, if our demand model were relatively simple, we might be willing to bypass the first two steps of the multistage validation procedure and might concentrate on the accuracy of the model's predictions. Whether we would be willing to skip steps one and two in verifying a particular model, in part, will depend on the cost of obtaining predictions with our model. If the model is characterized by (1) a small number of variables, (2) a small number of linear equations, (3) no stochastic variables, and (4) predictions for only one or two time periods, then we may be willing to concentrate on the third step of the procedure with a minimum of risk. But if we are dealing with a complex model consisting of a large number of nonlinear difference or differential equations and a large number of variables (some variables being stochastic), and the model is to be used to generate time paths of endogenous variables over extended periods of time, then the cost of omitting steps one and two of our procedure might be quite high. That is, it may be prudent to use steps one and two of the multistage procedure to detect errors in the model which otherwise might not become obvious until expensive computer runs have been made.

Thus, although most of our argument is relevant to the general problem of validating hypotheses or theories, the nature of computer simulation experiments makes the three-stage procedure particularly relevant to computer simulation models. This form of analysis is particularly useful when (1) it is extremely costly or impossible to observe the real-world processes that one is attempting to study, or (2) the observed system is so complex that it cannot be described by a set of equations for which it is possible to obtain analytical solutions that could be used for predictive purposes. Thus computer simulation is a more appropriate tool of analysis than techniques such as mathematical programming or marginal analysis when data against which predictions can be tested are not available and/or when predictions can be obtained only at great expense (in human time and/or computer time). In other words, computer simulation is most likely to be used when the savings derived from improving the model at earlier stages are most pronounced.

BIBLIOGRAPHY

1. Blaug, M. *Economic Theory in Retrospect.* Homewood, Ill.: Richard D. Irwin, 1962.
2. Burdick, Donald S., and Naylor, Thomas H. "Design of Computer Simulation Experiments for Industrial Systems," *Communications of the ACM,* **IX** (May 1966), 329-339.
3. Carnap, R. "Testability and Meaning," *Philosophy of Science,* **III** (1963).
4. Churchman, C. West. "An Analysis of the Concept of Simulation," *Symposium Simulation Models.* Austin C. Hoggatt and Frederick E. Balderston (eds). Cincinnati: South-Western Publishing Co., 1963.
5. Cohen, K. J. *Computer Models of the Shoe, Leather, Hide Sequence.* Englewood Cliffs, N. J.: Prentice-Hall, Inc., 1960.
6. Cohen, Kalman J., and Cyert, Richard M. "Computer Models in Dynamic Economics," *The Quarterly Journal of Economics,* **LXXV** (February 1961), 112-127.
7. Conway, R. W. "Some Tactical Problems in Digital Simulation," *Management Science,* **X** (October 1963), 47-61.
8. ———. *An Experimental Investigation of Priority Assignment in a Job Shop,* the RAND Corporation, RM-3789-PR (February 1964).
9. ———, Johnson, B. M., and Maxwell, W. L. "Some Problems of Digital Machine Simulation," *Management Science,* **VI** (October 1959), 92-110.
10. Cyert, Richard M. "A Description and Evaluation of Some Firm Simulations," *Proceedings of the IBM Scientific Computing Symposium on Simulation Models and Gaming.* White Plains, N. Y.: IBM, 1966.
11. ———, and March, James G. *A Behavioral Theory of the Firm.* Englewood Cliffs, N. J.: Prentice-Hall, Inc., 1963.
12. Fishman, George S., and Kiviat, Philip J. "The Analysis of Simulation-Generated Time Series," *Management Science,* **XIII** (March 1967), 525-557.
13. Friedman, Milton. *Essays in Positive Economics.* Chicago: University of Chicago Press, 1953.
14. Hutchison, T. W. *The Significance and Basic Postulates of Economic Theory.* London: Macmillan & Co., 1938.

15. King, E. P., and Smith, R. N. "Simulation of an Industrial Environment," *Proceedings of the IBM Scientific Computing Symposium on Simulation Models and Gaming.* White Plains, N. Y.: IMB, 1966.

16. Koopmans, Tjalling C. *Three Essays on the State of Economic Science.* New York: McGraw-Hill Book Co., 1957.

17. Naylor, Thomas H., Balintfy, Joseph L., Burdick, Donald S., and Chu, Kong. *Computer Simulation Techniques.* New York: John Wiley & Sons, 1966.

18. ———, Finger, J. M. "Verification of Computer Simulation Models,"*Management Science,* **XIV** (October 1967), 92-101.

19. ———. Wallace, W. H., and Sasser, W. E. "A Computer Simulation Model of the Textile Industry," *Journal of the American Statistical Association,* **LXII** (December 1967), 1338-1364.

20. ———, Wertz, Kenneth, and Wonnacott, Thomas. "Methods for Analyzing Data from Computer Simulation Experiments," *Communications of the ACM,* **X** (November 1967), 703-710.

21. ———, Wertz, Kenneth, and Wonnacott, Thomas. "Spectral Analysis of Data Generated by Simulation Experiments with Econometric Models," *Econometrica,* **XXXVII** (April 1969), 333-352.

22. Popper, Karl R. *The Logic of Scientific Discovery.* New York: Basic Books, 1959.

23. Reichenbach, Hans. *The Rise of Scientific Philosophy.* Berkeley: University of California Press, 1951.

24. Robbins, Lionel. *An Essay on the Nature and Significance of Economic Science.* London: Macmillan, 1935.

25. Siegel, Sidney. *Nonparametric Statistics.* New York: McGraw-Hill, 1956.

26. Sprowls, Clay. "Simulation and Management Control," *Management Controls*₅ *New Directions in Basic Research.* C. P. Bonini et al. (eds). New York: McGraw-Hill, 1964.

27. Teichroew, Daniel, and Lubin, John F. "Computer Simulation: Discussion of Techniques and Comparison of Languages," *Communications of the ACM,* **IX** (October 1966), 723-741.

28. Theil, H. *Economic Forecasts and Policy.* Amsterdam: North-Holland Publishing Co., 1961.

29. ———. *Optimal Decision Rules for Government and Industry.* Chicago: Rand McNally, 1964.

30. ———. *Applied Economic Forecasting.* Chicago: Rand McNally, 1966.

31. Van Horn, Richard. "Validation," *The Design of Computer Simulation Experiments.* Thomas H. Naylor (ed). Durham, N. C.: Duke University Press, 1969.

32. Walsh, John E. *Handbook of Nonparametric Statistics,* **I** and **II.** Princeton, N. J.: D. Van Nostrand Co., 1962, 1965.

Chapter 6 | The Design of
Computer Simulation Experiments[1]

EXPERIMENTAL DESIGN

The objective of any experimental investigation is to learn more about the system being investigated. As George Box [8] has pointed out, the aim of the experiment might be to explore and to describe the response surface over some region of interest in the factor space, or it might be to optimize the response over some operability region in the factor space. In either case, the basic feature of the experiment is the investigation of the response surface, using observations of the response at various factor levels as data.

Associated with each of the above-mentioned experimental objectives is a set of experimental designs. These designs have been created to provide not only economy in the required number of experimental trials but such additional qualities as minimum variance estimates, measures of the adequacy of the models, desirable confounding patterns, and ease of computation.

Since a computer simulation experiment is, indeed, an experiment, careful attention should be given to the problem of experimental design. In the following section, we describe an example simulation model. We then describe two different simulation experiments with the model that illustrate the use of several different experimental designs, including full factorial, fractional factorial, rotatable, and response surface designs.

AN EXAMPLE MODEL

Consider an inventory system in which daily demand D and production lead time LT are both stochastic variates with known probability distribu-

[1] This chapter is based, in part, on a previously published paper by J. S. Hunter and Thomas H. Naylor entitled "Experimental Designs for Computer Simulation Experiments" [26].

tions, given by $f(D)$ and $g(LT)$, respectively. (This model was previously described in Chapter 3.) The inventory level is reduced each day by the total demand for that day. When the inventory level becomes less than or equal to the reorder point ROP, then a production order is issued for an "optimum" order quantity EOQ. When a production order is filled, the number of units of the product ordered are added to the inventory stock. The total cost TC of operating the inventory system is the sum of the carrying, set-up, and shortage costs. Unit carrying, set-up, and shortage costs are given by C1, C2, and C3, respectively. The response surface for this relatively simple example is given by

$$TC = TC(C1,C2,C3,f(D), g(LT), EOQ, ROP) \qquad (6\text{-}1)$$

The parameters C1, C2, and C3 and the density function for demand are assumed to be given by market conditions and not subject to the control of the decision maker. The density function $g(LT)$ is fixed in the short-run by technology. EOQ and ROP are the only controllable decision variables (factors).

We wish to determine the effects of the seven factors in this model on the response variable TC. We define the factors or design variables as follows:

$$
\begin{aligned}
X_1 &= C1 & X_5 &= E(LT) \\
X_2 &= C2 & X_6 &= EOQ \\
X_3 &= C3 & X_7 &= ROP \\
X_4 &= E(D)
\end{aligned}
$$

where $E(D)$ and $E(LT)$ are the expected values, respectively, for demand and lead time. We run the simulation experiment once for the set of initial values of the seven factors. Next we vary the seven factors and observe (through additional simulation experiments) the effects on TC of different levels of each factor. Suppose that we consider two different levels of each factor. We then can use $+$ and $-$ signs to identify the two levels of each factor. For example, if the initial value of C1 was 100, we might wish to investigate X_1 equal to C1 $\pm \delta$ where $\delta = 25$. The effect of the ith factor on TC is estimated by $\overline{TC}_+ - \overline{TC}_-$ where the $\overline{TC}$'s are the average responses observed when X_i is at its $+$ and $-$ levels, respectively. If the stochastic variates D and LT had not been included in the model, the most important factor (over the ranges studied) could be quickly identified by the X_i with the largest effect. The presence of the stochastic variates D and LT requires that we replicate each simulation experiment several times. The average $\overline{TC}$ for each experiment then will be used as observations to determine the effects of different factors on the response variable.

In the following section we include a brief digression on the analysis of data generated by computer simulation experiments. Next, we describe two different types of simulation experiments with our example model: (1) an exploratory model, and (2) an optimization model. In each case, we describe several alternative experimental designs that may be appropriate for a given experiment.

DATA ANALYSIS

In a well-designed experiment consideration must be given to methods of analyzing the data once it is obtained. Most of the classical experimental design techniques described in the literature are used in the expectation that the data will be analyzed by one or both of these two methods: *analysis of variance* and *regression analysis*. The analysis of variance is a collection of techniques for data analysis that are appropriate when qualitative factors are present, although quantitative factors are not excluded. In Chapter 7, we describe the application of several analysis of variance techniques (F-test, multiple comparisons, and multiple ranking procedures) to computer simulation experiments. Regression analysis is a collection of techniques for data analysis that uses the numerical properties of the levels of quantitative factors. More will be said about regression analysis later in this chapter.

EXPLORATORY EXPERIMENTS

Suppose that with our inventory example we are interested in exploring the relationship between our seven factors [C1, C2, C3, E(D), E(LT), EOQ, and ROP] and the response variable TC. If this is the case, then several experimental designs are available for conducting exploratory simulation experiments with our model, so as to gain insight into the underlying mechanisms of the inventory system. We shall consider four different designs—full factorial designs, fractional factorial designs, rotatable designs, and response surface designs.

Full Factorial Designs

A full factorial design for our seven-factor experiment would involve selecting several values or *levels* for each of the seven factors in the experiment. By assigning to each factor one of its levels, we generate a design point. If all the design points obtainable in this way are used, we would have a (full) factorial design. Factorial designs [17, pp. 335 to 354] attempt to cover the relevant range of a factor by a series of uniformly spaced values.

The great advantage of [factorial designs] is [their] ability to map the entire response surface of systems with a small number of [factors]. The effectiveness of the method depends to a significant degree on the nature of the response surface. The gentler the slopes and the rounder the peaks and ridges, the more exactly does a [factorial design] of a given size portray the surface and approximate its highest points [25, p. 396].

The total number of design points in the full factorial design is the product of the numbers of levels for each factor. For example, a four-factor experiment with factor A at 2 levels, factor B at 2 levels, factor C at 3 levels, and factor D at 4 levels requires $2 \times 2 \times 3 \times 4 = 48$ design points. As the number of factors and the number of levels per factor increase, the number of design points required for the factorial grid increases markedly. If we have k factors with n values each, then the number of design points required is n^k. In our example model, which contains seven factors, if we considered only two levels of each factor, $2^7 = 128$ design points would be required for a full factorial design.

Suppose that each of the 128 design points consisted of a simulation run corresponding to 180 days of simulated experience with the inventory system. A conservative estimate of the amount of computer time required for a 180-day run might be about 15 seconds. (This estimate of computer time might well be much higher if the probability density functions of demand and lead time are very complex.) If each of the 128 runs is replicated (say 30 times) to reduce the effects of random error, then a full factorial experiment would require 16 hours of computer time.

Clearly, the full factorial design can require an unmanageably large number of design points if more than a very few factors are to be investigated.

Fractional Factorial Designs

Since a full factorial design for our example model leads to excessive amounts of computer time, we want to find other designs that require fewer design points but that do not cause us to forgo a great deal of information about the nature of the response function we are exploring with our simulation experiments. *Fractional factorial* designs enable us to accomplish this objective.

If we are willing to settle for a less-than-complete investigation, perhaps, including main effects and two-factor interactions, and excluding three-factor or higher-order interaction effects, there are designs that will accomplish our purpose and that require fewer trials than the full factorial. Fractional factorial designs, which include the Latin square and Greco-Latin square designs as special cases, are examples of designs that require only a fraction of the trials required by the full factorial design.

The major use of the fractional factorial designs is for screening, that is, for identifying the most important variable influencing a response. Sometimes they have been called "equal opportunity" designs, since they provide individual estimates of the main effect (and two-factor interactions if required) of all the competing variables with equal and maximum precision.

In any design that uses fewer trials than the full factorial, there will be some *confounding* of effects. A main effect, for example, may be confounded with one or more high-order interaction effects, that is, the statistic that measures a main effect will be identical to the statistic that measures certain of the interaction effects. Thus, the statistic in question may tell us that some effect is present, but it cannot tell us whether the main effect, the interaction effect, or some additive combination of the effects is present. Only if the interaction effect can be assumed to be zero (or, at least, negligibly small) are we justified in stating that the observed effect actually does estimate the main effect.

Of course, *every* design provides confounded (biased) estimates. For example, quadratic and cubic effects, if present, confound the estimates of the mean and main effects, respectively, whenever a two-level factorial design is employed. Trends, and other effects, confound estimates. Any phenomenon omitted from a fitted model will confound certain estimated parameters in the model regardless of the design used. Good fractional factorial designs are carefully arranged so that estimates of the effects thought to be important are confounded by effects thought to be unimportant.

Since experimenters are usually most interested in main effects, it is essential that main effects not be confounded with other main effects. In practically all of the commonly used fractional factorial designs, main effects are confounded with high-order interactions. Thus, if an experimenter uses one of these designs to measure main effects, he must be willing to assume, at least tentatively, that the interactions with which the main effects are confounded are zero or are quite small. Few experimenters are deterred from the use of fractional factorial designs by the necessity of such assumptions about high-order effects.

Much has been written on confounding in fractional factorial designs both in books and in articles in the professional journals. Tables of some of the available designs can be found in the book by Cochran and Cox [17], in a publication in the Applied Mathematics Series of the National Bureau of Standards [20] and, in [14], Bonini [2] has an example of a fractional factorial design employed in a computer simulation experiment.

Table 6-1a contains a fractional factorial design for our two-level, seven-factor inventory simulation experiment which contains only eight design points instead of the 128 required in a full factorial design. This design is called a 2^{7-4}_{III} fractional factorial design (the one-sixteenth replication of a 2-factorial design of resolution III). The fraction given in Table 6-1a is the smallest that can be chosen so that the estimates of the main effects of the variables are mutually orthogonal.[2]

Table 6-1a	Table 6-1b
The 2^{7-4}_{III} Fractional Factorial Design	The Complementary Fraction

X_1	X_2	X_3	X_4	X_5	X_6	X_7	X_1	X_2	X_3	X_4	X_5	X_6	X_7
−	−	−	+	+	+	−	+	+	+	−	−	−	+
+	−	−	−	−	+	+	−	+	+	+	+	−	−
−	+	−	−	+	−	+	+	−	+	+	−	+	−
+	+	−	+	−	−	−	−	−	+	−	+	+	+
−	−	+	+	−	−	+	+	+	−	−	+	+	−
+	−	+	−	−	−	−	−	+	−	+	−	+	+
−	+	+	−	−	+	−	+	−	−	+	+	−	+
+	+	+	+	+	+	+	−	−	−	−	−	−	−

If more information is needed, an additional eight-run 2^{7-4} fractional factorial can be employed, and the data from all runs can be analyzed. By combining fractions, opportunity exists to uncover information on various interactions between the factors. Additional fractions can be added, leading ultimately to the complete 2^7 design. However, the salient roles of the seven variables usually would be uncovered long before the full $2^7 = 128$ experiments were completed. One valuable second fraction is the complementary, or fold-over fraction, in which each run is the opposite of an earlier run, as illustrated in Table 6-1b. Further advantages occur if the entire 16 runs are planned initially and run in eight blocks of complementary pairs, for example,

$$− − − + + + −$$
$$+ + + − − − +$$

Many other blocking arrangements are possible.

If "interactions" between the factors on the response are anticipated, then estimates of these effects, in addition to the main effects, can be obtained by using a fractional factorial design of higher "resolution." The cost to the experimenter is more computer runs. A discussion of the resolution of fractional factorial designs, along with methods for constructing and for analyzing the designs, is given in [14].

[2] If $X_1'X_2 = 0$ in the model $Y = X_1B_1 + X_2B_2 + e$, then B_1 is said to be *orthogonal* to B_2.

If, for some reason, we find that it is necessary to investigate more than two levels of certain factors, then the 2^{k-p} fractional factorial designs can be quickly adapted to provide mixed-level fractional factorials. To illustrate, consider the column vectors X_6 and X_7 in the design of Table 6-1a. Viewed together, they provide four patterns of signs $(--)$, $(+-)$ and $(-+)$ and $(++)$. Let each pattern be associated with four levels $(-3, -1, 1, 3)$ of a new variable X_6'. The resulting mixed level $2^5 \times 4$ fractional factorial is displayed in Table 6-2a. If each pattern is associated with one of the three levels $(-1, 0, 1)$ of the new variable X_6'', we obtain the $2^5 \times 3$ fractional displayed in Table 6-2b.

Table 6-2a						Table 6-2b					
Fractional 4×2^5						Fractional 3×2^5					
X_1	X_2	X_3	X_4	X_5	X_6'	X_1	X_2	X_3	X_4	X_5	X_6''
−	−	−	+	+	−1	−	−	−	+	+	0
+	−	−	−	−	3	+	−	−	−	−	1
−	+	−	−	+	1	−	+	−	−	+	0
+	+	−	+	−	−3	+	+	−	+	−	−1
−	−	+	+	−	1	−	−	+	+	−	0
+	−	+	−	+	−3	+	−	+	−	−	−1
−	+	+	−	−	−1	−	+	+	−	−	0
+	+	+	+	+	3	+	+	+	+	+	1

These tables are merely two examples of the very large number of mixed level factorial designs of very desirable estimation qualities discussed in [1]. An important group of three-level fractional factorial designs is discussed in [10].

Rotatable Designs

If our mode of data analysis with our example model consists only of fitting a first-order regression equation to the data generated by the simulation experiment, then a two-level full factorial design or a fractional factorial design will provide sufficient precision to estimate the coefficients of the regression equation. (Recall that we have ruled out the full factorial design on the basis of computation time requirements.) However, if we fit a second-order polynomial (or higher-order polynomial) to our output data, then a fractional factorial design may lead to parameter estimates of the coefficients of the squared terms that have relatively low precision. Since a second-order polynomial in seven variables has 36 coefficients, the 2^{7-4}_{III}

fractional factorial design, which we previously described, would hardly be adequate. However, we may be able to find a second-order design that requires fewer than the 128 design points required for a 2^7 factorial design but more design points than the one-sixteenth replicate of a 2^7 factorial design of resolution III.

Rotatable designs were developed specifically for fitting second- (and higher-) order polynomials to output data. These designs exist for all values of k (the number of factors) and can be constructed by combining together the vertices of the regular or semiregular geometric figures plus center points. Rotatable designs guarantee that the standard deviation of the fitted response at any point in the factor space depends only on the distance of the point from the center and not on its direction. The design points, therefore, can be rotated about the center without changing the variance of the predicted response at any point on the fitted response surface. Rotatable designs require quantitative factors whereas factorial designs need not do so.

One design is formed from a *cube plus star plus center points*. If we take the origin as the center of the design, the cube portion will be a two-level full factorial with each factor at the levels $-a$ and $+a$. Writing k for the number of factors, we can designate the 2^k design points in the cube by $(\pm a, \pm a, \ldots, \pm a)$ where it is understood that each combination of plus signs and minus signs yields one of the points. The star portion consists of the $2k$ points $(\pm b, 0, \ldots, 0), (0, \pm b, 0, \ldots, 0), \ldots, (0, \ldots, 0, \pm b)$. The center points consist of n_0 runs at the center of the design, that is, the origin $(0, 0, \ldots, 0)$. The condition for rotatability is that $b/a = 2^{k/4}$. In our example experiment, we might use a fractional factorial in place of the 2^7 full factorial for the cube portion of the design. Draper and Herzberg [19] have described a second-order rotatable design for seven factors which requires 108 design points that may be suitable for our inventory model experiment.

Detailed information on rotatable designs can be found in Chapter 8A of Cochran and Cox [17] and in numerous journal articles [3,5,9,10,11,12, 13,15,19]. Austin Hoggatt [33] has used rotatable designs in his simulation experiments with marketing models.

Response Surface Designs

Suppose that in our example inventory model the parameters C1, C2, C3, E(D), and E(LT) are fixed and known and that we want to explore the relationship between our two decision variables EOQ and ROP and the response variable TC. We must find a response function that is a suitable approximation to the true response surface:

$$TC = TC(EOQ, ROP). \qquad (6\text{-}2)$$

The selection of approximating functional relationships has more often than not been from those that are linear in parameters because of the convenience of linear regression techniques. With this constraint the choice lies essentially between polynomials of higher and higher orders. For each order of the chosen approximation function, different types of experimental designs can be proposed.

Returning to our inventory model and using the notation that was introduced at the beginning of the paper, we might initially try to fit a first-order polynomial to the data generated by our simulation experiment as a first approximation of the true response function,

$$Y = \theta_0 + \theta_6 X_6 + \theta_7 X_7. \tag{6-3}$$

A good design is the full 2^2 factorial, repeated as illustrated by the filled in dots in Figure 6-1a. If the first-order model proves to be inadequate to represent the response over the ranges of X_6 and X_7 under study, then the design can be augmented by additional trials in X_6 and X_7, as illustrated by the open dots in Figure 6-1a and an empirical second-order polynomial fitted to the response:

$$Y = \theta_0 + \theta_6 X_6 + \theta_7 X_7 + \theta_{66} X_6^2 + \theta_{77} X_7^2 + \theta_{67} X_6 X_7. \tag{6-4}$$

Data from a series of runs, the fitted second-order model, and the resulting contours of the empirical response surface are shown in Figures 6-1a and 6-1b. The argument is *not* that the map of the system response provided by the design information exactly reproduces the actual response that could be determined at any point in the region of interest of X_6 and X_7. However, since it is usually true that the system response changes smoothly as variables such as X_6 and X_7 are varied, the picture is a representation of the response function and, in fact, is worth the proverbial thousand words. And obviously, the amount of experimentation (the number of times the full simulation model must be exercised) to provide this map is close to minimal.

What has been illustrated here is called response surface methodology (RSM) by experimental statisticians. First- and second-order models and associated designs are available for k variables. Excellent discussions, with examples, of response surface methods can be found in [7] and [16]. Further information on the experimental designs is given in [12,13], and [18]. The use of multidimensional maps of each of several response functions can often uncover, to the eye, relationships between responses that would defy all but the most exhaustive detailed investigations. Furthermore, through the use of canonical analysis of fitted second-order models [7], the redundancy of variables often becomes apparent as, for example, when some single canonical variable can replace two or more controlled variables.

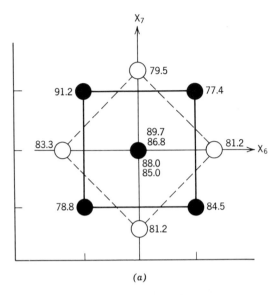

(a)

Figure 6-1a.   Octagon design.

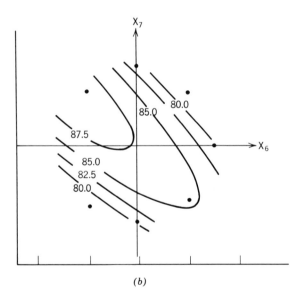

(b)

Figure 6-1b.   A fitted second-order model. $Y = 87.38 - 1.38X_6 + .36X_7 - 2.14X_6^2 - 3.09X_7^2 - 4.88X_6X_7$.

Also, with canonical analysis, we can ascertain the general shape of the response surface. Another important aspect of many response surface designs is that they may be blocked into subsets of runs and performed sequentially, the additional blocks being employed only when required.

If we had permitted all seven factors in our response function to vary rather than holding five of them constant, we would have found it necessary to resort to a fractional factorial or rotatable design instead of a full factorial design to fit the approximating polynomial.

Other Designs

At this point, it should come as no surprise to learn that a great many other experimental designs exist for exploratory experiments. Latin square, split plot, hierarchal, chain block, Youden squares, switchback, simplex, and balanced block designs all offer the opportunity for systematic and economical study of a response function. The literature associated with these designs is very extensive [4,17,18,22].

Once we have discovered *which* of the variables are most important and have described *how* these variables influence the response by means of our approximating empirical maps, we can concentrate on answering the question of *why* things appear as they do. Here we are likely to postulate nonpolynomial, nonlinear models and, perhaps, different competing models illustrative of competing theories. The construction of experimental designs for the problems of nonlinear models, and model discrimination, is undergoing rapid development. Interesting references are [15] and [24].

OPTIMIZATION EXPERIMENTS

If, on the other hand, our experimental objective is to find the levels of EOQ and ROP that minimize TC, then we must investigate the use of optimum seeking methods.

The method of steepest descent (or ascent in the case of maximization) is one of several major optimum seeking methods. We require a design point in the factor space as a starting value for the procedure. As a first step, we need a linear approximation, that is, an approximating hyperplane, to the response surface in the neighborhood of the starting value. Unless the response surface is a known function, we must explore the neighborhood of the starting value in order to fit an approximating hyperplane. A simplex, a fractional factorial, or a first-order rotatable design can be used to obtain a linear fit by least squares.

The next step is to explore along the direction of steepest descent as determined by the approximating hyperplane. Design points can be chosen along this direction until a point is reached at which no further progress seems likely. At this point, a new local exploration is performed with the possible result that a new direction of steepest descent will be obtained.

After several cycles of this process we are apt to reach a point at which the local linear fit is a nearly horizontal hyperplane with no direction of steepest descent. This will be the case if we have reached the bottom of a valley or hill or where the fitted hyperplane becomes inadequate to represent the response. Also it can happen if we have reached a saddle point that is a minimum in some directions but is a maximum in others. As a final step, therefore, we explore the neighborhood of the apparent minimum more thoroughly by fitting a local quadratic approximation to the response surface. This can be done by using a second-order rotatable design or, perhaps, a three-level fractional factorial design. If the approximating quadratic is positive definite, then we may have reached the minimum of the response surface.

One practical question, arising with the method of steepest descent, that may be of concern to management scientists is the step-size to take as we move in the direction of steepest descent. The trade-offs involve computer time and the risk of overshooting the mark and missing the minimum point on the response surface. If we choose a relatively small step-size, enormous amounts of computer time may be required to converge on an optimum. On the other hand, a larger step-size may reduce computation costs but may increase our chances of overshooting the optimum.

The single-factor method is another important optimum seeking method. In this method the level of a single-factor is varied while the levels of all other factors are held constant. When no further improvement is possible, the single factor is held fixed at its best level and another factor is chosen to be varied. After this single-factor search is performed for each factor in the experiment, the cycle begins again by varying the original factor once more. The process ends when no change in the level of any single factor leads to a decrease in the level of the response.

The single-factor method has, at least, two advantages when compared to the method of steepest descent. One is that it does not require local exploration at intermediate stages of the process. Since exploratory designs require many points, this could be a substantial saving. A second advantage for the single-factor method occurs when it is markedly easier to vary one factor at a time than it is to vary several factors simultaneously. This might be the case, for example, in an experiment using an engineering device (an analog computer, perhaps) where factor levels correspond to settings on a dial.

The single-factor method also has an important disadvantage when compared with the method of steepest descent. The search can move only in directions that are parallel to the coordinate axes. As a result, it is possible for the search to terminate on a ridge not parallel to any axis. This difficulty can be overcome by exploring the neighborhood of the apparent minimum by response surface methods.

Other optimum seeking methods exist, some of which combine the two approaches given above with methods for changing both the size of the design and the single-factor steps.

As a second example [30] of an optimization experiment, we consider Klein's well-known six-equation econometric model of the United States [27] and a Cobb-Douglas utility function. Although this model was previously described in Chapter 4, we repeat its specification here. The variables and equations for the model are listed below:

ENDOGENOUS VARIABLES

C_t = consumption in period t.

I_t = net investment in period t.

$W1_t$ = private wage bill in period t.

Y_t = national income in period t.

Π_t = non-wage income (profit) in period t.

K_t = capital stock at the end of period t.

POLICY VARIABLES

$W2_t$ = governmental wage bill in period t.

G_t = governmental demand in period t.

TX_t = business taxes in period t.

BEHAVIORAL EQUATIONS

Consumption function.

$$C_t = a_1 + a_2(W1_t + W2_t) + a_3\Pi_t + a_4\Pi_{t-1} + \mu_{1t}. \qquad (6\text{-}5)$$

Investment function.

$$I_t = b_1 + b_2\Pi_t + b_3\Pi_{t-1} + b_4K_{t-1} + \mu_{2t}. \qquad (6\text{-}6)$$

Demand-for-labor function.

$$W1_t = c_1 + c_2(Y_t + TX_t - W2_t) + c_3(Y_{t-1} + TX_{t-1} - W2_{t-1}) + c_4t + \mu_{3t}. \qquad (6\text{-}7)$$

IDENTITIES

National income equation.

$$Y_t = C_t + I_t + G_t - TX_t. \qquad (6\text{-}8)$$

Profit equation.

$$\Pi_t = Y_t - (W1_t + W2_t). \tag{6-9}$$

Capital stock equation.

$$K_t = K_{t-1} + I_t. \tag{6-10}$$

The μ-disturbances are assumed to have a multivariate normal distribution with zero mean and a given variance-covariance matrix.

Suppose that we are interested in evaluating the effects of our three policy variables (factors) on a single response variable, total utility,

$$TU = TU(W2,G,TX). \tag{6-11}$$

Assume that we are interested in a planning horizon of length T. The values of the policy variables are assumed to be fixed over a given planning horizon. That is, they do not vary between periods within T. Our simulation experiment consists of runs of length T for different values of the policy variables.

In each period during a given run, we solve for the six current endogenous variables in terms of the lagged endogenous variables, the policy variables, and the stochastic variates. The values of the lagged endogenous variables are the values generated in preceding periods. The stochastic variates are assumed to have been generated by a multivariate normal subroutine. Thus each run consists of the generation of T values for each of the six endogenous variables.

Following a procedure proposed by Fromm [21], we define a total utility function

$$TU = U1 + U2 \tag{6-12}$$

where U1 is the discounted sum of the utilities associated with each of the T periods of time,

$$U1 = \sum_{t=1}^{T} \frac{U_t}{(1+r)^t} \tag{6-13}$$

and r is the rate of time preference. U_t is the utility associated with the outcome of the tth period and is related to the values of the nine variables in period t by the following Cobb-Douglas utility function

$$U_t = \prod_{i=1}^{9} X_{it}^{\beta_i} \tag{6-14}$$

where

$X_{it} = A_{it}/C_{it},$
$A_{it} =$ simulated values of the ith variable in period t,

C_{it} = control value of the ith variable in period t,

β_i = proportional weight of the ith variable.

Our selection of a Cobb-Douglas utility function is obviously an arbitrary choice. We could have just as easily specified a CES, linear, or quadratic utility function. The control values are generated by a control run of length T in which the stochastic variates are supressed.

U2 is the utility of the variance of outcomes over T. It is also assumed to be a Cobb-Douglas function,

$$U2 = \prod_{i=1}^{9} (W_i)^{\beta_i} \tag{6-15}$$

where

$$W_i = \frac{\overline{A}_i}{S_i + \overline{A}_i} \tag{6-16}$$

and $\overline{A}_i$ and S_i are the sample mean and standard deviation of A_i,

$$\overline{A}_i = \frac{\sum_{t=1}^{T} A_{it}}{T} \tag{6-17}$$

$$S_i = \sqrt{\frac{\sum_{t=1}^{T} (A_{it} - \overline{A}_i)^2}{T-1}}. \tag{6-18}$$

Thus we observe that even for this relatively simple example the response surface

$$TU = TU(W2,G,TX) \tag{6-19}$$

is extremely complex. In fact, the only way in which the response function can be described explicitly is by considering the entire computer program for the simulations as the response function.

We have assumed for illustration that the variables W2, G, and TX are to be held fixed for the entire planning horizon and that our objective is to find the levels of these factors which will maximize total utility. Current real-world values of the factors might serve well as a starting point.

Among the RSM techniques that we have described previously, the steepest ascent method would be preferred to the single-factor method in this example for several reasons. First, with only three factors in the model, a two-level full factorial requires only eight design points. Thus, a local linear fit, which the method of steepest ascent requires, could be made economically. Second, it seems likely that the factors are strongly interrelated and that the response surface may have ridges running in directions not parallel to any coordinate axis in the factor space. For this type of response surface the method of steepest ascent usually works much better than the single-factor method. Finally, since this is a model for simulation by a digital computer, there is no particular advantage to varying the factors one at a time. (The book by Lavi and Vogl [28] suggests a number of other techniques, including conjugate gradient methods which might be used with this model.)

Once we have reached an apparent maximum, we would explore the vicinity with a second-order rotatable design centered at the point of maximum response and fit a quadratic function to our data. In our three-factor example, a cube-plus-star design with three center points would require $2^3 + 2 \cdot 3 + 3 = 17$ design points. The final step would be to perform a canonical reduction of our fitted quadratic to check whether the apparent maximum is a true maximum and to examine the sensitivity of the response to departures from the maximum point in various directions.

SOME PITFALLS AND CONTINGENCIES

As we have described several alternative experimental designs which may be used with computer simulation experiments, we now examine a number of practical problems that may arise in designing simulation experiments: (1) the problem of sample size, (2) the problem of too many factors, (3) the multiple response problem, (4) the problem of nonlinearity, (5) the problem of convergence, and (6) the problem of constrained optimization.

The Problem of Sample Size

The problem of sample size or stochastic convergence was previously defined in Chapter 2 and will not be repeated here. Recall that in Chapter 2, it was suggested that Monte Carlo or variance reduction techniques have been developed for reducing the sample size (that is, the number of replications of a simulation experiment) required to achieve a given level of statistical precision. Chapter 10 describes the application of several Monte Carlo techniques to a computer model of a queueing system.[3]

The Problem of Too Many Factors

We have previously alluded to the problem of "too many factors" in our discussion of factorial designs. Unfortunately, this problem is relevant not

[3] The reader also may wish to consult the papers by D. C. Handscomb and Jack P. Kleijnen in *The Design of Computer Simulation Experiments*, Thomas H. Naylor (ed). Durham, N.C.; Duke University Press, 1969.

only to factorial designs but also to other designs. Although high-speed computers and fractional factorial designs may partially alleviate this problem, they by no means eliminate it.

The Multiple Response Problem

The multiple response problem arises when we wish to observe many different response variables in a given experiment. The multiple response problem occurs frequently in computer simulation experiments in management science. In our inventory example there was only a single response variable—total cost. However, one can easily envisage a simulation experiment in which the decision maker is interested in several response variables, including output, cost, employment, profit, and so on. As we mentioned in Chapter 2, utility theory offers one possible solution to the multiple response problem. That is, if we can assign weights to the different output variables in a simulation experiment, we, in effect, can reduce the multiple responses to a common denominator, such as utility. We then have a single response—utility—which lends itself to analysis by the experimental designs described previously in this paper [21].

The Problem of Nonlinearity

When curve fitting is an integral part of the analysis of a response function, the problem of nonlinearity may arise. If the response function is merely nonlinear in variables, then polynomial approximations and various transformations may provide relatively easy solutions to the curve-fitting problem. If the response function is nonlinear in parameters, then the estimation problem becomes very difficult.

The Problem of Convergence

In our discussion of response surface designs, we described two optimum seeking methods. Under what conditions will a particular optimum seeking method converge on a global optimum? How quickly does the method converge? In many cases, the literature describing the convergence properties of the various optimum seeking techniques with response surface designs has been restricted to comparisons of techniques, using a few special example models. It is difficult to generalize on the convergence properties of alternative optimum seeking methods when one restricts himself to a small sample of special cases. There appears to be a need for experience with practical examples to help the users of optimum seeking methods to decide when a particular technique is more appropriate than another. It is well known that the whole question of nonconvexity and speed of convergence for optimum seeking methods needs further study.

Constrained Optimization

Constrained optimization of implicit response functions is an area which needs further investigation by researchers in the field of response surface methodology. This topic is particularly relevant to computer simulation experiments with models of economic systems.

SUMMARY

Successful learning requires: (1) the full use of prior knowledge in proposing useful models, and (2) good experimental strategies for gathering evidence useful for synthesis and conjecture. Our present experimental designs, and their methods of analysis, meet these requirements well. The mathematical models associated with the designs are very rich in the number of alternatives that are possible. The techniques for exposing the information in the data provided by the designs are well organized and usually are easy to perform. Thus experimental designs and their analyses directly enhance the remarkable acts of synthesis of new knowledge, and the conjecture of new ideas, that every experimenter covets.

To review, a simulation model is constructed in the hope that it will successfully mimic a real-world system. The model, as a consequence, may become very complicated and involved. However, our understanding will proceed only when we are able to synthesize the system in terms of simpler explanations. This synthesis will require initially the identification of the major variables affecting the responses and thus brings us to the problem of screening experimentation. Once the important variables are identified, we next must evolve terse empirical relationships, associating the leading variables with the responses. In essence, simple empirical models are superimposed on the larger detailed simulation model. The simpler models are useful for drawing general maps, for making broad inferences, and for identifying areas where more detailed models are required. Once an empirical understanding has been acquired, it becomes possible to postulate general laws and theories that any may be applicable not only for the particular system problem under study but for other similar systems. Of course, all that has been described is part and parcel of what is usually called "the scientific method." The use of experimental designs serves to make this learning process as economical in time and in resources as possible.

BIBLIOGRAPHY

1. Addelman, S. "Orthogonal Main-Effect Plans for Asymmetrical Factorial Experiments," *Technometrics,* **IV** (1962).
2. Bonini, Charles P. *Simulation of Information and Decision Systems in the Firm.* Englewood Cliffs, N. J.: Prentice-Hall, Inc., 1963.
3. Bose, R. C., and Carter, R. L. "Complete Representation in the Construction of Rotatable Designs," *Annals of Mathematical Statistics,* **XXX** (1959).
4. Bose, R. C., Clathworthy, W. H., and Shrinkhande, S. S. *Tables of Partially Balanced Designs with Two Associate Classes.* North Carolina Agricultural Experiment Station Technical Bulletin, Number 107 (1954).
5. Bose, R. C., and Draper, N. R. "Second Order Rotatable Designs in Three Dimensions," *Annals of Mathematical Statistics,* **XXX** (1959).
6. Box, G. E. P. "Multifactor Designs of First Order," *Biometrika,* **XXXIX** (1952), 49-57.
7. Box, G. E. P. "The Exploration and Exploitation of Response Surfaces: Some General Considerations and Examples," *Biometrics,* **X** (1954), 16-60.
8. Box, G. E. P. "Use of Statistical Methods in the Elucidation of Basic Mechanisms," *Biometrics,* **XIII** (1957).
9. Box, G. E. P., and Behnkin, D. W. "Simplex-Sum Designs: A Class of Second Order Rotatable Designs Derivable from Those of First Order," *Annals of Mathematical Statistics,* **XXXI** (1960).
10. Box, G. E. P., and Behnkin, D. W. "Some New Three Level Designs for the Study of Quantitative Variables," *Technometrics,* **II** (1960), 455-474.
11. Box, G. E. P., and Draper, N. R. "A Basis for the Selection of a Response Surface Design," *Journal of the American Statistical Association,* **LIV** (1959), 622-654.
12. Box, G. E. P., and Draper, N. R. "Choice of Second Order Rotatable Designs," *Biometrika,* **L** (1963), 335-352.
13. Box, G. E. P., and Hunter, J. S. "Multi-factor Experimental Designs for Exploring Response Surfaces," *Annals of Mathematical Statistics,* **XXVIII** (1957), 195-241.
14. Box, G. E. P., and Hunter, J. S. "The 2^{k-p} Fractional Factorial Designs Parts I and II," *Technometrics,* **III** (1961).
15. Box, G. E. P., and Hunter, William G. "The Experimental Study of Physical Mechanisms," *Technometrics,* **VII** (1965), 23-42.
16. Box, G. E. P., and Wilson, K. B. "On the Experimental Attainment of Optimum Conditions," *Journal of the Royal Statistical Society B,* **XIII** (1951), 1-45.
17. Cochran, W. G., and Cox, G. M. *Experimental Designs.* New York: John Wiley & Sons, 1957.
18. Davies, O. L. (ed). *Design and Analysis of Industrial Experiments.* New York: Hafner Publishing Co., 1960.
19. Draper, Norman R., and Herzberg, Agnes M. "Further Second Order Rotatable Designs," *Annals of Mathematical Statistics,* **XXXIX** (December 1968), 1995-2001.

20. "Fractional Factorial Designs for Factors at Two and Three Levels," U. S. Department of Commerce, National Bureau of Standards, *Applied Mathematics Series 58*, U. S. Government Printing Office, Washington, D. C. (September 1, 1961).

21. Fromm, Gary, and Taubman, Paul. *Policy Simulations with an Econometric Model*. Washington, D.C.: The Brookings Institution, 1968.

22. Herzberg, A. M., and Cox, D. R. "Recent Work on the Design of Experiments: A Bibliography and A Review," *Journal of the Royal Statistical Society A*, **CXXXII** (1969).

23. Hill, William J., and Hunter, William G. "A Review of Response Surface Methodology: A Literature Survey," *Technometrics*, **VIII** (November 1966), 571-590.

24. Hill, W. J., Hunter, W. G., and Wichern, D. W. "A Joint Design Criterion for the Dual Problem of Model Discrimination and Parameter Estimation," *Technometrics*, **X** (1968).

25. Hufschmidt, M. M. "Analysis of Simulation: Examination of Response Surface" *Design of Water-Resource Systems*, Arthur Maass et al (eds). Cambridge: Harvard University Press, 1966.

26. Hunter, J. S., and Naylor, Thomas H. "Experimental Designs for Computer Simulation Experiments," *Management Science*, **XVI** (March 1970).

27. Klein, L. R. *Economic Fluctuations in the United States, 1921-1941*. New York: John Wiley & Sons, 1950.

28. Lavi, A., and Vogl, T. P. *Recent Advances in Optimization Techniques*. New York: John Wiley & Sons, 1966.

29. Naylor, Thomas H., Balintfy, Joseph L., Burdick, Donald S., and Chu, Kong. *Computer Simulation Techniques*. New York: John Wiley & Sons, 1966.

30. Naylor, Thomas H., and Burdick, Donald S. "Response Surface Methods in Economics," *Review of the International Statistical Institute*, **XXXVII** (1969), 18-34.

31. Naylor, Thomas H., Burdick, Donald S., and Sasser, W. Earl. "Computer Simulation Experiments with Economic Systems: The Problem of Experimental Design," *Journal of the American Statistical Association*, **LXII** (December 1967), 1315-1337.

32. Plackett, R. L., and Burman, J. P. "The Design of Optimum Multifactorial Experiments," *Biometrika*, **XXXIII** (1946), 305-325.

22. Preston, Lee E., and Collins, Norman R. *Studies in a Simulated Market*. Research Program in Marketing, Graduate School of Business Administration, University of California, Berkeley, 1966.

34. Spendley, W., Hext, G. R., and Himsworth, F. R. "Sequential Application of Simplex Designs in Optimization and Evolutionary Operation," *Technometrics*, **IV** (1962).

Chapter 7 | Analysis of Variance

The major impetus behind the use of computer simulation by decision makers and policy makers is the possibility (and opportunity) of testing and of evaluating alternative decision rules, strategies, and economic policies before they are used in actual business and economic systems. Complete exploitation of simulation experiments implies a thorough analysis of the data thus generated. A preoccupation with model building among many experimenters simulating business and economic systems has unduly diverted attention from experimental design considerations, in general, and output analysis, in particular.

The principal aim of this chapter is to meet the problem of analyzing data that are generated by computer simulation experiments with models of business and economic systems. For this task we have selected three alternative forms of the analysis of variance which are particularly well-suited for comparing outputs of computer models, where those outputs represent the simulated results associated with alternative decision rules and policies. These techniques, in the order of their presentation, are as follows: the F-test, multiple comparison methods, and multiple ranking methods. Of course, other techniques exist—notably, sequential sampling methods and spectral analysis. (These two techniques are discussed in Chapters 8 and 9.)

With the aid of two example models—a model of a multiprocess firm and the Samuelson-Hicks [26,56] model—we shall attempt to illustrate, compare, and evaluate the analysis of variance techniques mentioned above. Following a brief exposition of each of the two models, we shall present the results of several simulation runs: that is, the data necessary for evaluating five alternative policies that are available to the decision makers. To this end, the output of the simulations will be subjected to an F-test, two different multiple comparison methods, and a multiple ranking procedure. Last, we shall discuss the relative advantages and shortcomings of each of these techniques as well as the necessary assumptions underlying their application to the analysis of data that are generated by computer simulation experiments.

A MODEL OF THE FIRM

We have chosen a relatively simple model of the firm developed by Chu and Naylor [13]. The assumptions underlying the model are summarized below.

1. The firm possesses a k-stage production process capable of manufacturing a single product. Without exception, each unit of final output of the firm must pass through all k of these stages in a particular order (see Figure 7-1).

2. Each process has its own separate production function that is independent of the production functions of the other k-1 processes.

3. The rate of output (production rate) of the jth process, Q_j ($j = 1, 2, \ldots, k$) during planning period TM is a random variable. Its probability density function $f_j(q)$ is completely determined by the level of factor inputs for process j during the planning period TM—which is to say that, by altering its allocation of productive inputs, the firm can alter the probability distributions of the Q_j. If $f_j(q)$ is determined, then obviously the expected value $E(Q_j)$ and variance $Var(Q_j)$ for process j are also determined.

4. Although the neoclassical production function was designed to measure Q_j, the quantity of output per unit time, it is more convenient in this model to use the reciprocal relationship, $ST_j = 1/Q_j$, where ST_j denotes the time required to produce one unit of output or one production order in the jth process ($j = 1, 2, \ldots, k$). The probability density function for ST_j and its parameters are completely determined by the level of factor inputs for process j. Therefore, for each process, ST_j may be treated as a random variable with a known probability density function $f_j(ST)$, expected value ET_j, and variance VT_j. In other words, the firm cannot

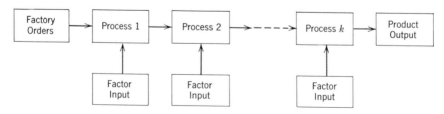

Figure 7.1.   A flow chart for a model of the firm.

completely control the value of ST_j, but it can affect ET_j or VT_j, or even $f_j(ST)$ by altering the rate of factor inputs for process j. Hence, for specified rates of factor input at the jth process, ST_j is a random variable that is not subject to further control by the firm.

5. The number of orders that arrive at the firm per unit time (or the quantity of output that can be sold per unit time at a particular price) is a random variable D with probability density function $f(d)$, expected value $E(D)$, and variance $Var(D)$. Hence, the firm cannot ordinarily [$Var(D) \neq 0$] predict with complete certainty the number of units that it can sell at a given price during TM. However, it is able to influence $f(d)$; $E(D)$, and $Var(D)$ by adjusting its expenditure strategies for advertising, marketing, and promotion. Demand is said to be a stochastic process, or equivalently, the time interval between the arrival of orders may be thought of as a stochastic process. In this model it is more convenient to think of the latter type of stochastic process. We define a random variable AT_i, the time interval between the arrival of the ith order and the $(i - 1)$th order, with a known probability density function $f(AT)$, expected value ET, and variance VT. Like the density function of demand, $f(AT)$ also is affected by advertising, marketing, and promotion strategies.

6. Once committed to a chosen rate of factor inputs, then the firm accepts all orders that are received throughout planning period TM, even though it may not be able to finish production (or possibly begin production) on all these orders in the period.

7. At the beginning of planning period, TM management must make two different types of decisions: (a) the ones pertaining to levels of expenditure for advertising and marketing and (b) the ones pertaining to factor input allocations for the k production processes. Recall that the former completely determine $f(d)$, $E(D)$, and $Var(D)$ over TM and the latter likewise govern $f_j(q)$, $E(Q_j)$, and $Var(Q_j)$ $(j = 1,2, \ldots , k)$.

We now consider the formulation of a mathematical model that describes our dynamic multiprocess firm. Let,

AT_i = the time interval between the arrival of the ith order and the $(i - 1)$th order, where an order is defined as the demand by a customer for the firm to produce one unit of final output and $i = 1, \ldots , m$. (7-1)

ST_{ij} = the process time for the ith order in the jth process, where $i = 1, \ldots , m$ and $j = 1, \ldots , k$. (7-2)

WT_{ij} = the amount of time that the ith order spends waiting to enter the jth process, where $i = 1, \ldots , m$ and $j = 1, \ldots, k$. (7-3)

DT_{ij} = the amount of time that the jth process remains idle while waiting for the ith order to arrive, where $i = 1, \ldots , m$ and $j = 1, \ldots, k$. (7-4)

$$T_{ij} = WT_{ij} + ST_{ij}, \quad i = 1, \ldots, m; j = 1, \ldots, k. \qquad (7\text{-}5)$$
$$= \text{the total time which the } i\text{th order spends at the } j\text{th process.}$$

When the first order arrives at the firm, that is, when $i = 1$, the following equations are assumed to describe the multiprocess system.

$$AT_1 = 0. \qquad (7\text{-}6)$$

$$DT_{11} = 0, \; DT_{12} = ST_{11}, \; \ldots, \; DT_{1k} = \sum_{j=1}^{k-1} ST_{1j}. \qquad (7\text{-}7)$$

$$WT_{11} = 0, \; WT_{12} = 0, \; \ldots, \; WT_{1k} = 0. \qquad (7\text{-}8)$$

$$T_{11} = ST_{11}, \; T_{12} = ST_{12}, \; \ldots, \; T_{1k} = ST_{1k}. \qquad (7\text{-}9)$$

For subsequent arrivals, that is, when $i = 2, 3, \ldots, m$, these equations must be modified accordingly. The T-equations become

$$
\begin{aligned}
T_{i1} &= WT_{i1} + ST_{i1} & i = 2, \ldots, m \\
T_{i2} &= WT_{i2} + ST_{i2} & i = 2, \ldots, m \\
&\;\;\bullet \\
&\;\;\bullet \qquad\qquad\qquad\qquad\qquad\qquad (7\text{-}10)\\
&\;\;\bullet \\
T_{ik} &= WT_{ik} + ST_{ik} & i = 2, \ldots, m
\end{aligned}
$$

Whether waiting time or idle time occurs at a particular process depends on the sign of the following differences, where $i = 2, \ldots, m$:

$$
\begin{aligned}
DIF_1 &= T_{i-1,1} - AT_i \\
DIF_2 &= (T_{i-1,1} + T_{i-1,2}) - (AT_i + WT_{i1} + ST_{i1}) \\
&\;\;\bullet \\
&\;\;\bullet \qquad\qquad\qquad\qquad\qquad\qquad\qquad (7\text{-}11)\\
&\;\;\bullet \\
DIF_k &= (T_{i-1,1} + T_{i-1,2} + \ldots + T_{i-1,k}) \\
&\quad - (AT_i + WT_{i1} + ST_{i1} + \ldots + WT_{i,k-1} + ST_{i,k-1}).
\end{aligned}
$$

If DIF_j is positive for the jth process, then idle time will be zero and waiting time will be equal to

$$WT_{ij} = DIF_j \qquad i = 2, \ldots, m; j = 1, \ldots, k. \qquad (7\text{-}12)$$

If DIF_j is negative for a particular process, then waiting time will be zero and idle time will be equal to

$$DT_{ij} = -DIF_j \qquad i = 2, \ldots, m; j = 1, \ldots, k. \qquad (7\text{-}13)$$

If DIF_j is equal to zero for a particular process, then both waiting time and idle time will be equal to zero for that process.

Furthermore, AT_i is assumed to be a random variable with probability density function $f(AT)$, expected value ET, and variance VT. And for each process, ST_{ij} is assumed to be a random variable with probability density function $f_j(ST_j)$, expected value ET_j, and variance VT_j.

Let us now endow the firm with more specific characteristics, having set forth the model. The length of the firm's planning horizon is three months (TM = 90 days) and is assumed to have been determined by the environment in which the firm exists instead of on the basis of statistical considerations. That is, the firm's decision makers are interested in making plans for the next 90 days—no more, no less.

The *response variable* or dependent variable in our simulation is profit. The *factors* in the experiment are (1) the expenditures for productive inputs (labor, raw materials, equipment, etc.), and (2) the expenditure for advertising, marketing, and promotion. As previously defined in the description of the model, both of these factors are *quantitative*. That is, in theory there exists a functional relationship between the numerical values of the levels of (1) expenditures for productive inputs and (2) expenditures for advertising, marketing and promotion, and the profitability of the firm. Although the firm's decision makers may choose from among an infinite number of levels for each factor, in practice, because of indivisibilities, institutional rigidities, incomplete information, and other reasons, the decision makers may restrict their factor-level decision to a finite number of levels. In our example model, we assume that the firm has simplified its factor-level decision to the point where it is considering only five different operating plans, each one featuring (1) a particular advertising and marketing strategy, (2) a particular allocation of inputs to the various stages of production, which we limit to four in number ($0 < k \leq 4$), and (3) a total cost, C. [We have already elaborated on points (1) and (2) in the preceding section; total costs appear in Table 7-1.] In other words, the firm's controllable quantitative factors have in effect been reduced to five levels of a single qualitative factor, that is, five operating plans or decision rules.

As a further simplification, we specify $f(d)$ and $f_j(q)$ to be Poisson distributions (arising from Poisson processes) for all five operating plans. This means that each operating plan consists of the specification (Table 7-1) of a total expenditure C and a set of values for the parameters E(D), E(Q₁), [sic] $E(Q_1)$, $E(Q_2)$, $E(Q_3)$, and $E(Q_4)$. For simulation purposes, it is convenient to take advantage of the well-known relationship between the *exponential* and *Poisson* distributions. It can be shown that if (1) the total number of events occurring during any given time interval is independent of the number of events that have already occurred prior to the beginning of the interval, and (2) the probability of an event occurring in the interval t to $t + \Delta t$ is approximately $\lambda \Delta t$ for all values of t (where λ is a constant), then (1) the

Table 7-1   Theoretical Values for Expected Demand and Expected Production Rates (in Units per Day) and Total Cost (in Dollars) for a Computer Model of the Firm.

Plans	Expected Demand Rate E(D)	Expected Production Rates				Total Cost C
		Process 1 $E(Q_1)$	Process 2 $E(Q_2)$	Process 3 $E(Q_3)$	Process 4 $E(Q_4)$	
I	3.00	3.33	3.75	4.00	3.50	$ 800
II	3.00	3.50	3.33	6.00	3.50	$ 800
III	3.00	5.00	4.25	6.00	5.00	$1250
IV	3.75	5.00	4.25	6.00	5.00	$1550
V	3.75	5.00	----	4.50	4.50	$1720

density function of the interval t between the occurrence of consecutive events is given by the negative exponential distribution,

$$f(t) = \lambda e^{-\lambda t}, \tag{7-14}$$

and the probability of x events occurring during time t is

$$f(x) = e^{-\lambda t} \frac{(\lambda t)^x}{x!} \qquad \text{for all } x \text{ and } t. \tag{7-15}$$

Translating this relationship into the language of our model, $f(d)$ and $f_j(q)$ are Poisson with parameters E(D), $E(Q_1)$, $E(Q_2)$, $E(Q_3)$, and $E(Q_4)$, respectively. The time interval between orders AT and the process times ST_j have negative exponential distributions with parameters,

$$\text{EAT} = 1/\text{E(D)} \tag{7-16}$$

$$\text{EST}_j = 1/\text{E}(Q_j) \qquad j = 1, 2, 3, 4 \tag{7-17}$$

The computer simulation experiment that we conducted with this model consisted of five runs, one for each operating plan. The parameters used— demand rate (in units per day), production rates (in units per day), and total cost—are tabulated in Table 7-1. Notice that plan V consists of three processes rather than four. A price P of $15 per unit of finished product is assumed to prevail throughout the experiment.

THE COMPUTER PROGRAM

Figure 7-2 contains a computer flow chart of the logic of our model of the firm. This flow chart will generate n replications of a given plan for our model. Each replication is run for TM units of time. The output of each replication is total profit:

$$\text{PROFIT} = \text{P} \cdot \text{Q} - \text{C} \qquad (7\text{-}18)$$

where P is price, Q is the number of units of product completed during time period TM, and C is total cost. The flow chart (and computer program) assumes that the availability of a computer subroutine for generating negative exponential variates with a given expected value.

In block 1 of Figure 7-2 the parameters K (total number of processes) and N (the number of replications of the simulation run) are read into the computer as input data. Next, the values of P, C, TM, EAT, and EST_j $(j = 1, \ldots, k)$ are read into the memory of the computer. These are the parameters for a given plan. Notice that EST_j is expressed as $\text{EST}(J)$ in the flow chart so as to conform with the FORTRAN computer programming language. Blocks 3 and 4 are initialization procedures in which L (an index for counting the number of replications) is set equal to one and Q (the number of units of output) is set equal to zero. In block 5, the process times are generated by the negative exponential subroutine. Next we compute idle time, waiting time, and total time for each process for the initial order according to (7-7), (7-8), and (7-9), respectively.

This program makes use of a simulated clock. The clock is set equal to idle time plus process time for process K in block 7. At the end of the planning horizon TM, the clock will have a value that is at least as great as TM. The arrival of a second order is indicated in block 8 by the generation of an arrival time AT, that is, the time which has elapsed between the arrival of order 1 and the arrival of order 2. Since a new order has been received, K additional process times must be generated in block 9. Block 10 increments total completed output by one.

B and D are set equal to T(1) and AT, respectively, in blocks 11 and 12. Blocks 13 through 21 are repeated K times, that is, once for each of the K production processes. In block 14, the appropriate difference indicated by equation system 7-11 is obtained. If WT(J) is positive, idle time will be equal to zero and waiting time will be equal to WT(J). If WT(J) is equal to zero, then both waiting time and idle time are equal to zero. If WT(J) is negative, waiting time will be equal to zero and idle time will be equal to $-$WT(J). In block 19, T(J) is calculated according to (7-10) for the jth process. B and D are recalculated in blocks 20 and 21 in accordance with (7-11). Clock time is updated in block 22.

If clock time is less than TM, then we return to block 8 and generate another interorder time and a set of K process times. However, if clock time is greater than or equal to TM, then we have completed one replication of the first simulation run. Total profit for that replication is calcu-

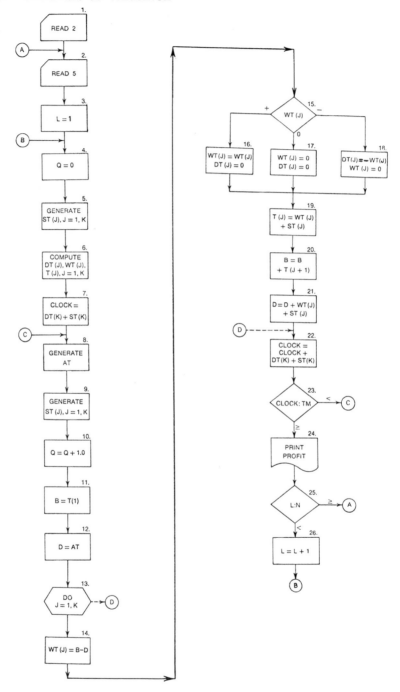

Figure 7-2.

lated according to (7-18) and printed on the output report. If the number of completed replications, L, is less than N, the number of replications required for the run, then L is increased by 1 and a new replication is begun in block 4. If the number of replications that have been completed is greater than or equal to N, then the run is terminated and a card is read in block 2 that contains the parameters for the next run.

The FORTRAN computer program corresponding to the flow chart in Figure 7-2 is displayed in Figure 7-3. Since there is almost a one-to-one correspondence between the statements of the FORTRAN program and the blocks in the flow chart, it will not be necessary to repeat the explanation of the logic of the program. However, a brief digression will be included to explain the FORTRAN subroutine for generating exponential variables.

A random variable, X, is said to have an exponential distribution if its density function is defined as

$$f(x) = \alpha e^{-\alpha x} \qquad (7\text{-}19)$$

for $\alpha > 0$ and $x \geq 0$.

The cumulative distribution function of X is

$$F(x) = \int_0^x \alpha e^{-\alpha t} \, dt = 1 - e^{-\alpha x} \qquad (7\text{-}20)$$

and the expected value and variance of X are given by the following formulas:

$$EX = \int_0^\infty x\alpha e^{-\alpha x} \, dx = 1/\alpha \qquad (7\text{-}21)$$

$$VX = \int_0^\infty (x - 1/\alpha)^2 \, \alpha e^{-\alpha x} \, dx = 1/\alpha^2 = (EX)^2. \qquad (7\text{-}22)$$

Since the exponential distribution has only one parameter α it is possible to express α as

$$\alpha = 1/EX. \qquad (7\text{-}23)$$

The generation of exponential random variables can be accomplished in a number of different ways. But since $F(x)$ exists in explicit form, the inverse transformation technique provides a straightforward method. Because of the symmetry of the uniform distribution, $F(x)$ and $1 - F(x)$ are interchangeable. Therefore

$$r = e^{-\alpha x} \qquad (7\text{-}24)$$

and, consequently,

$$x = -(1/\alpha) \log_e r = -EX \log_e r. \qquad (7\text{-}25)$$

```
 1   READ 2, K, N
 2   FØRMAT (2I2)
 3   DIMENSIØN EST(K), ST(K), T(K), WT(K), DT(K)
 4   READ 5, P, C, TM, EAT, (EST(J), J=1, K)
 5   FØRMAT (10F10.2)
 6   L=1
 7   Q=0.
 8   DØ 10 J=1, K
 9   CALL RAND (R)
10   ST(J)=-EST(J)*LØGF(R)
11   K1=K-1
12   DT(1)=0.
13   DØ 14 J=1, K1
14   DT(J+1)=DT(J)+ST(J)
15   DØ 17 J=1, K
16   WT(J)=0.
17   T(J)=ST(J)
18   CLØCK=DT(K)+ST(K)
19   CALL RAND (R)
20   AT=-EAT*LOGF(R)
21   DØ 23 J=1, K
22   CALL RAND (R)
23   ST(J)=-EST(J)*LØGF(R)
24   Q=Q+1.0
25   B=T(1)
26   D=AT
27   DØ 37 J=1, K
28   WT(J)=B-D
29   IF(WT(J))30, 30, 33
30   DT(J)=-WT(J)
31   WT(J)=0.
32   GØ TØ 34
33   DT(J)=0.
34   T(J)=WT(J)+ST(J)
35   B=B+T(J+1)
36   D=D+WT(J)+ST(J)
37   CØNTINUE
38   CLØCK=CLØCK+DT(K)+ST(K)
39   IF(CLØCK-TM) 19, 40, 40
40   PRØFIT=P*Q-C
41   PRINT 42, PRØFIT
42   FØRMAT (F10.2)
43   IF(L-N) 44, 4, 4
44   L=L+1
45   GØ TØ 7
46   END
```

Figure 7-3.   A computer program for a computer model of the firm.

Thus for each value of the pseudorandom number r, a unique value of x is determined, which will take only nonnegative values (since $\log_e r \leq 0$ for $0 \leq r \leq 1$), and will follow the exponential density function (7-19) with expected value EX. Although this technique seems very simple, remember that the computation of the natural logarithm on digital computers includes a power series expansion (or some equivalent approximation technique) for each uniform variable generated.

Two FORTRAN instructions are required to generate an exponential variable,

$$CALL\ RAND(R) \tag{7-26}$$

$$X\ =\ -EX*LOGF(R) \tag{7-27}$$

where RAND is a subroutine for generating uniformly distributed variables on the (0,1) interval and LOGF is a subroutine for taking the natural logarithm of a number. Both of these subroutines are available on nearly all of the digital computers that are in use today. The subroutine for generating exponential variables appears in statements 9 and 10, 19 and 20, and 22 and 23. These FORTRAN statements correspond to blocks 5, 8, and 9, respectively, of Figure 7-2.

VALIDATION

In Chapter 5, we suggested that in order to validate a computer model one must compare simulated data (data generated by the computer) with actual and historical data. Since our example model is a purely hypothetical model, this type of validation is clearly impossible. However, another alternative is available to us.

The steady-state properties of a single-channel, multistation queueing model with Poisson arrivals and service rates are available and can be used to check on the validity of the results of our simulation experiment. Normally, one would not perform a simulation experiment when an analytical solution exists for the problem to be solved. However, in the case of an expository treatment of simulation, an analytical solution provides a means of validating the results of the experiment. Our model can accommodate without complication any type of probability distribution or empirical distribution for both $f(d)$ and any number of $f_j(d)$, thus extending the reach of investigation into the realm where analytical solutions or approximations are too difficult to obtain.

Approximate expected total profit Π may be calculated analytically by the following formula for the case of Poisson demand and Poisson production processes [30,55]:

$$\Pi\ =\ \text{Expected Total Revenue–Expected Total Cost} \tag{7-28}$$

$$=\ P\left[E(D)\cdot TM\ -\ \sum_{j=1}^{k} \frac{E(D)/E(Q_j)}{1\ -\ E(D)/E(Q_j)} \right]\ -\ C$$

where

$E(D) \cdot TM$ = the expected number of orders which enter the sys-   (7-29)
tem or expected total demand during the planning
period.

$$\sum_{j=1}^{k} \frac{E(D)/E(Q_j)}{1 - E(D)/E(Q_j)}$$ = the expected number of units remaining   (7-30)
in the system either being processed or
waiting to be processed at the end of
the planning period.

$$E(D) \cdot TM - \sum_{j=1}^{k} \frac{E(D)/E(Q_j)}{1 - E(D)/E(Q_j)}$$ = the expected number of   (7-31)
completed orders or ex-
pected sales measured in
units during the planning
period.

P, TM, K, and C have already been defined. This formula for expected profit assumes $E(D)/E(Q_j) < 1$, and is merely an approximation, since it assumes that the system has reached a steady-state within 90 days.

Table 7-2 contains a comparison of the theoretical values of Π for each of the five plans with the sample means for each plan generated by the simulation experiment. The theoretical values were calculated from (7-28) and the data in Table 7-1. More will be said about this table later, but for the moment it will suffice to say that the sample means of profit for each of the five plans are very close to their corresponding theoretical values and, thus, tend to confirm the validity of the results of our simulation experiment.

THE EXPERIMENT[1]

The *initial conditions* for our experiment were identical for all replications of each simulation run. The system was assumed to be "empty" at the beginning of each replication for all five simulation runs [see (7-6) through (7-9)]. Activity was simulated for a period of 90 days, and total profit was calculated for the period. The simulation was repeated 50 times, using the given parameters for Plan I. (Repetition was accomplished by

[1] This section and the following section are based on the paper by Thomas H. Naylor, Kenneth Wertz, and Thomas Wonnacott entitled "Methods for Analyzing Data from Computer Simulation Experiments," *Communications of the ACM*, **X** (November 1967), 703-710.

Table 7-2   Output Data (Total Profit) Generated by Simulation Runs.

Plan Replication	I	II	III	IV	V
1	$ 3055	$ 3175	$ 2275	$ 3325	$ 3605
2	2665	3310	2470	3220	3335
3	2860	3280	2350	3250	3155
4	2995	2890	2665	2755	2855
5	2935	3220	2920	3130	3635
6	2875	2905	2530	3265	3140
7	3025	2635	3055	3355	3665
8	3115	2785	3085	3520	3140
9	2845	2515	2515	3220	3215
10	2965	2830	2500	3235	2945
11	2920	3085	2800	3265	3590
12	2890	2980	2245	2980	3125
13	3040	3145	2770	3070	2765
14	2920	2950	3010	2995	3680
15	3445	2845	2755	3490	3305
16	2845	2830	2710	3070	3470
17	3265	3055	2575	3145	3395
18	2815	2845	2770	3475	2840
19	3250	3055	2800	3505	3170
20	2890	3100	2890	3475	3290
21	3400	2830	2725	3610	3665
22	3040	2785	2830	3220	3140
23	3130	3145	2455	3130	3245
24	2755	3070	2995	3430	3140
25	2800	3025	2845	3145	2900
26	3055	2665	2905	3025	3155
27	2950	2965	2695	3490	3050
28	2845	3250	2755	2920	3170
29	3160	3100	2650	3445	3035
30	3130	3205	2875	3625	3095
31	2755	2815	2935	3445	3230
32	2920	2920	2905	3070	2945
33	2890	3190	2950	3505	2765
34	3145	2680	2575	3475	3020
35	2950	3010	2635	3685	3065
36	3205	2910	2290	3505	2930
37	3100	3430	2365	3085	2810
38	2950	2980	1855	3055	2825
39	3115	2935	2290	2905	3005
40	2695	3055	2590	3280	2825
41	2905	3250	2800	2995	2780
42	2650	2815	2425	3115	3050
43	3040	2695	2860	3265	3245
44	2800	2785	2695	3085	2780
45	2860	3070	2575	3565	3590
46	3205	3265	2770	2905	3350
47	2950	2830	2335	3415	2750
48	2740	3130	2800	3340	2855
49	3055	3310	2845	3295	2735
50	3010	3055	2845	3490	3125

altering the starting value of the pseudorandom number generator.) In a similar manner, 90-day runs, each repeated 50 times, were made for strategies II through V. The output data for the five simulation runs are tabulated in Table 7-2. For each sample of 50 observations, the sample mean and standard deviation were calculated and were tabulated in Table 7-3.

Table 7-3   Comparison of Approximate Expected Profit with Simulation Results for Five Alternative Plans for a Computer Model of the Firm

Plans	Approximate Expected Profit (Π)	Sample Mean of Profit ($\bar{X}$)	Sample Standard Deviation of Profit (s)
I	$2918.64	$2976.40	$175.83
II	$2918.64	$2992.30	$202.20
III	$2704.00	$2675.20	$250.51
IV	$3285.00	$3265.30	$221.81
V	$3147.50	$3131.90	$277.04

We now give our attention to the rationale underlying the sample sizes chosen for this experiment as well as to an analysis of some of the effects that these sample sizes have had on the experimental results.

The problem of sample size with computer simulation experiments is indeed complex. With computer simulation, sample size may be increased in two different ways: (1) the total length of the simulation run may be increased from, say, one month of simulated time to two months of simulated time; (2) runs of a given length may be replicated by using different sets of pseudorandom numbers.

First, consider the length of the simulation run. The length of the firm's planning horizon, 90 days, is assumed to be given. The choice of a suitable planning horizon is assumed to have been made by the firm's policy makers prior to and independent of the decision to use simulation as a mode of analysis. In other words, the length of the simulation run was not determined on the basis of statistical considerations.

Second, we consider the number of replications for each of our five simulation runs. We elected to use the same number of replications for each of the five simulation runs, because inequality of variances over the five operating plans has little effect on inferences about population means in the analysis of variance when the sample size is the same for all five operating plans [58, p. 345].

It is well known that the optimal sample size in analysis of variance depends on the answers one gives to the following three questions: (1) How large a shift in means do you wish to detect? (2) How much variability is present in the population? (3) What size risks are you willing to take? Power function charts for the specification of sample size in analysis of variance are available for determining n, the number of replications per plan for the following: (1) a given number of plans m; (2) a given population variance σ^2 for each plan; (3) a given level of significance α; and (4) a given power P to detect (5) a specified difference $\Pi_j - \Pi$ between the jth population mean and the grand mean.

Although it may be possible to specify a difference $\Pi_j - \Pi$, which we wish to detect for each plan, a level of significance, and a power for our experiment, meaningful estimates of the unknown parameter σ^2 are not as easy to obtain. Estimates of σ^2 must be based on past experimentation, a pilot study, or familiarity with the system being simulated. Matters are further complicated by the fact that there is reason to believe that the variance is not exactly the same for all five plans in our experiment. However, to obtain an idea of what n should be, we assume that

$$
\begin{aligned}
m &= 5 \\
\sigma &= 225 \\
\alpha &= .05 \\
P &= .90 \\
\Pi_j - \Pi &= 100 \qquad j = 1, 2 \\
& \; 0 \qquad\quad j = 3 \\
& -100 \qquad j = 4, 5.
\end{aligned}
$$

By using the power function charts described in [65, p. 104], we obtain a sample size of $n = 20$ for each plan. For $\sigma = 350$, and everything else held constant, we would obtain $n = 50$. To be safe, we have set the sample size at 50 replications per plan.

In the remainder of this chapter we shall apply the F-test, multiple comparisons, and multiple rankings to the data generated by the experiment mentioned above. Before considering these specific data analysis techniques, we must inquire about the accuracy of the sample means that appear in Table 7-3. This question can be answered, in part, by constructing 99 percent (or any other appropriate level) confidence intervals using the formula,

$$
\Pi = \overline{X} \pm zs/\sqrt{n} \tag{7-32}
$$

where $\overline{X}$ is the sample mean, s is the sample standard deviation, $n = 50$ is the sample size, z is the percentile of the normal distribution which leaves .5 percent probability in each tail, and Π is the true profit. (This formula is only an approximation, since s is used for σ.) By constructing 99 percent confidence intervals for each of the five plans, we obtain:

$$
\begin{array}{ll}
\text{Plan I} & 2912 < \Pi_1 < 3040 \\
\text{Plan II} & 2918 < \Pi_2 < 3065 \\
\text{Plan III} & 2584 < \Pi_3 < 2766 \\
\text{Plan IV} & 3185 < \Pi_4 < 3345 \\
\text{Plan V} & 3031 < \Pi_5 < 3233.
\end{array}
$$

The approximate (steady-state) true profits Π_j, in fact, are contained in these confidence intervals. We notice, however, that in plans I and II the steady-state Π_j come close to missing the confidence intervals. This is because these two plans involve the most congested queues (that take the longest to reach the steady-state) and, therefore, have their true Π_j approximated most poorly. A longer planning horizon (greater than 90 days) would have brought us closer to the steady-state and, doubtless, would have improved the accuracy of the approximate true profit in Table 7-3.

DATA ANALYSIS

The analysis of variance is a collection of techniques that are appropriate when the factors affecting the response are qualitative. We illustrate three different forms of the analysis of variance: the F-test [58], the multiple comparisons of Tukey [64] and Dunnett [15], and the multiple ranking procedure of Bechhofer, Dunnett, and Sobel [8].

All of these procedures were developed on three assumptions: (1) the independence of the statistical errors, (2) the equality of variance, and (3) normality. The first assumption is satisfied by the independence of the pseudorandom numbers. We know that the second and third assumptions are not exactly satisfied by our queueing model. The means of the five plans are slightly different (Table 7-3). The variances are doubtless different too, although the sample standard deviations in Table 7-3 indicate that the differences are slight. Profit fluctuates according to the number of orders arriving in 90 days, less the number of orders remaining in the system. Both of these numbers are approximately normally distributed (Poisson variates with large means are very nearly normal), so that we can expect the total profit to be approximately normal too. This expectation was borne out by sample histograms and data analysis.

However, all is not lost as a result of the departure from assumptions two and three of the analysis of variance. Certain procedures, such as the F-test, are known to be robust, that is, quite insensitive to departures from assumptions [58, pp. 331-368]. For example, Scheffé argues that, "inequality of variances in the cells of a layout has little effect on inferences about means if the cell numbers are equal, serious effects with unequal cell numbers," [58, p. 345]. For this reason we have chosen equal sample sizes for each of our five simulation runs. With regard to nonnormality, Scheffé concludes in Chapter 10 that "the effect of violation of the normality assumption is slight on inferences about means but dangerous on inferences about variances." Unfortunately, the robustness properties of multiple comparisons and multiple ranking procedures are not as well known as the ones of the simple F-test. We can safely hope that our departures from the assumptions of a common variance and normality are small enough not to seriously matter.

F-Test

We may wish to test the null hypothesis, H_0, that the expected profits for each of the five operating plans are equal; in symbols:

$$H_0: \Pi_1 = \Pi_2 = \ldots = \Pi_5$$

By employing the F-statistic, the decision rule for accepting or rejecting H_0 becomes the following:

$$\text{If } F \geq F_{\alpha, m-1, m(n-1)} \quad \text{reject } H_0$$
$$\text{Otherwise} \quad \text{accept } H_0$$

where F is the appropriate percentile of the F distribution, α is the significance level, $m = 5$ is the number of operating plans, and $n = 50$ is the number of replications per operating plan. If H_0 is accepted, then one tentatively concludes that the sample differences between plans are attributable to random fluctuations instead of to actual differences in population values (expected profits). On the other hand, if H_0 is rejected, then further analysis, such as multiple comparisons and multiple rankings, is recommended.

Since the pseudorandom numbers generated for the jth operating plan are independent of the ones for the other four plans, our experiment is analyzed as a single-factor experimental design. Let X_{ij} denote the total profit for the ith replication of plan j. $\overline{X}_{.j}$ is the average profit for plan j over all 50 replications. $\overline{X}_{..}$ is the grand average for all five plans over all 50 replications.

Table 7-4 contains a summary of the formulas necessary to compute the statistics used in the analysis of a single-factor experiment.

Table 7-4   Formulas for One Way Analysis of Variance

Source of Variation	Sum of Squares	Degrees of Freedom	Mean Square
Between Plans	$SS_{plans} = n \sum_{j=1}^{m} (\overline{X}_{.j} - \overline{X}_{..})^2$	$m-1$	$MS_p = SS_{plans}/m-1$
Error	$SS_{error} = \sum_{i=1}^{n} \sum_{j=1}^{m} (X_{ij} - \overline{X}_{.j})^2$	$m(n-1)$	$MS_e = SS_{error}/m(n-1)$
Total	$SS_{total} = \sum_{i=1}^{n} \sum_{j=1}^{m} (X_{ij} - \overline{X}_{..})^2$	$nm-1$	

The F statistic then is computed by the formula:

$$F = MS_p/MS_e.$$

By substituting the results of our experiment for the quantities in Table 7-4, we obtain Table 7-5. From the data in Table 7-5, we observe that $F = 46.6$, easily exceeding the critical value $F_{.05,4,245} = 2.21$. In this case F is even much greater than the critical value for $\alpha = .001$. Hence, the data generated by the simulation experiment do not support the null hypothesis that the expected profits are equal for each of the five strategies. One may check the decision to reject H_0 against Table 7-3, which shows that the approximate expected profits do indeed vary from plan to plan.

Since our objective was simply to illustrate the relevance of the F-test to the analysis of data from simulation experiments, we have considered only a special case—one-way analysis of variance. Consult one of several excellent textbooks on the analysis of variance for a description of two-way, three-way, and higher-order analysis of variance procedures. The books by Scheffé [58] and Winer [65] are helpful in this regard. In Chapter 8 we make use of three-way analysis of variance.

Table 7-5   Statistics for One-way Analysis of Variance

Source of Variation	Sum of Squares	Degrees of Freedom	Mean Square
Between Plans	9,677,758	4	2,419,440
Error	12,715,825	245	51,901
Total	22,393,583	249	

Multiple Comparisons

Typically, economic policy makers are interested not only in whether alternatives differ but also in *how* they differ. Multiple comparison and multiple ranking procedures often become tools relevant to meeting the latter query, since they have been designed specifically to attack questions of how means of many populations differ.

In contrast with the analysis of variance, multiple comparison methods emphasize the use of confidence intervals rather than the testing of hypotheses. Because in this chapter we have been concerned with the differences in population means, it may be tempting at this point to construct a number of 95 percent (say) confidence intervals for $\Pi_j - \Pi_J$.

$$(\overline{X}_j - \overline{X}_J) \pm t \cdot \sqrt{2MS_e/n} \qquad j, J = 1, 2, \ldots, m \qquad (7\text{-}33)$$

by employing the familiar Student's-t statistic. But a problem arises. The intervals developed in this manner are not all *simultaneously* true at the 95 percent level; indeed, the confidence level for the aggregate of intervals sinks considerably.

What is needed, therefore, is a way of constructing a *set* of confidence intervals that will all simultaneously be true with probability 95 percent. The May 1965 issue of *Technometrics* [20] contains a comprehensive review of alternative methods that have been proposed for solving this problem. For illustrative purposes, we shall discuss two of these methods and relate each of them to our simulation experiment: (1) Tukey's method [58,64,65], and (2) Dunnett's method [15]. The general form of these methods can be found in the appropriate references. In this chapter we shall give the specific form for *one-factor* experiments, although they are equally valid for many-factor experiments.

Tukey's method [58,64,65] will yield simultaneous confidence intervals (of the type previously described) for the differences between *all* pairs. With 95 percent probability, *all* of the following confidence intervals for $\Pi_j - \Pi_J$ are true:

$$(\overline{X}_{.j} - \overline{X}_{.J}) \pm q_{m,v}\sqrt{MS_e/n} \qquad j, J = 1, 2, 3, \ldots, m \qquad (7\text{-}34)$$

where $q_{m,v}$ is tabulated under the title "Distribution of the Studentized Range Statistic" [65], m is the number of sample means, and v is the number of degrees of freedom for MS_e, $m(n - 1)$ in the case of one-factor experiments. For the actual data generated by our single-factor computer simulation experiment, the formula for 95 percent confidence intervals is given by

$$(\overline{X}_{.j} - \overline{X}_{.J}) \pm q_{5,245}\sqrt{MS_e/n} = (\overline{X}_{.j} - \overline{X}_{.J}) \pm 3.86\sqrt{(51,901)/50}$$
$$= (\overline{X}_{.j} - \overline{X}_{.J}) \pm 124 \qquad j, J = 1, 2, 3, 4, 5 \qquad (7\text{-}35)$$

Table 7-6   Differences of Sample Means $(\bar{X}_{j.}-\bar{X}_{J.})$

j \ J	2	3	4	5
1	-15.9	301.2*	-288.9*	-155.5*
2	---	317.1*	-273.0*	-139.6*
3	---	---	-590.1*	-456.7*
4	---	---	---	-133.4*

Table 7-6 contains a tabulation of the differences between sample means for all 10 pairs of differences in our experiment. An asterisk (*) indicates that a particular difference exceeds the confidence allowance 124, thus making the difference "statistically significant," if this form of inference is desired. At the same time, and still covered by 95 percent certainty, we can make more subtle comparisons, technically called linear contrasts. For example, we can ask: "Does the difference $(\Pi_1 - \Pi_2)$ exceed the difference $(\Pi_2 - \Pi_3)$ and by how much?" "Do the first three means exceed the last two means on the average, and by how much?" If general linear contrasts are of more interest to the experimenter than the paired comparisons, then Scheffé's method [58] is usually preferred.

Dunnett's [15] method of multiple comparisons compares one specific mean, called the control mean, with all the others. In simulations of business and economic systems the control mean is usually the mean associated with the present operating plan, decision rule, or managerial strategy. Dunnett's multiple comparison procedure is summarized as follows: with 95 percent probability, all of the following confidence intervals for $\Pi_j - \Pi_c$ are true.

$$(\bar{X}_{.j} - \bar{X}_{.c}) \pm d\sqrt{2MS_e/n} \qquad j = 2, \ldots, m \qquad (7\text{-}36)$$

where,

Π_c = the control population mean,
$\bar{X}_{.c}$ = the control sample mean,
d = the percentile of Dunnett's t statistic [15,51] with degrees of freedom equal to $m(n - 1)$ for one-factor experiments.

In our simulation experiment we assume that plan I is the control plan and compare it with all the other plans. The formula for 95 percent confidence intervals is given by

$$(\overline{X}_{.j} - \overline{X}_{.c}) \pm 2.16\sqrt{[(2)(51{,}901)]/50} = (\overline{X}_{.j} - \overline{X}_{.c}) \pm 98.4$$
$$j = 2, 3, 4, 5. \qquad (7\text{-}37)$$

Table 7-7 contains a tabulation of the differences between sample means for comparisons between the control mean (plan I) and the means for plans II to V. Again an asterisk (*) indicates that a particular difference exceeds the confidence allowance 98.4, thus, making the difference statistically significant, if this form of inference is of interest.

Table 7-7   Differences of Sample Means $(\overline{X}_{.j} - \overline{X}_{.c})$

j	2	3	4	5
$(\overline{X}_{.j} - \overline{X}_{.c})$	15.9	-301.2*	288.9*	155.5*

Multiple Rankings

Frequently, the objective of computer simulation experiments with models of economic systems is to find the "best" policy or decision rule. Conventional tests of homogeneity, for instance, the F-test that k population means are equal, or Bartlett's test that k population variances are equal, do not provide the decision maker with the type of information necessary for decisions aimed at selecting the best plan or policy (for example, the policy that leads to the largest profit for a business firm, or the least amount of unemployment in the case of the economy as a whole).

Multiple ranking procedures are a direct approach to the solution of the problem of ranking alternatives, based on the empirical results obtained from some type of experiment whether it be a real-world experiment or a computer simulation experiment. The best rank of a set of economic policies or decision rules is simply the ranking of the sample means associated with the given policies or decision rules. However, because of random error, sample rankings may yield incorrect results. With what probability can we say that a ranking of sample means represents the true ranking of the population means? It is basically this question that multiple ranking procedures attempt to answer.

Historically, multiple ranking procedures can be traced back to the work of Bahadur [1] in 1950. He was one of the first statisticians to recognize the multiple ranking problem and to contribute to the theory of k sample problems. Among the early contributions to the literature in this field was Mosteller's work [38,39] with *slippage tests*.

Mosteller's procedure is a very simple nonparametric technique that is applicable only to one-factor balanced experiments. It is designed to test the null hypothesis that k populations are the same against the alternative hypothesis that one of the k populations "has slipped to the right of the rest" (is larger than the rest). On the basis of our own empirical results with this test [42], we are inclined to concur with Mosteller's own criticism of the test as lacking a desirable level of power. Other contributions to the literature on the theory of slippage tests include the work of Karlin and Truax [31], Kudo [33], and Paulson [44,45].

In 1954, Bechhofer [5] proposed a path-breaking procedure for selecting on the basis of sample means a single population from among k populations and for guaranteeing with probability P* that the selected population is the best (that is, has the highest mean), provided that some other condition on the parameters is satisfied. Since the terminology used by Bechhofer [5] is basic to many multiple ranking procedures, it will be helpful if we define some of the terms that are used throughout the remainder of this chapter.

We want to choose as the "best" population the population that yields the highest (or lowest) sample mean. We want to be assured with probability P* that we, indeed, have selected the correct population. If the best population differs only slightly from the next best population, then (because of random error) extremely large samples are required to detect such a small difference. However, our concern over not detecting the best population, when the difference between the best and the next best population is very small, may not be as great as it would be if this difference were very large. Therefore, we want to take that number of observations from each population so that the probability of a correct selection (CS) is at least P*, given that the difference δ between the best and next population is at least δ*. This may be stated mathematically as

$$\Pr(\text{CS} \mid \delta \geq \delta^*) \geq P^* \qquad (7\text{-}38)$$

where δ* and P* are specified by the decision maker.

If all but one of the populations have a mean equal to the mean of the "next best" population, then the means are said to be in the "least favorable configuration." If the means are not in this configuration, then the reliability criterion given by (7-38) is more easily satisfied. Since we do not know the true configuration, the reliability criterion must also be satisfied for the least favorable configuration [5, p. 23 and 6, p. 411].

With some of the multiple ranking procedures it is possible to find not only the best plan but also the following (and others unlisted):

1. The "best two" plans *without* regard to order.
2. The "best two" plans *with* regard to order.

3. The "best three" plans *without* regard to order.

4. The "best," "second best," "third best" (etc.) plan.

All of the multiple ranking procedures assume *independent observations*, and most of them assume *normally distributed observations*. In describing the existing multiple ranking procedures, it is convenient to divide them into two groups: (1) procedures assuming known variances, and (2) procedures assuming unknown variances.

The book by Bechhofer, Kiefer, and Sobel [9] contains a comprehensive survey of multiple ranking procedures that assume *known variances*. Unfortunately, the variance is usually *unknown* in most simulation experiments. For this reason the paper by Kleijnen and Naylor [32] can prove helpful to the reader. After surveying several multiple ranking procedures that assume *known* variances and *unknown* variances, Kleijnen and Naylor [32] critically evaluate the assumptions underlying the various ranking procedures and the extent to which these assumptions may or may not be violated when they are used with computer simulation experiments. Several modifications of existing multiple ranking procedures also are considered by Kleijnen and Naylor. The objective of these modifications is to circumvent some of the difficulties encountered when one or more of the assumptions that underlie existing multiple ranking procedures is violated.

To illustrate the applicability of multiple ranking procedures to the analysis of data from simulation experiments, we apply the Bechhofer, Dunnett, and Sobel [8] two-stage procedure to the output data from our example model of the firm. In Chapter 8, we shall apply a sequential multiple ranking procedure developed by Bechhofer and Blumenthal [7] to an inventory model.

We now consider a more detailed description of Bechhofer, Dunnett, and Sobel's two-sample multiple decision procedure for ranking means of *normal* populations with a *common unknown variance* [8] and the application of this procedure to our experiment. Using the notation of our experiment, we assume that for a given population (plan), j, X_{ij} is a normally and independently distributed random variable with expected value Π_j and common variance $\sigma_j^2 = \sigma^2$ ($j = 1, 2, \ldots, m$). We further assume that σ^2 and the Π_j are unknown. Denote the ranked Π_j by

$$\Pi_{[1]} \leq \Pi_{[2]} \leq \ldots \leq \Pi_{[m]} \qquad (7\text{-}39)$$

and the differences between the ranked means by

$$\delta_{ij} = \Pi_{[i]} - \Pi_{[j]} \ (i, j = 1, 2, \ldots, m). \qquad (7\text{-}40)$$

We do not know which population is associated with $\Pi_{[j]}$.

Assume that the experimental goal calls for the selection of the population having the largest expected value. (This is by no means the only goal that can be chosen.) Assume also that the experimenter specifies a parameter δ^* which is the smallest value of $\delta_{m,m-1}$ that he is willing to accept. In addition, the experimenter specifies the smallest acceptable value P for the probability of achieving his given goal when $\delta_{m,m-1} \geq \delta^*$.

Bechhofer, Dunnett, and Sobel's two-sample procedure consists of these five steps:

1. Take a first sample of N_1 observations from each of the m populations.

2. Calculate the mean square error, MS_e, which is an unbiased estimate of σ^2, having $v = m(n-1)$ degrees of freedom for $n = N_1$.

3. Take a second sample of $N_2 - N_1$ observations from each of the m populations, $N_2 = \max \{N_1, [2\,MS_e(h/\delta^*)^2]\}$, where the brackets [ ] denote the smallest integer equal to or greater than the rational number contained within the brackets, and h is obtained from Table 3 of Dunnett and Sobel [17] for the given values of v and P. If $2\,MS_e(h/\delta^*)^2 \leq N_1$, then no second sample is necessary and, therefore, $N_2 = N_1$.

4. For each population calculate the overall sample mean $\overline{X}_j$ where

$$\overline{X}_j = 1/N_2 \sum_{i=1}^{N_2} X_{ij} \qquad (j = 1, 2, \ldots, m). \qquad (7\text{-}41)$$

5. Denote the ranked values of $\overline{X}_j$ by

$$\overline{X}_{[1]} < \overline{X}_{[2]} < \cdots < \overline{X}_{[m]}. \qquad (7\text{-}42)$$

Rank the populations according to the ranking of the observed $\overline{X}_j$ and select the population that gives rise to $\overline{X}_{[m]}$ as the population having the largest population mean.

For our experiment, suppose that we want to select the plan having the largest expected profit and to guarantee that the probability of correctly choosing that population will be, at least, .90 when the difference between the plan with the highest expected profit and the plan with the second highest expected is $100.00. In other words, we are assuming that $P = .90$ and $\delta^* = 100$. We then let $N_1 = n = 50$ and calculate $MS_e = 51,901$. For $P = .90$ and $v = m(n-1) = 245$, we obtain $h = 1.58$ from Table 3 of [17]. Next we determine $\max \{N_1, [2\,MS_e(h/\delta^*)^2]\} = \max \{50, [2(51,901)(1.58/100)^2]\} = \max \{50, 26\} = 50$. Since $26 < 50$, no second sample is required, and $N_2 = N_1 = n = 50$. Sample means for $n = 50$ previously were calculated in Table 7-3. On the basis of the ranking of the sample means, we would select operating plan IV as the plan with the highest expected profit. If, in fact, the best operating plan has an expected profit that is $100.00 larger than the next best, we have, at least, a probability of 90 percent of correctly choosing it despite the random statistical fluctuations of sampling.

AN ECONOMETRIC MODEL

As a second example of the application of the F-test, multiple comparison methods, and of multiple ranking methods to evaluate the effects of alternative economic policies, we have chosen a stochastic version of the Samuelson-Hicks model [26,56]. The analytical properties of the Samuelson-Hicks model are well known and, as we shall demonstrate, can be used to check the results of our simulation experiments. Following a brief exposition of the model, we present the results of several simulation runs: that is, the data for evaluating the effects of five alternative economic policies on a single response variable—namely, the variance of national income.

The Samuelson-Hicks model has two principle attributes. First, it is a relatively simple model and is familiar to economists. Second, although its analytical properties are well known [19,27], it still possesses some of the characteristics of more complex econometric models which do not lend themselves to straightforward analytical solutions. The model consists of the following parameters, variables, and functional relationships:

PARAMETERS

b = accelerator coefficient,

c_1 = marginal propensity to consume in period $t - 1$, $0 < c_1 < 1$

c_2 = marginal propensity to consume in period $t - 2$, $0 < c_2 < 1$

g = governmental parameter.

EXOGENOUS VARIABLES

u_t and v_t = a stochastic variate with a known probability distribution, expected value, and variance.

ENDOGENOUS VARIABLES

C_t = consumption in period t.

I_t = investment in period t.

G_t = governmental expenditure in period t.

Y_t = national income in period t.

OPERATING CHARACTERISTICS

$$C_t = c_1 Y_{t-1} + c_2 Y_{t-2} + u_t. \qquad (7\text{-}43)$$

$$I_t = b(Y_{t-1} - Y_{t-2}) + v_t. \qquad (7\text{-}44)$$

$$G_t = g Y_{t-1}. \qquad (7\text{-}45)$$

IDENTITY

$$Y_t = C_t + I_t + G_t. \qquad (7\text{-}46)$$

By substituting the values of C_t, I_t, and G_t, given by (7-43), (7-44), and (7-45), respectively, into (7-46) we obtain

$$Y_t = w_t - a_1 Y_{t-1} - a_2 Y_{t-2} \qquad (7\text{-}47)$$

where

$$w_t = u_t + v_t, \tag{7-48}$$
$$a_1 = -(c_1 + b + g), \tag{7-49}$$
$$a_2 = b - c_2. \tag{7-50}$$

If we assume that national income is measured in terms of deviations y_t from its equilibrium value, then the final form of (7-47), which determines the time path of national income, is

$$y_t = w_t - a_1 Y_{t-1} - a_2 Y_{t-2} \tag{7-51}$$

Having described our example model in mathematical terms, let us now assign some arbitrary values to its parameters. We begin by assuming a planning horizon of length 200, that is, $t = 1, 2, \ldots, 200$. The starting values for national income in periods 1 and 2 are, respectively, 7.5 and 2.0. The parameters c_1 and c_2 have been assigned the values .375 and .300, respectively. The stochastic variates u_t and v_t are assumed to be independent normally distributed random variables with expected values equal to zero and variances equal, respectively, to 13.69 and 4.84. Therefore, the stochastic variate w_t is normally distributed with expected value equal to zero and variance equal to 18.53.

We assume that five alternative policies are under consideration and that each one has the following:

1. A *monetary policy* that assigns a particular value to the accelerator coefficient b.

2. A *fiscal policy* that assigns a particular value to the governmental parameter g.

The particular values assigned to b and g for policies I to V are displayed in Table 7-8.

Table 7-8   Accelerator Coefficient, Governmental Parameter, and Variance of National Income for Five Alternative Policies Using the Samuelson-Hicks Model

Policy	Accelerator Coefficient b	Governmental Parameter g	Variance of National Income σ_y^2
I	1.05	.250	504.9473
II	1.10	.125	245.2498
III	1.15	.050	242.6402
IV	1.15	.150	370.4739
V	1.15	.225	634.8269

THE COMPUTER PROGRAM

Figure 7-4 contains a flow chart for generating the time paths of the endogenous variables of the Samuelson-Hicks model on a computer. Block 1 of the flow chart contains a READ statement that causes the parameters b, c_1, c_2, and g to be read into the memory of the computer as well as the parameters describing the probability distributions of u_T and v_T and two initial values of Y_T. Block 2 indicates that blocks 2 through 5 will be repeated N times, where N is the length of the planning period to be simulated. Values of the stochastic variates u_T and v_T are generated in block 3 by the appropriate subroutines for the given probability distributions. In block 4, the values of our four endogenous variables are computed for time period T according to equations 11, 12, 13, and 10, respectively. Block 5 contains a PRINT statement that causes T, C_T, I_T, G_T, and Y_T to be printed at the end of each iteration.

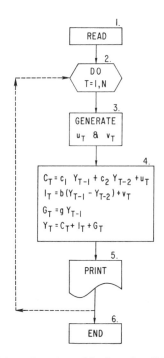

Figure 7-4.   A flow chart of the Samuelson-Hicks model.

VALIDATION

Since the theoretical properties of the Samuelson-Hicks model are completely known, we can use this information to validate our simulation results in the same manner that we validated the simulation results with our model of the firm.

It is possible to calculate the theoretical value of the variance of y_t for our model by the following formula:

$$\sigma_y{}^2 = \frac{(1 + a_2)}{(1 - a_2)[(1 + a_2)^2 - a_1{}^2]} \cdot \sigma_w{}^2 \tag{7-52}$$

where a_1 and a_2 were previously defined as $-(c_1 + b + g)$ and $(b - c_2)$, respectively. The theoretical variances for policies I to V have been tabulated in Table 7-8. Since the theoretical properties of our model are known, we shall make use of these known theoretical properties in evaluating the F-test, multiple comparisons, and multiple rankings as techniques for differentiating among the five policies on the basis of the output generated by our simulation experiment. However, we must point out that, for more complex econometric models, theoretical properties, such as the variance $\sigma_y{}^2$, are not likely to be known.

THE EXPERIMENT[2]

The computer simulation experiment that we conducted with the Samuelson-Hicks model consisted of five runs, one for each policy. In each run the economy was simulated for a period equal to 200 units (for example, days, months, etc.) of time and the sample variance of national income $s_y{}^2$ was calculated for the period. The simulation then was replicated 50 times (using the given values of b and g for policy I). Replication was accomplished by altering the starting value of the pseudorandom number generator used to generate w_t. In a similar manner, 200 time unit runs (each replicated 50 times) were made for policies II to V. The output data for the five simulation runs are tabulated in Table 7-9.

Before discussing the analysis of variance, it is appropriate that we make a data transformation which has been proposed by Scheffé [58, p. 83-87] and Bartlett and Kendall [3]. We let

$$X = \log_e s_y{}^2. \tag{7-53}$$

[2] This section and the following section are based on the paper by Thomas H. Naylor, Kenneth Wertz, and Thomas H. Wonnacott entitled "Some Methods for Evaluating the Effects of Economic Policies Using Simulation Experiments," *Review of the International Statistical Institute*, **XXXVI** (No. 2, 1968), 184-200.

Table 7-9

Policy Replication	I	II	III	IV	V
1	518.03	264.72	209.74	303.94	491.12
2	514.78	201.93	180.34	367.19	367.00
3	520.55	288.71	181.67	619.76	532.79
4	562.25	266.07	259.48	378.61	801.07
5	631.23	301.68	238.83	398.46	540.70
6	392.58	388.65	203.18	423.17	608.61
7	410.14	308.59	270.57	255.96	920.85
8	322.29	238.88	118.16	449.83	784.32
9	542.27	285.94	146.84	641.08	464.44
10	447.86	196.08	249.90	340.37	577.23
11	369.14	212.38	222.28	210.81	830.78
12	608.36	232.02	266.62	710.18	1191.43
13	437.04	212.32	215.34	397.86	773.94
14	560.41	194.78	252.75	311.20	614.08
15	531.10	220.74	208.57	453.51	508.59
16	252.10	150.32	250.11	386.83	523.44
17	211.54	183.44	204.82	322.61	508.11
18	347.87	282.88	310.09	283.35	596.50
19	284.48	335.60	204.27	438.55	660.12
20	551.72	154.39	156.26	326.22	383.36
21	467.34	308.35	194.31	324.60	762.33
22	560.71	344.94	183.81	384.14	589.08
23	470.01	184.41	229.91	489.75	668.67
24	280.65	222.75	248.92	203.54	510.39
25	481.93	178.65	214.29	236.69	643.74
26	367.83	157.43	247.41	234.44	752.61
27	490.75	228.68	174.88	269.75	458.71
28	457.76	384.75	223.56	306.21	550.67
29	583.86	224.90	323.59	527.87	680.72
30	616.71	199.48	252.73	397.58	809.30
31	457.04	296.48	162.10	461.04	790.36
32	354.83	196.85	261.66	231.78	981.49
33	370.54	248.08	194.33	278.60	889.04
34	666.73	224.96	198.89	281.06	331.99
35	279.39	182.93	299.43	387.97	496.50
36	350.34	255.73	261.52	332.36	624.81
37	506.35	250.83	271.75	265.28	497.78
38	420.31	243.10	302.10	542.32	460.45
39	683.65	375.18	209.05	226.61	225.61
40	190.68	330.83	162.05	508.61	458.44
41	477.02	336.21	461.50	342.45	859.12
42	583.41	212.38	258.94	299.65	955.53
43	339.04	170.17	287.80	475.66	502.05
44	242.07	234.73	231.94	365.29	596.06
45	431.44	122.26	237.82	506.39	565.43
46	478.73	377.65	213.87	274.32	639.02
47	336.11	231.59	175.80	485.06	723.43
48	446.46	215.56	298.86	337.24	516.64
49	636.11	199.19	196.38	267.38	412.59
50	528.00	251.88	323.41	251.88	633.61

This transformation has two advantages. First, X is more nearly normally distributed than s_y^2. Second, the variance of X tends to be constant over the five policies. In fact, the variance of X does not depend on its mean and is given by Scheffé [58, p. 84] as

$$\sigma_x^2 = \frac{2}{k} + \frac{\gamma_2}{k+1} \qquad (7\text{-}54)$$

where k is the equivalent number of degrees of freedom for s_y^2, and γ_2 is the kurtosis coefficient. Although k depends on the spectral shape, or equivalently, on the autocorrelation of y_t, one would not expect it to vary drastically from one policy to the next. In any case, homogeneity of the variance over the five policies is not a crucial assumption in the analysis of variance when the sample size is the same (50) for all five stabilization policies [58].

The five sample means and variances of X are given in Table 7-10, along with the population means given by Scheffé [58, p. 84] as

$$EX \doteq \log_e \sigma_y^2. \qquad (7\text{-}55)$$

This formula is based on a linear approximation of the logarithmic function. A more exact formula based on a quadratic approximation yields a slightly smaller value of EX,

$$EX \doteq \log_e \sigma_y^2 - 1/k \qquad (7\text{-}56)$$

where k is again the equivalent number of degrees of freedom of s_y^2. The sample means that are tabulated in Table 7-10 are all below their respective expected values because we have used the linear approximation for EX.

Table 7-10   Expected Value, Sample Mean, and Sample Variance of $X = \log_e s_y^2$ for Five Alternative Policies

Policy	Expected Value EX	Sample Mean $\overline{X}$	Sample Variance s_X^2
I	6.22	6.07	.0916
II	5.50	5.47	.0701
III	5.49	5.42	.0561
IV	5.91	5.87	.0912
V	6.45	6.39	.0930

DATA ANALYSIS

F-Test

We may wish to test the null hypothesis, H_0, that the variances of national income for each of the five stabilization policies are equal; in symbols

$$H_0: (\sigma_y{}^2)_1 = (\sigma_y{}^2)_2 = (\sigma_y{}^2)_3 = (\sigma_y{}^2)_4 = (\sigma_y{}^2)_5. \qquad (7\text{-}57)$$

The equivalent null hypothesis, using the transformed data, is

$$H_0: EX_1 = EX_2 = EX_3 = EX_4 = EX_5. \qquad (7\text{-}58)$$

By employing the F-statistic, the decision rule for accepting or rejecting H_0 becomes the following.

$$\begin{array}{ll} \text{If } F \geq F_{\alpha, m-1, m(n-1)} & \text{reject } H_0 \\ \text{Otherwise} & \text{accept } H_0 \end{array} \qquad (7\text{-}59)$$

where α is the significance level, $m = 5$ is the number of policies, and $n = 50$ is the number of replications per policy. If H_0 is accepted, then one tentatively concludes that the sample differences between policies are attributable to random fluctuations rather than to actual differences in population values (variances of y_t). On the other hand, if H_0 is rejected, then further analysis, such as multiple comparisons and multiple rankings, is recommended.

Let X_{ij} denote the logarithm of $s_y{}^2$ for the ith replication of policy j. $\overline{X}_j$ is the average value of $X = \log_e s_y{}^2$ for policy j over all 50 replications. $\overline{X}$ is the grand average for all 5 policies over all 50 replications. By substituting the results of our experiment for the quantities in Table 7-4, we obtain Table 7-11.

From the data in Table 7-11, $F = 104.06$, easily exceeding the critical value $F_{.05,4,245} = 2.21$. In this case, F is even much greater than the critical value for $\alpha = .001$. Hence, the data generated by the simulation experiment do

Table 7-11   Statistics for One-way Analysis of Variance

Source of Variation	Sum of Squares	Degrees of Freedom	Mean Square
Between policies	33.521	4	8.3803
Error	19.731	245	.08053
Total	53.252	249	

not support the null hypothesis that the variances of national income are equal for each of the five policies. One may check the decision to reject H_0 against Table 7-8, which shows that the variance of y_t does indeed differ from policy to policy.

Multiple Comparisons

Not unlike the analysis of variance, both multiple comparison and multiple ranking procedures are based on the normality assumption. Hence, we again must use the logarithmic transformation $X = \log_e (x_y{}^2)$. When we refer to the population mean and the sample mean of the jth stabilization policy, we shall be referring, respectively, to EX_j and $\overline{X}_j$ and *not* to Ey_j and $\overline{y}_j$.

Tukey's method will yield simultaneous confidence intervals (of the type previously described) for the differences between *all* pairs. With 95 percent probability, *all* of the followng confidence intervals are true:

$$(EX_j - EX_J) = (\overline{X}_j - \overline{X}_J) \pm q_{m,\nu}\sqrt{MS_e/n}$$
$$j, J = 1, 2, 3, \ldots, m \qquad (7\text{-}60)$$

where $q_{k,\nu}$ is tabulated under the title "Distribution of the Studentized Range Statistic" [65], and

$$m = \text{the number of sample means,}$$
$$\nu = \text{the number of degrees of freedom for } MS_e$$
$$= m(n - 1).$$

For the actual data generated by our single-factor computer simulation experiment, the formula for 95 percent confidence intervals is given by

$$(EX_j - EX_J) = (\overline{X}_j - \overline{X}_J) \pm q_{5,245} \sqrt{MS_e/n} \qquad (7\text{-}61)$$
$$= (\overline{X}_j - \overline{X}_J) \pm 3.86 \sqrt{.08053/50}$$
$$= (\overline{X}_j - \overline{X}_J) \pm .155 \simeq .16 \qquad j, J = 1, 2, 3, 4, 5.$$

Table 7-12 contains a tabulation of the differences between sample means for all 10 pairs of differences in our experiment. An asterisk (*) indicates that a particular difference exceeds the confidence allowance .16, thus, making the difference "statistiaclly significant," if this form of inference is desired.

To obtain inferences about $\sigma_y{}^2$ rather than X, we can substitute the value of EX given in (7-55) into (7-61) and obtain

$$\log_e (\sigma_y{}^2)_j - \log_e (\sigma_y{}^2)_J = (\overline{X}_j - \overline{X}_J) \pm .16 \qquad j, J = 1, 2, 3, 4, 5. \qquad (7\text{-}62)$$

or

Table 7-12   Differences of Sample Means $(\overline{X}_j\text{-}\overline{X}_J)$

j \ J	2	3	4	5
1	.60*	.65*	.20*	−.32*
2	---	.05	−.40*	−.92*
3	---	---	−.45*	−.97*
4	---	---	---	−.52*

$$\log_e (\sigma_y^2)_j/(\sigma_y^2)_J = (\overline{X}_j - \overline{X}_J) \pm .16 \qquad j, J = 1, 2, 3, 4, 5. \tag{7-63}$$

Taking the antilog of (7-63), we get

$$(\sigma_y^2)_j/(\sigma_y^2)_J = \exp [(\overline{X}_j - \overline{X}_J) \pm .16]. \tag{7-64}$$

As an example, consider the case when $j = 1$ and $J = 2$, that is, a comparison of policies I and II. Then $\overline{X}_1 - \overline{X}_2 = .60$, and (7-64) yields the following confidence limits:

$$e^{.44} < (\sigma_y^2)_1/(\sigma_y^2)_2 < e^{.76} \tag{7-65}$$

or

$$1.55 < (\sigma_y^2)_1/(\sigma_y^2)_2 < 2.14. \tag{7-66}$$

Following this procedure, we can formulate a table (see Table 7-13) of upper and lower confidence limits for the ratio $(\sigma_y^2)_j/(\sigma_y^2)_J$ for all j and J. Again, an asterisk is used to denote the rejection of the null hypothesis $(\sigma_y^2)_j = (\sigma_y^2)_J$.

Table 7-13   Upper (UCL) and Lower (LCL) Confidence Limits for $(\sigma_y^2)_j/(\sigma_y^2)_J$, Simultaneous for All j and J

j \ J		2	3	4	5
1	UCL	2.14*	2.25*	1.43*	.85*
1	LCL	1.55	1.63	1.04	.62
2	UCL		1.23	.79*	.47*
2	LCL		.90	.57	.34
3	UCL			.75*	.44*
3	LCL			.54	.32
4	UCL				.70*
4	LCL				.51

Multiple Rankings

To illustrate the applicability of multiple ranking procedures, we again make use of the Bechhofer, Dunnett, and Sobel [8] procedure, described earlier in this chapter.

For our experiment, suppose that we want to select the policy having the smallest variance and that we want to guarantee that the probability of correctly choosing that population will be at least .90 if, in fact, the logarithm of σ_y^2 of the best policy differs from the one of the next best policy by $-.10536$ (so that σ_y^2 of the best policy is .90 times as large as the next lowest σ_y^2). In other words, we are assuming that P = .90 and $\delta^* = -.10536$. We then let $N_1 = n = 50$ and calculate $\text{MS}_e = .08053$. For P = .90 and $\nu = m(n-1) = 245$ we obtain $h = 1.58$ from Table 3 of Dunnett and Sobel [17]. Next we determine max $\{N_1, [2 \text{ MS}_e(h/\delta^*)^2]\}$ = max $\{50,36\} = 50$. Since $36 < 50$, no second sample is required, and $N_2 = N_1 = n = 50$. Sample means for $n = 50$ were previously calculated in Table 7-10. On the basis of the ranking of the sample means, we would select policy III as the plan with the smallest variance of national income. If, in fact, the best policy has a variance σ_y^2 that is 90 percent as large as the variance of the second best policy, we have, at least, a probability of 90 percent of correctly choosing it despite random statistical fluctuations of sampling.

SUMMARY

With the aid of example models we have attempted to demonstrate the use of three alternative forms of the analysis of variance—the F-test, multiple comparisons, and multiple rankings—to analyze data generated by computer simulation experiments with economic systems. The differences in these three types of analysis of variance lie not so much in the assumptions underlying their use but, instead, with the types of experimental objectives with which they are most compatible. If one's experimental objective is to test the hypothesis that there is no difference between two or more plans or policies, then the F-test is an appropriate analytical tool. If one's objective is to obtain estimates of the sizes of these differences, then multiple comparisons are more appropriate. But if the object is to find with a specified degree of certainty the test plan, the second best plan, and so forth, then multiple ranking procedures represent the more direct approach. Caution, however, must be used to avoid the indiscriminate use of these techniques without due regard for the assumptions on which they are based. This is particularly true of the latter two techniques.

Finally, we observe that, although we have limited our analysis to a single-factor experiment, all of the techniques described in this chapter can be extended to experiments with many factors.

BIBLIOGRAPHY

1. Bahadur, R. R. "On the Problem in the Theory of k Populations," *Annals of Mathematical Statistics*, **XXI** (1950), 362-375.
2. Bartlett, M. S. *An Introduction to Stochastic Processes with Special Reference to Methods and Applications*. Cambridge: The University Press, 1962.
3. Bartlett, M. S., and Kendall, M. G. "The Statistical Analysis of Variance—Heterogeneity and the Logarithmic Transformation," *Journal of the Royal Statistical Society*, Series B, **VIII** (1946), 128-138.
4. Baumol, William J. "Pitfalls in Contracyclical Policies: Some Tools and Results," *Review of Economics and Statistics*, **XLIII** (February 1961), 21-26.
5. Bechhofer, R. E. "A Single Sample Multiple Decision Procedure for Ranking Means of Normal Populations with Known Variances," *Annals of Mathematical Statistics*, **XXV** (1954), 16-39.
6. Bechhofer, R. E. "A Sequential Multiple Decision Procedure for Selecting the Best One of Several Normal Populations with a Common Unknown Variance, and Its Use with Various Experimental Designs," *Biometrics*; **XIV** (1958), 408-429.
7. Bechhofer, R. E., and Blumenthal, Saul. "A Sequential Multiple-Decision Procedure for Selecting the Best One of Several Normal Populations with a Common Unknown Variance, II: Monte Carlo Sampling Results and New Computing Formulae," *Biometrics*, **XVIII** (March 1962), 52-67.
8. Bechhofer, R. E., Dunnett, C. W., and Sobel, M. "A Two-Sample Multiple Decision Procedure for Ranking Means of Normal Populations with a Common Unknown Variance," *Biometrika*, **XLI** (1954), 170-176.
9. Bechhofer, R. E., Kiefer, Jack, and Sobel, Milton. *Sequential Identification and Ranking Procedures*. Chicago: University of Chicago Press, 1968.
10. Bechhofer, R. E., and Sobel, M. "A Sequential Multiple Decision Procedure for Ranking Means of Normal Populations with Known Variances," *Annals of Mathematical Statistics*, **XXIV** (1953), 136-137.
11. Bechhofer, R. E., and Sobel, Milton. "A Single-Sample Multiple Decision Procedure for Ranking Variances of Normal Populations," *Annals of Mathematical Statistics*, **XXV** (1954), 273-289.
12. Chambers, M. L., and Jarratt, P. "Use of Double Sampling for Selecting Best Population," *Biometrika*, **LI** (1964), 49-64.
13. Chu, Kong, and Naylor, Thomas H. "A Dynamic Model of the Firm," *Management Science*, XI (May 1965), 736-750.
14. Dudewicz, E. J. "A Categorized Bibliography on Multiple-Decision (Ranking and Selection) Procedures," Department of Statistics, University of Rochester, November 1968.

15. Dunnett, C. W. "A Multiple Comparison Procedure for Comparing Several Treatments with a Control," *Journal of the American Statistical Association*, **L** (1955), 1096-1121.
16. Dunnett, C. W. "On Selecting the Largest of K Normal Population Means," *Journal of the Royal Statistical Society Series B* (1960), 1-40.
17. Dunnett, C. W., and Sobel, M. "A Bivariate Generalization of Student's t-Distribution, with Tables for Certain Special Cases," *Biometrika*, **XLI** (1954), 153-169.
18. Dunnett, C. W., and Sobel, M. "Approximations to the Probability Integral and Certain Percentage Points of a Multivariate Analogue of Student's t-Distribution," *Biometrika*, **XLII** (1955), 258-260.
19. Frisch, Ragnar. "Parametric Solution and Programming of the Hicksian Model." *Essays on Econometrics and Planning*. C. R. Rao (ed). New York: Pergamon Press, 1965.
20. Gupta, S. S. "On Some Multiple Decision (Selection and Ranking) Rules," *Technometrics*, **VII** (May 1965), 225-246.
21. Gupta, S. S., and Panchapakesan, S. "Multiple Ranking Procedures," *The Design of Computer Simulation Experiments*, Thomas H. Naylor (ed). Durham, N. C.: Duke University Press, 1969.
22. Gupta, S. S., and Sobel, M. "On a Statistic Which Arises in Selection and Ranking Problems," *Annals of Mathematical Statistics*, **XXVIII** (1957), 957-967.
23. Gupta, S. S., and Sobel, M. "On Selecting a Subset Which Contains All Populations Better than a Standard," *Annals of Mathematical Statistics*, **XXIX** (1958), 235-244.
24. Gupta, S. S., and Sobel, M. "On Selecting a Subset Containing the Population with the Smallest Variance," *Biometrika*, **XLIX** (1962a), 495-507.
25. Gupta, S. S., and Sobel, M. "On the Smallest of Several Correlated F Statistics," *Biometrika*, **XLIX** (1962), 509-523.
26. Hicks, J. R. *A Contribution to the Theory of the Trade Cycle*. Oxford: Clarendon Press, 1950.
27. Howrey, E. Philip. "Stabilization Policy in Linear Stochastic Systems," *Review of Economics and Statistics*, **XLIX** (August, 1967), 404-411.
28. Howrey, E. Philip. "Dynamic Properties of Stochastic Linear Econometric Models," Research Memo. No. 87, Econometric Research Program, Princeton University, 1967.
29. Huyett, M. J., and Sobel, M. "Selecting the Best One of Several Binomial Populations," *Bell System Technical Journal*, **XXXVI** (1957), 537-576.
30. Jackson, R. R. P. "Queueing Systems with Phase Type Service," *Operational Research Quarterly*, **V** (1954).
31. Karlin, S., and Truax, D. "Slippage Problems," *Annals of Mathematical Statistics*, **XXXI** (1960), 296-394.
32. Kleijnen, Jack P., and Naylor, Thomas H. "The Use of Multiple Ranking Procedures to Analyze Simulations of Business and Economic Systems," *Proceedings of the American Statistical Association*, August, 1969.

33. Kudo, Akio. "On the Invariant Multiple Decision Procedures," *Bulletin of the Mathematical Statistics Research Association of Statistical Science*, **VI** (1956), 57-68.

34. Lehmann, E. L. "A Theory of Some Multiple Decision Problems," *Annals of Mathematical Statistics*, **XXVIII** (1957), 1-25.

35. Lehmann, E. L. "Some Model I Problems of Selection," *Annals of Mathematical Statistics*, **XXXII** (1961), 990-1012.

36. Manser, Marilyn, Naylor, Thomas H., and Wertz, Kenneth. "The Effects of Alternative Plans for Allocating Federal Aid to Education to the States," *Proceedings of the American Statistical Association* (August 1969).

37. Maurice, R. "A Minimax Procedure for Choosing Between Two Populations Using Sequential Sampling," *Journal of the Royal Statistical Society Series B*, **XIX** (1957), 255-261.

38. Mosteller, Frederick. "A K-Sample Slippage Test for an Extreme Population," *Annals of Mathematical Statistics*, **XIX** (1948), 58-65.

39. Mosteller, Frederick, and Tukey, J. W. "Significance Levels for a K-Sample Slippage Test," Annals of Mathematical Statistics, **XXI** (1950), 120-123.

40. Naylor, Thomas H. (editor). *The Design of Computer Simulation Experiments*. Durham, N. C.: Duke University Press, 1969.

41. Naylor, Thomas H., Balintfy, Joseph L., Burdick, Donald S., and Chu, Kong. *Computer Simulation Techniques*. New York: John Wiley & Sons, 1966.

42. Naylor, Thomas H., Wertz, Kenneth, and Wonnacott, Thomas. "Methods for Analyzing Data from Computer Simulation Experiments," *Communications of the ACM*, **X** (November 1967), 703-710.

43. Naylor, Thomas H., Wertz, Kenneth, and Wonnacott, Thomas H. "Some Methods for Evaluating the Effects of Economic Policies Using Simulation Experiments," *Review of the International Statistical Institute*, **XXXVI** (No. 2, 1968), 184-200.

44. Paulson, Edward. "On the Comparison of Several Experimental Categories with a Control," *Annals of Mathematical Statistics*, **XXIII** (1952), 239-246.

45. Paulson, Edward. "An Optimum Solution to the K-Sample Slippage Problem for the Normal Distribution," *Annals of Mathematical Statistics*, **XXIII** (1952), 610-616.

46. Paulson, Edward. "A Sequential Procedure for Comparing Several Experimental Categories with a Standard or Control," *Annals of Mathematical Statistics*, **XXXIII** (1962), 438-443.

47. Paulson, Edward. "A Sequential Procedure for Choosing One of K Hypotheses Concerning the Unknown Mean of a Normal Distribution," *Annals of Mathematical Statistics*, **XXXIV** (1963), 549-554.

48. Paulson, Edward. "A Sequential Procedure for Selecting the Population with the Largest Mean for K Normal Populatons," *Annals of Mathematical Statistics*, **XXXV** (1964), 174-180.

49. Paulson, Edward. "Sequential Estimation and Closed Sequential Decision Procedures," *Annals of Mathematical Statistics*, **XXXV** (September 1964), 1048-1058.

50. Pfanzagl, J. "Ein Kobiniertes Test Und Klassifikations— Problem," *Metrika*, **II** (1959), 11-45.
51. Phillips, A. W. "Stabilization Policy in a Closed Economy," *Economic Journal*, **LXIX** (June 1954), 290-323.
52. Phillips, A. W. "Stabilization Policy and the Time-Form of Lagged Responses," *Economic Journal*, **LXXII** (June 1957), 265-277.
53. Ramberg, J. S. "A Comparison of the Performance Characteristics of Two Sequential Procedures for Ranking Means of Normal Populations," Technical Report No. 4, Department of Industrial Engineering, Cornell University, May 1966.
54. Robbins, H., Sobel, M., and Starr, N. "A Sequential Procedure for Selecting the Largest of K Means," *Annals of Mathematical Statistics*, **XXXIX** (1968), 88-92.
55. Saaty, Thomas L. *Elements of Queueing Theory*. New York: McGraw-Hill, 1961.
56. Samuelson, Paul A. "Interactions Between the Multiplier Analysis and the Principle of Acceleration," *Review of Economic Statistic*, **XII** (May 1938), 75-78.
57. Sasser, W. Earl *et al.* "A Sequential Sampling Simulation of an Inventory Model," Working Paper No. 17, Econometric System Simulation Program, Duke University, September 1, 1968.
58. Scheffé, Henry. *The Analysis of Variance*. New York: John Wiley & Sons, 1959.
59. Seal, K. C. "On a Class of Decision Procedures for Ranking Means of Normal Populations," *Annals of Mathematical Statistics*, **XXVI** (1955), 387-398.
60. Seal, K. C. "On Ranking Parameters of Scale in Type III Populations," *Journal of the American Statistical Association*, **LIII** (1958), 164-175.
61. Shirafuji, M. "Note on the Determination of the Replication Numbers for the Slippage Problem in r-Way Layout," *Bulletin of Mathematical Statistics*, **VII** (1956), 46-51.
62. Smith, Harry. "Regression Analysis and Analysis of Variance," *The Design of Computer Simulation Experiments*, Thomas H. Naylor (ed). Durham, N. C.: Duke University Press, 1969.
63. Somerville, P. N. "Some Problems of Optimum Sampling," *Biometrika*, **XLI** (1954), 420-429.
64. Tukey, J. W. "The Problem of Multiple Comparisons," Unpublished manuscript, Princeton University, 1953.
65. Winer, B. J. *Statistical Principles in Experimental Design*. New York: McGraw-Hill Book Co., 1962.

Chapter 8 | Sequential Sampling[1]

W. EARL SASSER, DANIEL A. GRAHAM, DONALD S. BURDICK AND
THOMAS H. NAYLOR

INTRODUCTION

In this chapter with the aid of an example model we describe the use of several sequential sampling techniques to analyze data generated by computer simulation experiments. The example model is a multi-item inventory model.

Since computer time is not a free gift of nature, data generated by computer simulation experiments are costly. The cost of experimentation may be greatly reduced, if at the end of each replication of the simulation experiment, the analyst balances the cost of additional replications (generated by the computer) against the expected gain in information from such replications. With computer simulation experiments, the objective of sequential sampling is to minimize the number of replications (sample size) necessary to obtain the information that is required from the experiment. Instead of setting in advance the number of replications to be generated, the sample size n is considered to be a random variable dependent on the outcome of the first $n-1$ replications. In terms of computer time, the cost of a simulation experiment is minimized by generating only enough observations to achieve the required results with predetermined accuracy.

For example, a sequential test with an inventory model could be designed to determine if the total costs associated with alternative inventory policies differ significantly. The sequential method sets a procedure for deciding at the ith observation whether to stop sampling or to continue sampling by taking the $(i + 1)$th observation. In hypothesis testing, for example, such

[1] This chapter is based on a paper by W. Earl Sasser, Donald S. Burdick, Daniel A. Graham, and Thomas H. Naylor entitled "The Application of Sequential Sampling to Simulation: An Example Inventory Model," which was previously published in the *Communications of the ACM*, **XV** (May 1970).

a procedure must specify for the ith observation a division of the i-dimensional space of all possible observations into three mutually exclusive and exhaustive sets: an area of preference A_i for accepting the hypothesis, an area of preference B_i for rejecting it, and an area of indifference C_i where no statement can be made about the hypothesis and further observations are necessary. The fundamental problem of the theory of sequential sampling is the one of a proper choice of the sets A_i, B_i, and C_i [50].

After describing a multi-item inventory model and the experiment to be conducted with the model, we shall outline four sequential sampling procedures: (1) a procedure for testing a hypothesis regarding the mean; (2) a procedure for comparing the means of k experimental categories with a control; (3) a multiple-decision procedure for selecting the best one of several populations, and (4) a heuristic procedure for selecting the best one of several populations. These procedures then are applied to simulation experiments with the given model.

AN INVENTORY MODEL

The multi-item inventory model described in this chapter is a modified version of an earlier model proposed by Balintfy [7]. The firm is assumed to carry an inventory consisting of n different items. The quantity of the ith item demanded on the tth day ($t = 1, \ldots, T$) is a random variable with a known probability distribution. Lead time is assumed to be equal to zero, that is, there is no time lapse between the placing of an order and the incrementing of the inventory levels by an amount equal to the economic order quantity for a particular item. The firm uses what Balintfy has called a *random joint-order policy*. That is, whenever the stock of a particular item reaches its reorder level or "must-order" point, then the inventory levels of the other $n - 1$ items are checked to determine whether the stocks of any of these items have fallen below what Balintfy calls the "can-order" point. Those items whose stocks are below the can-order point (but above the must-order point) are ordered jointly with the item whose stock has been depleted to the must-order point. The concept of a can-order point is merely a reflection of the fact that it may be feasible to reorder a given item before its stock is reduced to the must-order point. When the inventory level of an item is above its can-order point, it may not be technically or economically feasible to order any more of that item. Can-order points are usually determined by the availability of storage space.

At this juncture, it becomes necessary to introduce some mathematical notation. Our model consists of the following variables and parameters.

DEPENDENT VARIABLES

TOC = total cost of ordering.

TCC = total carrying cost.

TCOST = total cost.

DECISION VARIABLES

EOQ_i = economic order quantity for the ith inventory item, $i = 1, 2, \ldots, N$.

MOP_i = must-order point for the ith inventory item, $i = 1, 2, \ldots, N$.

COP_i = can-order point for the ith inventory item, $i = 1, 2, \ldots, N$.

RANDOM VARIABLES

D_{it} = a Poisson variate (with expected value ED_i) denoting the quantity of the ith item demanded on the tth day, $i = 1, 2, \ldots, N, t = 1, 2, \ldots, T$.

STATUS VARIABLES

INV_{it} = inventory level for the ith item at the end of the tth day, $i = 1, 2, \ldots, N, t = 1, 2, \ldots, T$.

NTO_i = number of times the ith item is ordered during T, $i = 1, 2, \ldots, N$.

TNJO = total number of joint orders during T.

PARAMETERS

FOC = fixed cost per joint-order, where a joint-order may include one or more items. This cost does not vary with the number of items in a joint-order.

VOC_i = variable cost of ordering the ith inventory item, $i = 1, 2, \ldots, N$.

CC_i = carrying cost per unit per day for the ith inventory item, $i = 1, 2, \ldots, N$.

As we have indicated above, there are three variables that are controllable by the firm's decision makers—economic order quantities, must-order points, and can-order points. Economic order quantities are calculated by the following formula:

$$EOQ_i = \sqrt{\frac{2 \cdot ED_i(FOC + VOC_i)}{CC_i}} \tag{8-1}$$

Notice that, although (8-1) is applicable for a single-item reorder policy, it is not applicable for a random joint-order policy. That is, the cost of ordering the ith item depends, in part, on the number of items that are ordered jointly with the ith item. Equation 8-1 does not take this factor into consideration. However, for our purposes (8-1) is an acceptable rule for the firm to use, since we are concerned primarily with exploring the effects of alternative can-order points and not with optimum economic order quantities. For the purpose of this experiment, (8-1) is just the arbitrary rule that is presently being used by the firm.

Since we have previously assumed that lead time is zero, the must-order points will be zero for all items. Assuming given economic order quantities for each item and given must-order points, the objective of our simulation experiment with this model is to determine the effects of alternative can-order points on total cost. Suppose that the firm is considering k different storage and warehousing configurations which will result in k different sets of can-order points. The firm is interested in knowing what effects, if any, these different can-order points will have on total cost.

Before turning to the computer flow chart for our model, we must specify three cost equations:

$$TOC = TNJO \cdot FOC + \sum_{i=1}^{n} (NTO_i \cdot VOC_i) \tag{8-2}$$

$$TCC = \sum_{i=1}^{N} \sum_{t=1}^{T} (INV_{it} \cdot CC_i) \tag{8-3}$$

$$TCOST = TOC + TCC \tag{8-4}$$

The computer flow chart for our model is displayed in Figure 8-1. The first step in the program is a READ statement that causes the input data T, N, MOP_i, COP_i, ED_i, CC_i, VOC_i, and FOC to be read into the computer. For our example, T is equal to 90 days and N is equal to 20 items. The must-order point is zero for all items. The can-order points are read into the computer as data. Table 8-1 contains the values for ED_i, CC_i, and VOC_i for all 20 items. The fixed joint-order cost FOC is assumed to be equal to $15.

After the input data are read into the computer, TOC, TCC, TCOST, INV_{it}, NTO_i, and TNJO are all set equal to zero. Next, demand is generated for each item by the appropriate Poisson subroutine. New inventory levels are calculated by subtracting daily demands from previous inventory levels. All items then are checked to determine whether the level of inventory of any item has reached the must-order point. If no item is to be ordered on a given day, carrying costs are updated and demand is generated for the next day. If, however, one item has reached the must-order point all N items are checked to determine whether their inventory levels are below the can-order point. Those items whose levels are below the can-order point are ordered. After carrying costs are calculated for a given day, this process is repeated for a total of T days. At the end of the simulation run, total cost is calculated.

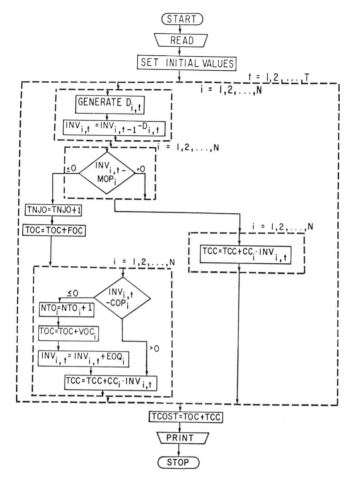

Figure 8-1.   A flow chart for a multi-item inventory model.

THE EXPERIMENT

The particular experiment conducted with the multi-item inventory model is aimed at testing the effects on total inventory cost of five different configurations of can-order points. (The objective of the experiment is strictly exploration and *not* optimization.) That is, the firm is considering five different plans for storing its inventory. Each of these five plans will result in the assignment of a particular set of can-order points to the items being carried in inventory.

Table 8-1   Expected Demand (ED$_i$), Carrying Cost (CC$_i$), and Variable Ordering Cost (VOC$_i$) for 20 Inventory Items

Item	ED$_i$	CC$_i$	VOC$_i$
1	2	$.005	1.30
2	4	.001	1.20
3	1	.002	1.40
4	2	.003	1.50
5	2	.001	1.90
6	6	.002	1.80
7	5	.009	1.80
8	9	.001	1.40
9	1	.004	1.60
10	2	.003	1.60
11	7	.004	1.00
12	6	.009	1.90
13	9	.002	1.00
14	9	.003	1.60
15	6	.006	1.80
16	4	.008	1.30
17	9	.010	1.00
18	4	.007	1.50
19	1	.001	1.30
20	4	.002	1.60

The firm is interested in evaluating its five can-order plans over a 90-day planning horizon. Therefore, 90-day simulation runs are made with the computer for each of the five plans. Each run is replicated to enable us to make probabilistic statements about the estimates of total cost that are associated with each of the five plans. Total inventory cost is analyzed for each of the five plans by using both sequential sampling methods and fixed sample-size methods. We then compare the two methods of data analysis in terms of the cost of computer time required to achieve a given level of statistical precision.

To investigate the bias resulting from the specification of the initial conditions of the model and the starting values of the random number generator, we performed a three-way analysis of variance test on the simulated data. We tested the effects of the five different can-order point plans (plans) with five different sets of beginning inventory levels (levels) and two different streams of random numbers (numbers). The results are tabulated in Table 8-2.

As expected, most of the variation beyond that of the grand mean can be attributed to the five different can-order point plans. However, one other statistic is significant at the .05 level—the plan-level interaction. This warns us of possible biases resulting from the use of a particular set of initial conditions with a particular plan. To gain further insight into these relationships, we compute the interaction table for the effect on total

Table 8-2   Three-Way Analysis of Variance Table

Source	Degrees of Freedom	Sum of Squares	Mean Square	Computed F-Statistic
Grand Mean	1	84,383,952.00		
Plans	4	2,686,619.00	671,654.75	649.40
Levels	4	6,745.95	1,686.49	1.63
Numbers	1	288.81	288.81	.28
Plans-Levels	16	50,380.80	3,148.80	3.04
Plans-Numbers	4	2,349.43	587.36	.57
Levels-Numbers	4	853.20	213.30	.21
Plans-Levels-Numbers	16	1,654.39	1,034.27	
TOTAL	50	87,147,746.75		

Table 8–3   Two-Factor Interaction Table for Plans and Beginning Inventory levels

Plans	Levels 1	2	3	4	5
1	72.93	9.63	−43.57	−36.82	−2.16
2	−2.12	2.60	−23.17	−9.46	32.14
3	6.59	18.12	−4.65	−30.23	10.17
4	−6.04	−6.62	23.91	15.19	−26.43
5	−71.35	−23.73	47.49	61.33	−13.72

inventory cost of plan i and initial inventory level j $(i, j = 1, \ldots, 5)$ where the interaction effect is defined as $\overline{X}_{ij} - \overline{X}_{i..} - \overline{X}_{.j.} + \overline{X}_{...}$. The results are tabulated in Table 8-3.

These calculations pinpoint the possible problem areas of our experiment. Notice that the first set of initial conditions in combination with plans 1 and 5 account for a considerable amount of the interaction between the plans and the beginning inventory levels.

These two cells (1,1) and (5,1) account for 41.3 percent of the variation as measured by the sum of squares all cells. [This calculation is easily made when one uses the knowledge that the plans-levels interaction sum of squares (from Table 8-2) is equal to twice the sum of squares of the entries in Table 8-3.] Therefore, the first set of initial conditions should be avoided with any experiments involving plans 1 or 5. If an experiment is run with this particular set of initial conditions, the results must be analyzed with these biases in mind. All of the following runs were made with the second set of initial conditions.

SEQUENTIAL ANALYSIS

Before considering the numerical results of our simulation experiments with the multi-item inventory model, we briefly summarize the four sequential procedures used to analyze the output data from the experiments. The first two procedures were developed by Paulson [42]. The third is due to Bechhofer and Blumenthal [9]. The fourth is a heuristic procedure.

1. Testing a Hypothesis Regarding the Mean [42]

Let X_1, X_2, . . . be a sequence of independent random variables with a common normal distribution with unknown mean μ and unknown variance σ^2. Suppose that we are interested in testing the null hypothesis H_0 that $\mu \leq \mu_0$ against the alternative hypothesis H_1 that $\mu > \mu_0$. Suppose further that we require a closed sequential procedure for testing H_0 so that P (rejecting $H_0 | \mu \leq \mu_0) \leq \alpha$ and P (accepting $H_0 | \mu > \mu_0 + \Delta) \leq \beta$. We begin by taking a sample of n_0 measurements and compute an estimate of the sampling variance

$$s^2 = \sum_{j=1}^{n_0} (X_j - \bar{x}_{n_0})^2/(n_0 - 1) \tag{8-5}$$

where n_0 is chosen so that

$$a(\delta) \leq 1.25 \log (1/\delta) \tag{8-6}$$

where

$$a(\delta) = [(1/\delta)^{2/f} - 1](f/2) \tag{8-7}$$

$$\delta = \min (\alpha, \beta) \tag{8-8}$$

$$f = n_0 - 1. \tag{8-9}$$

We then take measurements one at a time and stop the experiment and *reject H_0* as soon as

$$\sum_{j=1}^{n} (X_j - \mu_0 - \Delta/2) > s^2 a(\alpha)/2d - n(\Delta/2 - d) \tag{8-10}$$

and stop and *accept H_0* as soon as

$$\sum_{j=1}^{n} (X_j - \mu_0 - \Delta/2) < -s^2 a(\beta)/2d + n(\Delta/2 - d) \tag{8-11}$$

where

$$d = 3\Delta/8 \tag{8-12}$$

2. Comparing the Means of k Experimental Categories with a Control [42]

Let Π_0 denote the control category, and let $\Pi_1, \Pi_2, \ldots, \Pi_k$ denote the k experimental categories. X_{ij} denotes the jth measurement with category Π_i. Assume that for each j, X_{ij} is normally distributed with unknown mean μ_i and unknown variance σ^2, and that for all i and j ($i = 0, 1, \ldots, k$ and $j = 1, 2, \ldots$) all measures are independent. Π_i ($i = 1, 2, \ldots, k$) is said to be superior to the control if $\mu_i < \mu_0$. Consider the problem of finding a closed sequential procedure, for classifying each of the k experimental categories as superior or as not superior, which will satisfy the requirement that the probability is $\geq 1 - \alpha$ that all experimental categories with means $\geq \mu_0$ or $\leq \mu_0 - \Delta$ are classified correctly.

We begin by taking n_0 measurements from each of the $(k + 1)$ populations and compute an estimate of the sampling variance,

$$s^2 = \sum_{i=0}^{k} \sum_{j=1}^{n_0} (X_{ij} - \bar{x}_{in_0})^2 / (k + 1)(n_0 - 1) \tag{8-13}$$

where n_0 is chosen such that

$$a(\alpha) \leq 1.1 \log (1/\alpha) \tag{8-14}$$

where

$$a(\alpha) = [(1/\alpha)^{2/f} - 1](f/2), \tag{8-15}$$

$$f = (k + 1)(n_0 - 1). \tag{8-16}$$

We then take measurements one at a time. At the start of the experiment we start with one measurement on all $k + 1$ categories. At the jth stage ($j = 2, 3, \ldots$) we take one measurement with each of the experimental categories not yet classified. We classify an experimental category Π_i as *superior* as soon as

$$u_i = \bar{z}_{in} + d + [2s^2 a(\alpha)]/2dn < 0 \tag{8-17}$$

and classify Π_i as *not superior* as soon as

$$v_i = \bar{z}_{in} - d - [2s^2 a(\alpha)]/2dn > -\Delta \tag{8-18}$$

where

$$Z_{ij} = X_{ij} - X_{0j} \tag{8-19}$$

$$\bar{z}_{in} = \sum_{j=1}^{n} Z_{ij}/n \tag{8-20}$$

$$d = 3\Delta/8 \tag{8-21}$$

The experiment is terminated as soon as all categories are classified.

Paulson has also contributed four other sequential procedures [43]:
(1) a procedure for testing a hypothesis about the variance of a normal
distribution, (2) a procedure for deciding which of k nonoverlapping intervals contains the variance, (3) a procedure for testing a hypothesis
about the ratio of variances, and (4) a procedure for comparing the variances of k experimental categories with a standard or a control.

3. A Multiple-Decision Procedure for Selecting the Best One of Several Populations [9]

The procedure developed by Bechhofer and Blumenthal [9] is concerned
with selecting the population with the largest mean. Since our objective
is the selection of the set of can-order points that yields the lowest expected
total cost, it is necessary for us to multiply all of our sample values by -1
in order to apply the aforementioned procedure. We shall describe the
original version of the Bechhofer-Blumenthal procedure, although our
application of it uses data that has been premultiplied by -1.

Assume that the X_{ij} are normally and independently distributed random
variables with unknown population means μ_i and a common unknown
variance σ^2. The ranked population means are denoted by

$$\mu_{[1]} \leq \mu_{[2]} \leq \ldots \leq \mu_{[k]}. \tag{8-22}$$

It is not known which population is associated with $\mu_{[i]}$. The objective of
the experiment is to select the population associated with $\mu_{[k]}$. At the
outset of the experiment we specify two constants Δ^* and P^* ($0 < \Delta^* < \infty$,
$1/k < P^* < 1$). Let,

$$\Delta_{k,i} = \mu_{[k]} - \mu_{[i]} \qquad (i = 1, \ldots, k - 1) \tag{8-23}$$

Δ^* is the smallest value of $\Delta_{k,k-1}$ that is worth detecting, and P^* is the
smallest acceptable value of the probability P of achieving the goal when
$\Delta_{k,k-1} \geq \Delta^*$. The region $\Delta < \Delta^*$ is regarded as a zone of indifference, since
we do not care which plan is selected as best as long as its mean is within
Δ^* of the mean of lowest ranked plan.

We denote the sample sum based on the first n observations from the ith
population by Y_{in} ($i = 1, \ldots, k$), and the ranked Y_{in} by

$$Y_{[1]n} \leq Y_{[2]n} \leq \ldots \leq Y_{[k]n}. \tag{8-24}$$

At the nth stage of experimentation, take an observation from each of the
k populations. Starting with $n = 2$, compute the stopping statistic Z_n. If
$Z_n \leq (1 - P^*)/P^*$, stop experimentation and choose the population that
yields the largest sample sum, $Y_{[k]n}$, as the one having the largest popula-

tion mean. If $Z_n > (1 - P^*)/P^*$, take another observation from each of the k populations and compute Z_{n+1}. Continue in this manner until the rule calls for stopping. The stopping statistic is given by

$$Z_n = \sum_{i=1}^{k-1} L_{in} \qquad (8\text{-}25)$$

where

$$L_{in} = \left[\frac{(\text{SS}) + G - 2\Delta^* Y_{[k]n}}{(\text{SS}) + G - 2\Delta^* Y_{[i]n}} \right]^{-(f+k-1)/2} \qquad i = 1, 2, \ldots, k - 1 \quad (8\text{-}26)$$

$$G = \frac{\sum_{i=1}^{k} Y_{in}^2}{n} - \frac{\left(\sum_{i=1}^{k} Y_{in} \right)^2}{kn} + \frac{2\Delta^* \sum_{i=1}^{k} Y_{in}}{k} + \frac{n(k-1)(\Delta^*)^2}{k} \qquad (8\text{-}27)$$

and SS is the residual sum of squares with degrees of freedom $f = k(n - 1)$.

4 A Heuristic Approach to the Bechhofer Procedure

In selecting the "best" plan according to the Bechhofer procedure, we continue to sample from all populations throughout the experiment. It appears reasonable to expect that additional computational time would be saved by using a decision rule that eliminates the plans that are almost certain not to be the best. Our decision rule is as follows:

1. After drawing the nth observation from each of the k plans and subjecting the observations to the Bechhofer test, we simply compute the mean and standard deviation associated with each plan—computations that are quite trivial, since the Bechhofer procedure accumulates the sum of squares and squared sums for each plan.
2. For the plan that is ranked best at the nth stage of sampling, we compute the upper bound, UB_1, of the best plan by adding two standard deviations of this plan to its mean.
3. For each of the other plans, we compute a lower bound, LB_i, ($i = 2, \ldots, k$) by subtracting two standard deviations from each of these $k - 1$ plans.
4. Next, we take the $k - 1$ differences $D_i = LB_i - UB_1$ ($i = 2, \ldots, k$).
5. If D_i is greater than zero, we discontinue sampling from the ith plan at the $(n + 1)$st stage. If D_i is less than or equal to zero, we continue sampling from the ith plan at the $(n + 1)$st stage.

If our assumption of equal variances holds true for the five plans, we will drop a plan when it differs from the best plan by more than four standard deviations. Although we have not attempted any theoretical development of this heuristic approach, it appears to be conservative and likely to yield the same results as the Bechhofer procedure. Later we shall offer the results of our empirical work as evidence of its performance and computational cost savings.

ANALYSIS OF SIMULATION RESULTS

Four different sequential procedures were used to analyze the output data generated by the simulation experiments with our multi-item inventory model. For each method we have tabulated the cost of the computer time required to achieve given levels of statistical precision. We also have tabulated the cost of the computer time for using comparable fixed sample size methods. The computer costs of fixed sample size procedures versus sequential sampling procedures are compared.

1. Testing a Hypothesis Regarding the Mean

The first procedure that we utilized was Paulson's [42] sequential procedure for testing hypotheses about the mean. This test was applied to 90-day simulation runs with plan 1 only. (We could have selected any one of our five plans to illustrate the procedure.)

Intuitively, one would expect that sequential sampling would yield the best results when the true mean is not very close to the hypothesized mean. If our goal were to make sequential sampling look extremely favorable, we could bias the results by only testing hypotheses where the hypothesized values of the mean were at a considerable distance from the true mean. However, we have chosen to include what we consider to be a wide spectrum of hypothesized means to cover adequately the region less than, greater than, and very close to the true mean. (An estimate of the mean of the first plan after 150 observations is 1249.86 with a standard deviation of the mean of $36.73/\sqrt{150} = 3.00$.) We have calculated results for a one-tailed test of the mean of the form:

$$H_0: \mu \leq \mu_0$$
$$H_1: \mu > \mu_0$$

with μ_0 taking the values of 1150, 1200, 1225, 1250, 1275, 1300, and 1350.

For each hypothesis we have chosen 12 design points that represent various combinations of α, β, and Δ in an effort to display the sensitivity of this procedure to these three parameters. For each design point (DP), we have calculated the fixed sample size (FSS) required to yield the desired accuracy, given that the estimate of the sampling variance s^2 is obtained from an initial sample of n_0 observations. We have also recorded the fixed sample time (FST) which is the computer time in seconds (IBM 360/75) necessary to generate a sample of this size as well as the fixed sample cost (FSC). Notice that this fixed sample size is invariant with regard to the closeness of the hypothesized and true mean. Therefore, the fixed sample size and fixed sample time are applicable to all seven values of the hypothesized means. All of the above results are included in Table 8-4.

Table 8-4   Design Points for Simulation Runs with Plan 1

DP	α	β	Δ	η_0	s^2	FSS	FST	FSC
1	0.010	0.100	10.0	23	1659.27	150	210.03	$21.00
2	0.010	0.200	30.0	23	1088.67	16	22.27	2.23
3	0.010	0.300	10.0	23	1737.79	125	174.67	17.47
4	0.010	0.400	30.0	23	836.00	10	14.33	1.43
5	0.010	0.500	10.0	23	1260.81	70	97.88	9.79
6	0.010	0.600	30.0	23	1086.04	8	11.43	1.14
7	0.050	0.100	10.0	15	1645.70	125	174.67	17.47
8	0.050	0.200	30.0	15	768.55	10	14.13	1.41
9	0.050	0.300	10.0	15	985.26	50	69.92	6.99
10	0.050	0.400	30.0	15	1108.65	6	10.12	1.01
11	0.050	0.500	10.0	15	811.06	25	34.46	3.45
12	0.050	0.600	30.0	15	388.00	2	3.06	.31

In Tables 8-5 to 8-11, the results for each hypothesized mean are presented for each of the 12 design points. First, the fixed sample decision (FSD), which is made on the basis of the t-statistic computed from the sample of size FSS, is recorded as acceptance (A) or as rejection (R) of H_0. Next, the sequential sample size (SSS) that was required to yield the sequential sampling decision (SSD) is recorded. Also, the sequential sampling time (SST) is noted, followed by an estimate of the cost savings (CS) attributable to the reduced sequential sampling time. Observe that there are no costs associated with making the wrong decision. The cost savings measure the differences between the costs of the computer time (10¢/second) required to reach a decision by each procedure. An inspection of Tables 8-5 to 8-11 reveals that the sequential technique outperforms the fixed sample size procedure when we consider that our estimate of the

Table 8-5   Analysis of Simulation Results for Plan 1 with $\mu_0 = 1150$

DP	FSD	SSS	SSD	SST	CS
1	R	12	R	14.47	$19.56
2	R	3	R	3.61	1.87
3	R	11	R	13.26	16.14
4	R	3	R	3.63	1.05
5	R	9	R	10.89	8.70
6	R	3	R	3.58	.79
7	R	9	R	10.88	16.38
8	R	1	R	1.21	1.29
9	R	4	R	4.86	6.51
10	A	3	R	3.62	.65
11	R	3	R	3.64	3.08
12	A	1	R	1.20	.19

Table 8-6   Analysis of Simulation Results for Plan 1 with $\mu_0 = 1200$

DP	FSD	SSS	SSD	SST	CS
1	R	24	R	30.30	$17.97
2	R	7	R	8.61	1.37
3	R	28	R	35.34	13.93
4	R	2	R	2.46	1.17
5	R	19	R	23.87	7.40
6	A	7	R	9.87	.16
7	R	13	R	17.50	15.72
8	A	3	R	3.96	1.02
9	R	7	R	9.36	6.06
10	A	8	R	11.28	-.12
11	R	7	R	9.34	2.51
12	A	1	R	1.32	.17

Table 8-7   Analysis of Simulation Results for Plan 1 with $\mu_0 = 1225$

DP	FSD	SSS	SSD	SST	CS
1	R	59	R	90.21	$11.98
2	A	12	R	20.74	.15
3	R	48	R	72.50	10.22
4	A	13	R	17.47	-.33
5	R	44	R	66.97	3.09
6	A	2	A	3.20	.82
7	R	30	R	45.06	12.96
8	A	5	R	7.36	.68
9	R	17	R	25.81	4.41
10	A	9	R	12.48	-.24
11	R	22	R	27.40	.71
12	A	1	R	1.22	.18

Table 8-8   Analysis of Simulation Results for Plan 1 with $\mu_0 = 1250$

DP	FSD	SSS	SSD	SST	CS
1	A	46	A	57.62	$15.24
2	A	2	A	2.61	1.97
3	A	67	A	90.53	8.41
4	A	2	A	2.50	1.16
5	A	3	A	3.68	9.42
6	A	7	A	8.79	.26
7	A	38	A	49.11	12.56
8	A	5	A	6.77	.74
9	A	38	A	47.91	2.20
10	A	8	A	9.71	.04
11	A	16	A	20.43	1.40
12	A	1	A	1.23	.18

Table 8-9   Analysis of Simulation Results for Plan 1 with $\mu_0 = 1275$

DP	FSD	SSS	SSD	SST	CS
1	A	14	A	17.79	$19.22
2	A	4	A	4.85	1.74
3	A	12	A	14.64	16.00
4	A	2	A	2.43	1.17
5	A	3	A	3.72	9.42
6	A	1	A	1.35	1.01
7	A	12	A	15.91	15.88
8	A	2	A	2.67	1.15
9	A	7	A	9.34	6.06
10	A	2	A	2.67	.75
11	A	5	A	6.66	2.78
12	A	1	A	1.31	.18

Table 8-10   Analysis of Simulation Results for Plan 1 with $\mu_0 = 1300$

DP	FSD	SSS	SSD	SST	CS
1	A	10	A	12.23	$19.78
2	A	1	A	1.23	2.10
3	A	5	A	6.61	16.81
4	A	2	A	2.45	1.17
5	A	3	A	3.65	9.42
6	A	1	A	1.21	1.02
7	A	11	A	14.75	15.99
8	A	1	A	1.24	1.29
9	A	3	A	3.69	6.62
10	A	1	A	1.21	.89
11	A	2	A	2.46	3.20
12	A	1	A	1.25	.18

Table 8-11   Analysis of Simulation Results for Plan 1 with $\mu_0 = 1350$

DP	FSD	SSS	SSD	SST	CS
1	A	5	A	7.01	$20.30
2	A	1	A	1.32	2.10
3	A	3	A	3.85	17.08
4	A	1	A	1.26	1.29
5	A	1	A	1.28	.97
6	A	1	A	1.29	1.01
7	A	5	A	6.83	16.78
8	A	1	A	1.27	1.29
9	A	2	A	2.53	6.74
10	A	1	A	1.25	.89
11	A	1	A	1.29	3.32
12	A	1	A	1.26	.18

population mean after 150 observations is 1249.86. When the hypothesized mean is 1225, the sequential procedure accepts the null hypothesis at only one design point and the fixed sample size procedure "fails" by accepting the null hypothesis at each of the six design points where $\Delta = 30$. When $\mu_0 = 1200$, the fixed sample size procedure "fails" three times while the sequential procedure always rejects H_0. Even when μ_0 is as low as 1150, the fixed sample size procedure accepts H_0 at two design points. Our intuition proved correct with regard to the cost savings. The cost savings vary from $20.30 to $-.33$, but the larger savings are concentrated at the extreme values of the hypothesized means and the lower savings (in three instances negative savings) are clustered around the hypothesized values that are close to our estimate of the population mean. In assessing the relationship of cost to changes in the three parameters α, β, and Δ, we can formulate the following function:

$$CS = CS(\alpha, \beta, \Delta).$$

Our results indicate that the following partial derivatives generally hold true:

$$\frac{\partial CS}{\partial \alpha} < 0, \quad \frac{\partial CS}{\partial \beta} < 0, \quad \text{and} \quad \frac{\partial CS}{\partial \Delta} < 0.$$

Since the fixed sample size, FSS, can also be written in functional form as

$$FSS = FSS(\alpha, \beta, \Delta)$$

with

$$\frac{\partial FSS}{\partial \alpha} < 0, \quad \frac{\partial FSS}{\partial \beta} < 0 \quad \text{and} \quad \frac{\partial FSS}{\partial \Delta} < 0,$$

we, therefore, infer that any changes in α, β, and Δ that tend to increase the fixed sample size also tend to increase the cost saving.

We also experimented with various forms of cluster sampling in an effort to achieve further reductions in the cost of reaching a decision. However, we soon discovered that in the case of our particular model, the possibilities of cost savings by cluster sampling were unfavorable. This can be easily attributed to the length of time required to generate a cost observation from plan 1. This observation takes, on the average, 1.25 seconds, but the testing procedure requires less than .01 seconds. Therefore, any additional (more than the simple sequential scheme) observations that are required by a cluster approach are relatively costly. Certainly, this does not rule out the possibility of cluster sampling on a sequential basis for computer simulation experiments.

As the ratio

$$\frac{\text{time required for one observation}}{\text{time required for testing}}$$

decreases, a point is reached when such a sampling plan could economically be put into use. We leave this question as a topic for future research.

2. Comparing k Experimental Categories with a Control

In these tests we selected plan 1 as the control plan with which we were interested in comparing each of the other four plans. Our experiment consists of four tests of this type. Instead of setting a level of significance for each of the four tests, we set an α-level for the collection of comparisons in a particular test and consider the collection as a single decision under a multiple comparison procedure.

For the purposes of establishing a rough estimate of the required fixed sample size for this procedure, we shall use the method for determining the sample size for an overall F-test in the analysis of variance [54, p. 104]. In such a test the specified α-level sets an upper bound on the type 1 error. By drawing a suitably large sample from each plan, the power of the test with respect to a specific alternative hypothesis may be made as large as desired. Fixed sample sizes are obtained from [54, p. 658] for given Δ_i, k, and σ^2. Table 8-12 displays a representative sample of our empirical results with this test. For each of the four design points $(A, B, C,$ and $D)$, there are four comparisons to be made with the control plan. These comparisons (2 to 5) denote the following: 2, the results of the comparisons of plan 2 with plan 1; 3, the results of the comparisons of plan 3 with plan 1; 4, the results of the comparison of plan 4 with plan 1; and 5 denotes the results of the comparisons of the results of plan 5 with plan 1.

At all four design points (A,B,C,D) computational cost savings are available when the sequential procedure is chosen over the fixed sample size technique. We accumulated the computational time (in seconds) required for each of the four comparisons to obtain a single savings figure for each design point. Notice that the savings appear to bear the same relationship with α, β, and Δ that was present in the test of the mean.

An examination of the results reveals that the fixed sample procedure fails to detect a significant difference between plans 1 and 3 for any design

Table 8-12

Design Point	α	β	Δ	s^2	FSD^2	FSS	FST	SDD	SSS	SST	Cost Savings
A	.01	.10	20	1085.05			75.98			19.92	$5.61
A-2[3]					S	13		S	1		
A-3					*[1]	13		S	6		
A-4					I	13		I	1		
A-5					I	13		I	1		
B	.01	.30	20	1123.71			60.76			24.94	$3.58
B-2					S	10		S	1		
B-3					*[1]	10		S	8		
B-4					I	10		I	1		
B-5					I	10		I	1		
C	.05	.10	20	975.87			66.83			19.37	$4.75
C-2					S	11		S	1		
C-3					*[1]	11		I	6		
C-4					I	11		I	1		
C-5					I	11		I	1		
D	.05	.30	20	1449.28			49.12			42.37	$ .68
D-2					S	8		S	1		
D-3					*[1]	8		S	15		
D-4					I	8		I	1		
D-5					I	8		I	1		

[1] Not a significant difference at the .05 level.

[2] Decision is coded Superior (S) or Inferior (I).

[3] A-2 designates the comparison at design point A between the control and plan 2.

point. The inability of the fixed sample size procedure to detect a significant difference at the specified α and β levels can be attributed to the "rough" nature of the required sample size calculations.

The sequential procedure, because it is a "closed" procedure, always yields a decision. However, at design point C, plan 3 is classified as inferior to the control, although the opposite classification is obtained at the other design points. (Such decisions indicate the small degree of difference between the costs associated with the first and third plans.)

3. A Multiple-Decision Procedure for Selecting the Best One of Several Populations

At the first step in obtaining empirical results that display the computational efficiency of the sequential procedure, we must consider the sample size requirement of a single sample or nonsequential procedure. In this procedure the common number of observations from each plan is determined before experimentation begins. To obtain an estimate of this fixed sample size n, we rely on the work of Bechhofer [10]. The number of observations required is determined by the desired probability of a correct ranking when certain differences between population means are specified: Bechhofer has prepared tables to assist the experimenter in designing experiments for ranking means. Given (1) the smallest difference Δ^* that we desire to detect between the best and next best, (2) the probability P^* of successfully selecting the best population when the actual difference between the best and next best plans is greater than or equal to Δ^*, and (3) the common variance σ^2, we can go directly to Bechhofer's tables to determine the required fixed sample size. We have obtained an estimate of the variance from our prior results, as recorded in Table 8-12. The average variance of the four variance estimates of that table is approximately 1150. Selecting a value of 10 for Δ^*, we have presented the results of a range of probability levels with the fixed and sequential procedure in Table 8-13.

Table 8-13

Test	Δ^*	P	FSS	FSD	FST	SSS	SSD	SST	Computational Cost Saving
1	10	.8	35	Plan 2	210 sec	25	Plan 2	180 sec	$3.00
2	10	.9	49	Plan 2	300 sec	35	Plan 2	223 sec	6.70

Although our fixed sample size estimates are admittedly rough, we believe that the point is emphatically made that the sequential procedure allows one to obtain a decision with a desired statistical precision at a much lower cost.

4. A Heuristic Approach to Selecting the Best One of Several Populations

In this section we conclude our empirical findings with the results of our heuristic approach to the Bechhofer procedure. As we have noted previously, the costs associated with our five plans cover a broad range. Most of the plans are quickly eliminated from consideration as the best plan, which tends to make our heuristic approach appear quite favorable. We currently are investigating this approach in conjunction with a response surface exploration of plans whose costs are clustered close together. This testing should yield additional information about the reliability of the procedure.

For the purpose of comparison with the Bechhofer procedure, we chose the same two design points that we used in the above empirical work with the fixed sample and sequential procedures. With $\Delta_n = 10$ and $P^* = .8$, the heuristic procedure, just as the original procedure, selects plan 2 as superior with many fewer observations. Above, 25 observations were required from each of the five plans. Now, three observations are required from plans 2, 3, and 5 and only two from plans 1 and 4. This results in computational cost savings of $16.10. Similarly, for $P^* = .9$, the heuristic approach required four observations from plans 2 and 3, three from plan 5, and two from plans 1 and 4, but the Bechhofer procedure required 35 observations from all five plans. The resulting computational cost savings are $20.20.

CONCLUSIONS

Our purpose has been to present the case for sequential sampling techniques as a method for analyzing data from computer simulation experiments. The main criterion that we have investigated is the computational cost saving that is available by using sequential sampling. Our empirical results also display the computational efficiency of these techniques. We hope that the evidence is convincing enough for those currently using fixed sample size techniques to give serious consideration to sequential sampling. To those who have found the cost of statistical inference prohibitive, we have demonstrated that sequential sampling may be economically feasible.

BIBLIOGRAPHY

1. Amster, S. J. "A Modified Bayes Stopping Rule," *Annals of Mathematical Statistics*, **XXXIV** (1963), 1404-1413.
2. Anderson, T. W. "A Modification of the Sequential Probability Ratio Test to Reduce the Sample Size," *Annals of Mathematical Statistics*, **XXXI** (1960), 165-197.

3. Anscombe, F. J. "Large Sample Theory of Sequential Estimation," *Proceedings of the Cambridge Philosophic Society*, **XLVIII** (1952), 600-607.

4. Anscombe, F. J. "Sequential Estimation," *Journal of the Royal Statistical Society*, B, **XV** (1953), 1-29.

5. Armitage, P. "Restricted Sequential Procedures," *Biometrika*, **XLIV** (1957), 9-26.

6. Armitage, P. *Sequential Medical Trials*. Oxford: Blackwell Scientific Publications, 1960.

7. Balintfy, Joseph L. "On a Class of Multi-Item Inventory Problems," *Management Science*, **X** (January 1964), 287-297.

8. Bechhofer, R. E. "A Sequential Multiple Decision Procedure for Selecting The Best One of Several Normal Populations with a Colmon Unknown Variance, and Its Use with Varous Experimental Designs," *Biometrics*, **XIV** (1958), 408-429.

9. Bechhofer, R. E., and Blumenthal, Saul. "A Sequential Multiple-Decision Procedure for Selecting the Best One of Several Normal Populations with a Common Unknown Variance, II: Monte Carlo Sampling Results and New Computing Formulae," *Biometrics*, **XVIII** (March 1962), 52-67.

10. Bechhofer, R. E. "A Single-Sample Multiple Decision Procedure for Banking Means of Normal Populations with Known Variances," *Annals of Mathematical Statistics*, **XXV** (1954), 16-39.

11. Blackwell, D., and Girshick, M. A. *Theory of Games and Statistical Decisions*. New York: John Wiley & Sons, 1954.

12. Box, G. E. P., and Hunter, J. S. "The 2^{k-p} Fractional Factorial Designs, Part I," *Technometrics*, **III** (August 1961), 311-351.

13. Breakwell, J., and Chernoff, H. "Sequential Tests for the Mean of a Normal Distribution II (Large t)," *Annals of Mathematical Statistics*, **XXXV** (1964), 162-173.

14. Burdick, Donald S., and Naylor, Thomas H. "Response Surface Designs," *The Design of Computer Simulation Experiments*, Thomas H. Naylor (ed). Durham, N. C.: Duke University Press, 1969.

15. Burkholder, D. L. and Wijsman, R. A. "Optimum Properties and Admissibility of Sequential Tests," *Anneals of Mathematical Statistics*, **XXXIV** (1963).

16. Chernoff, H. "Sequential Tests for the Mean of a Normal Distribution II (Small t)," *Annals of Mathematical Statistics*, **XXXVI** (February 1965), 28-54.

17. Chernoff, H. "Sequential Tests for the Mean of a Normal Distribution IV (Discrete Case)," *Annals of Mathematical Statistics*, **XXXVI** (February 1965), 55-68.

18. Chernoff, H. "Sequential Designs," *The Design of Computer Simulation Experiments*, Thomas H. Naylor (ed). Durham, N. C.: Duke University Press, 1969.

19. Cox, D. R. "Sequential Tests for Composite Hypotheses," *Proceedings of the Cambridge Philosophical Society* (1952), 290-299.

20. Cox, D. R. "A Note on the Sequential Estimation of Means," *Proceedings of the Cambridge Philosophic Society*, **XLVIII** (1952b), 447-450.

21. Cox, D. R. "A Note on Tests of Homogeniety Applied After Sequential Sampling," *Journal of the Royal Statistical Society, B,* **XXII** (1960), 368-371.

22. Craig, C. C. "On a Class of Simple Sequential Tests on Means," *Technometrics,* **IV** (1962), 345-359.

23. Dvoretzky, A., Kiefer, J., and Wolfowitz, J. "Sequential Decision Problems for Processes with Continuous Time Parameter Problems of Estimation," *Annals of Mathematical Statistics,* **XXIV** (1953), 403-415.

24. Fan, C. T., Muller, Mervin E., and Rezucha, Ivan. "Development of Sampling Plans by Using Sequential (Item by Item) Selection Techniques and Digital Computers," *Journal of the American Statistical Association,* **LVII** (1962), 387-402.

25. Freeman, David, and Weiss, Lionel. "Sampling Plans Which Approximately Minimize the Maximum Expected Sample Size," *Journal of the American Statistical Association.* **LIX** (March 1964), 67-88.

26. Ghosh, M. N. "Bounds for Expected Sample Size in a SPR Test," *Journal of the Royal Statistical Society, B,* **XXII** (1960), 360-367.

27. Gilchrist, W. G. "Some Sequential Tests Using Range," *Journal of the Royal Statistical Society, B,* **XXIII** (1961).

28. Hajnal, J. "A Two-Sample Sequential t-Test," *Biometrika,* **XLVIII** (1961), 65-75.

29. Hall, W. J. "Some Sequential Analogs of Stein's Two-State Test," *Biometrika,* **XLIX** (1962), 367-378.

30. Jackson, J. E. "Bibliography on Sequential Analysis," *Journal of the American Statistical Association,* **LV** (1960), 516.

31. Jackson, J. E., and Bradley, R. A. "Sequential χ^2 and t-Tests and Their Application to an Acceptance Sampling Problem," *Technometrics,* **III** (1960), 519-534.

32. Johnson, N. L. "On the Choice of a Sequential Procedure," *Proceedings of the Biometric Society Symposium* (1960), 27-40, Leiden.

33. Kiefer, J. "Invariance, Minimax Sequential Estimation, and Continuous Time Processes," *Annals of Mathematical Statistics,* **XXVIII** (March 1957), 573-601.

34. Kiefer, J. "Sequential Minimax Search for a Maximum," *Proceedings of the American Mathematical Society* (June 1953), 502-506.

35. Kiefer, J., and Sacks, J. "Asymptotically Optimum Sequential Inference and Design," *Annals of Mathematical Statistics,* **XXXIV** (September 1963), 705-750.

36. Kiefer, J., and Weiss, L. "Some Properties of Generalized Sequential Probability Ratio Tests," *Annals of Mathematical Statistics,* **XXVIII** (1957), 57-75.

37. Kleijnen, Jack P. C., and Naylor, Thomas H. "The Use of Multiple Ranking Procedures to Analyze Simulations of Business and Economic Systems," *Proceedings of the American Statistical Association,* August, 1969.

38. Naylor, Thomas H. (ed). *The Design of Computer Simulation Experiments.* Durham, N. C.: Duke University Press, 1969.

39. Naylor, Thomas H., Balintfy, Joseph L., Burdick, Donald S., and Chu,

Kong. *Computer Simulation Techniques.* New York: John Wiley & Sons, 1966.

40. Naylor, Thomas H., Burdick, D. S., and Sasser, W. Earl. "Computer Simulation Experiments with Economic Systems: The Problem of Experimental Design," *Journal of the American Statistical Association,* **LXII** (December 1967), 1315-1337.

41. Naylor, Thomas H., Wertz, Kenneth, and Wonnacott, Thomas. "Methods for Analyzing Data From Computer Simulation Experiments," *Communications of the ACM,* **X** (November 1967), 703-710.

42. Paulson, Edward. "Sequential Estimation and Closed Sequential Decision Procedures," *Annals of Mathematical Statistics,* **XXXV** (September 1964), 1048-1058.

43. Paulson, E. "A Sequential Procedure for Choosing One of k Hypotheses Concerning the Unknown Mean of a Normal Distribution," *Annals of Mathematical Statistics,* **XXXIV** (1963), 549-554.

44. Paulson, E. "A Sequential Procedure for Selecting the Population with the Largest Mean from k Normal Populations," *Annals of Mathematical Statistics, XXXV* (1964), 174-180.

45. Paulson, E. "Sequential Procedures for Selecting the Best One of Several Binomial Populations," *Annals of Mathematical Statistics,* **XXXVIII** (1967), 117-123.

46. Ramberg, J. S. "A Comparison of the Performance Characteristics of Two Sequential Procedures for Ranking Means of Normal Populations," Technical Report No. 4, Department of Industrial Engineering, Cornell University, May 1966.

47. Robbins, H., Sobel, M., and Starr, N. "A Sequential Procedure for Selecting the Largest of k Means," *Annals of Mathematical Statistics,* **XXXIX** (1968), 88-92.

48. Sobel, M., and Huyett, M. J. "Selecting the Best One of Several Binomial Populations," *Bell System Technical Journal,* **XXXVI** 537-576.

49. Vagholkar, M. K., and Wetherill, G. B. "The Most Economical Binomial Sequential Probability Ratio Test," *Biometrika,* **XLVII** (1960), 103-109.

50. Wald, Abraham. *Sequential Analysis.* New York: John Wiley & Sons, 1947.

51. Weiss, L. "On Sequential Tests Which Minimize the Maximum Expected Sample Size," *Journal of the American Statistical Association,* **LVII** (1962), 551-566.

52. Wetherill, G. B. "Bayesian Sequential Analysis," *Biometrika,* **XLVIII** (1961), 281-292.

53. Wetherill, G. B. *Sequential Methods in Statistics.* New York: John Wiley & Sons, 1966.

54. Winer, B. J. *Statistical Principles in Experimental Design.* New York: McGraw-Hill, 1962.

55. Wolfowitz, J. "The Efficiency of Sequential Estimates and Wald's Equation for Sequential Processes," *Annals of Mathematical Statistics,* **XVIII** (1947), 215-230.

Chapter 9 | Spectral Analysis[1]

THOMAS H. NAYLOR, KENNETH WERTZ, and THOMAS H. WONNA-
COTT

INTRODUCTION

There are, at least, four reasons why one might want to consider spectral analysis as a technique for analyzing data generated by stimulation experiments with an economic model.

First. Data generated by simulation experiments are usually highly autocorrelated, for example, GNP in period t is likely to be highly correlated with GNP in period $t-k$. It is well known that when autocorrelation is present in sample data that the use of classical statistical estimating techniques (which assume the absence of autocorrelation) will lead to underestimates of sampling variances (which are unduly large) and inefficient predictions. Several methods are available for treating this problem:

1. Simply ignore autocorrelation and compute sample means and variances over time, thereby incurring the above-mentioned statistical problems.

2. Divide the sample record length into intervals that are longer than the interval of major autocorrelation and work with the observations on these supposedly independent intervals. This method suffers from the fact that, "the choices of sample record length and sampling interval seem to have neither enough prior nor posterior justification in most cases to make this choice much more than arbitrary" [10].

3. Replicate the simulation experiment and compute sample means and variances across the ensemble rather than over time. This method may lead to excessive computer running time and fail to yield the type of information that is desired about a particular time series.

[1] This chapter is based on a paper by Thomas H. Naylor, Kenneth Wertz, and Thomas H. Wonnacott entitled "Spectral Analysis of Data Generated by Simulation Experiments with Econometric Models," *Econometrica,* **XXXVII** (April 1969), 333-352.

4. Employ a sampling theory such as spectral analysis in which the probabilities of component outcomes in a time series depend on previous outcomes in the series.

With spectral analysis, the problems associated with methods (1) and (2) can be successfully avoided without replicating the experiment.

Second. "When one studies a stochastic process, he is interested in the average level of activity, deviations from this level, and how long these deviations last, once they occur," [10]. Spectral analysis provides this kind of information.

Third. With spectral analysis it is relatively easy to construct confidence bands and to test hypotheses for the purpose of comparing the simulated results of the use of two or more alternative economic policies. Frequently, it is impossible to detect differences in time series generated by simulation experiments when one restricts himself to simple graphical analysis.

Fourth. Spectral analysis also can be used as a technique for validating a model of an economic system. By comparing the estimated spectra of simulated data and corresponding real-world data, one can infer how well the simulation resembles the system that it was designed to emulate [10].[2]

AN EXAMPLE MODEL

To illustrate the application of spectral analysis to simulation experiments with economic models, we choose a stochastic version of the Samuelson-Hicks [22,43] multiplier-accelerator model as an example model. Although this model was previously described in Chapter 7, for convenience we shall repeat the specification of the parameters, variables, and functional relationships.

PARAMETERS

b = accelerator coefficient.   (9-1)

c_1 = marginal propensity to consume in period t-1, $0 < c_1 < 1$.   (9-2)

c_2 = marginal propensity to consume in period t-2, $0 < c_2 < 1$.   (9-3)

g = governmental parameter.   (9-4)

EXOGENOUS VARIABLES

u_t = a stochastic variate with a known probability distribution, expected value, and variance.   (9-5)

v_t = a stochastic variate with a known probability distribution, expected value, and variance.   (9-6)

---

[2] We discuss this topic in a different context in a later section. See also [33,34].

ENDOGENOUS VARIABLES

C_t = consumption in period t.		(9-7)
I_t = investment in period t.		(9-8)
G_t = governmental expenditure in period t.		(9-9)
Y_t = national income in period t.		(9-10)

OPERATING CHARACTERISTICS

$f(u_t)$ = probability density function of u_t.	(9-11)
$f(v_t)$ = probability density function of v_t.	(9-12)
$C_t = c_1 Y_{t-1} + c_2 Y_{t-2} + u_t.$	(9-13)
$I_t = b(T_{t-1} - Y_{t-2}) + v_t.$	(9-14)
$G_t = g Y_{t-1}.$	(9-15)

IDENTITY

$$Y_t = C_t + I_t + G_t. \tag{9-16}$$

By substituting the values of C_t, I_t, and G_t given by (9-13), (9-14), and (9-15), respectively, into (9-16), we obtain

$$Y_t = w_t - a_1 Y_{t-1} - a_2 Y_{t-2} \tag{9-17}$$

where

$$w_t = u_t + v_t, \tag{9-18}$$
$$a_1 = -(c_1 + b + g), \tag{9-19}$$
$$a_2 = b - c_2. \tag{9-20}$$

If we assume that national income is measured in terms of deviations y_t from its equilibrium value, then the final form of (9-17), which determines the time path of national income, is

$$y_t = w_t - a_1 y_{t-1} - a_2 y_{t-2}. \tag{9-21}$$

Equation 9-21 describes a second-order autoregressive process. The complete analytical solution for y_t is given by [3,23]:

$$y_t = k_1 r_1{}^t + k_2 r_2{}^t + \sum_{j=0}^{t-2} \lambda_j w_{t-j} \tag{9-22}$$

where r_1 and r_2 are the characteristic roots of (9-21), k_1 and k_2 are arbitrary constants determined by the initial conditions, and λ_j is given by

$$\lambda_j = \frac{r_1{}^{j+1} - r_2{}^{j+1}}{r_1 - r_2}. \tag{9-23}$$

The solution for the time path of national income is composed of two parts—a transient response and a stochastic response. The usual procedure for determining the dynamic properties of the solution of difference-equation models in economics is to suppress the stochastic part of the solution and to analyze only the deterministic solution. This is equivalent to looking at the expected value of the time path of national income in our model. Philip Howrey [23] has shown that disregarding the disturbance term in the Samuelson-Hicks model may be quite misleading. He has demonstrated that stabilization policies designed to increase the stability of the system by reducing the modulus of the roots, in fact, may increase the variance of the system.

If our model were a simultaneous equation model (and nonrecursive), nonlinear, and of higher order than two, then analytical solutions would become increasingly difficult, and the benefits from using a computer to generate the time paths of the endogenous variables would increase considerably. Although one clearly could perform experiments with our simple example model without a computer, it does illustrate many of the experimental design problems that are associated with more complex econometric models involving higher-order nonlinear systems of difference equations.

SIMULATION RUNS

Three separate simulation runs, each of which consisted of a sample size of 200, were made with the Samuelson-Hicks model. In each run u_t and v_t were assumed to be independent normally distributed random variables with expected values equal to zero and variances equal to σ_u^2 and σ_v^2, respectively.[3]

Run 1

The first simulation run consisted of the generation of 200 consecutive values of y_t, using the following parameters and starting values:

$$
\begin{aligned}
c_1 &= .375 & y_0 &= 7.0 \\
c_2 &= .300 & y_1 &= 2.5 \\
b &= 1.15 \\
g &= .05 \\
\sigma_u^2 + \sigma_v^2 &= 38.26
\end{aligned}
$$

then

$$
\begin{aligned}
a_1 &= -1.575, \\
a_2 &= .85, \\
\sigma_w^2 &= 38.26.
\end{aligned}
$$

[3] See Appendix B for a collection of FORTRAN subroutines for generating stochastic variates on a computer.

The output of Run 1 may be considered as the result of a given monetary policy ($b = 1.15$) and a given fiscal policy ($g = .05$) over time.

Run 2

The parameters of Run 2 are identical with those of Run 1 in nearly all respects; the only difference between the two runs lies in the stream of w_t's generated in each run. The set of w_t's generated in Run 2 are different from those generated in Run 1 even though they have the same mean, variance, and probability distribution. This result is achieved by simply changing the starting value of the pseudorandom number generator used in Run 2.

Run 3

The parameters and starting values for Run 3 are given by

$$
\begin{aligned}
c_1 &= .375 & y_0 &= 7.0 \\
c_2 &= .300 & y_1 &= 2.5 \\
b &= 1.05 \\
g &= .25 \\
\sigma_u{}^2 + \sigma_v{}^2 &= 38.26
\end{aligned}
$$

hence $a_1 = -1.675$ and $a_2 = .75$. Both the monetary policy ($b = 1.05$) and the fiscal policy ($g = .25$) used in Run 3 are different from their counterparts in Run 1.

THEORY OF SPECTRAL ANALYSIS

Since Granger and Hatanaka [14] and Nerlove [37] have previously presented and interpreted the theory of spectral analysis for economists, it will not be necessary to include a detailed treatment of this theory here. However, the definition of terms and the description of the spectral methods used to establish confidence intervals to analyze data generated by simulation experiments require that we, at least, review some of the basic elements of spectral theory. The references for a complete account of the theory of spectral analysis should be consulted.[4]

Spectral analysis considers data arranged in a series according to historical time. When one thus plots the movement of many economic variables through time, he often observes a remarkable degree of smoothness in the

[4] See Blackman and Tukey [4], Granger and Hatanaka [14], Grenander and Rosenblatt [16], Hannan [18], Jenkins [24], Nerlove [37], Parzen [39], Quenouille [41], Rosenblatt [42], Jenkins and Watts [25], Tukey [44], and Watts [45].

curve; that is, although a variable assumes values that are at different times relatively high and low, its path, nevertheless, progresses evenly enough to suggest that the current value of that variable is related to its past values. In short, the data of such a time series appear to be *auto-correlated*. It is essentially the quantification and the evaluation of this autocorrelation at which spectral analysis is aimed, after the data have been transformed into the frequency domain.[5]

The application of spectral analysis to a time series (whether it be actual or simulated) yields two types of information: (1) the magnitudes of deviations from the average level of a given activity, and (2) the period or length of these deviations, both of which require the transformation of the time series into the frequency domain. To obtain this information from a time series, we use the following notation.

Denote a particular stochastic generating process or ensemble by $\{X_t, t \epsilon T\}$, from which a "sample" time series $\{x_t, t = 1, 2, \ldots, n\}$ is taken. It is important to notice that $\{X_t\}$ will indicate the manner in which $\{x_t\}$ is formed for all t; but, because of its stochastic nature, $\{X_t\}$ cannot determine exactly the value of the series at any particular t. By studying the series, one attempts to approximate the structure of the generating process.

The generating process can be described (in part) in terms of its first and second moments.[6]

$$\mu_t = E[X_t] \tag{9-24}$$

$$\sigma_t{}^2 = E[(X_t - \mu_t)^2] \tag{9-25}$$

$$\gamma(t,s) = E[(X_t - \mu_t)(X_s - \mu_s)] \tag{9-26}$$

where E denotes the mathematical expectation across the ensemble, μ_t is the expected value (mean) of the process at time t, $\sigma_t{}^2$ is the variance of the process at time t, and $\gamma(t,s)$ is the autocovariance of the process between observations at times t and s.

Estimation of these parameters may be accomplished if one has M independent samples from $\{X_t\}$; that is, $\{x_t{}^k, k = 1, 2, \ldots, M\}$. By cutting

[5] There exist other methods than spectral analysis to quantify and to evaluate autocorrelation, notably a parametric representation by autoregressive or moving average processes. The relevance of these methods and others to the analysis of data generated by simulation experiments with econometric models has been treated in the paper by Watts [45].

[6] Throughout this Chapter, Greek letters will be used to denote parameters that characterize the stochastic process as a whole and the corresponding English letters to denote statistical estimators (random variables) based on a single time series.

across the ensemble at $t = t_0$, for example, one could calculate the ensemble average estimating μ_{t_0}:

$$\bar{x}_{t_0} = \frac{1}{M} \sum_{k=1}^{M} x_{t_0}{}^k. \tag{9-27}$$

Estimates of σ_t^2 and $\gamma(s,t)$ may be obtained in a similar fashion. Although it is usually impossible to sample across the ensemble in the case of economic time series in the "real world," with computer simulation it is possible to replicate a given series by simply altering the starting value of the pseudo-random number generator used to generate the series.

We consider a special class of series whose first and second moments are not functions of time; that is, there is no trend in the mean or variance of the series and its autocovariance is a function of time lag only. In symbols,

$$E[X_t] = \mu \tag{9-28}$$

$$E[(X_t - \mu)^2] = \sigma^2 \tag{9-29}$$

$$E[X_t - \mu)(X_s - \mu)] = \gamma(t - s) \qquad \text{for all } t,s \tag{9-30}$$
$$= \gamma_\tau$$

where $\tau = t - s$.

Estimates of these parameters can be obtained from a single time series by using, respectively, the following formulas,

$$\bar{x} = \frac{1}{n} \sum_{t=1}^{n} x_t \tag{9-31}$$

$$s^2 = \frac{1}{n} \sum_{t=1}^{n} (x_t - \bar{x})^2 \tag{9-32}$$

$$c_\tau = \frac{1}{n - \tau} \sum_{t=1}^{n-\tau} (x_t - \bar{x})(x_{t+\tau} - \bar{x}) \tag{9-33}$$

where $\gamma(0) = \sigma^2$ and $c_0 = s^2$.

Such series are sometimes called stationary in the wide sense or stationary to the second order.

The power spectrum is defined as the Fourier cosine transformation of the autocovariance

$$\phi(\omega) = \gamma_0 + 2 \sum_{\tau=1}^{\infty} \gamma_\tau \cos (\omega\tau) \qquad 0 \leq \omega \leq \pi. \tag{9-34}$$

The autocovariance may be recovered from the spectrum by means of the inverse transformation:

$$\gamma_\tau = \frac{1}{\pi} \int_0^\pi \phi(\omega) \cos(\omega\tau) \, d\omega \qquad \tau = 0, 1, 2, \ldots \qquad (9\text{-}35)$$

For the special case where $\tau = 0$, we obtain the variance as an integral of the spectrum:

$$\sigma^2 = \gamma_0 = \frac{1}{\pi} \int_0^\pi \phi(\omega) \, d\omega. \qquad (9\text{-}36)$$

Hence, we speak of the spectrum as the "decomposition" of the variance of a time series. Estimators of the power spectrum usually take the following form:

$$f(\omega_j) = \lambda_0 c_0 + 2 \sum_{\tau=1}^m \lambda_\tau c_\tau \cos(\omega_j \tau) \qquad (9\text{-}37)$$

where $f(\omega_j)$ is an estimate of the power spectrum averaged over a band of frequencies centered at ω_j, and

$$\omega_j = \frac{\pi j}{m} \qquad j = 0, 1, 2, \ldots, m, \qquad (9\text{-}38)$$

$$\lambda_\tau = \text{weights}, \qquad (9\text{-}39)$$

$$m = \text{number of frequency bands to be estimated.} \qquad (9\text{-}40)$$

The power spectrum gives the squared amplitude associated with oscillations at different frequencies ω; that is, the process is characterized in terms of independent additive contributions to the variance as they are located at each ω. Thus one plots $\phi(\omega)$ against (ω) in theory; $f(\omega_j)$ against ω_j in practice. A natural interpretation of a power spectrum is that if a band contributes a large proportion of the total variance, then it may be regarded as more important than a band where the power is less.

The selection of m (number of frequency bands) and n (sample size) must be made with care in order to balance the conflicting requirements of resolution and statistical stability [4]. Granger and Hatanaka [14] and Blackman and Tukey [4] have suggested some arbitrary guidelines for choosing values of m and n. The former advise that "the amount of data required before it becomes sensible to attempt to estimate a spectrum would seem to be greater than 100," although "crude spectra have occasionally been estimated with n as low as 80." These recommended levels would form an important barrier to investigators validating annual models whose data are of short duration. Of course, the problem is less binding for quarterly models. On the simulation side, the issue of sample size melds with considerations of experimental design which, as is shown in the next section, guided our choice of $n = 200$ and $m = 25$. In an earlier study [34], we used spectral analysis (with $n = 119$ and $m = 24$) to validate a nine-equation econometric model of the textile industry, using monthly data between 1953 and 1962. In this case, the value of n was determined entirely by data availability.

To obtain empirical estimates of the power spectrum, we have used a computer program developed by Karreman [26] (and modified for the IBM 360/75) which is based on the Tukey-Hanning estimator [4,13].

STATISTICAL PROPERTIES OF SPECTRA

In this section we carry out four objectives. First, we compute the spectral estimates for the series generated by Run 1, using the Samuelson-Hicks model, and examine some of the properties of these estimates. Second, we formulate confidence bands for the purpose of comparing the estimated spectrum generated by Run 1 with the corresponding theoretical spectrum for the Samuelson-Hicks model. Third, we formulate confidence bands for comparing the spectra of different computer runs by using the Samuelson-Hicks model. Fourth, we use spectral analysis to calculate the total variance of different series that are generated by the Samuelson-Hicks model and formulate confidence intervals for comparing the variances of these series.

At the outset, we observe that, for our selection of parameters, assumptions (9-28) to (9-30) are satisfied for the system (9-21). Many economic time series however, require intermediate treatment before spectral techniques become directly applicable. The methods for detecting and for removing a trending mean, as well as for handling a series whose variance and/or autocovariance changes through time, are discussed at length in [14]. Although most of these methods are familiar (for example, polynomial regression to remove a trend in mean), it must be admitted that the possible necessity of this intermediate step has probably made spectral analysis less attractive than other (but not perfectly substitutable) modes of analysis.

Without modifying our series, then, we pursue the four topics outlined for this section.

Figure 9-1 displays the estimated spectrum $f_1(\omega)$ for these ries generated by Run 1, using the Samuelson-Hicks model. (For convenience we use a logarithmic scale for the values of the spectrum.) The prominent peak in the empirical spectrum at $j = 4$ suggests that it is this frequence ω_4 (or one very near to it) that is making the largest contribution to the variance of the process. What further meaning is attached to this particular frequency point depends on the time dimensions of the data. For example, suppose that (1) the output of the Samuelson-Hicks model represented monthly data and that (2) we are interested in the annual cycle ($f = 1/12$). Since $\omega_j = j\pi/m$ and $\omega_j = 2\pi f$ and, therefore, $j = 2fm$, we may substitute for f and m in order to locate the annual component. In this example, it occurs at $j = 25/6 \simeq 4$, the approximate location, curiously enough, of the greatest power.

Figure 9-2 shows the theoretical and estimated spectra corresponding to Run 1 of the Samuelson-Hicks model. The theoretical spectrum $\phi_1(\omega)$ can be calculated from the formula [23],

$$\phi_1(\omega) = \sigma_W^2/T^2 \qquad 0 \le \omega \le \pi \tag{9-41}$$

where,

$$T = 1 + a_1 e^{-i\omega} + a_2 e^{-2i\omega}, \tag{9-42}$$

$$i = \sqrt{-1}. \tag{9-43}$$

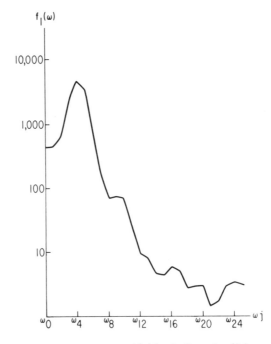

Figure 9-1.   Estimated spectrum $f_1(\omega)$ for the Samuelson-Hicks model (Run 1).

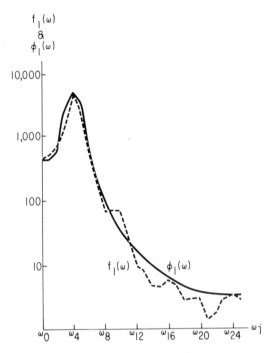

Figure 9-2. The comparison of the estimated spectrum $f_1(\omega)$ with the theoretical spectrum $\phi_1(\omega)$ for the Samuelson-Hicks model (Run 1).

The coefficients a_1 and a_2 were previously defined by $-(c_1 + b + g)$ and $(b - c_2)$. The *shape* of the spectrum is often as informative as a knowledge of the true power at a particular frequency.[7] For example, Figures 9-1 and 9-2 suggest that the lower frequencies (roughly $0 \leq \omega \leq \pi/3$) contribute much more to the variance of the process than do higher frequencies.

The work of Blackman and Tukey [4] informs us that spectral estimates $f(\omega_j)$ have desirable statistical properties, provided that the process X_t is Gaussian (normal). One property, in particular, the statistical independence of spectral estimates at nonadjacent frequencies, facilitates the interpretation of confidence intervals, a method of data analysis that is familiar to most economists.

If the theoretical spectrum is reasonably smooth [4], the distribution of $f(\omega_j)/\phi(\omega_j)$ is approximately χ_k^2/k with $k = 2n/m$ degrees of freedom.[8] Hence, to gain some information about $\phi(\omega_j)$ when the sample $f(\omega_j)$ are

---

[7] See [13] for an elaboration of this point.

[8] At the end points, $j = 0$ and $j = m$, the degrees of freedom drop to n/m. This applies for *all* estimated spectra throughout the paper.

available, one may construct a $(100-\alpha)$ percent confidence interval for $\phi(\omega_j)$.[9] Suppose that $\alpha = .05$; let $\chi^2_{.975,k}$ and $\chi^2_{.025,k}$ be the percentiles of the χ^2 distribution with k degrees of freedom leaving 2.5 percent in the lower and upper tails, respectively. Then

$$P_r\left(\frac{\chi^2_{.975,k}}{k} < \frac{f(\omega_j)}{\phi(\omega_j)} < \frac{\chi^2_{.025,k}}{k}\right) = .95. \tag{9-44}$$

Solving for $\phi(\omega_j)$,

$$P_r\left(\frac{f(\omega_j)}{\chi^2_{.025,k}/k} < \phi(\omega_j) < \frac{f(\omega_j)}{\chi^2_{.975,k}/k}\right) = .95. \tag{9-45}$$

The succession of confidence intervals at the frequency points ω_j $(j = 0, 1, \ldots, m)$, called a *confidence band*, is displayed in Figure 9-3, using the spectral estimates of the series generated by Run 1 of the Samuelson-Hicks model. The theoretical spectrum $\phi_1(\omega)$ is also plotted in Figure 9-3. We would normally expect about 5 percent of the confidence intervals in the confidence band to be in error. Reference to Figure 9-3, where our knowledge of the theoretical spectrum is utilized, reveals that 2 of the 26 intervals (ω_{10} and ω_{21}), or 7.7 percent do not cover the true values.

The simultaneous confidence band offers a slightly different method of analysis; it permits one to state with probability $100-\alpha$ that *all* of the confidence intervals are simultaneously true.

Let us sketch the development of this band for $\alpha = .05$.[10] If B_j denotes the error made on the jth frequency; and if we make $\Pr(B_j) = .05/m + 1)$ $(j = 0, 1, \ldots, m)$, then the probability of committing any error at all is

$$\Pr(B_0 \text{ or } B_1 \text{ or } \ldots \text{ or } B_m) \leq \Pr(B_0) + \Pr(B_1) + \ldots + \Pr(B_m)$$
$$= (m + 1)\,[(.05/(m + 1)] \tag{9-46}$$
$$= .05.$$

The crucial inequality above does not require independence or any other hypothesis; indeed, if the events B_j are mutually exclusive, then the expression becomes an equality.

Hence, when we allow an error rate of $.05/(m + 1)$ for each frequency (and, thus, a total error rate of .05 at most), then $.025/(m + 1) = .025/26 \simeq .001$ probability is left in each tail of the distribution. The simultaneous confidence band assumes the same form as the confidence band developed

---

[9] The reader may wish to contrast the interval developed in these pages with the interval described by Granger and Hatanaka [14].

[10] An extended discussion of this proof appears in [11].

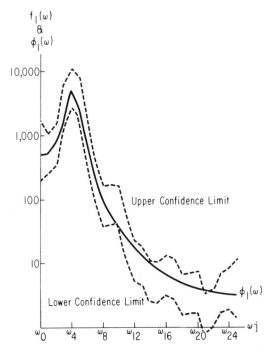

Figure 9-3. The confidence band for spectral estimates of Run 1 of the Samuelson-Hicks model.

previously, although the simultaneous band is obviously much wider than the latter. In symbols,

$$\Pr\left[\frac{f(\omega_j)}{\chi^2_{.001,k}/k} < \phi(\omega_j) < \frac{f(\omega_j)}{\chi^2_{.999,k}/k}\right] = .95. \tag{9-47}$$

$$j = 0, 1, \ldots, m.$$

Figure 9-4 depicts the 95 percent simultaneous confidence band and the theoretical spectrum for Run 1 with the Samuelson-Hicks model. This time all of the values of $\phi_1(\omega)$ lie within the confidence band.

In the introduction to this chapter, we asserted that the primary interest of economists in simulation stems from the fact that, with simulation, it may be possible to validate economic models and to compare the outcomes associated with alternative economic policies. Hence, economists are much more likely to be interested in constructing confidence bands to compare the estimated spectra of two series which are the result of the use of two different economic policies. Alternatively, economists may be interested in comparing the estimated spectrum of a series generated by a simulation

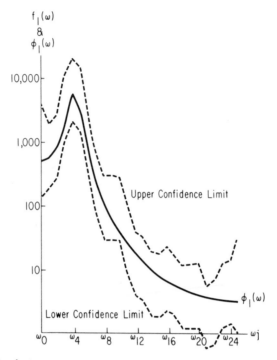

Figure 9-4. The simultaneous conficence band for spectral estimates of Run 1 of the Samuelson-Hicks model.

experiment with the estimated spectrum of the corresponding "real world" series as a means of verifying the results of the simulation.

Therefore, we next consider the comparison of two spectra via a confidence interval for the ratio $P_j = \phi_1(\omega_j)/\phi_2(\omega_j)$. Define $R_j = f_1(\omega_j)/f_2(\omega_j)$. We then obtain an F (variance-ratio) statistic

$$F_{k_1,k_2} = \frac{R_j}{P_j} = \frac{f_1(\omega_j)/\phi_1(\omega_j)}{f_2(\omega_j)/\phi_2(\omega_j)} \qquad (9\text{-}48)$$

where $k_1 = k_2 = 2n/m$ is the degrees of freedom for each of the two χ^2 variates. To arrive at a 95 percent confidence interval for P_j, let $F_{.,975,k_1,k_2}$, and $F_{.025,k_1,k_2}$ be the percentiles of the F distribution leaving .025 probability in the lower and upper tails, respectively. It follows that

$$\Pr\left(F_{.975,k_1,k_2} < \frac{R_j}{P_j} < F_{.025,k_1,k_2}\right) = .95. \qquad (9\text{-}49)$$

Solving for P_j, the 95 percent confidence interval becomes

$$\Pr\left(\frac{R_j}{F_{.025,k_1,k_2}} < P_j < \frac{R_j}{F_{.975,k_1,k_2}}\right) = .95. \qquad (9\text{-}50)$$

Of course, a 95 percent *simultaneous confidence band* may be derived for P_j, using nearly the same reasoning employed in the development of a 95 percent simultaneous confidence band for $\phi(\omega_j)$. The former may be expressed as

$$\Pr\left(\frac{R_j}{F_{.001,k_1,k_2}} < P_j < \frac{R_j}{F_{.999,k_1,k_2}}\right) = .95. \qquad (9\text{-}51)$$

For illustrative purposes we consider two examples. Suppose that we are interested in comparing the time path of national income generated by Run 1 (again using the Samuelson-Hicks model) with the time path of national income generated by Run 2. We recall that the only difference between Run 1 and Run 2 lies in the fact that we use a different starting value for the sequence of pseudorandom numbers that are used to generate the stochastic variate w_t. In other words, we know beforehand that the theoretical spectra of Runs 1 and 2 are identical, that is, $P = 1$. Figure 9-5 shows the simulated time paths of the two relevant series $\{y_t^{(1)}\}$ and $\{y_t^{(2)}\}$. A cursory glance at Figure 9-5 might lead one to conclude that the two series have little in common and are the result of the use of two different economic policies. Despite their apparent dissimilarity when inspected visually, the two series have been generated in exactly the same manner

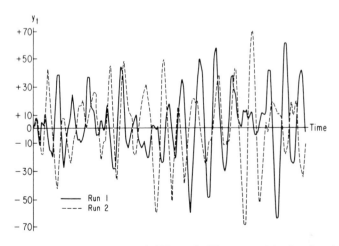

Figure 9-5.   The comparison of two series $\{y_t^{(1)}\}$ and $\{y_t^{(2)}\}$ generated by Runs 1 and 2, respec-
of the Samuelson-Hicks model.

(that is, the factor loadings are identical), with one exception—namely, different starting values were used for the random number generator which supplies the stochastic term w_t.

We now bring a measure of order to the two series by constructing a 95 percent simultaneous confidence band for P in Figure 9-6. As expected, the horizontal line $P = 1$ corresponding to the true ratio lies within the confidence band for all values of $(0 \leq \omega \leq \pi)$.

For a second example, we compare the time path of national income generated by Run 1 with that of Run 3. Recall that Run 3 represents the results of a change in monetary policy (accelerator coefficient) and a change in fiscal policy (governmental parameter). Constructing a 95 percent simultaneous confidence band for P in Figure 9-7, we observe that the graph of the horizontal oine $P = 1$ falls outside of the confidence band at ω_1, ω_2, ω_5, ω_{20}, ω_{22}, and ω_{24}, thus showing that the spectra, indeed, are different. As expected, the true ratio P, computed using formula 9-41, lies within the simultaneous confidence band, except at some high frequencies (ω_{20}, ω_{22}, ω_{24}), where "window leakage" [4] from the lower frequencies affects these weaker, and less important, frequencies. Figure 9-7 demonstrates even more specifically that the spectral *shapes* of Run 1 and Run 3

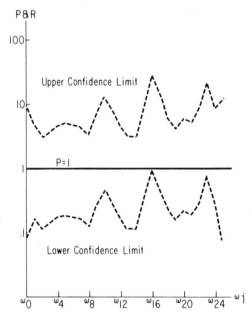

Figure 9-6.   The simultaneous confidence band for comparing the empirical spectra $f_1(\omega)$ and $f_2(\omega)$ of two series $\{y_t^{(1)}\}$ and $\{y_t^{(2)}\}$ generated by Runs 1 and 2, respectively, of the Samuelson-Hicks model.

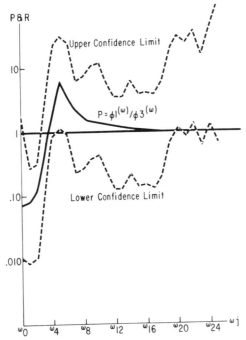

Figure 9-7. The simultaneous confidence band for comparing the empirical spectra $f_1(\omega)$ and $f_3(\omega)$ of two series $\{y_t^{(1)}\}$ and $\{y_t^{(3)}\}$ generated by Runs 1 and 3, respectively, of the Samuelson-Hicks model.

are different, because no horizontal line can be drawn that lies within the confidence band. If the spectral shapes were the same, that is, if $f_1(\omega) = k f_3(\omega)$, for some k, then the ratio P would equal k and its graph would be a horizontal line.

Thus far we have been concerned with the use of spectral analysis to decompose the variance of a time series into its frequency components [44]. We now consider the variance as a whole for a given time series. The natural estimator of σ^2, of course, is the sample variance s^2. Therefore, we would hope to use classical χ^2 or F-ratio statistics to analyze the variance of a given time series or two or more series. However, because *the time series is autocorrelated*, s^2, generally, does not have a χ^2 distribution with $(n-1)$ degrees of freedom. In a sense, the autocorrelation of the observations reduces the amount of information they provide about the variance, so that the number of degrees of freedom for s^2 is less than $(n-1)$. In fact, if the observations x_t are highly autocorrelated as in a pure sine wave, then s^2 has only 2 degrees of freedom [4, p. 21-25]. To determine, in general, the number of degrees of freedom for s^2, we resort to its spectral decomposition.

We begin by observing that (9-36) gives the theoretical variance σ^2 in terms of the spectrum ϕ. Similarly, the sample variance s^2 is given in terms of the estimated spectrum f:

$$s^2 = c_0 = \frac{1}{m}\left[\frac{f(0)}{2} + \sum_{j=1}^{m-1} f(\omega_j) + \frac{f(\pi)}{2}\right]. \tag{9-52}$$

This formula requires that the weight λ_0 in (9-37) be unity, a condition satisfied by every reasonable spectrum estimator.

Thus, s^2 is displayed as the sum of somewhat dependent terms,[11] each of which is a multiple of χ^2 on $2n/m$ degrees of freedom. Following a technique developed by Blackman and Tukey [4, p. 24], we can show that s^2 essentially[12] follows a χ^2 distribution with degrees of freedom approximated by

$$k = \frac{\left[\dfrac{f(0)}{2} + \sum\limits_{j=1}^{m-1} f(\omega_j) + \dfrac{f(\pi)}{2}\right]^2}{\dfrac{[f(0)]^2}{2} + \sum\limits_{j=1}^{m-1} [f(\omega_j)]^2 + \dfrac{[f(\pi)]^2}{2}} X(n/m). \tag{9-53}$$

We observe, in passing, that if the spectrum $f(\omega)$ is constant (corresponding to uncorrelated observations), then k reduces to n, which is approximately the correct value $n - 1$. Depending on the degree to which $f(\omega)$ is not constant (correlated observations), k will be reduced. Now that the distribution of s^2 is known, we can test σ^2 or can construct confidence intervals for one series alone or for a two-series comparison.

For example, to construct a confidence interval for σ_1^2/σ_2^2, the ratio of variances of two series, we notice that

$$F = \frac{n_1 s_1^2/\sigma_1^2 k_1}{n_2 s_2^2/\sigma_2^2 k_2} \tag{9-54}$$

has an F (variance-ratio) distribution with k_1, k_2 degrees of freedom. If we let $F_{k_1,k_2,.975}$ and $f_{k_1,k_2,.025}$ denote the percentiles which leave 2-1/2 percent of the probability in the lower and upper tails, respectively, then

$$\Pr\left(F_{k_1,k_2,.975} < \frac{n_1 s_1^2/\sigma_1^2 k_1}{n_2 s_2^2/\sigma_2^2 k_2} < F_{k_1,k_2,.025}\right) = .95. \tag{9-55}$$

[11] Blackman and Tukey [14] have shown that adjacent spectral estimates are correlated, but that nonadjacent estimates are practically uncorrelated.

[12] Strictly speaking, both here and in every other occurrence, it is ns^2/σ^2 that has a χ^2 distribution and not s^2.

Solving for σ_1^2/σ_2^2, we obtain our desired confidence interval:

$$\Pr\left(\frac{n_1 s_1^2 k_2}{n_2 s_2^2 k_1} \frac{1}{F_{k_1,k_2,.025}} < \sigma_1^2/\sigma_2^2 < \frac{n_1 s_1^2 k_2}{n_2 s_2^2 k_1} \frac{1}{F_{k_1,k_2,.975}}\right) = .95. \qquad (9\text{-}56)$$

For the comparison of Runs 1 and 2, the actual 95 percent confidence interval was computed to be

$$.429 < \sigma_1^2/\sigma_2^2 < 1.72 \qquad (9\text{-}57)$$

which contains the true value, unity.

SPECTRAL ANALYSIS: A LARGER ROLE?

In the previous discussion, we employed spectral analysis *in conjunction with an* econometric model, albeit a primitive one. Not all writers would cast spectral (and cross-spectral) analysis into so modest a role. Granger and Hatanaka apparently, would have these techniques become the primary guides in reshaping and in restating much economic theory, thus turning methodological biases away from "classical" model-building and toward more "advanced" modes of time-series analysis. We do not now champion the exclusiveness of either model-building or spectral techniques but insist that benefits can be derived from their joint and complementary use.

In addition to the outlets for compromise that are proposed in the sections above, it is important to bring this same notion to the issue of prediction. One sometimes hears that whereas econometric models can generate forecasts and that knowledge of the power spectrum cannot, the latter is of little relevance to forecasters. According to this argument, one also would be disposed to claim that it is the shovel that runs the earth, not man's understanding of cultivation, and, therefore, the latter is immaterial to farmers. Working from a different and more satisfactory premise—namely, *how* something is done affects *what* is done—we could contend that the spectral technique, as a tool of validation, may be pertinent to forecasters. Since, when an econometric model generates a series for a variable and that series yields a power spectrum which is fundamentally different from the spectrum of the actual data,[13] the simulator then learns that his model is defective, *at least*, along this dimension. What weight is to be attached to this information cannot be dictated, but an out-of-hand value of zero seems unwarranted. Until a model's predictive ability can be judged

[13] Of course, subject, to the problems of sample size and nonstationarity.

against actual data in future periods, its performance on tests of validation over past periods will certainly determine, to a great extent, how much confidence is to be given to the predicted levels, impact multipliers, and so on, that it currently produces.

SUMMARY

In this chapter, we demonstrate the potential value of spectral analysis as a technique for analyzing data generated by computer simulation experiments with economic models. By constructing the appropriate confidence bands, spectral analysis enables one to validate the output of simulation experiments and to compare the results of alternative economic policies that are associated with different series generated by an economic model.

The application of spectral analysis to series generated by computer simulation experiments differs from the application of spectral analysis to "real world" economic series in two ways. First, with computer simulation we are not subject to the same type of sample size limitations that one encounters with economic time series. Second, with computer simulation we can sample across the ensemble, an alternative that is rarely available with actual economic series. As yet, this opportunity has not been exploited by economists or simulators.

BIBLIOGRAPHY

1. Adelman, Irma, and Adelman, Frank L. "The Dynamic Properties of the Klein-Goldberger Model," *Econometrica*, **XXVII** (October 1959), 596-625.
2. Adelman, Irma. "Long Cycles—A Simulation Experiment," *Symposium on Simulation Models*. Austin C. Hogatt and Frederick E. Balderston (eds). Cincinnati: South-Western Publishing Co., 1963.
3. Bartlett, M. S. *An Introduction to Stochastic Processes with Special Reference to Methods and Applications*. Cambridge: The University Press, 1962.
4. Blackman, R. B., and Tukey, J. W. *The Measurement of Power Spectra*. New York: Dover Publications, Inc., 1958.
5. Burdick, Donald S., and Naylor, Thomas H. "Design of Computer Simulation Experiments for Industrial Systems," *Communications of the ACM*, **IX** (May 1966), 329-339.
6. Cunnyingham, J. "Spectral Analysis of Economic Time Series," Working Paper No. 16, United States Department of Commerce, Bureau of the Census, New York, 1963.
7. De Leeuw, Frank. "Financial Markets in Business Cycles: A Simulation Study," *American Economic Review*, **LIV** (May 1964), 309-323.

8. Duesenberry, James S., Eckstein, Otto, and Fromm, Gary. "A Simulation of the United States Economy in Recession," Econometrica, **XXVIII** (October 1960), 749-809.

9. Duesenberry, J. S., Fromm, G., Klein, L. R., and Kuh, E. *The Brookings Quarterly Econometric Model of the United States.* Chicago: Rand McNally & Co., 1965.

10. Fishman, George S., and Kiviat, Philip J. "The Analysis of Simulation-Generated Time Series," *Management Science*, **XIII** (March 1967), 525-557.

11. Fraser, D. A. S. *Nonparametric Methods in Statistics.* New York: John Wiley & Sons, 1957.

12. Fromm, Gary. "Recent Monetary Policy: An Econometric View," *National Banking Review*, **III** (March 1966), 299-306.

13. Granger, C. W. J. "The Typical Spectral Shape of an Economic Variable," *Econometrica*, **XXXIV** (January 1966), 150-161.

14. Granger, C. W. J., and Hatanaka, M. *Spectral Analysis of Economic Time Series.* Princeton, J. J.: Princeton University Press, 1964.

15. Granger, C. W. J., and Morgenstern, O. "Spectral Analysis of Stock Market Prices," *Kyklos*, **XVI** (1963), 1-27.

16. Grenander, U., and Rosenblatt, M. *Statistical Analysis of Stationary Time Series.* New York: John Wiley & Sons, 1957.

17. Gross, Donald, and Ray, Jack L. "A General Purpose Forecast Simulator," *Management Science*, **XI** (April 1965), 119-135.

18. Hannan, E. J. *Time Series Analysis.* New York: John Wiley & Sons, 1960.

19. Hannan, E. J. "Regression for Time Series," *Proceedings of the Symposium on Time Series Analysis.* Murray Rosenblatt (ed). New York: John Wiley & Sons, 1962.

20. Hatanaka, M. "A Spectral Analysis of Business Cycle Indicators: Lead-Lag in Terms of All Time Points," Princeton University, Econometric Research Program, Research Memorandum No. 53, 1963.

21. Hickman, Bert G. (ed). *Quantitative Planning of Economic Policy.* Washington, D. C.: The Brookings Institution, 1965.

22. Hicks, J. R. *A Contribution to the Theory of the Trade Cycle.* Oxford: Clarendon Press, 1950.

23. Howrey, E. Philip. "Stabilization Policy in Linear Stochastic Systems," *Review of Economics and Statistics*, **XLIX** (August 1967), 404-411.

24. Jenkins, G. M. "General Considerations in the Analysis of Spectra," *Technometrics*, **III** (May 1961), 133-166.

25. Jenkins, G. M., and Watts, D. G. *Spectral Analysis and Its Applications.* San Francisco: Holden-Day, 1968.

26. Karreman, Herman F. "Computer Programs for Spectral Analysis of Economic Time Series," Princeton University, Econometric Research Program, Research Memorandum No. 59, July 15, 1963.

27. Kendall, M. G. "On Autoregressive Time Series," *Biometrika*, **XXXIII** (August 1944), 105-122.

28. Lee, Y. W. *Statistical Theory of Communications*. New York: John Wiley & Sons, 1960.
29. Liu, Ta-Chung. "An Exploratory Quarterly Econometric Model of Effective Demand in the Postwar U. S. Economy," *Econometrica*, **XXXI** (July 1963), 301-348.
30. Malinvaud, E. *Statistical Methods of Econometrics*. Chicago: Rand McNally, 1966.
31. Naylor, Thomas H., Balintfy, Joseph L., Burkick, Donald S., and Chu, Kong. *Computer Simulation Techniques*. New York: John Wiley & Sons, 1966.
32. Naylor, Thomas H., Burdick, Donald S., and Sasser, W. Earl. "Computer Simulation Experiments with Economic Systems: The Problem of Experimental Design," *Journal of the American Statistical Association*, **LXII** (December 1967), 1315-1337.
33. Naylor, Thomas H., and Finger, J. M. "Verification of Computer Simulation Models," *Management Science*, **XIV** (October 1967), 92-101.
34. Naylor, Thomas H., Wallace, William H., and Sasser, W. Earl. "A Computer Simulation Model of the Textile Industry," *Journal of the American Statistical Association*, **LXII** (December 1967), 1338-1364.
35. Naylor, Thomas H., Wertz, Kenneth, and Wonnacott, Thomas. "Methods for Analyzing Data from Computer Simulation Experiments," *Communications of the ACM*, **X** (November 1967), 703-710.
36. Naylor, Thomas H., Wertz, Kennth, and Wonnacott, Thomas. "Some Methods for Evaluating the Effects of Economic Policies Using Simulation Experiments," *Review of the International Statistical Institute*, **XXXVI** (1968), 184-200.
37. Nerlove, M. "Spectral Analysis of Seasonal Adjustment Procedures," *Econometrica*, **XXXII** (1964), 241-286.
38. Nerlove, M. *Spectral Comparisons of Two Seasonal Adjustment Procedures*, Technical Report No. 2, National Science Foundation Grant GS-142, June 1, 1964.
39. Parzen, E. "Mathematical Considerations in the Estimation of Spectra," *Technometrics*, **III** (May 1961), 167-190.
40. Parzen, E. *Stochastic Processes*. San Francisco: Holden-Day, 1962.
41. Quenouille, M. H. *The Analysis of Multiple Time-Series*. New York: Hafner Publishing Co., 1957.
42. Rosenblatt, Murray. *Proceedings of the Symposium on Time Series Analysis*. New York: John Wiley & Sons, 1962.
43. Samuelson, Paul A. "Interactions Between the Multiplier Analysis and the Principle of Acceleration," *Review of Economic Statistics*, **XII** (May 1938), 75-78.
44. Tukey, John W. "Discussion, Emphasizing the Connection Between Analysis of Variance and Spectrum Analysis," *Technometrics*, **III** (May 1961), 191-219.
45. Watts, Donald. "Time Series Analysis," *Design of Computer Simulation Experiments*. Thomas H. Naylor (ed). Durham, N. C.: Duke University Press, 1969.
46. Wonnacott, Thomas. "Spectral Analysis Combining a Bartlett Window With an Associated Inner Window," *Technometrics*, **III** (May 1961), 237-245.

Chapter 10 | Variance Reduction[1]

WILLIAM A. MOY

INTRODUCTION

Numerous techniques have been proposed for increasing the sampling efficiency of Monte Carlo simulations above the one that is obtainable with simple random sampling. Some techniques have been applied in particle-physics applications with outstanding success [16]. Some have been applied to simple examples of operational problems [3,6,23]. But no applications of methods applicable to broad classes of operational problems have been reported.

The purpose of this chapter is to develop and to compare four such variance-reducing techniques in the simulation of certain types of queueing systems.

The systems to which we restrict our attention are characterized by regularly returning, after either a fixed time period or a fixed number of customers, to a known (generally empty) initial state. Many systems of practical importance are of this type. The classical tool-crib problem is an example, since the queue always is empty at the end of a work shift. For convenience, we refer to any such system as a "periodic queueing system."

The four techniques considered are (1) regression sampling, (2) anti-thetic-variate sampling, (3) stratified sampling, and (4) importance sampling. In each case, two alternative procedures for applying the technique are considered. One is completely independent of the system being simulated. The other is in some way dependent on the particular system being simulated. However, both are general purpose in that they may be applied in the simulation of any periodic queueing system.

---

[1] This Chapter was written by William A. Moy and is based on the paper that he presented at the symposium on "The Design of Computer Simulation Experiments," sponsored by the TIMS College on Simulation and Gaming which was held at Duke University on October 14 to 16, 1969. The paper was first published in *The Design of Computer Simulation Experiments*, Thomas H. Naylor (ed). Durham, N.C.: Duke Duke University Press, 1969.

PROBLEM FORMULATION

Define the sample space S_R by

$$S_R = \{\mathbf{R} = (R_1, \ldots, R_m): R_1 \tag{10-1}$$

is a random variable uniformly distributed in the
interval (0,1) and m is fixed and finite $\}$.

That is, S_R is the space of all random number vectors of length m.

Associated with every point $\mathbf{r}$ in S_R is a probability density $f(\mathbf{r})$. If each
of the elements in the random number vector are independent and identi-
cally distributed with

$$f(r_i) = \begin{cases} 1, 0 \leq r_i \leq 1 \\ 0, \text{ otherwise}, \end{cases} \tag{10-2}$$

then the joint probability density function is given by

$$f(\mathbf{r}) = \begin{cases} 1, 0 \leq r_i \leq 1 & \text{for all } i = 1, \ldots, m \\ 0, \text{ otherwise}. \end{cases} \tag{10-3}$$

Consider the random variable Y defined on S_R implicitly by a specified
computer program. By this we mean that given a random number vector
$\mathbf{R} = \mathbf{r}$, the computer program maps this random vector into a value of the
random variable Y. For generality, let this mapping be dependent on a
vector of input parameters $\boldsymbol{\gamma}$, that is, $Y = Y(\mathbf{r};\boldsymbol{\gamma})$. In this chapter, the
computer program, of course, will be a model of a periodic queueing
system.

Y could be either a vector-valued or scalar-valued function, but we shall
restrict our attention to scalar-valued functions only. For example, Y
might be the total customer waiting time during one period of the queueing
system, or the total cost of operating the system during one period.

We assume that the purpose of conducting the Monte Carlo simulation
is to estimate the expected value of Y, and to obtain as accurate an estimate
as possible with a given investment in computing cost. Formally, this
expectation is given by

$$E(Y) = \int_0^1 \ldots \int_0^1 Y(\mathbf{r})f(\mathbf{r}) \, d\mathbf{r}. \tag{10-4}$$

The usual procedure for estimating $E(Y)$ would be to generate a sample
of n random number vectors from the joint pdf $f(\mathbf{r})$, to compute the value
of Y for each, and to take the mean of these n observations of Y as the
estimate.

It must be realized that it is impossible to generate random number vectors that are truly random samples from $f(\mathbf{r})$, since each number is limited to a finite number of digits. However, no practical simulation will be pathological to the extent that this would make any significant difference. Since the integral form of $E(Y)$ is much easier to work with than the corresponding form involving a summation, we shall just assume that a random number vector generated by the computer is a random sample from $f(\mathbf{r})$.

Even though Y is seldom, if ever, known explicitly, we do have a freedom in specifying its form that, if recognized and exploited, may enable certain increases in the efficiency of the Monte Carlo technique. We must observe that the availability of this extra freedom is one of the main differences between experimenting on physical systems and experimenting on the simulation models of such systems.

In this chapter, this extra freedom is used in an elementary way. We simply require that in all simulation models (that is, computer programs) the correlation between each random number used in the simulation and the congestion caused by the simulated system event generated by that random number be positive and as large as possible.

Thus, if random numbers are used to generate service times in the running of the program, we require that large random numbers generate long service times. Similarly, in generating customer interarrival times, we require that large random numbers generate short interarrival times.

This procedure would insure, for example, that $Y(0)$, that is, the value of Y when $\mathbf{R} = (0, \ldots, 0)$ is the minimum value of Y, and $Y(1)$ is the maximum value.

The four alternatives to random sampling are presented in the next four sections. Experimental results follow.

REGRESSION SAMPLING

Consider the random variable Z defined on $S_{\mathbf{R}}$ by

$$Z(\mathbf{R};\mathbf{b}) = Y(\mathbf{R}) - X(\mathbf{R};\mathbf{b}) + E[X(\mathbf{R};\mathbf{b})] \qquad (10\text{-}5)$$

where $X(\mathbf{R};\mathbf{b})$—called the auxiliary variable—is a random variable defined on $S_{\mathbf{R}}$ which depends on K parameters given by the vector $\mathbf{b} = (b_1, \ldots, b_K)$. We require that the expectation of X be known numerically for any value of the parameter vector.

Clearly, $E(Z) = E(Y)$, and the variance of Z is given by

$$V(Z) = V(Y) + V(X) - 2 \operatorname{Cov}(X,Y). \qquad (10\text{-}6)$$

Suppose that, for a fixed total sample cost, either n_y random values of Y or n_z ($n_z \leq n_y$) random values of Z could be obtained. Sampling for Z will be preferred over simple random sampling if $V(z)/n_z < V(Y)/n_y$. A necessary condition for this inequality to be satisfied is that $\text{Cov}(X,Y)$ be large and positive or, in other words, that the correlation between X and Y be near $+1$.

The method proposed here is a generalization of a well-known sample-survey technique. The possibility of using this more restricted technique in Monte Carlo simulations has been recognized by several authors [16,17,18, 20,26]. However, none have indicated how the technique actually can be applied to specific Monte Carlo problems, and none have reported any results with real simulation models.

The problem of specifying the auxiliary variable may be considered in two phases: that of specifying a good form for $X(\mathbf{R};\mathbf{b})$ and that of specifying the parameter values for a specific application.

Consider the second problem first. Given $X(\mathbf{R};\mathbf{b})$ in parametric form, it is clear that $\mathbf{b}$ should be specified so that the variance of the estimate of $E(Y)$ is minimized. It can be shown [22] that under certain reasonable assumptions this criterion is equivalent to choosing the $\mathbf{b}$'s so as to minimize the sum of the squared differences between the x_i and the y_i values. Thus, given a sample of n observations, the optimum parameter values are given by the K equations:

$$\sum_{i=1}^{n} x_i \frac{\partial x_i}{\partial b_k} = \sum_{i=1}^{n} y_i \frac{\partial x_i}{\partial b_k}, \qquad k = 1, \ldots, K. \tag{10-7}$$

If b and $\bar{z} = (1/n)\, \Sigma z_i = (1/n)\, \Sigma[y_i - x_i + E(X)]$ are calculated from the same sample, then $\bar{z}$ will in general be a biased estimate of $E(Y)$ because of covariance terms. The amount of the bias usually will be unknown, although, in special cases, at least, it is known that $\bar{z}$ is a consistent estimator of $E(Y)$.

One approach to the elimination of the bias [17] is to split the sample into two or more groups; to estimate $\mathbf{b}_{\text{opt}}$ separately from each group, and to use the average of the estimates from all other groups in calculating the auxiliary variables for the observations within any group. The x_i and $\mathbf{b}$ within any group, thus, are independent and $\bar{z}$ gives an unbiased estimate of $E(Y)$.

The variance of $\bar{z}$ determined in this manner will be somewhat greater than $V(Z)/n$, but it still may be less than the corresponding $V(Y)/n$. We shall adopt this approach.

Limited experimental results [22] indicate that for samples of the size likely to be found in simulation studies, no improvement is obtained by using more than two groups. The experimental results reported in the section below used this approach with two groups of equal size.

To be a useful auxiliary variable, any candidate must pass three tests. First, the solution of the set of equations given by (10-7) for calculating the parameters from a sample must be computationally feasible. Second, given a set of parameter values, the calculation of the expected value of the variable also must be computationally feasible. Third, when applied to the simulation of a periodic queueing system, it must yield a variance reduction that is greater than could be obtained by simply devoting the same amount of extra effort to simple random sampling.

The imposed relationship between the random numbers used in generating the system events and the congestion caused by the events suggests that a system-independent auxiliary variable might be defined in terms of the sum or the average of the random numbers used in generating the observation. Examples of such auxiliary variables are

$$X(\mathbf{R};\mathbf{b}) = b_1 + b_2 \, \Sigma R_j \tag{10-8}$$

$$X(\mathbf{R};\mathbf{b}) = b_1 + b_2 \, \Sigma R_j + b_3 \, \Sigma R_j{}^2 \tag{10-9}$$

$$X(\mathbf{R};\mathbf{b}) = b_1 + b_2 \, \Sigma R_j + b_3 (\Sigma R_j)^2 \tag{10-10}$$

where the summations are for $j = 1, \ldots, m$. Each satisfies the first two requirements in the paragraph above.

System-dependent auxiliary variables may be defined in an endless number of ways. Two general types will be considered. The first includes auxiliary variables that are defined directly on the random numbers after they have been classified according to their use in the simulation. The second type includes the ones that are defined on the events generated by the random numbers instead of directly on the random numbers.

Suppose that the numbers in the random number vector $\mathbf{R}$ are regrouped so that the first m_1 of them are used to generate system events of type 1, the next m_2 are used to generate events of type 2, and so forth. Within each subgroup, let the numbers be listed in the order in which they are used. Let this vector of random numbers be designated $\mathbf{R}^*$, and let the vector $\mathbf{R}_1^*$ be the vector of the first m_1 numbers in $\mathbf{R}^*$, the vector $\mathbf{R}_2^*$, the next m_2 numbers in $\mathbf{R}^*$, and so on. Then both types of system-dependent auxiliary variables are special cases of an auxiliary variable of the form

$$X = f_1(\mathbf{R}_1^*) + f_2(\mathbf{R}_2^*) + \ldots + f_L(\mathbf{R}_L^*) \tag{10-11}$$

where $E[f_i(\mathbf{R}^*)]$ is known for all i.

For the first type of auxiliary variable to be considered, $f_i(\mathbf{R}_i^*)$ may be any function containing the random numbers and unknown parameters to be estimated from the sample observations.

For the second type, f_i will be a composite of two functions, say g_i and h_i, where h_i is the function that generates a system event of type i from a random number, and g_i is a function of such a system event whose parameters are estimated from the sample, that is, $f_i(\mathbf{R}_i^*) = g_i[h_i(\mathbf{R}_i^*)]$.

In general, each term of (10-11) will involve, at least, one unknown parameter that must be estimated from sample data. Since the solution of (10-7) becomes unwieldy if the number of parameters is large, say more than 10, L in (10-11) must be restricted.

If the number of event types generated in the simulation is small, this method may be applied directly. Otherwise, the effective value of L must be reduced through the elimination of terms that will likely have small effect on the correlation between X and Y or through the aggregation of terms likely to have similar parameter values. Our experience indicates that if the analyst applying the technique has adequate knowledge of the system being simulated, he can successfully perform this elimination or aggregation on an intuitive basis.

ANTITHETIC-VARIATE SAMPLING

Consider next a random variable Z defined by

$$Z(\mathbf{R}) = \alpha Y(\mathbf{R}) + (1 - \alpha) X(\mathbf{R}) \tag{10-12}$$

where $X(\mathbf{R})$ is any random variable whose expectation is known to be equal to $E(Y)$ and $0 < \alpha < 1$. The mean of Z is $E(Y)$, and the variance is given by

$$V(Z) = \alpha^2 V(Y) + (1 - \alpha)^2 V(X) + 2\alpha(1 - \alpha) \operatorname{Cov}(X,Y). \tag{10-13}$$

If the correlation between X and Y is sufficiently close to -1, it is clear that $V(Z)$ may be less then $V(Y)$ for a given sampling expenditure.

This method of sampling is known as the method of antithetic variates. It is a special case of general correlated sampling methods. It was first expounded in a paper by Hammersley and Morton [11] in 1956. It has since been discussed and expanded on in several other works by Hammersley and his collaborators [8,9,10,12,21], by Tukey [26], and by Page [23]. Marshall [20] also used the idea, but without referring to the technique by name.

The problem in applying this method in any simulation is to be able to find a suitable auxiliary variable X. In certain special cases, rather ingenious ways have been devised for specifying X. Marshall [20] gives one such example. But these methods lack generality.

A very simple system-independent method for obtaining X is to let $X(\mathbf{R}) = Y(\mathbf{R}^*)$ where the vector $\mathbf{R}^* = (1 - \mathbf{R})$. That is, the auxiliary variable is computed by rerunning the simulation, using the complements of the random numbers.

If the simulation model is such that the ith random number in each sequence will surely generate the same system event, then it is likely—and in some cases certain—that $\mathrm{Cov}(X,Y)$ will be negative. This is true regardless of whether the correlation between the random numbers and the congestion generated by them is forced to be positive for all types of system events.

If the simulation model is such that the ith random number in each sequence may not generate the same system event, then imposing the relationship between the random numbers and the events they generate may still cause $\mathrm{Cov}(X,Y)$ to be negative.

A potential advantage of regression sampling and antithetic-variate sampling over the two methods that follow is that they are essentially applied after the fact. That is, a Monte Carlo simulation is performed by using random sampling methods, and only then are the values of the auxiliary variable X calculated and the Z's obtained. These two stages are functionally completely independent, except that, in performing the random sampling, provisions must be made for obtaining data that will be needed later in calculating the X's.

Thus the simulation aspect of simple random sampling is preserved. In those cases where one wants to "observe" the simulated operation of the system in addition to estimating the expected value of some system property as accurately as possible, this may be an important consideration.

A second advantage is that they can be applied to any existing simulation program with only very minor changes.

STRATIFIED SAMPLING

Let $S_{\mathbf{R}}$ be partitioned into L mutually exclusive and exhaustive subspaces $S_1, S_2, \ldots, S_L$ called strata. From each stratum a random sample of size n_h is obtained, and the resulting values of the variable Y are averaged as $\bar{y}_h$. From these L values of $\bar{y}_h$ a pooled estimate of $E(Y)$ is obtained from

$$\bar{y}_{st} = \sum_{h=1}^{L} W_h \bar{y}_h \tag{10-14}$$

where W_h, the stratum weight, is the probability that a randomly selected R will be in stratum h.

It can be shown that $E(\bar{Y}_{st})$ is an unbiased estimate of the population mean μ of the random variable Y and, thus, that this procedure may be used as a substitute for simple random sampling. Such a sampling scheme is known as a stratified sampling procedure.

Stratified sampling is a commonly used technique in sample survey work. The general theory is given in many places. Among the most complete presentations are the books by Cochran [4], Dalenius [5], and Hansen, Hurwitz, and Madow [13,14]. The paper by Evans [7] is also very useful.

The use of stratified sampling in Monte Carlo simulations has been discussed by Albert [1], Clark [2], Ehrenfeld, and Ben-Tuvia [6], Kahn [17], and Tocher [25]. However, these discussions have all lacked generality, and no methods of stratification have yet been proposed that may be applied to practical digital computer simulations of queueing systems.

Assuming an infinite population, the variance of $\overline{Y}_{st}$ is given by

$$V(\overline{Y}_{st}) = \sum_{h=1}^{L} W_h^2 \sigma_h^2 / n_h \tag{10-15}$$

where σ_h^2 is the variance of Y over stratum h.

Consider an allocation of the total sample n among the strata so that n_h is proportional to the stratum weight, that is, $n_h = nW_h$. Denoting the estimate of $E(Y)$, obtained by this method of stratification as $\overline{Y}_{prop}$, it can be shown that

$$V(\overline{Y}_{prop}) = (1/n) \sum_{h=1}^{L} W_h \sigma_h^2 = \frac{V(Y)}{n} - \frac{\sigma_{\mu h}^2}{n} \tag{10-16}$$

where

$$\sigma_{\mu h}^2 = \sum_{h=1}^{L} W_h (\mu_h - \mu)^2$$

and μ_h is the expected value of Y over stratum h.

Notice that $V(\overline{Y}_{prop})$ will be less than the variance of Y obtained from random sampling unless $\mu_1 = \mu_2 = \ldots = \mu_L$ and that it can never be greater. Notice also that this equation implies that the stratification should be done so that the μ_h differ widely.

The variance of a stratified sampling estimate can be further reduced if the sample size in each stratum is made proportional to the stratum standard deviation. However, in practical sampling problems, the stratum standard deviations would not be known exactly, and estimates would have to be used. This would tend to increase the variance of $\overline{Y}$ and, in fact, might lead to poorer results than the ones that could be obtained with proportional allocation. For this reason, the discussion below will be limited to proportional allocation.

The general requirements that must be met by any stratified sampling plan are the following.

1. A stratification variable must be specified [5].
2. The probability function of the stratification variable must be known.
3. The number of strata must be specified [5].
4. The stratum limits must be specified in terms of the stratification variable.
5. The total sample size and the size of the sample to be taken from each stratum must be specified [5].
6. A method for randomly obtaining the sample from each stratum must be specified.

In order to *want* to use stratified sampling rather than simple random sampling, either (1) the variance of the parameter estimate obtained from stratified sampling must be less than the variance obtained from random sampling for a given total cost or (2), for a given fixed variance of the parameter estimate, the cost with stratified sampling must be less than the cost with random sampling.

Any random variable defined on the elements of the sample space S_R with known probability function is a possible stratification variable. A good stratification variable is one that is highly correlated with the variable Y, and whose cumulative distribution function $F(X)$ is known and readily solvable for X given a value of $F(X)$.

Consider the stratification variable:

$$X(R) = \sum_{i=1}^{m} \theta_i, \quad \text{where } \theta_i = \begin{cases} 1 \text{ if } R_i \geq C \\ 0 \text{ if } R_i < C \end{cases} \quad (0 < C < 1). \quad (10\text{-}17)$$

As a consequence of the imposed relationship between the random numbers and the congestion caused by the events they generate, it is likely that this stratification variable would be positively correlated with the total customer waiting time and, thus, might be a satisfactory stratification variable.

The probability distribution of this variable is the binomial with $p = (1 - C)$, that is,

$$P(X = k) = \binom{m}{k}(1 - C)^k C^{m-k}, \quad 0 < C < 1 \quad (10\text{-}18)$$
$$k = 0, \ldots, m.$$

The stratum weights and the conditional probability that X equals k, given that X is in stratum h, are easily obtained from this.

The generation of a random value of the stratification variable and the generation of a random number vector having the correct number of observations greater than C are also straightforward.

One potential difficulty with this scheme should be noted. The length of the random number vector must be constant. When the simulation program does not also require this, the vector length for this procedure must be fixed at, or slightly above, the largest value likely to be required. This may be difficult, since little or no information may be available for making a suitable choice. Furthermore, if the vector length is made longer than necessary, the advantage of stratification will be diminished.

System-dependent stratified sampling also can be conceived. The general approach would be to use a multidimensional stratification variable (vector) with each component the stratification variable for one event type or group of event types. These procedures, generally, would not be practical, however, since the number of strata must be kept small, say, less than 10, and the dimensionality of the stratification vector is thus restricted to at most three.

An alternative approach would be to select one or two event types or one or two classes of event types and to use the stratification scheme outlined above with just these events. This approach would tend to be successful if the events selected were highly correlated with Y.

IMPORTANCE SAMPLING

The final alternative to random sampling is obtained by substituting for the process under study a substitute process having the same expected value but smaller variance.

Define the random variable Z on S_R in terms of $Y(\mathbf{r})$, $f(\mathbf{r})$, and $f^*(\mathbf{r})$ by

$$Z(\mathbf{r}) = [Y(\mathbf{r})f(\mathbf{r})]/[f^*(\mathbf{r})] \qquad (10\text{-}19)$$

where $Y(\mathbf{r})$ is a random variable whose mean is to be estimated, $f(\mathbf{r})$ is the joint probability density function of $\mathbf{r}$, and $f^*(\mathbf{r})$ is a joint probability density function which is not zero for any $\mathbf{r}$.

Clearly, the expectation of Z with respect to the joint pdf f^* is equal to the expectation of Y with respect to the joint pdf f. Thus sampling from $f^*(\mathbf{r})$ and estimating $E(Z)$ represents an alternative procedure for estimating $E(Y)$.

The variance of Z is given by

$$V(Z) = \int_0^1 \cdots \int_0^1 \frac{Y^2(\mathbf{r})f^2(\mathbf{r})}{f^{*2}(\mathbf{r})} f^*(\mathbf{r})d\mathbf{r} - [E(Z)]^2. \qquad (10\text{-}20)$$

Notice that if $Y(r) \geq 0$ for all $\mathbf{r}$, this variance would be zero if $f^*(\mathbf{r})$ could be made equal to $Y(\mathbf{r})f(\mathbf{r})/E(Y)$. Thus the possibility of a large variance reduction is present if the pdf f^* is chosen judiciously.

The name, importance sampling, has been given to any such sampling procedure in which sampling is performed from a substitute joint probability function f^* and in which the variable Z is substituted for the variable of interest Y.

The main references to importance sampling are papers by Kahn and Marshall [18], Kahn [15,16,17], Marshall [19,20], Clark [3], and Ehrenfeld and Ben-Tuvia [6]. The application of importance sampling in the simulation of periodic queueing systems is not discussed in any of them, although Clark, and Ehrenfeld and Ben-Tuvia give expository examples of the use of importance sampling in simulating simple queueing systems.

As pointed out above, if f^* were optimally chosen, the variance of Z could be reduced to zero. However, to do this, the function Y and its expectation would have to be known, and sampling would be unnecessary.

Practically, the best that can be expected in the use of importance sampling is that a "good" form for f^* will be specified. This problem of specifying f^* may be considered in two parts: (1) that of specifying a good general form for f^* involving one or more parameters, and (2) that of specifying the parameters.

The requirements for a good parametric form for f^* in the simulation of periodic queueing systems can be deduced from the expression for the optimum f^*, that is, $f^*(\mathbf{r}) = Y(\mathbf{r})f(\mathbf{r})/E(Y)$.

Consider the two random number vectors $\mathbf{r}_0 = (0,0, \ldots, 0)$ and $\mathbf{r}_1 = (1, 1, \ldots, 1)$. For the simulation models of this paper $Y(\mathbf{r}_0) < Y(\mathbf{r}_1)$, and since $f(\mathbf{r}) = 1$ for all $\mathbf{r}$, $f^*(\mathbf{r}_0)$ should be less than $f^*(\mathbf{r}_1)$. Assuming that the random numbers are independently drawn so that

$$f^*(\mathbf{r}) = \prod_{i=1}^{m} f_i^*(r_i),$$

this would imply that $f_i^*(0)$ must be less than $f_i^*(1)$. In a similar manner it can be argued that $f_i^*(r)$ should be a nondecreasing function of r.

Two additional properties which a suitable substitute distribution must possess are: (1) it must be computationally feasible to generate a random value from the distribution, and (2) it must be computationally feasible to calculate $f^*(\mathbf{r})$ once the parameters have been specified.

A substitute probability density function that satisfies all these criteria and that gave the best results of those subjected to testing [22] is

$$f_i^*(r_i; \alpha_i) = \alpha_i^{r_i}[\ln (\alpha_i)]/(\alpha_i - 1) \qquad (10\text{-}21)$$

where α_i is a parameter used in generating the i random number. The experimental results are reported in the next section.

For each simulation model and substitute density function, there is an optimum parameter vector, say $\boldsymbol{\alpha}_0$, such that $V(Z; \boldsymbol{\alpha}_0) \leq V(Z; \boldsymbol{\alpha})$ as $\boldsymbol{\alpha}$ ranges over all values. The main problem in using importance sampling with a parametric form of the substitute distribution is thus in specifying $\boldsymbol{\alpha}$ so that, close to this maximum variance, reduction will be obtained.

In practical problems it would be impossible to provide separate estimates for each of the α's. There must be some aggregation. In the simplest case the same value would be used for all the α's. In other applications it might be desirable to use separate values of α for each type of system event.

The problem of obtaining a good estimate of $\boldsymbol{\alpha}_0$ can be approached in a variety of ways. Among them are the following.

1. Specify $\boldsymbol{\alpha}$ before sampling, using any available relevant information to improve the choice.

Clearly, this presents no theoretical difficulties, and if $V(Z; \boldsymbol{\alpha})$ turns out to be close to $V(Z; \boldsymbol{\alpha}_0)$—either because $\boldsymbol{\alpha}$ was close to $\boldsymbol{\alpha}_0$ or because $V(Z)$ was relatively insensitive to changes in $\boldsymbol{\alpha}$ in the interval in which $\boldsymbol{\alpha}$ and $\boldsymbol{\alpha}_0$ lie—this may be a good strategy to pursue.

The experimental results reported in [22] indicate that $\boldsymbol{\alpha}_0$ may be relatively constant for a particular simulation model, as the values of the system parameters change over relatively narrow ranges. This indicates that it may be possible to fairly accurately estimate $\boldsymbol{\alpha}_0$ from previous simulations of similar systems.

2. Apply double sampling, using the first sample to extimate $\boldsymbol{\alpha}_0$ and the second to estimate $E(Z)$.

Consider the case with $\alpha_1 = \alpha_2 = \ldots = \alpha_m = \alpha$. A necessary condition for obtaining the optimum parameter value is that $[\partial V(Z; \alpha)/\partial \alpha]|\alpha = \alpha_0$ vanish, in other words, that

$$\frac{\partial V(Z; \alpha)}{\partial \alpha} = \int_0^1 \cdots \int_0^1 \frac{Y^2(\mathbf{r})f^2(\mathbf{r}) \left[\dfrac{\partial f^*(\mathbf{r}; \alpha)}{\partial \alpha} \right]}{f^{*2}(\mathbf{r}; \alpha)} \, d\mathbf{r} = 0 \qquad (10\text{-}22)$$

assuming, of course, that $f^*(\mathbf{r}; \alpha)$ is differentiable.

This integral may be treated as defining the mean with respect to the pdf $f(\mathbf{r}; \alpha)$ of the random variable W defined on $S_{\mathbf{R}}$ by

$$W(\mathbf{r}; \alpha) = \frac{Y^2(\mathbf{r})f(\mathbf{r}) \left[\dfrac{-\partial f^*(\mathbf{r}; \alpha)}{\partial \alpha} \right]}{f^{*2}(\mathbf{r}; \alpha)}. \qquad (10\text{-}23)$$

More generally, we can write (10-22) in the following form:

$$\frac{\partial V(Z;\alpha)}{\partial \alpha} = \int_0^1 \cdots \int_0^1 \frac{Y^2(\mathbf{r})f^2(\mathbf{r})\left[\dfrac{-\partial f^*(\mathbf{r};\alpha)}{\partial \alpha}\right]}{f^{*2}(\mathbf{r};\alpha)} \frac{f^*(\mathbf{r};\alpha_1)}{f^*(\mathbf{r};\alpha_1)} \quad \text{(10-22a)}$$

where $f^*(\mathbf{r};\alpha_1)$ is the substitute pdf with a fixed value of the parameter. The integral then may be treated as defining the mean with respect to $f^*(\mathbf{r};\alpha_1)$ of a random variable defined on $S_{\mathbf{R}}$ by

$$W(\mathbf{r};\alpha) = \frac{Y^2(\mathbf{r})f^2(\mathbf{r})\left[\dfrac{-\partial f^*(\mathbf{r};\alpha)}{\partial \alpha}\right]}{f^{*2}(\mathbf{r};\alpha)f^*(\mathbf{r};\alpha_1)}. \quad \text{(10-23a)}$$

Since $Y(\mathbf{r})$ is unknown, (10-22) and (10-22a) cannot be used directly in estimating α_0. But, if sample data were available, α_0 could be estimated by equating the sample estimate of $E(W)$ to zero and solving for α. In a double sampling scheme, the first sample would be used for this purpose.

This procedure introduces a further restriction on the form of $f^*(\mathbf{r};\alpha)$, namely, that the solution of the equation $\bar{w} = 0$ for α must be computationally feasible. Many of the substitute density functions that we have considered have proved to be unsuitable because of this restriction.

The obvious problem with this form of double sampling is that sampling to estimate α_0 expends some of the resources that would otherwise be available for estimating $E(Y)$.

3. Apply double sampling, using the first sample to estimate α_0 but basing the estimate of $E(Y)$ on a combination of the two samples.

Suppose a sample of n_1 observations were obtained from a joint pdf $f^*(\mathbf{r};\alpha_1)$ and a second sample of n_2 observations were obtained from a joint pdf $f^*(\mathbf{r};\alpha_2)$. Then, if $\bar{Z}_1$ and $\bar{Z}_2$, respectively, are the sample means of the variables $Z_1 = Y(\mathbf{r})f(\mathbf{r})/f^*(\mathbf{r};\alpha_1)$ and $Z_2 = Y(\mathbf{r})f(\mathbf{r})/f^*(\mathbf{r};\alpha_2)$,

$$\bar{Z} = w_1\bar{Z}_1 + w_2\bar{Z}_2 \quad \text{(10-24)}$$

is an unbiased estimate of $E(Y)$ provided that w_1 and w_2 are independent of the sampling results and $w_1 + w_2 = 1$. In particular, let $\alpha_2 = \hat{\alpha}_0$ where $\hat{\alpha}_0$ is an estimate of α_0 that is calculated from the first sample, using the method of the second approach to estimating α_0 given above.

The difficulty with such a procedure is in estimating $V(\bar{Z})$ for use in confidence interval statements. This variance is given by

$$V(\bar{Z}) = w_1^2 V(\bar{Z})_1 + w_2^2 V(\bar{Z}_2) + 2w_1w_2 \operatorname{Cov}(\bar{Z}_1, \bar{Z}_2). \quad \text{(10-25)}$$

Estimates of $V(\bar{Z}_1)$ and $V(\bar{Z}_2)$ easily can be obtained from the samples, but an estimate of the covariance cannot be obtained from a single sample.

We conjecture, however, that the covariance will be negligible and can be neglected with little error. Limited experimental results reported in [10-22] seem to support this conjecture.

There remains the question of specifying w_1 and w_2. We suggest that crude, but perhaps satisfactory, first guesses for w_1 and w_2 could be obtained by ignoring the covariance term and optimizing $V(\bar{Z})$ with respect to w_1. The result is

$$w_1 = \frac{cn_1}{n_2 + cn_1} \qquad (10\text{-}26)$$

where n_1 and n_2, respectively, are the first and second sample sizes and c is an estimate of the ratio of $V(Z_2)/V(Z_1)$.

These three general approaches to estimating α_0 by no means exhaust the possibilities. In particular, we have not considered sequential procedures in which the estimate of α_0 is updated as each new simulation observation is calculated. These procedures, however, would compound the difficulties of obtaining unbiased estimates of $E(Y)$ and/or of estimating the variance of $\bar{Z}$.

Importance sampling with a single alpha is completely general purpose and system independent. With two or more alphas the procedure becomes system dependent.

A special form of system dependency is obtained by using substitute density functions for generating only a portion of the simulated event types. In this procedure the event types would be partitioned into two sets, with one containing all types in which the average event values are highly correlated with Y. Substitute density functions then would be used for generating the events of this set but not for the events of the other set. This procedure would yield a smaller variance reduction than could be obtained by using a separate substitute density function with each event type, but it also would be significantly less costly.

EXPERIMENTAL RESULTS

The value of any alternative sampling procedure in the simulation of periodic queueing systems can only be determined from many actual applications. As a start toward this evaluation, in this section we report on some experimental applications of the techniques described above in the simulation of six variations of a simple single-server system and in the simulation of a complex system that is more of the type likely to be encountered in practice.

The six variations of the single-server system, operating with a first-come first-served queue discipline, were obtained by varying the utilization factor ρ, the simulation period, and the forms of the service-time and interarrival-time distributions. The results obtained with the system-independent versions of the techniques described above are summarized in Table 10-1.

These results clearly show that all four techniques are capable of significantly decreasing variability in the simulations of simple queueing systems. They also indicate that the proposed method of stratified sampling is inferior to the other three methods and that the regression sampling method used is probably inferior to antithetic-variate sampling and importance sampling. In comparing antithetic-variate sampling to importance sampling in these applications, it must be noted that the former is the easiest to apply.

The second simulation model used in evaluating the candidate sampling techniques was a model of a hypothetical, but realistic, truck dock system. This model was motivated by the system studied by Schiller and Lavin [24]. The model is intended to represent the operation of a truck loading and unloading facility at a plant or warehouse operating on a one 8-hour shift per day basis and, we believe, is more or less typical of the type of periodic queueing problems to which Monte Carlo methods might be applied.

This model differs from the single-server model in the following important respects: (1) it consists of several servers in parallel; (2) each customer belongs to one of four distinct classes and each class has its own service time distribution; (3) service-time distributions are discrete; (4) the interarrival-time distribution varies over the simulation period reflecting start-up, shut-down, and "lunch-time" conditions; (5) service channels are closed during a "lunch period"; and (6) the simulation period is expressed in terms of a fixed time period—one simulated day—instead of in terms of a fixed number of customers.

The last difference is of special significance. It makes the number of random numbers used in obtaining a simulated observation a random variable rather than a constant and, as noted earlier, this poses certain additional difficulties in applying some of the sampling techniques.

Additional characteristics of the system are exponentially distributed service times, single queue, and first-come first-served queue discipline.

For this system we use as the variable of interest Y a cost function incorporating the total waiting time of all customers during the simulation period plus an overtime cost incurred by operating the facility beyond the end of the "shift" in order to complete service on all trucks that have arrived by an earlier deadline time.

Two versions of this model were used in the experiments: one with eight service channels and one with nine.

Table 10-1   Comparison of Variance Reductions Obtained with System Independent Methods Applied to the Single-Server Systems[a]

System Parameters				Regression Sampling[b] (Percent)	Antithetic-Variate Sampling[c] (Percent)	Stratified Sampling[d] (Percent)	Importance Sampling[e] (Percent)
ρ	Cust./Obs.	Arrival Dist.	Service Dist.				
0.8	50	Exp.	Exp.	36	36	26	44
0.8	200	Exp.	Exp.	30	49	18	54
0.6	50	Exp.	Exp.	23	43	36	47
1.0	50	Exp.	Exp.	47	46	15	43
0.8	50	Erlang $k=6$	Erlang $k=2$	27	0	18	33
0.8	50	Erlang $k=2$	Erlang $k=6$	22	72	26	53

[a] Sample sizes for these experiments were either 175 or 200 simulated observations except with regression sampling where 86 or 100 observations were used.

[b] With the auxiliary variable $x = b_1 + b_2 \Sigma R_i + b_3 (\Sigma R_i)^2$.

[c] Antithetic variates were obtained, using the complements of the random number vectors used in generating the random sampling estimates.

[d] With the stratification variable given by (10-17) with $C = 1/2$. For each system, samples were obtained for various numbers of strata between two and ten. The results reported are the best of these and were obtained with between two and six strata.

[e] With substitute density function $f^*(r) = \ln(\alpha) \alpha^r / (\alpha - 1)$.

Preliminary results with system-independent methods (Table 10-2) failed to show sampling efficiencies with either stratified sampling or importance sampling. We thus discarded these two methods.

Table 10-2   Comparisons of Variance Reductions Obtained with System-Independent Methods Applied to the Truck Dock System[a]

Number of Channels	Regression Sampling[b] (Percent)	Antithetic-Variate Sampling[c] (Percent)	Stratified Sampling[d]	Importance Sampling[e]
8	9	18	Increase	Increase
9	10	27	Increase	Increase

[a] Sample sizes were 180 with channels and 360 with 9 channels, except with regression sampling which was applied to the antithetic-variate sampling results also, thus, doubling the sample size.
[b] With the auxiliary variable $x = b_1 + b_2 \Sigma R_j + b_3 \Sigma R_j{}^2$.
[c] Antithetic variates were obtained by using the complements of the random number vectors used in generating the random sampling estimates.
[d] With the stratification variable given by (10-17) with $C = \frac{1}{2}$.
[e] With the substitute density function $f^*(\alpha) = \ln(\alpha)\alpha^r/(\alpha - 1)$.

A final series of experiments was run using both system-independent and system-dependent versions of regression sampling and antithetic-variate sampling plus system-dependent versions of importance sampling. The results are detailed in Table 10-3.

The auxiliary variables used in the four versions of regression sampling were as follows:

Method I. $X(R) = b_1 + b_2 \bar{R}_1 + b_3 \bar{R}_1{}^2$.
Method II. $X(R) = b_1 + b_2 \bar{R}_1$.
Method III. $X(R) = b_1 + b_2 \bar{A}_1$.
Method IV. $X(R) = b_1 + b_2 \bar{R}_1 + b_3 \bar{R}_2 + b_4 \bar{R}_3 + b_5 \bar{R}_4$.

Where $\bar{R}_1$, $\bar{R}_2$, $\bar{R}_3$, and $\bar{R}_4$ are the means of all random numbers used in generating, respectively, interarrival times, truck type, basic service times, and service-time additions based on the use being made of the truck; and $\bar{A}_1$ is the mean of all interarrival times.

Two versions of antithetic-variate sampling were used. In the version labeled "full" each antithetic observation was obtained by employing the complement of the random number vector that is used in generating the corresponding random sample. In the version labeled "partial" the comple-

Table 10-3　Average Variances, Variance Reductions Versus Random Sampling, Normalized Variance Reductions[1] and Computer Running Times (Minutes) Obtained with System-Dependent Methods Applied to the Truck-Dock System

Number of service channels	Sample size	Random sampling	Regression sampling				Antithetic-variate sampling		Importance sampling	
			Method I	Method II	Method III	Method IV	Full	Partial	One Parameter	Four Parameters
8	50	3087 -- -- .61	2585 16% 5% .69	2376 23% 14% .68	2542 18% 8% .68	2575 17% 2% .71	822 73% 73% .61	950 69% 67% .65	809 74% 73% .63	1296 58% 34% .96
	100	2496 -- -- 1.10	1606 36% 27% 1.24	1774 29% 20% 1.23	1948 22% 12% 1.23	1768 29% 18% 1.27	1034 59% 56% 1.16	1096 56% 50% 1.25	814 67% 63% 1.23	870 65% 37% 1.97
	200	2134 -- -- 2.17	1386 35% 27% 2.44	1527 28% 20% 2.43	1655 22% 13% 2.43	1513 29% 19% 2.48	975 54% 51% 2.31	986 54% 47% 2.48	718 66% 64% 2.35	749 65% 42% 3.63
9	50	712 -- -- .70	378 47% 41% .78	519 27% 14% .88	553 22% 14% .78	610 14% 1% .81	341 53% 61% .57	328 54% 60% .61	201 72% 76% .60	288 60% 47% .91
	100	813 -- -- 1.07	622 23% 13% 1.22	671 17% 7% 1.21	735 10% 2% 1.21	664 18% 5% 1.25	296 64% 61% 1.14	294 64% 59% 1.23	238 71% 68% 1.18	199 76% 61% 1.69
	200	712 -- -- 2.15	504 29% 20% 2.42	546 23% 14% 2.41	578 19% 9% 2.41	552 22% 11% 2.46	364 49% 45% 2.31	345 52% 43% 2.54	280 61% 57% 2.34	269 62% 36% 3.67

[1] Normalized variance reductions are estimated variance reductions corrected for the computing time differences. Specifically, normalized variance reduction = {1 − [(average variance of alternative sampling procedure) (computer running time of alternative sampling procedure)]/[(average variance of random sample)) (computer running time of random sample)]} 100 percent.

ments of the random numbers used in generating interarrival times in the random sample were utilized in generating interarrival times in the antithetic observation, but new random numbers were generated for the other three events.

The one-parameter version of importance sampling used a substitute pdf only for generating interarrival times. Other simulated events were generated, using uniformly distributed random numbers. The four-parameter version used a separate substitute pdf in generating each of the four types of system events. In each case, the sample was split into halves; random sampling was used for the first half; the parameter estimate(s) for the substitute pdf was calculated, and importance sampling was employed for the second half of the sample. The random and importance sample were then combined into a single estimate, using (10-24) and (10-26) with $c = .75$.

All variances shown are the average of ten samples. As indicated, each sample contained either 50, 100, or 200 observations, or simulated days, of system operation. Total computer-running times are shown. They were obtained from the internal clock on the CDC 3600.

CONCLUSIONS

The experimental results reported in Tables 10-1, 10-2, and 10-3 support the following tentative conclusions regarding the merits of the sampling techniques described in this paper, when they are applied in the simulation of periodic queueing systems.

1. Alternatives to random sampling exist that are generally applicable and significantly more efficient.

2. System-dependent methods are more efficient than system-independent methods.

3. System-dependent antithetic-variate sampling and system-dependent importance sampling are more efficient than correlated sampling.

4. Multi-parameter importance sampling is less efficient than single-parameter importance sampling. This is primarily because of the larger computing time needed for calculating parameter estimates.

BIBLIOGRAPHY

1. Albert, G. E. "A General Theory of Stochastic Estimates of the Neumann Series for the Solutions of Certain Fredholm Integral Equations and Related Series," *Symposium on Monte Carlo Methods*. Edited by H. A. Meyer. New York: John Wiley & Sons, Inc., 1956.

2. Clark, C. E. "The Utility of Statistics of Random Numbers," *Operations Research*, **VIII** (1960), 185-195.
3. Clark, C. E. "Importance Sampling in Monte Carlo Analyses," *Operations Research*, **IX** (1961), 603-620.
4. Cochran, W. G. *Sampling Techniques.* Second edition New York: John Wiley & Sons, Inc., 1963.
5. Dalenius, T. *Sampling in Sweden—Contributions to the Methods and Theories of Sample Survey Practice.* Stockholm: Almqvist and Wiksell, 1957.
6. Ehrenfeld, S., and Ben-Tuvia, S. "The Efficiency of Statistical Simulation Procedures," *Technometrics*, **IV** (1962), 257-275.
7. Evans, W. D. "On Stratification and Optimal Allocation," *Journal of the American Statistical Association*, **XLVI** (1951), 95-104.
8. Halton, J. H., and Handscomb, D. C. "A Method for Increasing the Efficiency of Monte Carlo Integration," *Journal of the Association for Computing Machinery*, **IV** (1957), 329-340.
9. Hammersley, J. M., and Handscomb, D. C. *Monte Carlo Methods.* New York: John Wiley & Sons, Inc., 1964.
10. Hammersley, J. M. and Mauldon, J. G. "General Principles of Antithetic Variates," *Proceedings, Cambridge Philosophical Society*, **LII** (1956), 476-481.
11. Hammersley, J. M., and Morton, K. W. "A New Monte Carlo Technique: Antithetic Variates," *Proceedings, Cambridge Philosophical Society*, **LII** (1956), 449-475.
12. Handscomb, D. C. "Proof of the Antithetic Variates Theorem for $n > 2$," *Proceedings, Cambridge Philosophical Society*, **LIV** (1958), 300-301.
13. Hansen, M. H., Hurwitz, W. N., and Madow, W. G. *Sample Survey Methods and Theory,* Vol. I: Methods and Applications. New York: John Wiley & Sons, Inc., 1953.
14. Hansen, M. H. *et al. Sample Survey Methods and Theory,* Vol. II: Theory. New York: John Wiley & Sons, Inc., 1953.
15. Kahn, H. "Modification of the Monte Carlo Method," *Scientific Computation Seminar Proceedings*, IBM Applied Science Department, (1949), 20-27.
16. Kahn, H. "Use of Different Monte Carlo Sampling Techniques," *Symposium on Monte Carlo Methods.* Edited by H. A. Meyer. New York: John Wiley & Sons, Inc., 1956.
17. Kahn, H. *Applications of Monte Carlo.* The RAND Corporation, RM-1237-AEC, 1956.
18. Kahn, H., and Marshall, A. "Methods of Reducing Sampling Size in Monte Carlo Computations," *Journal of the Operations Research Society of America*, **I** (1953), 263-278.
19. Marshall, A. W. "The Use of Multi-Stage Sampling Schemes in Monte Carlo Computations," *Symposium on Monte Carlo Methods.* Edited by H. A. Meyer. New York: John Wiley & Sons, Inc., 1956.
20. Marshall, A. W. *Experimentation by Simulation and Monte Carlo.* The RAND Corporation, Paper P-1174, 1958.

21. Morton, K. W. "A Generalization of the Antithetic Variate Method for Evaluating Integrals," *Journal of Mathematics and Physics*, **XXXVI** (1957), 289-293.

22. Moy, W. A. "Sampling Techniques for Increasing the Efficiency of Simulations of Queueing Systems." Unpublished Ph.D. dissertation, Northwestern University, Evanston, Ill., 1965.

23. Page, E. S. "On Monte Carlo Methods in Congestion Problems: II, Simulation of Queueing Systems," *Operations Research*, **XIII** (1965), 300-305.

24. Schiller, D. H. and Lavin, M. M. "The Determination of Requirements for Warehouse Dock Facilities," *Operations Research*, **IV** (1956), 231-243.

25. Tocher, K. D. *The Art of Simulation*. Princeton, N. J.: D. Van Nostrand Co., Inc., 1963.

26. Tukey, J. W. "Antithesis or Regression," *Proceedings, Cambridge Philosophical Society*, **LIII** (1957), 923-924.

Chapter 11 | Stopping Rules

With computer simulation we can conduct experiments with a given model either at a *particular point in time*, or we can conduct experiments over *extended periods of time*. In the former case, the simulation is said to be a *static* or *cross-section* simulation in which sampling takes place across the ensemble rather than over time. In the latter case, the simulation is said to be a *dynamic* or *time-series* simulation in which sampling takes place over time. A static simulation is achieved by replicating a given simulation run, that is, by changing the stream of pseudorandom numbers used to generate the stochastic variates of the model. A dynamic simulation results when we simply extend the length of a given simulation run over time without changing any of the conditions under which the simulation is being run. With a dynamic simulation we use only one long sequence of pseudorandom numbers instead of N different sequences of pseudorandom numbers.

We shall let N denote the number of *replications* of a static experiment and let T denote the *number of observations* or *periods of time* in a dynamic experiment. Whether we are conducting a static experiment or a dynamic experiment, a question arises as to how long the *sample record* must be in order to achieve a given level of statistical precision. A rule that determines the length of the sample record is called a *stopping rule*.

In the large majority of current simulations, the required sample record length is guessed at by using some rule such as "stop sampling when the parameter to be estimated does not change in the second decimal place when 1000 more samples are taken." The analyst must realize that makeshift rules such as this are dangerous, since he may be dealing with a parameter whose sample values converge to a steady state solution very slowly. Indeed, his estimate may be several hundred percent in error. Therefore it is necessary that adequate stopping rules be used in all simulations [15, p. 16].

The derivation of an appropriate stopping rule depends on whether or not the sample observations are correlated. In the case of static simulations we usually assume that the sample observations are independent. This independence can be guaranteed by the judicious choice of a pseudorandom number generator. However, the sample observations generated by a dynamic simulation experiment are likely to be highly autocorrelated.

In this chapter, we survey a number of different types of stopping rules that presently are available. First, we consider stopping rules that are appropriate with static simulations which are characterized by independent observations. Next, we treat stopping rules for dynamic simulations in which the sample observations are autocorrelated. In neither case is our objective to include an exhaustive list of stopping rules but, instead, to indicate the different types of stopping rules that are available.

INDEPENDENT OBSERVATIONS

First, we consider four fixed sample-size stopping rules in which the sample size is determined before the experiment is conducted. Each of these stopping rules assumes that the variance is *known*. Next, we describe several sequential sampling stopping rules in which the variance is assumed to be unknown.

Fixed-Sample-Size Rules

Estimation of the Population Mean

Suppose that we have a sample of N independent and identically distributed random variables $X_1, X_2, \ldots, X_N$ with *unknown mean* μ and *known variance* σ^2. Assume that we want to estimate the population mean μ and that we compute the unbiased estimator $\overline{X}$,

$$\overline{X} = \frac{1}{N} \sum_{i=i}^{N} X_i. \qquad (11\text{-}1)$$

We would like to find a stopping rule such that the probability of the true mean μ falling within the confidence interval

$$\overline{X} \pm Z_{\alpha/2}\sigma/\sqrt{N} \qquad (11\text{-}2)$$

is $(1 - \alpha)$ percent where σ is the standard deviation of X and $Z_{\alpha/2}$ is the percentile of the normal distribution that leaves $\alpha/2$ percent probability in each tail. If we specify the length of the confidence interval as

$$d = Z_{\alpha/2}\sigma/\sqrt{N} \qquad (11\text{-}3)$$

and if we know σ and can specify α, then we should stop sampling when

$$N = Z^2_{\alpha/2}\sigma^2/d^2. \tag{11-4}$$

Although the X_i's are not assumed to be normally distributed, the Central Limit Theorem permits us to assume that the distribution of $\overline{X}$ will be approximately normal, since the X_i's are independent and identically distributed.

Testing a Hypothesis about the Mean

If we want to test the null hypothesis that the population mean of a sequence of random variables is equal to μ_0 against the alternative hypothesis that $\mu \neq \mu_0$, then the optimal sample size depends on the following.

1. How large a difference between the true population mean and the hypothesized value do you wish to detect?
2. How much variability is present in the population?
3. What size risks are you willing to take?

Power function charts [34] for the specification of sample size for the test of hypotheses about population means are available for determining N, the number of replications of a static simulation experiment for (1) a given population variance σ^2, (2) a given level of significance α, and (3) a given power P to detect (4), a specified difference $\mu - \mu_0$ between the true population mean and the hypothesized value.

F-Test

In Chapter 7, we described the procedure for computing the stopping value N for a conventional F-test for testing the null hypothesis that the population means of k different populations are equal. Recall that the F-test assumes normality, independence, and a common variance.

Multiple Ranking Procedures

Suppose that we want to choose as the "best" population (among k populations) the population that has the largest population mean. We want to be assured with probability P^* that we, indeed, have selected the correct population. If the best population differs only slightly from the next best population, then (because of random error) extremely large samples are required to detect such a small difference. However, generally, our concern over not detecting the best population, when the difference between the best and the next best population is small, will not be as great as it would be if this difference were large. Therefore, we want to take that number of observations N from each population so that the probability of a correct selection (CS) is at least P*, given that the difference between the best and next best population is at least δ^*. This may be stated formally as

$$\Pr(\text{CS} \mid \delta \geq \delta^*) \geq \text{P*} \tag{11-5}$$

where δ^* and P* are specified by the decision maker. Bechhofer [4] has developed a procedure for determining a single population and for guaranteeing with probability P* that the selected population is "best," provided that the indifference quantity δ^* is specified. Bechhofer's procedure [4] assumes *normality* and a *common known variance* σ^2 for all k populations. In Chapter 7, we described an application of Bechhofer, Dunnett, and Sobel's [6] two-stage multiple ranking procedure. This procedure assumes *normality, unknown variances,* and *known variance ratios.* The paper by Kleijnen and Naylor [22] contains a comprehensive survey and a critical evaluation of multiple ranking procedures.

Sequential Sampling Rules

The rationale for the use of sequential sampling procedures with computer simulation experiments is set forth in the introduction to Chapter 8 and need not be repeated in this chapter. Chapter 8 demonstrates rather conclusively that it is possible to achieve substantial reductions in computer time by using sequential sampling stopping rules instead of fixed-sample-size rules.

Estimation of the Population Mean

Assume that we have a sample of independent and indentically distributed random variables $X_1, X_2, \ldots, X_n$ with *unknown mean* μ and unknown variance σ^2. We want to estimate the mean, and we compute

$$\overline{X} = \frac{1}{n} \sum_{i=i}^{n} X_i \tag{11-6}$$

and

$$s^2 = \frac{1}{n-1} \sum_{i=i}^{n} (X_i - \overline{X})^2 \tag{11-7}$$

which are the sample mean and variance. The problem is to find a stopping rule such that the probability of the true mean μ falling within the confidence interval

$$\overline{X} \pm Z_{\alpha/2} s / \sqrt{n} \tag{11-8}$$

is $(1 - \alpha)$ percent where $Z_{\alpha/2}$ is the percentile of the normal distribution which leaves $\alpha/2$ percent probability in each tail. If we specify the length of the confidence interval as

$$d = Z_{\alpha/2}s/\sqrt{n} \qquad (11\text{-}9)$$

then we should observe the sequence X_i, X_2, ... and stop sampling when

$$n = N = Z^2_{\alpha/2}s^2/d^2. \qquad (11\text{-}10)$$

This procedure is based on [15] and [16]. Anscombe [2] has proposed an alternative procedure that does not require the computation of the sample variance after each step. However, the expected sample size for Anscombe's method is more than four times as great as the expected sample size for the method that we have described. Therefore, it is not clear that either method is superior.

Like the fixed sample-size stopping rule for estimating population means, this method is also asymptotic and only holds true for large samples $(N \geq 50)$. Both the fixed-sample-size method and the sequential methods depend on the fact that

$$\sum_{i=i}^{n} X_i$$

has an approximately normal distribution with mean $n\mu$ and variance $n\sigma^2$ for large n, if the X_i are independent and identically distributed random variables with mean μ and variance σ^2 [15].

Testing a Hypothesis about the Mean

Let X_i, X_2, ... be a sequence of independent random variables with a common *normal* distribution with *unknown mean* μ and *unknown variance* σ^2. Paulson [27] has developed a sequential stopping rule for testing the null hypothesis H_0 that $\mu \leq \mu_0$ against the alternative hypothesis H_1 that $\mu > \mu_0$. This procedure is described in Chapter 8 and is applied to a simulation of a multi-item inventory system.

Comparing the Means of k Experimental Categories with a Control

In Chapter 8 we also describe a sequential stopping rule developed by Paulson [27] for comparing the means of k experimental categories with a control. This procedure also assumes *normality* and a common *unknown* variance.

A Multiple Ranking Procedure

Bechhofer and Blumenthal's [5] sequential sampling procedure for ranking the means of *normal* populations with *common unknown variance* is presented in Chapter 8, as well as the results of an example simulation experiment that uses the procedure.

AUTOCORRELATED OBSERVATIONS

Data generated by dynamic simulation experiments usually are highly autocorrelated, for example, national income generated by the Samuelson-Hicks model in period t is likely to be highly correlated with national income in period t-k. It is well known that when autocorrelation is present in sample observations that the use of classical sample-size rules (which assume the absence of autocorrelation) leads to the danger of underestimating the sample variances (which are unduly large) and, consequently, to taking too few observations to achieve the desired statistical precision. Several methods are available for treating this problem.

1. Simply ignore autocorrelation and use the stopping rules, previously described, that assume *independent* observations and, thereby, incur the above-mentioned statistical problems.

2. Divide the sample record length into intervals that are longer than the interval of major autocorrelation and work with the observations on these supposedly independent intervals. This approach suffers from the fact that, "the choices of sample record length and sampling interval seem to have neither enough prior nor posterior justification in most cases to make this choice much more than arbitrary" [14].

3. Replicate the simulation experiment and compute sample means and variances across the ensemble rather than over time. This method may lead to excessive compute running time and may fail to yield the type of information that is desired about the particular time series.

4. Use a method proposed by Gilman [15] that does take into consideration the presence of autocorrelation and requires that sampling stop when the variance of the sample mean falls below a predetermined level. When the sample observations are autocorrelated, the variance of the sample mean is

$$\sigma_{\bar{x}}^2 = (1/n^2) \text{ Var} \left(\sum_{i=1}^{n} X_i \right)$$

$$= (\sigma^2/n) + (2\sigma^2/n) \sum_{k=1}^{n-1} (1 - k/n) \rho(k) \qquad (11\text{-}11)$$

where $\rho(k)$ is the autocorrelation coefficient for terms of lag k. The stopping rule is: Stop sampling when

$$\sigma_{\bar{x}}^2 \leq M, \qquad (11\text{-}12)$$

where M is some constant. Unless the analyst has a great deal of knowledge about the system being simulated, the choice of M is completely arbitrary.

5. Employ a sampling theory, such as spectral analysis, in which the probabilities of component outcomes in a time series depend on previous outcomes in the series.

With spectral analysis the problems associated with methods (1) and (2) are successfully avoided without (3) replicating the experiment or (4) having to determine an arbitrary constant M. Fishman [12] has used spectral analysis to calculate what he calls the *equivalent independent observations* of a time series.

The variance of the sample mean computed from a set of independent observations is inversely proportional to the number of observations. This is not true for autocorrelated data. For sufficiently long sample records, however, one may show that the variance of the sample mean for autocorrelated data is inversely proportional to a fraction of the number of observations. This fractional factor depends on the autocorrelation properties of the process. By analogy with the independent case, it seems natural to regard this fraction of the number of observations as the number of *equivalent independent observations*.

To develop this analogy, we introduce the concept of the *correlation time* of a process. If a process is observed for a time interval equal to n correlation times, then one may show that, from the point of view of the variance of the sample mean, this time series is equivalent to collecting $n/2$ independent observations. Using the correlation time together with the observation interval, we can define the number of *equivalent independent observations* contained in an autocorrelated time series [12].

Further elaborating on the concept of equivalent independent observations, Fishman [12] states that, "If we can run the experiment long enough to use the large sample variance, then we can determine an equivalence between our results and those that would have been derived if we were analyzing independent observations." We made use of the concept of equivalent independent observations in Chapter 9 when we computed the equivalent degrees of freedom by using a procedure that was developed by Blackman and Tukey [7] to perform an analysis of variance with autocorrelated data.

BIBLIOGRAPHY

1. Anscombe, F. J. "Large Sample Theory of Sequential Estimation," *Proceedings of the Cambridge Philosophic Society*, **XLVIII** (1952), 600-607.
2. Anscombe, F. J. "Sequential Estimation," *Journal of the Royal Statistical Society, Series B*, **XV** (1953), 1-29.
3. Baker, A. C. "Properties of Some Tests in Sequential Analysis," *Biometrika*, **XXXVII** (1950), 334-346.
4. Bechhofer, R. E. "A Single Sample Multiple Procedure for Ranking Means of Normal Populations with Known Variances," *Annals of Mathematical Statistics*, **XXV** (1954), 16-39.
5. Bechhofer, R. E., and Blumenthal, Saul. "A Sequential Multiple-Decision

Procedure for Selecting the Best One of Several Normal Populations with a Common Unknown Variance, II: Monte Carlo Sampling Results and New Computing Formulae," *Biometrics*, **XVIII** (March 1962), 52-67.

6. Bechhofer, Robert E., Dunnett, C. W., and Sobel, M. "A Two-Sample Multiple Decision Procedure for Ranking Means of Normal Populations with a Common Unknown Variance," *Biometrika*, **XLI** (1954), 170-176.

7. Blackman, R. B., and Tukey, J. W. *The Measurement of Power Spectra*. New York: Dover Publications, Inc., 1958.

8. Brenner, M. E. "Selective Sampling—A Technique for Reducing Sample Size in Simulation of Decision-Making Problems," *Journal of Industrial Engineering*, **XIV** (November-December 1963), 291-296.

9. Brenner, Michael E. "A Relation Between Decision Making Penalty and Simulation Sample Size for Inventory Systems," *Operations Research*, **XIII** (May-June 1965), 433-443.

10. Conway, R. W. "Some Tactical Problems in Digital Simulation," *Management Science*, **X** (October 1963), 47-61.

11. Dubner, Harvey, and McCarthy, Edward, "Choice of Sample Size When Simulating Queueing Systems." Unpublished paper, 1969.

12. Fishman, George S. "Problems in the Statistical Analysis of Simulation Experiments; The Comparison of Means and the Length of Sample Records," *Communications of the ACM*, **X** (February 1967), 94-99.

13. Fishman, George S. "The Allocation of Computer Time in Comparing Simulation Experiments," *Operations Research*, **XVI** (March-April 1968).

14. Fishman, George S., and Kiviat, Philip J. "The Analysis of Simulation-Generated Time Series," *Management Science*, **XIII** (March 1967), 525-557.

15. Gilman, Michael J. "A Brief Survey of Stopping Rules in Monte Carlo Simulations," *Digest of the Second Conference on Applications of Simulation*, (December 2-4, 1968).

16. Gleser, L. J., Robbins, H., and Starr, N. "Some Asymptotic Properties of Fixed Width Sequential Confidence Intervals for the Mean of a Normal Population with Unknown Variance," Department of Mathematics, Columbia University Report, April 24, 1964.

17. Hammersley, J. M., and Handscomb, D. C. *Monte Carlo Methods*. New York: John Wiley & Sons, 1964.

18. Harling, John, "Simulation Techniques in Operations Research—A Review," *Operations Research*, **VI** (1958), 307-319.

19. Hauser, Norbert et al. "Design Problems in a Process Control Simulator," *Journal of Industrial Engineering*, **XVII** (February 1966), 79-86.

20. Hurtubise, Rolland A. "Sample Sizes and Confidence Intervals Associated with a Monte Carlo Simulation Model Possessing a Multinomial Output," *Simulation*, **X** (February 1969), 71-77.

21. Kabak, W. I. "Stopping Rules for Queueing Simulations," *Operations Research*, (March-April 1968).

22. Kleijnen, Jack P., and Naylor, Thomas H. "The Use of Multiple Ranking

Procedures to Analyze Business and Economic Systems," *Proceedings of the American Statistical Association* (August) 1969.

23. Ling, Timothy Y. "A Statistical Concept of Statics and Dynamics," *The Design of Computer Simulation Experiments*, Thomas H. Naylor (ed). Durham, N. C.: Duke University Press, 1969.

24. Naylor, Thomas H. (ed). *The Design of Computer Simulation Experiments*. Durham, N. C.: Duke University Press, 1969.

25. Naylor, Thomas H., Wertz, Kenneth, and Wonnacott, Thomas. "Methods for Analyzing Data from Computer Simulation Experiments," *Communications of the ACM*, **X** (November 1967), 703-710.

26. Naylor, Thomas H., Wertz, Kenneth, and Wonnacott, Thomas. "Spectral Analysis of Data Generated by Simulation Experiments with Econometric Models," *Econometrica*, **XXXVII** (April 1969), 333-352.

27. Paulson, Edward. "Sequential Estimation and Closed Sequential Decision Procedures," *Annals of Mathematical Statistics*, **XXXV** (September 1964), 1048-1058.

28. Ray, W. D. "Sequential Confidence Intervals for the Mean of a Normal Population with Unknown Variance," *Journal of the Royal Statistical Society, Series B*, **XIX** (1957), 133-43.

29. Sasser, W. Earl, Burdick, Donald S., Graham, Daniel A., and Naylor, Thomas H. "A Sequential Sampling Simulation Study of an Inventory Model," *Communications of the ACM*, XIII (May, 1970), 287-296.

30. Sen, K. P. "Some Non-Parametric Tests for *m*-Dependent Time Series," *Journal of the American Statistical Association*, LX (1965), 134-147.

31. Shreider, Y. A. *The Monte Carlo Method*. New York: Pergamon Press, 1965.

32. Tocher, K. D. *The Art of Simulation*. Princeton, N. J.: D. Van Nostrand Co., 1963.

33. Wetherill, G. B. *Sequential Methods in Statistics*. New York: John Wiley & Sons, 1966.

34. Winer, B. J. *Statistical Principles in Experimental Design*. New York: McGraw-Hill Book Co., 1962.

Chapter 12 | Simulation Versus Analytical Solutions: The Case of Econometric Models[1]

E. PHILIP HOWREY AND H. H. KELEJIAN

INTRODUCTION

In Chapter 1, we defined simulation as a numerical technique for conducting experiments with certain types of mathematical models, describing the behavior of a complex system on a digital computer. We further stated that simulation was a technique of "last resort" and should be used only when analytical techniques are not available for obtaining solutions to a given model. Unfortunately, in many cases, it is not obvious whether simulation or an analytical solution would be more appropriate for a particular model.

For example, take the case of, say a fourth-order nonlinear, stochastic difference equation model. On examining the model initially, an economist may conclude that the model may not have a known analytical solution. However, it may very well be that if the economist made a thorough search of the literature in mathematics or consulted with a mathematician, it might be possible to find an analytical solution to the model. A question arises as to whether it would be worth the time and effort to find an analytical solution if such a solution exists in the first place. It is quite possible

[1] This chapter is based on a paper that was presented at a symposium on "The Design of Computer Simulation Experiments," sponsored by the TIMS College on Simulation and Gaming at Duke University on October 14-16, 1968. The paper first appeared in *The Design of Computer Simulation Experiments*, edited by Thomas H. Naylor and published by the Duke University Press, Durham, North Carolina, 1969. The introductory section and the concluding section of this chapter were written by Thomas H. Naylor.

that a numerical solution or simulation of the model might provide the analyst with all of the information that he needs regarding the behavior of the particular system.

Throughout this book we have used numerous example models to illustrate simulation. Some of these models have known analytical solutions. For example, several of the queueing models and inventory models described in Chapter 3 have analytical solutions. In Chapter 7, we compared the output data generated by a simulation experiment with a multistage queueing model with the results obtained by an analytical solution as a means of validating the simulation experiment. In addition, the linear difference equation models including the cobweb models, the Samuelson-Hicks model, and the Klein six-equation model all have analytical solutions. Again, for expository purposes, it was convenient to use difference equation models with known analytical solutions to illustrate specific simulation techniques, for we then were able to check the results of our simulations.

In general, the whole question of when to use simulation rather than to search for an analytical solution is an open question—a question that needs a great deal more research. It is not likely that in the near future any general guidelines will be forthcoming to provide the practitioner with easy answers to this question. At best, we can only hope that useful guidelines will be forthcoming for particular classes of models, for example, inventory models, queueing models, or econometric models.

Howrey and Kelejian have taken an intial step in this direction for a particular class of models—*econometric models*. They have argued that, "the role of simulation as a tool of analysis of econometric models should be reconsidered." Four major points are made by Howrey and Kelejian:

1. Once a *linear* econometric model has been estimated and tested in terms of known distribution theory concerning parameter estimates, simulation experiments that are undertaken to investigate the model as an interrelated system yield *no additional information* about the validity of the model.

2. Although some of the dynamic properties of linear models can be inferred from simulation results, an analytical technique based on the model itself is available for this purpose.

3. The application of nonstochastic simulation procedures to econometric models that contain nonlinearities in the endogenous variables yields results that are not consistent with the properties of the reduced form of the model.

4. The results derived from the stochastic simulation of nonlinear systems are consistent with the corresponding reduced-form equations.

SIMULATION OF LINEAR MODELS

Consider the dynamic structural model,

$$y_t\Gamma = x_tB_1 + y_{t-1}B_2 + u_t, \qquad t = \ldots, -1, 0, 1, \ldots, \qquad (12\text{-}1)$$

where y_t is a $1 \times K$ vector of observations at time t on the endogenous variables; Γ is a $K \times K$ matrix of parameters; x_t is a $1 \times G$ vector of observations at time t on the exogenous variables; B_1 is a $G \times K$ matrix of parameters; y_{t-1} is the vector of lagged values of y_t; B_2 is a $K \times K$ matrix of parameters; u_t is a $1 \times K$ vector of disturbance terms at time t. The results, given subsequently, do not depend on the simple lag structure of model (12-1), since a higher-order system can be reduced to a first-order system with the introduction of appropriately defined artificial variables (see Baumol [2]). We assume that the disturbances and the exogenous variable have been generated by a stationary stochastic process so that for all t and s $E[u_t|x_s] = 0$; $E[u_t'u_t|x_s] = V_u$ where V_u is a $K \times K$ matrix of parameters that are independent of the elements of x_s; and that $E[u_t'u_s] = 0$ for $t \neq s$. Finally, we assume that the probability limits of the sample moments based on the elements of u_t and x_t are equal to their corresponding expectations.

Nonstochastic Simulation

Assuming that Γ^{-1} exists, the reduced-form system corresponding to (12-1) is

$$y_t = x_t\Pi_1 + y_{t-1}\Pi_2 + v_t, \qquad (12\text{-}2)$$

where $\Pi_1 = B_1\Gamma^{-1}$, $\Pi_2 = B_2\Gamma^{-1}$, and $v_t = u_t\Gamma^{-1}$. The assumptions described above imply that the parameters of (12-2) can be consistently estimated (see Goldberger [12, Chapter 7]). Let $\hat{\Pi}_i$ be a consistent estimate of Π_i ($i = 1, 2$) derived from a sample of size N so that $\hat{\Pi}_i = \Pi_i + \Delta_i$ where the matrix Δ_i converges in probability to the null matrix as the sample size increases without limit, that is, plim $\Delta_i = 0$. Using these definitions, the vectors of nonstochastically simulated values of the endogenous variables are defined as

$$\hat{y}_t^* = x_t\hat{\Pi}_1 + y_{t-1}^*\hat{\Pi}_2, \qquad t = 1, 2, \ldots \qquad (12\text{-}3)$$

$$\hat{y}_0^* = y_0.$$

That is, the simulated values of the endogenous variables are generated sequentially from the estimated reduced-form equations with the exogenous variables set equal to their historical values.

We now consider an investigation of the relationship between the historical values of the endogenous variables y_t and their simulated counterparts $\hat{y}_t^*$. Subtracting (12-2) from (12-3) yields the difference equation

$$\hat{y}_t^* - y_t = (\hat{y}_{t-1}^* - y_{t-1}) \Pi_2 + x_t \Delta_1 + \hat{y}_{t-1}^* \Delta_2 - v_t \qquad (12\text{-}4)$$

which has as its solution

$$\hat{y}_t^* = y_t + \sum_{j=1}^{t} [x_j \Delta_1 + \hat{y}_{j-1}^* \Delta_2 - v_j] \Pi_2^{t-j}. \qquad (12\text{-}5)$$

From this relationship between the simulated and historical values of the endogenous variables, it follows that, given t, y_0, and $X_t = (x_1, \ldots, x_t)$,

$$\text{plim } \hat{y}_t^* = y_t - \sum_{j=1}^{t} v_j \Pi_2^{t-j} = y_t^* \qquad (12\text{-}6)$$

where $y_0^* = y_0$, and $y_t^* = x_t \Pi_1 + y_{t-1}^* \Pi_2$ for $t \geq 1$. Then, it is clear from (12-6) that

$$E[y_t | X_t, y_0] = E[y_t^* | X_t, y_0] = y_t^*. \qquad (12\text{-}7)$$

The implication of (12-7) is that if (12-1) is correctly specified, the K scatter diagrams between the elements of y_t and the corresponding elements of $\hat{y}_t^*$, for large samples, should outline 45 degree lines. Therefore, the *inherent dynamic properties* of the process generating the elements of y_t can be inferred from an examination of the time paths of the elements of $\hat{y}_t^*$. It also would appear that the results given in (12-7) support the presumption of many authors that a rigorous test or validation of an econometric model can be carried out in terms of comparisons between the historical and simulated values of the endogenous variables (for example, see Goldberger [11, pp. 49-51], Holt (15), and Fromm and Taubman (10, Chapter 2)). This, however, is not the case. For even if Δ_1 and Δ_2 are ignored, it is clear from (12-5) that the difference between a particular element of y_t and the corresponding element of $\hat{y}_t^*$ is a disturbance term that is both autocorrelated and heteroskedastic. Therefore, the relationship between such elements should not be studied in terms of simple correlation analysis.

To derive a relationship between an observable function of y_t and one of $\hat{y}_t^*$, which contains a more manageable disturbance vector, consider the linear transformation $\ell [y_t] = y_t - y_{t-1} \hat{\Pi}_2$. We first observe from (12-3) that $\ell [\hat{y}_t^*] = x_t \hat{\Pi}_1$. It follows that the vectors $\hat{v}_t$ defined by

$$\hat{v}_t = \ell[y_t] - \ell[\hat{y}_t^*] \qquad (12\text{-}8)$$

are the reduced-form residuals of (12-2), that is, $\hat{v}_t = y_t - \hat{y}_t$ where $\hat{y}_t = x_t \hat{\Pi}_1 + y_{t-1} \hat{\Pi}_2$. This result demonstrates that once the classical regression tests concerning the parameters and the residuals of an econometric model have been carried out, the results of further tests of the model via comparisons of linear functions of the historical and simulated values of the endogenous variables over the period of estimation contain *no additional information* about the validity of the model. This means that even if each equation is estimated by a single-equation technique, the results of simulation experiments yield no information concerning the validity of the model as an interrelated system. Moreover, if observations outside the period of estimation are available, tests of the model using this information should be conducted in terms of the known multivariate distribution theory regarding forecasting and *not* in terms of ad hoc comparisons between historical and simulated values of the endogenous variables. For a comprehensive discussion of known econometric results concerning the appraisal of econometric models, see Christ [5, Chapter 10].

Stochastic Simulation

We now consider the case of stochastic simulation. That is, in each period a random variable is generated and added to a quantity such as $\hat{y}_t^*$. More formally, we define the vector of stochastically simulated values of the endogenous variables at time t as $\hat{y}_t^s$ where

$$\hat{y}_t^s = x_t\hat{\Pi}_1 + \hat{y}_{t-1}^s\hat{\Pi}_2 + \epsilon_t, \qquad t = 1, 2, \ldots \tag{12-9}$$

$$\hat{y}_0^s = y_0,$$

where ϵ_t is a $1 \times K$ vector of disturbances at time t generated by the experimenter. The distribution of ϵ_t is identical to that estimated for the reduced-form vector v_t. We assume that ϵ_t is independent of v_s and x_s for all t and s.

Consider now the large-sample counterpart of (12-9), that is, set $\hat{\Pi}_1 = \Pi_1$ and $\hat{\Pi}_2 = \Pi_2$. Then it is clear from (12-2) and (12-9) that the process generating $\hat{y}_t^s$ is identical to the one generating the historical values y_t. Therefore, an examination of the time paths of the elements of $\hat{y}_t^s$ should yield information concerning the properties of the process generating the elements of y_t. However, it does not follow that the elements of $\hat{y}_t^s$, on the average, will be good predictors of the corresponding elements of y_t. In fact, the structure of the relationships between the elements of y_t and the ones of $\hat{y}_t^s$ is similar to that of a model of errors of measurement. Therefore, it follows that if the elements of y_t are regressed on the corresponding element of $\hat{y}_t^s$, the slope of the regression line will be less than unity.

The analogy with the errors of measurement model is readily apparent from a comparison of the solution of y_t from (12-2) with the solution of $\hat{y}_t^s$

from the large-sample counterpart of (12-9). These two solutions can be written as

$$y_t = C(x_1, \ldots, x_t, y_0) + \sum_{j=1}^{t} v_j \Pi_2^{t-j} \tag{12-10}$$

$$\hat{y}_t{}^s = C(x_i, \ldots, x_t, y_0) + \sum_{j=1}^{t} \epsilon_j \Pi_2^{t-j} \tag{12-11}$$

where

$$C(x_1, x_2, \ldots, x_t, y_0) = y_0 \Pi_2{}^t + \sum_{j=1}^{t} x_j \Pi_1 \Pi_2^{t-j}. \tag{12-12}$$

On substitution of (12-11) into (12-10), a relationship between the historical and simulated values of the endogenous variables is obtained:

$$y_t = \hat{y}_t{}^s + \phi_t; \quad \phi_t = \sum_{j=1}^{t} (v_j - \epsilon_j) \Pi_2^{t-j}. \tag{12-13}$$

To investigate the relationships between the elements of y_t and the ones of $\hat{y}_t{}^s$, we now derive the covariance matrix $\Omega_t = E[(\hat{y}_t{}^s) \, '\phi_t]$. To do this, we first notice from (12-9) that, if the small-sample errors in $\hat{\Pi}_1$ and $\hat{\Pi}_2$ are ignored,

$$E[(\hat{y}_t{}^s) \, '\epsilon_{t-j}] = (\Pi_2{}^j) \, 'V_\epsilon, \quad j = 0, 1, \ldots, t - 1, \tag{12-14}$$

where $V_\epsilon = E[\epsilon_t' \epsilon_t]$. The assumptions underlying (12-9) imply that

$$E[(\hat{y}_t{}^s) \, 'v_{t-j}] = 0, \quad j = 0, 1, \ldots, t - 1. \tag{12-15}$$

Therefore, from (12-14), (12-15), and the definition of ϕ_t in (12-13), we have

$$\Omega_t = E[(\hat{y}_t{}^s) \, '\phi_t] = - \sum_{j=1}^{t} (\Pi_2^{t-j}) \, 'V_\epsilon \Pi_2^{t-j}. \tag{12-16}$$

Provided that the econometric model is stable, that is, the characteristic roots of Π_2 lie inside the unit circle in the complex plane, this covariance matrix converges as $t \to \infty$.

This property of Ω_t can be verified by observing that (12-16) implies that Ω_t is generated by

$$\Omega_t = V_\epsilon + \Pi_2' \Omega_{t-1} \Pi_2. \tag{12-16A}$$

Moreover, since Ω_t is symmetric, it has a modified square root so that the homogeneous part of the difference equation (12-16A) can be written as

$$K_t' K_t = \Pi_2' K_{t-1}' K_{t-1} \Pi_2. \tag{12-16B}$$

It is clear that Ω_t will converge to the matrix Ω, obtained by solving $\Omega - \Pi_2^2 \Omega \Pi_2 = V_\epsilon$, provided that the solution of the homogeneous system (12-16B) converges to the null matrix. If the characteristic roots of Π_2 are less than unity in absolute value, the matrix K_t generated by

$$K_t = K_{t-1}\Pi_2 \qquad (12\text{-}16\text{C})$$

will converge to the null matrix for any set of initial conditions. Thus the stability of the econometric model guarantees convergence of the co-variance matrix Ω_t.

Since V_ϵ is a variance-covariance matrix, it must be positive definite. Therefore, the diagonal elements of a matrix, such as $-(\Pi_2{}^i)'V_\epsilon\Pi_2{}^i$ must be negative. It follows from (12-16) that the diagonal elements of Ω_t are negative which, in turn, implies that each element of $\hat{y}_t{}^s$ is negatively correlated with the corresponding element in ϕ_t. Hence, from (12-13) and the standard results concerning errors of measurement as described, for example, by Johnston [19, pp. 148-50], we observe that, if the elements of y_t are regressed on the corresponding elements of $\hat{y}_t{}^s$, the slope of the estimated lines will be less than unity. Moreover, the scatter diagrams between the elements of y_t and those of $\hat{y}_t{}^s$ will not outline 45 degree lines. Therefore, even though the process generating $\hat{y}_t{}^s$ is identical to the one generating y_t, the elements of $\hat{y}_t{}^s$, on the average, will fail to predict consistently the corresponding elements of y_t.

SIMULATION OF NONLINEAR MODELS

In this section we specify a structural model that is nonlinear in the endogenous variables but linear in the parameters [9]. The reduced-form equations are derived and compared to the process that generates the simulated values of the endogenous variables. On the basis of this comparison, it is found that the simulated values can be expected to *diverge systematically* from the corresponding historical values.

Consider the model

$$y_t = x_t H_1 + F(y_t, y_{t-1}, x_t) H_2 + R(y_{t-1}, x_t) H_3 + u_t \qquad (12\text{-}17)$$

where y_t, x_t, y_{t-1}, and u_t are exactly as defined in (12-1); H_1, H_2, and H_3 are, respectively, $G \times K$, $M_1 \times K$, and $M_2 \times K$ matrices of parameters; $F(y_t, y_{t-1}, x_t)$ is a $1 \times M_1$ vector of observations at time t on M_1 functions $f_{it} = f_i(y_t, y_{t-1}, x_t)$. Each of these functions is assumed to depend on, at least, one of the endogenous variables (elements of y_t) and an arbitrary number of predetermined variables. In addition, at least, one of the functions of f_{it} is assumed to be nonlinear in one or more of the endogenous variables. Similarly, $R(y_{t-1},x_t)$ is a $1 \times M_2$ vector of observations on M_2 functions $r_{it} = r_i(y_{t-1},x_t)$. We retain the assumptions underlying (12-1) concerning the stochastic process that generates the elements of x_t and u_t. Finally, in order to interpret the K equations of (12-17) as structural equations for the K variables in y_t, we assume that if f_{it} contains the jth element of y_t, then the i, jth element of M_2 is zero. Without this assumption, the equations in (12-17) would not be linear in H_1, H_2, and H_3.

Reduced-Form Equations

Consider the functions f_{it}, $i = 1, 2, \ldots, M_1$. Each of these functions can be considered a random variable. Then because the mathematical expectation of one variable conditional on a set of others is, in general, a function of those conditioning variables, we have

$$E[f_{it}|x_t,y_{t-1}] = s_{it}, \qquad i = 1, \ldots, M_1, \tag{12-18}$$

where s_{it} is a function of the elements of x_t and y_{t-1}, that is, $s_{it} = s_i(x_t,y_{t-1})$. (A sufficient condition for the function f_{it} to have finite moments is that these functions have finite range, a condition which is satisfied in most econometric models.) It is clear from (12-18) that f_{it} can be expressed as

$$f_{it} = s_{it} + w_{it}, \qquad i = 1, \ldots, M_1, \tag{12-19}$$

where w_{it} is a stochastic element so that $E[w_{it}|x_t,y_{t-1}] = 0$ (see Wold [25]. By using (12-19), we observe that

$$F(y_t,y_{t-1},x_t) = S(y_{t-1},x_t) + W_t, \tag{12-20}$$

where $S(y_{t-1},x_t)$ and W_t are $1 \times M_1$ vectors whose ith elements, respectively, are s_{it} and w_{it}. Substituting (12-20) into (12-17), we have

$$y_t = x_t H_1 + S(y_{t-1},x_t) H_2 + R(y_{t-1},x_t) H_3 + e_t = J(y_{t-1},x_t) + e_t, \tag{12-21}$$

where $e_t = u_t + W_t H_2$. It is clear that $E[e_t|x_t,y_{t-1}] = 0$ and, thus, that $E[y_t|x_t,y_{t-1}] = J(y_{t-1},x_t)$. We, therefore, define the system of equations in (12-21) as the reduced-form equations for the elements of y_t in terms of the elements of x_t and y_{t-1}.

It should be evident that the equations in (12-21) *do not* represent the solution of the system in (12-17) for the endogenous variables in terms of the elements of x_t, y_{t-1}, and linear combinations of the structural disturbances in u_t. For instance, assume that the solution of the system for the ith element of y_t, say y_{it}, in terms of the elements of x_t, y_{t-1}, and the structural disturbances is given by

$$y_{it} = y_i(x_t,y_{t-1},u_t), \qquad i = 1, 2, \ldots, K. \tag{12-22}$$

Because the endogenous variables do not appear in the same functional form in all equations, the functions y_i, in general, will be nonlinear. Then the ith element of $J(y_{t-1}, x_t)$, say $j_{it} = j_i(y_{t-1}, x_t)$, is obtained by assuming

$$E[y_i(x_t, y_{t-1}, u_t) \mid x_t, y_{t-1}] = j_{it}. \tag{12-23}$$

Clearly, an additive linear function of the disturbances is not the only function that has a mean conditional on given values of the elements of x_t and y_{t-1}.

An example may help to clarify and extend the above argument. Consider the explicit but simplified version of the original system:

$$y_{1t} = b_1 x_t + u_{1t}. \tag{12-24}$$

$$y_{2t} = b_2 y_{1t-1} + b_3 \exp(y_{1t}) + u_{2t}, \tag{12-25}$$

where the disturbances u_{it} ($i = 1, 2$) are normally distributed with means zero, variances σ_i^2, and covariance $\sigma_{12} \neq 0$. Assume that each u_{it} is not autocorrelated and, furthermore, is independent of x_t.

The solution of (12-24) and (12-25) for y_{2t} in terms of the predetermined variables and the disturbances is

$$y_{2t} = b_2 y_{1t-1} + b_3 \exp(b_1 x_t) \exp(u_{1t}) + u_{2t}. \tag{12-26}$$

Then, because $E[\exp(u_{1t}) \mid x_t, y_{1t-1}] = \exp(\sigma_1^2/2)$, we notice that

$$\exp(u_{1t}) = \exp(\sigma_1^2/2) + u_{3t}, \tag{12-27}$$

where $E[u_{3t} \mid x_t, y_{1t-1}] = 0$. Substituting (12-27) into (12-26), we obtain the reduced-form equation for y_{2t}:

$$y_{2t} = b_2 y_{1t-1} + b_4 \exp(b_1 x_t) + z_t, \tag{12-28}$$

where $b_4 = b_3 \exp(\sigma_1^2/2)$, and the reduced-form disturbance $z_t = u_{2t} + b_3 \exp(b_1 x_t) u_{3t}$. It is clear that $E[z_t \mid x_t, y_{1t-1}] = 0$.

In comparing (12-28) with (12-26), we observe that the deterministic part of the reduced-form equation, obtained by setting $z_t = 0$, cannot be derived from (12-26) by setting the structural disturbances u_{1t} and u_{2t} equal to zero. In brief, the reduced-form equation for y_{2t} is *not* a solution of the system. A related point is that the reduced-form disturbance z_t is *not* a linear function of the structural disturbances. Indeed, it is clear that z_t is heteroskedastic with respect to x_t, even though the structural disturbances are homoskedastic. Finally, it should be noted that, in general, if the structural disturbances of an econometric model are assumed to be uncorrelated instead of independently distributed over time, the reduced-form disturbances will be autocorrelated, since nonlinear functions of uncorrelated variables are generally correlated. Thus, the properties of the reduced-form disturbances should not be inferred from those of the structural disturbances.

Nonstochastic Simulation

In order to simplify the argument that follows, but leaving the results intact, we ignore the problem of estimation and assume, instead, that the parameter matrices H_1, H_2, and H_3 are known. Since consistent estimation procedures have been developed for models such as (12-17) (see Eisenpress and Greenstadt [7] and Kelejian [21]), this amounts to a large-sample analysis of the simulation results.

The $1 \times K$ vector of simulated values Y_t^* is defined as

$$y_t^* = x_t H_1 + F(y_t^*, y_{t-1}^*, x_t) H_2 + R(y_{t-1}^*, x_t) H_3, \qquad t = 1, \ldots, \qquad (12\text{-}29)$$
$$y_0^* = y_0.$$

The solution of (12-29) for y_t^*, $t = 1, \ldots$, usually is obtained by numerical and sequential methods (see Evans and Klein [8, pp. 39-39]). For instance, given y_0^* and x_1, the system in (12-29) is first solved by iterative procedures for y_1^*. Then, given x_2 and y_1^*, y_2^* is obtained, and so on. Thus, let y_t^* be expressed in general as

$$y_t^* = T_1(y_{t-1}^*, x_t) \qquad (12\text{-}30)$$

where $T_1(y_{t-1}^*, x_t)$ is a $1 \times K$ vector whose ith element is the solution of the system (12-29) corresponding to the ith element of y_t^*. Assume now that the solution of the original structural system (12-17) is

$$y_t = T_2(y_{t-1}, x_t, u_t). \qquad (12\text{-}31)$$

Then it is clear that

$$y_t^* = T_2(y_{t-1}^*, x_t, 0) = T_1(y_{t-1}^*, x_t). \qquad (12\text{-}32)$$

In comparing the process (12-32), generating the vectors of simulated values, with the process (12-21), generating the vectors of historical values of the endogenous variables, two points should be noted. First, because the K functions of $T_1(y_{t-1}^*, x_t)$ are not equal to those of $J(y_{t-1}, x_t)$, multiplier analysis based on nonstochastic simulation yields results *that do not apply* to the corresponding historical values. (For an example of multiplier analysis in a nonlinear system, based on simulated results, see Evans and Kelin [8, pp. 48-49, and Chapter 5]. See also Fromm and Taubman [10, Chapter 2].) That is, in general,

$$\frac{\partial y_t^*}{\partial y_{t-1}^*, x_t} \neq \frac{\partial E[y_t, y_{t-1} = y_{t-1}^*, x_t]}{\partial y_{t-1}^*, x_t} \qquad (12\text{-}33)$$

where, generally, if $p = (p_1, \ldots, p_m)$ and $q = (q_1, \ldots, q_n)$, then $\partial p/\partial q$ is an $m \times n$ matrix whose i, jth element is $\partial p_i/\partial q_j$.

The second point to note is that the elements of y_t^* can be expected to diverge systematically from the corresponding elements of y_t. More explicitly, from (12-30) to (12-32) it can be shown that unless the disturbance vector u_t is degenerate in the sense that all the moments of its elements are zero,

$$E[(y_t - y_t^*)\,|\,y_0, X_t] = \theta(y_0, X_t) \neq 0, \tag{12-34}$$

where $X_t = (x_1, \ldots, x_t)$ and $\theta(y_0, X_t)$ is a $1 \times K$ vector of functions of the elements of y_0 and X_t. Therefore, one would not expect the K scatter diagrams between the elements of y_t and of y_t^* to outline 45 degree lines. Indeed, simulation over a period in which the elements of x_t show a trend could lead to an *increasing divergence* between the elements of y_t and those of y_t^*; even though the econometric model (12-17) is properly specified. It is clear, therefore, that nonlinear models such as (12-17) should *not be validated* in terms of comparisons between the elements of y_t and those of y_t^*. As in the linear case, validation should be carried out in terms of the multivariate distribution theory, corresponding to the estimates of the structural parameters and the various tests for randomness that concern the *structural disturbances.*

The results given above suggest that the properties of dynamic nonlinear models should not be studied in terms of nonstochastic simulation procedures. Essentially, the reason for this is that such simulation results are based on the solutions of the structural equations, but these solutions are not the reduced-form equations. Now, because of the difficulties involved in obtaining analytical solutions to a system of nonlinear equations and then in performing the integrations necessary to obtain the conditional expectations, the reduced-form equations in (12-21), generally, will be unknown. Hence, some approximation is necessary.

One possibility is to obtain points on the reduced-form equations via stochastic simulation. For instance, let v_t be a $1 \times K$ vector of disturbances at time t which are generated by the experimenter and which have a distribution identical to the structural disturbances u_t. Then the stochastically simulated values of the endogenous variables are defined in terms of (12-29) with the exception that v_t, for $t \geq 1$, is added to the right-hand side of that equation. In this case, it is clear that the solution of the resulting equation for y_t^*, now denoted as y_t^{**}, would be

$$y_t^{**} = T_2(y_{t-1}^{**}, x_t, v_t), \qquad t = 1, \ldots. \tag{12-35}$$

Therefore, if the time path of x_t is *held constant*, and y_t^{**} is repeatedly generated, the ensemble averages of the elements of y_t^{**} would be determined by the reduced-form equations:

$$\operatorname{plim} N^{-1} \sum_{i=1}^{T} T_2[y_{t-1}^{**}(i), x_t, v_t(i)] = J(y_{t-1}^{**}, x_t), \qquad (12\text{-}36)$$

where $y_{t-1}^{**}(i)$ and $v_t(i)$ are the vectors of values of y_{t-1}^{**} and v_t corresponding to the ith simulation. Therefore, the properties of the reduced-form equations may be studied in terms of the simulation results corresponding to different time paths of x_t (see Nagar [24] for an example of stochastic simulation). However, it should be clear that one would not validate a nonlinear model in terms of comparisons between the elements of y_t and those of y_t^{**}. The reason for this is that the difference between these vectors is a vector of variables that are autocorrelated, heteroskedastic and, in general, will have a distribution that is not known.

If stochastic simulation is not feasible, an alternative approach is to assume that each reduced-form equation can be approximated by a polynomial. More explicitly, the ith element of $J(y_{t-1}, x_t)$, j_{it}, may be expressed as

$$j_{it} = p_{it}^{d_i} + \delta_{it}^{d_i}, \qquad (12\text{-}37)$$

where $p_{it}^{d_i}$ is a polynomial of degree d_i in the elements of x_t and y_{t-1}, and $\delta_{it}^{d_i}$ is the remainder in the approximation. Assume now that $\delta_{it}^{d_i} \to 0$ as $d_i \to \infty$. Then, for sufficiently large d_i, we have from (12-21)

$$y_{it} = p_{it}^{d_i} + e_{it} \qquad (12\text{-}38)$$

where e_{it} is the ith element of e_t. Since $E[e_{it} | y_{t-1}, x_t] = 0$ the ordinary least-squares estimate of $p_{it}^{d_i}$, say $\hat{p}_{it}^{d_i}$, would, as $e_i \to \infty$, be a consistent estimate of $E[y_{it} | y_{t-1}, x_t]$. Therefore, the multipliers relating y_{it} to the predetermined variable could be approximated *analytically* by

$$\frac{\partial \hat{p}_{it}^{d_i}}{\partial y_{t-1}, x_t} = \frac{\partial E[y_{it} | (y_{t-1}, x_t)]}{\partial y_{t-1}, x_t}. \qquad (12\text{-}39)$$

DYNAMIC PROPERTIES OF STOCHASTIC LINEAR SYSTEMS

We previously suggested that the inherent dynamic properties of a linear system can be inferred from the simulated time paths of the endogenous variables of the model, even though there need not be a close correspondence between the simulated and historical values of the endogenous variables. The very fact that the simulated and historical values of the variables need not correspond indicates that it is the dynamic properties of the simulation paths, and not these paths themselves, that are of primary interest. However, the results of simulation experiments are difficult to interpret because of sampling variability. Therefore, it is desirable to consider analytical methods which are not subject to sampling variability that can be used to infer the dynamic properties of a stochastic system. In this section, we show that the dynamic properties of a model can be studied analytically in terms of the spectral representation of the solution of a system of stochastic linear difference equations. The method is applied to a simple econometric model, and the use of the implied dynamic characteristics for an investigation of the validity of the model is considered.

Final Form and Solution of a Linear Model

Consider again the reduced-form equations (12-9) that are used in stochastic simulation. For expository purposes, this system is rewritten as

$$A(L)z_t = Bx'_t + \epsilon'_t \qquad (12\text{-}40)$$

where $z'_t = \hat{y}_t{}^s$, $B = \hat{\Pi}'_2$, and $A(L) = I - \hat{\Pi}'_1 L$ with L defined as the lag operator. The final form of the system, the framework within which the dynamic properties of an econometric model are usually analyzed, can be derived as follows. Let the $K \times K$ λ-matrix $a(\lambda)$ denote the adjoint of $A(\lambda)$, and let $\Delta(\lambda) = |A(\lambda)|$ denote the determinantal polynomial of $A(\lambda)$. Premultiplying (12-40) by $a(L)$ yields the final form of the econometric model:

$$\|\Delta(L)\|z_t = a(L) Bx'_t + a(L) \epsilon'_t \qquad (12\text{-}41)$$

where $\|\Delta(L)\|$ is a matrix with $\Delta(L)$ on the main diagonal and zeros everywhere else. The final form [11] is, thus, a system of stochastic difference equations, each equation of which has the same autoregressive part $\Delta(L)$.

The method of solving a system of linear difference equations with constant coefficients, such as (12-41), is well known [2,23]. The complete solution is composed of a particular solution of the original system and a general solution of the homogenous system, obtained by deleting $Bx'_t + \epsilon'_t$ from (12-40). A particular solution can be written formally at sight, namely,

$$z_t = \frac{a(L)}{\Delta(L)} Bx'_t + \frac{a(L)}{\Delta(L)} \epsilon'_t. \qquad (12\text{-}42)$$

The complete solution, thus, is given by

$$z_t = C\Lambda^t + \frac{a(L)}{\Delta(L)} Bx'_t + \frac{a(L)}{\Delta(L)} \epsilon'_t \qquad (12\text{-}43)$$

where C is a $K \times n$ matrix of constants determined by the initial conditions and Λ is an n-dimensional vector $\lambda^n \Delta(\lambda^{-1}) = 0$. (If there are repeated roots of the determinantal equation, some of the columns of C may contain powers of t.)

The complete solution, thus, consists of three parts: a so-called transient response $C\Lambda^t$ which, provided that the system is stable, approaches zero as t increases; a component of the particular solution $[a(L)/\Delta(L)]\ Bx'_t$, corresponding to the exogenous variables; and a component of the particular solution $[a(L)/\Delta(L)]\ \epsilon'_t$, corresponding to the disturbance terms. The usual method of determining the dynamic properties of the solution is to suppress the stochastic part of the solution and to analyze only the deterministic solution [11,22]. This is equivalent to looking at the expected value of the time path of the endogenous variables of the system, given the exogenous variables.

Two kinds of information are obtained from the deterministic system. The values of the roots of the determinantal equation yield information about the modulus and periodicity of the transient response. If the roots are all less than unity in absolute value, the system is stable and approaches the particular solution from any set of initial conditions. If complex roots occur, this is usually taken as an indication that the system will tend to oscillate. The periodicity and rate of damping of the sinusoidal components contributed by complex roots can be ascertained from these roots. Dynamic multipliers may be calculated to determine the response of the endogenous variables to changes in the exogenous variables.

There is little doubt that these methods provide interesting and useful information about the system of equations. For short-term forecasting and the formulation of discretionary stabilization policy, these techniques may provide a sufficient characterization of the dynamic properties of the model. If, however, the longer-term properties of the model are to be investigated, it may not be reasonable to disregard the impact of the disturbance terms on the time paths of the endogenous variables. (Haavelmo [13] has pointed out the inadequacy of a comparison of the solution of the deterministic system with the observed series of observations for testing dynamic theories.) Neither of the above techniques provides information about the magnitude or correlation properties of deviations from the expected value of the time path. In the discussion that follows attention will be focused on the contribution of the disturbance terms to the time paths of the variables in the model.

Spectral Representation of Solution

An analytical description of the properties of the stochastic response of a system of difference equations can be based on the spectral representation of a stochastic process. (A good introduction to spectral representations is contained in Yaglom [26]). Suppose that the disturbances in the model $\epsilon_{jt}(j = 1, 2, \ldots, K)$, are generated by a wide-sense stationary process; that is, the means, variances, and lagged covariances of the disturbances are independent of time. Then the disturbance process has the spectral representation

$$\epsilon_t' = \int_{-\pi}^{\pi} e^{i\omega t} \, dU(\omega) \tag{12-44}$$

where $dU(\omega)$ is a $K \times 1$ vector of stochastic functions and $i = \sqrt{-1}$. It is easy to verify that the spectrum matrix of the disturbance process is given by [26, p. 43]

$$f(\omega) = E[dU(\omega) \, dU^*(\omega)] \tag{12-45}$$

where dU^* is the conjugate transpose of dU.

Returning to the complete solution of the linear econometric model given by (12-43), the particular solution corresponding to the disturbance terms can now be written as

$$z_t = \frac{a(L)}{\Delta(L)} \int_{-\pi}^{\pi} e^{i\omega t} \, dU(\omega) \tag{12-46}$$

where ϵ_t' has now been replaced by its spectral representation. Interchanging the order of the operations in this expression leads directly to

$$z_t = \int_{-\pi}^{\pi} e^{i\omega t} \, T(\omega) \, dU(\omega) \tag{12-47}$$

where $T(\omega) = a(e^{-i\omega})/\Delta(e^{-i\omega})$ is the $K \times K$ *transfer matrix* obtained by operating on $e^{i\omega t}$ by a $(L)/\Delta(L)$. The interchange of operations involved in going from (12-46) to (12-47) is permissible provided that each of the elements in the matrix $[a(L)/\Delta(L)] \, e^{i\omega t}$ converges absolutely. This will be true if the roots of the determinantal equation $\lambda_n \Delta(\lambda^{-1}) = 0$ are of modulus less than one so that the system is stable. Provided that this is the case, this last expression indicates that the kernel of the z_t process is $dZ(\omega) = T(\omega) \, dU(\omega)$.

The spectral matrix $F(\omega) = [F_{ij}(\omega)]$ of the endogenous variables now is obtained by using (12-45) with the appropriate substitutions:

$$F(\omega) = E[dZ(\omega) \, dZ^*(\omega)] = E[T(\omega) \, dU(\omega) \, dU^*(\omega) \, T^*(\omega)]$$
$$= T(\omega) \, f(\omega) \, T^*(\omega). \tag{12-48A}$$

The spectral matrix, each element of which is a function of angular frequency ω, provides a compact description of the second-moment properties of the stochastic model. The elements along the main diagonal are the power spectra of the endogenous variables, and the off-diagonal elements are the cross-spectra, relating the corresponding endogenous variables. Observe that if the covariance functions of the endogenous variables are of direct interest, they may be obtained by transforming the spectral matrix $F(\omega)$:

$$\gamma_{jk}(s) = \int_{-\pi}^{\pi} e^{-i\omega s} F_{jk}(\omega)\, d\omega. \tag{12-48}$$

The use of (12-45), (12-48), and this transformation provides a computationally simple scheme for obtaining these covariance functions.

Application of Spectral Method

To illustrate the application of the spectral representation of the solution of a stochastic system, the method is applied to Klein's Model I. This model, described in Klein [22], consists of three behavioral equations that relate to consumption expenditure, investment expenditure, and the private wage bill, and three identities. The complete six-equation system is as follows.

$$C = 17.7 + .02\Pi + .87(W_1 + W_2) + u_1.$$
$$I = 22.6 + .08\Pi + .68\Pi_{-1} - .17K_{-1} + u_2.$$
$$W_1 = 1.5 + .43(Y + T - W_2) + .15(Y + T - W_2)_{-1}$$
$$+ .13(t - 1931) + u_3. \tag{12-49}$$
$$Y + T = C + I + G.$$
$$Y = \Pi + W_1 + W_2.$$
$$\Delta K = I.$$

The endogenous variables include consumption C, nonwage income Π, the private wage bill W_1, net investment I, the capital stock at the beginning of the year K_{-1}, and income Y. The exogenous variables are government wage payments W_2, business taxes T, government expenditure G, and time t in years. All variables are measured in constant dollars, and the parameters were estimated by the method of limited information maximum likelihood from annual data for 1921 to 1941.

The first step in the derivation of the spectrum matrix of the system is the computation of the spectrum matrix of the disturbance process. On the assumption that the residuals are serially uncorrelated, the spectrum matrix of the residuals is

$$f(\omega) = \hat{\Sigma}/2\pi = \frac{1}{2\pi}\begin{bmatrix} 1.69 & 0.50 & -0.47 & 0 & 0 & 0 \\ 0.50 & 2.05 & 0.29 & 0 & 0 & 0 \\ -0.47 & 0.29 & 0.59 & 0 & 0 & 0 \\ 0 & 0 & 0 & 0 & 0 & 0 \\ 0 & 0 & 0 & 0 & 0 & 0 \\ 0 & 0 & 0 & 0 & 0 & 0 \end{bmatrix} \tag{12-50}$$

The nonzero entries in this matrix are estimates of the variances and co-variances of the disturbances (u_1, u_2, u_3) given by Klein [22, p. 72]. The transfer matrix $T(\omega)$ then is obtained by inverting the complex-valued matrix $A(e^{i\omega})$ where

$$A(e^{-i\omega}) = \begin{bmatrix} 1 & 0-.87 & 0 & -.02 & 0 \\ 0 & 1 & 0 & 0 & -.08-.68e^{-i\omega} & -.17e^{-i\omega} \\ 0 & 0 & 1 & -.43-.15e^{-i\omega} & 0 & 0 \\ -1 & -1 & 0 & 1 & 0 & 0 \\ 0 & 0 & 1 & -1 & 1 & 0 \\ 0 & -1 & 0 & 0 & 0 & 1-e^{-i\omega} \end{bmatrix}$$

(12-51)

for selected values of $\omega(0 \leq \omega \leq \pi)$. Finally, the spectrum matrix is obtained by using (12-48).

The power spectra of the endogenous variables implied by Klein's model I are contained on the main diagonal of the matrix $T(\omega) f(\omega) T^*(\omega)$ where $T(\omega) = A(\omega)^{-1}$. The power spectra of C, I, and Y are given in Table 1. The significance and interpretation of the power spectra derive from the

Table 12-1   Power Spectra of Construction, Investment, and Income Implied by Klein's Model I

Frequency Cycles per year	Power		
	Consumption	Investment	Income
0/40	0.88	0.00	0.88
1/40	1.82	0.52	3.69
2/40	5.23	2.54	14.32
3/40	9.09	5.26	27.51
4/40	7.05	4.51	22.39
5/40	4.07	2.80	13.31
6/40	2.44	1.77	8.06
7/40	1.60	1.19	5.23
8/40	1.14	0.85	3.62
9/40	0.87	0.64	2.64
10/40	0.70	0.49	2.02
11/40	0.60	0.40	1.60
12/40	0.53	0.32	1.31
13/40	0.49	0.27	1.11
14/40	0.46	0.24	0.96
15/40	0.44	0.21	0.85
16/40	0.42	0.19	0.77
17/40	0.41	0.17	0.72
18/40	0.40	0.16	0.69
19/40	0.40	0.16	0.67
20/40	0.40	0.15	0.66

fact that the spectrum provides a decomposition of the variance by frequency components, that is,

$$\gamma_{ii} = \int_{-\pi}^{\pi} F_{ii}(\omega) \, d\omega \qquad (12\text{-}52)$$

where γ_{ii} denotes the variance of the ith endogenous variable in the system. The results in Table 12-1, thus, indicate that the response of these endogenous variables of this system to random disturbances exhibits a fairly regular oscillation with a period of approximately 13.3 years.

By way of comparison, the characteristic roots of the system are .292, and .704 ± .344i. The pair of complex roots has a period of 14 years subject to a damping factor of .784. Thus the periodic response to random disturbances could have been anticipated from an examination of the characteristic roots of the system. However, notice that the existence of complex characteristic roots is neither a necessary nor a sufficient condition for the implied power spectra to exhibit an interior relative maximum. (Howrey [16] has shown that the existence of complex roots does not necessarily imply that the power spectrum has an interior maximum, and Chow [3] has shown that an interior maximum can exist even though the characteristic roots are all real.) The inference of the dynamic characteristic roots, therefore, is somewhat difficult. This example indicates that the power spectrum does provide a useful description of the stochastic response of the system. (For additional examples of the use of spectrum-analytic techniques to describe the dynamic properties of an econometric model, refer to Howrey [17] and Chow and Levitan [4].)

Spectral Representation in Validation

A question that arises quite naturally at this point is the extent to which the usefulness of the spectral representation is limited to a description of the solution of a system of stochastic equations. In particular, it may be of interest to consider the applicability of the spectral representation to tests of the validity of the model. A rather obvious procedure that suggests itself at this point is a comparison of the power spectra implied by the model $F(\omega)$ with the power spectra $\hat{F}(\omega)$, estimated directly from the series of observations on the endogenous variables. Significant differences between the two then might be taken as an indication that the model is not correctly specified.

An alternative time-domain approach might involve a comparison of the average distance between observed peaks of the endogenous variables with the mean distance between peaks implied by the model. This is the approach taken, for example, by Adelman and Adelman [1]. On the assumption that the disturbance process is normal, the mean distance between peaks can be calculated from the covariance functions [18]. In view of the relationship given in (12-48A), the covariance functions, in turn, can be computed from the spectrum matrix. It follows that the observations on the comparison of the estimated and implied power spectra also hold true for a comparison of the estimated mean distance between peaks and the mean distance implied by the econometric model.

Two points should be observed in connection with this approach. First, if the model contains no exogenous variables, this procedure is tantamount to a test of the hypothesis that the residuals $(\hat{\epsilon}_1, \ldots, \hat{\epsilon}_T)$ obtained by operating on the realization $\{z_t\}$ by $A(L)$ is not significantly different from white noise. Although this procedure has the advantage that the estimated spectrum may be suggestive of a more appropriate model if the original formulation is not adequate, it does not represent an advance beyond the classical tests of significance of regression analysis, which include tests of the independence of the estimated residuals.

The second point is that additional complications arise if there are any exogenous variables in the system, which is the usual case in economic models. Returning to the complete solution of the model, given in (12-43), the limiting value of the solution depends on both the disturbance process and the exogenous variables. Thus, it is the spectral representation of

$$z_t = \frac{a(L)}{\Delta(L)} [Bx_t' + \epsilon_t'] \tag{12-53}$$

that should be compared with the direct spectrum estimate $\hat{F}(\omega)$. Therefore, to carry out the test in this case the spectrum matrix of the process $\{x_t'\}$ must be obtained. Once again, however, the test reduces to a check of the ability of the filter $A(L)$ to reduce $z_t - Bx_t'$ to a sequence of uncorrelated disturbance vectors. We, thus, are left with the conclusion that, although the spectral representation of the solution of a system of equations is of interest for descriptive purposes, its use for testing the validity of the model appears to be rather limited.

CONCLUSIONS

That computer simulation yields little in the way of additional information about either the validity of *linear* econometric models or their dynamic properties is well known to most economists. Howrey and Kelejian have very succinctly demonstrated that all of the information that can be obtained about the validity and dynamic behavior of *linear* econometric models through the use of simulation also can be derived from existing analytical techniques. But, in spite of this fact, simulation still may prove to be a useful tool for examining the properties of linear econometric models. The reasons are as follows. First, from a computational standpoint, it may be much easier to generate numerical solutions to higher-order difference equation models instead of applying the more sophisticated analytical tools suggested by Howrey and Kelejian (for example, the calculation of characteristic roots and power spectra). Second, the interpretation of the simulated time paths of econometric models may prove to be more straightforward than the interpretation of the analytical solutions described by Howrey and Kelejian. Third, if one is performing exploratory experiments with a model and is making frequent changes in the model, then the amount of information provided by simulation may be all that is required to evaluate the model. A more rigorous analysis that uses one of the above-mentioned analytical procedures simply may not be appropriate.

Howrey and Kelejian's conclusion that with nonstochastic, nonlinear econometric models the simulated values can be expected to diverge systematically from their historical values is a matter of possible serious consequences for econometricians. What is the relative magnitude of this systematic divergence in the case of existing nonlinear econometric models? How serious is this problem? To answer these questions in a meaningful way will require extensive empirical investigation with a variety of different types of econometric models.

In summary, Howrey and Kelejian have provided us with some excellent guidelines as to when to use analytical solutions versus simulation with econometric models. Let us hope that more work of this type will soon be forthcoming for other types of models, for instance queueing, production, and inventory.

BIBLIOGRAPHY

1. Adelman, Irma and Frank. "The Dynamic Properties of the Klein-Goldberger Model," *Econometrica* **XXVII** (October 1959), 596-625.
2. Baumol, W. J. *Economic Dynamics: An Introduction.* New York: Macmillan Co., 1959.
3. Chow, G. C. "The Acceleration Principle and the Nature of Business Cycles," *Quarterly Journal of Economics* (August 1968), 403-418.
4. Chow, G. C., and Levitan, R. E. "Nature of Business Cycles Implicit in a Linear Econometric Model," IBM Research Report RC 2085, Thomas J. Watson Research Center, Yorktown Heights, New York, 1968.
5. Christ, C. F. *Econometric Models and Methods.* New York: John Wiley & Sons, 1966.

6. Duesenberry, J. *et al. The Brookings Quarterly Econometric Model of the United States.* Amsterdam: North-Holland Publishing Co., 1965.

7. Eisenpress, H., and Greenstadt, J. "The Estimation of Nonlinear Econometric Systems," *Econometrica* **XXXIV** (October 1966) 851-861.

8. Evans, M. K., and Klein, L. R. *The Wharton Econometric Forecasting Model.* Philadelphia: Economics Research Unit, Department of Economics, Wharton School of Finance and Commerce, 1967.

9. Fisher, F. *The Identification Problem in Econometrics.* New York: McGraw-Hill Book Co., 1966.

10. Fromm, G., and Taubman, P. *Policy Simulations With an Econometric Model.* Washington, D. C.: The Brookings Institute, 1968.

11. Goldberger, A. S. *Impact Multipliers and Dynamic Properties of the Klein-Goldberger Model.* Amsterdam: North-Holland Publishing Co., 1959.

12. Goldberger, A. S. *Econometric Theory.* New York: John Wiley & Sons, 1964.

13. Haavelmo, T. "The Inadequacy of Testing Dynamic Theory by Comparing Theoretical Solutions and Observed Cycles," *Econometrica* **VIII** (October 1940), 312-321.

14. Hadley, G.*Linear Algebra.* Reading, Mass.: Addison-Wesley Publishing Co.,1961.

15. Holt, C. "Validation and Application of Macroeconomic Models Using Computer Simulation," 637-650. *The Brookings Quarterly Econometric Model of the United States.* Edited by J. S. Duesenberry *et al.* Amsterdam: North-Holland Publishing Co., 1965.

16. Howrey, E. P. "Stabilization Policy in Linear Stochastic Systems," *Review of Economics and Statistics* **XLIX** (August 1967), 404-411.

17. Howrey, E. P. "Stochastic Properties of the Klein-Goldberger Model," R.M. No. 88, Econometric Research Program, Princeton University, Princeton, N. J., 1967.

18. Howrey, E. P. "A Spectrum Analysis of the Long-Swing Hypothesis," *International Economic Review* (June 1968), 228-252.

19. Johnston, J. *Econometric Methods.* New York: McGraw-Hill Book Co., 1963.

20. Kendall, M. G., and Stuart, A. *The Advanced Theory of Statistics, II.* New York: Hafner Publishing Co., 1961.

21. Kelejian, H. H. "Two Stage Least Squares and Nonlinear Systems," Working Paper No. 8, Princeton: Industrial Relations Section, Princeton University, 1968.

22. Klein, L. R. *Economic Fluctuations in the United States: 1921-1941.* New York: John Wiley & Sons, 1950.

23. McManus, M. "Dynamic Cournot-Type Oligopoly Models: A Correction," *Review of Economic Studies* (October 1962), 337-339.

24. Nagar, A. L. "Stochastic Simulation of the Brookings Econometric Model," paper presented at the San Francisco Meetings of the Econometric Society, December 1966.

25. Wold, H. "A Generalization of Causal Chain Models: (Part III of a Triptych of Causal Chain Systems)," *Econometrica* **XXVIII** (April 1960), 443-463.

26. Yaglom, A. M. *An Introduction to the Theory of Stationary Random Functions.* Englewood Cliffs, N. J.: Prentice-Hall, 1962.

Chapter 13 | A Computer Model

of the Tobacco Industry[1]

JOHN M. VERNON, NORFLEET W. RIVES, AND THOMAS H. NAYLOR

NTRODUCTION

In this chapter we describe an econometric model of the American tobacco industry for the period 1949 to 1966. The model contains 19 equations and is divided into three major blocks: (A) leaf production, (B) leaf price, and (C) cigarettes.

The objective of the model is to explain the behavior of the tobacco industry over an 18-year period. Ultimately, we hope to use the model to perform policy simulation experiments to evaluate the effects of alternative governmental and managerial policies on the behavior of the industry.

We begin with a brief description of the industry. Next, we discuss the theoretical specification of the model and the statistically estimated equations. We conclude with some example simulation results that provide additional evidence of the validity of the model for explaining the behavior of the tobacco industry over the period 1949 to 1966.

DESCRIPTION OF THE INDUSTRY

The *tobacco industry*, as we shall use the term, includes the growers of flue-cured tobacco leaf, the auction-warehouse system wherein the leaf is sold to the cigarette manufacturers, and the manufacture and sale of

[1] This chapter is based on a paper by John M. Vernon, Norfleet W. Rives, and Thomas H. Naylor, entitled "An Econometric Model of the Tobacco Industry," *Review of Economics and Statistics*, **LI** (May 1969), 149-157. The paper was presented previously at the International Meeting of the Institute of Management Sciences in Cleveland, Ohio, on September 12, 1968.

cigarettes to the public. We ignore the manufacture of other tobacco products.

There are a number of other types of tobacco leaf, for example, Burley, Maryland, fire-cured, and so on, which we have elected to ignore.[2] Our justification is that flue-cured leaf is the most important in cigarette production. One estimate has placed the average blend of all domestic cigarettes as 49 percent flue-cured and 37 percent Burley [26, Table 18]. Table 13-1 shows acreage and leaf productions for the years 1960 to 1967. Flue-cured is produced mainly in North Carolina, South Carolina, Virginia, and Georgia.

Table 13-1   Leaf Production and Acreage in United States and Puerto Rico 1960 to 1967

Leaf Production and Acreage in U.S. and Puerto Rico, 1960-1967

Crop Year	Total of Acreage	All Tobacco Production (1000 lbs)	Flue-Cured Acreage	Production (1000 lbs)
1960	1,169710	1,971,355	691,760	1,250,635
1961	1,201,010	2,091,773	698,470	1,257,891
1962	1,252,230	2,350,130	729,800	1,408,448
1963	1,205,430	2,375,559	694,470	1,371,462
1964	1,108,370	2,265,628	627,570	1,387,804
1965	993,650	1,870,483	562,300	1,058,970
1966	985,970	1,900,431	609,300	1,108,970
1967	989,340	2,018,699	626,860	1,267,851

Source. United States Department of Agriculture Consumer and Marketing Service. Annual *Report on Tobacco Statistics, 1967*, Table 1.

Flue-cured leaf markets open annually in July and August. The leaf is brought by the growers to the auction warehouses. It then is placed in flat baskets and arranged in rows on the auction floor.

When the auction begins, the auctioneer, the warehouseman and his clerks walk along one side of the row, the buyers' representatives on the other side. The warehouseman begins the proceedings with a starting bid on a particular pile of tobacco. The auctioneer then takes up his chant, the buyers recording their bids by nods, winks or gestures until the maximum bid consummates the sale [20, p. 258].

[2] We are currently working toward the incorporation of the Burley leaf market into the model.

The selling side of the leaf market consists of a very large number of growers.[3] However, the buying side is quite different. Tobacco buyers are either representatives of the domestic cigarette manufacturers or are buyers for export. Table 13-2 is included to give an indication of the concentration of the cigarette manufacturing industry. The buying side of the leaf market reasonably can be classified as oligopsonistic. A number of studies have been made in an effort to determine the extent to which the buying side behaves competitively [16,20,25]. The results are inconclusive, although one hypothesis which has been put forth is that of "percentage buying" [16]. This hypothesis states that the buyers are more concerned with insuring that other buyers pay the same price for leaf inputs than they are in obtaining the minimum (oligopsonistic) price. Given this behavioral pattern, it becomes more acceptable to estimate a demand function for tobacco.

Table 13-3 is presented to indicate the importance of foreign trade in both tobacco leaf and cigarettes. Of the total imports of tobacco leaf, about 80 percent is for use in the manufacture of cigarettes. The remainder is

[3] For example, the number of acreage allotments under the government control program for flue-cured leaf in 1967 was 194, 475 [26, Table 5].

Table 13-2   Market Shares of Domestic Cigarette Sales 1966

Market Shares of Domestic Cigarette Sales - 1966

Firm	Market Share in Percent
R.J. Reynolds	32.6
American Tobacco	24.4
Brown & Williamson	14.0
Philip Morris	10.8
P. Lorillard	9.1
Liggett & Meyers	8.8
U.S. Tobacco	0.1
Larus & Brother	0.1
Stephans Brothers	0.1
Total	100.0

Source. *Printers' Ink*, 1966.

used for cigar manufacture. Foreign leaf accounts for about 12 percent of the tobacco in an average domestic cigarette. And, of total flue-cured leaf produced in 1967 in the United States, about one-third was exported.

Table 13-3 Tobacco Foreign Trade of the United States in 1967

Tobacco Foreign Trade of U.S. in 1967

	Exports	Imports
Flue-Cured (1000lbs)	427,435	
Burley (1000lbs)	46,060	
Other types (1000lbs)	98,780	
Total	572,275	196,700
Cigarettes (millions)	23,652.0	12.1

Source. United States Department of Agriculture Consumer and Marketing Service. *Annual Report on Tobacco Statistics, 1967,* Table 35.

Since 1933, the United States Government has intervened in the operation of the tobacco leaf market [3]. This intervention consists of two basic controls: (1) output restriction, and (2) support prices. The existence of these controls has created an effective monopoly on the selling side of the leaf market. In fact, the controls often are justified on the grounds that monopoly power is necessary to offset oligopsony on the buying side. In any event, the most difficult problem that we have encountered in building the model has been the treatment of the two government control or policy variables, namely, acreage allotment, AL, and support price, SP. We now consider the econometric model.

THE MODEL

The variables of the model are defined below. Further explanation of the variables is given in the discussion of the individual equations.

VARIABLES[4]

Endogenous Variables

AFR   Free market acreage   Artificial Series—Estimated
                    (acres)

[4] All pounds are in farm-sales equivalent weights. All variables refer to the current year *t*, unless otherwise indicated.

AVAL	Acre value (dollars)	From identity
AFRMAL	Free market acreage less allotment (acres)	From identity
UND	Underage (acres)	From identity
A	Actual acreage (acres)	Annual flue-cured acres. *Source. Annual Report on Tobacco Statistics.*
Q	Leaf production (1000 lbs)	Annual flue-cured leaf produced. *Source. Annual Report on Tobacco Statistics*
QNET	Leaf production less leaf pledged (1000 lbs)	From identity
SQNET	Ratio of net leaf supply to domestic disappearance (Usage)	From identity
SQ	Ratio of leaf supply less exports only to domestic disappearance (Usage)	From identity
PACT	Leaf price (cents)	Average annual flue-cured price. *Source. Annual Report on Tobacco Statistics*
PFR	Free market leaf price (cents)	Artificial Series—Estimated
SPMFP	Support price minus free market price (cents)	From identity
T	Leaf pledged by growers at support price (1000 lbs)	*Source. Agricultural Statistics*
CCON	Cigarette consumption (billions cigarettes)	Annual domestic cigarette consumption. *Source. Agricultural Statistics*
CPRO	Cigarette production (billions cigarettes)	*Source. Agricultural Statistics*
LFPCIG	Leaf per cigarette (lbs/1000 cigarettes)	*Source. Annual Report on Tobacco Statistics*
CDIS	Disappearance (Usage) into cigarette production (1000 lbs)	*Source. Annual Report on Tobacco Statistics*
DDISP	Domestic leaf disappearance (Usage) (1000 lbs)	*Annual amount of leaf which disappears from stock. Source. Annual Report on Tobacco Statistics*

STK | Stock of leaf at end of crop year (1000 lbs) | *Source. Annual Report on Tobacco Statistics*

Exogenous Variables

OTHDIS | Disappearance into other products (1000 lbs) | *Source. Annual Report on Tobacco Statistics*

PCAPY | Disposable income per capita (dollars) | *Source. Economic Report of the President*

RDISY | Real disposable income (billions dollars) | *Source. Economic Report of the President*

RPCIG | Real price of cigarettes retail (cents/pack) | Average cigarette price deflated by consumer price index. *Source. Bureau of Labor Statistics.*

TIME | Time | 1949 = 1

TXFWD | Tax free withdrawals and exports (billions cigarettes) | *Source. Agricultural Statistics*

WPX | Wholesale price index | *Source. Economic Report of the President*

X | Exports of leaf (1000 lbs) | *Source. Annual Report on Tobacco Statistics*

YPA | Yield per acre (lbs) | Average annual amount of flue-cured leaf produced per acre. *Source. Annual Report on Tobacco Statistics*

Policy Variables

AL | Allotment of acres (acres) | *Source. Annual Report on Tobacco Statistics*

LBDMY | Dummy variable for first year poundage program | Equals 1 in 1965 and zero otherwise

SBDMY | Dummy variable for Soil Bank | Equals 1 in 1957, 1958 and zero otherwise

SP | Support price (cents) | *Source. Annual Report on Tobacco Statistics*

The model consists of 19 equations that represent the tobacco industry for the period 1949 to 1966. Since the model is recursive, the seven behavioral equations were estimated by ordinary least squares.[5] The remain-

---

[5] These seven equations include (13-1), (13-4), (13-10), (13-11), (13-13), (13-14), and (13-16). Two of these equations describe the behavior of artificial, or hypothetical, endogenous variables. The construction of two equations, (13-1) and (13-11), is described fully in the following sections.

ing 12 equations are identities. For convenience, we consider the model in three blocks. The first block of six equations explains total leaf production and the effect of the government restruction on output. The second block, (13-7) to (13-13), describes the determination of leaf price and the effect of the government support price. The third block, (13-14) to (13-19), is concerned with the cigarette manufacturing portion of the industry.

To illustrate the order in which the blocks must be solved and to provide an initial overview of the model, we include a flow chart (Figure 13-1). As indicated in the chart, Blocks 1 and 3 must be solved first for the values of Q and DDISP, and then Block 2 may be solved for the remaining variables.[6] Bars are placed over predetermined variables.

1. Leaf Production

The justification for treating leaf production separately from price determination is that the tobacco leaf market is of the cobweb type. That is, price and production are not determined simultaneously. Instead, production depends on *lagged* price and can be determined first. Since price depends on current production, it can logically be determined after production has been fixed. In more concrete terms, tobacco growers decide on leaf production in the spring, based on the price received for the crop in the preceding fall. The tobacco then is harvested in July and August and taken to market. Since the growers normally have no storage capability, the leaf production is thrown on the market in perfectly inelastic supply (modified somewhat by the control program).

We find it useful to treat the average amount of leaf produced per acre, YPA, as exogenous to the model. That is, YPA depends mainly on weather, technical change and, since 1965, YPA has been subject to governmental limitation. If price is multiplied by YPA, we obtain the variable acre-value, AVAL. Consequently, we view the grower as possessing a supply function of acreage, A, which responds to the lagged price of acres, or AVAL_{t-1}. Under free market conditions, we would like to estimate the acreage equation $A = f(\text{AVAL}_{t-1})$. For example, the line OB in Figure 13-2 could represent such an equation.

There would be no problem in estimating OB if we had reason to believe that all observable points actually lie on OB. Unfortunately, we have reason to believe otherwise. If the government set the allotment for acraege

---

[6] Equation 13-2, the definitional equation of the variable AVAL, could have logically been placed in Block 2 rather than in Block 1, since its current value cannot be found until Block 2 is solved. However, only the *lagged* value of AVAL is needed in any other equations, and we prefer to place it in Block 1 for economic reasons.

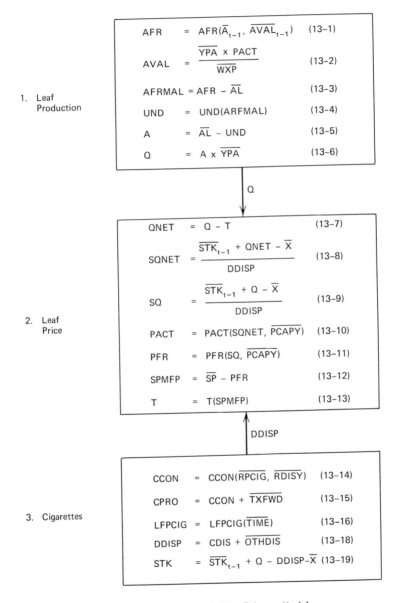

1. Leaf Production

$$AFR = AFR(\overline{A}_{t-1}, \overline{AVAL}_{t-1}) \qquad (13\text{-}1)$$

$$AVAL = \frac{\overline{YPA} \times PACT}{\overline{WXP}} \qquad (13\text{-}2)$$

$$AFRMAL = AFR - \overline{AL} \qquad (13\text{-}3)$$

$$UND = UND(ARFMAL) \qquad (13\text{-}4)$$

$$A = \overline{AL} - UND \qquad (13\text{-}5)$$

$$Q = A \times \overline{YPA} \qquad (13\text{-}6)$$

Q

2. Leaf Price

$$QNET = Q - T \qquad (13\text{-}7)$$

$$SQNET = \frac{\overline{STK}_{t-1} + QNET - \overline{X}}{DDISP} \qquad (13\text{-}8)$$

$$SQ = \frac{\overline{STK}_{t-1} + Q - \overline{X}}{DDISP} \qquad (13\text{-}9)$$

$$PACT = PACT(SQNET, \overline{PCAPY}) \qquad (13\text{-}10)$$

$$PFR = PFR(SQ, \overline{PCAPY}) \qquad (13\text{-}11)$$

$$SPMFP = \overline{SP} - PFR \qquad (13\text{-}12)$$

$$T = T(SPMFP) \qquad (13\text{-}13)$$

$DDISP$

3. Cigarettes

$$CCON = CCON(\overline{RPCIG}, \overline{RDISY}) \qquad (13\text{-}14)$$

$$CPRO = CCON + \overline{TXFWD} \qquad (13\text{-}15)$$

$$LFPCIG = LFPCIG(\overline{TIME}) \qquad (13\text{-}16)$$

$$DDISP = CDIS + \overline{OTHDIS} \qquad (13\text{-}18)$$

$$STK = \overline{STK}_{t-1} + Q - DDISP - \overline{X} \qquad (13\text{-}19)$$

Figure 13-1.   A flow chart of the Tobacco Model.

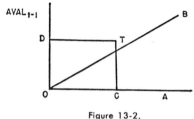

Figure 13-2.

at OC acres when AVAL_{t-1} was OD, then the point observed in that year was point T. Clearly, point T does not lie on the acreage supply equation.

To avoid this difficulty, we employ a strategy proposed by Johnson [12] in a study of the Burley market. Instead of attempting to estimate A, we estimate the difference between A and acreage allotment AL. This difference or underage, UND, is the number of acres not planted even though they are permitted by the allotment. The hypothesis is that UND will be lower the greater is the economic incentive to growers. Although Johnson used the lagged price of leaf as the economic incentive variable, we use a different approach. Before describing this approach we point out that the use of lagged price appears to have the defect that AL is not accounted for. That is, UND might be zero in year 1 and 500 in year 2, even though the lagged price was constant, simply because the level of AL varied.

Our strategy is to estimate a hypothetical free market acreage, AFR, and to use the excess of AFR over AL as a measure of the growers' incentive to reduce UND. The AFR equation is estimated by using 1910 to 1930 data. Thus, since the government control program did not go into effect until after 1933, the 1910 to 1930 data points should all lie on the line OB in Figure 13-1. Of course, in using the equation we must make the rather strong assumption that the structure of supply has not changed over this long period of time. The excellent statistical results for these equations offer some support for this assumption.

Based on the hypothesis that A depends on the *expected* AVAL, we can develop A as a function of A_{t-1} and AVAL_{t-1} [4, p. 206]. Equation 13-1 is the acreage equation estimated with 1910 to 1930 data. Since it will be used in the model to generate acreages for the 1949-1966 period that would have occurred had the free market structure of 1910 to 1930 prevailed, we label it the free market acreage equation. The only other behavioral equation in the first six is (13-4), the underage equation. We have already discussed the explanation for regressing UND on the excess of AFR over AL, or AFRMAL. As hypothesized, the coefficient of AFRMAL is negative and is statistically significant.

One further point should be made about the UND equation. Two dummy variables were used to account for the unusual events affecting UND. One dummy variable represents the effect of the Soil Bank program, which was in effect in 1956, 1957, and 1958. Since the program was announced too late in 1956 to affect growers' decisions, the dummy variable SBDMY represents 1957 and 1958 only. The second dummy variable, LBDMY, represents the effect of a change in allotment after planting was over in 1965. The original allotment was set at 515,425 acres in December 1964. However, in May 1965, the allotment was increased to 607,335 acres as a result of the passage of a new governmental control program (the new program permits control of poundage as well as of acreage).

FREE-MARKET ACREAGE

$$\log \text{AFR} = -1.2098 + 0.8566 \log \overline{A}_{t-1} + 0.4825 \log \overline{\text{AVAL}}_{t-1} \qquad (13\text{-}1)$$
$$(0.6066) \quad (0.0683) \qquad\qquad (0.1242)$$

$\overline{R}^2 = 0.9150$
$\text{DW} = 2.3247$ \qquad\qquad (1910-1930)
$\text{SE} = 0.1302$

ACRE VALUE

$$\text{AVAL} = \frac{\overline{\text{YPA}} \times \text{PACT}}{\overline{\text{WPX}}} \qquad (13\text{-}2)$$

FREE-MARKET ACREAGE LESS ALLOTMENT

$$\text{AFRMAL} = \text{AFR} - \overline{\text{AL}} \qquad (13\text{-}3)$$

UNDERAGE

$$\text{UND} = 26.9640 - 0.0160 \text{ AFRMAL} + 46.3971 \text{ SBDMY}$$
$$(6.6716) \quad (0.0085) \qquad\qquad (5.2275)$$
$$+ 33.6419 \text{ LBDMY} \qquad (13\text{-}4)$$
$$(7.5373)$$

$\overline{R}^2 = 0.8296$
$\text{DW} = 1.5642$ \qquad\qquad (1949-1966)
$\text{SE} = 6.8986$

ACTUAL ACREAGE

$$A = \overline{\text{AL}} - \text{UND} \qquad (13\text{-}5)$$

LEAF PRODUCTION

$$Q = A \times \overline{\text{YPA}} \qquad (13\text{-}6)$$

2. Leaf Price

In (13-7) to (13-13), we attempt to integrate the government support price for leaf into the determination of price. The essence of this part of the model is that the amount of leaf pledged by growers at the support price, T, and the market price of leaf, PACT, are mutually dependent. That is, PACT depends on T and T depends on PACT.

The statement that T depends on PACT requires further explanation. As suggested by Johnson [12], we hypothesize that T depends on the difference between SP and the hypothetical free market price, PFR. Thus, PFR is analogous to AFR, since it represents what the price would have been if the government control program had not been in effect. Since we use the parameter estimates from the PACT equation to generate the artificial PFR series (described below), it is in this special sense that we view T and PACT as simultaneously determined. Although we would prefer a simultaneous estimation of the T and PACT equations, this is not possible because of the nonexistence of actual data on PFR.

We now turn to (13-10), the PACT equation, in order to explain the derivation of the free market price, PFR. First, however, we must describe the explanatory variables used.

A number of studies of the tobacco industry [8,15,20,15] have all found that an important variable in explaining price is a variable resembling our SQNET. This variable is the ratio of the total supply of leaf available to total usage of leaf, or disappearance. As such, SQNET represents an inventory stock to sales ratio concept. Cigarette manufacturers often have stated that they seek to maintain a ratio of total supply of leaf to current usage of about 2.5 to 1 [20]. A main reason for these large inventories is the 2 to 3 year aging requirement of tobacco leaf. The numerator of the variable SQNET is equal to the sum of the stock of tobacco on hand at the beginning of the market period and the leaf production minus exports and minus the tobacco pledged under the support program, T. The numerator then is divided by the current domestic usage of tobacco leaf, DDISP. The expectation that the coefficient of this variable in the PACT equation is negative is confirmed by the statistical results.

The second variable, PCAPY, is an income variable that accounts for shifts in demand over the period. It has a positive coefficient, as expected. Perhaps, the most serious omission is a variable to account for the quality of leaf. Unfortunately, we have been unable to obtain such a variable.

The derivation of PFR from (13-10) is accomplished by setting T equal to zero. That is, if the government is not intervening in the market, total pledges of leaf will be zero. Hence, (13-11) is simply (13-10) with T set equal to zero. PFR is always less than PACT, as expected.

Equation 13-13 is the T equation. The goodness-of-fit of this equation, as measured by the coefficient of determination, is poorer than for any of the other equations. However, the regression coefficient is of the expected sign and is statistically significant. We also should mention that in *estimating* the equation, a value of PFR was used that differs slightly from the PFR given in (13-11). The "adjusted" PFR used was determined by first calculating a predicted *difference* between PACT and PFR for each year by subtracting (13-11) from (13-10). Then the predicted difference was subtracted from the observed market price to obtain the "adjusted" PFR.

LEAF PRODUCTION LESS LEAF PLEDGED

$$\text{QNET} = \text{Q} - \text{T} \tag{13-7}$$

RATIO OF NET LEAF SUPPLY TO DOMESTIC DISAPPEARANCE

$$\text{SQNET} = \frac{\overline{\text{STK}}_{t-1} + \text{QNET} - \overline{\text{X}}}{\text{DDISP}} \tag{13-8}$$

RATIO OF LEAF SUPPLY LESS EXPORTS TO DISAPPEARANCE

$$\text{SQ} = \frac{\overline{\text{STK}}_{t-1} + \text{Q} - \overline{\text{X}}}{\text{DDISP}} \tag{13-9}$$

ACTUAL LEAF PRICE

$$\log \text{PACT} = -0.2833 \log \text{SQNET} + 0.5858 \log \overline{\text{PCAPY}} \tag{13-10}$$
$$(0.1108) \qquad\qquad (0.0189)$$

$$\overline{\text{R}}^2 = 0.7873$$
$$\text{DW} = 1.6657 \qquad (1949\text{-}1966)$$
$$\text{SE} = 0.0435$$

FREE-MARKET LEAF PRICE

$$\log \text{PFR} = -0.2833 \log \text{SQ} + 0.5858 \log \overline{\text{PCAPY}} \tag{13-11}$$

Note. PFR is an artificial series derived by using parameter estimates in (14-10). Actual data on PFR do not exist.

SUPPORT PRICE LESS FREE-MARKET PRICE

$$\text{SPMFP} = \overline{\text{SP}} - \text{PFR} \tag{13-12}$$

LEAF PLEDGED UNDER SUPPORT PROGRAM

$$\log \text{T} = 5.4038 + 0.1472 \text{ SPMFP} \tag{13-13}$$
$$(0.1609) \quad (0.0352)$$

$$\overline{\text{R}}^2 = 0.4922$$
$$\text{DW} = 1.2729 \qquad (1949\text{-}1966)$$
$$\text{SE} = 0.4393$$

3. Cigarettes

Equation 13-14 is the demand function for cigarettes. In view of the oligopolistic pricing behavior of the cigarette manufacturers, it seems reasonable to take the price of cigarettes as exogenous. However, this is one part of the model that we expect to improve later by adding equations and, perhaps, by treating price as endogenous.

The demand function displays properties similar to the ones that have been obtained by a number of other investigators. For example, the price elasticity of demand for cigarettes is -0.43 and the income elasticity is 0.77. According to Sackrin [21], other analyses have shown that the price elasticity of demand for cigarettes is between -0.3 and -0.4, and the income elasticity of demand about 0.5. A dummy variable used to represent the 1964 Surgeon General's report on the link between cancer and smoking proved to be insignificant.

The other estimated equation in this block is the technical relation between leaf disappearance and cigarette production. Thus (13-16) is a regression of tobacco leaf per cigarette, LFPCIG, on time. It reveals that LFPCIG is declining exponentially at about 3 percent per year. The ratio of flue-cured leaf price to Burley price also was tried as an independent variable, but it proved to be statistically insignificant.

DOMESTIC CIGARETTE CONSUMPTION

$$\log \text{CCON} = -0.4250 \log \overline{\text{RPCIG}} + 0.7721 \log \overline{\text{RDISY}} \quad (13\text{-}14)$$
$$\quad\quad\quad\quad (0.1349) \quad\quad\quad\quad\quad (0.0765)$$

$$\overline{R}^2 = 0.9094$$
$$\text{DW} = 0.5900 \quad\quad\quad (1949\text{-}1966)$$
$$\text{SE} = 0.0467$$

CIGARETTE PRODUCTION

$$\text{CPRO} = 20 \times \text{CCON} + \overline{\text{TXFWD}} \quad\quad\quad (13\text{-}15)$$

LEAF PER 1000 CIGARETTES

$$\log \text{LFPCIG} = 0.6161 - 0.0289 \overline{\text{TIME}} \quad\quad (13\text{-}16)$$
$$\quad\quad\quad\quad (0.0156 \quad (0.0017)$$

$$\overline{R}^2 = 0.9531$$
$$\text{DW} = 1.3836 \quad\quad\quad (1949\text{-}1966)$$
$$\text{SE} = 0.0286$$

DISAPPEARANCE INTO CIGARETTE PRODUCTION

$$\text{CDIS} = (\text{LFPCIG} \times \text{CPRO}) 1000 \quad\quad (13\text{-}17)$$

DOMESTIC LEAF DISAPPEARANCE

$$\text{DDISP} = \text{CDIS} + \overline{\text{OTHDIS}} \quad\quad\quad (13\text{-}18)$$

LEAF STOCK

$$STK = \overline{STK}_{t-1} + Q - DDISP - \overline{X} \qquad (13\text{-}19)$$

SIMULATIONS

To gain additional insight regarding the validity of our model, we treated it as a closed-loop simulation model. That is, for given starting values of the lagged endogenous variables and given values of the exogenous variables and the policy variables, we solved the model each period for the current values of the 19 endogenous variables. The values of the endogenous variables generated in one period were fed back into the model in future periods in the form of lagged endogenous variables. The error terms in the behavioral equations were suppressed. In this manner, we generated the time paths for the 19 endogenous variables over the period 1949 to 1966.

The simulations were run on an IBM 360/75 computer with the aid of PROGRAM SIMULATE—a simulation language developed at the University of Wisconsin for conducting simulation experiments with econometric models.

Figures 13-3 to 13-8 contain graphs of six of the variables whose time paths were simulated. For the purpose of comparisons, the actual time paths of these six variables are also plotted. On the basis of these graphical comparisons of the simulated output of the model and the actual time paths of the corresponding variables, we conclude that our model does a reasonably good job of simulating the behavior of the tobacco industry between the years 1949 and 1966. It remains to be seen how well the model will predict the future.

Of course, a number of more sophisticated techniques exist for validating simulation models. For example, in an earlier study of the textile industry,

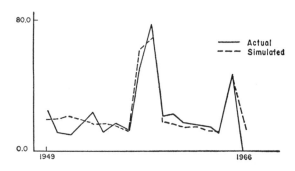

Figure 13-3.   Flue-cured underage (1000 acres).

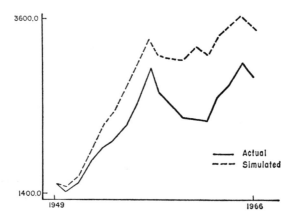

Figure 13-4. Stocks of flue-cured tobacco leaf (1000 lbs).

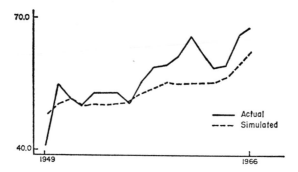

Figure 13-5. The actual price of flue-cured tobacco leaf (cents).

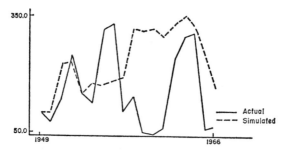

Figure 13-6. The volume of flue-cured tobacco leaf pledged by growers at the support price
(1000 lbs).

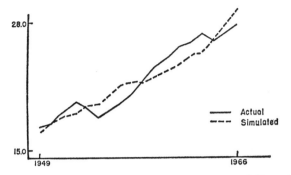

Figure 13-7.   The domestic cigarette consumption in the United States (billions of cigarettes).

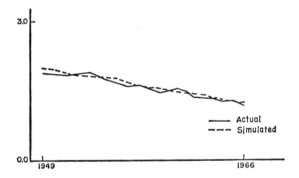

Figure 13-8.   Flue-cured tobacco leaf per 1000 cigarettes (lbs/1000 cigarettes, ratio estimate).

Naylor, Sasser, and Wallace [17] used spectral analysis and analysis of variance to validate an econometric model. (See Chapter 5 for a discussion of other validation procedures that may be relevant to this model.)

BIBLIOGRAPHY

1. *An Economic Impact Study of the Tobacco Industry.* Arlington, Va.: C.E.I.R., Inc., 1964.
2. Benedict, Murray R., and Stine, Oscar C. *The Agricultural Commodity Programs.* New York: The Twentiety Century Fund, 1956.
3. Brooks, R. C., and Williamson, J. C., Jr. *Flue-Cured Tobacco Programs, 1933-1958.* A. E. Information Series No. 66, North Carolina State College, Raleigh, 1958.
5. Christ, Carl F. *Econometric Models and Methods.* New York: John Wiley & Sons, Inc., 1966.

5. Cohen, Kalman J. *Computer Models of the Shoe, Leather, Hide Sequence.* Englewood Cliffs, N. J.: Prentice-Hall, 1960.
6. Cyert, Richard M., and March, James G. *A Behavioral Theory of the Firm.* Englewood Cliffs, N. J.: Prentice-Hall, 1963.
7. Gage, Charles F. *American Tobacco: Types, Uses, Markets.* United States Department of Agriculture. Bureau of Agricultural Economics. Circular No. 249. (January 1933).
8. Goris, Hendricke. *Price-Determining Factors in American Tobacco Markets.* Amsterdam: North Holland, 1954.
9. Haenszel, William, Shimkin, Michael B. and Miller, Herman P. *Tobacco Smoking Patterns in the United States.* United States Department of Health, Education and Welfare. United States Public Health Service. Public Health Monograph No. 45 (May 1956).
10. Heady, Earl O., and Dillion, John L. *Agricultural Production Functions.* Ames, Iowa: Iowa State University Press, 1961.
11. Heady, Earl O., and Tweeten, Luther G. *Resource Demand and Structure of the Agricultural Industry.* Ames, Iowa: Iowa State University Press, 1963.
12. Johnson, Glenn L. *Burley Tobacco Control Programs.* Bulletin 580, Kentucky Agricultural Experiment Station, Lexington, February 1952.
13. Johnston, J. *Econometric Methods.* New York: McGraw-Hill, 1963.
14. Fisher, F. M. *A Priori Information and Time Series Analysis.* Amsterdam: North-Holland, 1962.
15. Fisher, William H. *Economics of Flue-Cured Tobacco.* Federal Reserve Bank of Richmond, 1945.
16. Jackson, Elmo L. *The Pricing of Cigarette Tobaccos.* Gainesville, Fla.: University of Florida Press, 1955.
17. Naylor, Thomas H., Wallace, William H., and Sasser, W. Earl. "A Computer Simulation Model of the Textile Industry," *Journal of the American Statistical Association,* **LX** (December 1967), 1338-1364.
18. Naylor, Thomas H. *et al. Computer Simulation Techniques.* New York: John Wiley & Sons, 1966.
19. Nerlove, Marc. *The Dynamics of Supply; Estimation of Farmers' Response to Price.* Baltimore: The Johns Hopkins Press, 1958.
20. Nicholls, William H. *Price Policies in the Cigarette Industry.* Nashville, Tenn.: Vanderbilt University Press, 1951.
21. Sackrin, S. M. "Factors Affecting the Demand for Cigarettes," *Agricultural Economics Research.* United States Department of Agriculture. Economic Research Service, Vol. **XIV** (July 1962).
22. Sanderson, Fred H. *Methods of Crop Forecasting.* (Harvard Economic Studies No. 93) Cambridge: Harvard University Press, 1954.
23. Suits, Daniel B. "An Econometric Model of the Watermelon Market," *Journal of Farm Economics,* **XXXVII** (May 1955).
24. Suits, Daniel B. and Koizumi, Susuma. "The Dynamics of the Onion Market," *Journal of Farm Economics,* **XXXVIII** (May 1956).
25. Tennant, Richard B. *The American Cigarette Industry.* New Haven: Yale University Press, 1950.

26. United States Department of Agriculture. Consumer and Marketing Service. *Annual Report on Tobacco Statistics*. (Selected years, 1946-1967.)
27. United States Department of Agriculture. *Agricultural Statistics*, 1967 and selected previous years. Washington: United States Government Printing Office, 1967.
28. Williamson, J. C., Jr., and Brooks, R. C. *Poundage Quota Controls for Flue-Cured Tobacco*. A. E. Information Series No. 83, North Carolina State College, Raleigh, 1961.

Chapter 14 | Effects of Alternative Policies for Allocating Federal Aid for Education to the States: A Computer Simulation[1]

MARILYN MANSER, THOMAS H. NAYLOR, AND KENNETH WERTZ

INTRODUCTION

This chapter describes an econometric model that attempts to explain per capita expenditures for education by the states (in the United States). A computer simulation experiment was conducted with the model to determine the effects of six alternative federal schemes for allocating funds for educational purposes to the states.

THE MODEL

Our approach to the question of expenditure determinants regards the governmental unit that is responsible for dispensing funds as the center of analysis. Or, more precisely, it is the decision-making procedure of such a unit that is of initial interest, since by examining it, one could be *led to* the consideration of variables that are influential in setting expenditure levels. such factors then enjoy a common element.

It is our hypothesis that, at least, three factors are prominent to the state official or the committee that is responsible for drafting the budget for expenditures on education: (1) the amount spent on education by the state (including federal payments) in the previous year; (2) the amount of

[1] This chapter is based on a paper by Marilyn Manser, Thomas H. Naylor, and Kenneth Wertz, entitled "Effects of Alternative Policies for Allocating Federal Aid for Education," *Simulation and Games*, I (June, 1970), 134–154.

federal payments for education to the state in the previous year; and (3) the amount spent on education by neighboring states in the previous year.

All factors are regarded on a per capita basis.

$$S_t^i = a^i S_{t-1}^i + b^i G_{t-1}^i + c^i N_{t-1}^i + B_t^i \qquad (14\text{-}1)$$

where i denotes the ith state $(i = 1, \ldots, 48)$ and

S_t^i = the amount spent per capita on education by state i in year t. (14-2)

G_t^i = the amount of federal payments per capita for education in state i in period t. (14-3)

N_t^i = a neighborhood variable representing the amount spent per capita on education by states which are neighbors of state i in period t. (14-4)

E_t^i = a stochastic error term. (14-5)

The subscript t refers to the years 1951 to 1965.

The use of the variable S_{t-1}^i assumes that the decision makers base this year's budget on last year's budget. Wildavsky [30] has argued that "The largest determining factor of the size and content of this year's budget is last year's budget. Most of the budget is a product of previous decisions." Among the reasons for this phenomenon are that a large number of commitments are made years ahead of time and that many items are standard and are simply reenacted each year unless there is a special reason to challenge them. Davis, Dempster, and Wildavsky [6] concur that "By far the most important aid to calculation is the incremental method."

Although federal payments to states do not constitute a very large portion of the latter's educational outlay (about 6.8 percent), their receipt does offer some flexibility in financing.

The importance of federal aid for specific programs cannot be denied . . . While not true from the taxpayer's point of view, federal aid can be regarded as "outside money" from the point of view of the state and local government, and its availability should be expected to have a direct effect on raising state and local expenditure levels [23].

A state might reduce its own effort by substituting federal funds for its own; or simply spend the amount received; or be induced to spend even more than the amount received ("stimulation"). Since the S^i series are *not* net of the G^i series, one could identify the probable existence of one of three alternatives above by examining whether $b < 1$; $b \simeq 1$; or $b > 1$, respectively.

The inclusion of the variable N_t^i in the model supposes that states are in some manner influenced by the expenditure patterns of neighboring states.

Although the extent to which voters are aware of, and react to, tax-rate and expenditure differentials within an area, and the extent to which businesses assess the quality of public services when making relocation decisions are fields in which definitive research is lacking, the hypothesis that the expenditure differentials between adjacent states should not be so great as to be highly conspicuous seems intuitively reasonable. It also would be reasonable for state officials to search for clues as to what educational services they should be providing by scanning what is being done around them.

In this model, the neighborhood effect is specified as follows:

$$N_t{}^i = \sum_{j=1}^{48} W_j{}^i \cdot S_t{}^j, \tag{14-6}$$

where $W_j{}^i$ = the fraction of state i's land perimeter that adjoins state j. The portions of a state's boundary that touch the sea or a foreign country are not regarded as contributing to the state's land perimeter. Obviously, if state i does not border on state j, $W_j{}^i = 0.0$.

Admittedly, it may be possible to come up with a better specification of $N_t{}^i$, but whatever the form of the neighborhood variable, it is important to do the following.

. . . explicitly recognize the interactions among governments, both at the same level and at different levels. A fully articulated theory of public expenditure would explain the expenditures of one government, not only as a result of conditions prevailing within its boundaries, but also as a consequence of expenditures by other governments. Such a system could only be solved simultaneously for all units [18].

Regional differences, on a broader scope, have been investigated in various ways in empirical studies. For example, Shapiro [25] considered (1) the southern states and (2) the northern and western states as two separate regions and substantiated the hypotheses that certain socioeconomic factors operate to determine the levels of expenditure regardless of region and that the relative importance of these explanatory factors will not be the same. Our model is unique in considering a state-by-state rather than a broader regional effect and in representing this effect by a meaningful numerical variable instead of a dummy variable.

Several problems arose in estimating the parameters of the model. For every state there is a problem of multicollinearity. The simple correlation coefficients between the variables are quite high. The simple correlation coefficient between $S_t{}^i$ and $N_t{}^i$ was greater than .90 in almost every case. This could produce large sampling variances and a high R^2 with all t-tests failing. An attempt to inject extraneous information into the data via a technique described by Goldberger [12] proved to be unsuccessful. However, if these patterns of multicollinearity can be assumed to continue, at least, for the short period for which projections are to be made, then the equations still may be useful. And in this situation, the ordinary least-squares estimators are still unbiased and consistent.

The simultaneous presence of a lagged endogenous variable S_{t-1}^i and autocorrelated error terms may yield biased, inconsistent parameter estimates [15]. Consequently, we used a modified version of the Cochrane-Orcutt iterative technique to estimate the parameters of the model [21].

The results of the regressions for each of the 48 states appear in Table 14-1. If the t-statistic indicates that a coefficient is significant at the .1 level, the coefficient is denoted by an asterisk in Table 14-1. (The Durbin-Watson statistic, which appears in Table 14-1, is of limited value, since it can be shown that the presence of a lagged endogenous variable will cause it to be biased toward 2.00.)

Table 14-1   Regression Results, Model of State Expenditures for Education by State

State	Regression Coefficient			Statistical Values		
	a	b	c	Standard Error	R^2	D.W.[a]
1. Ala.	0.3106*	1.0025*	0.7192*	3.0736	.9591	1.982
2. Ariz.	0.9972*	−0.0059	0.0710	5.7458	.9379	1.798
3. Ark.	−0.2248	−0.4180	1.1196*	2.5760	.9534	2.044
4. Calif.	1.0802*	0.9001	−0.0665	2.5170	.9766	1.963
5. Colo.	1.0482*	0.1893	0.0356	3.1798	.9806	2.016
6. Conn.	0.8952*	−4.9766	0.4874	2.5420	.9557	2.031
7. Del.	0.3042	−7.3108	3.2573*	16.5892	.7543	1.719
8. Fla.	0.6280*	0.7420	0.3919*	3.8221	.9192	1.851
9. Ga.	0.2955*	1.4735	0.7335*	2.3524	.9673	1.788
10. Idaho	0.7167*	−1.4857*	0.3000*	2.2319	.9777	2.002
11. Ill.	−0.6872*	6.6989*	0.9173*	2.4995	.9673	1.825
12. Ind.	0.7107*	1.6718	0.3993	2.6353	.9824	1.914
13. Iowa	0.7340*	0.5835	0.2699	1.9725	.9786	1.949
14. Kans.	0.3499	−0.3451	0.7735*	2.9698	.9528	1.956
15. Ky.	1.0468*	−3.2248*	0.2738*	3.6778	.9665	1.991
16. La.	1.1837*	−0.1592	−0.1680	4.0730	.9525	1.985
17. Maine	0.9538*	1.8288	0.0516	2.1772	.9676	1.602
18. Md.	0.8464*	1.4295	0.1052	3.6505	.9481	2.132
19. Mass.	0.0329	2.4742	0.4930*	1.7659	.9516	1.892
20. Mich.	0.6941*	−2.6788	0.9864	3.3104	.9661	1.807

State	Regression Coefficient			Statistical Values		
	a	b	c	Standard Error	R^2	D.W.[a]
21. Minn.	0.7393*	0.6564	0.4294	2.3290	.9865	2.116
22. Miss.	0.5581*	−1.0673	0.5467*	4.3368	.9379	2.000
23. Mo.	−0.0886	−1.2537	1.1267*	2.2662	.9671	1.533
24. Mont.	0.3055*	1.7247*	0.6318*	3.9512	.9312	1.587
25. Nebr.	0.7278*	0.1723	0.1770	1.6966	.9393	1.646
26. Nev.	0.4881*	−6.7840*	1.0162*	8.5777	.8988	2.556
27. N. H.	0.4987*	−0.0187	0.4383*	2.0775	.9457	1.141
28. N. J.	0.8334*	−2.7092	0.1890*	2.1466	.9356	1.758
29. N. Mex.	0.8952*	0.3022	0.3086	9.7610	.8973	1.917
30. N. Y.	1.1349*	−4.6460	0.1834	2.6157	.9863	1.954
31. N. C.	0.4898*	2.2784	0.5546*	3.5304	.9511	1.779
32. N. Dak.	−0.5770*	3.4794	1.5320*	4.5963	.9471	1.809
33. Ohio	0.9291*	−0.0971	0.0858	1.0859	.9784	2.003
34. Okla.	0.5806*	0.2230	0.5658*	3.7960	.9378	1.502
35. Ore.	0.2297	0.3361	0.7298*	1.9074	.9920	1.978
36. Pa.	0.1208	−10.4398*	1.4258*	3.6834	.9349	2.054
37. R. I.	0.8090*	0.8501	0.3011	4.3529	.9264	2.167
38. S. C.	1.1385*	6.4303*	−0.3981*	6.3539	.5080	2.020
39. S. Dak.	0.7269*	1.1123	0.1808	2.1208	.9722	1.364
40. Tenn.	0.8583*	−1.2080*	0.2721*	1.0551	.9922	2.087
41. Tex.	1.1730*	−1.8102*	−0.0033	3.7511	.9321	2.209
42. Utah	0.4171*	2.5673*	0.4683*	5.7335	.9694	2.059
43. Vt.	0.6053*	−0.0901	0.6735*	5.2427	.9358	1.934
44. Va.	0.2698*	−0.2677	0.6633*	1.0437	.9911	2.249
45. Wash.	0.6544*	−0.7675	0.7923	3.9302	.9827	1.774
46. W. Va.	1.0006*	0.5125	0.0496	2.4023	.9663	2.049
47. Wisc.	0.3800	3.5474*	0.2458*	1.7620	.9914	2.082
48. Wyo.	0.6228*	2.9402*	0.4243	8.1878	.8281	2.236

[a] Statistics for the Durbin-Watson test.

Source. Data for the regressions are from the *Compendium of State Government Finances in 19xx* (1950 to 1966).

This model might be criticized on the grounds that it excludes the variable personal income per capita which has been found to be significant in many studies. For example, Jerry Miner [18] found with his model of local expenditures on education that "The levels of state per capita income are the most important positive determinant of total per capita expenditures."

We originally included per capita personal income in the model, partially because of the weight of tradition, but we were forced to drop it because of severe problems with multicollinearity. This omission may not seem quite so surprising when the fact that this model represents a different methodology than the one of previous studies is taken into account. Here, it is the decision-making process itself which is of primary importance. Another difference is that this model explains state, rather than local, expenditures, whereas local expenditures are of primary importance in many of the models that include income as an important explanatory variable. Since the pattern of income distribution among the states changes only very slowly, the omission should not cause any problems with the simulations, which cover a relatively short period of time—seven years. Break [3], for example, refers to the ". . . extent to which population growth and income growth have been matched geographically, thereby producing a high degree of stability in per capita interstate income differentials."

THE POLICY ALTERNATIVES

In theory, there are an infinite number of alternative policies available to federal policy makers for allocating federal funds for education to the states. In practice, because political and institutional constraints, the number of policy alternatives available may be reduced to a relatively small number. Since we are concerned not so much with a particular set of policies but, instead, with a general methodology for testing the effects of any given allocation policy, we shall consider only six somewhat arbitrary policies. The reader, no doubt, can think of numerous other policies which also might be feasible.

To illustrate the methodology, we shall choose a particular measure of effectiveness by which to compare the effects of the six policies. The measure that we have chosen is the ratio of total state educational expenditures to federal payments to the states for education. The rationale for this measure of effectiveness is that the policy makers are concerned with the extent to which different federal allocation schemes motivate the states to spend their own funds for education. We do not claim that this is the only criterion that federal policy makers consider in allocating federal aid to education among the states, but that it is an important one. The methodology that we shall describe is general and can easily be extended to include other criteria, for instance, the distribution of per capita income.

The ratio of total state educational expenditures to total federal payments to the states for education over a period of n years is given by Z where

$$Z = \frac{\sum_{t=1}^{n} \sum_{i=1}^{48} S_t{}^i P_t{}^i}{\sum_{t=1}^{n} \sum_{i=1}^{48} G_t{}^i P_t{}^i} \tag{14-7}$$

and $P_t{}^i$ denotes the population of the ith state in year t.

We shall be concerned with the effects of six different allocation plans on Z for the seven-year period beginning in 1966 and ending in 1972. The plans are defined as follows.

Plan 1. This plan is the control plan, and it calls for increases in federal payments to state i at the rate $\bar{g}_i$ where $\bar{g}_i$ is the average growth rate of G^i for the past five years. Therefore,

$$G_t{}^i = (1 + \bar{g}_i) G_{t-1}^i$$

Plan 2. Under this plan, federal payments to state i are increased by 3 percent over the payments it would have received under the control plan. Hence,

$$G_t{}^i = (1.03)(1 + \bar{g}_i) G_{t-1}^i$$

Plans 3 and 4 allocate federal aid to each state on the basis of its use of federal funds by utilizing the coefficient b in the regression equation. Osman [22] has considered the question of whether federal aid has been mainly a substitute for state and local funds, or whether expenditures from state and local revenue sources have been increased as a result. He defines stimulation as ". . . an increase in state and local expenditures on a given function *from their own revenues* as a result of federal aid to that function." In our model, stimulation occurs if b is greater than one. If b is greater than zero but less than or equal to one, increased federal aid leads to an increase in expenditures but to no stimulation. If b is less than zero, increased federal aid to that state leads to a decrease in per capita expenditure. Osman [22], by using a regression equation to explain the average level of per capita expenditure on education for the United States as a whole by state and local governments, found that, "A high degree of federal stimulation is implied by the large regression coefficient for aid to education. Each added dollar of federal aid was associated with a $5.11 increase in state-local expenditures." An examination of Table 14-1 reveals that our model yields no such large-scale stimulation effect. The coefficient b is greater than one for only 15 states and is negative for 22 states.

Plan 3. If $b > 1$, increase the rate of federal aid by 7 percent,

$$G_t{}^i = (1.07)(1 + \bar{g}_i)\, G_{t-1}^i,$$

if $b < 1$, decrease the rate of federal payments by 2 percent,

$$G_t{}^i = (.98)(1 + \bar{g}_i)\, G_{t-1}^i.$$

Plan 4. This plan is similar to Plan 3 except that it does not penalize states that are not stimulated to spend more than they receive, even though they do increase their total expenditures as a result of federal aid. If $b > 1$, increase the rate of federal payments by 3 percent

$$G_t{}^i = (1.03)(1 + \bar{g}_i)\, G_{t-1}^i.$$

If $0 \le b \le 1$, federal aid is identical to that of the control plan (Plan 1),

$$G_t{}^i = (1 + \bar{g}_i)\, G_{t-1}^i.$$

If $b < 0$, federal aid is decreased by 2 percent,

$$G_t{}^i = (.98)(1 + \bar{g}_i)\, G_{t-1}^i.$$

Plans 5 and 6 attempt to reward the states that are in some sense "leaders" and, thus, indirectly to stimulate expenditures in states that are "followers." Suppose then we let C denote the set of states for which the coefficient c in the model is significant at the .1 level. For each state, the percentage of its boundary which touches a state or states that are in set C was computed.

Plan 5. Under this plan, federal payments are increased by 6 percent to the 20 states that are characterized by the fact that, at least, 60 percent of their boundaries adjoin states for which the neighborhood variable c is significant.

Plan 6. Federal payments are increased by 3 percent to the 31 states for which, at least, 50 percent of their boundaries adjoin states for which the neighborhood variable is significant.

POLICY SIMULATIONS

To test the effects of the six allocation plans on Z, the state-federal educational expenditure ratio, we conducted policy simulation experiments with our model for a seven-year period (1966 to 1972). For a given plan, we solved for S^i each period in terms of (1) the value of S^i generated by the model in the preceding period, (2) the value of G_{t-1}^i, as given by the particular plan, (3) the value of the neighborhood variable, and (4) the stochastic error term. We assumed that the error terms were normally distributed with expected value equal to zero and standard deviation equal to the standard error of the estimate. For each plan we ran the simulation seven years and calculated Z. The population variables used to calculate Z were obtained by the following formula.

$$P_t{}^i = (1 + \bar{p}_i)\, P_{t-1}^i \qquad (14\text{-}8)$$

where $\bar{p}_i$ is the average growth rate of P^i for 1961 to 1965.

There are two reasons for making the simulations stochastic. First, by including the stochastic variable $E_t{}^i$, we consider the random effects that have not been explained by our model. Second, we now can say something about the degree of confidence that we have in any inferences that we might make about the differences in the effects of the six policies on the state-federal educational expenditure ratio. For each plan, we replicated the simulation experiment 30 times. The output data for the simulation experiment are shown in Table 14-2. Each column contains 30 different values of the state-federal educational expenditure ratio Z, one for each replication of the experiment.

The sample means ($\bar{Z}_j$) for each of the six plans appear in Table 14-3.

DATA ANALYSIS

To analyze the output data generated by our simulation experiment, we make use of the methodological scheme outlined in Chapter 7. Specifically, we consider three different forms of the analysis of variance to analyze the effects of the six different allocation plans on the state-federal education expenditure ratio. These forms are (1) the F-test, (2) multiple comparisons, and (3) a multiple ranking procedure.

F-Test

Suppose that we wish to test the null hypothesis H_0 that the expected state-federal education expenditure ratios for each of the six allocation plans are equal. By employing the F-statistic, the decision rule for accepting or rejecting H_0 becomes

> If $F \geq F_{\alpha, k-1, k(n-1)}$ reject H_0.
> Otherwise   accept H_0.

Table 14-2 State-Federal Education Expenditure Ratios Generated by Simulation Runs Using Six Alternative Federal Allocation Plans

Repli- cation	Plan 1	Plan 2	Plan 3	Plan 4	Plan 5	Plan 6
1	7.0254	6.1703	7.5007	7.4588	6.4170	6.4481
2	7.0478	6.1266	7.3887	7.5018	6.1476	6.4800
3	7.2901	6.0814	7.4198	7.3659	6.2329	6.4187
4	7.1757	6.2612	7.6622	7.3906	6.2582	6.5162
5	7.1121	6.0832	7.4388	7.3559	6.3575	6.3398
6	7.0894	6.1578	7.4383	7.4262	6.2568	6.3380
7	7.0956	6.1413	7.4057	7.5080	6.1207	6.5207
8	7.1343	6.2165	7.3320	7.3453	6.3083	6.2997
9	7.0875	6.0831	7.3667	7.2335	6.2236	6.4266
10	7.3412	6.0439	7.4069	7.4431	6.2305	6.3733
11	7.2635	6.2207	7.3199	7.4494	6.1685	6.4087
12	7.1019	6.2667	7.4871	7.3100	6.1259	6.3993
13	7.1972	6.1859	7.4515	7.4006	6.1946	6.4003
14	7.1002	6.2268	7.4627	7.4020	6.3366	6.5150
15	7.1981	6.1509	7.3867	7.5635	6.2792	6.4534
16	7.0442	6.3245	7.5353	7.5604	6.1267	6.3962
17	7.2412	6.2768	7.3525	7.2819	6.1952	6.4440
18	7.2094	6.2547	7.3677	7.4073	6.2639	6.4058
19	7.1272	6.3520	7.3758	7.3768	6.3634	6.5386
20	7.1217	6.0537	7.4606	7.5633	6.1874	6.5350
21	7.0542	6.1846	7.3678	7.5095	6.1515	6.6129
22	7.2079	6.1877	7.3996	7.3473	6.3798	6.2814
23	7.0578	6.2004	7.3519	7.5017	6.2349	6.3486
24	7.1097	6.2044	7.4310	7.4995	6.2489	6.5805
25	7.1639	6.1920	7.4131	7.5051	6.2013	6.6457
26	7.1649	6.1917	7.3806	7.3840	6.2848	6.3958
27	7.0864	6.1242	7.5250	7.3544	6.4350	6.2790
28	6.8535	6.0441	7.4556	7.5425	6.3191	6.4868
29	6.0634	6.0798	7.5304	7.3991	6.1877	6.4319
30	7.0778	6.1980	7.3278	7.4291	6.3199	6.6603

Table 14-3 Sample Means $(\bar{Z}_j)$ for Six Alternative Allocation Plans

Plan	Sample Mean $(\bar{Z}_j)$
1	7.1281
2	6.1762
3	7.4247
4	7.4272
5	6.2519
6	6.4423

where F is the appropriate percentile of the F-distribution, α is the level of significance, $k = 6$ the number of plans, and $n = 30$ is the number of replications per operating plan. If H_0 is accepted, then one tentatively concludes that the sample differences between plans are attributable to random fluctuations rather than to actual differences in the state-federal expenditure ratios.

The F-statistic is computed by the formula:

$$F = \text{MS}_p/\text{MS}_e$$

where MS_p is the mean square between plans and MS_e is the mean square error. Table 14-4 contains the results of a one-way analysis of variance of the output data that appear in Table 14-2. From the data in Table 14-4, we see that $F = 1349.8$, easily exceeding the critical value of the .005 percent level of significance, $F_{.005,5,174} = 3.35$. Hence, the data generated by the simulation experiment do not support the null hypothesis that the expected state-federal expenditure ratios are equal for each of the six plans.

Table 14-4   Statistics for One-Way Analysis of Variance

Source of Variation	Sum of Squares	Degrsee of Freedom	Mean Square
Between plans	51.252450	5	10.250490
Error	1.321367	174	0.007594
Total	52.573817	179	

Multiple Comparisons

Typically, economic policy makers are interested not only in whether alternatives differ but also in *how* they differ. This suggests the use of confidence intervals.

Because our concern is with differences in population means, we construct a *set* of confidence intervals that will all simultaneously be true with probability 95 percent. Tukey's method [19,20] will yield simultaneous confidence intervals (of the type previously described) for the differences between *all* pairs. With 95 percent probability, *all* of the following confidence intervals for $\text{EZ}_j - \text{EZ}_J$ are true:

$$(\bar{Z}_j - \bar{Z}_J) \pm q_{m,\nu} \sqrt{\frac{\text{MS}_e}{n}} \qquad j,J = 1, 2, 3, \ldots, m$$

where $q_{m,\nu}$ is tabulated under the title "Distribution of the Studentized Range Statistic," and

m = the number of sample means,
ν = the number of degrees of freedom for MS_e, $m(n-1)$
in the case of one-factor experiments.

For the actual data generated by our single-factor computer simulation experiment the formula for 95 percent confidence intervals is given by

$$(\bar{Z}_j - \bar{Z}_J) \pm .006448 \qquad j, J = 1, \ldots, 6$$

Table 14-5 contains a tabulation of the differences between sample means for all 15 pairs of differences in our experiment. An asterisk (*) indicates that a particular difference exceeds the confidence allowance .006448, thus, making the difference "statistically significant," if this form of inference is desired. Notice that all of the differences are significant except the difference in sample means between Plans 3 and 4.

Table 14-5   Differences of Sample Means, $\bar{Z}_i - \bar{Z}_J$

j	J	2	3	4	5	6
1		0.9519*	−0.2966*	−0.2991*	0.8762*	0.6858*
2		–	−1.2485*	−1.2510*	−0.0757*	−0.2661*
3		–	–	−0.0025	1.1728*	0.9824
4		–	–	–	1.1753*	0.9849*
5		–	–	–	–	−0.1904*

Since our analysis has shown that there is no significant difference between Plans 3 and 4, by using the state-federal education expenditure ratio as a criterion, we can drop one of the two plans from consideration before proceeding with our analysis. We arbitrarily drop Plan 3.

Multiple Ranking

For our experiment, suppose that we want to select the plan having the largest state-federal expenditure ratio and to guarantee that the probability of correctly choosing that population will be, at least, .90 when the difference between the plan with the highest expected state-federal expenditure ratio and the plan with the second highest expected state-federal expenditure ratio is .1. This suggests the use of the Bechhofer, Dunnett, and Sobel [1] procedure, which was described in Chapter 7. In other words, we are assuming that P = .90 and $\delta^* = .1$. We then let $N_1 = n = 30$ and calculate $MS_e = .006971$ from Table 14-6. For $P = .90$ and $\nu = m(n - 1) =$ 145, we obtain $h = 2.59$ from Table 3 of [7]. Next we determine

$$\{\max N_1, [2\ MS_e(h/\delta^*)^2]\}$$
$$= \max\ \{30,[2(.006971)(2.59/.1)^2]\},$$
$$= \max\ \{30,9\} = 30.$$

Since $9 < 30$, no second sample is required and $N_2 = N_1 = n = 30$. Sample means for $n = 30$ previously were calculated in Table 14-3. On the basis of the ranking of the sample means, we would select Allocation Plan 4 as the plan with the highest expected state-federal education expenditure ratio. If, in fact, the best plan has an expected state-federal expenditure ratio that differs from the next best by .1, we have, at least, a probability of 90 percent of correctly choosing it despite the random statistical fluctuations of sampling.

Table 14-6   Statistics for One-Way Analysis of Variance for Simulation Excluding Plan 3

Source of Variation	Sum of Squares	Degrees of Freedom	Mean Square
Between plans	37.665330	4	9.416334
Error	1.010830	145	0.006871
Total	38.676160	149	

BIBLIOGRAPHY

1. Bechhofer, R. E., Dunnett, C. W., and Sobel, M. "A Two-Sample Multiple Decision Procedure for Ranking Means of Normal Populations with a Common Unknown Variance," *Biometrika*, **XLI** (1954), 170-176.
2. Brazer, Harvey E. "The Federal Government and State-Local Finances," *National Tax Journal*, **XX** (2) (June 1967), 155-164.
3. Break, George F. *Intergovernmental Fiscal Relations in the United States.* Washington: The Brookings Institute, 1967.
4. Buchanan, James M. *The Public Finances.* Homewood, Ill.: Richard D. Irwin, Inc., 1965.
5. Burkhead, Jesse. *Public School Finance.* Syracuse: Syracuse University Press, 1964.
6. Davis, Otto A., Dempster, M. A. H., and Wildavsky, Aaron. "A Theory of the Budgetary Process," *American Political Science Review*, **LX** (September 1966), 529-547.
7. Dunnett, C. W., and Sobel, M. "A Bivariate Generalization of Student's T-Distribution with Tables for Certain Special Cases," *Biometrika*, **XLI** (1954).

8. Fabricant, Solomon. *Trend of Government Activity Since 1900.* New York: National Bureau of Economic Research, Inc., 1952.

9. Fisher, Glenn. "Determinants of State and Local Government Expenditure: A Preliminary Analysis," *National Tax Journal,* **XIV** (December 1961), 349-355.

10. Fisher, Glenn. "Interstate Variation in State and Local Government Expenditures," *National Tax Journal,* **XVII** (March 1964), 57-74.

11. Gillespie, W. Irwin. "Effect of Public Expenditures on the Distribution of Income," *Essays in Fiscal Federalism.* Edited by R. A. Musgrave. Washington: The Brookings Institute, 122-186.

12. Goldberger, Arthur S. *Econometric Theory.* New York: John Wiley & Sons, Inc., 1964.

13. Haskell, M. A. "Federal Grants and the Income Density Effect," *National Tax Journal,* **XV** (March 1962), 105-108.

14. Isard, Walter. *Methods of Regional Analysis.* Cambridge: The M.I.T. Press, 1960.

15. Johnston, J. *Econometric Methods.* New York: McGraw-Hill Book Co., Inc., 1963.

16. Malinvaud, E. *Statistical Methods of Econometrics.* Chicago: Rand McNally and Company, 1966.

17. Maxwell, James A. *Financing State and Local Governments.* Washington: The Brookings Institution, 1965.

18. Miner, Jerry. *Social and Economic Factors in Spending for Public Education.* Syracuse: Syracuse University Press, 1963.

19. Naylor, Thomas H., Wertz, Kenneth, and Wonnacott, Thomas H. "Methods for Analyzing Data from Computer Simulation Experiments," *Communications of the ACM,* **X** (November 1967), 703-710.

20. Naylor, Thomas H., Wertz, K., and Wonnacott, T. "Some Methods for Evaluating the Effects of Economic Policies Using Simulation Experiments," *Review of the International Statistical Institute,* **XXXVI** (1968), 184-200.

21. Norman, M. R. "OLS Autoregressive Program," Economics Research Units, University of Pennsylvania.

22. Osman, Jack. "The Dual Impact of Federal Aid on State and Local Government Expenditures," *National Tax Journal,* **XIX** (December 1966), 362-372.

23. Sacks, S., and Harris, Robert. "The Determinants of State and Local Government Expenditures and Intergovernmental Flows of Funds," *National Tax Journal,* **XVII** (March 1964), 75-85.

24. Sargent, Thomas J. "Some Evidence on the Small Sample Properties of Distributed Lag Estimators in the Presence of Autocorrelated Disturbances," *Review of Economics and Statistics,* **XLX** (February 1968), 87-95.

25. Shapiro, Sherman. "Some Socioeconomic Determinants of Expenditures for Education: Southern and Other States Compared," *Comparative Education Review,* **VI** (October 1962), 160-166.

26. Tiebout, Charles. "A Pure Theory of Local Expenditures," *Journal of Political Economy*, **LXIV** (October 1956), 416-424.

27. U. S. Bureau of the Budget. *The Budget of the United States Government for the Fiscal Year Ending June 30, 1966.* Washington: U. S. Government Printing Office, 1966.

28. U. S. Bureau of the Census. *Compendium of State Government Finances in 1965* (1950 to 1965).

29. Weisbrod, Burton. *External Benefits of Education.* Princeton, N. J.: Industrial Relations Section, Princeton University, 1964.

30. Wildavsky, Aaron. *The Politics of the Budgetary Process.* Boston: Little, Brown and Company, 1964.

Chapter 15 | A Model of the

United States Monetary Sector[1]

JAMES M. BOUGHTON AND THOMAS H. NAYLOR

INTRODUCTION

This chapter describes an econometric model of the monetary sector of the United States economy. Computer simulation techniques are used to validate the model and to test the effects of several alternative monetary policies on the behavior of a set of target variables. Unlike its predecessors—the Brookings Model [9] and the F.R.B.-M.I.T. Model [9]—this model was specifically designed to trace through the transmission of monetary policies to the proximate and intermediate targets of the Federal Reserve, principally through the commercial banking system. Although previous simulation studies with monetary models (including the work of deLeeuw [7], deLeeuw and Gramlich [9], and Fromm and Taubman [12]) have focused on a small number of different monetary policies (usually two or three), we shall consider seven of these policies in order to study the similarities and the differences in the tools available to the Federal Reserve. Also by examining several different intermediate targets, we shall be able to examine the independence of those targets and the consequences of using each one of them.

The 17 equations of the model explain movements in six intermediate policy targets: currency, demand deposits, time deposits, interest rates on government bonds and on mortgage loans, and the volume of mortgage loans. (Although the last item is not usually included in such a list, it is clear from policy actions during the 1966 credit crunch that availabilityof funds to the housing market is, indeed, a high priority target.) The remain-

[1] This chapter is based on a paper by James M. Boughton and Thomas H. Naylor entitled "Simulation Experiments with a Monetary Policy Model," which was published in *Applied Economics*, II (August, 1970).

ing 10 equations explain the "status" variables that are necessary for understanding the transmission of policy to the targets. Basically, these status variables are the short-term money market guides, or the proximate targets, of the Federal Reserve: member bank reserves and subdivisions thereof, commercial loan volume, activity in federal funds, and short-term interest rates.

The predetermined variables in the model, aside from the lagged values of endogenous variables, fall into two groups: policy instruments and non-monetary variables from other economic sectors. The latter group includes GNP, disposable personal income, business investment, and housing starts. The policy instruments include the central open-market variable, unborrowed reserves plus currency, the discount rate, ceiling rates on time deposits and on FHA-insured loans, required reserve ratios, and two Treasury-controlled variables—government demand deposit balances and the maturity structure of the federal debt.

VARIABLES

The data used to estimate the parameters of the model are all seasonally unadjusted, except for disposable income, which is available only in adjusted form. All monetary variables are in billions of dollars, and interest rates are in decimal form. The model consists of 17 endogenous variables (including six intermediate policy targets and 11 status variables), 10 policy instruments, and five exogenous variables. These variables are defined below.

TARGET VARIABLES

Financial Assets

CURR	Currency	Currency liabilities of the Treasury and Federal Reserve Banks, less currency holdings of commercial banks. *Source. Federal Reserve Bulletin.*
DD	Demand deposits	Demand deposits in member banks, net of cash items in process of collection and demand deposits due from domestic commercial banks. *Source. Board of Governors of the Federal Reserve System, "Aggregate Reserves and Member Bank Deposits," Release G.10 of the Division of Research and Statistics.*

| ML | Mortgage loans | New mortgage loans of all Savings and Loan Associations. *Source. Business Statistics* and *Survey of Current Business.* |
| TD | Time deposits | Time and savings deposits in member banks. *Source.* Same as DD. |

Interest Rates

| RM_{GL} | Bond rate | Market yield on Treasury securities maturing or callable in 10 years or more. *Source.* Unpublished data appendix to [8] and *Federal Reserve Bulletin.* |
| RM_{ML} | Mortgage loan rate | Rates charged for conventional first mortgage loans on new residential construction. *Source.* Federal Reserve Bank of Atlanta and *Federal Reserve Bulletin.* |

STATUS VARIABLES

Financial Assets

CL	Commercial loans	Commercial and industrial loans made by weekly reporting member banks. *Source. Federal Reserve Bulletin.*
FF	Federal funds loans	Gross purchases of Federal funds by 46 major Reserve City Banks. *Source. Federal Reserve Bulletin.*
RES_B	Reserves, borrowed	Reserves borrowed by member banks from the Federal Reserve. *Source.* Same as DD.
RES_E	Reserves, excess	Excess reserves of member banks. *Source.* Same as DD.
RES_F	Reserves, free	Free reserves of all member banks. *Source.* Same as DD.
RES_R	Reserves, required	Required reserves for all member banks. *Source.* Same as DD.
RES_T	Reserves, total	Total reserves held by all member banks. *Source.* Same as DD.

Interest Rates

| RM_{CL} | Commercial loan rate | Rates charged by banks on short-term business loans. *Source. Federal Reserve Bulletin.* |

RM_{FF} Federal funds rate   Average rates charged by major banks for purchase of Federal funds. *Source. Federal Reserve Bulletin.*

RM_{GS} Treasury bill rate   Market yield on 91-day Treasury bills. *Source.* Unpublished data appendix to [8] and *Federal Reserve Bulletin.*

RM_{TD} Time deposit rate   Yield on time deposits at commercial banks. *Source.* Unpublished data appendix to [8] and [17].

POLICY INSTRUMENTS

Financial Assets

BF_L Long-term debt   Outstanding Treasury bonds. *Source. Federal Reserve Bulletin.*

BF_{PUB} Total debt   Total publicly-held marketable Treasury debt. *Source. Federal Reserve Bulletin.*

BF_S Short-term debt   Outstanding Treasury bills. *Source. Federal Reserve Bulletin.*

DD_{GF} Government deposits   United States Government-owned demand deposits. *Source.* Same as DD.

RES_{NBC} Reserves, unborrowed, plus currency   Unborrowed reserves plus currency as defined above for CURR. *Source.* Same as DD and *Federal Reserve Bulletin.*

RRR_{DD} Reserve ratio on DD   Reserve ratio required against time deposits. *Source. Federal Reserve Bulletin.*

RRR_{TD} Reserve ratio on TD   Reserve ratio required against time deposits. *Source. Federal Reserve Bulletin.*

Interest Rates

RM_{FHA} FHA ceiling   Federal Housing Administration limit on interest rates charged for mortgage loans insured by it. *Source. Savings and Loan Fact Book.*

RM_{FRB} Federal Reserve discount rate   Discount rate at the Federal Reserve Bank of New York. *Source. Federal Reserve Bulletin.*

RM_{TDM} Ceiling on RM_{TD} Maximum rate payable on time and savings deposits at commercial banks, under Regulation Q of the Federal

Reserve Board of Governors. A weighted average of ceilings applicable to different types of deposits. *Source. Federal Reserve Bulletin.*

EXOGENOUS VARIABLES

HU_{STS}	Housing starts	New housing units started; privately owned dwellings only. In millions of units. *Source. Business Statistics.*
I_{BSNS}	Investment	Business expenditures on new plant and equipment, plus net changes in inventories. *Source. National Income* and *Product Accounts of the United States.*
Q_i	Seasonal dummies	Quarterly dummies for seasonal adjustment. $Q_i = 1$ in the ith quarter of each year, and $Q_i = 0$ otherwise.
W	Public wealth	Public wealth, computed as an average of recent values of GNP.
Y_D	Disposable income	Disposable personal income, seasonally adjusted at annual rates. *Source. Business Statistics.*

THE MODEL

All regressions were estimated by two-stage least squares. For each behavioral equation the time period over which the equation was estimated is listed along with the adjusted value of R^2; the Durbin-Watson statistic (DW), and the standard error of the estimate (SE). Standard errors for each coefficient are listed in parentheses below the coefficients. The model consists of 13 behavioral equations and four identities. The equations are listed below.

BEHAVIORAL EQUATIONS

Currency Holdings

$$\Delta CURR = -0.2186 - 0.1662\,CURR_{-1} - 0.0299\,DD - 0.00047\,RM_{TD}W$$
$$(.0514) \qquad (.0082) \qquad (.00025)$$

$$+0.1723\,RES_{NBC} - 0.3913\,Q_1 - 0.0133\,Q_2 + 0.1860\,Q_3$$
$$(.0380)$$

$$+ 0.2186\,Q_4 \qquad\qquad (15\text{-}1)$$

$$\bar{R}^2 = .80$$
$$DW = 1.11 \qquad\qquad (1951\ I\text{-}1966\ IV)$$
$$SE = 0.17$$

Demand Deposit Holdings

$$\Delta DD = -2.0338 - 0.1674\, DD_{-1} - 0.0104\, RM_{TD}W - 0.0039\, RM_{GS}W$$
$$ (.0636) \qquad\qquad (.0075) \qquad\qquad (.0011)$$

$$+ 0.2569\, RES_{NBC} + 0.0287\, Y_D + 0.0623\, Q_1$$
$$(.0510) \qquad\qquad (.0203)$$

$$- 1.6449\, Q_2 - 0.4512\, Q_3 + 2.0338\, Q_4 \qquad\qquad (15\text{-}2)$$

$\bar{R}^2 = .88$
DW $= 1.54$ (1951 I-1966 IV)
SE $= 0.57$

Time Deposit Holdings

$$\Delta TD = -10.1473 - 0.0444\, TD_{-1} + 0.0132\, RM_{TD}W \qquad (15\text{-}3)$$
$$ (.0392) \qquad\qquad (.0035)$$

$$- 0.0086\, RM_{GS}W + 0.2811\, RES_{NBC} + 0.3524\, Q_1$$
$$(.0015) \qquad\qquad (.1727)$$

$$+ 0.3290\, Q_2 - 0.0192\, Q_3 - 0.6622\, Q_4$$

$\bar{R}^2 = .73$
DW $= 1.04$ (1951 I-1966 IV)
SE $= .73$

Volume of Commercial Loans

$$\Delta CL = -3.9925 - .1198\, CL_{-1} - .0558\, \Delta(RM_{GS}RES_R) \qquad (15\text{-}4)$$
$$ (2.0180) \quad (.0419) \qquad\quad (.0395)$$

$$+ .1752\, \Delta(RM_{CL}RES_R) + .2957\, RES_T + .3184\, I_{BSNS}$$
$$(.1130) \qquad\qquad\qquad (.1724) \qquad\quad (.0712)$$

$$- .4542\, Q_1 + .0646\, Q_2 - .0762\, Q_3 + .4658\, Q_4$$

$\bar{R}^2 = .56$
DW $= 2.17$ (1951 I-1966 IV)
SE $= .71$

Borrowed Bank Reserves

$$\Delta RES_B = -.6611\, (RES_B)_{-1} + .0051\, RM_{FRB}RES_R - .0593\, FF$$
$$ (.0655) \qquad\qquad (.0011) \qquad\qquad (.0331)$$

$$- .3191\, RES_F \qquad\qquad\qquad\qquad\qquad\qquad (15\text{-}5)$$
$$(.0385)$$

$\bar{R}^2 = .82$
DW $= 1.75$ (1960 I-1966 IV)
SE $= .04$

Borrowed Federal Funds

$$\Delta FF = -.8449 - .6543\ FF_{-1} + .0270\ RM_{FF}RES_R + 1.1851\ RES_F$$
$$(.2239)\quad(.1279)\qquad(.0050)\qquad\qquad(.2790)$$

$\bar{R}^2 = .53$
$DW = 2.18$ (1960 I-1966 IV)
$SE = .13$

Volume of Mortgage Loans

$$\Delta ML = -8.3084 - .4527\ ML_{-1} + .0401\ RM_{ML}W - .0394\ RM_{CL}W$$
$$(2.9035)\quad(.0539)\qquad(.0125)\qquad\quad(.0096)$$
$$+ .0690\ HU_{STS}W \qquad\qquad\qquad\qquad (15\text{-}7)$$
$$(.0052)$$

$\bar{R}^2 = .86$
$DW = .97$ (1957 II-1966 IV)
$SE = .91$

Interest Rate on Treasury Bills

$$\Delta RM_{GS} = -0.0060\ (RM_{GS})_{-1} + 0.9023\ \Delta RM_{FRB}$$
$$\phantom{\Delta RM_{GS} =}(.0106)\qquad\qquad(.1631)$$
$$\phantom{\Delta RM_{GS} =}- 9.1861\ \Delta(RES_F/RES_R) + 2.6417\ \Delta(BF_S/BF_{PUB})\quad(15\text{-}8)$$
$$\phantom{\Delta RM_{GS} =}(4.3077)\qquad\qquad\qquad(1.0752)$$

$\bar{R}^2 = .65$
$DW = 1.81$ (1951 I-1966 IV)
$SE = .22$

Interest Rate on Treasury Bonds

$$\Delta RM_{GL} = -.1947 + .2481\ \Delta RM_{GS} - .0429\ (RM_{GL})_{-1}\qquad(15\text{-}9)$$
$$\phantom{\Delta RM_{GL} =}(.0372)\qquad\qquad(.0222)$$
$$\phantom{\Delta RM_{GL} =}+ 1.7912\ CL/(DD + TD) - 1.1063\ \Delta(BF_L/BF_{PUB})$$
$$\phantom{\Delta RM_{GL} =}(.8379)\qquad\qquad\qquad(.8771)$$
$$\phantom{\Delta RM_{GL} =}+ .0200\ Q_1 + .0207\ Q_2 + .0179\ Q_3 - .0586\ Q_4$$

$\bar{R}^2 = .51$
$DW = 2.19$ (1951 I-1966 IV)
$SE = .09$

Interest Rate on Time Deposits

$$\Delta RM_{TD} = -.1208 - .0046\ (RM_{TD})_{-1} + .2747\ \Delta RM_{TDM} \qquad (15\text{-}10)$$
$$\phantom{\Delta RM_{TD} = } (.0469)\quad (.0048)\qquad\qquad (.0224)$$
$$+ .8361\ CL/(DD + TD)$$
$$(.2567)$$

$$\bar{R}^2 = .73$$
$$DW = 2.05 \qquad\qquad (1951\ \text{I-}1966\ \text{IV})$$
$$SE = .03$$

Interest Rate on Commercial Loans

$$\Delta RM_{CL} = -.4692 - .0660\ (RM_{CL})_{-1} + .4621\ \Delta RM_{FRB} \qquad (15\text{-}11)$$
$$\phantom{\Delta RM_{CL} = } (.1544)\quad (.0228)\qquad\qquad (.0551)$$
$$+ 3.9316\ CL/(DD + TD)$$
$$(1.0147)$$

$$\bar{R}^2 = .58$$
$$DW = 1.81 \qquad\qquad (1951\ \text{I-}1966\ \text{IV})$$
$$SE = .10$$

Interest Rate on Federal Funds

$$\Delta RM_{FF} = .0035\ (RM_{FF})_{-1} + .4367\ \Delta RM_{GS} + .7345\ \Delta RM_{FRB} \quad (15\text{-}12)$$
$$\phantom{\Delta RM_{FF} = } (.0087)\qquad\qquad (.1201)\qquad\qquad (.1792)$$

$$\bar{R}^2 = .79$$
$$DW = 1.60 \qquad\qquad (1955\ \text{II-}1966\ \text{IV})$$
$$SE = .18$$

Interest Rate on Mortgage Loans

$$\Delta RM_{ML} = -.2090\ (RM_{ML})_{-1} + .1344\ \Delta RM_{GS} + .2320\ RM_{FHA} \quad (15\text{-}13)$$
$$\phantom{\Delta RM_{ML} = } (.0754)\qquad\qquad (.0276)\qquad\qquad (.0829)$$

$$\bar{R}^2 = .53$$
$$DW = .81 \qquad\qquad (1957\ \text{II-}1966\ \text{IV})$$
$$SE = .07$$

IDENTITIES

Required Reserves

$$RES_R = RRR_{DD}(DD + DD_{GF}) + RRR_{TD}TD \qquad (15\text{-}14)$$

Free Reserves

$$RES_F = RES_{NBC} - CURR - RES_R \qquad (15\text{-}15)$$

Excess Reserves

$$RES_E = RES_F + RES_B \qquad (15\text{-}16)$$

Total Reserves

$$RES_T = RES_R + RES_E \qquad (15\text{-}17)$$

ANALYSIS OF THE MODEL

Equation 15-1 gives an idea of the general form of all of the equations. The left-hand side is the one-period change in currency, and the first right-hand term is the level of the dependent variable, lagged one quarter.

The second term on the right is demand deposits—the other component of the money supply, along with currency. In the absence of a useful series on the implicit interest rate on demand deposits, this term is to be regarded as a measure of the substitution effect between CURR and DD.

The third term is the interest rate on time deposits, multiplied by public wealth. The time deposit rate is included as the price of a substitute good and, as expected, it has a negative coefficient. It is multiplied by wealth in order to transform it into dollars, so as to reflect general price changes. This satisfies the postulate that asset demands are not subject to a money illusion: that they are homogenous of degree zero with respect to general price changes.

There is no direct price variable in this equation simply because currency has no measurable price; more exactly, its price is identically zero. In later equations, the own price is included whenever possible.

The fourth term in (15-1) is the open-market variable, RES_{NBC}. This is included as an essential link between policy and currency holdings. Finally, the equation contains quarterly dummies for seasonal adjustment; the coefficients reflect the expected seasonal pattern in currency requirements.

The form of the demand-deposit equation (15-2) is very similar to the one for currency. The time deposit rate is included and has a somewhat higher coefficient than in the first equation, as would be expected. The bill rate is significant and, in fact, adds a great deal of explanatory power to the equation. As before, RES_{NBC} (unborrowed reserves plus currency) is included to establish the basic policy linkage. Disposable income, which did nothing for currency, is helpful in explaining demand deposits in standard Cambridge fashion (a rise in income requiring a rise in the money supply).

The time-deposit equation (15-3) contains nothing that is unfamiliar. For the first time, however, we have the "own" interest rate in measurable form. The coefficient, of course, is positive and is approximately equal in absolute value to the sum of the cross-effects in (15-1) and (15-2).

The time-deposit rate itself is explained in (15-10). The principal explanatory variable is the maximum rate that banks are permitted to pay under Regulation Q of the Federal Reserve. The inclusion of this term alone accounts for nearly 70 percent of the variance of RM_{TD}. The loan-deposit ratio is also included, to reflect the pressures on the banking system that lead to increases in both RM_{TDM} and RM_{TD}.

There are three different loan markets in the model, comprising six equations. The functions of these markets can be described briefly. First, there are two equations expressing the market for commercial loans. They are included because the ratio of commercial loans to total deposits forms one of the main internal constraints on bank asset expansion. There is also a market for mortgage loans. This is included because policy actions in the past few years have shown that an adequate flow of funds into this market is a prime policy objective. Finally, there is a market for government securities, given by the equations for short- and long-term interest rates on these assets. This market is included because Treasury securities are the principal medium through which policy is transmitted into the banking system.

The heart of the model is the market for bank reserves, expressed in (15-5), (15-14), and (15-15). The process of reserve determination is controlled by the open-market variable, RES_{NBC}. The function of the model is to show how changes in RES_{NBC} are distributed among its components: currency holdings, required reserves, and free reserves. Required reserves are given by identity (15-14) and by the reduced-form relations for deposits, in which RES_{NBC} plays an important role. The addition of the behavioral equation for currency completes the system, and the level of free reserves is given as a residual.

To illustrate this process, consider the case of reserve contraction by the Federal Reserve. RES_{NBC} falls, bringing reductions in the supplies of currency, demand deposits, and time deposits. Required reserves fall, and the entire model—interest rates included—will equilibrate to restore desired levels of free reserves.

This model eliminates the concept of banks demanding "free" or excess reserves, because these reserves are not, from the view of the banker, quantities that are demandable. Bankers can borrow reserves from one or more sources and, if they borrow from outside the sector, they will create reserves temporarily. But the "demandable" quantities to the banker are securities discounted at the Federal Reserve and the funds that are borrowed from other banks (federal funds). For example, if a bank finds that it will be deficient in reserves during a given period, it may borrow reserves either from the Federal Reserve or from another bank. For the banking system as a whole, the choice is between (a) increasing reserve volume by borrowing from the Federal Reserve and (b) increasing the rate of use of existing reserves by activating the interbank market for federal funds. In either case, the aggregate level of free reserves is unaffected, and the level of excess reserves is altered exactly by the volume of discounting.

This particular taxonomy is desirable because it divides reserves into three components that are determined in three quite different ways, isolating the different determinants of total reserves:

1. Required reserves are determined by public demand for bank deposits and by the reserve ratios set by the Federal Reserve. Indirectly, of course, they are strongly affected by other Federal Reserve policies.

2. Free reserves are determined by the difference between the volume of unborrowed reserves plus currency supplied by the Federal Reserve, on the one hand, and the volume needed for currency demands and required reserves, on the other.

3. Borrowed reserves are determined by bank demands, subject to the explicit and implicit restrictions of the Federal Reserve.

VALIDATION

Having formulated an econometric model of the monetary sector and having estimated its parameters, we now must consider the question of the validity of the model before we use it to conduct monetary policy simulation experiments. Specifically, we are concerned with the degree to which the simulated time paths of the endogenous variables of the model conform to the actual observed time paths. That is, we simulate the behavior of the monetary sector by solving each quarter for the values of the 17 endogenous variables in terms of the given values of the policy variables and exogenous variables and the values of the lagged endogenous variables generated in previous periods. We then compare the simulated output of the model with the actual observed values of the time paths of the targets and the status variables. Tables 15-1 to 15-5 contain graphical comparisons of the simulated time series and the observed values of the six target variables of our model over the seven-year period beginning in 1960 and ending in 1966. A casual observation of these results would lead us to the tentative conclusion that our simulations conform reasonably well to the observed data. The major exception seems to be that when the mortgage loan market crumbled in 1965 and 1966 under the pressure of historically high interest rates, the simulations miscalculated both the interest-rate pressure and the consequent decline. Of course, we recognize that, in order to say anything definitive about the validity of our model, we should subject our simulation results to more rigorous "goodness of fit" tests [24]. Chapter 5 describes a number of different goodness of fit tests for validating computer simulation models.

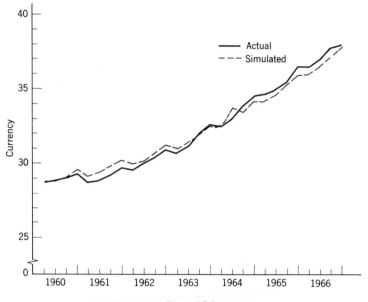

Figure 15-1.

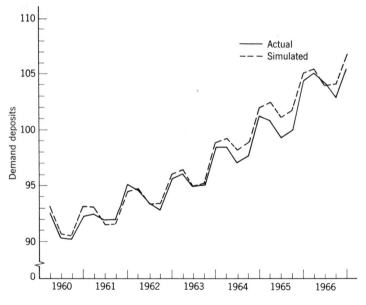

Figure 15-2.

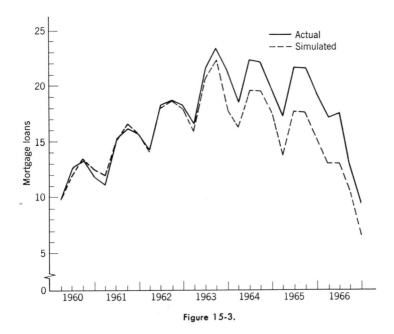

Figure 15-3.

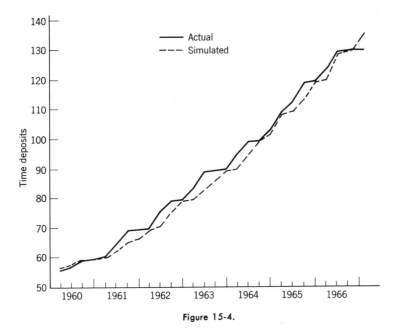

Figure 15-4.

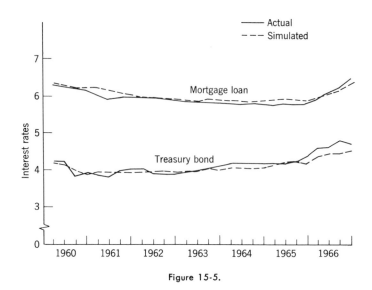

Figure 15-5.

POLICY SIMULATIONS[2]

Within the context of our model, the Federal Reserve has five basic policy tools at its disposal: the supply of reserves, the discount rate, the Regulation Q ceiling, and the reserve requirements on both time and demand deposits. In addition to these instruments, the Federal Housing Administration has one policy tool, the ceiling rate on FHA-insured mortgages. And also the Treasury can vary the maturity structure of the federal debt. The policy simulations that we have performed afford us an opportunity to test for the independence of these instruments. There are two basic limitations to our approach: first, no statistical tests have been made on the simulation results, and second, we have not attempted to compare the magnitudes of changes made in different policies. Therefore, we have tried to compare the directions in which the endogenous variables are pushed when policies are changed, and to determine from this whether the same sort of response could have been produced by a different policy action.

The results of the policy simulations are summarized in the eight tables at the end of this chapter. Table 15-1 lists the simulated values of the endogenous variables from the control run, and the other seven tables show the deviations from the control-run values which result from the various policy actions.

[2] All of the simulations described in this chapter were run with PROGRAM SIMULATE.

Table 15-1 Control Run: Simulated Values of All Endogenous Variables with No Monetary Policy Changes

	1964:3	1964:4	1965:1	1965:2	1965:3	1965:4	1966:1	1966:2	1966:3	1966:4
Targets										
CURR	33.69	34.39	34.40	34.84	35.51	36.21	36.23	36.73	37.44	38.07
DD	97.75	100.84	101.44	100.21	100.81	104.18	104.67	103.32	103.51	106.09
ML	22.09	20.44	17.04	21.46	21.68	19.63	17.74	17.68	15.37	11.47
TD	100.36	103.09	106.61	109.88	112.99	116.02	120.22	124.47	128.44	131.62
RM_{GL}	4.10	4.09	4.15	4.22	4.23	4.18	4.33	4.40	4.48	4.55
RM_{ML}	5.77	5.80	5.84	5.86	5.85	5.83	5.91	6.01	6.10	6.25
Status Variables										
CL	39.16	41.49	43.39	44.97	46.32	49.08	51.57	54.07	55.50	58.57
FF	1.93	2.18	2.57	2.16	1.93	2.64	3.13	3.08	2.79	2.26
RES_B	0.26	0.27	0.26	0.45	0.56	0.35	0.32	0.38	0.50	0.72
RES_F	0.23	0.25	0.33	-0.18	-0.25	0.41	0.36	0.17	-0.10	-0.53
RES_R	20.38	20.86	21.07	21.33	21.44	21.38	21.91	22.00	22.25	22.56
RM_{CL}	4.97	5.06	5.22	5.25	5.28	5.41	5.65	5.74	5.83	5.95
RM_{FF}	3.45	3.67	3.98	4.04	4.02	4.06	4.45	4.45	4.47	4.55
RM_{GS}	3.42	3.61	3.84	4.02	4.01	3.88	4.22	4.25	4.33	4.54
RM_{TD}	3.43	3.59	3.62	3.67	3.71	3.76	4.03	4.09	4.15	4.20

The first policy change was a $500 million decrease in the supply of unborrowed reserves plus currency (RES_{NBC})—the primary policy tool of the Federal Open Market Committee of the Federal Reserve System. The level of this variable, through a multiplier process, should control the levels of outstanding financial assets within some degree of tolerance. The effects of changes here are well known, through extensive treatment in the literature and through the previous monetary policy simulation studies. There are, however, a few new wrinkles to be pointed out (see Table 15-2 below). First, the volume of new mortgage loans is affected only after a fairly long lag. The initial response of ML is an increase of approximately $150 million, as funds shift out of the banking system into other institutions. This increase is not wiped out in our model until about six quarters later, after which mortgage loans fall steadily along with other assets.

The second point is that interest rates, particularly those on Treasury bills and federal funds, rise initially but return to their control-run levels after a very few quarters. This suggests that these rates are responding to the rate of change in the money stock, rather than to its absolute level.

It may also be of interest to observe the changes in the level and in the distribution of total bank reserves. Initially, most of the decrease in reserve supply is absorbed by reductions in free reserves, offset by increases in the borrowing of reserves. Over the span of the simulation, the levels of RES_F and RES_B are restored to their normal paths. By the end of the period, the $500 million decrease in RES_{NBC} has brought about a $340 million reduction in currency holdings, a $180 million reduction in required reserves, and a $20 million increase in free reserves.

Raising the Discount Rate (Table 15-3) reduces deposits in the expected way, and quite strongly. The effect, furthermore, is sustained over the full period. There is a small increase in currency holdings, reducing the size of the monetary multipliers. The net effect is that a $500 million decrease in RES_{NBC} and a one-half point increase in the discount rate have roughly the same impact on the conventionally defined money supply. The discount rate, however, brings about a far greater change in the broad money supply (including time deposits) than does the given reduction in the supply of reserves.

The key to the differences in the two streams of alterations seems to be that raising the discount rate causes other interest rates to rise also; this is particularly true of the federal funds and the Treasury bill rates. Changing the supply of reserves has only a small and temporary effect on rates in our model. Thus asset levels that are particularly dependent on interest rates are affected more sharply by the discount rate increase than by the reserve squeeze. Time deposits fall markedly. Commercial loan volume actually increases initially, until the credit rationing takes its toll. The mortgage

Table 15-2   Effects on Monetary Variables of a $500 Million Decrease in the Supply of Unborrowed Reserves Plus Currency

	1964:3	1964:4	1965:1	1965:2	1965:3	1965:4	1966:1	1966:2	1966:3	1966:4
Targets										
CURR	-0.08	-0.14	-0.19	-0.23	-0.26	-0.28	-0.30	-0.31	-0.33	-0.34
DD	-0.22	-0.38	-0.49	-0.57	-0.53	-0.67	-0.69	-0.71	-0.72	-0.72
ML	0.15	0.19	0.17	0.12	0.07	0.01	-0.04	-0.10	-0.16	-0.22
TD	-0.35	-0.63	-0.86	-1.04	-1.19	-1.31	-1.41	-1.49	-1.55	-1.60
RM_{GL}	0.04	0.03	0.02	0.01	0.00	0.00	-0.00	-0.00	-0.00	0.00
RM_{ML}	0.02	0.01	0.00	0.00	-0.00	-0.00	-0.01	-0.01	-0.01	-0.00
Status Variables										
CL	-0.32	-0.32	-0.32	-0.31	-0.30	-0.30	-0.29	-0.29	-0.29	-0.29
FF	-0.40	-0.44	-0.38	-0.30	-0.23	-0.17	-0.12	-0.08	-0.05	-0.02
RES_B	0.14	0.16	0.14	0.11	0.08	0.05	0.03	0.02	0.00	-0.01
RES_F	-0.37	-0.27	-0.20	-0.14	-0.10	-0.06	-0.04	-0.01	0.00	0.02
RES_R	-0.05	-0.09	-0.11	-0.13	-0.15	-0.16	-0.17	-0.17	-0.18	-0.18
RM_{CL}	-0.00	-0.01	-0.01	-0.01	-0.00	-0.00	0.00	0.01	0.01	0.01
RM_{FF}	0.07	0.05	0.04	0.03	0.02	0.01	0.00	0.00	0.00	-0.01
RM_{GS}	0.17	0.12	0.08	0.06	0.04	0.02	0.01	0.00	0.00	-0.01
RM_{TD}	-0.00	-0.00	-0.00	-0.00	-0.00	-0.00	0.00	0.00	0.00	0.00

Table 15-3 Effects on Monetary Variables of a One-half Percent Increase in the Discount Rate

	1964:3	1964:4	1965:1	1965:2	1965:3	1965:4	1966:1	1966:2	1966:3	1966:4
Targets										
CURR	0.01	0.02	0.03	0.05	0.07	0.08	0.10	0.12	0.13	0.15
DD	-0.25	-0.45	-0.61	-0.75	-0.87	-0.98	-1.07	-1.15	-1.23	-1.30
ML	-1.04	-1.69	-2.10	-2.38	-2.58	-2.75	-2.89	-3.01	-3.13	-3.25
TD	-0.53	-1.02	-1.46	-1.88	-2.26	-2.62	-2.96	-3.28	-3.57	-3.85
RM_{GL}	0.11	0.11	0.10	0.10	0.10	0.10	0.10	0.10	0.10	0.11
RM_{ML}	0.06	0.04	0.03	0.02	0.02	0.01	0.01	0.01	0.00	0.00
Status Variables										
CL	0.33	0.26	0.19	0.12	0.05	-0.02	-0.08	-0.15	-0.21	-0.27
FF	0.36	0.53	0.61	0.66	0.69	0.71	0.73	0.74	0.76	0.79
RES_B	0.01	-0.01	-0.03	-0.04	-0.06	-0.07	-0.08	-0.08	-0.09	-0.10
RES_F	0.05	0.09	0.12	0.14	0.16	0.17	0.19	0.20	0.21	0.23
RES_R	-0.06	-0.11	-0.16	-0.19	-0.23	-0.26	-0.29	-0.31	-0.34	-0.37
RM_{CL}	0.24	0.24	0.23	0.23	0.23	0.23	0.23	0.23	0.23	0.23
RM_{FF}	0.55	0.54	0.53	0.53	0.52	0.52	0.51	0.51	0.50	0.50
RM_{GS}	0.43	0.41	0.39	0.38	0.37	0.36	0.36	0.35	0.34	0.34
RM_{TD}	0.00	0.00	0.01	0.01	0.01	0.02	0.02	0.02	0.03	0.03

loan volume, by contrast, falls immediately and steadily. This is attributed to the dependence of the mortgage loan rate on the FHA ceiling; when the discount rate rises, rates on commercial loans rise more rapidly than those on mortgage loans, bringing a shift in favor of the more profitable assets.

As for reserve changes, the level of unborrowed reserves is lowered only to the extent of the induced currency drain, but the distribution shifts in favor of free reserves as deposits fall. The volume of borrowing (RES_B) falls accordingly, and the trading of reserves in the funds market (FF) increases.

The raising of the ceiling rate on time deposits (Table 15-4) causes an increase in the average yield on time deposits (RM_{TD}) and a shift in asset holdings from demand deposits to time deposits, but it leaves the rest of the system virtually unaffected. No other interest rate changes perceptibly, and currency and reserve distributions are affected only slightly. There is some shifting out of business loans into mortgages, in line with the relative increase in time deposits.

Analyzing the net impact of an increase in RM_{TDM} depends entirely on whether one uses the conventional or the broad money supply as his portfolio measure. The narrow definition leads to the conclusion that policy has tightened; after four quarters, the money stock has fallen by more than $600 million. But in the same period, the Friedmanian concept of money shows a $460 million *increase*, for a net swing of more than a billion dollars. Furthermore, if interest-rate patterns are the guide, then there appears to be virtually no effect from the policy change.

The effects of a change in the FHA ceiling, RM_{FHA}, are isolated in the mortgage market (Table 15-5). In part, this isolation is an unrealistic result of our omitting the real sectors of the economy from the simulation. Changes in the flow or mortgage funds will produce changes in the housing market which, in turn, might ultimately feed back into the financial sector. If included, however, this effect probably would not be very strong except after a very long lag.

The reduction of RM_{FHA} by 50 basis points has an immediate impact of reducing the average rate changed on all mortgages by about 12 basis points and of drawing some $670 million dollars in funds out of the market. Over the course of the 10-period simulation, the drop in the interest rate steadily converges on the one-half point drop in the ceiling. Also, there is a very significant drop in the flow of funds through the mortgage market. After one year, the volume of new loans is about $3.5 billion below what it would have been without the policy change; by the end of the run, the flow of funds has virtually dried up.

This simulation, then, confirms our intuitive feeling that the volume of new mortgage loans is critically sensitive to the ability of lenders to charge

Table 15-4   Effects on Monetary Variables of a One-half Percent Increase in the Time Deposit Rate Ceiling

	1964:3	1964:4	1965:1	1965:2	1965:3	1965:4	1966:1	1966:2	1966:3	1966:4
Targets										
CURR	-0.00	-0.00	0.00	0.01	0.02	0.03	0.04	0.05	0.07	0.08
DD	-0.20	-0.37	-0.50	-0.62	-0.72	-0.81	-0.88	-0.94	-1.00	-1.06
ML	-0.01	-0.01	0.00	0.03	0.07	0.12	0.19	0.27	0.37	0.48
TD	0.27	0.55	0.82	1.07	1.31	1.55	1.77	1.97	2.15	2.31
RM_{GL}	-0.00	-0.00	-0.01	-0.01	-0.01	-0.01	-0.01	-0.01	-0.01	-0.01
RM_{ML}	-0.00	-0.00	-0.00	-0.00	-0.00	-0.00	0.00	0.00	0.00	0.00
Status Variables										
CL	-0.00	-0.02	-0.04	-0.06	-0.09	-0.12	-0.15	-0.19	-0.22	-0.24
FF	0.02	0.04	0.06	0.06	0.06	0.04	0.03	0.02	-0.01	-0.04
RES_B	-0.01	-0.02	-0.02	-0.03	-0.03	-0.02	-0.02	-0.01	-0.00	0.01
RES_F	0.02	0.04	0.04	0.04	0.04	0.03	0.02	0.02	-0.00	-0.03
RES_R	-0.02	-0.04	-0.05	-0.05	-0.06	-0.06	-0.07	-0.07	-0.06	-0.05
RM_{CL}	-0.00	-0.00	-0.00	-0.01	-0.01	-0.01	-0.02	-0.03	-0.03	-0.04
RM_{FF}	-0.00	-0.01	-0.01	-0.01	-0.01	-0.00	-0.00	-0.01	0.00	0.01
RM_{GS}	-0.01	-0.02	-0.02	-0.02	-0.02	-0.01	-0.01	-0.01	0.00	0.01
RM_{TD}	0.14	0.14	0.14	0.13	0.13	0.13	0.13	0.13	0.12	0.12

Table 15-5 Effects on Monetary Variables of a One-half Percent Decrease in the Ceiling Rate for FHA Mortgages

	1964:3	1964:4	1965:1	1965:2	1965:3	1965:4	1966:1	1966:2	1966:3	1966:4
Targets										
CURR	0.00	0.00	0.00	0.00	0.00	0.00	0.00	0.00	0.00	0.00
DD	0.00	0.00	0.00	0.00	0.00	0.00	0.00	0.00	0.00	0.00
ML	-0.67	-1.60	-2.56	-3.46	-4.26	-4.99	-5.62	-6.17	-6.64	-7.07
TD	0.00	0.00	0.00	0.00	0.00	0.00	0.00	0.00	0.00	0.00
RM_{GL}	0.00	0.00	0.00	0.00	0.00	0.00	0.00	0.00	0.00	0.00
RM_{ML}	-0.12	-0.21	-0.28	-0.34	-0.38	-0.42	-0.45	-0.47	-0.49	-0.50
Status Variables										
CL	0.00	0.00	0.00	0.00	0.00	0.00	0.00	0.00	0.00	0.00
FF	0.00	0.00	0.00	0.00	0.00	0.00	0.00	0.00	0.00	0.00
RES_B	0.00	0.00	0.00	0.00	0.00	0.00	0.00	0.00	0.00	0.00
RES_F	0.00	0.00	0.00	0.00	0.00	0.00	0.00	0.00	0.00	0.00
RES_R	0.00	0.00	0.00	0.00	0.00	0.00	0.00	0.00	0.00	0.00
RM_{CL}	0.00	0.00	0.00	0.00	0.00	0.00	0.00	0.00	0.00	0.00
RM_{FF}	0.00	0.00	0.00	0.00	0.00	0.00	0.00	0.00	0.00	0.00
RM_{GS}	0.00	0.00	0.00	0.00	0.00	0.00	0.00	0.00	0.00	0.00
RM_{TD}	0.00	0.00	0.00	0.00	0.00	0.00	0.00	0.00	0.00	0.00

rates that are competitive with the ones that are available on alternative uses of assets. This ability, in turn, is dependent to a large degree on the level of the FHA ceiling rate.[3]

The next two simulations show the effects of changing the reserve requirements on demand deposits (Table 15-6) and on time deposits (Table 15-7). These two variables enter the model only through the identity defining required reserves (15-14); consequently, the two sets of effects are practically identical. Since, almost certainly, there would be some shifting between the two types of deposits if one requirement were changed independently of the other, it would seem desirable to find a way to incorporate this effect into the model. To date, this has not been feasible.

The most striking feature of Tables 15-6 and 15-7 is that the changes in monetary assets, CURR, DD, and TD, are almost identical to the ones produced by a one-half point increase in the discount rate for the entire period. There would seem to be little reason to expect this, since other effects show a rather different pattern. The primary effect, of course, is the substitution of borrowed for free reserves which necessarily results from the conversion of free reserves into required balances. Federal funds trading falls accordingly, and interest rates are pushed upward. However, the model does seem to permit too much of the adjustment to be absorbed in the reserve positions of banks, so that commercial loans, for example, continue to rise throughout the period in spite of the falling levels of deposits. In short, this type of model is not very well suited for analyzing the impact of variables that enter only through identities without behavioral implications.

For our final simulation, we shortened the maturity structure of the federal debt (Table 15-8) by increasing the ratio of Treasury bills to the total outstanding debt by one percentage point and by simultaneously decreasing the ratio of bonds to total debt by the same figure. That is, BF_S/BF_{PUB}, which appears in the equation for the bill rate, rises slightly, while BF_L/BF_{PUB}, appearing in the bond rate equation, falls. For a constant level of debt, this implies that the Treasury has shifted \$2 billion from bonds into bills. Table 15-8 reveals that this shift has almost no effect on our model. Interest rates rise somewhat, and deposits fall slightly to offset the increase in liquidity brought about by the shift to short-term securities. This leads to the tentative conclusion that this form of debt management has little effect on the monetary sector, although there might be effects on investment and aggregate demand which would feed back into the sector in a full model of the economy.

[3] The implication here that changes in the FHA ceiling have a strong effect on conventional mortgages as well is supported by a recent paper by David S. Huang and Michael D. McCarthy, "Simulation of the Home Mortgage Market in the Late Sixties, *"Review of Economics and Statistics,* **XLIV** (November 1967), 441-450.

Table 15-6 Effects on Monetary Variables of a One-Half Percent Increase in the Reserve Requirements on Demand Deposits

	1964:3	1964:4	1965:1	1965:2	1965:3	1965:4	1966:1	1966:2	1966:3	1966:4
Targets										
CURR	0.01	0.02	0.03	0.05	0.07	0.08	0.10	0.12	0.13	0.15
DD	-0.25	-0.45	-0.62	-0.76	-0.89	-1.01	-1.13	-1.23	-1.33	-1.48
ML	0.28	0.27	0.09	-0.21	-0.57	-0.98	-1.44	-1.94	-2.47	-3.02
TD	-0.53	-1.02	-1.46	-1.85	-2.20	-2.55	-2.84	-3.09	-3.30	-3.40
RM_{GL}	0.11	0.11	0.11	0.11	0.12	0.13	0.14	0.15	0.16	0.17
RM_{ML}	0.06	0.04	0.03	0.02	0.02	0.01	0.01	0.00	0.00	-0.00
Status Variables										
CL	0.30	0.47	0.65	0.82	0.97	1.11	1.26	1.37	1.47	1.56
FF	-0.96	-1.28	-1.35	-1.37	-1.37	-1.36	-1.33	-1.31	-1.29	-1.28
RES_B	0.39	0.53	0.58	0.59	0.59	0.58	0.58	0.57	0.56	0.55
RES_F	-0.98	-0.97	-0.94	-0.93	-0.91	-0.90	-0.89	-0.87	-0.85	-0.84
RES_R	0.97	0.95	0.90	0.88	0.84	0.82	0.79	0.75	0.72	0.70
RM_{CL}	0.01	0.02	0.04	0.07	0.09	0.12	0.15	0.18	0.22	0.25
RM_{FF}	0.19	0.18	0.17	0.16	0.15	0.16	0.15	0.14	0.14	0.13
RM_{GS}	0.43	0.41	0.39	0.37	0.36	0.37	0.35	0.34	0.32	0.31
RM_{TD}	0.00	0.01	0.01	0.01	0.02	0.03	0.04	0.05	0.05	0.09

Table 15-7   Effects on Monetary Variables of a One-Half Percent Increase in the Reserve Requirements on Time Deposits

	1964:3	1964:4	1965:1	1965:2	1965:3	1965:4	1966:1	1966:2	1966:3	1966:4
Targets										
CURR	0.01	0.02	0.03	0.05	0.07	0.08	0.10	0.12	0.14	0.16
DD	-0.24	-0.44	-0.61	-0.75	-0.89	-1.03	-1.16	-1.30	-1.43	-1.60
ML	0.27	0.27	0.09	-0.19	-0.54	-0.94	-1.40	-1.91	-2.46	-3.06
TD	-0.51	-0.98	-1.43	-1.83	-2.20	-2.58	-2.92	-3.24	-3.52	-3.70
RM_{GL}	0.11	0.10	0.11	0.11	0.12	0.13	0.15	0.16	0.17	0.19
RM_{ML}	0.06	0.04	0.03	0.02	0.02	0.02	0.01	0.01	0.01	0.00
Status Variables										
CL	0.29	0.45	0.64	0.81	0.98	1.13	1.31	1.45	1.59	1.72
FF	-0.93	-1.24	-1.34	-1.38	-1.41	-1.43	-1.45	-1.47	-1.50	-1.52
RES_B	0.37	0.52	0.57	0.59	0.61	0.61	0.63	0.64	0.65	0.65
RES_F	-0.95	-0.94	-0.93	-0.94	-0.95	-0.96	-0.98	-1.00	-1.01	-1.02
RES_R	0.94	0.92	0.90	0.89	0.88	0.88	0.88	0.88	0.87	0.86
RM_{CL}	0.01	0.02	0.04	0.06	0.09	0.12	0.15	0.19	0.22	0.26
RM_{FF}	0.18	0.17	0.17	0.16	0.16	0.17	0.16	0.16	0.16	0.16
RM_{GS}	0.41	0.40	0.39	0.38	0.38	0.39	0.39	0.39	0.38	0.37
RM_{TD}	0.00	0.00	0.01	0.01	0.02	0.03	0.04	0.05	0.06	0.09

Table 15-8 Effects on Monetary Variables of a Shortening of the Maturity Structure of the Federal Debt

	1964:3	1964:4	1965:1	1965:2	1965:3	1965:4	1966:1	1966:2	1966:3	1966:4
Targets										
CURR	0.00	0.00	0.00	0.00	0.00	0.00	0.01	0.01	0.01	0.01
DD	-0.01	-0.03	-0.03	-0.04	-0.05	-0.05	-0.06	-0.06	-0.07	-0.07
ML	0.02	0.03	0.03	0.03	0.03	0.02	0.01	0.00	-0.01	-0.02
TD	-0.03	-0.06	-0.09	-0.11	-0.14	-0.16	-0.18	-0.20	-0.22	-0.24
RM_{GL}	0.02	0.02	0.01	0.01	0.01	0.01	0.01	0.01	0.01	0.01
RM_{ML}	0.00	0.00	0.00	0.00	0.00	0.00	0.00	0.00	0.00	0.00
Status Variables										
CL	-0.03	-0.03	-0.03	-0.03	-0.03	-0.03	-0.03	-0.03	-0.03	-0.03
FF	0.01	0.01	0.02	0.02	0.02	0.02	0.02	0.02	0.03	0.03
RES_B	-0.00	-0.00	-0.00	-0.01	-0.01	-0.01	-0.01	-0.01	-0.01	-0.01
RES_F	0.00	0.01	0.01	0.01	0.01	0.01	0.01	0.01	0.01	0.01
RES_R	-0.00	-0.01	-0.01	-0.01	-0.01	-0.01	-0.02	-0.02	-0.02	-0.02
RM_{CL}	-0.00	-0.00	-0.00	-0.00	-0.00	-0.00	0.00	0.00	0.00	0.00
RM_{FF}	0.01	0.01	0.01	0.01	0.01	0.01	0.01	0.01	0.01	0.01
RM_{GS}	0.03	0.02	0.02	0.02	0.02	0.02	0.02	0.02	0.02	0.02
RM_{TD}	-0.00	-0.00	-0.00	-0.00	-0.00	-0.00	0.00	0.00	0.00	0.00

These simulations demonstrate a wide range of results from policies that appear to be relatively homogeneous in nature. The test that we have formulated centers on the intermediate targets of the Federal Reserve; it is quite possible that the effects of policies on more distantly related targets, such as aggregate demand, would be less sharply differentiated. Similarly, the model shows that the effects of different policies on the proximate targets, such as bank reserve positions, are radically different from one another. Nonetheless, we can draw the following conclusions with respect to the monetary targets.

1. Open-market operations may be used to alter both the conventionally defined and the broadly defined money supply, while having only a temporary effect on interest rates and only a mild effect on the volume and distribution of loans.

2. The discount rate has a much greater effect on the broad money supply than on the conventional stock. Its effects on interest rates and asset composition are more sustained than the ones that result from open-market operations. The use of the discount rate, then, creates a number of side effects that are not observable under FOMC actions.

3. The primary effects of changes in the maximum time-deposit rates are distributional. Asset holdings shift between demand and time deposits and between short- and long-term loans, but the net effects on credit and liquidity are not very great.

4. The maximum rates for FHA-insured mortgages have a major impact on the mortgage market, with respect to both rates and volume. Any effects that this process might have on the banking system are not revealed in our model.

5. Reserve requirement changes, as manifested in this model, have an effect that is more akin to the effects of discount policy than to those of open-market operations. Interest rates and time-deposit volume are heavily influenced here. Standard textbook theory holds that reserve-requirement changes accomplish nothing that cannot be accomplished by other instruments; certainly, these simulations support that theory.

6. Debt management policies seem to have very little effect on the monetary sector. Any effect emanating from this type of policy must work through the real sectors of the economy or, at least, in some way not specified in this particular model.

Thus there appear to be, at least, three independent policy tools at the disposal of the Federal Reserve: open-market operations, Regulation Q, and the discount rate. This conclusion, however, is based on the hypothesis that the Federal Reserve is interested in influencing all of its intermediate targets in some way. If, instead, it is interested only in altering the conventional money supply without regard to side effects, then any policy will serve just as well as any other.

Although the conclusions presented above are less definite than we would like them to be, they do, hopefully, shed light on the interrelationships among monetary policies. To form more definite conclusions, we would have to conduct stochastic simulations with a full complement of statistical tests, in the context of a model of the complete economy, including a measure of the policy makers' preference functions. And, finally, we would need to conduct a more rigorous comparison of policy inputs—perhaps, along the lines suggested by Fromm and Taubman [12, pp. 84-88]. That type of analysis, then, will form the next major stage of this continuing research project.

BIBLIOGRAPHY

1. Anderson, Leonall C., and Levine, Jules M. "A Test of Money Market Conditions as a Means of Short-Run Monetary Management," *National Banking Review*, **IV** (September 1966), 41-51.
2. Board of Governors of the Federal Reserve System. *The Federal Funds Market*, Washington, D. C. (1959).
3. Boughton, James M., *et al.* "A Policy Model of the United States Monetary Sector," *Southern Economical Journal*, **XXXV** (April 1969).
4. Brainard, William C., and Tobin, James. "Pitfalls in Financial Model Building," American Economic Review, **LVIII** (May 1968), 99-122.
5. Bryan, William R. "Bank Adjustments to Monetary Policy: Alternative Estimates of the Lag," *American Economic Review*, **LVII** (September 1967), 855-864.
6. deLeeuw, Frank. "The Demand for Money: Speed of Adjustment, Interest Rates, and Wealth," *Staff Economic Studies*, Board of Governors of the Federal Reserve System, 1965.
7. deLeeuw, Frank. "Financial Markets in Business Cycles: A Simulation Study," *American Economic Review*, **LIV** (May 1964), 309-323.
8. deLeeuw, Frank. "A Model of Financial Behavior," in J. Duesenberry and others (ed.), *The Brookings Quarterly Econometric Model of the United States*. Chicago: Rand McNally, 1965.
9. deLeeuw, Frank, and Gramlich, Edward. "The Federal Reserve—M.I.T. Econometric Model," *Federal Reserve Bulletin*, **LIV** (January 1968), 11-40.
10. Friedman, Milton. *Studies in the Quantity Theory of Money*. Chicago: University of Chicago Press, 1956.
11. Fromm, Gary. "Recent Monetary Policy: an Econometric View," *National Banking Review*, **III** (March 1966), 299-306.
12. Fromm, Gary, and Taubman, Paul. *Policy Simulations with an Econometric Model*. Washington, D. C.: The Brookings Institution, 1968.

13. Goldfeld, Stephen M. *Commercial Bank Behavior and Economic Activity.* Amsterdam: North-Holland, 1966.
14. Chase, Samuel B., Jr., and Gramley, Lyle E. "Time Deposits in Monetary Analysis," *Federal Reserve Bulletin,* **LI** (October 1965), 1380-1406.
15. Hamburger, Michael J., and Latta, Cynthia M. "The Term Structure of Interest Rates: Some Additional Evidence" (unpublished manuscript presented at meetings of the Federal Reserve System Committee on Financial Analysis, April 17-18, 1967).
16. Hendershott, Patric H. "The Demand for Money: Speed of Adjustment, Interest Rates, and Wealth—A Sequel," *Staff Economic Studies,* Board of Governors of the Federal Reserve System, 1966.
17. Hendershott, Patric H. "Recent Development of the Financial Sector of Econometric Models," *Journal of Finance,* **XXIII** (March 1968), 41-65.
18. Jones, David M. "The Demand for Money: A Review of the Empirical Literature," *Staff Economic Studies,* Board of Governors of the Federal Reserve System, 1966.
19. Koyck, L. M. *Distributed Lags and Investment Analysis.* Amsterdam: North-Holland, 1954.
20. Malinvaud, E. *Statistical Methods of Econometrics.* Chicago: Rand McNally, 1966.
21. Modigliani, Franco, and Sutch, Richard. "Innovations in Interest Rate Policy," *American Economic Review,* **LVI** (May 1966), 178-197.
22. Naylor, Thomas H., Balintfy, Joseph L., Burdick, Donald S., and Chu, Kong. *Computer Simulation Techniques.* New York: John Wiley & Sons, 1966.
23. Naylor, Thomas H., Burdick, Donald S., and Sasser, W. Earl. "Computer Simulation Experiments with Economic Systems: The Problem of Experimental Design," *Journal of the American Statistical Association,* **LXII** (December 1967), 1315-1337.
24. Naylor, Thomas H., and Finger, J. M. "Verification of Computer Simulation Models," *Management Science,* **XIV** (October 1967), 92-101.
25. Naylor, Thomas H., Wallace, William H., and Sasser, W. Earl. "A Computer Simulation Model of the Textile Industry," *Journal of the American Statistical Association,* **LXII** (December 1967), 1338-1364.
26. Naylor, Thomas H., Wertz, Kenneth, and Wonnacott, Thomas. "Spectral Analysis of Data Generated by Simulation Experiments with Econometric Models," *Econometrica,* **XXXVII** (April 1969), 333-352.
27. Nichols, Dorothy M. *Trading in Federal Funds,* Board of Governors of the Federal Reserve System, 1965.
28. Teigen, Ronald L. "An Aggregated Quarterly Model of the U. S. Monetary Sector, 1953-1964," *Proceedings of the Conference on Targets and Indicators of Monetary Policy,* forthcoming publication.
29. Teigen, Ronald L. "Demand and Supply Functions for Money in the United States: Some Structural Estimates," *Econometrica,* **XXXII** (October 1964), 476-509.
30. U. S. House of Representatives. *To Eliminate Unsound Competition for Savings and Time Deposits.* Hearings before the Committee on Banking and Currency, Washington, D. C., 1966.

Appendix A | Pseudorandom
Number Generators

INTRODUCTION

In Chapter 2, we describe the important role that uniformly distributed random variables play in the generation of random variables drawn from *other* probability distributions such as the normal, Poisson, and binomial distributions. A number of techniques now exist for generating uniformly distributed random variables r (where $0 \leq r \leq 1$) with a digital computer. The numbers generated by these computer subroutines are called pseudorandom numbers because, although they are generated from a completely deterministic formula by a digital computer, their statistical properties coincide with the statistical properties of numbers generated by an idealized chance device that selects numbers from the unit interval (0,1) independently and with all numbers equally likely. Provided that these pseudorandom numbers can pass the set of statistical tests (frequency tests, autocorrelation test, lagged product test, runs test, gap test, and so on) implied by an idealized chance device, then these pseudorandom numbers can be treated as "truly" random numbers even though they are not.

Before describing several pseudorandom number generators we propose several criteria that should be satisfied by an *ideal* pseudorandom number generator. An ideal pseudorandom number generator should yield sequences of numbers that are (1) uniformly distributed, (2) statistically independent, (3) reproducible, and (4) nonrepeating for any desired length. Furthermore, such a generator should also be capable of (5) generating random numbers at high rates of speed, yet of (6) requiring a minimum amount of computer memory capacity. The congruential methods described in this chapter come closer to satisfying *all* of these criteria than any other known method of generating random numbers.

In this appendix we shall describe several specific methods for generating pseudorandom numbers with a computer. They include the following: (1) the multiplicative method, (2) the mixed method, and (3) the combination method. After describing these procedures and some of their properties, we then consider the problem of autocorrelated pseudorandom numbers and the various tests that are available for testing the "randomness" of pseudorandom numbers.

CONGRUENTIAL METHODS[1]

As we have previously indicated, congruential methods for generating random numbers are completely deterministic because the arithmetic processes that are involved in the calculations uniquely determine each term in a sequence of numbers. In fact, formulas are available for calculating in advance the exact value of the ith number in a sequence of numbers $\{n_0, n_1, n_2, \ldots, n_i, \ldots\}$ before the sequence is actually generated. Although these processes are not random processes at all, pragmatic grounds dictate that we treat them as though they were if the sequences that result consistently pass a certain number of statistical tests designed to test various properties of random variates. For example, if it can be shown that the numbers in a sequence appear to be uniformly distributed and statistically independent, then the process can be assumed to be random even though it is deterministic. (It can be shown that congruential methods satisfy both of these requirements reasonably well.) Properties (3) and (6) of the above-mentioned requirements of random number generators are automatically satisfied by the application of congruential methods because the sequences generated by these methods are completely reproducible and require only a minimum amount of memory capacity on a computer. Properties (4) and (5) are the only requirements whose degree of satisfaction depends entirely on the properties of the methods applied. These properties will be analyzed in the following pages.

The congruential methods for generating pseudorandom numbers are based on the mathematical concept of *congruence*. Two integers a and b are said to be *congruent modulo m* if their difference is an integral multiple of m. The congruence relation is expressed by the notation $a \equiv b \pmod{m}$, which reads "a is congruent to b modulo m." This means that $a - b$ is divisible by m and that a and b yield identical remainders when divided by $|m|$. For example, $1897 \equiv 7 \pmod 5$ and $4339 \equiv 39 \pmod{10^2}$.

The following recursive formula is basic to all congruential methods

$$n_{i+1} \equiv \lambda n_i + \mu \pmod m \qquad \text{(A-1)}$$

[1] For a complete treatment of the theory underlying congruential methods, see Chapter 3 of the book by Thomas H. Naylor, Joseph L. Balintfy, Donald S. Burdick, and Kong Chu entitled *Computer Simulation Techniques* [47]. The following texts on number theory may also be helpful [4,48,59].

where n_i, λ, μ, and m are all nonnegative integers. Expanding (A-1) for $i = 0,1,2, \ldots$ we obtain

$$n_1 \equiv \lambda n_0 + \mu \ (\text{mod } m)$$

$$n_2 \equiv \lambda n_1 + \mu = \lambda^2 n_0 + (\lambda + 1) \mu \ (\text{mod } m)$$

$$n_3 \equiv \lambda^3 n_0 + (\lambda^2 + \lambda + 1) \mu = \lambda^3 n_0 + \frac{\mu(\lambda^3 - 1)}{(\lambda - 1)} \ (\text{mod } m) \quad \text{(A-2)}$$

. . . .

$$n_i \equiv \lambda^i n_0 + \frac{\mu(\lambda^i - 1)}{(\lambda - 1)} \ (\text{mod } m).$$

Given an initial *starting value* n_0, a *constant multiplier* λ, and an *additive constant* μ, then (A-2) yields a congruence relationship (modulo m) for any value of i over the sequence $\{n_1, n_2, \ldots, n_i, \ldots\}$. The subsequent terms of $\{n_i\}$ as determined by (A-2) are all integers forming a sequence of residues modulo m. This, in turn, implies that $n_i < m$ for all n_i. From the integers in the sequence $\{n_i\}$, rational numbers in the unit interval $(0,1)$ can be obtained by forming the sequence $\{r_i\} = \{n_i/m\}$.

We now consider the question of whether there exists a smallest positive value of i, $i = h$, so that $n_h = n_0$ where h is the period of the sequence $\{n_i\}$. If such an h does exist, what conditions can be imposed on n_0, λ, μ, and m so that the period of $\{n_i\}$ is as large as possible? Our interest in this problem stems from the fact that if $n_i = n_0$ for some $i = h$, then $n_{h+1} = n_1, n_{h+2} = n_2$, and so on. That is, the sequence of pseudorandom numbers will repeat itself after a period equal to h.

It can be shown [47] that such an h always exists and that its maximum value depends on m. This is equivalent to saying that it is impossible to obtain nonrepeating sequences by congruential methods. In practice, however, the period of a sequence can be set satisfactorily high by choosing a sufficiently large modulus or by other techniques [19].

The Multiplicative Method

The *multiplicative congruential method* computes a sequence $\{n_i\}$ of nonnegative integers less than m by means of the congruence relation:

$$n_{i+1} \equiv \lambda n_i \ (\text{mod } m). \quad \text{(A-3)}$$

This method is merely a special case of congruence relation (A-1) where $\mu = 0$. The multiplicative method has been found to behave quite well statistically. That is, with the proper choice of the multiplier λ and the starting value n_0, it is possible to generate sequences of numbers that are uncorrelated and uniformly distributed [10,15,19]. Furthermore, by imposing certain conditions on λ and n_0 we can insure a maximum period for sequences generated by this method. Since the method is completely deterministic, the sequences are completely reproducible. This method requires a minimum amount of computer memory capacity. Computationally the method merely requires that we take the product of two numbers that can be accomplished at high rates of speed with modern digital computers.

Most computerized versions of the multiplicative congruential method employ a modulus $m = p^e$, representing the word size of the computer, where p denotes the number of numerals in the number system used by the computer and e denotes the number of digits in a word. For binary computers $p = 2$, and for decimal computers $p = 10$. On variable word-length computers the value of e is left to the programmer's discretion, whereas on fixed-word length computers e is a constant. The symbols b and d will be used in place of e to denote binary and decimal digits, respectively.

There are two reasons for choosing $m = p^e$. First, reduction modulo m is accomplished by truncating and retaining only the low-order e digits; and second, conversion to the unit interval (to obtain uniformly distributed variates) involves only moving the binary or decimal point to the left of the number. By the proper choice of m, these divisions can be circumvented.

Since most computers use either a binary or a decimal number system, we consider the multiplicative method for each of these two number systems. In both cases, we are concerned with generating sequences of nonnegative integers (less than p^e) by means of the congruence relation.

$$n_{i+1} \equiv \lambda n_i \ (\mathrm{mod} \ p^e) \tag{A-4}$$

We discuss for both cases the conditions that may be imposed on the constant multiplier λ and the starting value n_0 to assure maximal periods for sequences generated by this method.

Binary Computers

For binary computers we choose $m = 2^b$, where b is the number of binary digits (bits) in a word. The maximum attainable period with the multiplicative method is $h = 2^{b-2}$. The multiplicative procedure for generating pseudorandom numbers with a binary computer may be summarized as follows.

1. Choose any odd number as a starting value n_0.
2. Choose an integer $\lambda = 8t + 3$, where t is any positive integer for a constant multiplier.

3. Compute λn_0 by using fixed-point integer arithmetic. This product will consist of $2b$ bits, from which the high-order b bits are discarded, and the low-order b bits represent n_1.

4. Calculate $r_1 = n_1/2^b$ to obtain a uniformly distributed random variable defined on the unit interval.

5. Each successive random number n_{i+1} is obtained from the low-order bits of the product λn_i.

Consider the following illustrative example taken from [47] in which b is assumed to be equal to 4. The multiplicative procedure will produce 4 random numbers ($h = 2^{4-2} = 4$) before repeating.

1. Choose $n_0 = 7$. This is equivalent to $n_0 = 0111$ in binary form.

2. For $t = 1$, then λ is either equal to 11 or 5. We choose $\lambda = 5$ or $\lambda = 0101$ in binary form.

3. $\lambda n_0 = (0101)(0111) = 00100011$. Therefore, $n_1 = 0011$ and $r_1 = 3/16 = 0.1875$.

4. $\lambda n_1 = (0101)(0011) = 00001111$. Therefore, $n_2 = 1111$ and $r_2 = 15/16 = 0.9375$.

5. $\lambda n_2 = (0101)(1111) = 01001011$. Therefore, $n_3 = 1011$ and $r_3 = 11/16 = 0.6875$.

6. $\lambda n_3 = (0101)(1011) = 00110111$. Therefore, $n_4 = 0111 = n_0$ and $r_4 = 7/16 = 0.4375$.

The following multiplicative generator has been widely used on the IBM SYSTEM/360 and binary computers with a 32-bit word size. It has a constant multiplier $\lambda = 5^{13} = 1{,}220{,}703{,}125$, a starting value $n_0 = 5^{13}$, and a modulus $m = 2^{31} - 1$. The FORTRAN subroutine for this generator is given below.[2]

```
      SUBROUTINE RAND (N1,N,R)
1     N = 1220703125*N1
2     IF(N) 3,4,4
3     N = N + 214783647 + 1
4     N1 = N
5     R = N
6     R = R*0.4656613E - 9
7     RETURN
8     END
```

The symbols N1, N, and R are substituted in the FORTRAN subroutine, respectively, for n_0, n, and r. To execute the subroutine we make use of the following statement:

---

[2] This subroutine appears in Geoffrey Gordon's book entitled *System Simulation* published by Prentice-Hall, Inc., Englewood Cliffs, N.J., 1969.

CALL RAND (N1,N,R).

The subroutine yields both floating-point and fixed-point integer random numbers. N is a random integer between 1 and $2^{31} - 1$ and R is a floating-point random number between 0 and 1. (There are 31 bits available for computation in the 32-bit general register of the IBM SYSTEM/360. One bit is a sign bit.)

In statement 1, the starting value n_0 is multiplied by λ the constant multiplier. Statement 2 provides a check for the possibility of a negative value of N. Statement 3 has the effect of inverting the sign of N if the highest-order bit (which is the sign bit) is negative. In statement 4, N1 is set equal to N in preparation for the next execution. Statements 5 and 6 convert N into a floating-point variable.

If more than one sequence of random numbers is required, then we can read in different starting values N1, N2, N3, . . . Alternatively, if we want to repeat the sequence, then we can simply reset N1 to its original value within the main program.

This particular generator has been subjected to extensive empirical testing and has been found to perform quite well. The paper by Gorenstein [20] reports on the statistical properties of this generator.

Lewis, Goodman, and Miller [14] have presented empirical results for another multiplicative congruential generator with $\lambda = 7^5 = 16807$ and $m = 2^{31} - 1$. This generator also gives satisfactory statistical results [41]. A program for this generator written in SYSTEM/360 assembler language is described in (41).

Decimal Computers

For a decimal computer we choose $m = 10^d$, where d is the number of decimal digits in a word. The maximum attainable period is $h = 5 \times 10^{d-2}$. The multiplicative procedure for generating pseudorandom numbers with a decimal computer may be summarized as follows.

1. Choose any odd integer not divisible by 5 as a starting value n_0.

2. Choose an integer $\lambda = 200t + p$ for a constant multiplier, where t is any integer and p is any of the values 3, 11, 13, 19, 21, 27, 29, 37, 53, 59, 61, 67, 69, 77, 83, 91.

3. Compute λn_0 by using fixed-point integer arithmetic. This product will consist of $2d$ digits, from which the high-order d digits are discarded, and the low-order digits are the value of n_1.

4. The decimal point may be shifted d digits to the left to convert the random number (which is an integer) into a uniformly distributed random variable defined over the unit interval ($r_1 = n_1/10^d$).

5. Each successive random number n_{i+1} is obtained from the low-order digits of the product λn_i.

Consider the following illustrative example taken from [47] in which d is assumed to be equal to 4. The multiplicative procedure will produce 500 random numbers ($h = 5 \times 10^{4-2} = 500$) before repeating.

1. Choose $n_0 = 5379$.
2. For $t = 0$ and $p = 91$, then λ is either equal to $+91$ or -91. We choose $+91$.
3. $\lambda n_0 = (91)(5379) = 00489489$. Therefore, $n_1 = 9489$ and $r_1 = 0.9489$.
4. $\lambda n_1 = (91)(9489) = 00863499$. Therefore, $n_2 = 3499$ and $r_2 = 0.3499$.
5. $\lambda n_2 = (91)(3499) = 00318409$. Therefore, $n_3 = 8409$ and $r_3 = 0.8409$.
6. $\lambda n_3 = (91)(8409) = 00765219$. Therefore, $n_4 = 5219$ and $r_4 = 0.5219$.

The example shows that the low-order digits are far from random. With multiplicative generators only the highest-order digit position has full period, and the period decreases for the lower-order digits. Therefore, if a random number smaller than word size is required, the higher-order digits should be used.

The Mixed Method

The *mixed congruential method* computes a sequence $\{n_i\}$ of nonnegative integers less than m by means of the congruence relation given by (A-1),

$$n_{i+1} \equiv \lambda n_i + \mu \pmod{m}. \tag{A-5}$$

This method differs from the multiplicative procedure in that μ is not assumed to be equal to zero. The advantage of the *mixed congruential method* is that, with the proper choice of λ and μ, it is possible to obtain sequences with a period that covers the full set of m different numbers. That is, it is possible to obtain a period $h = 2^b$ in the case of a binary computer and a period $h = 10^d$ in the case of a decimal computer. From a computational standpoint, the method requires an extra addition operation that is not required with the multiplicative method.

Another alleged advantage of the mixed congruential method is that with the proper choice of μ it is possible to minimize serial correlation [9,53]. Empirical results with the mixed method have failed to demonstrate its superiority over the multiplicative method from the standpoint of randomness and the absence of serial correlation. "There is at present no method of generation of pseudouniform sequences better than the simple multiplicative congruence method with a carefully chosen multiplier" [10].

The conditions imposed on λ and μ in order to achieve a full period $(h = m)$ may be summarized as follows.

1. μ is relatively prime to m.
2. $\lambda \equiv 1 \pmod{p}$ if p is a prime factor of m.
3. $\lambda \equiv 1 \pmod{4}$ if 4 is a factor of m.

The practical interpretation of these conditions is given below.

Binary Computers

To achieve a full period $h = m = 2^b$, the parameter μ must be an odd number and λ must satisfy the congruence relationship

$$\lambda \equiv 1 \pmod{4} \tag{A-6}$$

which can be achieved by setting

$$\lambda = 2^k + 1 \tag{A-7}$$

for $k \geq 2$. Any positive integer can be selected for the starting value n_0. However, the above-mentioned conditions are not sufficient for assuming that sequences generated by the mixed congruential method will be statistically satisfactory. Only by empirical testing can we have confidence in the statistical properties of sequences that are generated by the mixed congruential method. The systematic testing of mixed generators on binary computers has been described in [10,29,42].

Decimal Computers

To generate a sequence of pseudorandom numbers with full period $(h = m = 10^d)$, the constant μ must be a positive odd integer not divisible by 5 and the multiplier λ must satisfy the condition

$$\lambda \equiv 1 \pmod{20} \tag{A-8}$$

or, equivalently,

$$\lambda = 10^k + 1 \tag{A-9}$$

for $k > 1$. Again, these conditions are not sufficient to guarantee acceptable statistical properties for sequences of pseudorandom numbers that are generated by the mixed congruential method. Empirical results with mixed congruential generators, using decimal computers, are described in [1].

Each digit in the random numbers generated by this method (including the last digit in a word) has a full period. This property makes small-word sizes and higher speeds possible when the length of the period is not a significant requirement.

THE COMBINATION METHOD

Several years after their discovery, congruential methods came under attack in the literature [9,15,25,34,42,51,61] on the grounds that the numbers generated by these methods were not statistically satisfactory. It was shown that autocorrelation was, indeed, a serious problem with several of these generators. As a result of these findings, several new versions of the congruential methods called *combination methods* were suggested in the literature.

MacLaren and Marsaglia [42] have suggested a combination method in which a mixed congruential generator computes indexes that determine which random number from p previously stored numbers should be next in the sequence. The p numbers $n_1, n_2, \ldots, n_i, \ldots, n_p$ are generated by the multiplicative congruential method in such a manner that the ith number is replaced by a new n_i value if i is the index generated by the mixed method. The combination method passed *all* of the statistical tests which were applied to it. The disadvantages of this method are that it requires 128 words of memory and that you must generate two random numbers in order to get one number that you are actually going to use.

An alternative method of generating pseudorandom numbers based on the combination of two congruential generators has been proposed by Westlake [60]. It retains two of the desirable features of congruential generators, namely, the long cycle and the ease of implementation with a digital computer. Unlike the combination method proposed by MacLaren and Marsaglia [42], Westlake's method does not require the retention in computer memory of a table of generated numbers. The generator also yielded completely satisfactory results on a fairly stringent series of statistical tests.

Recently, Marsaglia and Bray [45] have described a combination method that involves three congruential generators. In describing their combination generator, Marsaglia and Bray [45] stated that, "short and fast programs will result even if three generators are mixed. One to fill, say, 128 storage locations, one to choose a location from the 128, and a third thrown in just to appease the gods of chance. Why be half (or two-thirds) safe?" Marsaglia and Bray present FORTRAN subroutines for their generator for the IBM 360, IBM 7094, and the UNIVAC 1108.

The initial enthusiasm for combination generators has been dampened by the publication of the paper by Coveyou and Macpherson [10]. They concluded that any multiplicative generator is satisfactory (statistically) if its multiplier meets certain Fourier analysis criteria. On the other hand, Marsaglia [44] argues that every multiplicative generator has a defect that makes it unsuitable for certain Monte Carlo problems—points produced in the unit n-cube fall into a relatively small number of parallel hyperplanes.

AUTOCORRELATION

We have previously alluded to the problem of serial correlation or autocorrelation with sequences of pseudorandom numbers generated by the multiplicative and mixed congruential generators. A number of studies [9,15,25,34,42,51,61] have shown that an improper choice of λ or μ may lead to sequences of numbers that are highly autocorrelated. Since we use pseudorandom numbers to generate random variables from given probability distributions (Appendix B), it follows that if we use autocorrelated pseudorandom numbers we shall obtain autocorrelated random variables. If we apply classical statistical techniques to random variables that are highly autocorrelated, we may underestimate the variance of the random variable and, therefore, make incorrect inferences about the system that is being investigated.

Coveyou and Macpherson [10] have written an extremely useful paper which attempts to put the problem of autocorrelation in perspective. Their conclusions are summarized below.

1. There is at present no method of generation of pseudo-uniform sequences better than the simple multiplicative congruence method with a carefully chosen multiplier.

2. The multiplier λ should *not* be close to a simple rational multiple of m; if it is, the basic congruence shows that appreciable serial correlation will result.

3. The multiplier λ should *not* be close to a simple rational multiple of the square root of m; even though this choice may produce very small correlation between adjacent pairs, serious difficulties result in the triplet distribution.

4. The multiplier λ should not be chosen with a small number of ones in the binary representation to facilitate "shift and add" techniques; if the number of ones is small enough to do any good, "small" solutions of the basic congruence again will lead to trouble.

5. Above all, the multiplier λ must be adequately large.

6. The choice of a multiplier must be made more carefully for computers of short word length; it may be necessary to use multiple precision arith-

metic for computers (such as the IBM 360) with short word length in order to ensure unquestionably good statistical performance.

Coveyou and Macpherson [10] analyzed the autocorrelation properties of 28 different congruential generators in their paper. The paper by Gelder [15] has also investigated the autocorrelation properties of several congruential generators.

STATISTICAL TESTS

The statistical properties of pseudorandom numbers generated by the methods outlined in the previous section should coincide with the statistical properties of numbers generated by an idealized chance device that selects numbers from the unit interval (0,1) independently and with all numbers equally likely. Clearly, the pseudorandom numbers that are produced by computer programs are not random in this sense, since they are completely determined by the starting data and have limited precision. But as long as our pseudorandom numbers can pass the set of statistical tests implied by the idealized chance device mentioned above, these pseudorandom numbers can be treated as "truly" random numbers, even though they are not.

Chapter 3 of the book by Naylor, Balintfy, Burdick, and Chu [47] contains a comprehensive survey of the statistical tests that are available for testing the randomness of pseudorandom numbers. These tests include (1) the frequency test, (2) serial correlation tests, (3) the lagged product test, (4) tests of runs, (5) the gap test, (6) the maximum test, and (7) the poker test.

The multiplicative generator, which we described earlier in this chapter, with $\lambda = 5^{13}$ and $n_0 = 5^{13}$ has been subjected to extensive statistical testing by Gorenstein [20]. Among the tests used by Gorenstein were (1) the moments test, (2) the run test, (3) and χ^2 test for a uniform distribution, (4) the serial test, (5) the χ^2 test for independence of sequences, and (6) tests of derived vector sequences. The particular multiplicative generator in question performed very well when subjected to these tests. MacLaren and Marsaglia [42] applied similar tests to their combination method which also yielded satisfactory results.

The selection of the appropriate statistical tests for pseudorandom numbers is always limited by a set of desiderata for a given generator and by a particular application. It is advisable, however, for the user to design his own statistical tests if certain functions or properties of the random numbers that are not covered here are going to be crucial in the evaluation or validation of results.

BIBLIOGRAPHY

1. Allard J. L., Dobell, A. R., and Hull, T. E. "Mixed Congruential Random Number Generators for Decimal Machines," *Journal of the ACM*, **X** (1963), 131-141.
2. Anderson, R. L. "Distribution of the Serial Correlation Coefficient," *Annals of Mathematical Statistics*, **XIII** (March 1942), 1-33.
3. Barnett, V. D. "The Behavior of Pseudo-Random Sequences Generated on Computers by the Multiplicative Congruential Method," *Mathematical Computations*, **XVI** (January 1962), 63-69.
4. Birkhoff, G., and MacLane, S. A. *A Survey of Modern Algebra*. New York: Macmillan, 1953.
5. Canavos, George C. "A Comparative Analysis of Two Concepts in the Generation of Uniform Pseudorandom Numbers," *Proceedings of the ACM 22nd National Conference*. Washington: Thompson Book Co., 1967.
6. Certaine, J. E. "On Sequences of Pseudo-Random Numbers of Maximal Length," *Journal of the ACM*, **V** (1958), 353-356.
7. Chambers, R. P. "Random Number Generation on Digital Computers," *IEEE Spectrum*, **IV** (February 1967), 48-56.
8. Clark C. E. "The Utility of Statistics of Random Numbers," *Operations Research*, **VIII** (March-April 1960), 185-195.
9. Coveyou, R. R. "Serial Correlation in the Generation of Pseudo-random Numbers: Monte Carlo Calculation," *Journal of the ACM*, **VII** (January 1960), 72-74.
10. Coveyou, R. R., and Macpherson, R. D. "Fourier Analysis of Uniform Random Number Generators," *Journal of the ACM*, **XIV** (January 1967), 100-119.
11. Downham, D. Y., and Roberts, F. D. K. "Multiplicative Congruential Pseudo-Random Number Generators," *Computer Journal*, **X** (May 1967), 74-77.
12. Forsythe, G. E. "Generation and Testing of Random Digits at the National Bureau of Standards, Los Angeles," in *Monte Carlo Method*. National Bureau of Standards Applied Mathematics Series No. 12, Washington, D. C., 1951.
13. Franklin, J. N. "Deterministic Simulation of Random Processes," *Math. Comput.*, **XVII** (1963), 28-59.
14. Gebhardt, F. "Generating Pseudo-Random Numbers by Shuffling a Fibonacci Sequence," *Math. Comp.*, **XXI** (October 1967), 708-709.
15. Gelder, A. Van. "Some Results in Pseudo-Random Number Generation," *Journal of the ACM*, **XIV** (October 1967), 785-792.
16. Gill, A. "On a Weight Distribution Problem, With Application to the Design of Stochastic Generators," *Journal of the ACM*, **X** (1963).
17. Good, I. J. "The Serial Test for Sampling Numbers and Other Tests for Randomness," *Proceedings of the Cambridge Philosophical Society*, **XLIX** (1953), 276-284.
18. Good, I. J. "On the Serial Test for Random Sequences," *Annals of Mathematical Statistics*, **XXVIII** (1957), 262-264.

19. Gorenstein, S. "Another Pseudorandom Number Generator," *Communications of the ACM*, **IX** (October 1966), 711.

20. Gorenstein, S. "Testing a Random Number Generator," *Communications of the ACM*, **X** (February 1967), 111-118.

21. Green, B. F. *Digital Computers in Research*. New York: McGraw-Hill, 1963.

22. Green, B. F., Smith, J., and Klem, L. "Empirical Tests of an Additive Random Number Generator," *Journal of the ACM*, **VI** (1959), 527-537.

23. Greenberger, M. "An a Priori Determination of Serial Correlation in Computer Generated Random Numbers," *Mathematics of Computations*, **XV** (1961), 383-389.

24. Greenberger, M. "Notes on a New Pseudo-Random Number Generator," *Journal of the ACM*, **VIII** (April 1961), 163-167.

25. Greenberger, M. "Method in Randomness," *Communications of the ACM*, **VIII**, (1965), 177-179.

26. Holz, B. W., and Clark, C. E. "Tests of Randomness of the Bits of a Set of Pseudorandom Numbers," Operations Research Office, December 1958.

27. Hull, T. E. "Random-Number Generation and Monte-Carlo Methods," *Digital Computer User's Handbook*. Edited by M. Klerer and G. Korn. New York: McGraw-Hill Book Co., 1967.

28. Hull, T. E., and Dobell, A. R. "Random Number Generators," *SIAM Review*, **IV** (July 1962), 230-254.

29. Hull, T. E., and Dobell, A. R. "Mixed Congruential Random Number Generators for Binary Machines," *Journal of the ACM*, **XI** (1964), 31-41.

30. Hutchinson, D. W. "A New Uniform Pseudorandom Number Generator," *Communications of the ACM*, **IX** (June 1966), 432-433.

31. IBM Corporation. "Random Number Generation and Testing," IBM Reference Manual C20-8011, IBM Technical Publication, White Plains, New York, 1959.

32. Itzelsberger, G. "Some Experiences with the Poker Test of Investigating Pseudo-Random-Numbers," *Digital Simulation in Operational Research*. Edited by S. H. Hollingdale. New York: American Elsevier Pub. Co., 1967.

33. Jagerman, D. L. "The Autocorrelation Function of a Sequence Uniformly Distributed Modulo 1," *Annals of Mathematical Statistics*, **XXXIV** (1963), 1243-1252.

34. Jansson, B. "Autocorrelations Between Pseudo-Random Numbers," *Nordisk Tidskr. Informations-Behandling*, **IV** (1964), 6-27.

35. Jansson, B. *Random Number Generators*. Stockholm: Victor Petersons Bokindus-triab, 1966.

36. Kendall, M. G., and Smith, B. B. "Randomness and Random Sampling Numbers," *Journal of the Royal Statistical Society*, **CI** (1938), 147-166.

37. Korn, G. A. *Random-Process Simulation and Measurements*. New York: McGraw-Hill, 1966.

38. Kuhen, H. G. "A 48-Bit Pseudo-Random Number Generator," *Communications of the ACM*, **IV** (1961), 350-352.

39. Lehmer, D. H. "Mathematical Methods in Large-Scale Computing Units," *Annals Computer Laboratory Harvard University*, **XXVI** (1951), 141-146.
40. Lehmer, D. H. "Random Number Generation on the BRL High Speed Computing Machines," *Math. Rev.*, **XV** (1954), 559.
41. Lewis, P. A. W., Goodman, A. S., and Miller, J. M. "A Pseudo-Random Number Generator for the System/360," *IBM Systems Journal*, **VIII** (No. 2, 1969), 136-146.
42. MacLaren, M. D., and Marsaglia, G. "Uniform Random Number Generators," *Journal of the ACM*, **XII** (1965), 83-89.
43. Marsaglia, G. "Generating Discrete Random Variables in a Computer," *Communications of the ACM*, **VI** (January 1963), 37-38.
44. Marsaglia, G. "Random Numbers Fall Mainly in the Planes," *Proc. Nat. Acad. Sci.*, **LX** (September 1968).
45. Marsaglia, George, and Bray, T. A. "One-Line Random Number Generators and Their Use in Combinations," *Communications of the ACM*, **XI** (November 1968), 757-759.
46. Marsaglia, G., and MacLaren, M. D. "A Fast Procedure for Generating Normal Random Variables," *Communications of the ACM*, **VII** (1964), 4-10.
47. Naylor, Thomas H., Balintfy, Joseph L., Burdick, Donald S., and Chu, Kong. *Computer Simulation Techniques*. New York: John Wiley & Sons, 1966.
48. Ore, O. *Number Theory and Its History*. New York: McGraw-Hill, 1948.
49. Page, E. S. "The Generation of Pseudo-Random Numbers," *Digital Simulation in Operational Research*. Edited by S. H. Hollingdale. New York: American Elsevier Pub. Co., 1967.
50. Payne, W. H., Rabung, J. R., and Bogyo, T. P. "Coding the Lehmer Pseudo-Random Number Generator," *Communications of the ACM*, **XII** (February 1969), 85-86.
51. Peach, P. "Bias in Pseudo-Random Numbers," *Journal of the American Statistical Association*, **LVI** (1961), 610-618.
52. Rand Corporation. *One Million Random Digits and 100,000 Normal Deviates*. Glencoe, Ill.: Free Press, 1965.
53. Rotenberg, A. "A New Pseudo-Random Number Generator," *Journal of the ACM*, **VII** (1960), 75-79.
54. Stockmal, F. "Calculations with Pseudo-Random Numbers," *Journal of the ACM*, **XI** (January 1964), 41-52.
55. Taussky, O., and Todd, J. "Generation and Testing of Pseudo-Random Numbers," *Symposium on Monte Carlo Methods*, H. A. Meyer (ed). New York: John Wiley, 1956.
56. Tausworthe, R. C. "Random Numbers Generated by Linear Recurrence Modulo Two," *Math. Comput.*, **XIX** (1965), 201-209.
57. Tocher, K. D. "The Application of Automatic Computers to Sampling Experiments," *Journal of the Royal Statistical Society B*, **XVI** (1954), 39-61.
58. Tocher, K. D. *The Art of Simulation*. Princeton, N. J.: Van Nostrand, 1963.
59. Uspensky, James V., and Heaslet, M. A. *Elementary Number Theory*. New York: McGraw-Hill, 1939.

60. Westlake, W. J. "A Uniform Random Number Generator Based on the Combination of Two Congruential Generators," *Journal of the ACM*, **XIV** (April 1967), 337-340.
61. Whittlesey, J. R. B. "A Comparison of the Correlation Behavior of Random Number Generators for the IBM 360," *Communications of the ACM*, **XI** (September 1968), 641-644.

Appendix B | Random Variable Generators

INTRODUCTION

In this appendix we describe a number of computer subroutines for generating random variables from several of the more widely used probability distributions. We consider five continuous distributions and five discrete distributions. For each distribution we specify either the density function or the probability function, depending on whether the distribution is continuous or discrete. In addition, the parameters, expected value, and variance, for each distribution are given. We also present a FORTRAN subroutine for generating random variables for each of the distributions. These subroutines assume the availability of a pseudorandom number generator that can be called by the following FORTRAN instruction:

$$\text{CALL RAND(R)}. \tag{B-1}$$

Since we do not present the relevant theory that underlies each of these generators, we refer the interested reader to Chapter 4 of *Computer Simulation Techniques* [27] by Naylor, Balintfy, Burdick, and Chu. This reference also contains an exhaustive list of probability distributions and generators, including many distributions that are not presented in this Appendix.

CONTINUOUS PROBABILITY DISTRIBUTIONS

In considering stochastic processes that involve either continuous or discrete random variables, we define a function $F(x)$ called the *cumulative distribution function* of x, which denotes the probability that a random variable X takes on the value of x or less. If the random variable is discrete, then x takes on specific values, and $F(x)$ is a step function. If $F(x)$ is continuous over the domain of x, it is possible to differentiate this function and define $f(x) = dF(x)/dx$. The derivative $f(x)$ is called a *probability density function*. The cumulative distribution function can be stated mathematically as

$$F(x) = P(X \le x) = \int_{-\infty}^{x} f(t)\, dt \tag{B-2}$$

where $F(x)$ is defined over the range $0 \leq F(x) \leq 1$, and $f(t)$ represents the value of the probability density function of the random variable X when $X = t$.

UNIFORM DISTRIBUTION

$$Density\ Function\colon f(x) = \begin{cases} \dfrac{1}{b-a} & a < x < b \\ 0 & \text{otherwise,} \end{cases} \tag{B-3}$$

Parameters: a and b

$$Expected\ Value\colon EX = \int_a^b \frac{1}{b-a} x\, dx = \frac{b+a}{2} \tag{B-4}$$

$$Variance\colon^1 VX = \int_a^b \frac{(x-EX)^2}{b-a}\, dx = \frac{(b-a)^2}{12} \tag{B-5}$$

FORTRAN Subroutine:

```
    SUBRØUTINE UNIFRM (A,B,X)
1   CALL RAND (R)
2   X = A + (B - A) * R
3   RETURN
4   END
```

NORMAL DISTRIBUTION

$$Density\ Function\colon f(x) = \frac{\exp\left[-\,(x-\mu_x)^2/2\sigma_x^2\right]}{\sigma_x\sqrt{2\pi}}, \quad -\infty < x < \infty, \tag{B-6}$$

Parameters: μ_x and σ_x

Expected Value: $EX = \mu_x$

Variance: $VX = \sigma_x^2$ and $STDX = \sigma_x$.

FORTRAN Subroutine:

```
    SUBROUTINE NORMAL (EX, STDX,X)
1   SUM = 0.0
2   DO 4 I = 1, 12
3   CALL RAND (R)
4   SUM = SUM + R
5   X = STDX * (SUM - 6.) + EX
6   RETURN
7   END
```

MULTIVARIATE NORMAL DISTRIBUTION

$$Density\ Function\colon f(\mathbf{x}) = |2\pi\mathbf{V}|^{-1/2} \exp\left[-\tfrac{1}{2}(\mathbf{x}-\mathbf{\mu})'\mathbf{V}^{-1}(\mathbf{x}-\mathbf{\mu})\right], \tag{B-7}$$

[1] In order to avoid confusion with FORTRAN subscripted variables we use the symbols EX and VX to denote, respectively, the expected value and variance of X rather than the customary E(X) and Var (X).

where $\mathbf{x}$ is an n-dimensional random normal vector, $\boldsymbol{\mu}$ is an n-dimensional vector, $\mathbf{V}$ is an $n \times n$ matrix, and $|2\pi\mathbf{V}|$ is the determinant of the $2\pi\mathbf{V}$ matrix.

Parameters: $\boldsymbol{\mu}$ and $\mathbf{V}$.

Expected Value: $\mathrm{E}(x) = \boldsymbol{\mu}$, where $\boldsymbol{\mu}$ is the mean vector.

Variance-Covariance Matrix:

$$V = \mathrm{E}[(\mathbf{x} - \boldsymbol{\mu}) \cdot (\mathbf{x} - \boldsymbol{\mu})'] = \begin{bmatrix} \sigma^2{}_{11} \cdots \sigma^2{}_{1n} \\ \cdots\cdots\cdots \\ \sigma^2{}_{nl} \cdots \sigma^2{}_{nn} \end{bmatrix} \tag{B-8}$$

where $\sigma_{ii}{}^2$ denotes the variance of the ith random variable and $\sigma_{ij}{}^2$ denotes the covariance between the ith random variable and the jth random variable.

FORTRAN Subroutine:[2]

```
1   SUBRØUTINE MVN (V, EX, N, X, K5, D, Z, SUM2)
2   DIMENSIØN V(N,N), EX(N), X(N), D(N,N), Z(N), SUM2(N)
3   IF (K5-1) 4,4,29
4   DØ 7 J1  = 1,N
5   X(J1)  = 0.0
6   DØ 7 J2  = 1,N
7   D(J1,J2)  = 0.0
8.  DØ 9 I  = 1,N
9   D(I,1)  = V(I,1)/V(1,1) ** .5
10  DØ 28 I  = 2, N
11  SUM  = 0.0
12  K1  = I-1
13  DØ 14 K  = 1,K1
14  SUM  = SUM + D(I,K) * D(I,K)
15  CK  = V(I,I) - SUM
16  IF (CK) 17,17,18
17  STØP
18  D(I,I)  = SQRT(CK)
19  IF(I-N) 20,28,28
20  K1  = I
21  DØ 27 J  = 2,K1
22  SUM1  = 0.0
23  K2  = J-1
24  DØ 25 K  = 1,K2
25  SUM1  = SUM1 + D(I+1,K)
26  D(I+1,J)  = (V(I+1,J) - SUM1) / D(J,J)
27  CØNTINUE
28  CØNTINUE
29  DØ 31 I  = 1,N
30  SUM2(I)  = 0.0
31  CALL NORMAL (0.0, 1.0, Z(I))
32  DØ 34 I  = 1,N
33  DØ 34 J  = 1,N
34  SUM2(I)  = SUM2(I) + D(I,J) * Z(J)
35  DØ 36 I  = 1,N
36  X(I)  = SUM2(I) + EX(I)
37  RETURN
38  END
```

[2] This subroutine was contributed by Professor W. Earl Sasser of the Harvard Business School, and it is based on a method proposed by Scheuer and Stoller [29]. The theory underlying this procedure also appears in [27, pp. 97-99].

K5 must be set equal to one in the main program the first time MVN is called. It must not be equal to one, thereafter.

The papers by McCarthy [14] and Nagar [26] describe the use of multivariate normal generators to generate the stochastic error terms for simultaneous-equation econometric models. They suggest two computational alternatives when the variance-covariance matrix of the least-squares estimated structural disturbances Σ is singular, that is, when the number of sample observations is less than the number of equations.

EXPONENTIAL DISTRIBUTION

Density Function: $f(x) = \alpha e^{-\alpha x}$ (B-9)

for $\alpha > 0$ and $x \geq 0$.

Parameter: α

Expected Value: $\text{EX} = \displaystyle\int_0^\infty x\alpha e^{-\alpha x}dx = \dfrac{1}{\alpha}$ (B-10)

Variance: $\text{VX} = \displaystyle\int_0^\infty \left(x - \dfrac{1}{\alpha}\right)^2 \alpha e^{-\alpha x}dx = \dfrac{1}{\alpha^2} = (\text{EX})^2.$ (B-11)

FORTRAN Subroutine:

```
      SUBRØUTINE EXPENT (EX,X)
1     CALL RAND (R)
2     X =  -EX * LØG (R)
3     RETURN
4     END
```

LOG(R) is a FORTRAN function for taking the natural logarithm of R.

THE GAMMA DISTRIBUTION

Density Function: $f(x) = \dfrac{\alpha^k x^{(k-1)} e^{-\alpha x}}{(k - 1)!}$ (B-12)

where $\alpha > 0$, $k > 0$, and x are nonnegative.

Parameters: α and k

Expected Value: $\text{EX} = \dfrac{k}{\alpha}.$

Variance: $\text{VX} = \dfrac{k}{\alpha^2}.$

FORTRAN Subroutine:

```
      SUBROUTINE GAMMA (K,A,X)
1     TR  =  1.0
2     DØ 4 I  = 1,K
3     CALL RAND (R)
4     TR  =  TR*R
5     X  =  -LØG (TR)/A
6     RETURN
7     END
```

A is the FORTRAN symbol for α.

Other Distributions

A number of other distributions can be generated by subroutines which take advantage of the relationship between these distributions and the distributions described previously in this section. For example, procedures for generating χ^2, t, and F distributions are straightforward extensions of the procedure for generating normal variates [27, pp. 96–97]. The lognormal generator [27, pp. 99-101] also is based on the normal distribution. Hyperexponential, generalized exponential (or Pearson XI type), and Weibull generators can be derived from the exponential generator [27, pp. 85-86]. The beta and Dirichlet distributions are extensions of the gamma distribution [27, pp. 89-90). These distributions are described in Chapter 4 of [27], and techniques are presented for generating random variables from these distributions.

DISCRETE PROBABILITY DISTRIBUTIONS

The cumulative probability distribution for a discrete random variable X is defined in a manner similar to (B-2).

$$F(x) \; = \; \mathrm{P}(X \leq x) \; = \; \sum_{x=0}^{x} f(x), \tag{B-13}$$

where $f(x)$ is the frequency or *probability function* of X defined for integer x values such that

$$f(x) \; = \; \mathrm{P}(X \; = \; x) \tag{B-14}$$

for $x = 0, 1, 2, \ldots$.

GEOMETRIC DISTRIBUTION

Probability Function: $f(x) \; = \; pq^x \qquad x = 0, 1, 2, \ldots$. $\hspace{2cm}$ (B-15)

Parameters: p and q where $0 \leq p \leq 1$ and $q = 1 - p$.

Expected Value: $\text{EX} = \dfrac{q}{p}$

Variance: $\text{VX} = \dfrac{q}{p^2} = \dfrac{\text{EX}}{p}$.

FORTRAN Subroutine: The geometric distribution is a special case of the Pascal distribution with $k = 1$. A FORTRAN subroutine for the Pascal distribution is described in the following section. Geometric variates can be generated by the Pascal subroutine by setting $k = 1$.

PASCAL DISTRIBUTION

Probability Function: $f(x) = \begin{pmatrix} k + x - 1 \\ x \end{pmatrix} p^k q^x \qquad x = 0, 1, 2, \ldots$ (B-16)

Parameters: k, p, and q where k is an integer, $0 \leq p \leq 1$, and $q = 1 - p$.

Expected Value: $\text{EX} = \dfrac{kq}{p}$

Variance: $\text{VX} = \dfrac{kq}{p^2}$.

FORTRAN Subroutine:

```
      SUBRØUTINE PASCAL (K, Q, X)
1     TR  =  1.0
2     QR  =  LØG(Q)
3     DØ 5 I  =  1,K
4     CALL RAND (R)
5     TR  =  TR*R
6     NX  =  LØG(TR)/QR
7     X = NX
8     RETURN
9     END
```

BINOMIAL DISTRIBUTION

Probability Function: $f(x) = \begin{pmatrix} n \\ x \end{pmatrix} p^x q^{n-x}$ (B-17)

where x is an integer defined on the finite interval, $0, 1, 2, \ldots n$, and $q = (1 - p)$.

Parameters: n, p, and q where $0 \leq p \leq 1$.

Expected Value: $\text{EX} = np$

Variance: $VX = npq$.

FORTRAN Subroutine:

```
      SUBRØUTINE BINØM (N, P, X)
   1  X = 0.0
   2  DØ 6 I = 1, N
   3  CALL RAND (R)
   4  IF (R-P) 5,5,6
   5  X = X + 1.0
   6  CØNTINUE
   7  RETURN
   8  END
```

HYPERGEOMETRIC DISTRIBUTION

Probability Function: $f(x) = \dfrac{\dbinom{Np}{x}\dbinom{Nq}{n-x}}{\dbinom{N}{n}} \quad \begin{array}{l} 0 \leq x \leq Np \\ 0 \leq n - x \leq Nq, \end{array}$ (B-18)

where x, n, and N are integers.

Parameters: n, N, p, and q where $0 \leq p \leq 1$ and $p + q = 1$.

Expected Value: $EX = np$

Variance: $VX = npq\left(\dfrac{N-n}{N-1}\right)$.

FORTRAN Subroutine:

```
      SUBRØUTINE HYPGEØ (TN, NS, P, X)
   1  X = 0.0
   2  DØ 10 I = 1, NS
   3  CALL RAND (R)
   4  IF (R-P) 5,5,8
   5  S = 1.0
   6  X = X + 1.0
   7  GØ TØ 9
   8  S = 0.0
   9  P = (TN*P-S)/(TN-1.0)
  10  TN = TN - 1.0
  11  RETURN
  12  END
```

The symbols TN and NS are FORTRAN symbols for N and n, respectively.

POISSON DISTRIBUTION

Probability Function: $f(x) = e^{-\lambda}\left(\dfrac{\lambda^x}{x!}\right) \qquad x = 0, 1, 2, \ldots \lambda > 0,$ (B-19)

Parameter: λ

Expected Value: $EX = \lambda$

Variance: $VX = \lambda$.

FORTRAN Subroutine:

```
          SUBRØUTINE PØISSN (P, X)
 1   X  =  0.0
 2   B  =  EXP (-P)
 3   TR =  1.0
 4   CALL RAND (R)
 5   TR =  TR*R
 6   If (TR-B) 9,7,7
 7   X  =  X + 1.0
 8   GØ TØ 4
 9   RETURN
10   END
```

EXP (X) is a FORTRAN function denoting e^x. P is the FORTRAN symbol for λ.

BIBLIOGRAPHY

1. Aitchison, J., and Brown, J. A. C. *The Lognormal Distribution.* Cambridge: Cambridge University Press, 1957.
2. Anderson, T. W. *An Introduction to Multivariate Statistical Analysis.* New York: John Wiley & Sons, 1958.
3. Box, G. E. P., and Muller, M. E. "A Note on the Generation of Normal Deviates," *Annals of Mathematical Statistics,* **XXVIII** (1958), 610-611.
4. Brockmeyer, E., Halstrom, H. L., and Jensen, A. *The Life Works of A. E. Erlang.* Copenhagen: Copenhagen Telephone Co., 1948.
5. Brown, R. G. *Statistical Forecasting for Inventory Control.* New York: McGraw-Hill Book Co., 1959.
6. Brown, R. G. *Smoothing, Forecasting and Prediction of Discrete Time Series.* Englewood Cliffs, N J.: Prentice-Hall, Inc., 1963.
7. Burr, Irving W. "A Useful Approximation of the Normal Distribution Function, with Application to Simulation," *Technometrics,* **IX** (November 1967).
8. Butler, James W. "Machine Sampling from Given Probability Distribution," in *Symposium on Monte Carlo Methods.* New York: John Wiley & Sons, Inc., 1954, 249-264.
9. Cramer, Harold. *Mathematical Methods of Statistics.* Princeton: Princeton University Press, 1957.
10. Feller, William. *An Introduction to Probability Theory and Its Application.* New York: John Wiley & Sons, 1950.
11. Galliher, Herbert P. "Simulation of Random Processes," *Notes on Operations Research 1959.* Cambridge: The Technology Press, Massachusetts Institute of Technology, 1959.
12. Gupta, S. S. "Probability Integrals of Multivariate Normal and Multivariate t," *Anneals of Mathematical Statistics,* **XXXIV** (1963).

13. Hammersley, J. M., and Handscomb, D. C. *Monte Carlo Methods*. NewYork: John Wiley & Sons, 1964.

14. McCarthy, Michael D. "Some Notes on the Generation of Pseudo Structural Errors for Use in Stochastic Simulation Studies," Conference on Econometric Models of Cyclical Behavior, Harvard University, November 14-15, 1969.

15. Maguire, B. A., Pearson, E. S., and Jensen, A. "The Time Intervals Between Industrial Accidents," *Biometrika*, **XXXIX** (1952), 168-180.

16. Marsaglia, G. *On Generating Exponentially Distributed Random Variables*. Seattle: Boeing Scientific Res. Labs., 1960.

17. Marsaglia, G. "Generating Exponential Random Variables," *The Annals of Mathematical Statistics*, **XXXII** (1961), 899-900.

18. Marsaglia, G. *Uniform Distributions Over a Simplex*. Seattle: Boeing Scientific Res. Labs., 1961.

19. Marsaglia, G. *Improving the Polar Method for Generating a Pair of Normal Random Variables*. Seattle: Boeing Scientific Res. Labs., 1962.

20. Marsaglia, G. "Generating Discrete Random Variables in a Computer," *Communications of the ACM*, **VI** (January 1963), 37-38.

21. Marsaglia, G. *Generating Variables from the Tail of the Normal Distribution*. Seattle: Boeing Scientific Res. Labs., 1963.

22. Marsaglia, G. *Still Another Method for Producing Normal Variables on a Computer*. Seattle: Boeing Scientific Res. Labs., 1965.

23. Marsaglia, G., and Bray, T. A. *A Small Procedure for Generating Normal Random Variables*. Seattle: Boeing Scientific Res. Labs., 1962.

24. Marsaglia, G., and MacLaren, M. D. "A Fast Procedure for Generating Normal Random Variables," *Communications of the ACM*, **VII** (1964), 4-10.

25. Muller, Mervin E. "A Comparison of Methods for Generating Normal Deviates on Digital Computers," *Journal of the Association for Computing Machinery*, **VI** (1959), 376-383.

26. Nagar, A. L. "Stochastic Simulations of the Brookings Econometric Model," *The Brookings Model: Some Further Results*, J. S. Duesenberry *et al* (ed). Chicago: Rand McNally, 1969.

27. Naylor, Thomas H., Balintfy, Joseph L., Burdick, Donald S., and Chu, Kong. *Computer Simulation Techniques*. New York: John Wiley & Sons, 1966.

28. Parzen, Emanuel. *Modern Probability Theory and its Applications*. New York: John Wiley & Sons, Inc., 1960.

29. Scheuer, Ernest, and Stoller, David S. "On the Generation of Normal Random Vectors," *Technometrics*, **IV** (May 1962), 278-281.

30. Teichroew, Daniel. "A History of Distribution Sampling Prior to the Era of the Computer and Its Relevance to Simulation," *American Statistical Association Journal* (March 1965), 27-49.

31. Tocher, K. D. "The Application of Automatic Computers to Sampling Experiments," *Journal of the Royal Statistical Society* B, **XVI** (1954), 39-61.

32. Tocher, K. D. *The Art of Simulation*. Princeton, N.J.: Van Nostrand, 1963.

33. Von Neumann, John. "Various Techniques in Connection with Random Digits," in *Monte Carlo Methods*, National Bureau of Standards, Applied Math. Series 12 (1951), 36-38.
34. Wilks, S. S. *Mathematical Statistics*. New York: John Wiley & Sons, 1962.
35. Yagil, S. "Generation of Input Data for Simulations," *IBM Systems Journal*, **II** (1963), 288-296.

Appendix C | *Simulation Languages*[1]

PHILIP J. KIVIAT

INTRODUCTION

Simulation programming languages are designed to assist analysts in the design, programming, and analysis of simulation models. This appendix discusses basic simulation concepts, presents arguments for the use of simulation languages, discusses the four languages GPSS, SIMSCRIPT II, SIMULA, and CSL, summarizes their basic features, and comments on the probable future course of events in simulation language research and development.

Simulation languages are shown to assist in the design of simulation models through their "world view," to expedite computer programming through their special purpose, high-level statements, and to encourage proper model analysis through their data collection, analysis, and reporting features. Ten particularly important simulation programming language features are identified: modeling a system's static state, modeling system dynamics, statistical sampling, data collection, analysis and display, monitoring and debugging, initialization and language usability. Examples of each of the four simulation languages, GPSS, SIMSCRIPT II, SIMULA, and CSL, are used to illustrate how these features are implemented in different languages.

The future development of simulation programming languages is shown to be dependent on advances in the fields of computer languages, computer graphics, and time sharing. Some current research is noted and outstanding research areas are identified.

[1] This appendix has been reproduced with the permission of Philip J. Kiviat and the RAND Corporation. It was originally published by The RAND Corporation as Memorandum RM-5883-PR in January, 1969 and was entitled "Digital Computer Simulation: Computer Programming Languages." Mr. Kiviat is now President of Simulation Associates, Inc., 1263 Westwood Blvd., Los Angeles, California.

Some Definitions

A reader who is completely unfamiliar with digital computers and the basic concepts of computer programming should consult an introductory computer programming text before going any further. References [1] and [22] are good texts for the purpose. Those who are familiar with computers and who, at least, are aware of the basic concepts of programming should be able to follow this Appendix without additional preparation.

A *computer programming language* is a set of symbols recognizable by a computer, or by a computer program, that denote operations a programmer wishes a computer to perform. At the lowest level, a *basic machine language* (BML) program is a string of symbols that corresponds directly to machine functions, such as adding two numbers, storing a number, and transferring to an address. At a higher level, an *assembly language* (AL) program is a string of mnemonic symbols that correspond to machine language functions and are translatable into a basic machine language program by an *assembly program* or *assembler*. Simple assemblers do little but substitute basic machine language codes for mnemonics and assign computer addresses to variable names and labels. Sophisticated assemblers can recognize additional symbols (macros) and construct complicated basic machine language programs from them.

A *compiler* is a program that accepts statements written in a usually complex, high-level *compiler language* (CL) and translates them into either assembly language or basic machine language programs—which in turn, at least in the case of CL to AL translation, may be reduced to more basic programs. Compilation is much more complex than assembly, as it involves a higher level of understanding of program organization, much richer input languages, and semantic as well as syntactic analysis and processing.

An *interpreter* is a program that accepts input symbols and, instead of translating them into computer instructions for subsequent processing, directly executes the operations they denote. For this reason, an *interpretive language* (IL) can look like a BML, an AL, a CL or anything else. Interpretive language symbols are not commands to construct a program to do something, as are assembly language and compiler language commands, but commands to do the thing itself. Consequently, even though programs written in a CL aud IL may look identical, they call for sharply different actions by the programs that "understand" them, and different techniques are employed in writing them.

For all but basic machine language and interpretive programs, a distinction must be drawn between the program submitted to the computer, the *source language program*, and the program executed[2] by the computer,

---

[2] Excluding modifications made during loading.

the *object program*. An assembler that accepts mnemonic basic machine codes as its input and translates them into numerical basic machine codes has the mnemonics as its source language and the numerical basic codes as its object language. A compiler that accepts Englishlike language statements as its input and translates them into assembly language mnemonics, which in turn, are, translated into numerical basic machine codes, has the Englishlike language as its source language and the numerical basic codes as its object language. An interpreter that operates by reading, interpreting, and operating directly on source codes has no object code. Every time an interpretive program is executed, a translation takes place. This differs from what is done by assemblers and compilers where translation takes place only once, from source to object language and, thus, enables the subsequent running of object programs without translation.

Basic machine language and assembly language programs suffer in that they are specific to a particular computer. Since their symbols correspond to particular computer operations, programs written in BML or an AL are meaningful only in the computer for which they are designed. As such, they can be regarded as *machine oriented languages* (MOL).

Most compilers and interpreters can be classified as *problem oriented languages* (POL). As such, they differ from BML and AL, which reflect computer hardware functions and have no problem orientation. A POL written for a particular problem area contains symbols (language statements) appropriate for formulating solutions to typical problems in that area. A POL is able to express problem solutions in *computer independent notation*, using a probram that "understands" the POL to translate the problem solution expressed in source language to a BML object program or to execute it interpretively.

Figure 1 illustrates a BML, and AL, and two POLs. Each example shows the statement or statements (symbols) that must be written to express the same programming operation, the addition of three numbers.

The point of the discussion thus far has been to establish the definitions of BML, AL, CL, MOL, POL, assembler, compiler, and interpreter. With-

BML	AL: FAP	POL: FORTRAN	POL: COBOL
+050000... +040000... +040000... +060100...	CLA A ADD B ADD C STO X	X = A+B+C	ADD A,B TO C GIVING X

Figure 1.   A programming example.

out these definitions, it is impossible to understand the historical evolution of simulation programming languages or their basic characteristics.

A *simulation programming language* (SPL) is a POL with special features. Simulation being a problem-solving activity with its own needs, programming languages have been written to make special features available to simulation programmers at a POL level. Historically, this has been an evolutionary process. SPLs have developed gradually from AL programs with special features, through extended commercially available POLs, to sophisticated, special-purpose SPLs. A discussion of these special features is necessary to place the development process in perspective and to introduce the topics that follow. More complete histories of simulation programming languages and the development of simulation concepts can be found in [35], [36], [42], [43], [46], [60], and [61].

Principal Features of Simulation Languages

Simulation, as defined in [34], is a technique used for reproducing the dynamic behavior of a system as it operates in time.

To represent and to reproduce system behavior, features that are not normally found or adequately emphasized in most programming languages are needed. These features have the following characteristics:

(1) They provide data representations that permit straightforward and efficient modeling,

(2) They permit the facile portrayal and reproduction of dynamics within a modeled system.

(3) They are oriented to the study of stochastic systems, that is they contain procedures for the generation and analysis of random variables, and time series.

The first feature calls for data structures more elaborate than the typical unsubscripted-subscripted variable organizations found in, say, FORTRAN and ALGOL. Data structures must be richer in two ways: They must be capable of complex organization, as in tree structures, lists, and sets; and they must be able to store varieties of data, such as numbers, both integer and real, double-precision and complex, character strings of both fixed and variable length, and data structure references. As data structures exist only so that they can be manipulated, statements must be available that (1) assist in initializing a system data base (as we may call the collection of data that describe a system); (2) permit manipulations on the data, such as adding elements, changing data values, altering data structures, and monitoring data flows; and (3) enable communication between the modeler and the data. PL/I, the newest general-purpose POL, pays great attention to data structures, although not as much as some people would like [29]. ALGOL 68, the revised version of ALGOL 60, also leans in this direction [18]. Activity in the CODASYL committee charged with improving COBOL shows that they too are aware of the importance of this topic [55].

The second feature deals with modeling formalisms, both definitional and executable, that permit the simulation of dynamic, interactive systems. Statements that deal with time-dependent descriptions of changes in system state, and mechanisms that organize the execution of various system-state-change programs so that the dynamics of a system are represented correctly, are an integral part of every SPL.

The third feature stems from the fact that the world is constantly changing in a stochastic manner. Things do not happen regularly and deterministically, but randomly and with variation. Procedures are needed that generate so-called pseudorandom variates from different statistical distributions and from empirical sampling distributions, so that real-world variability can be represented. Procedures also are needed for processing data generated by simulation models in order to make sense out of the masses of statistical data they produce [21].

The history of simulation-oriented programming languages, noted above, points out that there is no one form a simulation language must take, nor any one accepted method of implementing such a language. An SPL can be an AL with special instructions in the form of macros that perform simulation-oriented tasks, a CL with special statements that perform essentially the same tasks, or an IL with statements similar to the ones found in simulation-oriented CLs and ALs but with an entirely different implementation. Here, it is sufficient merely to point out the principal characteristics of all SPLs, thus, providing a base for discussing why SPLs are needed and for understanding some pros and cons of using specialized SPLs and general POLs for simulation.

Reasons for Having SPLs

The two most frequently cited reasons for having simulation programming languages are (1) programming convenience, and (2) concept articulation. The former is important in the actual writing of computer programs, the latter in the modeling phase and in the overall approach taken to system experimentation.

It is difficult to say which of the two is more important. Certainly, many simulation projects have never gotten off the ground or, at least, were not completed on time, because of programming difficulties. But then, other projects have failed because their models were poorly conceived and designed, making the programming difficult and the required experimentation impossible, or nearly so. If it were necessary to choose, concept articulation probably should be ranked first, since any statements or features provided by a simulation programming language must exist within a conceptual framework.

Succeeding sections examine a number of simulation programming concepts and describe how they are implemented in different SPLs. Some models also are described, with comments on how various conceptual frameworks help or hinder their analysis and examination.

It is fair to say at this point, before going through this demonstration and without documented proof, that SPLs have contributed to the success of simulation as an experimental technique, and that the two features, programming convenience and concept articulation, are the major reasons for this success. SPLs provide languages for describing and modeling systems—languages composed of concepts central to simulation. Before these concepts were articulated, there were no words with which to describe simulation tasks, and without words there was no communication—at least, no communication of the intensity and scope that is found today.

A third substantial reason for having higher-level SPLs has come about through their use as communication and documentation devices. When written in Englishlike languages, simulations can be explained to project managers and nonprogramming-oriented users much more easily than when they are written in hieroglyphic ALs. Explanation and debugging are easier when a program can be read instead of having to be deciphered.

Reasons for Using Existing POLs

Cogent arguments, both technical and operational, have been advanced for avoiding SPLs and sticking with tried-and-true algebraic compilers. Technical objections dwell mostly on object program efficiency, debugging facilities, and the like. Some of the operational objections are the noted inadequacy of SPL documentation, the lack of transferability of SPL programs across different computers, and the difficulty of correcting SPL compiler errors.

Most of these points are valid, although their edge of truth is often exceedingly thin. It is almost necessarily true that specialized simulation programming languages are less efficient in certain aspects than more general algebraic compilers. Because an SPL is designed for one purpose, it is less efficient for another. No single programming language can be all things to all men, at least, not today. Painful experience is proving this to be true. SPLs should be used where their advantages outweigh their disadvantages, but they should not be criticized for their limitations alone.

An SPL should be criticized if it does something poorly that it was designed to do, that is, a simulation-oriented task, but not if it is inefficient in a peripheral nonsimulation-oriented task.

But technical criticisms are the least of the arguments levied against SPLs by people seeking to justify their use of existing algebraic POLS. The most serious and justifiable criticisms are the ones that pertain to the use of individual SPLs. Unlike the commonly used POLs, such as FORTRAN, ALGOL, and COBOL, which are produced and maintained by computer manufacturers, SPLs, with few exceptions, have been produced by individual organizations for their own purposes and have been released to the public more as a convenience and as an intellectual gesture than as a profitable business venture. The latter are too often poorly documented, larded with undiscovered errors, and set up to operate on nonstandard systems or, at least on systems different from the ones that a typical user seems to have. Although attractive intellectually, they often have been rejected because it is simply too much trouble to get them working.[3] In a programming community that is accustomed to having computer manufacturers do all the compiler support work, most companies are not set up to do these things themselves.

The answer has been, "Stick to FORTRAN or something similar." It is easy to sympathize with this attitude, but it is unwise to agree in all cases. For a small organization with limited programming resources, doing a small amount of simulation work according to this strategy is probably justifiable; difficulties can be eased somewhat by using languages such as GASP and FORSIM IV, which are actually FORTRAN programming packages [19], [37], [53]. Large organizations that have adequate programming resources and do a considerable amount of simulation work are probably fooling themselves when they avoid investing resources in an SPL and stick to a standard POL. One reason they often decide to do so is that the direct costs to install and maintain a SPL are visible, although the incremental costs incurred by using a POL are hidden and not easily calculated. This is the worst kind of false economy. Another often-heard excuse is that programmers and analysts are unwilling to learn a new programming language. If so, they should reform. When they learn to use an SPL, they are doing far more than learning a new programming language; they are learning concepts especially structured for simulation modeling and programming—concepts that do not even exist in nonsimulation-oriented POLs.

[3] The exception is GPSS, which IBM introduced and has maintained, supported, and redesigned three times since 1962.

Today, the designers of simulation programming languages are paying much more attention to their users than they have in the past, and computer manufacturers are supporting SPLs much more readily. Although the era of the independently produced SPL is not past, it has probably seen its heyday. Problems of system compatibility and compiler support will diminish in the future, and most operational problems will fade or vanish. But there is no escaping the need to learn new languages; our only choice is whether to volunteer or to be drafted.

SIMULATION PROGRAMMING CONCEPTS

Every SPL has a small number of special simulation-oriented features. The way they are elaborated and implemented makes particular SPLs difficult or easy to use, programmer- or analyst-oriented, and so on. They support the concepts embodied in the definition of simulation used in this series of Memoranda: the use of a numerical model to study the behavior of a system as it operates over time.

By taking the key words in this definition one at a time, we set forth the basic SPL requirements:

Use . . . to study the behavior: an SPL must provide facilities for performing experiments, for presenting experimental results, for prescribing experimental conditions, and so on.

Numerical model . . . of a system: an SPL must provide facilities for describing the structure of a great variety of systems. Representations are needed for describing the objects found in systems, their qualities and properties, and the relationships between them.

Operates over time: an SPL must provide facilities for describing dynamic relationships within systems and for operating the system representation in such a way that the dynamic aspects of system behavior are reproduced.

This section concentrates first on concepts that are related to the descriptions of a system's static structure and next on concepts that are related to representing system dynamics.

Describing a System: The Static Structure

The static structure of a simulation model is a time-independent framework within which system states are defined. System states are possible configurations in which a system can be; in numerical models, different system states are represented by different data patterns. Dynamic system processes act and interact within a static data structure, changing data values and, thereby, changing system states.

A definition of a system points out characteristics that are important in establishing a static system structure: a system is an interacting collection of objects in a closed environment, the boundaries of which are clearly stated. Every system:

a. contains identifiable classes of objects,
b. which can vary in number,
c. have varying numbers of identifying characteristics,
d. and are related to one another and to the environment in changeable, although prescribed ways.

Simulation programming languages must be able to do the following.

1. Define the classes of objects within a system
2. Adjust the number of these objects as conditions within the system vary
3. Define the characteristics or properties that can both describe and differentiate objects of the same class, and declare (numerical) codes for them, and
4. Relate objects to one another and to their common environment.

These requirements are not unique to SPLS; they are also found in languages and programs associated with information retrieval and management information systems.

Although it might be interesting to examine all SPLs and to contrast the particular ways in which they express structural concepts, it would hardly be practical. First, they are too numerous; second, many are simply dialects—lineal descendants or near relatives of a small number of seminal languages. In the interests of economy and clarity, only the basic concepts of these languages are discussed here. Excellent discussions of the features and pros and cons of the most widely used simulation languages can be found in [43], [60], [61], [64], and [66].

Identification of Objects and Object Characteristics

All SPLs view the "real world" in pretty much the same way, and they reflect this view in the data structures they provide for representing systems. Basically, systems are composed of classes of different kinds of objects that are unique and can be identified by distinguishing characteristics. Objects are referred to by names such as entity, object, transaction, resource, facility, storage, variable, machine, equipment, process, and element. Object characteristics are referred to by names such as attribute, parameter, state, and descriptor. In some languages, all objects are passive, that is, things happen to them; in some languages, objects are active as well, that is, they flow through a system and initiate actions.

Table 1 lists several popular SPLs and shows the concept names and formulisms associated with each.

Table 1   Identification Methods

Language	Concepts	Example
SIMSCRIPT [33, 39, 45]	Entity, Attribute	AGE(MAN) read AGE OF MAN
SIMULA [13, 14, 59]	Process, Attribute	AGE attribute of current process MAN
GPSS [23, 24, 26]	Transaction, Parameter	P1 first parameter of current transaction
CSL [7, 9, 11]	Entity, Property	LOAD(SHIP) read LOAD OF SHIP

Relationships between Objects

There is a class relationship between objects in all SPLs; several objects have different distinguishing characteristics and are in that sense unique, but have a common bond in being of the same type. For example, in a system containing a class of objects of the type SHIP, two ships may have the names MARY and ELISABETH. The objects are different yet related.

This form of relationship rarely is strong enough for all purposes, and it must be supplemented. It is almost always necessary to be able to relate objects, of the same and different classes, having restricted physical or logical relations in common. For example, it might be necessary to identify all SHIPs of a particular tonnage or all SHIPs berthed in a particular port.

To this end, all SPLs define relationship mechanisms. Names such as set, queue, list, chain, group, file, and storage are used to describe them. Each language has operators of varying power that place objects in, and remove them from, relationship structures, that determine whether several objects are in particular relationships to each other, and so on.

Table 2 lists the relationship concepts of the languages shown in Table 1.

Table 2   Relationship Methods

Language	Concept	Example
SIMSCRIPT	Set	FILE MAN FIRST IN SET(I); insert MAN into SET(I)
SIMULA	Set	PRCD(X,MAN); precede element X with element MAN in the set to which X belongs
GPSS	User chain group	LINK I, FIFO; put current transaction first in Chain I
CSL	Set	MAN.3 HEAD SET(I); put the third man at the head of Set I

Generation of Objects

Some languages deal only with fixed data structures that are allocated either during compilation or at the start of execution. These structures represent fixed numbers of objects of different classes. Other languages allow both fixed and varying numbers of objects. There is a great deal of variety in the way different languages handle the generation of objects. The methods are related both to the "world view" of the language and the way in which the language is expressed, that is, as a compiler, an interpreter, or a POL program package. Many of the differences between SIMSCRIPT and SIMULA can be traced to compiler features that have little to do with simulation per se. The block-structure/procedure orientation of SIMULA, which is rooted in ALGOL, has influenced the way processes are generated and the way they communicate with one another. The global-variable/local-variable/subroutine orientation of SIMSCRIPT, which is rooted in FORTRAN, has similarly influenced the way entities are generated and the way they communicate with one another. In these two cases, the differences are profound. A SIMULA process contains both a data structure and an activity program; a SIMSCRIPT entity holds only a data structure and is linked indirectly to an event subroutine.

Table 3 describes several object generation methods.

Table 3   Generation Methods

Language	Concept	Example
SIMSCRIPT	Generate a new entity whenever one is needed	CREATE A MAN CALLED HENRY
SIMULA	Generate a new process whenever one is needed	HENRY:= new MAN
GPSS	Generate a new transaction with some specified time between successive generations	GENERATE 10,3
CSL	Does not exist	--

Of necessity, these illustrations are sketchy and not indicative of the wealth of descriptive, relational, and operational facilities offered by the languages quoted. This is not altogether bad, as our purpose here is to impart a flavor for the ways in which SPLs describe static system structures and is not to teach or to compare the features of particular languages. Those who are interested in the specifics of individual languages should refer to their respective programming manuals.

Describing a System: The Dynamic Structure

Although a model's static structure sets the stage for simulation, its dynamic structure makes this possible. The dynamics of system behavior in all SPLs is represented procedurally, that is, by computer programs. Although desirable, no nonprocedural SPLs have yet been invented, although substantial success toward this end has been achieved in limited areas [25].

At present, two SPLs have achieved widespread prominence and use in the United States, and two others have achieved similar prominence in Europe and Great Britain. They are GPSS, SIMSCRIPT, SIMULA, and CSL, respectively. Interestingly enough, each presents a different view of system dynamics. To understand why this is true, a historical rather than functional discussion is appropriate.

The Concept of Simulated Time

Soon after academics and practitioners recognized that the simulations of industrial and military processes could be conducted on digital computers, they started to separate the simulation-oriented portions of computer programs from the parts that describe the processes being simulated. A simulation vocabulary was developed; the first word in it was probably "clock." Program structures began to reflect the concepts that were embodied in the vocabulary.

Since time and its representation are the essence of simulation, it was natural for it to be the first item of concern. If one could represent the passage of time within a computer program and could associate the execution of programs with specific points in this simulated time, one could claim to have a time-dependent simulation program.

The first *simulation clocks* imitated the behavior of real ones. They were counters that "ticked" in unit increments that represented seconds, minutes, hours, or days, providing a pulse for simulation programs. Each time the clock ticked, a *simulation control program* looked around to see what could happen at that instant in simulated time. What could happen could be determined in two ways: (1) by predetermined instruction, or (2) by search. Before discussing these two techniques, we must describe simulation control programs.

The Structure of Simulation Control Programs

The heart of every simulation program, and every SPL, is a time control program. This program is referred to in various publications as a clockworks, a simulation executive, a timing mechanism, a sequencing set, and the like. Its functions are always the same: to advance simulation time and to select a subprogram for execution that performs a specified simulation activity.

Thus, every simulation program has a hierarchical structure. At the top sits the time-control program, at an intermediate level sit simulation-oriented routines, at the bottom sit routines that do basic housekeeping functions such as input, output, and the computation of mathematical functions. Every SPL provides a time-control program; when using an SPL, a simulation programmer does not have to write one himself—or even worse, invent one.

Depending on how the time-control program works, a simulation programmer may or may not have to use special statements to interact with the timing mechanism. Most simulation languages contain one or more statements that permit a programmer to organize system activities in a time-dependent manner. Later, this section will describe several different simulation control program schemes and the ways in which a programmer interacts with them.

First, it must be understood that every simulation program is composed of blocks of statements that deal with specific system activities. These blocks may be complete routines[4] or parts of routines. They have been called events, activities, blocks, processes, and segments. The distinctions between them will be clarified presently; at the moment it is only necessary to understand that a simulation program is composed of identifiable models that deal with different simulation situations.

A simulation control program can select a portion of code to execute in either of two ways: (1) by predetermined instruction, or (2) by search. Regardless of how the result is determined, the effect is the same: the execution of an appropriate block of code. Figure 2 blocks out the basic structure of every simulation program. Simulation starts at I, where a model is initialized with sufficient data to describe its initial system state and the processes that are in motion within it. Based on information computed in the "next event" block, S switches to the code block that corresponds to the proper simulation activity.

The "search" method of next-event selection relies on the fact that, when a system operates, it moves from state to state in a predetermined manner. The times at which state changes occur may be random, and they represent the effects of statistically varying situations, but basic cause-and-effect relations still hold true. Given that a system is in state "A," it will always move into state "B" if certain conditions hold true; code block AB,

---

[4] The words routine, subroutine, program, subprogram, and procedure are used here interchangeably.

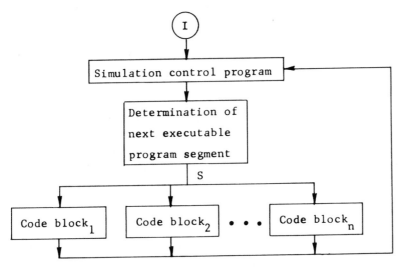

Figure 2. Basic simulation structure.

say, must always be executed to effect the change. A search method relies on descriptions of activity-producing system states and a scanner that examines system-state data to determine whether a state change can take place at any particular clock pulse.

When a state change can be made, the code block representing it alters data values to reflect the change. Since many system changes take place over a period of time, some of the data changes are to "entity clocks." These clocks are set to the simulated time at which a state change is considered completed. When the control program finds that an "entity clock" has the same time as the master simulation clock, it performs the activity associated with that clock, for example, relegating a working machine to idleness or causing an emptying tank to run dry. State changes that happen instantaneously, either when a code block is executed or as the result of some entity clocks equaling the simulation clock, cause new code blocks to be executed, new entity clocks to be set, . . ., cause the system activities to be reexamined.

The efficiency of this rather basic scheme was first improved by eliminating the uniform clock pulse. Since, in many simulations, events do not occur on every clock pulse but randomly in time, a great deal of computer time can be lost in scanning for things to do each time the clock is advanced one increment. It is more efficient to specify the time at which the *next event* is to occur and to advance the clock to this time. As nothing can happen before this time, it is unnecessary to search for altered system states. By definition of the next event, no entity clock can have an earlier time. At best, it can only be equal to the next event time.

The term "next-event simulation" was given to simulation programs that stepped from event time to event time, passing over increments of time in which no state changes occurred. *All modern SPLs use the next-event technique.* The term *critical event* often is used in the same spirit.

Two SPLs that do employ search are GSP [62] and CSL. In both, the *activity* is the basic dynamic unit. An activity is a program composed of a test section and an action section. Whenever simulation time is advanced, all activity programs are scanned for possible performance. If all test conditions in an activity are met, state-changing and time-setting instructions in the action section are executed; if, at least, one test condition is not met, the action instructions are passed over. A cyclic scanning of activity programs insures that all possibilities are examined and all interactions are accounted for.

In addition to the *activities scan*, GSP incorporates an *event scheduling* mechanism that enables an activity to specify that some system event is to take place at a determined time in the future. Events that are not affected by other events, that is, are not heavily interactive, can be treated more efficiently this way, as repeated scanning is not required to determine when they can be done.

When an activity scan is not employed, as is the case in GPSS, SIM-SCRIPT, and SIMULA, all system events must be predetermined and scheduled. The activity-scan and event-scheduling approaches are different solutions to the same problem; an activity scan is efficient for highly interactive processes that involve a fixed number of entities, for example, multiresource assignment problems in shops that produce homogeneous products; event scheduling is efficient for less interactive processes that involve large numbers of entities, for example, simulations of job shops that produce special-order products. Efficiency must be treated as a multidimensional quality, of course. We must speak of modeling efficiency and programming efficiency, as well as computer running-time efficiency.

The differences between activity-scanning and event-scheduling orientations can be pointed out best by procedural descriptions.

EVENT SELECTION PROCEDURES

Consider a simple shop situation in which a man and a machine must work together to produce a part. Each has an independent behavior in that the man starts and ends his day, takes coffee breaks, and goes to lunch without regard for how the machine is performing, and the machine suffers breakdowns and power failures without regard for what the man may be doing.

The Activity Scanning Approach. An activity approach to simulating the processing of a part in this man-machine shop specifies the conditions for a job to start processing, and the actions that take place when these conditions are met:

Test section:	if part is available AND if machine is idle AND if man is idle THEN do Action section OTHERWISE return to timing mechanism

Action section:	put man in committed state
	put machine in committed state
	determine time man will be engaged
	determine time machine will be engaged
	set man-clock to time man will become
	    available
	set machine-clock to time machine will become
	    available
	return to timing mechanism

Emphasis is on the activity of producing the part, not on the individual roles of the man and the machine. Periodic scanning of the activity finds instances when all three conditions hold true.

The Event Scheduling Approach. An event scheduling approach to the same problem requires that three programs be written, one for the man, one for the machine, and one for the part. The programs contain both test and action statements, and are "menus" for situations that can take place whenever a state-change event occurs. For example, one event in the simulation of the above man-machine shop would be the return of a man to the idle state from whatever activity in which he might have been engaged. The routine that represents the "man becomes idle" event might look like the following:

Test section:	if part is available AND if machine is idle THEN do Action section$_1$ OTHERWISE do Action section $_2$
Action section$_1$:	put man in committed state put machine in committed state determine time man will be engaged determine time machine will be engaged schedule return of man to availability schedule return of machine to availability return to timing mechanism
Action section$_2$:	put man in idle state return to timing mechanism

Although these two program protocols may look similar, they are quite different. The event program is executed only when a state change occurs; the activity program, on the other hand, is examined at each timing cycle to see if a state change can take place. Furthermore, the activity contains logic for the availability of part, man, and machine, but three event programs must be written for the return of a man, machine, and part— testing, respectively, that a machine and part, man and part, and man and machine are available.

Neither approach is clearly superior to the other; each has its advantages in some situations. Differences among SPLs that use one approach or another usually stem from their authors' attempts to design a language suited to the particular class of problems they study and, hence, gain modeling, programming, and execution efficiency.

The Process Interaction Approach. One of the difficulties of the event approach is its division of the logic of an operating system into small parts. The activity approach seems to suffer less from this criticism. A third approach, called the process, attempts to combine the efficiencies of event scheduling with the concise notation of activity scanning.

A *process* can be defined as a set of events that are associated with a system behavior description. The events are interrelated by special scheduling statements, such as DELAY, WAIT, and WAIT UNTIL, that interrupt the execution of a subprogram until a specified period of time has passed or a stated set of conditions hold true. DELAY and WAIT are *time-oriented* and are effected through event scheduling techniques. WAIT UNTIL, being *condition-oriented*, requires an activity-scan approach. A process description thereby combines the run-time efficiency of event scheduling with the modeling efficiency of activity scanning. SIMULA in a process-oriented language that has had several years of successful experience and has undergone one revision [16]. GPSS is a process-oriented language with a longer history and an even more widespread acceptance. Although it is flow-chart-oriented instead of statement-oriented, the basic process concepts that are expressed here apply to it.

A key feature of process-orientation is that a single program is made to act as though it were several programs, independently controlled either by activity-type scans or event scheduling. Each process has several points at which it interacts with other processes. Each process can have several active phases; each active phase of a process is an event. This is different from pure event or activity approaches that allow an interaction only when all the actions associated with an event or activity have been completed, for example, when they return to the timing mechanism.

The programming feature that makes this scheme possible is the reactivation point, which is essentially a pointer that tells a process routine where to start execution after some time-delay command has been executed. Figure 2 illustrates the concepts of *interaction point* and *reactivation point* for prototype event, activity, and process routines.

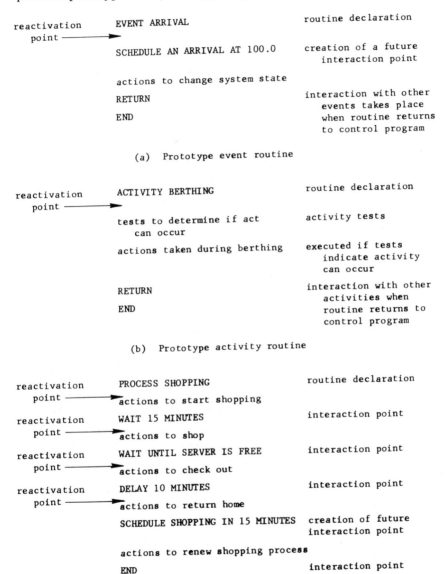

reactivation point ———▸

EVENT ARRIVAL   routine declaration

SCHEDULE AN ARRIVAL AT 100.0   creation of a future
                                              interaction point

actions to change system state

RETURN   interaction with other
                                              events takes place
END   when routine returns
                                              to control program

(a) Prototype event routine

reactivation point ———▸

ACTIVITY BERTHING   routine declaration

tests to determine if act   activity tests
    can occur
actions taken during berthing   executed if tests
                                              indicate activity
                                              can occur

RETURN   interaction with other
                                              activities when
END   routine returns to
                                              control program

(b) Prototype activity routine

reactivation point ———▸
PROCESS SHOPPING   routine declaration
actions to start shopping

reactivation point ———▸
WAIT 15 MINUTES   interaction point
actions to shop

reactivation point ———▸
WAIT UNTIL SERVER IS FREE   interaction point
actions to check out

reactivation point ———▸
DELAY 10 MINUTES   interaction point
actions to return home

SCHEDULE SHOPPING IN 15 MINUTES   creation of future
                                              interaction point

actions to renew shopping process

END   interaction point

(c) Prototype process routine

Figure 3. Concepts of interaction point and reactivation point.

In Figure 3a, there is one reactivation point and one interaction point. An event routine always starts at the same executable statement and, while it may have several physical RETURN statements, only one can be executed in any activation. When it is executed, it returns control to the master control program, which selects the next event (previously scheduled) to occur. All actions taken within the event routine occur at the same simulated time, independently of other events. The event is not totally divorced from other events, as all events share the same system data.

In Figure 3b, there is again only one reactivation point and one logical interaction point. If an activities test section permits them to take place, all actions occur at the same simulated time.

Figure 3c presents a sharply different picture, with many reactivation and interaction points.

Figures 3a, b, and c show that reactivation and interaction points always come in pairs. A minute's reflection will show that this has to be true. At each interaction point a reactivation point is defined, which is the place execution will start when the indicated time delay elaspes or the condition being sought occurs. Within a process routine, all actions do not necessarily take place at the same simulated time, but through a series of active and passive phases.

The reader should be able to see the differences between the event, activity, and process prototypes and should be able to get a qualitative feel for how these three differ.

Each modeling scheme has distinct virtues. Each can be shown to be advantageous in some situations and disadvantageous in others. There are no rules for selecting one scheme over another in given situations, nor is it likely that any such rules will ever be stated. The universe of possible simulation models is so large and so diverse that undoubtedly, there would have to be more exceptions than firm rules. Several points, however, are clear:

1. A language employing event scheduling gives a modeler precise control over the execution of programs.

2. A language employing activity scanning simplifies modeling multi-resources systems by allowing conditional statements of resource availability to be specified in one place.

3. A process-oriented language reduces the number of "overhead" statements a programmer has to write, since he can combine many event subprograms in one process routine. In addition, the overall flow of a system is clear, as all logic is contained in one routine instead of in several.

On the other hand, there is nothing one scheme can do that another cannot. Questions of feasibility must be separated from questions of efficiency. Also, as more experience is gained with the languages that employ these schemes, more efficient algorithms will be developed and efficiency, per se, will become less of a problem. Eventually, modeling esthetics will become an overriding consideration.

Table 4 categorizes many of the SPLs that are used today according to the dynamic modeling scheme they employ.

Table 4   SPL Dynamic Modeling Schemes

Event-oriented Languages	Activity-oriented Languages[a]	Process-oriented Languages
GASP	AS [51]	GPSS
SEAL [56]	CSL	NSS [50]
SIMCOM [58]	ESP [65]	OPS [27]
SIMPAC [2]	FORSIM-IV	SIMPLE [17]
SIMSCRIPT	GSP	SIMULA
SIMTRAN [5]	MILITRAN [48]	SLANG [32]
	SILLY [57]	SOL [41]
	SIMON [31]	SPL [52]

[a] Some of these languages are not "pure," for example GSP and MILITRAN have both activity-scan and event-selection phases. The principal orientation is as indicated, however.

SIMULATION PROGRAMMING LANGUAGE FEATURES

Specifying System Structure

Every SPL must have a way of describing system structure in both its static and dynamic aspects. Table 5 summarizes the principal features needed for this description.

Representing Statistical Phenomena

To model the real world, one must have a way of modeling random factors and effects. It is necessary to model uncertainty and variability with equal ease.

Uncertainty enters into models in statements such as the following.

In situation X, 15 percent of the time Y will occur and 85 percent of the time Z will occur. Given that a system is in state X, some probabilistic mechanism is required to select either state Y or state Z as the next state.

Table 5   System Modeling Features

Statements to:

Define classes of objects within a system
Adjust the number of objects within a class as system
    conditions change
Define properties of system objects
Describe relationships among system objects
Define activities, events, or processes
Organize events or processes

Programs to:

Select activity, event, or process subprograms for execution
Advance simulation time

Variability enters into models in, for instance, these statements:

The time to travel from A to B has an exponential distribution with a mean of 3 hours, or the number of customers expected to arrive per hour has a Poisson distribution with a mean of 6. A probablistic mechanism must be available for generating samples from statistical distributions.

In reproducing variability or uncertainty, a simulation model must have a way of *generating random variables*. A basic feature of every SPL is a random-number generator. Additional features are programs that transform random numbers into variates from various statistical distributions and that perform related sampling tasks.

A process is random if predictions about its future behavior cannot be improved from a knowledge of its past behavior. A sequence of numbers is a random sequence if there is no correlation between the numbers, that is, if there is no way to predict one number from another. Random numbers are needed to introduce uncertainty and variability into models, but because of the kinds of experiments that are performed with simulation models, truly random sequences of numbers are not adequate. One must have reproducible sequences of numbers that, for all intents and purposes, are random as far as their statistical properties are concerned.

Pseudorandom numbers, as reproducible streams of randomlike numbers are called, are generated by mathematical formulas in such a way that they appear to be random. Since they are not random, but come from deterministic series, they can only approximate the independence of truly random number sequences. Every simulation study calls for verification of random-number generators to insure that the statistical properties are adequate for the experiment being performed [20]. Every SPL must have a procedure for generating statistically acceptable sequences of pseudorandom numbers.

Pseudorandom number sequences always consist of numbers that are statistically independent and that are uniformly distributed between 0 and 1. Generation of a pseudorandom number produces a real number somewhere in this range.

Pseudorandom numbers can be used directly for statistical sampling tasks. They can represent probabilities in a decision sense or in a sampling sense. The model statement,

Make decision D_1 60 percent of the time,
Make decision D_2 40 percent of the time,

can be implemented in an SPL by generating a pseudorandom number and by testing whether it lies between 0.0 and 0.60. If it is, decision D_1 is taken; if it is not, decision D_2 is taken. For a sufficiently large number of samples, D_1 will be selected 60 percent of the time, but the individual selections of D_1 or D_2 will be independent of previous selections.

The model statement,

Produce product P_1 20 percent of the time,
Produce product P_2 10 percent of the time,
Produce product P_3 15 percent of the time,
Produce product P_4 20 percent of the time,
Produce product P_5 35 percent of the time,

can be implemented in a similar way by sampling from a cumulative probability distribution. A random product code can be drawn from the above product mix by putting the product frequency data into, for example, this table:

Product type	Cumulative probability
1	0.20
2	0.30
3	0.45
4	0.65
5	1.00

In this table, the difference between the successive cumulative probability values is the probability of producing a particular product; for example, product 3 is produced $0.45 - 0.30 = 0.15$ or 15 percent of the time. When a pseudorandom number is generated and matched against the table, a random product selection is made. For example, generating the number 0.42 selects product 3. Since numbers between 0.30 and 0.45 will be generated 15 percent of the time, 15 percent of the product numbers generated will be type 3.

Although this type of sampling is useful for empirical frequency distributions, it is less useful for sampling from statistical distributions such as the exponential and normal. To use a table look-up procedure like the one described above and to sample accurately in the tails of a statistical distribution, large tables must be stored. Generally, a simulation cannot afford the tables needing the storage for model data and program. Algorithms rather than table look-up procedures are used.

Sampling algorithms are of many kinds. Some distributions are easily represented by exact mathematical formulas; some must be approximated. All sampling methods operate in the same way insofar as they transform a pseudorandom number to a number from a particular statistical distribution. References 10, 49, and 63 discuss these procedures in detail. As simulation is almost always performed by using sampling: procedures that can generate samples from standard statistical distributions are mandatory in an SPL.

In conducting sampling experiments, which is what simulations really are, one is interested in control and precision as well as the accuracy of representation. The topics dealt with thus far have all been concerned with representation.

Control is necessary when one is using simulation to test and to compare alternative rules, procedures, or qualities of equipment. When several simulation runs are made that differ only in one carefully altered aspect, it is important that all other aspects remain constant. One must be able to introduce changes only where they are desired. This is one of the reasons for requiring reproducible random-number streams. A feature that aids in this is the provision of multiple streams of pseudorandom numbers. Having more than one stream enables parts of a model to operate independently, as far as data generation is concerned, and not to influence other parts. For example, when studying decision rules for assigning men to jobs, one does not want to influence the generation of jobs inadvertently. Multiple pseudorandom number streams increase a programmer's control over a model.

One also wants to be able to control the generation of random numbers if by doing so, one can reduce the variability of simulation generated performance figures. For example, it is always desirable to make the variance of the estimate of the average length of a waiting line within a simulation model as small as possible. The reduction of sample variance is a statistical rather than a programming problem in all but one respect; a programmer should be able to control the generation of pseudorandom numbers if this is required. One known way to reduce variance is to use antithetic variates in separate simulation runs; this is discussed in [20]. As the generation of a stream of variates that are antithetic to a given stream involves no more than a simple subtraction,[5] this feature should be present in an SPL.

Table 6 summarizes the minimum statistical sampling features that an SPL should have.

Table 6   Statistical Sampling Features

Pseudorandom number generation
    Multiple random-number streams
    Antithetic variates
Sampling from empirical table look-up distributions
Sampling from theoretical statistical distributions

Data Collection, Analysis, and Display

The performance of a simulated system can be studied in several ways [34]. The dynamic of the system's behavior can be traced by looking at plots of relevant simulation variables as they change over time. The aggregate performance can be studied by looking at statistical analyses of simulation generated data; means, variances, minima, maxima, and histograms are usually produced for such summaries.

Ideally, an SPL should automatically produce all data collection, analysis, and display. Unfortunately, this cannot always be done, since format requirements differ among organizations and display media vary— what is possible on a plotter may not be possible on a line printer or a typewriter. Also, efficiencies are gained if certain data are not analyzed. There is no virtue in producing frequency counts of variables that are not of direct interest to a simulation experimenter.

There are several topics to discuss in this general area: (1) how data collection is specified, (2) what data collection facilities should be provided, (3) how display media can be used, (4) how display formats are specified, and (5) what data analyses should be performed.

Data Collection Specification

The best one can say of a data collection specification is that it is un-obtrusive. Although data collection is necessary, statements that collect data are not per se part of a simulation model's logic, and they should not obscure the operations of a model in any way. People find that debugging is difficult enough without having to deal with errors caused by statements that are intended only to observe the behavior of a model.

---

[5] If r is a generated pseudorandom number, its antithetic variate is $1 - r$.

The ultimate in unobtrusiveness is to have no specification statements whatever. Being free from them, clearly eliminates any difficulties that they may cause when reading or debugging a simulation program code. Unfortunately, having no specification, means that every possible piece of data must be collected in every possible way, at the risk of neglecting to collect something an analyst may want. In small models this is probably worthwhile. In large models it can lead to unacceptable increases in core storage requirements and in program running times. GPSS collects certain data automatically and allows a programmer to collect other data himself; GASP does something similar.

A reasonable alternative is a linguistically natural set of data collection statements that can be applied globally to a model. Being linguistically natural, they will be easy to use and will be clearly differentiable from other types of programming statements. Being globally applicable, they need to be written only once instead of at each place a particular item of data to be collected appears.

Barring this, data can be collected through explicit procedural program statements. Data-collection specification statements of this sort are no different from normal variable assignment statements or from subroutine calls. They are the easiest to implement in an SPL, but the most obtrusive and difficult with which to deal. Most SPLS provide facilities of this kind. SIMSCRIPT II [39] has a capability for global data-collection specification.

Data Collection Facilities

One must be able to collect a variety of data, since one should be able to compute all the statistics an analyst might want about a simulation variable. This includes counts of the number of times a variable changes value, sums, sums of squares, maxima and minima of these values, histograms over specified intervals, cross-products of specified variables, time-integrated sums and sums of squares for time-dependent data, and time-series displays. Simulation is a statistical tool, and statistically useful data are required to use it.

Naturally, some data are easier to collect than others. Table 7 lists the minimum data one should be able to collect. These data should be easily collectable with specialized statements. One should be able to collect any other data without extreme difficulty. An important feature of an SPL is that it allow reasonably free access to all model data.

Data Analysis

One should not have to program the analysis of data for standard statistical calculations, such as the computations of means and variances.

Tqble 7   Data Collection Features

Number of observations, maxima, and minima for all variables
Sums and sums of squares for time-independent variables
Time-weighted sums and sums of squares for time-dependent variables
Variable value histograms for time-independent variables
Time-in-state histograms for time-dependent variables
Time-series plots over specified time intervals

If global specifications are employed, names attached to statistical quantities should invoke calculations when the names are mentioned. If data collection statements are used, standard functions should operate on named data to compute the necessary quantities.

Table 8 shows the minimum analysis one should be able to perform from collected data. If the data are present, one also would like to have functions that compute correlation coefficients and spectra [21].

Table 8   Data Analysis Features

Means
Variances and standard deviations
Frequency distributions

Display Media

Standard statistical information is easily printed on typewriters and line printers. Time series plots and histograms are enhanced by graphic display. As this type of information derives most of its impact from visual observation, there is little reason it should not be presented this way. Advanced SPLs should have routines for charting results, either by simulating a plotter on a line printer or by displaying results directly on a plotter [13], [23], [62].

Today, with a growing number of large-scale computing systems making use of cathode-ray-tube displays (CRTs), these devices are being used more and more for displaying simulation output [54]. Two situations lend themselves to CRT application.

In the first situation, the CRT is used only to produce attractively formatted graphs and reports. The device is not viewed on-line; pictures are made and used in lieu of printed reports. There is no doubt that programmers can use enhanced graphical capabilities if given the opportunity. Generally, no changes need be made to a SPL to let them do so, other than providing the access to general system software routines. To be specific, a programmer should be able to call library plotting routines from a SIM-SCRIPT or GPSS program.

The second situation is the more glamorous, with output produced on-line as a program is executed. Given a language and an operating system that lets a programmer interrupt a running program, alter system param-eters and variables, and then continue simulating where he left off, an entirely new type of simulation debugging and experimentation is possible. This type of interactive, adaptive dialogue between model and programmer makes on-line, evolutionary model design possible, changes the economics of sequential, optimum-seeking experimentation, and adds a valuable dimension to program debugging. Several researchers, at The RAND Corporation and elsewhere, are currently working in this area [17], [30].

Specification of Display Formats

There are probably as many types of output statements as there are people who write programming languages. Each type, being a little differ-ent, emphasizes one or more aspects of output control at the expense of others. Styles range from no specification at all (GPSS), through format-free statements (SIMSCRIPT II) and formatted statements (CSL), to special report forms (SIMSCRIPT). There are times when each style has its merits, and a fully equipped SPL will have a variety of output display statements.

Four types of display statements that exist in present-day SPLs are as follows:

1. *Automatic output in a standard format (GPSS, GASP).*

   This is a time-saver for the programmer and a boon in reasonable small models where all data can be displayed at a reasonable cost.

   It does not force a beginning simulation programmer to deal explicitly with output.

   It is only as good as the exhaustiveness of its contents.

   It is often unsatisfactory for formal reports, forcing subsequent typing and graph preparation.

2. *Format-free output (SIMSCRIPT II).*

   This enables a programmer to control the display of information without regard for formats.

   It is adequate only if it covers all the data structures in a language.

   It is more useful for debugging, error message reporting, and printing during program checkout.

3. *Formatted output (CSL).*

This requires the most programmer knowledge, but provides the maximum control of information display.

It is traditionally the most difficult part of many programming languages, insofar as the greatest number of errors are made by novice programmers in format statements.

4. *Report Generators (SIMSCRIPT, GSP).*

They are the easiest way of producing specially designed reports.

They must have a complete complement of control facilities to cover all report situations.

They can be a nuisance to use in very simple situations.

They usually generate an extremely large amount of object code.

They are efficient from a programming standpoint, but not from a core-consumption point of view.

Since the production of reports is the primary task of all programs, whether they are run for checkout, for display of computed results, or for the preparation of elaborate management reports and charts, a good SPL should contain statements adapted to all display situations. Referring to our discussion of data collection, a programmer should not have to spend a great deal of his time writing output statements. He should be able to concentrate on model construction and programming, and not have to dwell at length on conventional output tasks. However, he should be able to spend time on sophisticated output statements to produce displays that are unusual or that deal with exotic display devices.

Monitoring and Debugging

Two essential requirements of all SPLs can be served by the same set of programming facilities. SPLs should be able to assist in,

1. Program debugging; and in
2. Monitoring system dynamics.

Debugging can be difficult in high-level programming languages, as there is generally a great deal of difference between source and object codes. Errors can be detected during compilation and execution that are only distantly related to source-language commands. Moreover, when an SPL is translated into an intermediate POL, as was originally done in SIMSCRIPT and CSL, execution error messages are often related to the intermediate language and not to the programmer's source statements.

These messages, although meaningful to an expert, can mislead a novice SPL programmer.

Debugging also is difficult because the flow of control in a simulation is stochastically determined. Moreover, it can be difficult to obtain a record of the flow of control, since an SPL-designed "timing routine" or other form of control program is the originating point for all event calls. In some languages, it is impossible to do so. Without program flow information, and information about the system state at various times, some simulation program errors can be found only by luck.

The debugging features that an SPL should provide are listed in Table 9.

Table 9   Debugging Features

Report compile and excute-time errors by source statement related messages;

Display complete program flow status when an execute-time error occurs. This means displaying the entry points and relevant parameters for all function and subroutine calls in effect at the time of the error;

Provide access to control information between event executions. This allows event-tracing during all or selected parts of a program, and use of control information in program diagnostic routines.

These same facilities are needed for monitoring system dynamics. As one use of simulation is the study of system behavior, one must be able to view sequences of events and their relevant data to observe system reactions to different inputs and different system states. Event-tracing is an important tool for this kind of study.

In an event-oriented SPL, debugging and monitoring features, undoubtedly, will be implemented differently from the same or similar features in activity- or process-oriented SPLs. This is not important. The basic issue is whether a basic facility exists for assisting in program debugging and for doing program monitoring.

Initialization

Because simulation is the movement of a system model through simulated time by changing its state descriptions, it is important that an SPL provide a convenient mechanism for specifying initial system states. In simulations dedicated to studying start-up or transient conditions, a convenient mechanism for doing this is mandatory; in simulations that only analyze steady-stage system performance, it is still necessary to start off at some feasible system configuration.

Some SPLs start simulation in an "empty and idle state" as their normal condition and require special efforts to establish other conditions. They rely either on standard input statements, formatted or unformatted, to read in data under program control or on preliminary programs that set the system in a predetermined state.

An alternative to these procedures is a special form that reduces the initialization task to filling out a form instead of writing a program. Although adequate in a large number of situations, this alternative suffers from being inflexible. As with the preparation of simulation reports, the correct answer lies in a mixture of initialization alternatives.

Another aspect of initialization is the ability to save the state of a system during a simulation run and reinitialize the system to this state at a later time. This facility is crucial in the simulation of extremely large systems, and in conducting sequential experiments. One should be able to save all the information about a program, including relevant data on the status of external storage devices and peripheral equipment, and to restore it on command at a later date.

Other Features

There are a number of nonoperational features that must be considered when designing or selecting an SPL. A manager or analyst is interested in program readability; communication of the structure, assumptions, and operations of a model are important if the model is to be used correctly. A manager also is interested in execution efficiency; simulations can require large numbers of experimental runs, and the cost per run must be low enough to make a project economical. On the other hand, a manager must balance the costs of producing a program against program execution costs. Complex modeling languages may compile and execute less efficiently than simpler languages, but they make problems solvable in a shorter period of time. If total problem-solving time is important rather than computer time costs, the evaluation criteria change.

SPL documentation is important to applications and system programmers. An applications programmer needs a good instruction manual to learn a language and to use as a reference guide. As an SPL becomes more complex the need for good documentation increases. Systems programmers need documentation to be able to maintain an SPL. This documentation must allow them to install the language in the computing system; with today's complex, hard-tailored systems this is becoming more difficult. It also must provide enough information for them to make modifications in the SPL itself as translator errors are discovered. It is less important that users be able to modify an SPL, either to change the form of statements or to add new ones, but this can be an important consideration in certain instances. Some languages, in fact, are designed to do this easily [16], [38], [50].

SOME EXAMPLES OF SPLS

This section illustrates four SPLs: SIMSCRIPT II, an event-oriented language; SIMULA, a process-oriented language; CSL, an activity-oriented language; and GPSS, a transaction-oriented language.[6] With the exception of the SIMSCRIPT II example, which appears for the first time in this chapter, the illustrations are taken from published descriptions of the respective languages. The examples differ in detail and specificity, but they are nevertheless representative of the concepts that the languages employ. As they have been taken from other sources with only a surface editing, they also differ greatly in style and format.

Because the SIMSCRIPT II example was written especially for this chapter, it is the most detailed and illustrates the greatest number of features. Consequently, there may be a tendency to judge SIMSCRIPT II a superior language. However, such a judgment should not be made solely on the basis of these examples. Ideally, they should all be comparable and not bias the sought-after end, which is the explication of their different approaches to providing the SPL features that are discussed in the pre-ceding section. We can only hope that our inability to procure "equally representative" examples will not detract from our purpose.

The concepts that the languages employ have all been described in previous sections and readers should be able to follow the examples without a thorough understanding of each. The format of the following subsections is in three parts: the description of a model, the simulation program for the model, the discussion of the program.

Simscript II: An Event-Oriented Language

The model used in this example is the "executive-secretary system" described in [34]. The program conforms as closely as possible to the descricption given in [34] and the flow charts of its events.

The Model

We assume that executives in an office system have two types of tasks: they process incoming communications (invoices, requests for bids, price

---

[6] Although GPSS is process-oriented, in the sense that its models take a synoptic view of systems, its basic orientation is with the flow of transactions instead of with the occurrence of processes.

queries) and handle interoffice correspondence. The tasks are not independent of one another; the former are produced by mechanisms external to the office system, the latter arise during daily operations. As they result in similar actions, we can treat both the same way, through an event that "discovers" a task. Other events assign tasks to secretaries, schedule coffee breaks and departures for lunch, and handle the review of completed secretarial tasks. Table 10 lists the objects that "live" in the office system—which we shall call entities from here on—and their attributes.

Table 10   System Entities and Their Attributes

Executive	Secretary	Task
Position: Manager Senior Junior State: Busy Available On break	Skill in typing: words/minute errors/100 words Skill in dictation: words/minute errors/100 words Skill in office work: general rating 1-100 State: Busy Available On break	Type: Invoice Price quotation Bid Telephone Dictation Typing Characteristics: Time Secretarial requirements Probability of requiring a follow-up task

Given the static structure defined in Table 10, the nature of the task-discovery event, and some logic not yet described, we can construct a flow-chart model of the actions that take place when a request enters the system. This model is illustrated in Figure 4. Numbers to the left of each flow-chart block refers to comments in the body of the text that describe the operations which take place within the block. The SIMSCRIPT II program for the model follows the flow charts and their description. The flow charts and their respective programs differ somewhat as the flow charts are simplified for clarity.

Block 1 is the entry point to the flow chart. It contains a name that will be used in subsequent flow charts to refer to the "task request" event. The directed arrow leading from it is a symbol commonly used to indicate a path and direction of flow.

Block 2 is a decision block that splits the logical flow, depending on the kind of request that has just occurred. To understand how this block operates, we must understand the concept of an event occurrence.

An event occurs when its "time arrives," the time having been previously recorded by an internal scheduling block or observed on an input data card. The precise mechanism that accomplishes these tasks need not be

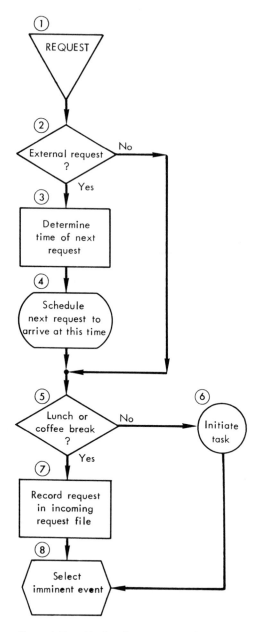

Figure 4. Event Number 1: request to perform a task.

stated here. It suffices if the reader understands that there is some mechanism operating in the background of the simulation program, observing data cards and previously scheduled events, ordering them by their event times, and "popping them up" when their time arrives. This, in fact, is the function of the event selection block (Block 8). Notice that every event terminates with an event selection block. It is in event selection blocks that time discriminations are made, events selected, and the simulation clock advanced.

When a request event is popped up, the simulation program has access to information associated with it, for example, how it was caused. The model is able to look at this information and take action on it.

If the request is for an internally generated task, the flow chart leads directly to Block 5, where a question is asked to determine if office workers are available to process the request. If the request is for an externally generated task, the program pauses in Blocks 3 and 4 to read information about the next arrival from an external data source, and to schedule its arrival at some future time. When it does so, it records a memo of a request arrival and its time on a calendar of events scheduled to occur. This calendar is part of the selection mechanism employed in sequencing events and in advancing simulation time. These operations are performed by the SIMSCRIPT II system and do not have to be programmed explicitly.

By the time the program arrives at Block 5, it is through with scheduling future events and is concerned with processing the request that has just arrived. Since real offices do not work continuously, but pause for lunch and coffee breaks during the day, the model asks if such a period is in progress. If it is, the request cannot be processed immediately but must be filed for later handling. If the request can be processed, Block 6 transfers control to a routine that does so. The routine will return to the request event when it finishes processing the task.

Block 7 records a request that cannot be handled in a backlog file; it might be an in-basket in real life. The file entry is made so that when the office workers return to their desks they observe the tasks that have accumulated while they were gone.

Block 8 directs the simulation program to select an event from the time-ordered file of scheduled events. It might be another request or the completion of a previous task. When the next event is selected, it may or may not indicate a simulation time advance. If it does not, we think of it and the event just completed as occurring simultaneously; although they are processed in series on the computer, there is no time advance, and they are considered as happening at the same time.

Initiating a Task

Once the system has accepted a request, a match must be made between it and the resources needed to fill it. A routine is written to do this; its logic is shown in Figure 5. First a search is made for an executive. If one is found who is free and can handle the request, a secretary is obtained if needed.

Block 1, as always, is an entry block giving the symbolic name of the routine.

Block 2 starts the match between a task and its resources by asking if the request just entered calls for a particular executive, for example, there has been a telephone call for a certain person or a request for a price quotation from a specialist in a certain area. If no particular executive is called for, Block 1 passes flow to Block 3, where an executive is selected. If a certain person is requested, flow proceeds to Block 4, where a test is made to determine if this person is available.

Block 3 is typical of a functional block whose description is short but whose programming content might be large. A procedure to select an executive can be brief, for example, managers can do everything, senior executives can do everything except give price quotations, junior executives can only answer the telephone; or it can be long and elaborate, for example, an executive is selected whose personal qualifications as listed in his personnel file match the requirements of the task according to a complex and computationally intricate formula. Many of a simulation model's key assumptions are built into blocks like this one.

When an executive is selected, Block 3 transfers to Block 4, the block to which control is passed if a particular executive is called for.

Block 4 asks if the executive requested in Block 2 or selected in Block 3 is available. It does so by examining the executive's state (status code); if the code is "available," the executive is free to handle the request, if it is "busy" or "on break," he is not. Once again, as in Block 2, the flow logic is split depending on the answer to this question.

If the selected executive is available, flow passes to Block 8, where the processing of the task continues. Before we consider these actions, we must discuss what happens if the executive is not available.

Block 5 asks if a substitute is available for a busy executive, implying that a substitution can be made and that a procedure exists for finding one. This situation is a little like that of Block 3, where an executive is selected for a particular type of task. Block 5 could be expanded to a series of blocks that describe a procedure for selecting a substitute, testing for his availability, selecting another substitute if necessary, and so on, until all possible candidates are tried and are accepted or rejected. In our simplified model

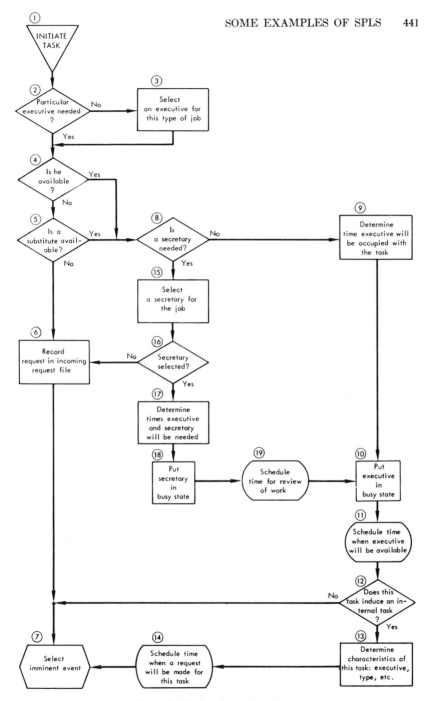

Figure 5. Initiation of a task routine.

we do not do this. We only indicate that if a substitute cannot be found, control passes to Block 6, which files the unprocessed task.

Block 6 of this event is identical to Block 7 of the request event; it files information about the request for later processing. This block appears in the simulation model whenever a request cannot be processed and must be "remembered."

In Block 7 control is passed via an event-selection block back to the "timekeeping" mechanism of the simulation program. Since the current request cannot be processed, the model must look at its calendar of scheduled events to determine what to do next.

Returning to the case where an executive is available to process a request, we ask next in Block 8 if a secretary is also needed. She will be if the request is for dictation or for some task where instructions must be given; she will not be if the task is simply answering a telephone call. This question can be answered in a number of ways in an operating computer program; as with most questions of this type, we leave the description of decision making at the macro level, namely, that a decision must be made.

Block 9 starts the flow path for the case where a request can be honored by an executive alone; it determines the amount of time he will spend on the task.

Block 10 puts the executive in a "busy" state so that he cannot be called on to do another task while he is working on this one. He will remain in this state until the "executive available" event occurs; this is scheduled in Block 11 to happen after the lapse of the previously determined amount of time.

Before it proceeds with the simulation, the model must ask if processing this task, for example, answering a phone call, induces another task, for example, writing a memo. This is done in Block 12. If a task is not induced, flow passes to Block 7, where the model is instructed to select another event and to proceed with the simulation. If a task is induced, Block 13 determines its characteristics and passes them on to Block 14, where the induced task is scheduled to be requested. Flow then proceeds to Block 7.

If, back in Block 8, we found that a secretary was needed to work along with the executive, control would have passed to Block 15, where a secretary must be selected before a task starts. This logic can pair a particular secretary with an executive, pool all secretaries so that they are available to all executives, or employ some immediate scheme. As was done in selecting an executive, when a secretary is chosen, her status code must be tested to ascertain if she is available.

Block 16 performs this test. Like Block 5, it can be considered a macro block in which alternatives and availabilities are tested until a decision is reached. If a secretary is not available, a request cannot be processed and must be filed along with other unprocessed requests.

Once a secretary is found, Blocks 17, 18, and 19 determine the time the executive and secretary will spend on the job, put the secretary in the "busy" state, and schedule the time when her work will be reviewed. It is not necessary that the executive and the secretary work together on the task for the same period of time; separate events are provided to schedule their release from the task at different times. The release times can be the same, however, if the task is a cooperative effort.

Block 19 transfers control to Block 10 after completing its function, picking up at a part of the flow chart that we have already seen. The reader should be able to understand why and how this is done.

Review of a Secretarial Task

One of the office rules is that every task a secretary performs must be reviewed. When a secretary finishes a task she brings it to the attention of the executive who initiated it. If he is not available, she waits.[7] If he is available, he reviews the work and either accepts it or notes corrections that must be made before another review. The logic of the review event is shown in Figure 6.

Block 1, as usual, names the event. Block 2 asks a question about executive availability and transfers to Block 3 or 5, depending on the answer.

Block 3 records the review task in the task backlog file if the executive is busy. The task is filed along with incoming requests that were filed for reasons that we observed in previous flow charts. Block 4 calls on the simulation timing mechanism to select the next scheduled event. The secretary is not assigned an "available" state, but remains "busy," waiting for the executive to become free and to review her work.

Block 5 is another macro block, hiding what might be an enormous amount of logic behind the label "executive review of secretary's work."

Block 6 branches on the previously computed review decision. If the task has been done satisfactorily, the secretary is scheduled to become available immediately (Block 9).

An unsatisfactory task has its correction time computed in Block 7 and its review rescheduled in Block 8.

With reference to this event, it is important to observe its hidden basic assumptions: a review task takes no time, and a secretary stays with a

---

[7] This may not be good office practice, but it is a feature of our example.

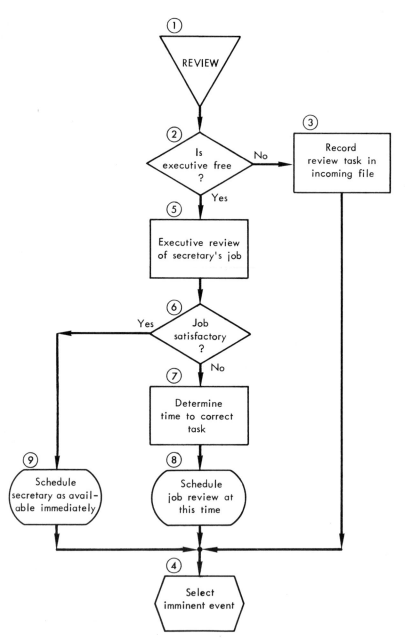

Figure 6. Event Number 2: review of a secretarial task.

job until it gets reviewed. These assumptions can be easily changed to allow secretaries to do other work while waiting for reviews, to cause executives to spend time making large-scale corrections, and so on.

Executive Available at the End of a Task

This event marks the completion of an executive activity. It returns an executive to an "available" state and determines his next action: another task, a break for coffee or lunch, or an idle (discretionary time) period. The event logic is shown in Figure 7.

Block 1 names the event. Block 2 puts the executive in an available state and asks questions about the next executive actions. These questions are asked in a specific order and imply certain things. From the logic of the event, we observe that a lunch or coffee break cannot start until a current job is completed, but it will be taken when it is due regardless of task backlogs. This is important, as it assumes a priority sequence imposed by the order in which questions are asked and not by explicit priority statements.

Block 3, which decides if a break is due, also contains hidden logic. When one considers the connections between events and the way in which the model operates, he notices that if an executive is idle (in the "available" state) and a break time occurs, there is no mechanism that alerts him of this. By the way the model is constructed, breaks can be taken only after the completion of jobs. This will have little practical effect if (a) the work rate is high in the office so that there are no long periods of idle time possible, or (b) the logic of Block 3 looks ahead and starts a break early if one is almost due. This small difficulty has been put in the model to acquaint the reader with problems that can occur when one sets out to build a model from scratch.

If a break is due or in progress, Block 4 places the executive in the "break" state, Block 5 determines its duration, Block 6 schedules the executive's return to an availability condition (by executing this same event some time in the future after the simulation clock has advanced past the break point), and Block 7 returns control to the event selection mechanism.

If a break is not due, the model must decide whether the executive should be left in the available stage or assigned to a waiting task. It does this by looking, in Block 8, at the file in which we have been putting requests that could not be processed. If the file is empty, the executive is left alone and control is passed to Block 7 to select the next event.

If the file is not empty, the model must select a job. If there is only one job in the file, there is no problem. If there is more than one, there is a conflict situation that must be resolved. Conflict is usually resolved by

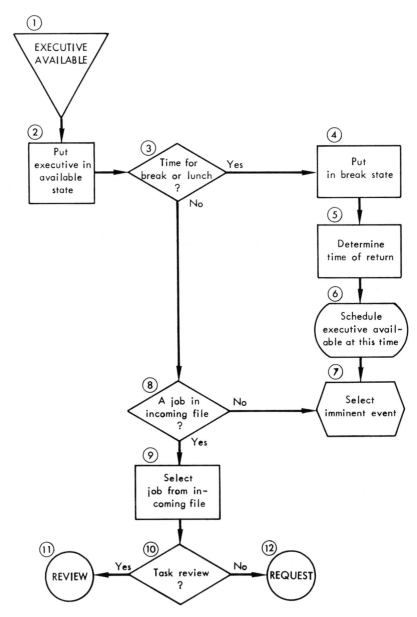

Figure 7. Event Number 3: available of an executive at the end of a task.

priority rules that assign values to different types of jobs; a job is selected that has the highest (or perhaps lowest) value. In cases with ties, multiple ranking criteria are used, possible criteria that might be used in this model are the time a job arrives in the system, the skill level required to process a job, and so on. The issue of selection rules is complex, and a model that merely says "select a job" hides a great deal of work that must be done to develop an operating model. For example, few organizations have well-articulated and formalized priority rules, and a modeler may have his hands full merely trying to find out the "rules of the game."

Once a task has been selected, however, it is relatively simple to route the executive to the proper flow chart to process it. This is shown in Blocks 10, 11, and 12.

Secretary Available at the End of a Task

This event is similar to event 3 in both its intent and its form. When a secretary is released from a task, she becomes available and is either sent on a break, put on a backlogged jog, or left idle, depending on current conditions. Blocks 1 to 10 in the flow chart of Figure 8 correspond to similar blocks in Figure 7 and need not be commented on here.

Description of the Program

Rather than describe the SIMSCRIPT II program in detail, we discuss only the statements that highlight the SPL features mentioned in previous sections. The purpose of the examples is to show how various languages implement simulation programming concepts, not to describe the languages themselves. Those who wish to understand the examples and the languages more fully can do so by studying their respective programming manuals.

The *preamble* to the subprograms that make up the SIMSCRIPT II model declares the static system structure of the model, using the entity-attribute-set organization framework; declares the events that compose the dynamic structure; defines special properties of the two structures, such as the mode of attributes, the ranking of sets, and the priority order of events; and specifies data-collection and analysis tasks. The preamble is a set of global declarations that describe the system being simulated to the SIMSCRIPT II compiler. In the case of the data-collection and analysis statements and some debugging statements not illustrated in the example, the preamble also specifies tasks that the compiler is to perform.

The main routine provides overall simulation experiment control. It calls on a programmer-written routine to initialize the static system state and to provide events for the timing routine that will set the model in motion. The START SIMULATION statement removes the first scheduled event

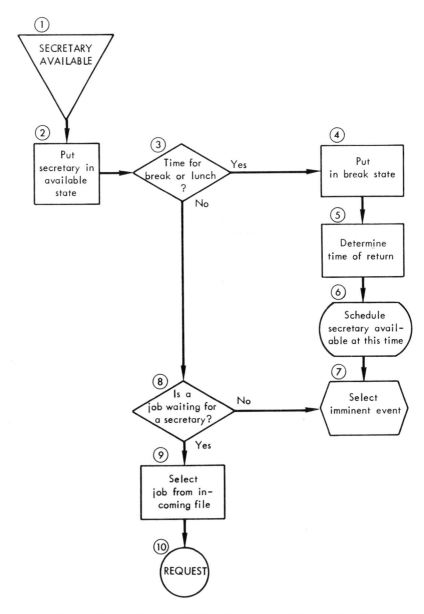

Figure 8. Event number 4: availability of a secretary at the end of a task.

```
PREAMBLE
NORMALLY MODE IS INTEGER
''DECLARATION OF STATIC SYSTEM STRUCTURE
THE SYSTEM OWNS A REQUEST.FILE
PERMANENT ENTITIES....
    EVERY EXECUTIVE HAS A POSITION AND A STATE
    EVERY SECRETARY HAS A STATUS
    EVERY TASK.TYPE HAS A TASK.TIME, A NEED, AND
        AN INDUCE.PROBABILITY
    EVERY SECRETARY, TASK.TYPE HAS A SKILL.FACTOR
        DEFINE TASK.TIME, INDUCE.PROBABILITY AND
            SKILL.FACTOR AS REAL VARIABLES
TEMPORARY ENTITIES....
    EVERY TASK HAS A WHO, A WHAT AND A DELAY.TYPE
        AND MAY BELONG TO THE REQUEST.FILE
''DECLARATION OF DYNAMIC SYSTEM STRUCTURE
EVENT NOTICES....
    EVERY REQUEST HAS AN EXEC AND A CLASS
    EVERY REVIEW HAS AN EX AND A SEC
    EVERY EXECUTIVE.AVAILABLE HAS AN EX1
    EVERY SECRETARY.AVAILABLE HAS A SEC1
EXTERNAL EVENTS ARE REQUEST AND END.OF.SIMULATION
BREAK REVIEW TIES BY HIGH EX THEN BY LOW SEC
PRIORITY ORDER ''OF EVENTS'' IS REQUEST, REVIEW, SECRETARY.AVAILABLE,
    EXECUTIVE.AVAILABLE AND END.OF.SIMULATION
''OTHER DECLARATIONS
DEFINE OFFICE.STATUS AS AN INTEGER FUNCTION
DEFINE INDUCE.TYPE, SECRETARY.REQUIRED.CLASS AND
    SUM.REQUESTS AS INTEGER VARIABLES
DEFINE SATISFACTORY AS A REAL VARIABLE
DEFINE IDLE TO MEAN 0
DEFINE WORKING TO MEAN 1
DEFINE BREAK TO MEAN 2
''DATA COLLECTION AND ANALYSIS DECLARATIONS
ACCUMULATE AVG.BACKLOG AS THE MEAN AND
    STD.BCKLOG AS THE STD.DEV OF N.REQUEST.FILE,
ACCUMULATE STATE.EST(0 TO 2 BY 1)AS THE HISTOGRAM
    OF STATE
ACCUMULATE STATUS.EST(0 TO 2 BY 1)AS THE HISTOGRAM
    OF STATUS
END
```

```
                    MAIN ''THIS ROUTINE CONTROLS THE SIMULATION EXPERIMENT
'INITIALIZE' CALL INITIALIZATION ''TO ESTABLISH THE INITIAL SYSTEM STATE
                    START SIMULATION ''BY SELECTING THE FIRST EVENT
                    ''WHEN SIMULATION RUN IS ENDED CONTROL PASSES HERE
                    IF DATA IS ENDED, STOP
                    OTHERWISE...''GET SET FOR ANOTHER RUN
                        UNTIL REQUEST.FILE IS EMPTY, DO
                            REMOVE THE FIRST TASK FROM THE REQUEST.FILE
                            DESTROY THE TASK
                        LOOP
                    GO INITIALIZE ''FOR THE NEXT EXPERIMENT
                    END




                    ROUTINE FOR INITIALIZATION
                    READ N.EXECUTIVE    CREATE EACH EXECUTIVE
                    READ N.SECRETARY    CREATE EACH SECRETARY
                    READ N.TASK.TYPE    CREATE EACH TASK.TYPE
                    FOR EACH EXECUTIVE, DO READ POSITION(EXECUTIVE) AND
                        STATE(EXECUTIVE) RESET TOTALS OF STATE LOOP
                    FOR EACH SECRETARY, DO
                        READ STATUS(SECRETARY) RESET TOTALS OF STATUS
                        ALSO FOR EACH TASK.TYPE, READ SKILL.FACTOR(SECRETARY, TASK.TYPE),
                            TASK.TIME(TASK.TYPE), NEED(TASK.TYPE),
                            INDUCE.PROBABILITY(TASK.TYPE)
                    LOOP
                    READ INDUCE.TYPE, SECRETARY.REQUIRED.CLASS AND SATISFACTORY
                    RESET TOTALS OF N.REQUEST.FILE
                    END




                    EVENT REQUEST GIVEN EXEC AND CLASS SAVING THE EVENT NOTICE
                    ADD 1 TO SUM.REQUESTS ''COUNT NUMBER OF TASK REQUESTS
                    IF REQUEST IS EXTERNAL, READ EXEC AND CLASS ''FROM A DATA CARD
                    REGARDLESS...''PROCESS THE REQUEST
                    IF OFFICE.STATUS=WORKING,
                        NOW INITIATE.TASK GIVING EXEC AND CLASS    GO AHEAD
                    OTHERWISE...''FILE THE REQUEST UNTIL THE BREAK IS OVER
                        CREATE A TASK      ''TO ACT AS A MEMO
                        LET WHO=EXEC       ''RECORD WHO THE REQUEST WAS FOR
                        LET WHAT=CLASS     ''RECORD THE TYPE OF TASK
                        LET DELAY.TYPE=0 ''RECORD THAT THE MEMO REPRESENTS A REQUEST
                            ''RECEIVED DURING A BREAK PERIOD
                        FILE THE TASK IN THE REQUEST.FILE
        'AHEAD'     DESTROY THE REQUEST
                    RETURN ''TO THE TIMING ROUTINE
                    END
```

```
              ROUTINE TO INITIATE.TASK GIVEN EXECUTIVE AND CLASS
              DEFINE EXEC.TIME AND SEC.TIME AS REAL VARIABLES
              IF EXECUTIVE,   "NO EXECUTIVE HAS BEEN SPECIFIED, SELECT ONE
                  FOR EACH EXECUTIVE WITH STATE=IDLE AND POSITION GE NEED(CLASS),
                      FIND THE FIRST CASE
                  IF FOUND, GO TO 'SEC.TEST'
                  ELSE...''NO EXECUTIVE AVAILABLE FOR THIS TASK
'NO.EXEC'             LET .D=1  ''INDICATING THE TASK IS WAITING FOR AN EXECUTIVE
'NO.WORKER'          CREATE A TASK    LET WHO=0     LET WHAT=CLASS
                        LET DELAY.TYPE=D
                     FILE THE TASK IN THE REQUEST.FILE
                     RETURN   ''TO THE TIMING ROUTINE
              ELSE...''AN EXECUTIVE HAS BEEN REQUESTED

              IF STATE ¬ =IDLE,
                  ''REQUESTED EXECUTIVE IS BUSY, LOOK FOR SUBSTITUTE
                  CALL SUBSTITUTION GIVING EXECUTIVE YIELDING EXECUTIVE
              THEN IF EXECUTIVE=0, ''NO SUBSTITUTE CAN BE FOUND
                  GO TO NO.EXEC
              ELSE ''AN EXECUTIVE IS AVAILABLE, IS A SECRETARY REQUIRED?
'SEC.TEST' IF CLASS >= SECRETARY.REQUIRED.CLASS,
                  ''A SECRETARY IS REQUIRED FOR THIS TASK
                  PERFORM SECRETARY.SELECTION YIELDING SECRETARY
                  IF SECRETARY=0, ''NO SECRETARY IS AVAILABLE FOR TASK
                     LET D=2 ''INDICATING THE TASK IS WAITING FOR A SECRETARY
                     GO TO NO.WORKER
                  ELSE...''DETERMINE TIME EXECUTIVE AND SECRETARY WORK
                  LET EXEC.TIME=EXPONENTIAL.F(TASK.TIME(CLASS),1)
                  LET SEC.TIME=EXEC.TIME + EXPONENTIAL.F(TASK.TIME(CLASS),1)*
                                        SKILL.FACTOR(SECRETARY,CLASS)
                  LET STATUS=WORKING ''SET THE SECRETARY IN THE WORKING STATE
                  SCHEDULE A REVIEW (EXECUTIVE, SECRETARY) IN SEC.TIME MINUTES
              REGARDLESS...
              IF EXEC.TIME=0 ''EXECUTIVE IS WORKING ALONE AND MUST COMPUTE
                 ''HIS TIME
                  LET EXEC.TIME=2*EXPONENTIAL.F(TASK.TIME(CLASS),1)
              REGARDLESS...
              LET STATE=WORKING ''SET THE EXECUTIVE IN THE WORKING STATE
              SCHEDULE AN EXECUTIVE.AVAILABLE(EXECUTIVE) IN EXEC.TIME MINUTES
              IF CLASS > INDUCE.TYPE, ''CHECK FOR AN INDUCED TASK
                  CREATE A REQUEST CALLED INDUCED
                  LET EXEC(INDUCED)=EXECUTIVE
                  LET CLASS(INDUCED)=CLASS-1
                  SCHEDULE THE REQUEST CALLED INDUCED IN UNIFORM.F(0.0,1.0,1) HOURS
              REGARDLESS
              RETURN ''TO THE TIMING ROUTINE
              END
```

```
ROUTINE SUBSTITUTION GIVEN EXEC YIELDING EXEC1
''FIND THE FIRST IDLE EXECUTIVE WITH AT LEAST THE SAME RANK
FOR EACH EXECUTIVE WITH STATE=IDLE AND POSITION >
    POSITION(EXEC), FIND EXEC1=THE FIRST EXECUTIVE
IF NONE, LET EXEC1=0
REGARDLESS    RETURN ''TO THE CALLING PROGRAM
END




ROUTINE FOR SECRETARY.SELECTION YIELDING SECRETARY
''FIND THE FIRST IDLE SECRETARY
FOR EACH SECRETARY WITH STATUS=IDLE, FIND THE FIRST CASE
IF NONE, LET SECRETARY=0
REGARDLESS    RETURN ''TO THE CALLING PROGRAM
END




EVENT REVIEW GIVEN EXECUTIVE AND SECRETARY
IF STATE ¬=IDLE, ''EXECUTIVE BUSY, CANNOT REVIEW JOB
    CREATE A TASK
    LET WHO=EXECUTIVE    LET WHAT=SECRETARY
    LET DELAY.TYPE=3 ''INDICATING A DELAYED REVIEW
    FILE THE TASK IN THE REQUEST.FILE
    DESTROY THE REVIEW
    GO RETURN
ELSE...''EXECUTIVE REVIEWS SECRETARY'S WORK
IF RANDOM.F(2) LE SATISFACTORY,
    ''TASK HAS BEEN PERFORMED SATISFACTORILY
    SCHEDULE A SECRETARY.AVAILABLE(SECRETARY) NOW
    GO RETURN
ELSE...''TASK MUST BE CORRECTED
    RESCHEDULE THIS REVIEW IN 15 MINUTES
'RETURN'  RETURN ''TO THE TIMING ROUTINE
    END
```

```
EVENT EXECUTIVE.AVAILABLE GIVEN EXECUTIVE
LET STATE=IDLE ''PUT EXECUTIVE IN THE IDLE STATE
IF OFFICE.STATUS ¬=WORKING,
    ''A BREAK PERIOD IS IN PROGRESS
    LET STATE=BREAK ''PUT THE EXECUTIVE IN THE BREAK STATE
    RESCHEDULE THIS EXECUTIVE.AVAILABLE AT TRUNC.F(TIME.V)+1
    GO RETURN
OTHERWISE...''EXECUTIVE IS FREE TO WORK ON BACKLOGGED TASKS
IF REQUEST.FILE IS EMPTY, GO RETURN
ELSE...''FIND TASKS NEEDING EXECUTIVE ATTENTION
FOR EACH TASK IN THE REQUEST.FILE WITH DELAY.TYPE¬=2
    FIND THE FIRST CASE ''NOT WAITING FOR A SECRETARY
IF NONE, GO RETURN ''NO BACKLOGGED EXECUTIVE JOBS
ELSE...''EXAMPLE TASK
    REMOVE THE TASK FROM THE REQUEST.FILE
IF DELAY.TYPE=0 OR DELAY.TYPE=1, ''WAIT IS TO START A NEW TASK
    CREATE A REQUEST    SUBTRACT 1 FROM SUM.REQUESTS
    SCHEDULE THE REQUEST(WHO, WHAT)NOW
    GO AHEAD
ELSE ''TASK IS A SECRETARY REVIEW, THE VARIABLE "WHAT"
    ''IS USED FOR THE SECRETARY IDENTIFICATION
    SCHEDULE A REVIEW(WHO, WHAT)NEXT
'AHEAD'   DESTROY THIS TASK
'RETURN'  RETURN ''TO THE TIMING ROUTINE
          END
```

```
EVENT SECRETARY.AVAILABLE GIVEN SECRETARY
LET STATUS=IDLE ''PUT SECRETARY IN THE IDLE STATE
IF OFFICE.STATUS ¬ =WORKING,
    ''A BREAK PERIOD IS IN PROGRESS
    LET STATUS=BREAK ''PUT THE SECRETARY IN THE BREAK STATE
    SCHEDULE THIS SECRETARY.AVAILABLE AT TRUNC.F(TIME.V)+1
    GO RETURN
ELSE...''SECRETARY IS FREE TO WORK ON BACKLOGGED TASKS
IF THE REQUEST.FILE IS EMPTY, GO RETURN
ELSE...''FIND TASKS NEEDING SECRETARIAL ATTENTION
FOR EACH TASK IN THE REQUEST.FILE WITH DELAY.TYPE=2,
    FIND THE FIRST CASE
IF NONE, GO RETURN ''NO TASKS WAITING FOR A SECRETARY
ELSE...
REMOVE THE TASK FROM THE REQUEST.FILE
CREATE A REQUEST    SUBTRACT 1 FROM SUM.REQUESTS
SCHEDULE THE REQUEST(WHO, WHAT)NOW
DESTROY THIS TASK
'RETURN'  RETURN ''TO THE TIMING ROUTINE
          END
```

```
            EVENT END.OF.SIMULATION
            NOW REPORT
            FOR I=1 TO EVENTS.V, ''EMPTY THE EVENTS LIST
            UNTIL EV.S(I) IS EMPTY, DO
                REMOVE THE FIRST J FROM EV.S(I)
                GO TO REQ OR REV OR SEC OR EXEC PER I
                'REQ' DESTROY THE REQUEST CALLED J
                       GO LOOP
                'REV' DESTROY THE REVIEW CALLED J
                       GO LOOP            .
                'SEC' DESTROY THE SECRETARY.AVAILABLE CALLED J
                       GO LOOP
                'EXEC' DESTROY THE EXECUTIVE.AVAILABLE CALLED J
'LOOP'      LOOP
            RETURN ''TO THE TIMING ROUTINE
            END




            ROUTINE FOR OFFICE.STATUS
            DEFINE T AS A REAL VARIABLE
            LET T=MOD.F(TIME.V,24)
            IF 12 = HOUR.F(TIME.V) OR 10.75 < T < 11 OR
            .15.75 < T < 16, RETURN WITH 0 ''INDICATING BREAK IN PROGRESS
            ELSE RETURN WITH 1 ''INDICATING OFFICE NOW WORKING
            END




            ROUTINE REPORT
            START NEW PAGE
            PRINT 2 LINES WITH AVG.BACKLOG AND STD.BACKLOG THUS
                AVERAGE BACKLOG IS **.** TASKS
                STD.DEV        IS   *.**
            SKIP 3 OUTPUT LINES
            BEGIN REPORT
            BEGIN HEADING
            PRINT 2 LINES THUS
                ANALYSIS OF EXECUTIVE STATUS
                   IDLE    WORKING    BREAK
            END ''HEADING
            FOR EACH EXECUTIVE, PRINT 1 LINE WITH STATE.EST(EXECUTIVE,1)/
                TIME.V, STATE,EST(EXECUTIVE,2)/TIME.V, STATE.EST(EXECUTIVE,3)/
                TIME.V AS FOLLOWS
                  *.**       *.**       *.**
            END ''REPORT
            SKIP 3 OUTPUT LINES
            BEGIN REPORT
            BEGIN HEADING
            PRINT 2 LINES THUS
                ANALYSIS OF SECRETARY STATUS
                   IDLE    WORKING    BREAK
            END ''HEADING
```

```
FOR EACH SECRETARY, PRINT 1 LINE WITH STATUS.EST(SECRETARY,1)/
    TIME.V, STATUS.EST(SECRETARY,2)/TIME.V, STATUS.EST(SECRETARY,3)/
    TIME.V AS FOLLOWS
        *.**    *.**    *.**
END ''REPORT
SKIP 5 OUTPUT LINES
PRINT 1 LINE WITH SUM.REQUESTS AND TIME.V LIKE THIS
    ***REQUESTS WERE PROCESSED IN ****.* SIMULATED DAYS
RETURN ''TO CALLING PROGRAM
END
```

(the initialized event with the earliest event time) from the file of scheduled events and starts the simulation by transferring program control to it.

Eventually, either by running out of data or by programmer action, all events are processed, no new ones are created, and control passes from the timing routine (represented by the START SIMULATION statement) to the statement that follows it. If there are no more data, the sequence of experiments is terminated. If there are more data, the system is initialized for another run.

The two routines MAIN and INITIALIZATION illustrate the primary features SIMSCRIPT II provides for controlling simulation experiments.

In the next routine, an event named REQUEST, the features of interest are the statements CREATE, FILE, and DESTROY. The CREATE statement generates a new entity of the class TASK whenever it is executed; this statement is SIMSCRIPT II's way of dynamically allocating storage to system entities as they are needed. The DESTROY statement takes a named entity, REQUEST in this example, and returns it to a pool of free data storage, providing space for the subsequent creation of additional entities. The FILE statement takes a named entity and puts it in a set along with other entities. In this example an entity named TASK is put in a set named REQUEST.FILE.

In the routine INITIATE.TASK, the features to note are IF and FOR statements that perform logical tests and searches, the statistical function EXPONENTIAL.F, and the event-scheduling statements. The IF and FOR statements are SIMSCRIPT II's way of dealing with the common programming problem of determining the state of objects, or of the system itself, and of selecting among objects according to stated criteria. The statistical function indicates the way sampling is done to represent statistically varying phenomena. The last argument in the EXPONENTIAL.F function-call selects one of ten built-in number streams; if the argument is negative, the antithetic variate of the generated pseudorandom number is used. The SCHEDULE statements are the basic mechanism for specifying events that are to occur in the future. When a SCHEDULE statement is executed, an entity, called an event notice, of a specified type is put in a time-ordered file that is ordered by the schedule time; when the simulation clock advances to this time, the event is executed and is said to "occur."

The event routines EXECUTIVE.AVAILABLE and SECRETARY. AVAILABLE contain REMOVE statements. These statements retrieve entities from sets according to criteria that are either implied or specified in the preamble. One of the functions of the preamble is to specify such things as the relationship that entities in sets have to one another.

The REPORT routine illustrates SIMSCRIPT II's facilities for generating reports. No output is collected, analyzed, or printed automatically by SIMSCRIPT II. Instead, the data-collection and analysis statements of the preamble and the report specification features pictured are used to tailor reports to simulation experiment requirements.

Naturally, this brief explanation has not made the program clear in all its details—that was not its intent. Rather, its purpose is to show how SIMSCRIPT II provides the simulation-oriented features discussed previously. All three of the examples below follow this same pattern.

SIMULA: A Process-Oriented Language

This example has been taken from Chapter 13 of [13].[8] Its model is similar to the ones used in many SPL descriptions and, aside from terminology, structurally very similar to the SIMSCRIPT II model just presented. The program is quite different.

The Model

A job consists of machine groups, each containing a given number of identical machines in parallel. The system is described from a machine point of view, that is, the products flowing through the system are represented by processes that are passive data records. The machines operate on the products by remote accessing.

The products consist of *orders*, each for a given number of product *units* of the same *type*. There is a fixed number of product types. For each type, there is a unique routing and given processing times.

For each machine group (number *mg*) there is a set *avail* [*mg*] of idle machines and a set *que* [*mg*], which is a product queue common to the machines in this group. The products are processed one *batch* at a time. A batch consists of a given number of units, which must belong to the same order. The batch size depends on the product type and the machine group.

A product queue is regarded as a queue of *orders*. The queue discipline is essentially first-in-first-out, the position of an order in the queue being defined by the arrival of the first unit of that order. However, if there is less than an acceptable batch of units of a given order waiting in the queue, that is, if the batch size is too small as yet, the next order is tried.

[8] Courtesy of the Norwegian Computing Center.

The last units of an order are accepted as a batch, even if the number of units is less than the ordinary minimum batch size. If a machine finds no acceptable batch in the product queue, it waits until more units arrive.

Although the individual pieces of product are "units," a unit is not treated as an individual item in the present model. For a given *order* and a given *step* that is, machine group, in its schedule, we define an *opart* (order part) record to represent the group of units currently involved in that step. The units are either in processing or waiting to be processed at the corresponding machine group.

An order is represented by a collection of opart records. The sum of units in each opart is equal to the number of units in the order. Each opart is a member of a product queue. If a machine group occurs more than once in the schedule of a product type, there may be more than one opart of the same order in the product queue of that machine group.

Among the attributes of an opart record are the following integers: the order number, *ono*, the product *type*, the *step*, the number of units waiting, *nw*, and the number of units in processing, *np*. The flow of units in the system is effected by counting up and down the attributes nw and np of opart records.

An opart record is generated at the time when the first batch of units of an order arrive at a machine group. It is entered at the end of the corresponding product queue. The opart will remain a member of this queue until the last unit has entered processing. It will drop out of the system when the last unit has finished processing. A Boolean attribute *last* is needed to specify whether a given opart contains the last units of the order involved in this step.

At a given time the units of an order may be distributed on several machine groups. There will be an opart record[9] for each of them. An opart process[9] will reference the one at the next step, that is, machine group, through an *element* attribute "successor." An order is thus represented by a simple chain of opart records. The one at the head has no successor, the one at the tail has its attribute "last" equal to *true*. The chain "moves" through the system by growing new heads and dropping off tails.

Figure 9 shows three consecutive steps in the schedule of products of a given type. A product queue consists of oparts (circles) connected by vertical lines. Oparts belonging to the same order are connected by horizontal lines. Machines are represented by squares. A dotted line between an opart and a machine indicates a batch of units in processing. When the batch of the third opart in que [j] is finished, a new opart receiving this batch will be generated and included in que[k].

---

[9] The terms "record" and "process" both refer to the data structure associated with a particular group of units.

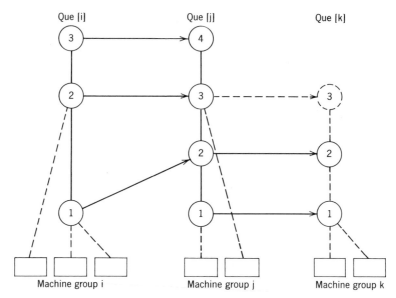

Figure 9. Flow of products through the shop

The Program

The following program fragment is part of the head of a SIMULA block describing the above system. A machine activity is given. For clarity, only statements essential for the behavior of the model are shown. The program is not complete. Underlined words are SIMULA keywords.

1. *set array* que, avail [1:nmg]; *integer* U;
2. *integer procedure* nextm (type, step); *integer* type, step; . . . . ;
3. *real procedure* ptime (type, step); *integer* type, step; . . . . ;
4. *integer procedure* bsize (type, mg); *integer* type, mg; . . . . ;
5. *activity* opart (ono, type, step, nw, np, last, successor);
6.   *integer* ono, type, step, nw, np;
7.   *Boolean* last; *element* successor;
8. *activity* machine (mg); *integer* mg;
9.   *begin integer* batch, next; *Boolean* B; *element* X;
10. serve: X:=head (que[mg]);
11.   *for* X:=suc (X) *while* exist (X) *do*
12.   *inspect* X *when* opart *do*
13.   *begin* batch:=bsize (type, mg);
14.   *if* nw < batch *then begin*
15.   *if* last *then* batch :=nw *else go to* no *end*;

16.   nw := nw − batch; np := np + batch;
17.   *if* last ∧ nw = 0 *then* remove (X);
18.   *activate* first (avail[mg]);
19.   hold (batch x ptime (type, step)xuniform (0.9, 1.1, U));
20.   np := np − batch; B := last ∧ nw + np = 0;
21.   next := nextm (type, step);
22.   *inspect* successor *when* opart *do*
23.   *begin* nw := nw + batch; last := B *end*
24.   *otherwise begin* successor :=
25.   *new* opart (ono, type, step + 1, batch, 0, B, *none*);
26.   include (successor, que [next]) *end*;
27.   *activate* first (avail [next]);
28.   *go to* serve;
29. no: *end*;
30.   wait (avail [mg]); remove (current); *go to* serve *end*;

Description of the Program

Line 1	The sets contain oparts and idle machines, respectively. The variable U defines a pseudorandom number stream (line 19).
Lines 2–4	The functions "nextm" and "ptime" specify the next machine group and the current processing time for a given product type and step in the schedule. "bsize" determines the batch size, given the product type and machine group number. The three functions are left unspecified, that is, their programs are not shown.
Lines 5–7	The meanings of the attributes of opart processes have been explained in the model description. The activity body[10] is a dummy statement: an opart process is a data record with no associated actions.
Line 8	The machine activity extends to and includes line 30. The parameter mg is the machine group number. Machines belonging to the same group are completely similar.
Line 9	"batch" is the size of the current batch of units, "next" is the number of the next machine group for the units currently being processed, the meaning of "B" is explained below (line 20), and "X" is used for scanning.

[10] In the SIMULA nomenclature, a process is a dynamic structure of an activity, that is, an activity is a process prototype.

Line 10   Prepare for scanning the appropriate product queue. Select the first opart in que[mg].

Line 11   Scan. The controlled statement is itself a connection statement[11] (lines 12 to 29).

Line 12   There is only one connection branch (lines 12 to 29). Since a product queue contains only opart records, connection must become effective. The attributes of the connected opart are accessible inside the connection block.

Line 13   Compute the standard batch size.

Lines 14, 15   A smaller batch accepted only if the opart is at the tail end of the chain. In this case "nw" is nonzero (see line 17), and the units are the last ones of the order. Otherwise the next opart is tried by branching to the end of the set inspection loop.

Line 16   The "batch" units are transferred from the waiting state to the in-processing state by reducing nw and increasing np.

Line 17   The opart is removed from the product queue when processing has started on the last units of the order.

Line 18   The current machine has found an acceptable batch of units and has updated the product queue. There may be enough units left for another batch; therefore, the next available machine in this group (mg) is activated. If there is no idle machine, the set avail[mg] is empty and the statement has no effect. See also lines 27 and 30.

Line 19   The expected processing time is proportional to the number of units in the batch. The actual processing time is uniformly distributed in the interval +10 percent around the expected value. The sequence of pseudo-random drawings is determined by the initial value of the variable U.

Line 20   Processing is finished; np is reduced. The Boolean variable B gets the value *true* if, and only if, the last units of an order have now been processed. In that case the connected opart should drop off the chain at this system

---

[11] "Connection" is a means of accessing local variables from outside the block in which they are defined. In this instance, attributes of the oparts stored in que[mg] are being referenced.

time (see comments to line 28). It follows that B is always the correct (next) value of the attribute "last" of the succeeding opart (lines 23, 25).

Line 21	Compute the number of the machine group to receive the current batch of units.

Line 22   The *element* attribute "successor" is inspected. The connection statement, lines 22 to 26, has two branches.

Line 23   This is a connection block, executed if "successor" refers to an opart. The latter is a member of the product queue of the next machine group. It receives the processed batch of units, which are entered in the waiting state. The attribute "last" is updated. Notice that the attributes referenced in this inner connection block are those belonging to the successor to the opart connected outside (X).

Lines 24, 25   If the connected opart (X) is at the head of the chain, the value of "successor" is assumed equal to *none*, and *otherwise* branch is taken. A new opart is generated, and a reference to it is stored in "successor." The new opart has the same "ono" and "type" as the old one, and its "step" is one greater. It has "batch" units in the waiting state and none in processing. Its attribute "last" is equal to "B." Since the new opart has become the head of the chain, its "successor" should be equal to *none*. Notice that the initial value of "last" may well be *true*, for example, if the order contains a single unit.

Line 26   The new opart is included at the end of the product queue of the next machine group.

Line 27   The current machine has now transferred a batch of units to the product queue of next machine group. Therefore, the first available machine (if any) of that group is activated. If that machine finds an acceptable batch, it will activate the next machine in the same group (line 18). This takes care of the case in which the batch transferred is larger than the standard batch size of the next machine group for this type of product.

Line 28   The machine immediately returns to the beginning of its operation rule to look for another acceptable batch, starting at the front end of the product queue. At this point, if B is *true*, the connected opart is empty of units and will not be referenced any more. We can regard it as having dropped off the chain. It is easy to demonstrate, however, that the opart will physically leave the system, that is, its reference count is reduced to zero. The possible stored references are: (1) The variable X and the connection pointer "opart" of this machine or another one of the same group. The *go to* statement leads out of the connection block, which deletes the connection pointer. X is given another value in line 10. Any other machine referencing this opart would have to be suspended in line 19, which is impossible since np is zero (refer to the second statement of line 16).

(2) Set membership in que[mg]. The opart must have been removed from the queue (by this machine or another one) since "last" is *true* and nw is now zero (line 17).

(3) The attribute "successor" of the opart preceding this one in the chain. The first opart of this order to enter the systems has no predecessor. Provided that this first one drops out when it is empty, our conclusion follows by induction (see below).

Line 29   The end of the connection block and of the statement controlled by the *for* clause in line 11.

Line 30   If, after having searched the entire product queue, the machine has found no acceptable batch, it includes itself in the appropriate "avail" set and goes passive. Its local sequence control remains within the wait statement as long as the machine is in the passive state. When the machine is eventually activated (by another machine: line 27 or 18), it removes itself from the "avail" set and returns to scan the product queue. The "avail" sets are operated in the first-in-first-out fashion.

The mechanism for feeding orders into the system is not shown above. This is typically done by the Main Program or by one or more "arrival" processes, which generate a pattern of orders, either specified in detail by input data, or by random drawing according to given relative average frequencies of product types and other sizes.

An arrival pattern defined completely "at random" is likely to cause severely fluctuating product queues, if the load on the system is near the maximum. The following is a simple way of rearranging the input pattern in order to achieve a more uniform load. The algorithm is particularly effective if there are different "bottlenecks" for the different types of products.

31. *activity* arrival (type, mgl, pt);
32.   *integer* type, mgl; *real* pt;
33. *begin integer* units;
34. loop: select (units, type); id := id + 1;
35.   include (*new* opart (id, type, 1, units, 0, *true*, *none*), que[mgl]);
36.   *activate* first (avail [mgl]);
37.   hold (ptxunits); *go to* loop *end*;
38. *procedure* select (n, type); *value* type; *integer* n, type; . . .;
39. *integer* id;

Line 31	There will be one "arrival" process for each product type. "mgl" is the number of the first machine group in the schedule of this type of product. "pt" is a stipulated "average processing time" per unit, chosen so as to obtain a wanted average throughput of units of this type (see line 37).
Line 34	The procedure "select" should choose the size, "units," of the next order of the given type, for example, by random drawing or by searching a given arrival pattern for the next order of this type. "id" is a nonlocal integer variable used for numbering the orders consecutively.
Line 35	An order is entered by generating an opart record that contains all the units of the order. The units are initially in the waiting state. The order is filed into the appropriate product queue. The set membership is the only reference to the opart stored by the arrival process. Consequently, this opart will leave the system when it becomes empty of units, as assumed earlier (line 28).[12]
Line 36	A machine in the appropriate group is notified of the arrival of an order.
Line 37	The next order of the same type is scheduled to arrive after a waiting time proportional to the size of this order which ensures a uniform load of units (of each type).

[12] In SIMULA, process records that are no longer needed, that is, are not referenced by any other process, are automatically returned to available storage. This contrasts with the DESTROY statement used by SIMSCRIPT for the same task.

The "output" of units from the system can conveniently be arranged by routing all products to a dummy machine group at the end of the schedule. It contains one or more "terminal machines" (not shown here), which may perform observational functions, for instance the recording of the completion of orders.

The dynamic setup of the system is a separate task, since initially the Main Program is the only process present. The Main Program should generate (and activate) all processes that are "permanent" parts of the system, such as machines, arrival processes, and observational processes. The system can be stated empty of products. However, a "steady" state can be reached in a shorter time if orders (opart records) are generated and distributed over the product queues in suitable quantities.

Experimental results are obtained by *observing* and by *reporting* the behavior of the system. Three different classes of outputs can be distinguished:

1. *On-line reporting.* Quantities describing the current state of the system can be printed out, for example, with regular system time intervals: lengths of product queues in terms of units waiting, the total number of units in the system, the number of idle machines in each group, and so on. A more detailed online reporting may be required for program debugging.

2. *Accumulated machine statistics.* By observing the system over an extended period of system time, averages, extrema, histograms, and so on, can be formed. Quantities observed can be queue lengths, idle times, throughputs, and so on. The accumulation of data could be performed by the machine processes themselves.

Example. To accumulate a frequency histogram of the idle periods of different lengths for individual machines, insert the following statements on either side of the "wait" statement of line 30.

"tidle := time" and "histo(T, H, time − tidle, 1)," where "tidle" is a local *real* variable, and T and H are arrays. T[i] are *real* numbers that partition observed idle periods (time − tidle) into classes according to their lengths, and H[i] are integers equal to the number of occurrences in each class. The system procedure "histo" will increase H(i) by one (the last parameter), where i is the smallest integer such that T[i] is greater than or equal to the idle period, "time − tidle." T and H together thus define a frequency histogram, where T[i] − T[i − 1] is the width of the ith column, and H[i] is the column length.

3. *Accumulated order statistics.* During the lifetime of an opart record, the "history" of an order at a given machine group can be accumulated

and recorded in attributes of the opart. The following are examples of data that can be found.

The arrival of the first unit of the order at this machine group is equal to the time at which the opart is generated. The departure time of the last unit is equal to the time at which the variable B gets the value *true* (line 20 of a machine connecting the opart).

The sum of waiting times for every unit of the order in this queue is equal to the integral with respect to system time of the quantity nw (which is a step function of time). The integral can be computed by the system procedure "accum." The statements "nw := nw $\pm$ batch" (lines 16 and 23) are replaced by "accum (anw, tnw, nw, $\pm$ batch)," where the *real* variables anw and tnw are additional attributes of the opart process, with initial values zero and "time," respectively. The procedure will update nw and accumulate the integral in anw. It is equivalent to the statements: anw := anw $+$ nw x (time $-$ tnw); tnw : = time; nw = nw $\pm$ batch.

It is worth noticing that arrival times, waiting times, and the like, in general, cannot be found for individual units, unless the units are treated as individuals in the program. Neither can the maximum waiting time for units in an order. The average waiting time, however, is equal to the above time integral divided by the number of units in the order.

The complete history of an order in the shop is the collection of data recorded in the different oparts of the order. These data can be written out on an external storage medium at the end of the lifetime of each opart. That is, an output record could be written out before line 28, whenever B is *true*, containing items such as the order number, ono, the sum of waiting times, anw, the current system time, and so on. When the simulation has been completed, the data records can be read back in, sorted according to order numbers, and processed to obtain information concerning the complete order, such as the total transit time, total waiting time, and so forth.

The same information can be obtained by retaining the complete opart chain in the system until the order is out of the shop; however, this requires more memory space. The chain can be retained by making the arrival process include the initial opart in an auxiliary set, or by having a pointer from the opart currently at the head of the chain back to the initial one. The opart chain can be processed by the terminal machine. (The order is completely through the shop at the time when the attribute "last" of the opart in the terminal product queue gets the value *true*.) In the former case, the terminal machine also should remove the appropriate opart from the auxiliary set, in order to get rid of the opart chain.

CSL: An Activity-Oriented Language

This example has been taken from [11].[13] However, unlike the two previous models, it is indicative of the kinds of models industrial firms construct to solve practical operating problems.

The Model

This example is a simulation of the operation of a simple port, which consists of an outer deep-water harbor and a series of berths. Each berth can hold one large ship, which can berth only at full tide, or three small ships, which can also move at half-tide. The tide runs in a 12-hour sequence, out for several hours, half-tide for an hour.

A distribution of unloading times for large ships is available as data, and unloading times for small ships are normally distributed. Interarrival time are negative exponentially distributed.

The program is to record the waiting times of large and small ships and the times for which the berths are empty. The purpose of the simulation might be to study the operation as a basis for experiments to find a more efficient way of scheduling the working of the port, or to determine the effect of providing extra berths. The scheduling used in this model is a simple first-in first-out scheme.

Description of the Program

The comments embedded in the program document its micro behavior rather well. What is not obvious from the program is its macro behavior, that is, how activities are controlled, initiated, and performed.

The CONTROL segment of the program has four tasks: it defines global variables, it defines functions, it defines global FORMAT and LINGEN statements, and it specifies activities through the sector list. Of these tasks, only the last is important to us now. Notice that the CONTROL segment of CSL is similar to the SIMSCRIPT II preamble.

A short discussion of how time is represented within CSL models and how simulation is carried out should clarify the operations of the program.

Interactions in a real system are dependent on time and the system moves through time. Therefore it is necessary to have some means of representing time in a simulation program. Time values are held in variables called T-cells. T-cells may arise in two ways; they are either defined as integer cells or arrays, or as cells attached to their names with "T." For example, if the class of ships is defined thus:

---

[13] Courtesy of the IBM United Kingdom Data Centre.

The Program

PORT SIMULATION   EXAMPLE PROGRAM

```
      CONTROL
      CLASS TIME SHIP.100 BERTH.4
C           DEFINE CLASSES OF 100 SHIPS AND 4 BERTHS
      SET OCEAN HARBOUR LARGE SMALL FREE PART FULL
      SET SHIPIN(BERTH)
C           DEFINE THE SETS REQUIRED, INCLUDING AN ARRAY OF AS
C           MANY SETS AS THERE ARE BERTHS, SHIPIN(X) WILL HOLD
C           A LIST OF THE NAMES OF SHIPS IN BERTH X
      NAME S B
      INTEGER TIDE TLARGE TSMALL
      TIME CHANGE ARRIVE FINISH
C           DEFINE TWO NAME VARIABLES, AN INTEGER VARIABLE TO
C           SHOW THE STATE OF THE TIDE, AND ADDITIONAL TIME
C           CELLS. ALSO TWO INTEGERS TO HOLD TOTAL ARRIVALS
C           OF LARGE AND SMALL SHIPS RESPECTIVELY.
      HIST LARGEQ 25,2,5  SMALLQ 25,2,5  IDLE 25,2,5
      HIST UNLOD 20,3,5
C           DEFINE THE HISTOGRAMS REQUIRED. LARGEQ HAS 25
C           CELLS WITH RANGE 0-4 (MIDPOINT 2), 5-9,10-14 ETC.
C           UNLOD WILL CONTAIN THE UNLOADING TIME DISTRIBUTION
C           FOR LARGE SHIPS.
      INITL
      ACTIVITIES
      TIDES ARRVL BTHL BTHS DBTH ENDING
C           SPECIFY THE LIST OF SECTORS (ACTIVITIES)
      END


      SECTOR INITL
      T.FINISH=24000
      T.CHANGE=7
      T.ARRIVE=0
      TIDE=0
C           THIS SECTOR IS ENTERED ONLY ONCE AND SETS UP THE
C           INITIAL STATE OF THE MODEL. T.FINISH REFERS TO THE
C           TIME AT WHICH SIMULATION IS TO FINISH, T.CHANGE TO
C           THE TIME AT WHICH THE TIDE NEXT CHANGES AND TIDE
C           SHOWS THE STATE OF THE TIDE AS FOLLOWS -
C           0    TIDE OUT    1 HALF IN    2 TIDE FULL    3 HALF IN
C           T.ARRIVAL SHOWS THE TIME BEFORE THE NEXT ARRIVAL OF
C           A SHIP AT THE PORT.
      FOR X = 1,SHIP
        SHIP.X INTO OCEAN
      FOR X = 1,BERTH
        BERTH.X INTO FREE
        T.BERTH.X=0
```

```
C           INITIALLY ALL SHIPS ARE IN OCEAN
C           AND ALL BERTHS FREE
      READ (5,10) UNLOD
C           READ IN THE DISTRIBUTION GIVEN AS DATA.
10    FORMAT (I4)
      END



      SECTOR TIDES
C           THIS SECTOR IS CONCERNED WITH TIDE CHANGES
      T.CHANGE EQ 0
C           WHICH CAN ONLY OCCUR WHEN THEY ARE DUE
      TIDE+1
      GOTO (10,20,10,30) TIDE
C           CHANGE TIDE MARKER AND RESET TIME CELL FOR NEXT
C           CHANGE
10    T.CHANGE=1
      GOTO 60
20    T.CHANGE=3
      GOTO 60
30    T.CHANGE=7
      TIDE=0
60    DUMMY
C           AND RETURN TO CONTROL SEGMENT
      END



      SECTOR ARRVL
C           THIS SECTOR IS CONCERNED WITH ARRIVALS OF SHIPS
14    T.ARRIVE EQ 0
C           WHICH CAN ONLY OCCUR WHEN ONE IS DUE
      FIND S OCEAN FIRST &15
      S FROM OCEAN INTO HARBOUR
      T.S=0
C           FIND THE FIRST SHIP IN THE OCEAN MOVE IT TO THE
C           HARBOUR AND ZERO ITS TIME CELL
      T.ARRIVE=NEGEXP(7)
C           SAMPLE THE TIME TO THE NEXT ARRIVAL
      UNIFORM(SYSTEMSTREAM) GT 0.75 &13
      S INTO LARGE
      TLARGE+1
      GOTO 14
13    S INTO SMALL
      TSMALL+1
      GOTO 14
C           A QUARTER OF THE SHIPS ARE LARGE, OTHERS SMALL.
C           GO BACK TO START OF SECTOR IN CASE NEGEXP HAS
C           GIVEN A ZERO SAMPLE
15    WRITE(6,100) T.FINISH,CLOCK
100   LINGEN
```

```
1  NOT ENOUGH SHIPS IN MODEL - SIMULATION TERMINATED
2  TIME LEFT ***** TIME ELAPSED *****
  T.FINISH = 0
C     IF A SHIP IS NOT FOUND IN OCEAN, WRITE MESSAGE
C     AND SET T.FINISH SO THAT SIMULATION CEASES IN
C     SECTOR ENDNG.
GOTO ENDNG.
END



      SECTOR BTHL
C           THIS SECTOR IS CONCERNED WITH BERTHING LARGE SHIPS
      TIDE EQ 2
      FIND B FREE ANY
      FIND S HARBOUR FIRST
        S IN LARGE
C           THE TIDE MUST BE FULL, THERE MUST BE A FREE BERTH
C           AND A LARGE SHIP WAITING IN THE HARBOUR
      ENTER -T.S,LARGEQ
C           WHEN THE SHIP ENTERED THE HARBOUR ITS TIME CELL
C           WAS SET TO ZERO.  SINCE THEN IT HAS BEEN REDUCED
C           AT EACH TIME ADVANCE AND SO -T.S IS THE WAITING-
C           TIME OF THE SHIP.  THIS IS RECORDED IN THE
C           HISTOGRAM
      B FROM FREE INTO FULL
      S FROM HARBOUR INTO SHIPIN(B)
C           THE BERTH IS NOW FULL AND THE SHIP MOVES FROM THE
C           HARBOUR INTO THE BERTH
      ENTER -T.B,IDLE
C           JUST AS -T.S SHOWED THE SHIPS WAITING TIME SO -T.B
C           SHOWS THE BERTH IDLE TIME
      T.S=SAMPLE(UNLOD)
C           SAMPLE AN UNLOADING TIME FOR THE SHIP
      RECYCLE
C           CAUSE ANOTHER PASS THROUGH THE SECTORS (BECAUSE
C           MORE THAN ONE SHIP MIGHT BERTH AT THE SAME TIME)
      END



      SECTOR BTHS
C           THIS SECTOR IS CONCERNED WITH BERTHING SMALL SHIPS
C           AND IS SIMILAR TO THE PREVIOUS ONE
      TIDE GE 1
      FIND S HARBOUR FIRST
        S IN SMALL
      FIND B PART ANY &20
C           THE SHIP IS MOVED TO A PARTLY FULL BERTH IF THERE
C           IS ONE
      SHIPIN(B) EQ 2  &30
      B FROM PART INTO FULL
C           IF THE BERTH ALREADY HAS TWO SHIPS IN IT, IT NOW
C           BECOMES FULL
      GOTO 30
```

```
20      FIND B FREE ANY
        B FROM FREE INTO PART
C            IF NO PARTLY FULL BERTH WAS FOUND, SEEK A FREE
C            BERTH WHICH NOW BECOMES PARTLY FULL
        ENTER -T.B,IDLE
C            RECORD IDLE TIME
30      ENTER -T.S,SMALLQ
        T.S=DEVIATE(5.0,20.0)
        S FROM HARBOUR INTO SHIPIN(B)
        RECYCLE
C            AS IN BERTHING OF LARGE SHIPS
        END


        SECTOR DBTH
C            THIS SECTOR IS CONCERNED WITH DEBERTHING
        TIDE NE 0
C            THE TIDE CANNOT BE OUT
        FOR X = 1,BERTH
C            DEAL WITH EACH BERTH SEPARATELY IN TURN
20          FOR S SHIPIN(X) FIRST        &15
                T.S LE 0
                CHAIN
                  S IN SMALL
                  OR S IN LARGE
                  TIDE EQ 2
                DUMMY*
C            FIND A SHIP IN THE BERTH WHICH IS READY TO LEAVE
C            (TIME CELL HAS BEEN REDUCED TO ZERO OR BEYOND BY
C            TIME ADVANCE) AND WHICH CAN DO SO AT THE PRESENT
C            STATE OF THE TIDE.  IF NONE - GO ON TO TRY THE
C            NEXT BERTH
        RECYCLE
C            SET RECYCLE SWITCH TO TRY SECTORS AGAIN BEFORE
C            TIME ADVANCE (IN PARTICULAR BERTHING SECTORS
C            MAY NOW SUCCEED)
        S FROM SHIPIN(X) INTO OCEAN
        S IN LARGE      &16
        S FROM LARGE
        T.BERTH.X=0
        BERTH.X FROM FULL INTO FREE
        GOTO 15
C            IF SHIP LEAVING IS LARGE BERTH IS NOW FREE.
C            ZERO ITS TIME CELL SO THAT IDLE TIME CAN BE
C            COMPUTED LATER.  THEN GO TO NEXT BERTH.
16      S FROM SMALL
        SHIPIN(X) EQ 0      &17
        BERTH.X FROM PART INTO FREE
        TO.BERTH.X=0
        GOTO 15
```

---

*DUMMY is a statement that does nothing when executed.

```
C              SIMILARLY IF SHIP LEAVING IS SMALL AND NOW THERE
C              ARE NONE LEFT IN THE BERTH.
17      SHIPIN(X) EQ 2      &20
        BERTH.X FROM FULL INTO PART
        GOTO 20
C              IF SMALL SHIP IS LEAVING AND BERTH WAS PREVIOUSLY
C              FULL, RECORD FACT THAT IT IS NOW ONLY PARTLY FULL
C              IN EITHER CASE GO BACK TO SEE IF ANY MORE SHIPS
C              ARE READY TO LEAVE THIS SAME BERTH
15      DUMMY
        DUMMY
        END



        SECTOR ENDNG
C              THIS SECTOR IS CONCERNED WITH OUTPUT OF RESULTS
        T.FINISH EQ 0
C              WHICH IS TO BE DONE AFTER TIME HAS BEEN ADVANCED
C              SO THAT T.FINISH HAS BECOME ZERO
        WRITE(6,100)
100     LINGEN SKIP PAGE
    1       PORT SIMULATION RESULTS
        WRITE(6,101)
101     LINGEN SKIP 2
    1       TOTAL     LARGE     SMALL
        WRITE(6,102) (TLARGE+TSMALL),TLARGE,TSMALL
102     LINGEN SKIP 1
    1       *****    *****     *****     SHIPS ENTERED HARBOUR
        J=0
        FOR S HARBOUR
         S IN LARGE     &10
         J+1
10      DUMMY
        K=HARBOUR-J
        WRITE(6,103)(J+K),J,K
103     LINGEN SKIP 1
    1       *****    *****     *****     SHIPS LEFT IN HARBOUR
        L=LARGE-J
        M=SMALL-K
        WRITE(6,104)(L+M),L,M
104     LINGEN SKIP 1
    1       *****    *****     *****     SHIPS STILL IN BERTHS
        TLARGE-J
        TSMALL-K
C              CALCULATE NUMBERS OF SHIPS THAT HAVE LEFT HARBOUR
        WRITE(6,100)
        WRITE(6,200)
200     LINGEN SKIP 2
    1       CELL RANGE     LARGEQ     SMALLQ     IDLETIME
        Y=0
        J=0
        K=0
```

```
      FOR X=1,25
          WRITE(6,300) Y,(Y+4),LARGEQ(X),SMALLQ(X),IDLE(X)
          Y+5
          J+LARGEQ(X)
          K+SMALLQ(X)
          DUMMY
      LONGL=TLARGE-J
      LONGS=TSMALL-K
C             TLARGE NOW HAS TOTAL NUMBER OF LARGE SHIPS WHICH
C             HAVE LEFT THE HARBOUR.  J HOLDS THE TOTAL NUMBER
C             OF ENTRIES IN THE HISTOGRAM.  THEREFORE TLARGE - J
C             IS THE NUMBER OF SHIPS WHOSE WAITING TIMES WERE
C             OUTSIDE THE RANGE OF THE HISTOGRAM
      WRITE(6,400) LONGL,LONGS
      STOP
300   LINGEN SKIP 1
    1     *** TO ***     *****     *****     *****
400   LINGEN SKIP 1
    1     OVER           *****     *****
      END
```

CLASS TIME SHIP .100

then this serves to define entity names as above, and also 100 T-cells addressed as T.SHIP.1, . . ., T.SHIP.100. An array of integer T-cells could be defined as

TIME BREAKDOWNS (10)

T-cells have all the properties of other integer cells and may participate normally in arithmetic and tests. Their time-advancing properties are additional.

Time advancement is performed in a repeated two-stage process as follows. Stage 1 scans all T-cells to find the smallest positive nonzero value in any cell. This is regarded as the time of the next event, or the time at which an event is next able to arise in the system. The program is now advanced to this position in time by subtracting this value from all T-cells. This completes stage 1.

In stage 2 the program itself is entered. The user must specify his program as a series of individual routines called activities, and phase 2 consists of an attempt to obey each of the activities in turn. Each activity describes the rules relating to the performance of one kind of activity in the system; for example, that of unberthing a ship.

The program statements in an activity normally begin with a series of tests to find out whether the activity can be initiated; they may be tests on T-cells to ascertain whether, for instance, any ships are due to leave a berth. Following the opening tests are the statements that actually carry out the work of the activity, for example, arithmetic and set-manipulation statements.

The actual question of division of the program into activities is governed by individual programming style. The activities must clearly cover all possible courses of action available in the system, but this is not the whole story. For instance, in the example program the berthings of large and small ships are handled as separate activities. The orders in them are largely duplicate; should they, therefore, be combined in one? This is purely a question of taste and, as such, is unresovable on logical grounds.

The structure of a CSL test now can be more fully explained. The most frequent use of a test is at the start of an activity; under these circumstances, if the test fails, it may be assumed that the activity cannot be carried out.

For this reason, the customary operation of computer test orders has been changed; a test failure leads to transfer of control, usually to the next activity, whereas in the case of success the next statement is obeyed. To provide more detailed control of flow, a statement label may be specified, for example,

$$DATA \ (10) \ EQ \ 4 \ \& \ 87.$$

In the event of failure, control goes to the statement labeled 87.[14]

The second phase, it will be noticed, consists of an attempt to obey all the activities specified in the system. Apparently, this involves much redundant effort, as at most points in time one or two activities only are likely to be entered successfully and the rest will be abandoned after a test or two; but a closer analysis shows that computing time to carry out work of this kind must be expended in any simulation programming system, whether or not it is carried out under direct control of the programmer. Therefore, it seems most useful to make the necessary testing explicit and under the user's control.

When all the activities have been entered, the normal procedure is that a return to phase 1 takes place, and time is further advanced. This procedure is not in itself sufficient; activities are interlinked and the completion of one activity may enable the initiation of another. For example, the unberthing of one ship will free a berth that another may use. The user can control this in two ways: first, by careful choice of the order in which activities are specified, and second, by the use of a special recycling device to cause further attempts to obey the activities to be made.

GPSS/360: A Transaction-Flow Language

A simple harbor model is used to illustrate GPSS. Although it is identical to the CSL model, the match is close enough to provide a feel for how the languages represent similar systems. The example is taken from [24].[15]

[14] An & before a number indicates that it is a statement label.

The Model

Ships arrive at a small port with a known arrival pattern. While in port, the ships unload some of their cargo, taking a certain amount of time, and then proceed on their voyages. Since there is only one pier, a ship must wait if it arrives while another is unloading. If several ships are waiting, the one that arrived first will be unloaded first. Of interest here is the total amount of time a ship will spend in port, including the time spent waiting for the pier to become available.

[15] Reprinted by permission from (H20-0304-1 General Purpose Simulation System/360 Introductory User's Manual), 1967, and (H20-0186-1 General Purpose Simulation System/360 Application Description), 1966, by International Business Machines Corporation.

The gross behavior of the system can be pictured quite simply as follows:

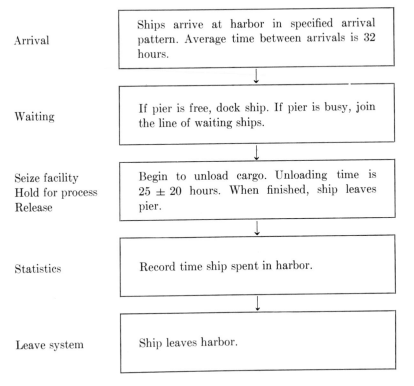

Arrival	Ships arrive at harbor in specified arrival pattern. Average time between arrivals is 32 hours.
Waiting	If pier is free, dock ship. If pier is busy, join the line of waiting ships.
Seize facility Hold for process Release	Begin to unload cargo. Unloading time is 25 ± 20 hours. When finished, ship leaves pier.
Statistics	Record time ship spent in harbor.
Leave system	Ship leaves harbor.

The Program

Unlike most SPLs, GPSS has two representations, a flow chart and a coding form language. The flow-chart model of the simple harbor system is shown in Figure 10.

The coding form, or statement language model, is shown in Figure 11. There is a direct correspondence between its statements and the flow chart symbols of Figure 10.

Description of the Program

The dynamic entities in GPSS are called "transactions." These represent the units of traffic, such as ships in this example. They are "created" and "destroyed" as required during the simulation run, and can be thought of as moving through the system causing actions to occur. Associated with each transaction are a number of parameters, to which the user can assign values to represent characteristics of the transaction. For example, a transaction representing a ship might carry the amount of cargo it is to unload in a parameter. This number then could be used in the simulator logic to determine how long the unloading operation would take. Transactions can be related to one another by placing them in groups that can be searched, scanned, and modified.

Entities of the second class represent elements of system equipment that are acted on by transactions. These include facilities, stores, and logic switches. A facility can handle only one transaction at a time and could represent the pier in the example given. It represents a potential bottleneck. A store can handle several transactions concurrently, and could be used to represent a parking lot or a typing pool. A logic switch is a two-state indicator that can be set by one transaction to modify the flow of other transactions. It could model a traffic light or the "next window" sign of a bank teller.

To measure system behavior, two types of statistical entities are defined: queues and tables. Each queue maintains a list of transactions delayed at one or more points in the system, and it keeps a record of the average number of transactions delayed and the length of these delays. A table may be used to collect any sort of frequency distribution desired. These two entities provide a major portion of the GPSS output.

The operational entities, called "blocks," constitute the fourth and final class. Like the blocks of a diagram, they provide the logic of a system, instructing the transactions where to go and what to do next. These blocks, in conjunction with the other three classes of entities identified above, constitute the language of GPSS.

To provide input for the simulation, control, and definition cards are prepared from a flow chart of the system. This constitutes the model in GPSS language. Once the system model is loaded, the GPSS program generates and moves transactions from block to block according to timing information and to the logical rules incorporated in the blocks themselves. Each movement is designated to occur at a particular point in time. The

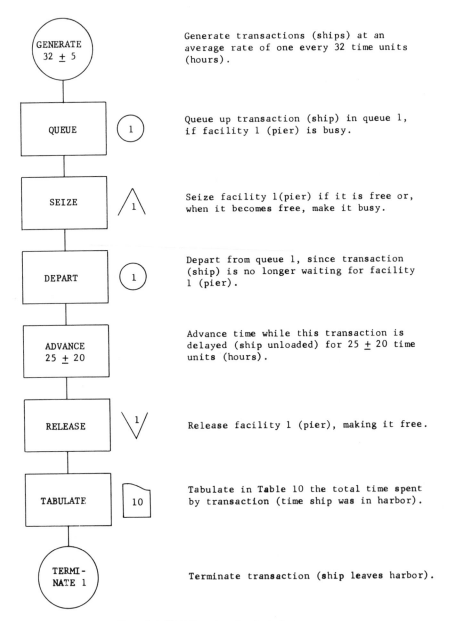

GENERATE 32 ± 5 — Generate transactions (ships) at an average rate of one every 32 time units (hours).

QUEUE 1 — Queue up transaction (ship) in queue 1, if facility 1 (pier) is busy.

SEIZE 1 — Seize facility 1(pier) if it is free or, when it becomes free, make it busy.

DEPART 1 — Depart from queue 1, since transaction (ship) is no longer waiting for facility 1 (pier).

ADVANCE 25 ± 20 — Advance time while this transaction is delayed (ship unloaded) for 25 ± 20 time units (hours).

RELEASE 1 — Release facility 1 (pier), making it free.

TABULATE 10 — Tabulate in Table 10 the total time spent by transaction (time ship was in harbor).

TERMINATE 1 — Terminate transaction (ship leaves harbor).

Figure 10. GPSS flow chart for simple harbor system.

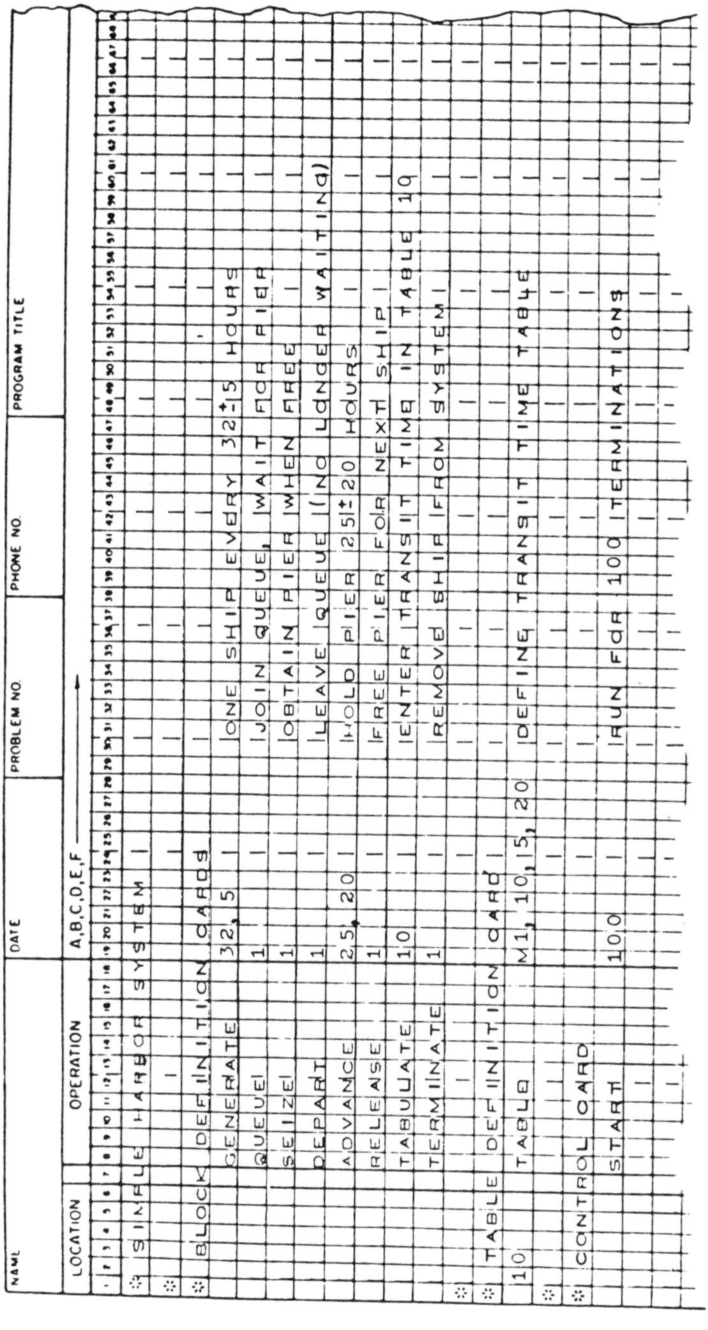

NAME | DATE | PROBLEM NO. | PHONE NO. | PROGRAM TITLE

LOCATION | OPERATION | A,B,C,D,E,F

```
* SIMPLE HARBOR SYSTEM
*
* BLOCK DEFINITION CARDS
      GENERATE   32,5          ONE SHIP EVERY 32±5 HOURS
      QUEUE      1             JOIN QUEUE, WAIT FOR PIER
      SEIZE      1             OBTAIN PIER WHEN FREE
      DEPART     1             LEAVE QUEUE (NO LONGER WAITING)
      ADVANCE    25,20         HOLD PIER 25±20 HOURS
      RELEASE    1             FREE PIER FOR NEXT SHIP
      TABULATE   10            ENTER TRANSIT TIME IN TABLE 10
      TERMINATE  1             REMOVE SHIP FROM SYSTEM
*
* TABLE DEFINITION CARD
10    TABLE      M1,10,5,20    DEFINE TRANSIT TIME TABLE
*
* CONTROL CARD
      START      100           RUN FOR 100 TERMINATIONS
```

Figure 11. GPSS Harbor Model.

program automatically maintains a record of these times and executes the movements in their correct time sequence. When actions cannot be performed at the originally scheduled time—for example, when a required facility is already in use—processing temporarily ceases for that transaction. The program automatically maintains a status of the condition causing the delay, and as soon as it changes, the transaction is activated again.

Summary

Four different SPLs have been presented to give the reader a helpful glance at different concepts, features, and language styles in use today. Except for SIMULA, the examples illustrate the latest releases of the languages.[16] SIMULA 67 has been discussed in public [16], but since no written material was available at the time this chapter was written, an example of it is not included.

As these examples are small and simple, they do not illustrate all, or even necessarily the best, features of all four languages. Some languages fare better than others in these short destinations. It should be kept in mind that the author's intent has not been language instruction, but a broad-based review. No language selections should be based on the details of this section alone. Still, it will be a useful exercise to look back and see how the different languages handle similar operations such as time control, entity generation, random sampling, and set manipulation.

CURRENT SPL RESEARCH

SPL research currently is being conducted in nonprofit corporations, universities, the research organizations of computer manufacturers and computer software companies, industrial research organizations, and some military staff groups. With only a little simplification, one can say that this research falls in either of two general categories: the development of new simulation concepts, and the development of improved simulation systems. The two are quite different, yet, since all SPL projects seem to combine some elements of each, few people would say that they are doing strictly one or the other. Researchers developing new concepts make advances in operating systems; experimenters developing new operating systems find new concepts arising from their work. Although few projects can qualify as either pure concept development or pure operating system design, this distinction is made in the following discussion.

---

[16] To be fair, it must be stated that, of the four examples presented, the one describing GPSS/360 is the least representative of the power of its full language. The complete GPSS/360 language contains 14 entity and 43 block types.

Research on Simulation Concepts

The 1967 IFIPS Working Conference on Simulation Languages [8] produced several important papers on SPL design.[17] Several of them described modifications to existing languages, others described new languages based on the refinements of existing concepts. The spirit of the conference, however, was evolution rather than revolution.

Despite the fact that many SPLs are in use today, there have been only a few instances in which a language introduced concepts that were significantly different from the ones of its predecessors. The languages best known for introducing new simulation concepts are the following: GSP, GPSS, SIMSCRIPT, SOL, SIMULA, and SIMPAC.

As far as we know, no completely new simulation concepts are being developed today. Most language research is aimed at unifying existing language concepts (NSS [50] is an integration of SIMSCRIPT and SIMULA with some original ideas added[18]), extending an accepted language (SIMSCRIPT II extends SIMSCRIPT as SIMULA 67 extends SIMULA), or writing a compiler for an existing language in a widely used procedural programming language (SPL [52] is being written in PL/I and is derived from SIMULA and SOL). A good deal of work being done throughout the programming community on date-base concepts is finding its way into simulation languages (for example, SIMULA 67 and SIMSCRIPT II) and general-purpose programming languages (reference variable extensions to PL/I and ALGOL 68). Many concepts exploited in SPLs for some time, at present, are being integrated into COBOL.

There will always be room for this kind of research. Programming being what it is, it has no theoretical limit, and there will always be opportunities for improvements, refinements, and extensions. Until a standard simulation programming language evolves, if that day ever comes, people will be rewriting SPLs in new languages, will be discovering new ways to do old things better, and will be making evolutionary changes in concepts and implementations.

A fertile field for SPL research is language concepts. One area in particular that has hardly been touched is the integration of discrete-event and continuous-time simulation. Today, continuous-time simulation is conducted on both analog and digital computers, with a trend toward increased use on digital and hybrid machines [6]. The languages used for simulating continuous systems on digital computers differ greatly from

---

[17] IFIPS is the International Federation of Information Processing Societies.
[18] The most notable one is a sophisticated version of the WAIT UNTIL command of SOL.

the SPLs that we have been discussing. There is almost no relationship between discrete-event and continuous-time SPLs. This is a sad and hopefully short-term condition that will be alleviated when more research effort is expended on language integration.

A second promising area is the synthesis of modeling languages with procedures for performing statistical experiments and the analysis of their results. Although some work has been published on efficient statistical analysis and experimentation techniques [20], [49], no simulation programming languages presently contain these procedures. In part, this is because little research has been done on identifying and developing statistical procedures that are adapted especially to simulation studies. As this area receives more attention, however, both from researchers and practitioners, language designers will begin to consider experimentation, and analyses as well as modeling and true "simulation systems" will be developed. Statisticians, language designers, simulation analysts, and computer programmers will contribute jointly to these efforts.

In speaking of evolution in simulation concepts and in attempting to predict the future from the past, one can be guided by these facts:

1. Activity- and event-oriented SPLs merged at roughly the same time. GSP, CSL, GPSS, and SIMSCRIPT were developed more or less in parallel.

2. Process-oriented SPLs came later. SOL and SIMULA evolved from the above languages and ALGOL.

3. Current research is attempting to unify and extend the activity-, event-, and process-orientations [8].

4. Interest in the statistical analyses and interpretation of simulation results seems to be growing more rapidly each year.

It seems a good bet that research in simulation modeling concepts will continue for some time. A great many modeling techniques still seem forced and artificial; there is much room for improvement in programming techniques. Topics that are well identified as needing research attention are: decision specification—decision tables have not been used in SPLs; simultaneity—parallel interactions are currently difficult to account for; synchronous and asynchronous behavior specification— richer vocabularies for synchronizing system processes and for executing activities asynchronously are required; data-base definition—we are still far from being able to specify complex state descriptions simply and elegantly; data-base management—efficient ways of partitioning data bases and of unifying them without complication remain to be worked out. For some solutions to these problems, see [4], [15], and [47].

Research on Operating Systems and Mechanisms

As simulation is an experimental technique, people are always interested in making simulation programs easier to use. The standard way of performing a simulation experiment today is to make a series of experimental runs at different system parameter settings by submitting a set of programs and data decks for batch processing. Although this procedure does the job, it has several serious defects: (1) program development and debugging is slow and painful; (2) more program runs than necessary are usually made because of the rigidity of a scheme which requires that a program be run completely before any information about its behavior can be obtained and used; and (3) it is difficult to get a feel for system dynamics by looking at a sequence of after-the-fact system-state snapshots. Systems are being designed today that assist in each of these areas. These systems use interactive languages, time-sharing, and graphics.

Interactive Languages

The best-known interactive SPL is OPS-3 [27]. This language was designed and implemented at M.I.T. and was used successfully to demonstrate the feasibility of interactive modeling. Operating in a time-shared environment under the M.I.T. Compatible Time Sharing System (CTSS), OPS-3 provides a user with on-line, interactive communication between himself and a programming system. By using it, one can, in a single sitting, compose a program, test and modify it, expand and embellish it, and prepare it for subsequent production use. That interactive languages will become standard in the future is a fact established by OPS-3, JOSS,[19] BASIC, RUSH, and other interactive languages. Greenberger and Jones [28] have specified in great detail the features of an elegant interactive simulation system.

Time-sharing is not mandatory for interactive man-machine dialogue, as the above discussion might imply. At M.I.T., and SPL named SIMPLE is being designed and programmed to operate on an IBM 1130 computer [17]. On such a small machine, it is economically feasible to allow one person to have full use, even though the computer is inactive a great deal of the time. Time-sharing allows multiple users to fully utilize a computer, but it is not necessary for an interactive language.

In the future, widely used SPLs, undoubtedly, will have two modes of operation. They will be able to be used interactively to build models; for this, either incremental compilation or interpretation will be used. They also will be capable of efficient code generation through optimizing com-

[19] JOSS is the trademark and service mark of The RAND Corporation for its computer program and services using that program.

pilation. This is necessary if large simulation studies that require lengthy experimental runs are to be made economically.

Time-Sharing

Time-sharing enters into simulation in that it makes certain things possible, such as interactive modeling. During model construction and testing, when programmer-program interaction is important, time-sharing makes interaction economical. Time-sharing also can be useful during model utilization, when production runs are made. When it is necessary to study a model's behavior, instead of running it merely to derive steady-state statistics, time-sharing can offer substantial benefits; when a man can enter a program from a console, watch its performance, and either leave it alone, stop it permanently, or stop it temporarily to adjust some parameters and start again, a new plateau in the use of simulation will be reached. It then will become possible for man to enter into the exploratory and experimental process more completely and more efficiently than he can in today's batch environment. For this reason, substantial future research will be devoted to this area. The SIMPLE language mentioned above, in fact, is designed to do this. IBM's continuous-time simulation language, CSMP, operates in this mode today [12].

Graphics

A considerable amount of simulation-oriented graphics research is going on right now. At the Norden Division of United Aircraft, an IBM 2250 is used to modify source language GPSS programs and to view their output in graphical form [54]. At The Rand Corporation, the Grail system and the RAND Tablet are used to construct GPSS programs on-line from hand-drawn flow charts [30]. At M.I.T., the SIMPLE project is using graphics for man-computer interaction during modeling and experimentation. Papers have been written on the use of graphics in simulation modeling and on the use of existing graphics packages for analyzing simulation-generated output [44].

There is little doubt that interactive modeling is carried out better with a CRT device than with a typewriter or line printer. When designing programs, flow charts and other symbolic notation can be displayed. For analyzing performance data, graphs provide more insight than do lists of numbers. The growing use of line-printer plotting simulators testifies to the utility of graphic output.

Research in SPL graphics will take several directions in the future. Graphical input is an area of great interest that is just getting started. Graphical output is on a far firmer footing and has had some operational success. The difficult thing about incorporating graphics in an SPL is its ultimate dependence on graphic hardware and software that are not properly part of a simulation language. Statements in SPLs that perform graphical tasks, for a long time, will be computer-system dependent, and not independent concepts. Graphical research also will prosper for interactive modeling and program modification. The successes and benefits claimed to date virtually insure this.

THE FUTURE OF SPLS

The preceding section has demonstrated that a great deal of research remains to be done. We are far from knowing all there is to know about simulation, both in concept and in practice. It will be a long time before we come to a point where we wish to standardize on a single language, and, hence, change from a dynamic era of research and development to one of slow evolution.

The greatest challenge today lies in unifying discrete-event and continuous-time simulation languages. Some think that this cannot be done. Some think it should not be done. Certainly, we know little about how to do it.[20]

The researcher faced with the selection of a research project in the simulation language area does not lack alternatives. There are still advances to be made in modeling concepts; our ways of modeling both static and dynamic structures are incomplete. And, certainly, the fields of interactive compilers and/or interpreters and graphics are exciting ones and in the mainstream of modern programming research.

Today, the manager or programmer faced with the task of selecting an SPL does not always have a clear choice. His choice will probably be less clear in the future, as languages are drawing closer together on many issues, but remaining apart on others. It is our hope that this chapter will make some language selection choices easier and more objective and that will provide some direction to SPL research.

[20] A recent publication, D. A. Fahrland, "Combined Discrete-Event/Continuous Systems Simulation," SCR-68-16, Case Western Reserve University Systems Research Center, July 1968, may provide the needed impetus to initiate a constructive dialogue on this topic.

Checklist of Features for SPL Evaluation

Feature	Comments
Modeling a system's static state	Simulation programming languages must be able to: (1) define the classes of objects within a system, (2) adjust the number of these objects as conditions within the system vary,

Checklist of Features for SPF Evaluation — Continued

Feature	Comments
Modeling a system's static state—Continued	(3) define characteristics or properties that can both describe and differentiate objects of the same class, and declare numerical codes for them, (4) relate objects to one another and to their common environment.
Modeling system dynamics	The heart of every simulation program, and every SPL is a time control program. Its functions are always the same: to advance simulation time and to select for execution a program that performs a specified simulation activity. An SPL must contain such a program, statements that define events, activities or processes, and statements that organize these events, activities or processes.

Statistical sampling	Pseudorandom number generation
	     Multiple random number streams
	     Antithetic variates
	 Sampling from empirical table look-up distributions
	 Sampling from theoretical statistical distributions

Data collection specification	The nicest thing one can say about a data collection specification is that it is unobstrusive. While data collection is necessary, statements that are written to obtain data but are not themselves part of a simulation model's logic, should not obscure the operations of a model in any way.
Data analysis	Means Variances and Standard Deviations Frequency Distributions
Data collection	Number of observations, maxima and minima for all variables Sums, and sums of squares for time-independent variables Time-weighted sums, and sums of squares for time-dependent variables Variable value histograms for time-independent variables Time-in-state histograms for time-dependent variables Time series plots over specified time intervals

Checklist of Features for SPF Evalution — Continued

Feature	Comments
Display formats	Since the production of reports is the primary task of all programs, whether they are run for program checkout, for the display of computed results, or for the preparation of elaborate management reports and charts, a good SPL should contain statements adapted to all display situations. (1) Automatic output in standard format (2) Format-free output (3) Formatted output (4) Report generators
Monitoring and debugging	Reporting execute-time errors by source statement related messages Displaying complete program flow status when an execute-time error occurs. This means displaying the entry points and relevant parameters for all function and subroutine calls in effect at the time of the error. Accessing control information between event executions. This allows event tracing during all or selected parts of a program, and use of control information in program diagnostic routines.
Initialization	A simulation is essentially the movement of a system model through simulated time by changing its state descriptions, it is important that an SPL provide a convenient mechanism for specifying initial states. This can be done either by: (a) A special initialization form; or (b) convenient data input statements and formats. One should also be able to save all the information about a program, including relevant data on the status of external storage devices and periphera equipment and restore it on command.

Other	Program readability
	Execution efficiency
	Modeling efficiency
	Documentation
	    for instruction
	    for installation
	    for maintenance

BIBLIOGRAPHY

1. Arden, B. W. *An Introduction to Digital Computing.* Reading, Mass.: Addison-Wesley, 1963.
2. Bennett, R. P. *et al.* "SIMPAC User's Manual," System Development Corporation, TM-602/000/00, April 1962.
3. Blunden, G. P., and Krasnow, H. S. "The Process Concept as a Basis for Simulation Modeling," *Simulation,* **IX** (August 1967), 89-94.
4. Blunden, G. P. "On Implicit Interaction in Process Models," IFIP Working Conference on Simulation Languages, Oslo, Norway, 1967.
5. Braddock, D. M., Dowling, C. R., and Rochelson, K. "SIMTRAN—A Simulation Programming System for the IBM 7030," IBM SDD, Poughkeepsie, N. Y., July 1965.
6. Brennan, R. D. "Continuous System Modeling Programs: State-of-the-Art and Prospectus for Development," IFIP Working Conference on Simulation Languages, Oslo, Norway, 1967.
7. Buxton, J. N., and Laski, J. G. "Control and Simulation Language," *Computer Journal,* **V** (1962).
8. Buxton, J. N. (ed). *Proceedings of the IFIP Working Conference On Simulation Languages.* Amsterdam: North-Holland, 1968.
9. Clementson, A. T. "Extended Control and Simulation Language," *Computer Journal,* **IX** (November 1966).
10. Colker, A. *et al. The Generation of Random Samples from Common Statistical Distributions,* United States Steel Corporation, Applied Research Laboratory Report 25.17-016(1), November 1962.
11. IBM United Kingdom Limited Data Centre, *CSL User's Manual,* London, 1966.
12. IBM Corporation, *Continuous System Modeling Program (CSMP/360): Application Description,* H20-0240, 1967.
13. Dahl, O. J., and Nygaard, K. "The SIMULA Language," Report from the Norwegian Computing Center, May 1965.
14. Dahl, O. J., and Nygaard, K. "SIMULA—An ALGOL—Based Simulation Language," *Communications of the ACM,* **IX** (September 1966), 671.
15. Dahl, O. J., and Nygaard, K. "Class and Subclass Declarations," IFIP Working Conference on Simulation Languages, Oslo, Norway, 1967.
16. Dahl, O. J., Myhrhaug, B., and Nygaard, K. "Some Features on the SIMULA 67 Language," *Proceedings of the Second Conference on Applications of Simulation,* New York, December 2-4, 1968.
17. Donovan, J. J., Alsop, J. W., and Jones, M. M. "A Graphical Facility for an Interactive Simulation System," *Proceedings of IFIPS Congress,* 1968.
18. "Draft Report on the Algorithmic Language ALGOL 68," IFIP Working Group on ALGOL, WG.2.1, February 1968.
19. Famolari, E. "FORSIM IV User's Guide," SR-99, The Mitre Corp., February 1964.
20. Fishman, G. S., and Kiviat, P. J. *Digital Computer Simulation: Statistical Considerations,* The RAND Corp., RM-5387-PR, November 1967.

21. Fishman, G. S., and Kiviat, P. J. "The Analysis of Simulation Generated Time Series," *Management Science*, **XVIII** (March 1967), 527-557.
22. Galler, B. F. *The Language of Computers*. New York: McGraw-Hill, 1962.
23. IBM, *General Purpose Simulation System/360 User's Manual*, H20-0326-2, 1967.
24. IBM, *General Purpose Simulation/360: Application Description*, H20-0186-1, 1966.
25. Ginsberg, A. S., Markowitz, H. M., and Oldfather, P. M. *Programming by Questionnaire*, The RAND Corp., RM-4460-PR, April 1965.
26. Gordon, G. "A General Purpose Systems Simulator, " *IBM Systems Journal*, **I** (1962).
27. Greenberger, M. *et al. On-Line Computation and Simulation: The OPS-3 System*. Cambridge, Mass.: M.I.T. Press, 1965.
28. Greenberger, M., and Jones, M. "On-Line Incremental Simulation," IFIP Working Conference on Simulation Languages, Oslo, Norway, 1967.
29. IBM, *IBM Operating System/360, PL/1: Language Specifications*, File No. S-360-29, Form (28-6571-1), 1967.
30. Haverty, J. P. *Grail/GPSS, Graphic On-Line Modeling*, The RAND Corporation, P-3838, January 1968.
31. Jills, P. R. "SIMON-A Computer Simulation Language in ALGOL," *Digital Simulation in Operation Research*, S. H. Hollingdale (ed). New York: American Elsevier Co., 1967.
32. Kalinichenko, L. A. "SLANG—Computer Description and Simulation-Oriented Experimental Programming Language," IFIP Working Conference on Simulation Languages, Oslo, Norway, 1967.
33. Karr, H. W., Kleine, H., Markowitz, H. M. "SIMSCRIPT 1.5," Consolidated Analysis Centers, CACI 65-INT-1, Santa Monica, California, June 1965.
34. Kiviat, P. J. *Digital Computer Simulation: Modeling Concepts*, The RAND Corp., RM-5378-PR, August 1967.
35. Kiviat, P. J. "Development of Discrete Digital Simulation Languages," *SIMULATION*, **VIII** (February 1967).
36. Kiviat, P. J. "Development of New Digital Simulation Languages," *Journal of Industrial Engineering*, **XVII** (November 1966).
37. Kiviat, P. J. "GASP—A General Activity Simulation Program," Project No. 90.17-019(2), Applied Research Laboratory, U.S. Steel Corp., Monroeville, Pa., July 1963.
38. Kiviat, P. J. *Introduction to the SIMSCRIPT II Programming Language*, The RAND Corp., P-3314, February 1966.
39. Kiviat, P. J., Villanueva, R., and Markowitz, H. M. *The SIMSCRIPT II Programming Language*. Englewood Cliffs, N. J.: Prentice-Hall, 1968.
40. Kiviat, P. J. *Simulation Language Report Generators*, The RAND Corp., P-3349, April 1966.
41. Knuth, D. C., and McNeley, J. L. "SOL—A Symbolic Language for General—Purpose System Simulation," *IEEE Transactions on Electronic Computers*, August 1964.

42. Krasnow, H. S. "Dynamic Representation in Discrete Interaction Simulation Languages," *Digital Simulation in Operational Research*, S. H. Hollingdale (ed). New York: American Elsevier Co., 1967.

43. Krasnow, H. S., and Merikallio, R. A. "The Past, Present and Future of Simulation Languages," *Management Science*, **XI** (November 1964), 236-267.

44. Lackner, M. R. "Graphic Forms for Modeling and Simulation" IFIP Working Conference on Simulation Languages, Oslo, Norway, 1967.

45. Markowitz, H. M., Karr, H. W., and Hausner, B. *SIMSCRIPT: A Simulation Programming Language.* Englewood Cliffs, N. J.: Prentice-Hall, 1963.

46. McNeley, J. L. "Simulation Languages," *SIMULATION*, **IX** (August 1967), 95-98.

47. McNeley, J. L. "Compound Declarations," IFIP Working Conference on Simulation Languages, Oslo, Norway, 1967.

48. Systems Research Group, Inc. *MILITRAN Programming Manual*, Report ESD-TDR-64-320, June 1964.

49. Naylor, Thomas H., Balintfy, Joseph L., Burdick, Donald S., and Chu, Kong. *Computer Simulation Techniques.* New York: John Wiley, 1966.

50. Parente, R. J. "A Language for Dynamic System Description," IBM Advanced System Development Division Technical Report 17-180, 1966.

51. Parslow, R. D. "AS: An ALGOL Simulation Language," IFIP Working Conference on Simulation Languages, Oslo, Norway, 1967.

52. Petrone, L. "On a Simulation Language Completely Defined Onto the Programming Language PL/I," IFIP Working Conference on Simulation Languages, Oslo, Norway, 1967.

53. Pritsker, A. A. B., and Kiviat, P. J. *Simulation with GASP II: A FORTRAN Based Simulation Language.* Englewood Cliffs, N. J.: Prentice-Hall, 1969.

54. Reitman, J. "GPSS/360 Norden, The Unbounded and Displayed GPSS," *Proceedings of SHARE XXX*, Houston, Texas, February 29 1968.

55. Report to the CODASYL COBOL Committee. *COBOL Extensions to Handle Data Bases*, Data Base Task Group. January 1968.

56. IBM. *Simulation Evaluation and Analysis Language (SEAL), System Reference Manual*, January 17, 1968.

57. United States Steel Corporation. *Simulation Language and Library (SILLY)*, Engineering and Scientific Computer Services, February 1968.

58. General Electric Company. *SIMCOM User's Guide*, Information Systems Operations, TR-65-2-149010, 1964.

59. UNIVAC. *SIMULA Programmer's Reference Manual*, UP-7556, 1967.

60. Teichroew, D., and Lubin, J. F. "Computer Simulation: Discussion of Techniques and Comparison of Languages," *Communications of the ACM*, **IX** (October 1966), 723-741.

61. Tocher, K. D. "Review of Simulation Languages," *Ooperational Research Quarterly*, **XVI** (June 1965), 189-218.

62. Tocher, K. D., and Hopkins, D. A. "Handbook of the General Simulation Program, II," Report 118/ORD 10/TECH, United Steel Companies, Ltd., Sheffield, England, June 1964.

63. Tocher, K. D. *The Art of Simulation.* Princeton, N. J.: D. Van Nostrand, 1963.
64. Weinert, A. E. "A SIMSCRIPT-FORTRAN Case Study," *Communications of the ACM*, **X** (December 1967), 784-792.
65. Williams, J. W. J. "The Elliott Simulator Package (ESP)," *Computer Journal*, **VI** (January 1964), 328-331.
66. Young, Karen. "A User's Experience with Three Simulation Languages (GPSS, SIMSCRIPT and SIMPAC)," System Development Corporation, TM-1755/000/00,/1963.

Author Index

Abe, D. K., 83
Ackerman, S. S., 59, 83
Addelman, S., 183
Adelman, F. L., 147, 266, 316, 318
Adelman, Irma, 147, 266, 316, 318
Aitchison, J., 403
Albert, G. E., 276, 287
Allard, J. L., 392
Allen, R. G. D., 147
Alsop, J. W., 486
Amster, S. J., 243
Amstutz, A. E., 61, 83
Anderson, L. C., 379
Anderson, T. W., 243, 403
Ando, A. K., 147
Anscombe, F. J., 244, 296
Ansoff, H. I., 107, 147
Arden, B. W., 486
Armitage, P., 244
Asimow, M., 87

Bahadur, R. R., 205, 219
Baker, A. C., 296
Baker, C. T., 53, 59, 83, 85
Balderston, F. E., 124, 147
Balintfy, J. L., 11, 38, 58, 86, 151, 164, 184,
    221, 224, 244, 245, 268, 382, 391, 394,
    396, 404, 488
Barnett, V. D., 392
Bartlett, M. S., 219, 266
Baumol, W. J., 83, 147, 219, 318
Bechhofer, R. E., 35, 36, 200, 206–208,
    218–219, 230, 232–234, 242–243, 244,
    293, 294, 296, 297, 349, 350
Behnkin, D. W., 183
Benedict, M. R., 335
Bennett, R. P., 486

Ben-Tuvia, S., 276, 279, 288
Beracha, H. H., 83
Berman, E. B., 53, 83
Birkhoff, G., 392
Blackman, R. B., 36, 251, 254, 257, 264,
    266, 296, 297
Blackwell, D., 244
Blaug, M., 155, 163
Blumenthal, S., 207, 219, 230, 232, 244, 294,
    296
Blunden, G. P., 486
Bogyo, T. P., 394
Bonini, C. P., 36, 41, 84, 99, 105–106, 147,
    169, 183
Boschan, Charlotte, 150
Bose, R. C., 183
Boughton, J. M., 353, 379
Box, G. E. P., 27, 36, 165, 183, 244, 403
Braddock, D. M., 486
Bradley, R. A., 245
Brainard, W. C., 379
Bray, T. A., 389, 394, 404
Brazer, H. E., 350
Break, G. F., 350
Breakwell, J., 244
Brennan, R. D., 486
Brenner, M. E., 53, 84, 297
Brockmeyer, E., 403
Brooks, R. C., 335
Brown, D. E., 84
Brown, J. A. C., 403
Brown, R. G., 403
Bryan, W. R., 379
Buchanan, J. M., 350
Bulkin, M. H., 59, 84
Burdick, D. S., 11, 22, 27, 36, 38, 58, 86, 151,
    163, 164, 184, 221, 223, 244, 245, 266, 268,
    391, 394, 396, 404, 488

491

Burkhead, J., 350
Burkholder, D. L., 244
Burman, J. P., 184
Burns, A. F., 148
Burr, I. W., 403
Butler, J. W., 403
Buxton, J. N., 486

Canavos, G. C., 392
Carlson, B. R., 107, 148
Carnap, R., 163
Carter, R. L., 183
Certaine, J. E., 392
Chambers, M. L., 219
Chambers, R. P., 392
Chase, S. B., Jr., 380
Chernoff, H., 22, 35, 36, 244
Christ, C. F., 12, 303, 318, 335
Chow, G. C., 148, 316, 318
Chu, K., 11, 38, 41, 44, 48, 58, 84, 86, 148, 151, 164, 184, 186, 219, 221, 245, 268, 391, 394, 396, 404, 488
Churchman, C. W., 163
Clark, C. E., 276, 279, 288, 393
Clarkson, G. P. E., 61, 84, 111, 148
Clathworthy, W. H., 183
Clementson, A. T., 486
Cochran, W. G., 26, 27, 36, 169, 172, 183, 276, 288
Cohen, K. J., 8, 41, 84, 99, 105, 111, 113, 119, 122, 148, 160, 163, 336
Colker, A., 486
Colley, J. L., 84
Collins, N. R., 126, 151, 184
Conway, R. W., 59, 84, 163, 297
Cooper, R. L., 148
Cournot, A., 96, 97
Coveyou, R. R., 389, 390, 391, 392
Cox, D. R., 27, 37, 184, 244, 245
Cox, G. M., 26, 27, 36, 169, 172, 183
Craig, C. C., 245
Cramer, H., 403
Cunningham, J., 266
Cyert, R. M., 36, 41, 84, 96, 99, 100–105, 111, 148, 159, 160, 163, 336

Dahl, O. J., 36, 486
Dalenius, T., 276, 288
Davies, O. L., 183
Davis, O. A., 339, 350

Day, R. L., 61, 84
De Leeuw, F., 148, 266, 353, 379
Dempster, M. A. H., 339, 350
Dickens, J. H., 84
Dill, W. R., 85
Dillion, J. L., 336
Dobell, A. R., 392, 393
Donovan, J. J., 486
Doppelt, N., 85
Dowling, C. R., 486
Downham, D. Y., 392
Draper, N. R., 29, 37, 172, 183
Dubner, H., 297
Dudewicz, E. J., 219
Duesenberry, J. S., 85, 148, 267, 319
Dunnett, C. W., 35, 36, 200, 203, 204, 207– 208, 218–219, 220, 293, 297, 349, 350
Dvoretzky, A., 245
Dzielinski, B. P., 41, 53, 59, 83, 85

Eckstein, O., 267
Edgeworth, F. Y., 96
Ehrenfeld, S., 276, 279, 288
Eisenpress, H., 319
Elton, E. J., 84
Engle, R. F., 148
Evans, M. K., 37, 85, 139, 142, 148, 149, 150, 308, 319
Evans, W. D., 276, 288

Fabricant, S., 351
Fahrland, D. A., 483
Famolari, E., 486
Fan, C. T., 245
Feigenbaum, E. A., 96, 100, 101, 148
Feller, W., 403
Fey, W. R., 107, 149
Finger, J. M., 38, 153, 268
Fisher, F. M., 319, 336
Fisher, G., 351
Fisher, W. H., 336
Fishman, G. S., 37, 163, 267, 296, 297, 486, 487
Forrester, J. W., 85, 107, 149
Forsythe, G. E., 392
Fraser, D. A. S., 267
Franklin, J. N., 392
Frazier, G. D., 84
Freeman, D., 245
Friedman, L., 87

Friedman, M., 155, 156, 163, 379
Frisch, Ragnar, 220
Fromm, G., 28, 37, 85, 142, 148, 149, 178, 184, 267, 302, 308, 319, 353, 379

Gage, C. F., 336
Galler, B. F., 487
Galliher, H. P., 43, 85, 403
Gebhardt, F., 392
Geisler, M. A., 41, 53, 85
Gelder, A. Van, 392
Geraci, V. J., 149
Gere, W. S., 59, 85
Gershefski, G. W., 64, 85
Ghosh, M. N., 245
Gilchrist, W. G., 245
Gillespie, R. W., 107
Gillespie, W. I., 150, 351
Gilman, M. J., 295, 297
Ginsberg, A. S., 487
Girshick, M. A., 244
Gleser, L. J., 297
Goldberger, A. S., 145, 149, 150, 302, 319, 340, 351
Goldfeld, S. M., 380
Good, I. J., 392
Goodman, A. S., 386, 394
Gordon, G., 385, 487
Gorenstein, S., 386, 391, 393
Goris, H., 336
Graham, D. A., 223
Gramley, L. E., 380
Gramlich, E., 148, 353, 379
Granger, C. W. J., 37, 251, 254, 258, 265, 267
Graves, R. L., 87
Green, B. F., 393
Green, G., 149
Greenberger, M., 393, 487
Greenstadt, J., 319
Grenander, U., 251, 267
Gross, D., 85, 267
Gupta, S. S., 22, 35, 37, 220, 403

Haavelmo, T., 319
Hadley, G., 319
Haenszel, W., 336
Haitovsky, Y., 148
Hajnal, J., 245
Hall, W. J., 245
Halstrom, L., 403

Halton, J. H., 288
Hamburger, M. J., 86, 380
Hammersley, J. M., 25, 26, 37, 274, 288, 297, 404
Handscomb, D. C., 25, 26, 37, 180, 288, 297, 404
Hannan, E. J., 251, 267
Hansen, M. H., 276, 288
Harling, J., 297
Harris, R., 351
Haskell, M. A., 351
Hatanaka, M., 37, 251, 254, 258, 265, 267
Hauser, N., 297, 488
Haverty, J. P., 487
Heady, E. O., 336
Heaslet, M. A., 394
Heller, J., 59, 85
Hendershott, P. H., 380
Henshaw, R. C., 85
Hertz, D. B., 61, 62, 63, 85
Herzberg, A. M., 27, 37, 172, 183, 184
Hext, G. R., 184
Hickman, B. G., 267
Hicks, J. R., 85, 149, 185, 209–212, 220, 248–250, 255–265, 267
Hill, W. J., 27, 37, 184
Himsworth, F. R., 184
Hirsch, A. A., 150
Hoggatt, A. C., 93, 113, 124, 147, 149, 172
Holland, E. P., 107, 150
Holt, C. C., 37, 141, 150, 302, 319
Holz, B. W., 393
Hopkins, D. A., 488
Howrey, E. P., 37, 129, 143, 146, 147, 150, 220, 250, 267, 299, 316, 319
Huang, D. S., 374
Hufschmidt, M. M., 27, 37, 184
Hull, T. E., 392, 393
Hunter, J. S., 2, 22, 26, 165, 183, 184, 244
Hunter, W. G., 27, 37, 183, 184
Hurst, E. G., 59, 85
Hurtubise, R. A., 297
Hurwitz, W. N., 276, 288
Hutchinson, D. W., 393
Hutchison, T. W., 155, 163
Huyett, M. J., 220, 246

Isard, W., 351
Itzelsberger, G., 393

Jackson, E. L., 336

Jackson, J. E., 245
Jackson, J. R., 59, 85, 86
Jackson, R. R. P., 220
Jagerman, D. L., 393
Jansson, B., 393
Jarmain, W. E., 107, 150
Jarratt, P., 219
Jenkins, G. M., 37, 251, 267
Jensen, A., 403, 404
Jills, P. R., 487
Johnson, G. L., 336
Johnson, N. L., 245
Johnston, J., 150, 319, 336, 351
Jones, D. M., 380
Jones, M., 487
Jones, M. M., 486
Jorgenson, Dale W., 148

Kabak, W. I., 297
Kagdis, J., 86
Kahn, H., 276, 279, 288
Kalinchenko, L. A., 487
Kant, I., 154, 157
Karlin, S., 206, 220
Karr, H. W., 487, 488
Karreman, H. F., 255, 267
Kelejian, H. H., 37, 129, 143, 146, 147, 150, 299, 319
Kendall, M. G., 219, 267, 319, 393
Kiefer, J., 207, 219, 245
King, E. P., 164
Kiviat, P. J., 37, 38, 39, 163, 267, 297, 406, 486, 487, 488
Kleijnen, J. P., 35, 38, 180, 207, 220, 245, 293, 297
Klein, L. R., 85, 128, 139, 142, 147, 149, 150, 177, 184, 267, 308, 314–315, 319
Kleine, H., 487
Klem, L., 393
Knuth, D. C., 487
Koizumi, S., 336
Koopmans, T. C., 164
Korn, G. A., 393
Koyck, L. M., 380
Krasnow, H. S., 38, 486, 488
Kudo, A., 206, 221
Kuehn, A. A., 61, 86
Kuh, E., 85, 148, 267
Kuhen, H. G., 393

Lackner, M. R., 86, 488
Laski, J. G., 486

Latta, Cyntheia M., 380
Lavi, A., 180, 184
Lavin, M. M., 289
Lawless, R. M., 86
Lee, Y. W., 268
Le Grande, E., 86
Lehmann, E. L., 221
Lehmer, D. H., 394
Levine, J. M., 379
Levitan, R. E., 316, 318
Lewis, P. A. W., 386, 394
Liebenberg, M., 150
Ling, T. Y., 38, 298
Liu, T. C., 148, 150, 268
Lubin, J. F., 164, 488

McCarthy, E., 297
McCarthy, M. D., 374, 399, 404
Machlup, F., 150
McKay, G., 111
McKenney, J. L., 86
MacLane, S. A., 392
MacLaren, M. D., 389, 391, 394
McManus, M., 319
McNeley, J. L., 487, 488
Macpherson, R. D., 389, 390, 391, 392
Madow, W. G., 276, 288
Maguire, B. A., 404
Malinvaud, E., 150, 268, 351, 380
Malone, J. M., 38
Manne, A. S., 53, 85, 86
Manser, Marilyn, 221, 338
March, J. G., 36, 41, 84, 97, 99, 100–105, 148, 159, 336
Markowitz, H. M., 38, 487, 488
Marsaglia, G., 389, 391, 394, 404
Marshall, A. W., 274, 279, 288
Mattessich, R., 61, 64, 86
Mauldon, J. G., 288
Maurice, R., 221
Maxwell, J. A., 351
Meir, R. C., 86
Merikallio, R. A., 488
Meyer, H. A., 287
Miller, H., 336
Miller, J. M., 386, 394
Miner, J., 343, 351
Modigliani, F., 147, 380
Monty, G., 53, 86
Montgomory, D. B., 59, 86
Moore, G. H., 148, 150
Morgenstern, O., 267

Morton, K. W., 274, 288, 289
Moss, J. H., 86
Mosteller, F., 205, 206, 221
Moy, W. A., 38, 269, 289
Muller, M. E., 245, 403, 404
Muth, J. F., 41, 59, 86
Muyen, A. R., 53, 86
Myhrhaug, B., 36, 486

Naddor, E., 41, 53
Nagar, A. L., 150, 310, 319, 399, 404
Naylor, T. H., 11, 22, 26, 27, 35, 36, 37, 38,
    39, 41, 44, 58, 84, 86, 87, 88, 113, 119,
    151, 153, 160, 164, 165, 184, 186, 196,
    353, 380, 394, 396, 404, 488
Nelson, R. T., 59, 87
Nerlove, M., 251, 268, 336
Neumann, J. von, 405
Newell, W. T., 86
Nicholls, W. H., 336
Nichols, Dorothy M., 380
Nord, O. C., 107, 151
Norman, M. R., 351
Nygaard, K., 36, 486

Oldfather, P. M., 487
Orcutt, G. H., 87, 151
Ore, O., 394
Osman, J., 344, 351
Overholt, J. L., 26, 38

Packer, A. H., 53
Packer, D. W., 87, 107, 151
Page, E. S., 274, 289, 394
Panchapapkesan, S., 37, 220
Parente, R. J., 488
Parslow, R. D., 488
Parzen, E., 39, 251, 268, 404
Paulson, E., 206, 221, 230, 232, 234, 246,
    294, 298
Payne, W. H., 394
Peach, P., 394
Pearson, E. S., 404
Petrone, L., 488
Pfanzagl, J., 222
Phillips, A. W., 222
Plackett, R. L., 184
Popkin, P., 150
Popper, K. R., 154, 164
Preston, L. E., 126, 151, 184
Pritsker, A. A. B., 39, 59, 87, 488

Pugh, A. L., 39, 107, 109, 151

Quenouille, M. H., 251, 268

Rabung, J. R., 394
Ramberg, J. S., 222, 246
Rasche, R., 147
Ray, J., 85, 267
Ray, W. D., 298
Reichenbach, H., 21, 39, 151, 155, 164
Reitman, J., 488
Rezucha, I., 245
Rhenman, E., 84
Rives, N. W., 88, 152, 320
Robbins, H., 222, 246, 297
Robbins, L., 164
Roberts, E. B., 107, 151
Roberts, F. D. K., 392
Robinson, Joan, 87, 151
Rochelson, K., 486
Rosenblatt, M., 251, 267, 268
Rotenberg, A., 394
Rowe, A. J., 87

Saaty, T. L., 87, 222
Sackrin, S. M., 336
Sacks, J., 245
Sacks, S., 351
Salveson, M. E., 59, 87
Samuelson, P. A., 87, 151, 185, 209–212,
    222, 249–250, 255–265, 268
Sandeman, J., 59, 87
Sanderson, F. H., 336
Sargent, T. J., 351
Sasieni, M., 87
Sasser, W., 38, 113, 119, 151, 152, 160, 164,
    184, 222, 223, 246, 268, 298, 336, 398
Scheffé, H., 39, 201, 202, 204, 214, 222
Scheuer, E., 38, 404
Schiller, D. H., 289
Schriber, T. J., 39
Seal, K. C., 222
Sen, K. P., 298
Shapiro, S., 340, 351
Shimkin, M. B., 336
Shirafuji, M., 222
Shreider, Y. A., 298
Shrinkhande, S. S., 183
Shubik, M., 111, 152
Siegel, S., 160, 164
Simon, H. A., 84, 111, 148

Slevin, D. P., 107, 147
Smith, B. B., 393
Smith, H., 22, 29, 37, 39, 222
Smith, J., 393
Smith, R. N., 164
Sobel, M., 35, 36, 200, 207–208, 218–219, 220, 222, 246, 293, 297, 349, 350
Somerville, P. N., 222
Spendley, W., 184
Sprowls, R. C., 87, 153, 164
Starr, N., 222, 246, 297
Steinhoff, H. W., 84
Stekler, H. O., 152
Stine, O. C., 335
Stockmal, F., 394
Stoller, D. S., 398, 404
Stuart, A., 319
Suits, D. B., 152, 336

Taubman, P., 37, 85, 149, 184, 302, 308, 319, 353, 379
Taussky, O., 394
Tausworthe, R. C., 394
Teichroew, D., 164, 488
Teigen, R. L., 380
Tennant, R. B., 336
Theil, H., 161, 164
Thompson, G. L., 41, 59, 86, 87
Thorelli, H. B., 87
Tiebout, C., 352
Tobin, J., 379
Tocher, K. D., 276, 289, 298, 394, 404, 488, 489
Todd, J., 394
Tonge, F. M., 59, 87
Treyz, G. I., 148, 152
Trilling, D. R., 59, 87
Truax, D., 206, 220
Tukey, J. W., 36, 39, 200, 203, 216, 221–222, 251, 254, 255, 257, 264, 266, 268, 274, 289, 296–297, 348
Tweeten, L. G., 336

Urban, G. L., 59, 86

Uspensky, J. V., 394

Vagholkar, M. K., 246
Van Horn, R., 22, 39, 164
Vernon, J. M., 41, 87, 88, 151, 152, 320
Villanueva, R., 38, 487
Vogl, T. P., 180, 184

Wald, A., 39, 246
Wallace, W. H., 38, 113, 119, 151, 160, 164, 268, 336
Walsh, J. E., 36, 39, 160, 164
Watts, D., 22, 39, 251, 267, 268
Weinert, A. E., 489
Weisbrod, B., 352
Weiss, L., 61, 88, 245, 246
Weitz, H., 61, 88
Wells, W. D., 61, 88
Wertz, K., 38, 151, 164, 196, 212, 221, 246, 247, 268, 298, 338, 351
Westlake, W. J., 389, 394
Wetherill, G. B., 246, 298
Whittlesey, J. R. B., 395
Wichern, D. W., 184
Wijsman, R. A., 244
Wildavsky, A., 339, 350, 352
Wilks, S. S., 405
Williams, J. W. J., 489
Williamson, J. C., 335, 337
Wilson, K. B., 36, 183
Winer, B. J., 202, 222, 246, 298
Wismer, D. A., 107, 152
Wold, H., 319
Wolfowitz, J., 246
Wonnacott, T., 38, 151, 164, 196, 212, 221, 246, 247, 268, 298, 351

Yagil, S., 405
Yaglom, A. M., 319
Yance, J. V., 152
Yaspin, A., 87
Young, Karen, 489
Yurow, J. A., 111, 152

Zarnowitz, V., 150

Subject Index

Activity oriented language, 420–421, 424–425, 436, 466
ALGOL, 15–16, 409, 412, 416, 480
ALGOL 60, 410
ALGOL 68, 410, 479
Analysis of variance, 29–35, 160, 167, 185–222, 228–229, 263–265, 346–350
Analytical solutions, 3–5, 47, 51, 143, 195–196, 212, 256–257, 299–337
Anheuser-Busch model, 68–71
Antithetic-variate sampling, 25, 274–275, 284–287
Approximating hyperplane, 172–176
Apriorism, 154–155
AS, 425
Assembler, 407
Assembly language, 407
Autocorrelation, 35, 160–161, 247–248, 251–255, 263–264, 295–296, 390–391

Balanced block design, 175
BASIC, 481
Basic machine language (BML), 407
Beta distribution, 400
Binary computers, 384–386, 388–390
Binomial distribution, 401–402
Boise Cascade model, 65
Bonini model, 105–106, 169
Brookings model, 142, 144–145, 353
Business games, 73–83

Canonical analysis, 173, 176, 180
Carnegie Tech Game, 73–74, 83
Central limit theorem, 20, 292
Chi-square distribution, 20, 257–259, 400
Chi-square test, 160, 257–259
Cigarette demand, 332–333

Clarkson model, 61–62
Clock, 47, 54–55, 191, 417–425
Cobb-Douglas function, 177–179
COBOL, 410, 412, 479
Cobweb model, 89–93
Compiler, 407
Compiler language (CL), 407
Computer independent notation, 408
Computer programming, 15–21, 190–195, 406–489
Computer programming language, 406–489
Computer simulation, definition, 2–6
  methodology, 11–39
  rationale, 6–10
  relation to scientific method, 6–8
Concomitant observations, 23–24
Confidence band, 258–263
Confidence interval, 34, 199–200, 203–205, 216–217, 291, 293, 348–349
Congruential methods, 382–395
  combination, 389–390
  mixed, 387–388
  multiplicative, 383–387
Constrained optimization, 182
Continuous probability distributions, 17–20, 396–400
  beta, 400
  chi-square, 20, 257–259, 400
  Dirichlet, 400
  exponential, 47, 51, 189–196, 399
  F distribution, 20, 260–265, 400
  gamma, 399–400
  Gaussian, *see* Continuous probability distributions, normal
  generalized exponential, 400
  hyperexponential, 400
  lognormal, 400

497

multivariate normal, 129, 132, 397–398
normal, 20, 200–201, 292, 397
Pearson XI, *see* Continuous probability
    distributions, generalized exponential
t distribution, 20, 400
uniform, 18–20, 397
Weibull, 400
Corning Glass model, 65
Corporate models, 68–73, 112
CSL, 406, 466–473
CTSS, 481
Cumulative distribution function, 17–19,
    396–397

Data analysis, 29–36, 133–137, 167, 185–
    268, 346–350, 429–433
analysis of variance, 29–35, 160, 167,
    185–221
F-test, 34, 201–202, 215–216, 292, 346–
    348
multiple comparisons, 34, 203–205, 216–
    217, 348–349
multiple rankings, 34–35, 205–208, 218,
    232–233, 242, 292–293, 294, 349–350
nonparametric methods, 36, 160
regression analysis, 27, 29, 160, 167
sequential sampling, 35, 223–246, 293–
    294
spectral analysis, 35, 160–161, 247–268,
    295–296, 312–317
Data generation, 16–21, 193–195, 396–
    405, 425–429
Decimal computers, 386–388
Density function, 17–19, 190, 193, 396–
    397
Dirichlet distribution, 400
Discrete probability distributions, 21, 400–
    403
binomial, 401–402
empirical, 21
geometric, 400–401
hypergeometric, 402
Markov chains, 42–43
Pascal, 401
Poisson, 47, 51, 189–190, 402–403
Dow Chemical model, 65
Duopoly models, 96–99, 100–101
Dynamic simulation, 6, 143, 146, 147, 290,
    310–317, 417–425
DYNAMO, 107–111

Econometric models, 113–124, 126–147
inadequate estimation techniques, 146–147
large-scale, 142–143
linear, 136–139, 301–305, 310–317
nonlinear, 139–141, 305–310
perverse results, 143, 146
simulation versus analytical solutions, 143
solutions, 136–141
unstable coefficients, 147
Econometric problems, 143–147
Econometrics, 113–124, 126–147, 320–337,
    338–343, 353–363
Economic models, 89–152, 177–179, 186–
    190, 209–210, 248–250, 299–319, 320–
    337, 338–343, 353–380
behavioral, 99–106
cobweb, 89–93
competitive industry, 93–96
department store, 101–105
duopoly, 96–99, 100–101
econometric, 113–124, 126–147, 177–179,
    209–210, 248–250, 299–319, 320–337,
    338–343, 353–380
economy, 126–147, 177–179, 209–210,
    248–250, 353–380
firm, 89–113, 186–190
Industrial Dynamics, 107–111
industry, 113–126, 320–337
linear, 128–133, 136–139, 301–305, 310–
    317
lumber industry, 124–126
macrodynamic, 126–147, 177–179, 209–
    210, 248–250, 299–319, 353–380
macroeconometric, 126–147, 177–179, 209–
    210, 248–250, 299–319, 353–380
management game, 73–83
monopoly, 105
nonlinear, 139–141, 305–310
oligopoly, 101
Samuelson-Hicks, 209–212, 248–250
shoe industry, 119–124
solutions, 136–141
textile industry, 113–125
tobacco industry, 320–337
United States economy, 128–133, 142–143,
    177–179, 353–380
Economic systems, 89–152, 177–179, 186–
    190, 209–210, 248–250, 299–319, 320–
    337, 338–343, 353–380
Economic theory, 111–113, 126–127

Empirical distributions, 21
Empiricism, 155
Endogenous variables, 2, 12–15, 45
Equivalent degrees of freedom, 263–264, 296
Equivalent independent observations, 296
Error checking, 16, 141, 433–435
ESP, 425
Event-oriented language, 421–422, 424–425, 436–456
Exogenous variables, 2, 12–15, 45
Experimental design, 5, 22–29, 133, 165–184, 196–200
Experimental design problems, 24–29, 180–182
  constrained optimization, 182
  motive, 27–28
  multiple response, 28–29, 181
  nonlinearity, 181
  size, 26–27, 180–181
  stochastic convergence, 24–26, 180
Experimental designs, 165–184
  exploratory, 27, 167–175
  fractional-factorial, 26, 168–171
  full factorial, 26, 167–168
  optimization, 27, 175–180
  response surface, 26–27, 172–175, 175–180
  rotatable, 171–172
Exponential distribution, 47, 51, 189–196, 399

Factor analysis, 160
Factors, 3–4, 23–24, 26–27, 166–175
Factor selection, 26–27, 167–172, 180–181
F distribution, 20, 260–265, 400
Federal aid for education, 338–352
Federal Reserve Board, 12, 353–363, 366–379
Financial models, 61–68
Firm, models of, 89–113, 186–190
Flow chart, 15, 46, 192
Forecasting, 158
FORSIM, 412, 425
FORTRAN, 15–17, 19–21, 43, 190–195, 385, 397–403, 409, 412, 416
Fractional factorial design, 168–171
F.R.B.-M.I.T. model, 353
F-test, 34, 201–202, 215–216, 292, 346–348
Full factorial design, 26, 167–168

Gaming, *see* Operational gaming
Gamma distribution, 399–400
GASP, 412–425
Gaussian distribution, *see* Normal distribution
Gauss-Seidel method, 139–141
Generalized exponential distribution, 400
General purpose compilers, 15–16
Generation of stochastic random variables, 16–21, 193–195, 396–405
Geometric distribution, 400–401
Goodness of fit, 22, 159–161, 259–263
GPSS, 15, 406, 420, 473–478
Graphics, 482–483
Greco-Latin square designs, 26
GSP, 425, 480

Harvard Game, 83
Hertz model, 62–63
Historical verification, 21, 119–125, 158, 333–335, 363–366
Hyperexponential distribution, 400
Hypergeometric distribution, 402

IBM model, 70
IBS SYSTEM/360, 15, 473
Importance sampling, 25–26, 278–282, 284–287
Independence, 34, 200, 291–293
Industrial Dynamics, 107–111
Industry, models of, 113–126, 320–337
Initial conditions, 6, 16, 228–229
Interaction, 32–33, 168–171, 228–229
Interactive language, 481–482
Interpreter, 407
Interpretive language (IL), 407
Inventory models, 52–57, 165–167, 224–227
Inverse transformation method, 17–20, 193–195

Job-shop problem, 57–59
JOSS, 481

Kolmogorov-Smirnov test, 160

Latin square designs, 26, 175
Linear models, 128–133, 136–139, 301–305, 310–317
Logical positivism, 155
Lognormal distribution, 400

Machine breakdown model, 57
Macrodynamic models, 126−147, 177−179, 209−210, 248−250, 299−319, 353−380
Main effects, 31−33, 168−171
Management game, 73−83
Management science models, 40−88
  corporate, 68−73, 112
  finance, 61−68
  inventory, 52−57, 165−167, 224−227
  management games, 73−83
  marketing, 59−61
  Markov chain, 42−43
  production, 57−59, 186−190
  queueing, 44−52, 186−190, 436−447, 456−458, 466, 474−475
Marketing models, 59−61
Markov chains, 42−43
Mathematical models, 2−6, 12−15
Matrix inversion, 131−132, 136−139
Mattessich model, 64
MILITRAN, 425
Model evaluation, 14−15
Model formulation, 2−6, 12−15
Monetary model, 353−380
Monetary policy simulation, 353−380
Monte Carlo techniques, 6, 10, 25−26, 269−289
Multiple comparisons, 34, 203−205, 216−217, 348−349
Multiple ranking procedures, 34−35, 205−208, 218, 232−233, 242, 292−293, 294, 349−350
Multistage validation, 156−158
Multivariate normal distribution, 129, 132, 397−398

Newton-Raphson method, 141
Newton's method, 141
Nonlinear models, 139−141, 305−310
Nonparametric methods, 36, 160
Normal distribution, 20, 200−201, 292, 397
NSS, 425
Number theory, 382

OBE model, 142
Object program, 407−408
Oligopoly models, 101
Operating system, 481
Operational gaming, 73−83
OPS, 425

OPS−3, 481
Ordinary least squares, 117, 325, 340−341
Output reports, 16, 429−433

Parameter estimation, 12, 15, 117, 270, 291, 293−294, 325, 340−341, 357
Pascal distribution, 401
Pearson XI distribution, see Generalized exponential distribution
Pillsbury model, 59
PL/I, 15, 479
Poisson distribution, 47, 51, 189−190, 402−403
Policy simulation, 1−2, 12, 133−138, 196−200, 210−214, 227−229, 343−346, 366−379
Policy targets, 354−355
Policy variables, 1−2, 12, 133−138, 196−200, 210−214, 227−229, 343−346, 366−379
Polynomial, 173−176, 180−181
Positive economics, 155−156
Prediction, 21−22, 156
Problem formulation, 11−12, 128
Problem oriented language (POL), 408−413
Process oriented language, 422−425, 456−465
Production models, 57−59, 186−190
Programming, 15−21, 43, 190−195, 385, 397−403, 406−489
PROGRAM SIMULATE, see SIMULATE
Pseudorandom numbers, 17−21, 193−195, 198, 200, 228, 251, 270−271, 381−405
  combination method, 389−390
  congruential methods, 382−395
  definition, 17, 381
  mixed congruential method, 387−388
  multiplicative congruential method, 383−387
  number theory, 382
  serial correlation, 390
  statistical tests, 17, 391

Queueing models, 44−52, 186−190, 436−447, 456−458, 466, 474−475
  multichannel, 48−52
  single-channel, multistation, 48, 186−190
  single-station, 44−48

Random number, 17−21, 193−195, 198, 200, 228, 251, 270−271, 381−405
Random number generators, 17−21, 193−195, 381−405
Random variable, 17−21, 193−195, 396−405
Random variate, 17−21, 193−195, 396−405
Rationalism, 154−155

Recursive models, 117, 325
Reduced form, 131, 138–139, 301, 306
Regression analysis, 27, 29, 146–147, 160
Regression sampling, 25, 271–274, 284–287
Replications, 24–25, 35, 196–200, 223–224, 247–248, 269–289, 290–294
Response, 3, 23
Response surface, 3, 26–27, 172–180
Rotatable design, 171–172
RSM, 173
RUSH, 481

Sample size, 24–25, 35, 196–200, 223–224, 247–248, 269–289, 290–294
Scheduling models, 57–59
Scientific method, 6–9, 153–158
Scientific philosophy, 22, 153–158
SEAL, 425
Sequential sampling, 35, 223–246, 293–294
Serial correlation, 35, 160–161, 247–248, 251–255, 263–264, 295–296, 390–391
SILLY, 425
SIMCOM, 425
SIMON, 425
SIMPAC, 425
SIMPLE, 425
Simplex design, 175
SIMSCRIPT II, 14–16, 406, 416, 417, 420, 432–433, 436–456
SIMTRAN, 425
SIMULA, 406, 416, 417, 456–465
SIMULATE, 141, 333, 366
Simulation, definition, 2–6
  methodology, 11–39
  properties, 4–6
  rationale, 6–10
Simulation clock, 47, 54–55, 191, 417–425
Simulation control program, 417–425
Simulation languages, 14, 15, 16, 141, 406–489
Simulation models, 2–6, 12–15
  deterministic, 6
  dynamic, 4, 6, 143, 146, 147, 290, 310–317, 417–425
  static, 6, 290, 413–416
  stochastic, 6, 129–130
Simulation programming language (SPL), 409–489
Simulation versus analytical solutions, 143
Simultaneous confidence band, 258–263

Simultaneous confidence interval, 203–205, 216–217, 348–349
Single-factor method, 28
SLANG, 425
SOL, 425, 479, 480
Source program language, 409–489
Spectral analysis, 35, 160–161, 247–268, 295–296, 312–317
SPL, 409–489
Starting conditions, 6, 16, 228–229
Static simulation, 6, 290, 413–416
Stationary stochastic process, 253
Statistical independence, 34, 200, 291–293
Statistical tests of pseudorandom numbers, 17, 391
  frequency tests, 391
  gap test, 391
  lagged product tests, 391
  maximum test, 391
  poker test, 391
  serial test, 391
  tests of runs, 391
Status variables, 45, 54
Steepest ascent, 28, 175–180
Stochastic convergence, 24–26, 180, 269–289, 290–296
Stochastic variables, 6, 16–21, 193–195, 396–405
Stopping rules, 290–298
Stratified sampling, 25–26, 275–278, 284–287
Sun Oil Corporate Model, 64–67
Synthetic apriorism, 154–155

t distribution, 20, 400
Textile models, 113–125
Theil's inequality coefficient, 161
Time series, 6, 35, 247–268, 295–296
Time sharing, 482
Tobacco industry, 320–337
Transaction flow language, 473–478
Transaction matrix, 42–43
Two-stage least squares, 146, 357

U.C.L.A.-Michigan State Game, 83
Ultraempiricism, 155
Uniform distribution, 17–20, 381–382, 397
Uniform-grid method, 28
Utility theory, 28–29, 177–181

Validation, 21–22, 153–164, 195–196,
    248, 259–265, 333–335, 363–366
Variance-covariance matrix, 129, 397–398
Variance reduction techniques, 25–26, 269–
    289
Verification, 21–22, 153–164, 195–196, 248,
    259–265, 333–335, 363–366

Waiting line models, 44–53, 186–190, 436–447,

456–458, 466, 474–475
Weibull distribution, 400
Wharton model, 142–143

XEROX model, 72–73

Youden squares design, 175